Systems Programming
Designing and Developing
Distributed Applications

Systems Programming
Designing and Developing
Distributed Applications

Richard John Anthony
Reader in self-managing computer systems
University of Greenwich, UK

AMSTERDAM • BOSTON • HEIDELBERG • LONDON
NEW YORK • OXFORD • PARIS • SAN DIEGO
SAN FRANCISCO • SINGAPORE • SYDNEY • TOKYO
Morgan Kaufmann is an imprint of Elsevier

Morgan Kaufmann is an imprint of Elsevier
225 Wyman Street, Waltham, MA, 02451, USA

Library of Congress Cataloging-in-Publication Data
A catalog record for this book is available from the Library of Congress.

British Library Cataloguing in Publication Data
A catalogue record for this book is available from the British Library.

ISBN: 978-0-12-800729-7

For information on all MK publications
visit our website at www.mkp.com

Working together
to grow libraries in
developing countries

www.elsevier.com • www.bookaid.org

To Maxine, Elaine, Darrell, my mother Ellen and in memory of my father Norman

Contents

Preface

This book provides a comprehensive introduction to designing and developing distributed applications. The main emphasis is on the communication aspects of multicomponent systems, and the ways in which the design of such systems is impacted by, and impacts on, the behavior of the underlying operating systems, networks, and protocols.

The backdrop for this book is the increasing dependence of business, and society in general, on distributed systems and applications. There is an accompanying increasing need for well-trained engineers who can deliver high quality solutions. This requires strong design skills and best practice implementation techniques as well as a big picture view in which the engineer appreciates the way in which applications will use the resources of the system and be impacted by the configuration and behavior of the host system as a whole.

An integrated approach is taken, which cuts across several traditional computer science disciplines including operating systems, networking, distributed systems, and programming, and places the required background and theory into application and systems contexts with a variety of worked examples. The book is multidimensional; it has a problem-solving style and achieves a balance between theoretical underpinning and practitioner focus through development of application use cases of distributed applications.

Through embedded practical activities, the reader actually participates in the content, performing experiments and running simulations as they go. During these activities, dynamic aspects of systems are presented in animated and dynamic ways which convey far more information, and make complex aspects of systems accessible. Most of the accompanying experiments and simulations are user-configurable to support what-if investigation and give the reader an opportunity to gain an in-depth understanding. Practical programming challenges cover a wide range of aspects of systems. Several of these involve building full working distributed applications; these are made accessible through the provision of well-documented sample source code and clear guided tasks to add functionality and build systems by extending the sample code.

THE ORIGIN AND PURPOSE OF THIS BOOK

Designing and developing distributed applications is a hybrid topic in computer science, fundamentally based on concepts and mechanisms which are drawn from several of the traditional core subject areas which include networking, operating systems, distributed systems (theoretical, rather than developmental), and software engineering. The vast majority of high quality texts currently available focus on one of these subject areas with clear traditionally established boundaries in their scope. The majority of these books are primarily theoretical in style and approach.

At the outset of writing this book, I had been teaching a practical-oriented course in the area of distributed applications for many years and was very aware of the lack of a single book that comprehensively covered the subject matter of designing and developing distributed applications, with a strong practical emphasis. In effect, what I wanted was a standalone guide that would serve as a primary text for my own course and for others like it. I also wanted a book that would be accessible to my students, who are a diverse group with different levels of experience and confidence. I wanted, with a single book, to encourage those who are just starting out in software engineering, while equally satisfying the needs of more experienced learners who require more advanced challenges. My course already had a theory-meets-practice emphasis which had worked well for 13 years and was well received by students. On several occasions, when discussing the lack of availability of a suitable course text book, students had suggested I write one myself based directly on the course.

This book fills a clearly identified gap in provision. It provides an integrative text that relates the various underlying concepts together in a self-contained way so that a reader can appreciate the big picture view across systems, while also understanding the key underpinning theory and being able to explore with supported practical activities, all from one self-contained source. As such, the book is differentiated from other mainstream texts which tend to map onto one of the traditional subject areas and also tend to have a more theoretical basis.

The book has been designed to support courses which teach distributed applications design with a theory-meets-practice emphasis. The main focus is on application development and the supporting knowledge necessary to ensure high quality outcomes in this regard, and has been organized so as to naturally bridge across several areas of computer science. As such, it does not attempt to develop as much breadth in those areas as a traditionally organized text (for example, just focusing on networking, or operating systems) would be expected to do. Rather, it provides the very important integration across these disciplines. The primary design is focused on providing accessible example-based coverage of key aspects of distributed systems and applications, with detailed discussion supported by case studies, interactive teaching and learning tools, and practical activities. A main goal was to facilitate readers to understand practical examples of socket-based applications and to start to develop their own applications as a guided parallel track to the reading of the book.

The theoretical aspects of the book and the majority of mechanistic aspects covered are transferrable across languages, but there are implementation aspects which have language-dependent interpretation. Sample code is therefore provided in three popular programming languages to maximize accessibility: C++, Java, and C#.

The supplemental resources code base is extensive, including sample code for the various in-text examples, starting points, and sample solutions for the end-of-chapter programming tasks, and full source code for all three of the case studies.

The supplemental resources also include special editions of the author's established Workbenches suite of teaching and learning tools. These are used in some of the in-text activities and can also be used on a broader basis of self-guided or tutor-guided exploration of topics, or can be used to bring the subject matter to life in lectures or laboratory settings. The concept of the Workbenches was inspired by the need to represent dynamic aspects of systems in realistic and accessible ways. Any tutor who has attempted to teach scheduling (as one example of the very many dynamic aspects covered) with a series of static diagrams will appreciate the limitations of the approach in terms of the difficulty to convey the true richness of the behavior that can be exhibited. The Workbenches were specifically designed to overcome these limitations when teaching dynamic or complex aspects of systems. The user-configured practical experiments and user-configured simulations cover a wide range of topics in networking, distributed systems, and operating systems. The chapter texts link to these activities and provide guidance to the reader to map the practical learning to the underpinning theoretical concepts.

The style of the book, with its strong emphasis on guided practical exploration of the core theory, makes it suitable as a self-study guide as well as a course companion text.

THE INTENDED AUDIENCE

The book has been designed to have a very wide appeal. The target audience includes

- Teachers of distributed systems who require a self-contained course text with in-built practical activities, programming exercises, and case studies which they can use as the basis of an interesting and inspiring course.
- Students studying application development and requiring a book which links together the many different facets of distributed systems, operating systems, and networking, with numerous clearly explained practical examples and a rich repository of sample code.
- Experienced programmers who are new to designing and developing distributed applications and/ or socket programming, or perhaps need a quick-start resource to get a distributed application project off the ground.
- Trainee programmers learning any of C++, Java, or C# and requiring the additional challenge of writing network applications with sockets.
- Sockets-level programmers familiar with one of the languages supported by the book {C++, Java, C#} and requiring an example-based resource to facilitate cross-training to one of the other languages.
- Students studying other areas of computer science and requiring a basic grounding in distributed systems in the form of a self-study guide with a practical emphasis.

THE ORGANIZATION OF THE BOOK

The book has a core section of four chapters which look at the background concepts, technical requirements, challenges presented, as well as the techniques and supporting mechanisms necessary to build distributed applications. Four specific viewpoints have been chosen so as to divide the material into related categories which are significant from a design and operational perspective. This approach enables a structured and detailed examination of the underlying concepts and mechanisms of systems, which cuts across the boundaries of the traditional teaching subjects.

The following Chapter 6 is set at the higher level of distributed systems themselves. This chapter does the important job of integrating the ideas, concepts, and mechanisms discussed in the earlier core chapters into the context of entire systems, and identifies the services needed to ensure those systems are high quality in terms of their functional and nonfunctional requirements.

All of the chapters have a practical emphasis, with in-built experiments and practical exploration activities and there is a case study that runs through all of the core chapters, integrating and cross-linking them. However, to address the wide scope of architectures, structures, behaviours, and operating contexts of distributed applications, a final chapter provides two further, fully operational and clearly documented case studies accompanied by full code.

The Introduction chapter motivates the book and the integrative systems approach that has been taken. It provides a brief historical perspective on the rise of distributed computing and its significance in a modern context. It provides a short foundation of some key topics which are covered in depth later in the book, but are necessary for the reader to have a basic appreciation at the outset. This includes the general characteristics of distributed systems; the main benefits of distributed systems; key challenges that must be overcome when building distributed applications; metrics for measuring the quality and performance of distributed systems; and an introduction to the main forms of transparency. This chapter also introduces the three case studies, the supplementary material available at the book's companion Web site, the in-text practical activities, and the Workbenches suite of interactive teaching and learning tools.

The Process view chapter examines the ways in which processes are managed and how this influences communications at the low level. It deals with aspects such as process scheduling and blocking, message buffering and delivery, the use of ports and sockets, and the mechanism of process binding to a port which thus enables the operating system to manage communications at the computer level on behalf of its local processes. This chapter also deals with concepts of multiprocessing environments, threads, and operating system resources such as timers.

The Communication view chapter examines the ways networks and communication protocols operate and how the functionalities and behavior of these impact on the design and behavior of applications. This viewpoint is concerned with topics which include communication mechanisms and the different modes of communication, e.g., unicast, multicast, and broadcast, and the way such choices can impact on the behavior, performance, and scalability of applications. The functionality and features of the TCP and UDP transport-layer protocols are described, and compared in terms of performance, latency, and overheads. Low-level details of communication are examined from a developer viewpoint, including the role and operation of the socket API primitives. The remote procedure call and remote method invocation higher-level communication mechanisms are also examined.

The Resource view chapter examines the nature of the resources of computer systems and how they are used in facilitating communication within distributed applications. Physical resources of interest are processing capacity, network communication bandwidth, and memory. The discussion focuses on the need to be efficient with the use of these finite resources which directly impact on the performance and scalability of applications and the system itself. Memory is also discussed in the context of buffers for the assembly, sending, and receiving of messages.

The Architecture view chapter examines the structures of distributed systems and applications. The main focus is on the various models for dividing the logic of an application into several functional components and the ways in which these components interconnect and interact. The chapter also considers the ways in which the components of systems are mapped onto the underlying resources of the system and the additional functional requirements that arise from such mapping, for example, the need for flexible run-time configuration. The various architectural models are discussed in terms of their impact on key nonfunctional quality measures such as scalability, robustness, efficiency, and transparency.

The Distributed Systems chapter follows the four core viewpoint chapters. Distributed systems form a backdrop for these chapters as they each deal with a specific set of supporting theoretical aspects, concepts, and mechanisms. This chapter is set at a level higher and focuses on the distributed systems themselves, their key features and functional requirements, and the specific challenges associated with their design and development. The distributed systems chapter thereby puts the content of the core chapters into the wider systems perspective and discusses issues that arise from the distribution itself, as well as techniques to address these issues. The provision of transparency is key to achieving quality in distributed applications. For this reason, transparency is a theme that runs through all the chapters, in relation to the various topics covered, and is also a main focal aspect of the discussion of the case studies. To further reinforce the importance of transparency, it is covered as a subject in its own right, in depth in this chapter. Ten important forms of transparency are defined and explored in terms of their significance and the way in which they impact on systems and applications. Techniques to facilitate the provision of these forms of transparency are explained. This chapter also describes common services, middleware, and technologies that support interoperability in heterogeneous environments.

The final chapter "Case studies—putting it all together" relates together the content of the previous chapters in the form of a pair of detailed distributed application case studies which are used as vehicles to illustrate many of the various issues, challenges, techniques, and mechanisms discussed earlier. The goal is to provide an integrative aspect, in which applications are examined through their entire life cycle. This chapter has a problem-solving approach and is based around provided working applications, their source code, and detailed documentation. The presentation of these applications makes and reinforces links between theory and practice, making references to earlier chapters as necessary.

IN-TEXT ACTIVITIES

A series of practical activities are embedded throughout the text of chapters 2–6 to reinforce key concepts through experimentation. Each activity is based on a specific concept or mechanism which the activity places into a systems or application context.

HOW TO USE THE BOOK

The book has been designed to flexibly support a wide variety of users with different requirements. Suggested uses include:

As an essential course text. This was the primary motivation for writing the book. The book has been based on a successful course on designing and building distributed applications. There is in-depth coverage of the central theme of distributed applications, supported by detailed practical activities, working examples, case studies, end-of-chapter questions, and programming challenges with solutions. The book also includes a wide range of foundational and supporting technical material including concepts, issues, mechanisms, and strategies relating to aspects of systems that need to be understood.

Due to a combination of the cross-cutting integrative approach taken, and the extensive resource base provided, the book provides an ideal course guide; tutors can flexibly structure courses around the book depending on the technical depth that they wish to achieve and the experience level of their students. The source code for the example programs are provided at the book's resources Web site, in three languages: C++, Java, and C#.

The Workbench-based activities can be used as demonstrators during lectures, or as guided exercises in either the classroom or as directed self-study. These can be used to illustrate dynamic behavior through inter alia simulations of scheduling, thread priority, or deadlock (which are all notoriously difficult to convey to students when only static diagram representations are used). Live simulations can be used in exciting ways by pausing the simulation and asking the audience what they think will happen next, or by running the simulations with different settings to show how certain configuration affects behavior.

The network experiments can be used to demonstrate setting up of communications between processes and sending messages across. This can be used to explore the use of the socket primitives, aspects of performance such as blocking and buffering, and also the behavior of the transport protocols TCP and UDP. For example, you can explore the TCP bind-listen-connect-accept sequence necessary to set up a connection, dynamically with real processes, in a lecture setting.

You can also use the Workbench activities to set a wide variety of student laboratory exercises or homework, for example, to evaluate efficiency in communication, scenarios where communication deadlock may occur, or perhaps to use the detailed statistics generated to compare scheduling algorithms in terms of efficiency, fairness, or throughput.

The Distributed Systems Workbench will enable you to (for example) set up an election algorithm experiment that runs on all of the computers in a laboratory. Students can examine scenarios such as terminating the current master process and predicting the next behavior. You can start multiple master process instances and see how the algorithm resolves the situation. The provided logger application will capture the run-time sequence of process state changes for subsequent analysis. Another example is to explore the client–server game application and to ask students to attempt to reverse engineer the message sequence that occurs based on observed behavior; challenges such as this are very good to encourage deeper enquiry.

The use cases are all fully working and can be translated into learning and evaluation exercises, or used as a basis on which to build larger projects.

The end-of-chapter programming exercises can be used as assessed activities or tutorial activities. You can use them as provided, or elaborate on the challenge depending on the level of experience of your students.

As a self-teach guide. The book is an ideal guide for independent study; a large amount of technical documentation is provided to accompany the practical aspects of the content which enables you to use the book in a self-teach manner, and be able to check your progress as you go along against the sample solutions (for the programming challenges), explanations of expected outcomes (for the in-text activities), and answers to end-of-chapter questions. The experiments and simulations provided by the Workbenches are user-configurable and repeatable so that you can work at your own pace and explore as deep as you need. One of the main original motivators for the development of the Workbenches was the realization that we all learn at different rates, and what one person gets immediately others may struggle with at first. Therefore, the Workbenches support personalized/progressive learning.

By providing sample application code in three popular languages, the book also serves as a sort of Rosetta stone for the use of the socket API and the transport layer protocols (TCP and UDP). Once you understand the implementation in one of the languages, you can use the examples to relate across the different languages. This is particularly helpful where, for example, you are developing a system that has some components developed in one language (for example, the server side could be C++) and some components developed in another language (for example, the client side could be developed in C#). The final case study in Chapter 7 purposefully emphasizes this aspect of heterogeneity and interoperability. The use cases are a powerful study resource for self-learning target setting and reflection, enabling you to master each of them one by one over whatever time line suits your needs and initial experience.

As a secondary text. The book has an integrative cross-cutting theme which sits across the traditional subject areas of networking, operating systems, programming, and distributed systems theory. The book, with its clear explanations and strong practical emphasis, is an ideal supplemental text to spice up courses where the primary focus is one of (networking, application development, or operating systems), with the addition of the various activities and programming exercises. It has a quite different style to the more traditional tightly focused and often primarily theoretical-oriented texts and would be good to use side by side with other specialized texts to give students a variety of information sources and to help fill some of the gaps where the taught subject matter overlaps other subject areas (an aspect this book excels in).

The Workbench-based activities are all suitable for standalone piecemeal use. For example, you may choose to only use a subset of the activities of the Operating Systems Workbench (or one of the others) to bring to life some specific aspects of the course content that students struggle with, or simply to break up a long sequence of presentation slides with a live experiment or simulation.

As a reference text with practical examples. The book covers a wide range of topics within the subject areas of distributed systems, networking, programming, and operating systems. The book is distinguished from mainstream alternatives by its extensive range of practical examples and source code resources. It therefore serves as a reference guide with a twist. For a significant proportion of the topics, you will find related guided practical activities or programming challenges with solutions or contextualization in the form of one or more of the use cases.

THE SUPPORT MATERIALS

The book is supplied with supplementary materials provided via a companion Web site. The URL is http://booksite.elsevier.com/9780128007297.

The materials are organized on the Web site in a way which maps onto the various chapters in the book. There are several types of resources which include:

Sample program code. Sample code is provided for the in-text activities and examples where relevant, the use-case applications, and sample solutions for the programming exercises. The sample code can be used in several ways:

- In most cases, complete application source code is provided. This enables readers to study the entire application logic and to relate it to the explanation in the text. There are cases where the text provides brief code snippets to explain a key point; the reader can then examine the full application code to put the snippet into perspective with the application logic. Much of the sample code is provided in three languages: C++, Java, C#.
- The sample application code can be used as a starting point on which to develop solutions to the end-of-chapter resources; guidance as to which is the most appropriate resource to use is given in such cases.
- There are also some specific sample solutions to the end of chapter programming exercises, in cases where the solution is not already exemplified elsewhere in the resources.

Executable files. Many of the applications are also provided in executable form. This enables readers to run applications and study their behavior without having to first compile them. This is particularly important when following the in-text activities and examples to minimize interruption when switching between reading and the practical work.

The Workbenches teaching and learning tools. The book is accompanied by a suite of sophisticated interactive teaching and learning applications (called Workbenches) that the author has developed over a period of 13 years to promote student-centred and flexible approaches to teaching and learning, and to enable students to work remotely, interactively, and at their own pace. The Networking Workbench, Operating Systems Workbench, and Distributed Systems Workbench provide combinations of configurable simulations, emulations, and implementations to facilitate experimentation with many of the underlying concepts of systems. The Workbenches have been tried and tested with many cohorts of students and are used as complementary support to several courses by several lecturers at

Acknowledgments

I would like to express my sincere gratitude to the technical reviewers for taking the time to carefully read the material and for providing some very valuable feedback and suggestions.

I would also like to thank the editorial team at Morgan Kaufmann for their advice and guidance through the process of planning and writing the book.

Many thanks also to the numerous past students of my systems programming course who have provided feedback on the course structure and content either directly through comments and suggestions or indirectly through their keen participation as evidenced by the fantastic work achieved. Thanks especially to those students over the years who suggested that I should write the book; I finally did it.

There are also many colleagues, friends, and family who have provided encouragement. In particular, I am eternally grateful to my lovely Maxine who has been extremely patient and supportive and who has brought very many cups of tea to the study.

INTRODUCTION

CHAPTER CONTENTS

This book is a self-contained introduction to designing and developing distributed applications. It brings together the essential supporting theory from several key subject areas and places the material into the context of real-world applications and scenarios with numerous clearly explained examples. There is a strong practical emphasis throughout the entire book, involving programming exercises and experiments for the reader to engage in, as well as three detailed fully functional case studies, one of which runs through the four core chapters, places theory aspects into application perspectives, and cross-links across the various themes of the chapters. The book is an ideal companion text for undergraduate degree courses.

This chapter introduces the book, its structure, the way the technical material is organized, and the motivation behind this. It provides a historical perspective and explains the significance of distributed systems in modern computing. It also explains the integrative, cross-discipline nature of the presentation and the underlying "systems thinking" approach. It describes and justifies the way that material has been presented from four carefully selected viewpoints (ways of looking at systems, structure, organization, and behavior). These viewpoints have been chosen to overcome the artificial boundaries that are introduced when material is divided for the purposes of teaching into traditional categorizations of operating systems, networking, distributed systems, and programming; whereas many of the key concepts pertinent to distributed systems overlap several of these areas or reside in the margins between these areas.

The overall goal of the book is to furnish the reader with a rounded understanding of the architecture and communication aspects of systems, and also the theoretical underpinning necessary to understand the various design choices available and to be able to appreciate the consequences of the various design decisions and tradeoffs. Upon reaching the end of this book, the reader will be equipped to design and build their first distributed application.

The technical content is brought alive through an interactive style which incorporates practical activities, examples, sample code, analogies, exercises, and case studies. Many practical experiments and simulation activities are provided by a special edition of the author's established Workbenches teaching and learning resources suite. Application examples are provided throughout the book to put the conceptual aspects into perspective. These are backed up by extensive source code and a mix of theory and practice exercises to enhance both skills and supporting knowledge.

1.1 RATIONALE

1.1.1 THE TRADITIONAL APPROACH TO TEACHING COMPUTER SCIENCE

Computer science is an extremely broad field of knowledge, encompassing diverse topics which include systems architectures, systems analysis, data structures, programming languages, software engineering techniques, operating systems, networking and communication among many others.

Traditionally, the subject material within computer science has been divided into these topic areas (disciplines) for the pragmatic purposes of teaching at universities. Hence, a student will study Operating Systems as one particular subject, Networking as another, and Programming as another. This model works well in general, and has been widely implemented as a means of structuring learning in this field.

However, there are many aspects of computer systems which cut across the boundaries of several of these disciplines, and cannot be fully appreciated from the viewpoint of any single one of these disciplines; so to gain a deep understanding of the way systems work, it is necessary to study systems holistically across several disciplines simultaneously. One very important example where a cross-discipline approach is needed is the development of distributed applications.

To develop a distributed application (i.e. one in which multiple software components communicate and cooperate to solve an application problem), the developer needs to have programming skills and knowledge of a variety of related and supporting activities including requirements analysis, design, and testing techniques. However, successful design of this class of application also requires a level of expertise in each of several disciplines: networking knowledge (especially protocols, ports, addressing, and binding), operating systems theory (including process scheduling, process memory space and buffer management, and operating system handling of incoming messages), and distributed systems concepts (such as architecture, transparency, name services, election algorithms, and mechanisms to support replication and data consistency). Critically, an in-depth appreciation of the ways that these areas of knowledge interact and overlap is needed, for example, the way in which the operating systems scheduling of processes interacts with the blocking or non-blocking behavior of network sockets and the implications of this for application performance and responsiveness and efficiency of system resource usage. In addition, the initial requirements analysis can only be performed with due diligence if the developer has the ability to form a big-picture view of systems and is not focussing on simply achieving connectivity between parts, hoping to add detail subsequently on an incremental basis, which can lead to unreliable, inefficient or scale-limited systems (a problem that tends to occur if the developer has knowledge compartmentalized within the various disciplines). This is a situation where the whole is significantly greater than the sum of the parts; having segmented pools of knowledge in the areas of operating systems, networking, distributed systems theory, and programming is not sufficient to design and build high-quality distributed systems and applications.

There are in reality no rigid boundaries between the traditional disciplines of computer science, but rather these are overlapping subsets of the wider field. The development of almost any application or system that could be built requires aspects of understanding from several of these disciplines integrated to some extent. A systems approach addresses the problem of topics lying within the overlapping boundaries of several subject areas, and thus potentially only being covered briefly or being covered in distinctly different ways in particular classes. This can have the outcome that students don't manage to connect up the various references to the same thing, or relate how an aspect covered in one course relates to or impacts on another aspect in another course. Mainstream teaching will continue along the traditional lines, fundamentally because it is an established way to provide the essential foundational building blocks of knowledge and skill. However, there is also plenty of scope for integrative courses that take a systems approach to build on the knowledge and skills provided by more traditional courses and give students an understanding of how the various concepts interrelate and must be integrated to develop whole systems.

1.1.2 **THE SYSTEMS APPROACH TAKEN IN THIS BOOK**

The main purpose of this book is to provide a self-contained introduction to designing and developing distributed applications, including the necessary aspects of operating systems, networking, distributed systems, and programming, and the interaction between these aspects is necessary to understand and develop such applications.

Rather than to anchor one of the traditional specific disciplines within computer science, much of the content necessarily occupies the space where several of these disciplines overlap, such as operating systems and networking (e.g. inter-process communication, the impact of scheduling behavior on processes using blocking versus nonblocking sockets, buffer management for communicating processes, and distributed deadlock); networking and programming (e.g. understanding the correct usage of the socket API and socket-level options, maintaining connection state, and achieving graceful disconnection); operating systems and programming in a network context (e.g. understanding the relationships between the various addressing constructs (process id, ports, sockets, and IP addresses), sockets API exception handling, and achieving asynchronous operation within a process using threads or combining timers and nonblocking sockets); and distributed systems and networking (e.g. understanding how higher-level distributed applications are built on the services provided by networks and network protocols).

The core technical content of the book is presented from four viewpoints (the process view, the communication view, the resource view, and the architecture view) which have been carefully chosen to best reflect the different types and levels of organization and activity in systems and thus maximize the accessibility of the book. I find that some students will understand a particular concept clearly when it is explained from a certain angle, while others will understand it only superficially, but will gain a much better grasp of the same concept when a second example is given, approaching and reinforcing from a different angle. This is the approach that has been applied here. Communications between components in modern computing systems is a complex topic, influenced and impacted by many aspects of systems design and behavior. The development of applications which are distributed is further complexified by the architectures of the underlying systems, and of the architectures of the applications themselves, including the functional split across components and the connectivity between the components. By tackling the core material from several angles, the book gives readers the maximum opportunity to understand in depth, and to make associations between the various parts of systems and the roles they play in facilitating communication within distributed applications. Ultimately, readers will be able to design and develop distributed applications and be able to understand the consequences of their design decisions.

Chapter 2: Process View

The first of the four core chapters presents the process view. This examines the ways in which processes are managed and how this influences communications at the low level, dealing with aspects such as process scheduling and blocking, message buffering and delivery, the use of ports and sockets, and the way in which process binding to a port operates, and thus enables the operating system to manage communications at the computer level, on behalf of its host processes. This chapter also deals with concepts of multiprocessing environments, threads, and operating system resources such as timers.

Chapter 3: Communication View

This chapter examines the ways networks and communication protocols operate and how the functionalities and behavior of these impact on the design and behavior of applications. This viewpoint is concerned with topics which include communication mechanisms and the different modes of communication, e.g., unicast, multicast, and broadcast, and the way this choice can impact on the behavior, performance, and scalability of applications. The functionality and features of the TCP and UDP transport-layer protocols are described, and compared in terms of performance, latency, and overheads. Low-level details of communication are examined from a developer viewpoint, including the role and operation of the socket API primitives. The remote procedure call and remote method invocation higher-level communication mechanisms are also examined.

Chapter 4: Resource View

This chapter examines the nature of the resources of computer systems and how they are used in facilitating communication within distributed systems. Physical resources of interest are processing capacity, network communication bandwidth, and memory. For the first two, the discussion focuses on the need to be efficient with, and not waste, these limited resources which directly impact on performance and scalability of applications and the system itself. Memory is discussed in the context of buffers for the assembly and storage of messages prior to sending (at the sender side), and for holding messages after receipt (at the receiver side) while the contents are processed. Also, important is the differentiation between process-space memory and system-space memory and how this is used by the operating system to manage processes, especially with respect to the receipt of messages by the operating system on behalf of local processes and subsequent delivery of the messages to the processes when they issue a receive primitive. The need for and operation of virtual memory is examined in detail.

Chapter 5: Architecture View

This chapter examines the structures of distributed systems and applications. The main focus is on the various models for dividing the logic of an application into several functional components and the ways in which these components interconnect and interact. The chapter also considers the ways in which the components of systems are mapped onto the underlying resources of the system and the additional functional requirements that arise from such mapping, for example, the need for flexible run-time configuration. The various architectural models are discussed in terms of their impact on key nonfunctional quality aspects such as scalability, robustness, efficiency, and transparency.

Chapter 6: Distributed Systems

Distributed systems form a backdrop for the four core viewpoint chapters, each of which deals with a specific set of theoretical aspects, concepts, and mechanisms. These are followed by a chapter which focuses on the distributed systems themselves, their key features and functional requirements, and the specific challenges associated with their design and development. This chapter thereby puts the content of the core chapters into the wider systems perspective and discusses issues that arise from the distribution itself, as well as techniques to address these issues.

The provision of transparency is key to achieving quality in distributed applications. For this reason, transparency is a theme that runs through all the chapters, in relation to the various topics covered, and is also a main focal aspect of the discussion of the main case study. To further reinforce the importance of transparency, it is covered in its own right, in depth, in this chapter. Ten important forms of transparency are defined and explored in terms of their significance and the way in which they impact on systems and applications. Techniques to facilitate the provision of these forms of transparency are discussed. This chapter also describes common services, middleware, and technologies that support interoperability in heterogeneous environments.

Chapter 7: Case Studies—Putting it All Together

This chapter brings together the content of the previous chapters in the form of a pair of fully detailed distributed application case studies which are used as vehicles to illustrate many of the various issues, challenges, techniques, and mechanisms discussed earlier.

The goal is to provide an integrative aspect, in which applications are examined through their entire life cycle. This chapter has a problem-solving approach and is based around provided working applications, their source code, and detailed documentation. The presentation of these applications makes and reinforces links between theory and practice, making references to earlier chapters as necessary.

1.2 THE SIGNIFICANCE OF NETWORKING AND DISTRIBUTED SYSTEMS IN MODERN COMPUTING—A BRIEF HISTORICAL PERSPECTIVE

My career began in the early 1980s, as a microprocessor technician at a local university. Computer systems were very different then to what is available now. Computers were isolated systems without network connections. Microprocessors were recently on the scene and the "IBM PC" was just about to arrive. There was no such thing as a computer virus. Mainframe computers were the dominant type of computing system for business. They really did look like those systems you see in old films with large removable disk drives that resembled top-loader washing machines, and large units the size of wardrobes with tape reels spinning back and forth on the front. These systems required a team of operators to change tapes and disks to meet users' requirements, and this use model required that much of the processing was performed in batch mode, in which users submitted a job request and the actual processing was performed sometime, possibly hours, later.

Let me briefly take you back to that time. As part of my job, I built several complete microprocessor-based computer systems from scratch. The technology was manageable by a single person who could understand and develop all aspects of the system, the hardware, the operating software, and the applications that run on them. I was the designer of both hardware and software and used advanced (for their day) microprocessors such as the Zilog Z80 and various latest technologies from Motorola and Intel. I built the motherboard as well as the power supply, wrote the operating system (well the monitor system as it was), and wrote the applications that ran on the systems. I was responsible for testing and bug fixing at all levels of hardware and software. I was both the operator and the user at the same time. The complexity of the entire system was a mere fraction of the complexity of modern systems.

The advent of the microprocessor was a very significant milestone in the evolution of computing. It brought about many major changes and has led to the current situation of ubiquitous computing on a global scale. As a direct result, my modern-day students are faced with multicomponent multilayered interconnected systems, incredibly complex (in both their design and behavior) to the extent that no single individual can be expected to fully understand all aspects of them.

The "PC" (personal computer) concept was established in 1981 with the arrival of IBM's Personal Computer. Up until this point, there had been a wide variety of desk-top computer offerings from a variety of manufacturers, but each had a different architecture and operating system. This represented risk for businesses as well as for software developers as there was a lack of consistency and it was difficult to make a commitment to a particular technology. The original IBM PC was relatively expensive, but it had an open and easy-to-copy hardware architecture. This enabled a variety of competitors to build "IBM-compatible" machines (sometimes called "PC clones") which for the most part were considerably cheaper alternatives with acceptable quality. The fact that they had the same architecture, including the central processor (the Intel 8086 family of devices), meant that they all could support the same operating system (the most popular of the three that were available for the PC being Microsoft's Disk Operating System) and thus could run the same applications. This consistent approach was the key to success of the PC and quite soon these systems were established in very many businesses and many people started buying them for home use too. This was, over the next few years, a true revolution in computing.

Perhaps the most dramatic development since the PC arrived has been the advent of networking. Once the personal computer concept had caught on, and with it the incredibly important notion of standardization at the platform level, there was an increasing need to pass data from one system to another. To achieve something resembling wide-area networking, we actually used to put floppy magnetic disks in the post in those days, while our version of local area networking was to save a file onto a floppy disk in one computer, remove the disk, walk to the desk of a colleague, and place the disk into their computer so that they could access the required file.

Local Area Networking (LAN) technologies started to become commercially available in the mid 1980s and were becoming commonplace by the end of the 1980s. Initially, the cost of wiring up buildings and the per-computer cost of connecting were quite high, so it was common for organizations to have labs of computers in which only a small number were connected to the network. It was also common to have isolated networks scattered about which provided local access to server systems (e.g. file servers) and shared resources such as printers, but were not connected to the wider systems.

Prior to the widespread implementation of LANs, the basic concepts of wide-area networking were already being established. Serial connections could be used to connect computers on a one-to-one basis, much the same as connecting a computer to a printer. A pair of MoDem (Modulator-Demodulator) devices could be placed one at each end of a phone line and thus extend the serial connection between the computers to anywhere that had a phone connection; although, this was cumbersome and had to use low data transmission rates to achieve an acceptable level of reliability.

The Internet is a wide-area network that had already existed in earlier forms since the 1970s, but was not used commercially, and was not yet available to the public at large. University mainframe computer systems were connected by various systems including the Joint Academic NETwork (JANET) in the United Kingdom.

Once the cost of per-computer connection was reduced into double digit sums, there was a rush to connect just about every computer to a LAN. I remember negotiating a deal across several departments of the university I worked for so that we could place a combined order for about 300 network adapter cards for all our PCs and thus make a large bulk saving on cost. Can you imagine the transformational effect of moving from a collection of hundreds of isolated PCs to a large networked infrastructure in a short timeframe? When you consider scaling this up across many universities and businesses simultaneously, you start to realize the impact networking had. Not only were the computers within organizations being connected to LANs in very large numbers but also the organizations were connecting their internal LANs to the Internet (which became much more accessible as the demand to connect brought about service provision companies and the cost of connecting reduced dramatically).

Suddenly, you could transmit data between remote locations, or log in to remote computers and access resources, from the computer on your desk. Initially, wide-area networking was dominated by e-mail and remote connections using Telnet or rlogin, while local area networking was dominated by resource sharing and file transfers. Once the infrastructure was commonplace and the number of users reached a critical mass, there was a sustained increase in the variety of applications that used network communications, and as bandwidths increased and reliability improved, this gave rise to the now common e-commerce and media-streaming applications not previously feasible.

Distributed systems can be considered an evolutionary step beyond applications that simply use network connections directly. Early networked applications suffered from a lack of transparency. For example, users would have to know the address of the other computer and the protocol being used and would have no way to ensure the application was running at the remote end. Such applications required that users have significant knowledge about the system configuration and did not scale well. Distributed systems employ a number of techniques and services to hide the details of the underlying network (e.g. to allow the various components of the system to automatically locate each other, and may even automatically start up remote services if not already running when a request is made). The user need not know details such as the architecture of the service or the number of or location of its components. The fundamental goal of distributed system design is to hide its internal detail, architecture, location of components, etc., from users, making the system of parts appear as a single coherent whole. This increases usability and reliability.

In recent years, distributed systems have come to dominate almost all business computing, including e-commerce, and also in the form of online banking, online stock brokerage, and a wide range of other Internet-based services, and also a large fraction of nonbusiness computing too, including gaming and e-government. Almost all applications are either distributed or at least use the services of networks in some form; an example of this latter category is a word processor which runs on the local computer but saves a file on a network drive (one that is held on a file server rather than the local machine), and which uses the Internet to access a remotely located help file. A question I ask my students at the beginning of each course is to consider the applications they use most commonly and to think about the underlying communication requirements of these. Ask yourself how many applications you have used this week which operate entirely on a single platform without any communication with another system?

When I first taught distributed systems concepts, I did so using the future tense to describe how they would become increasingly dominant due to their various characteristics and benefits. Now they are one of the most common types of software system in use. I can appreciate the number of lower-level activities that takes place behind the scenes to carry out seemingly simple (from the user perspective) operations. I am aware of the underlying complexity involved and realize just how impressive the achievement of transparency has become, such that for most of the time users are totally unaware of this underlying complexity and of the distribution itself.

This section has set the scene for this book. Distributed systems are here to stay and will be ever more dominant in all walks of our increasingly online and information-dependent lives. It is important to understand the complexities of these systems and to appreciate the need for careful design and development by an army of well informed and highly skilled engineers. This book contributes to this effort by providing a solid introduction to the key concepts and challenges involved.

1.3 **INTRODUCTION TO DISTRIBUTED SYSTEMS**

This section provides an essential concise background to distributed systems. This serves as a brief primer and sets the scene for the four core chapters. Distributed systems concepts are discussed throughout the book, forming a backdrop to the core chapters and are examined in depth in Chapter 6. There are also three distributed application case studies, one of which runs throughout the core chapters and the remaining two are presented in depth in Chapter 7.

A distributed computing system is one where the resources used by applications are spread across numerous computers which are connected by a network. Various services are provided to facilitate the operation of distributed applications. This is in contrast to the simpler centralized model of computing in which resources are located on a single computer and the processing work can be carried out without any communication with, or dependency on, other computers.

A distributed application is one in which the program logic is spread across two or more software components which may execute on different computers within a distributed system. The components have to communicate and coordinate their actions in order to carry out the computing task of the application.

1.3.1 **BENEFITS AND CHALLENGES OF DISTRIBUTED SYSTEMS**

The distributed computer system approach has several important benefits which arise from the ability to use several computers simultaneously in cooperative ways. These benefits include:

- The ability to scale up the system (because additional resources can be added incrementally).
- The ability to make the system reliable (because there can be multiple copies of resources and services spread around the system, faults which prevent access to one replica instance of a resource or service can be masked by using another instance).
- The ability to achieve high performance (because the computation workload can be spread across multiple processing entities).
- The ability to geographically distribute processing and resources based on application-specific requirements and user locality.

However, the fact that applications execute across several computers simultaneously also gives rise to a number of significant challenges for distributed computing. Some of the main challenges which must be understood and overcome when building distributed systems include:

- Distributed systems exhibit several forms of complexity, in terms of their structure, the communication and control relationships between components, and the behavior that results. This complexity increases with the scale of the system and makes it difficult to test systems and predict their behavior.
- Services and resources can be replicated; this requires special management to ensure that the load is spread across the resources and to ensure that updates to resources are propagated to all instances.
- Dynamic configuration changes can occur, both in the system resources and in the workload placed on the system. This can lead to abrupt changes in availability and performance.
- Resources can be dispersed and moved throughout the system but processes need to be able to find them on demand. Access to resources must therefore be facilitated by naming schemes and support services which allow for resources to be found automatically.

- Multiple processes access shared resources. Such access must be regulated through the use of special mechanisms to ensure that the resources remain consistent. Updates of a particular resource may need to be serialized to ensure that each update is carried out to completion without interference from other accesses.

1.3.2 **THE NATURE OF DISTRIBUTION**

Distributed systems can vary in character depending on which aspects of systems are distributed and the way in which the distribution is achieved. Aspects of systems which can be distributed include:

- **Files**: Distributed file systems were one of the earliest forms of distribution and are commonplace now. Files can be spread across the system to share the service load over multiple file server processes. Files can also be replicated with copies located at multiple file server instances to provide greater accessibility and robustness if a single copy of a file is destroyed.
- **Data**: Distributed databases allow geographical dispersion of data so that it is local to the users who need it; this achieves lower access latency. The distribution also spreads the load across multiple servers and as with file services, database contents can also be replicated for robustness and increased availability.
- **Operating System**: The operating system can be distributed across multiple computers. The goal is to provide an abstract single computer system image in which a process appears to execute without direct binding to any particular host computer. Of course the actual process instructions are physically executed on one particular host, but the details of this are masked by the process-to-operating system interface. Middleware essentially achieves the same thing at one level higher, i.e., middleware is a virtual service layer that sits on top of traditional node-centric operating systems to provide a single system abstraction to processes.
- Security and authentication mechanisms can be distributed across computers to ensure consistency and prevent weak entry points. The benefits include the fact that having consistent management of the security across whole systems facilitates better oversight and control.
- **Workload**: Processing tasks can be spread across the processing resources dynamically to share (even out) the load. The main goal is to improve overall performance by taking load from heavily utilized resources and placing it on underutilized resources. Great care must be taken to ensure that such schemes remain stable under all workload conditions (i.e. that load oscillation does not occur) and that the overheads of using such a scheme (the monitoring, management, and task transfer actions that occur) do not outweigh the benefits.
- Support services (services which support the operation of distributed systems) such as name services, event notification schemes, and systems management services can themselves be distributed to improve their own effectiveness.
- User applications can be functionally divided into multiple components and these components are distributed within a system for a wide variety of reasons. Typically, there will be a user-local component (which provides the user interface as well as some local processing and user-specific data storage and management), and one or more user-remote parts which are located adjacent to shared data and other resources. This aspect of distribution is the primary focus of this book.

1.3.3 **SOFTWARE ARCHITECTURES FOR DISTRIBUTED APPLICATIONS**

The architecture of an application is the structure by which its various components are interconnected. This is a very important factor which impacts on the overall quality and performance. There are several main aspects that affect the structure of software systems; these include:

- The number of types of components.
- The number of instances of each component type.
- The cardinality and intensity of interconnections between the component instances, with other components of the same type and/or of other types.
- Whether connectivity is statically decided or determined dynamically based on the configuration of the run-time system and/or the application context.

The simplest distributed systems comprise two components. When these are of the same type (i.e. each component has the same functionality and purpose), the architecture is described as peer-to-peer. Peer-to-peer applications often rely on ad hoc connectivity as components are dynamically discovered and also depart the system independently; this is especially the case in mobile computing applications in which peer-to-peer computing is particularly popular.

Client server applications comprise two distinct component types, where server components provide some sort of service to the client components, usually on an on-demand basis driven by the client. The smallest client server applications comprise a single component of each type. There can be multiple instances of either component type and most business applications that have this architecture have a relatively high ratio of clients to servers. This works on the basis of statistical multiplexing because client lifetimes tend to be short and collectively the requests they make to the server are dispersed over time.

Applications that comprise three or more types of components are termed three-tier or multi-tier applications. The basic approach is to divide functionality on a finer-grained basis than with two-tier applications such as client server. The various areas of functionality (such as the user interface aspect, the security aspect, the database management aspect, and the core business logic aspect) can be separated each into one or more separate components. This leads to flexible systems where different types of components can be replicated independently of the other types or relocated to balance availability and workload in the system.

Hybrid architectures can be created which combine concepts from the basic models. For example, in client server applications, the client components do not interact directly with each other and in many applications they do not interact at all. Where there is communication between clients, it occurs indirectly via the server. A hybrid could be created where clients communicate directly with other clients, i.e. adding a peer-to-peer aspect, but in such cases, great care must be taken to manage the trade-off between the added value to the application and the increased complexity and interaction intensity. In general, keeping the interaction intensity as low as possible and using hierarchical architectures rather than flat schemes leads to good outcomes in terms of scalability, maintainability, and extensibility of applications.

1.3.4 **METRICS FOR MEASURING THE QUALITY OF DISTRIBUTED SYSTEMS AND APPLICATIONS**

Requirements of distributed applications fall into two categories: those that are related to the functional behavior of the application and those which are related to the overall quality of the application in terms of aspects such as responsiveness and robustness. The latter are called nonfunctional requirements because they cannot be implemented as functions. For example, you cannot write a software function called "responsiveness" which can control this characteristic; instead, characteristics such as responsiveness are achieved through the design of the entire system. There is a cyclic relationship in which almost all functional–behavior parts of an application will typically contribute to the achievement of the nonfunctional aspects, which in turn influence the quality by which the functional requirements are met. It is thus very important that all stages of the design and development of distributed applications place very high importance on the nonfunctional requirements. In some respects, it is even more important to emphasize the nonfunctional requirements because the functional requirements are more likely to be self-defining and thus less likely to be overlooked. For example, a functional requirement such as "back up all transaction logs at the end of each day" can be clearly stated and specific mechanisms can be identified and implemented. The functionality can be easily tested and checked for conformance. However, it is not so straightforward to specify and to ensure the achievement of the nonfunctional requirements such as scalability and robustness.

The functional requirements are application-specific and can relate to behavior or outcomes such as sequencing of activities, computational outputs, control actions, security restrictions, and so forth. These must be defined precisely in the context of a particular application, along with clear test specifications so that the developers can confirm the correct interpretation of the requirement and that the end-result operates correctly.

Nonfunctional requirements are less clearly defined generally and open to interpretation to some extent. Typical nonfunctional requirements include scalability, availability, robustness, responsiveness, and transparency. While all of these requirements contribute to the measure of quality of the distributed application, it is transparency which is considered to be the most important in general. Transparency can be described at the highest level as "hiding the details of the multiplicity and distribution of components such that users are presented with the illusion of a single system." Transparency provision at the system level also reduces the burden on application developers so that they can focus their efforts on the business logic of the application and not have to deal with all the vast array of technical issues arising because of distribution. For example, the availability of a name service removes the need for developers to build name-to-address resolution mechanisms into applications, thus reducing the complexity of applications as well as reducing development time and cost.

Transparency is a main cross-cutting theme in this book and various aspects of it are discussed in depth in several places. It is such a broad concept that it is subdivided into several forms, each of which plays a different role in achieving high quality systems.

1.3.5 INTRODUCTION TO TRANSPARENCY

Transparency can be categorized into a variety of forms which are briefly introduced below. Transparency is discussed in greater detail throughout the book. It is discussed contextually in relation to the various topics covered in the four core chapters, and is covered in significant depth as a subject in its own right in Chapter 6.

1.3.5.1 Access Transparency

Access transparency requires that objects are accessed with the same operations regardless of whether they are local or remote. That is, the interface to access a particular object should be consistent for that object, no matter where it is actually stored in the system.

1.3.5.2 Location Transparency

Location transparency is the ability to access objects without knowledge of their location. This is usually achieved by making access requests based on an object's name or ID which is known by the application making the request. A service within the system then resolves this name or ID reference into a current location.

1.3.5.3 Replication Transparency

Replication transparency is the ability to create multiple copies of objects without any effect of the replication seen by applications that use the objects. It should not be possible for an application to determine the number of replicas, or to be able to see the identities of specific replica instances. All copies of a replicated data resource, such as files, should be maintained such that they have the same contents and thus any operation applied to one replica must yield the same results as if applied to any other replica.

1.3.5.4 Concurrency Transparency

Concurrency transparency requires that concurrent processes can share objects without interference. This means that the system should provide each user with the illusion that they have exclusive access to the objects. Mechanisms must be in place to ensure that the consistency of shared data resources is maintained despite being accessed and updated by multiple processes.

1.3.5.5 Migration Transparency

Migration transparency requires that data objects can be moved without affecting the operation of applications that use those objects, and that processes can be moved without affecting their operations or results.

1.3.5.6 Failure Transparency

Failure transparency requires that faults are concealed such that applications can continue to function without any impact on behavior or correctness arising from the fault.

1.3.5.7 Scaling Transparency

Scaling transparency requires that it should be possible to scale up an application, service, or system without changing the underlying system structure or algorithms. Achieving this is largely dependent on efficient design, in terms of the use of resources, and especially in terms of the intensity of communication.

1.3.5.8 Performance Transparency

Performance transparency requires that the performance of systems should degrade gracefully as the load on the system increases. Consistency of performance is important for predictability and is a significant factor in determining the quality of the user experience.

1.3.5.9 Distribution Transparency

Distribution transparency requires that the presence of the network and the physical separation of components are hidden such that distributed application components operate as though they are all local to each other (i.e. running on the same computer) and, therefore, do not need to be concerned with details of network connections and addresses.

1.3.5.10 Implementation Transparency

Implementation transparency means hiding the details of the ways in which components are implemented. For example, this can include enabling applications to comprise components developed in different languages in which case, it is necessary to ensure that the semantics of communication, such as in method calls, is preserved when these components interoperate.

1.3.5.11 Achieving Transparency

The relative importance of the various forms of transparency is system-dependent and also application-dependent within systems. However, access and location transparencies can be considered as generic requirements in any distributed system. Sometimes, the provision of these two forms of transparency is a prerequisite step toward the provision of other forms (such as migration transparency and failure transparency). Some of the transparency forms will not be necessary in all systems; for example, if all parts of applications are developed with the same language and run on the same platform type, then implementation transparency becomes irrelevant.

   The various forms of transparency are achieved in different ways, but in general this is resultant of a combination of the design of the applications themselves as well as the provision of appropriate support services at the system level. A very important example of such a service is a name service, which is the basis for the provision of location transparency in many systems.

1.4 INTRODUCTION TO THE CASE STUDIES

Distributed applications are multifaceted multicomponent software which can exhibit rich and complex behaviors. It is therefore very important to anchor theoretical and mechanistic aspects to relevant examples of real applications. The writing of this book has been inspired by an undergraduate course entitled Systems Programming that has been developed and delivered over a period of 13 years. This course has a theory-meets-practice emphasis in which the lecture sessions introduce and discuss the various theory, concepts, and mechanisms, and then the students go into the laboratory to carry out programming tasks applying and investigating the concepts. A favorite coursework task for this course has been the design and development of a distributed game; specifically for the coursework, it must be a game with a client server architecture that can be played across a network. The students are free to choose the game that they will implement, and it is made clear to the students that the assessment is fundamentally concerned with the communication and software-architecture aspects, and not, for example, concerned with graphical interface design (although many have been impressive in this regard too). By choosing their own game, the students take ownership and engage strongly in the task. The game theme certainly injects a lot of fun into the laboratory sessions, and I am certainly a keen advocate of making learning fun, but it should also be appreciated that the functional and nonfunctional requirements of a distributed game are similar to those of many distributed business applications and thus the learning outcomes are highly transferable.

1.4.1 THE MAIN (DISTRIBUTED GAME) CASE STUDY

In keeping with the coursework theme described above, the main case study application used in the book is a distributed version of the game Tic-Tac-Toe (also known as Noughts-and-Crosses). The business logic and control logic for this game has been functionally divided across the client and server components. Multiple players, each using an instance of the client component, can connect to the game server and select other players to challenge in a game. The actual game logic is not particularly complex, and thus it does not distract from the architectural and communication aspects that are the main focus of the case study.

The case study runs through the core chapters of the book (the four viewpoints), placing the theory and concepts into an application context and also providing continuity and important cross-linking between those chapters. This approach facilitates reflection across the different viewpoints and facilitates understanding of some of the design challenges and the potential conflicts between the various design requirements that can arise when developing distributed applications.

The Tic-Tac-Toe game has been built into the Distributed Systems Workbench (see later in this chapter) so that you can explore the behavior of the application as you follow the case study explanation throughout the book. The entire source code is provided as part of the accompanying resources.

Figure 1.1 shows the distributed game in use; there are two client processes connected to a server process and a game is in play between the two clients, mediated by the server. For demonstration purposes, the game has been designed so that all components can run on a single computer, as was

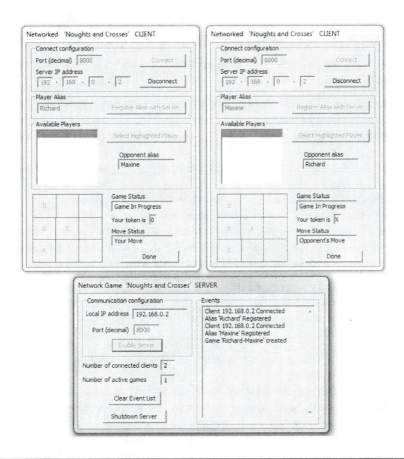

FIGURE 1.1

The Tic-Tac-Toe game in play.

the case in the scenario illustrated. However, the normal use mode of the game is to run the different components on different computers.

1.4.2 THE ADDITIONAL CASE STUDIES

Due to the very wide scope of distributed systems, additional case studies are necessary to ensure that a variety of architectures, functionalities, and communication techniques are evaluated. Two additional case studies are therefore provided in the final chapter. These are covered in depth taking the reader through the development life cycle and including activities ranging from requirements analysis through to testing.

The first of these case studies is a time-service client which accesses the standard NIST time service using the Network Time Protocol. The second case study is an Event Notification Service (ENS), complete with a sample distributed application comprising event publisher and consumer components which communicate indirectly via the ENS. The application components have been developed in a variety of languages to facilitate exploration of interoperability and issues relating to heterogeneous systems.

1.5 INTRODUCTION TO SUPPLEMENTARY MATERIAL AND EXERCISES

A significant amount of supplementary material accompanies this book. The supplementary material falls into several categories:

- Three complete case studies with full source code and detailed documentation.
- Extensive sample code and executable code to support practical activities in chapters and to support the programming challenges (including starting points for development and example solutions).
- Special editions of the established Workbenches suite of teaching and learning tools (see later in this chapter).
- Detailed documentation accompanying the Workbenches, describing further experiments and exploitation of the supported concepts and mechanisms.
- Teaching support materials including student coursework task specifications and introductory laboratory exercises to familiarize students with the basics of communication using the TCP and UDP protocols; these are based on provided sample code which students can extend.

Due to the complex and dynamic nature of distributed systems, it can be challenging to convey details of their behavior, and the way in which design choices impact this behavior, to students. Inconsistencies can arise in the way students perceive different descriptions of behavior presented to them, for example:

- The theoretical behavior of a system (for example, as you might read in a book, instruction manual, or lecture presentation).
- An individual's expectation of behavior, based on extrapolation of experience in other systems, or previous experience with the same system but with different configuration.
- The observed behavior of a system when an empirical experiment is carried out; especially since this can be sensitive to the system configuration and exact method of carrying out the experiment and thus typically the results obtained require some skill in their interpretation.

To understand in depth, the student needs to be able to see the way in which applications' behavior is affected by the combination of its configuration and its run-time environment. This highlights why this book is structured as it is, with practical activities interspersed throughout. There is a risk when studying complex systems of gaining a superficial understanding based on a subset of the theory, without appreciating the underlying reasons for why systems are as they are, and behave as they do. The inclusion of experiments to provide a practical grounding for the theory concepts and to make links between observed phenomenon and the underlying causes is therefore very important (see next section).

1.5.1 IN-TEXT ACTIVITIES

In-text activities are embedded into the main text of the book and form an important part of the theory-meets-practice approach. These practical activities are tightly integrated with the relevant sections of the discussion, and are intended to be carried out as a parallel activity to reading the book. The activities are identified using activity boxes which set them out in a consistent format, comprising:

- An explanation of the activity, the intended learning outcomes, and its relevance to the particular section of the book.
- Identification of which supplementary material is required.
- Description of the method for carrying out the activity.
- Evaluation, including discussion of the outcomes, results observed, and their implications.
- Reflection, questions and/or challenges to encourage further independent investigation and to reinforce understanding.

Activity I1 provides an example of the format of the in-text activities and explains how to access the book's supporting resources from the companion Web site.

ACTIVITY I1: ACCESSING THE SUPPLEMENTARY MATERIAL

The four core chapters (the process view, the communication view, the resource view, the architecture view) and the distributed systems chapter each contain embedded practical activities which should, where possible be completed as the book is read. These activities have been designed to anchor key concepts and to allow the reader to explore more broadly, as many of the activities involve configurable experiments or simulations which support what-if exploration.

The activities are set out in a consistent format with identified learning outcomes, a clear method, expected results, and reflection. This first activity introduces the style of the subsequent activities which are embedded into the text of the other chapters. It has the same layout as those activities.

Prerequisites: Any specific prerequisites for the activity will be identified here; this activity has none.

Learning Outcomes
1. Familiarization with the style and purpose of the in-text activities.
2. Familiarization with the support resources.

Method: This activity is carried out in two steps:
1. Locate and visit the book's online resources Web site.
    i.   The book's online Web site is located at: http://booksite.elsevier.com/9780128007297.
    ii. The resources are accessible via the "Resources" tab at the bottom of the page.
2. Copy resources locally to your computer.

Please note that all materials, programs, source code, and documentation are provided as is, in good faith but without guarantee or warranty. They are provided with the best intention of being a valuable resource to aid investigation and understanding of the text book that they accompany.

The recommended way to use the supporting resources is to create a separate folder named "SystemsProgramming" on your computer to hold the resources that relate to each chapter, and to copy the resources across in their entirety.
Notes:

- Obtaining all of the resources at the outset will make the reading of the book flow smoothly without the interruption of regularly having to revisit the Web site.

- The executable applications, including the Workbenches are designed to be downloaded onto your computer before running.

Expected Outcome
At the end of this activity, you should be aware of the nature and extent of the supporting resources available. You should know how to copy the resources to your own computer to facilitate their use.

Reflection
For each of the subsequent activities, there is a short reflection section which provides encouragement and steering for additional experimentation and evaluation.

1.6 THE WORKBENCHES SUITE OF INTERACTIVE TEACHING AND LEARNING TOOLS

The book is accompanied by a suite of sophisticated interactive teaching and learning applications (called Workbenches) that the author has developed over a period of 13 years to promote student-centered and flexible approaches to teaching and learning, and to enable students to work remotely, interactively and at their own pace. The Networking Workbench, Operating Systems Workbench, and Distributed Systems Workbench provide combinations of configurable simulations, emulations, and implementations to facilitate experimentation with many of the underlying concepts of systems. The Workbenches have been tried and tested with many cohorts of students and are used as complementary support to several courses by several lecturers at present. Specific technical content in the book is linked to particular exercises and experiments which can be carried out using the Workbench software tools. For example, there are specific experiments in the Networking Workbench that deal with addressing, buffering, blocking versus nonblocking socket IO modes, and the operation of the TCP and UDP protocols.

The motivation for developing the Workbenches came from my experience of teaching aspects of computer systems which are fundamentally dynamic in their behavior. It is very difficult to convey the dynamic aspects of systems such as communication (e.g. connectivity, message sequence), scheduling, or message buffering with traditional teaching techniques, especially in a classroom environment. It is also problematic to move too soon to a program-developmental approach, as inexperienced programmers get bogged down with the problems of programming itself (syntax errors, programming concepts, etc.) and often the networking or distributed systems learning outcomes are not reached or fully developed due to slow progression.

The Workbenches were developed to fill these gaps. Lecturers can demonstrate concepts with live experiments and simulations in lectures for example, and students can explore the behaviors of protocols and mechanisms in live experiments but without actually having to write the underlying code. A series of progressive activities have been developed to accompany the workbench engines, and have been very well received by students. Specific advantages of the Workbenches include:

- The replacement of *static* representations of systems and systems behavior with *dynamic*, interactive, user-configured simulations (showing how components interact and also the temporal relationships within those interactions).
- Readers can learn at their own pace, with configurable and repeatable experiments.
- The Workbenches can be used in lectures and tutorials to demonstrate concepts as well as in the laboratory and unsupervised, and thus reinforce the nature of the book as an ideal course guide.
- The Workbenches are accompanied by progressive laboratory exercises, designed to encourage analysis and critical thinking. As such, the tools bring the content of the book to life, and allow the reader to see first-hand the behaviors and effects of the various operating systems mechanisms, distributed systems mechanisms, and networking protocols.

A special Systems Programming edition of the Workbenches has been released specifically to accompany this book. This edition is also referred to as release 3.1.

1.6.1 OPERATING SYSTEMS WORKBENCH 3.1 "SYSTEMS PROGRAMMING EDITION"

Configurable simulations of process scheduling and scheduling algorithms; threads, thread priorities, thread locking, and mutual exclusion; deadlock; and memory management and virtual memory.

1.6.2 THE NETWORKING WORKBENCH 3.1 "SYSTEMS PROGRAMMING EDITION"

Practical experimentation with the UDP and TCP protocols; ports, addressing, binding, blocking and nonblocking socket IO modes; message buffering; unicast, multicast, and broadcast modes of communication; communication deadlock (distributed deadlock); and DNS name resolution.

1.6.3 DISTRIBUTED SYSTEMS WORKBENCH 3.1 "SYSTEMS PROGRAMMING EDITION"

Practical experimentation with an election algorithm; a directory service; a client server application (the distributed game that forms the main case study); one-way communication; and the Network Time Protocol (the network time service client case study in the final chapter).

1.7 SAMPLE CODE AND RELATED EXERCISES
1.7.1 SOURCE CODE, IN C++, C#, AND JAVA

There are numerous complete applications and also some skeletal code which are used as a starting point for readers to get begin developing their own applications, as well as serving as the basis and starting point for some of the end of chapter exercises. There are examples written in various languages and the event notification server case study purposefully demonstrates interoperability between components developed using three different languages.

1.7.2 APPLICATION DEVELOPMENT EXERCISES

Chapters 2–7 include application development exercises related to the specific chapter's content. Working examples are provided and, in some cases, these lead on from the in-text activities, so readers will already be familiar with the functionality of the application. The general approach encouraged is to start by examining the provided sample code and to relate the application's behavior to the program logic. Understanding can be enhanced by compiling and single-stepping through the sample code instructions. Once a clear understanding has been achieved, the second step is to extend the functionality of the application by adding new features as set out in the specific task. Sample solutions are provided where appropriate.

THE PROCESS VIEW

CHAPTER CONTENTS

2.1 RATIONALE AND OVERVIEW

The process is the ultimate endpoint of communication in distributed systems. Within a particular system or application, multiple processes execute as separate entities, scheduled by the operating system. However, for these processes to act cooperatively and coherently to solve application problems, they need to communicate. Understanding the nature of processes and the way they interact with the operating system is a key prerequisite to designing systems of processes that communicate to build higher-level structures and thus solve application-level problems of distributed systems.

The abbreviation IO will be used when discussing input and output in generic contexts.

2.2 PROCESSES

This section examines the nature of processes and the way in which they are managed by operating systems. In particular, the focus is on the way in which input and output (IO) from devices is mapped onto the IO steams of a process and the way in which interprocess communication (IPC) is achieved with pipelines.

2.2.1 BASIC CONCEPTS

It is first necessary to introduce the basic concepts of processes and their interaction with systems. This sets the scene for the subsequent deeper investigation.

We start with the definition of a program.

A program is a list of instructions together with structure and sequence information to control the order in which the instructions are carried out.

Now let us consider the definition of a process.

A process is the running instance of a program.

This means that when we run (or execute) a program, a process is created (see below).

The most important distinction between a program and a process is that a program does not *do* anything; rather, it is a description of *how to do* something. When a process is created, it will carry out the instructions of the related program.

A set of instructions that are supplied with home-assembly furniture are a useful analogy to a computer program. They provide a sequenced (numbered) set of individual steps describing how to assemble the furniture. The furniture will not be assembled just because of the existence of the instructions. It is only when someone actually carries out the instructions, in the correct order, that the furniture gets built. The act of following the instructions step by step is analogous to the computer process.

Another important relationship between a program and a process is that the same program can be run (executed) many times, each time giving rise to a unique process. We can extend the home-assembly furniture analogy to illustrate; each set of furniture is delivered with a copy of the instructions (i.e., the same "program"), but these are instantiated (i.e., the instructions are carried out) at many different times and in different places, possibly overlapping in time such that two people may be building their furniture at the same time—unbeknownst to each other.

2.2.2 CREATING A PROCESS

The first step is to write a program that expresses the logic required to solve a particular problem. The program will be written in a programming language of your choice, for example, C++ or C#, enabling you to use a syntax that is suitably expressive to represent high-level ideas such as reading input from a keyboard device, manipulating data values, and displaying output on a display screen.

A compiler is then used to convert your human-friendly high-level instructions into low-level instructions that the microprocessor understands (thus the low-level instruction sequence that the compiler generates is called machine code). Things can go wrong at this point in two main ways. Syntax errors are those errors that break the rules of the language being used. Examples of syntax errors include misspelled variable names or keywords, incorrect parameter types, or incorrect numbers of parameters being passed to methods and many other similar mistakes (if you have done even a little programming, you can probably list at least three more types of syntax error that you have made yourself). These errors are automatically detected by the compiler and error messages are provided to enable you to locate and fix the problems. Thus, there should be no ongoing issues arising from syntax once you get the code to compile.

Semantic errors are errors in the presentation of your logic. In other words, the meaning as expressed by the logic of the program code is not the intended meaning of the programmer. These errors are potentially far more serious because generally, there will be no way for the compiler to detect them. For example, consider that you have three integer variables A, B, and C and you intend to perform the calculation C = A - B but you accidentally type C = B - A instead! The compiler will not find any errors in your code as it is syntactically correct, and the compiler certainly has no knowledge of the way your program is supposed to work and does not care what actual value or meaning is ascribed to variables A, B, and C. Semantic errors must be prevented by careful design and discipline during implementation and are detected by vigilance on the part of the developer, and this must be supported by a rigorous testing regime.

Let us assume we now have a logically correct program that has been compiled and stored in a file in the form of machine code that the microprocessor hardware can understand. This type of file is commonly referred to as an executable file, because you can "execute" (run) it by providing its name to the operating system. Some systems identify such files with a particular filename extension, for example, the Microsoft Windows system uses the extension ".exe".

It is important to consider the mechanism for executing a program. A program is a list of instructions stored in a file. When we run a program, the operating system reads the list of instructions and creates a process that comprises an in-memory version of the instructions, the variables used in the program, and some other metadata concerning, for example, which instruction is to be executed next. Collectively, this is called the process image and the metadata and variables (i.e., the changeable parts of the image) are called the process state, as the values of these describe, and are dependent on, the state of the process (i.e., the progress of the process through the set of instructions, characterized by the specific sequence of input values in this run-instance of the program). The state is what differentiates several processes of the same program. The operating system will identify the process with a unique *Process IDentifier* (PID). This is necessary because there can be many processes running at the same time in a modern computer system and the operating system has to keep track of the process in terms of, among other things, who owns it, how much processing resource it is using, and which IO devices it is using.

The semantics (logic) represented by the sequence of actions arising from the running of the process is the same as that expressed in the program. For example, if the program adds two numbers first and then doubles the result, the process will perform these actions in the same order and will provide an answer predictable by someone who knows both the program logic and the input values used.

Consider the simplest program execution scenario as illustrated in Figure 2.1.

Figure 2.1 shows the pseudocode for a very simple process. Pseudocode is a way of representing the main logical actions of the program, in a near-natural language way, yet still unambiguously, that is independent of any particular programming language. Pseudocode does not contain the full level of detail that would be provided if the actual program were provided in a particular language such as C++, C#, or Java, but rather is used as an aid to explain the overall function and behavior of programs.

The program illustrated in Figure 2.1 is a very restricted case. The processing itself can be anything you like, but with no input and no output, the program cannot be useful, because the user cannot influence its behavior and the program cannot signal its results to the user.

A more useful scenario is illustrated in Figure 2.2.

```
Start
  Do some processing
End
```

FIGURE 2.1

Pseudocode for a simple process.

```
Start
  Get input
  Do some processing
  Produce output
End
```

FIGURE 2.2

Pseudocode of a simple process with input and output.

This is still conceptually very simple, but now, there is a way to steer the processing to do something useful (the input) and a way to find out the result (the output).

Perhaps the easiest way to build a mental picture of what is happening is to assume that the input device is a keyboard and the output device is the display screen. We could write a program Adder with the logic shown in Figure 2.3.

If I type the number 3 and then the number 6 (the two input values), the output on the display screen will be 9.

More accurately, a process gets its input from an *input stream* and sends its output to an *output stream*. The process when running does not directly control or access devices such as the keyboard and display screen; it is the operating system's job to pass values to and from such devices. Therefore, we could express the logic of program Adder as shown in Figure 2.4.

When the program runs, the operating system can (by default) map the keyboard device to the input stream and the display screen to the output stream.

Let's define a second program Doubler (see Figure 2.5).

We can run the program Doubler, creating a process with the input stream connected to the keyboard and the output stream connected to the display screen. If I type the number 5 (the input), the output on the screen will be 10.

```
Start
    Read a number from the keyboard, store it in variable X
    Read a number from the keyboard, store it in variable Y
    Add X + Y and store the result in variable Z
    Write Z on the display screen
End
```

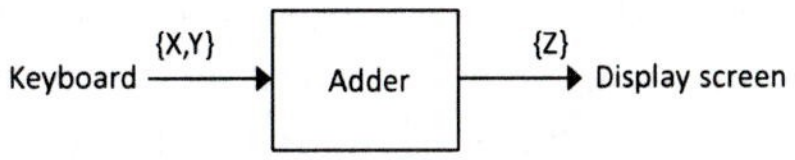

Keyboard —{X,Y}→ [Adder] —{Z}→ Display screen

FIGURE 2.3

Two aspects of the process, the pseudocode and a block representation, which shows the process with its inputs and outputs.

```
Start
    Read a number from the input stream, store it in variable X
    Read a number from the input stream, store it in variable Y
    Add X + Y and store the result in variable Z
    Write Z on the output stream
End
```

Input stream —{X,Y}→ [Adder] —{Z}→ Output stream

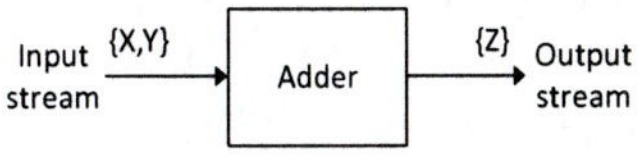

FIGURE 2.4

The Adder process with its input and output streams.

```
Start
    Read a number from the input stream, store it in variable V
    Multiply V * 2 and store result in variable W
    Write W on the output stream
End
```

Input stream —{V}→ [Doubler] —{W}→ Output stream

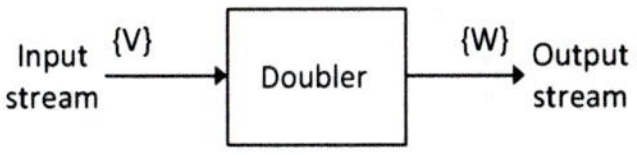

FIGURE 2.5

The Doubler process; pseudocode and representation with input and output streams.

The concept of IO streams gives rise to the possibility that the IO can be connected to many different sources or devices and does not even have to involve the user directly. Instead of the variable W being displayed on the screen, it could be used as the input to another calculation, in another process. Thus, the output of one process becomes the input to another. This is called a pipeline (as it is a connector between two processes, through which data can flow) and is one form of IPC. We use the pipe symbol | to represent this connection between processes. The pipeline is implemented by connecting the output stream of one process to the input stream of another. Notice that it is the operating system that actually performs this connection, and not the processes themselves.

The Adder and Doubler processes could be connected such that the output of Adder becomes the input to Doubler, by connecting the appropriate steams. In this scenario, the input stream for process Adder is mapped to the keyboard, and the output stream for process Doubler is mapped to the display screen. However, the output stream for Adder is now connected to the input stream for Doubler, via a pipeline.

Using the pipe notation, we can write Adder | Doubler.

This is illustrated in Figure 2.6.

If I type the number 3 and then the number 6 (the two input values), the output on the display screen will be 18. The output of process Adder is still 9, but this is not exposed to the outside world (we can call this a *partial result* as the overall computation is not yet complete). Process Doubler takes the value 9 from process Adder and doubles it, giving the value 18, which is then displayed on the screen.

We have reached the first practical activity of this chapter. The activities are each set out in the form of an experiment, with identified learning outcomes and a method to follow.

I have specifically taken the approach of including carefully scoped practical tasks that the reader can carry out as they read the text because the learning outcomes are better reinforced by actually having the hands-on experience. The practical tasks are designed to reinforce the theoretical concepts introduced in the main text. Many of the practical tasks also support and encourage your own exploration by changing parameters or configuration to ask what-if questions.

The presentation of the activities also reports expected outcomes and provides guidance for reflection and in some cases suggestions for further exploration. This is so that readers who are unable to run the experiments at the time of reading can still follow the text.

The first Activity P1 provides an opportunity to investigate IPC using pipes.

The example in Activity P1 is simple, yet nevertheless extremely valuable. It demonstrates several important concepts that are dealt with in later sections:

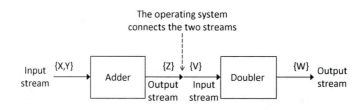

FIGURE 2.6

The Adder and Doubler processes connected by a pipe.

ACTIVITY P1 EXPLORING SIMPLE PROGRAMS, INPUT AND OUTPUT STREAMS, AND PIPELINES

Prerequisites

The instructions below assume that you have previously performed Activity I1 in Chapter 1. This activity places the necessary supplemental resources on your default disk drive (usually C:) in the directory SystemsProgramming. Alternatively, you can manually copy the resources and locate them in a convenient place on your computer and amend the instructions below according to the installation path name used.

Learning Outcomes

This activity illustrates several important concepts that have been discussed up to this point:

1. How a process is created as the running instance of a program by running the program at the command line
2. How the operating system maps input and output devices to the process
3. How two processes can be chained together using a pipeline

Method

This activity is carried out in three steps:

1. Run the Adder.exe program in a command window. Navigate to the ProcessView subfolder of the SystemsProgramming directory and then execute the Adder program by typing Adder.exe followed by the Enter key. The program will now run as a process. It waits until two numbers have been typed (each one followed by the Enter key) and then adds the numbers and displays the result, before exiting.
2. Run the Doubler.exe program in the same manner as for the Adder.exe program in step 1. The process waits for a single number to be typed (followed by the Enter key) and then doubles the number and displays the result, before exiting.
3. Run the Adder and Doubler programs in a pipeline. The goal is to take two numbers input by the user and to display double the sum of the two numbers. We can write this formulaically as:

$$Z = 2 * (X + Y)$$

where X and Y are the numbers entered by the user and Z is the result that is displayed. For example, if $X = 16$ and $Y = 18$, the value of Z will be 68.

The command-line syntax to achieve this is Adder | Doubler.

The first process will wait for two numbers to be typed by the user. The output of the Adder process will be automatically mapped onto the input of the Doubler process (because the | was used), and the Doubler process will double the value it receives, which is then output to the display screen.

The image below shows the results when the three steps above are followed:

ACTIVITY P1 EXPLORING SIMPLE PROGRAMS, INPUT AND OUTPUT STREAMS, AND PIPELINES—Cont'd

Expected Outcome

For each of the first two steps, you will see that the program was executed as a process that follows the logic of the program (see the source code in file Adder.cpp and also Doubler.cpp). Notice that by default, the operating system automatically mapped the keyboard as the input device and the display screen as the output device although this was not specified in the program. You will also see how the operating system remaps the input and output streams of the processes when the pipeline is used. The individual programs are used as building blocks to construct more complex logic.

Reflection

1. Study the source code of the two programs and read the built-in comments.
2. Think about the different roles of the programmer who wrote the two programs, the operating system, and the user who types the command line and provides the input and how each influence the end result. It is important to realize that the overall behavior seen in this activity is a result of a combination of the program logic, the operating system control of execution, and the user's input data.

---

1. Processes can communicate; for example, the output from one process can become the input to another process.
2. In order for processes to communicate, there needs to be a mechanism to facilitate this. In the simple scenario here, the operating system facilitates the IPC by using the pipeline mechanism as a connector between the output stream of one process and the input stream of the other.
3. Higher-level functionality can be built up from simpler logic building blocks. In the example, the externally visible logic is to add two numbers and double the result; the user sees the final result on the display screen and does not need to know how it was achieved. This is the concept of modularity and is necessary to achieve sophisticated behavior in systems while keeping the complexity of individual logical elements to manageable levels.

2.3 PROCESS SCHEDULING

This section examines the role the operating system plays in managing the resources of the system and scheduling processes.

A process is "run" by having its instructions executed in the central processing unit (CPU). Traditionally, general-purpose computers have had a single CPU, which had a single core (the core is the part that actually executes a process). It is becoming common in modern systems to have multiple CPUs and/or for each CPU to have multiple cores. Since each core can run a single process, a multiple core system can run multiple processes at the same time. For the purpose of limiting the complexity of the discussion in this book, we shall assume the simpler, single-core architecture, which means that only a single process can actually execute instructions at any instant (i.e., only one process is running at a time).

The most fundamental role of an operating system is to manage the resources of the system. The CPU is the primary resource, as no work can be done without it. Thus, an important aspect of resource management is controlling usage of the CPU (better known as process scheduling). Modern operating systems have a special component, the scheduler, which is specifically responsible for managing the processes in the system and selecting which one should run at any given moment. This is the most obvious and direct form of interaction between processes and the operating system, although indirect interaction also arises through the way in which the operating system controls the other resources that a particular process may be using.

Early computers were very expensive and thus were shared by large communities of users. A large mainframe computer may have been shared across a whole university, for example. A common way to accommodate the needs of many users was to operate in "batch mode." This required that users submit their programs to be run into a "batch queue" and the system operators would oversee the running of these programs one by one. In terms of resource management, it is very simple; each process is given the entire resources of the computer, until either the task completes or a run-time limit may be imposed. The downside of this approach is that a program may be held in the queue for several hours. Many programs were run in overnight batches, which meant that the results of the run were not available until the next day.

The Apollo space missions to the moon in the 1960s and 1970s provide an interesting example of the early use of computers in critical control applications. The processing power of the onboard Apollo Guidance Computer[1] (AGC) was a mere fraction of that of modern systems, often likened simplistically to that of a modern desktop calculator, although through sophisticated design, the limited processing power of this computer was used very effectively. The single-core AGC had a real-time scheduler, which could support eight processes simultaneously; each had to yield if another higher-priority task was waiting. The system also supported timer-driven periodic tasks within processes. This was a relatively simple system by today's standards, although the real-time aspects would still be challenging from a design and test viewpoint. In particular, this was a closed system in which all task types were known in advance and simulations of the various workload combinations could be run predeployment to ensure correctness in terms of timing and resource usage. Some modern systems are closed in this way, in particular embedded systems such as the controller in your washing machine or the engine management system in your car (see below). However, the general-purpose computers that include desktop computers, servers in racks, smartphones, and tablets are open and can run programs that the user chooses, in any combination; thus, the scheduler must be able to ensure efficient use of resources and also to protect the quality of service (QoS) requirements of tasks in respect to, for example, responsiveness.

Some current embedded systems provide useful examples of a fixed-purpose computer. Such a system only performs a design-time specified function and therefore does not need to switch between multiple applications. Consider, for example, the computer system that is embedded into a typical washing machine. All of the functionality has been predecided at design time. The user can provide inputs via the controls on the user interface, such as setting the wash temperature or the spin speed, and thus configure the behavior but cannot change the functionality. There is a single program preloaded

---

[1]The actual technical specification of the Apollo Guidance Computer, in use from 1966 until 1975, was a 16-bit processor based on discrete resistor-transistor logic (which predates the superior transistor-transistor logic) and operated at a frequency of 2 MHz. It had 2 kB RAM (which is used to hold variable values, as well as system control information such as the stack) and 36 kB read-only memory, ROM (which is used to store the program code and constant data values). In its day, this represented state-of-the-art technology. For purposes of understanding the performance increases and the cost reduction that has occurred since the time of the Apollo missions, an Atmel ATmega32 microcontroller is an 8-bit single chip computer that operates at 16 MHz and has 2 kB RAM and 33 kB ROM (actually 32k Flash memory, which can be used in the same way as ROM, plus 1 kB of ROM) and costs less than £5 at the time of writing.

ACTIVITY P2 EXAMINE LIST OF PROCESSES ON THE COMPUTER (FOR WINDOWS OPERATING SYSTEMS)

Prerequisites
Requires a Microsoft Windows operating system.

Learning Outcomes
1. To gain an understanding of the typical number of and variety of processes present on a typical general-purpose computer
2. To gain an appreciation of the complexity of activity in multiprocessing environment
3. To gain an appreciation of the need for and importance of scheduling

Method
This activity is performed in two parts, using two different tools to inspect the set of processes running on the computer.

Part 1
Start the Task Manager by pressing the Control, Alt, and Delete keys simultaneously and select "Start Task Manager" from the options presented. Then, select the Applications tab and view the results, followed by the Processes tab, and also view the results. Make sure the "Show processes for all users" checkbox is checked, so that you see everything that is present. Note that this procedure may vary across different versions of the Microsoft operating systems.

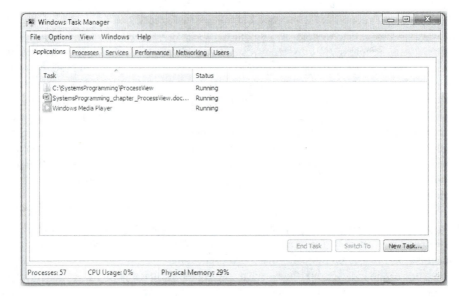

Expected Outcome for Part 1
You will see a new window that contains a list of the applications running on the computer, or a list of the processes present, depending on which tab is selected. Examples from my own computer (which has the Windows 7 Professional operating system) are shown. The first screenshot shows the list of applications, and the second screenshot shows the list of processes.

ACTIVITY P2 EXAMINE LIST OF PROCESSES ON THE COMPUTER (FOR WINDOWS OPERATING SYSTEMS)—Cont'd

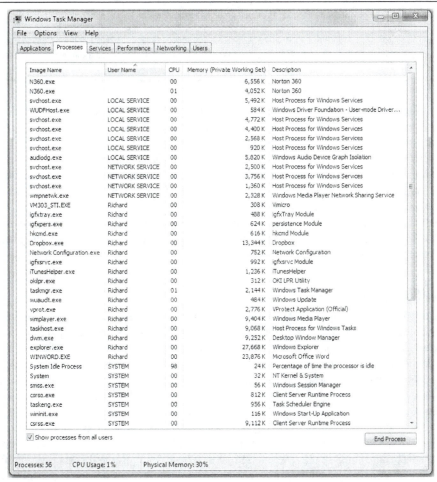

Part 2

Explore the processes present in the system using the TASKLIST command run from a command window. This command gives a different presentation of information than that provided by the Task Manager. Type TASKLIST /? to see the list of parameters that can be used. Explore the results achieved using some of these configuration parameters to see what can you find out about the processes in the system and their current state.

Reflection

You will probably have a good idea which applications are running already (after all, you are the user), so the list of applications will be of no surprise to you. In the examples from my computer, you can see that I was editing a chapter from this book while listening to a CD via the media player application.

However, you will probably see a long list of processes when selecting the Processes tab. Look closely at these processes; is this what you expected? Do you have any idea what all these are doing or why they are needed?

ACTIVITY P2 EXAMINE LIST OF PROCESSES ON THE COMPUTER (FOR WINDOWS OPERATING SYSTEMS)—Cont'd

Note that many of the processes running are "system" processes that are either part of the operating system or otherwise related to resource management; device drivers are a good example of this.

Note especially the "System Idle Process," which in the example above "runs" for 98% of the time. This pseudoprocess runs when no real processes are ready to run, and the share of CPU time it gets is often used as an inverse indication of the overall load on the computer.

---

into these systems, and this program runs as the sole process. Many embedded systems platforms have very limited resources (especially in terms of having a small memory and low processing speed) and thus cannot afford the additional overheads of having an operating system.

Now, bearing in mind how many processes are active on your computer, consider how many processes can run at any given time. For older systems, this is likely to be just 1. For newer systems, which are "dual core," for example, the answer is 2, or 4 if it is "quad core." Even if we had perhaps 32 cores, we would typically still have more processes than cores.

Fundamentally, the need for scheduling is that there tend to be more processes active on a computer than there are processor units, which can deal with them. If this is the case, then something has to arbitrate; this is one of the most important things the operating system does.

2.3.1 SCHEDULING CONCEPTS

Several different scheduling techniques (algorithms) have been devised. These have different characteristics, the most important differentiator being the basis on which tasks are selected to run.

Given that generally there are more processes than processors, the processes can be said to be competing for the processor. To put it another way, the processes each have work to do and it is important that they eventually complete their work, but at any given moment, some of these may be more important, or urgent than others. The scheduler must ensure that wherever possible, the processor is always being used by a process, so that resource is not wasted. The performance of the scheduler is therefore most commonly discussed in terms of the resulting efficiency of the system, and this is measured in terms of the percentage of time that the processing unit is kept busy. "Keeping the processor busy" is commonly expressed as the primary goal of the scheduler. Figures 2.7 and 2.8 illustrate this concept of efficiency.

As shown in Figure 2.7, schedule A uses 8 of the 10 processor timeslots and is thus 80% efficient. The two timeslots that were not used are lost, that resource cannot be reclaimed. Another way to think of this situation is that this system is performing 80% of the work that it could possibly do, so is doing work at 80% of its maximum possible rate.

Figure 2.8 shows the ideal scenario in which every timeslot is used and is thus 100% efficient. This system is performing as much work as it could possibly do, so is operating its maximum possible rate.

FIGURE 2.7

Schedule A uses 8 out of 10 timeslots (a system with three processes).

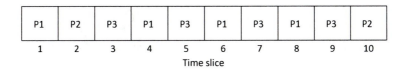

FIGURE 2.8

Schedule B uses 10 out of 10 timeslots (a system with three processes).

2.3.1.1 Time Slices and Quanta

A preemptive scheduler will allow a particular process to run for a short amount of time called a quantum (or time slice). After this amount of time, the process is placed back in the ready queue and another process is placed into the run state (i.e., the scheduler ensures that the processes take turns to run).

The size of a quantum has to be selected carefully. Each time the operating system makes a scheduling decision, it is itself using the processor. This is because the operating system comprises one or more processes and it has to use system processing time to do its own computations in order to decide which process to run and actually move them from state to state; this is called context switching and the time taken is the scheduling overhead. If the quanta are too short, the operating system has to perform scheduling activities more frequently, and thus, the overheads are higher as a proportion of total system processing resource.

On the other hand, if the quanta are too long, the other processes in the ready queue must wait longer between turns, and there is a risk that the users of the system will notice a lack of responsiveness in the applications to which these processes belong.

Figure 2.9 illustrates the effects of quanta size on the total scheduling overheads. Part (a) of the figure shows the situation that arises with very short quanta. The interleaving of processes is very fine, which is good for responsiveness. This means that the amount of time a process must wait before its next quanta of run time is short and thus the process appears to be running continuously to an observer such as a human user who operates on a much slower timeline. To understand this aspect, consider, as analogy, how a movie works. Many frames per second (typically 24 or more) are flashed before the human eye, but the human visual system (the eye and its brain interface) cannot differentiate between the separate frames at this speed and thus interpret the series of frames as a continuous moving image. If the frame rate is reduced to less than about 12 frames per second, a human can perceive them as a series of separate flash-

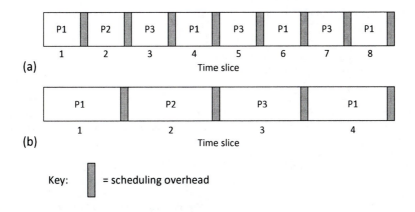

FIGURE 2.9

Quantum size and scheduling overheads.

ing images. In processing systems, shorter quanta give rise to more frequent scheduling activities, which absorbs some of the processing resource. The proportion of this overhead as a fraction of total processing time available increases as the quanta get smaller, and thus, the system can do less useful work in a given time period, so the optimal context switching rate is not simply the fastest rate that can be achieved.

In part (b) of Figure 2.9, the quanta have been increased to approximately double the size of those shown in part a. This increases the coarseness of the process interleaving and could impact on the responsiveness of tasks, especially those that have deadlines or real-time constraints associated with their work. To get an initial understanding of the way this can materialize, imagine a user interface that has a jerky response, where it seems to freeze momentarily between dealing with your input. This jerky response could be a symptom that the process that controls the user interface is not getting a sufficient share of processing time or that the processing time is not being shared on a sufficiently fine-grained basis. Despite the impacts on task responsiveness that can arise with having larger quanta, they are more efficient because the operating system's scheduling activities occur less frequently, thus absorbing a smaller proportion of overall processing resource; for the scenario shown, the scheduling overhead for system (b) is half that of system (a).

Choosing the size of the time quantum is an optimization problem between on the one hand the overall processing efficiency and on the other hand the responsiveness of tasks. To some extent, the ideal value depends on the nature of the applications running in the system. Real-time systems (i.e., ones that have applications with a time-based functionality or dependency, such as streaming video where each frame must be processed with strict timing requirements) generally need to use shorter quanta to achieve finer interleaving and thus ensure the internal deadlines of applications are not missed. Specific scheduling issues arising from deadlines or real-time constraints of processes will be discussed in more detail later.

ACTIVITY P3 EXAMINING SCHEDULING BEHAVIOR WITH REAL PROCESSES—INTRODUCTORY

Prerequisites

The instructions below assume that you have obtained the necessary supplemental resources as explained in Activity P1.

Learning Outcomes

This activity explores the way in which the scheduler facilitates running several processes at the same time:
1. To understand that many processes can be active in a system at the same time
2. To understand how the scheduler creates an illusion that multiple processes are actually running at the same time, by interleaving them on a small timescale
3. To gain experience of command-line arguments
4. To gain experience of using batch files to run applications

Method

This activity is carried out in three parts, using a simple program that writes characters to the screen on a periodic basis, to illustrate some aspects of how the scheduler manages processes.

Part 1
1. Run the PeriodicOutput.exe program in a command window. Navigate to the "ProcessView" subfolder and then execute the PeriodicOutput program by typing PeriodicOutput.exe followed by the Enter key. The program will now run as a process. It will print an error message because it needs some additional information to be typed after the program name. Extra information provided in this way is termed "command-line arguments" and is a very useful and important way of controlling the execution of a program.
2. Look at the error message produced. It is telling us that we must provide two additional pieces of information, which are the length of the time interval (in ms) between printing characters on the display screen and the character that will be printed at the end-of-each time interval.
3. Run the PeriodicOutput.exe program again, this time providing the required command-line parameters.

ACTIVITY P3 EXAMINING SCHEDULING BEHAVIOR WITH REAL PROCESSES—INTRODUCTORY—Cont'd

For example, if you type PeriodicOutput 1000 A, the program will print a series of A's, one each second (1000ms).

As another example, if you type PeriodicOutput 100 B, the program will print a series of B's, one every 1/10th of a second.

Experiment with some other values. Notice that the program will always run for 10s (10,000ms) in total, so the number of characters printed will always be 10,000 divided by the first parameter value. Examine the source code for this program (which is provided as part of the supplemental resources) and relate the program's behavior to the instructions.

Expected Outcome for Part 1

The screenshot below shows the output for a couple of different parameter settings. So far, we have only run one process at a time.

Part 2

1. We will now run several copies of the PeriodicOutput.exe program at the same time. To do this, we shall use a batch file. A batch file is a script containing a series of commands to be executed by the system; for the purpose of this activity, you can think of it as a metaprogram that allows us to specify how programs will be executed. The batch file we shall use is called "PeriodicOutput_Starter.bat". You can examine the contents of this file by typing "cat PeriodicOutput_Starter.bat" at the command prompt. You will see that this file contains three lines of text, each of which is a command that causes the operating system to start a copy of the PeriodicOutput.exe program, with slightly different parameters.
2. Run the batch file by typing its name, followed by the Enter key. Observe what happens.

Expected Outcome for Part 2

You should see the three processes running simultaneously, evidenced by the fact that their outputs are interleaved such that you see an "ABCABC" pattern (perfect interleaving is not guaranteed and thus the pattern may vary). The screenshot below shows the typical output you should get.

ACTIVITY P3 EXAMINING SCHEDULING BEHAVIOR WITH REAL PROCESSES—INTRODUCTORY—Cont'd

The batch file sets the intervals between printing characters to 20 ms for each of the three processes. This is on a similar scale to the size of a typical scheduling quantum and yields quite a regular interleaving (which arises because the three processes spend a relatively long time "sleeping" between their brief single-character-at-a-time output activity, giving the scheduler plenty of time to manage other activities in the system).

Part 3

Experiment with different settings by editing the batch file (use a simple text editor such as Notepad, and do not use a word processor as this may add special characters, which confuse the command interpreter part of the operating system). Try changing the time interval, or adding a few extra processes. In particular, try a shorter character printing interval for the three processes, such as 5 ms. The faster the rate of activity in the three processes, the less likely it becomes that the scheduler will achieve the regular interleaving we saw in part 2 above. Because the computer has other processes running (as we saw in Activity P2), we may not see a perfect interleaved pattern, and if we run the batch file several times, we should expect slightly different results each time; it is important that you realize why this is.

Reflection

You have seen that the simple interleaving achieved by running three processes from a batch file can lead to a regular pattern when the system is not stressed (i.e., when the processes spend most of their time blocked because they perform IO, between short episodes of running and becoming blocked once again). Essentially, there is sufficient spare CPU capacity in this configuration that each process gets the processing time it needs, without spending long in the ready state.

However, depending on the further experimentation you carried out in part 3, you will probably have found that the regularity of the interleaving in fact depends on the number of, and behavior of, other processes in the system. In this experiment, we have not stated any specific requirement of synchrony between the three processes (i.e., the operating system has no knowledge that a regular interleaving pattern is required), so irregularity in the pattern would be acceptable.

In addition to gaining an understanding of the behavior of scheduling, you should have also gained a level of competence with regard to configuring and running processes, the use of command-line arguments and batch files, and an understanding of the effects of the scheduler.

An interesting observation is that while over the past couple of decades central processor operating speeds (the number of CPU cycles per second) have increased dramatically, the typical range of scheduling quantum sizes has remained generally unchanged. One main reason for this is that the complexity of systems and the applications that run on them have also increased at high rates, requiring more processing to achieve their rich functionality. The underlying trade-off between responsiveness (smaller quantum size) and low overheads (larger quantum size) remains, regardless of how fast the CPU operates. Quantum sizes in modern systems are typically in the range of about 10 ms to about 200 ms, although smaller quanta (down to about 1 ms) are used on very fast platforms. A range of quantum sizes can be used as a means of implementing process priority; this works on the simple basis that higher-priority processes should receive a greater share of the processing resource available. Of course, if processes are IO-intensive, they get blocked when they perform IO regardless of priority.

Another main factor why quantum sizes have not reduced in line with technological advances is that human perception of responsiveness has not changed. It is important from a usability viewpoint that interactive processes respond to user actions (such as typing a key or moving the mouse) in a timely way, ideally to achieve the illusion that the user's application is running continuously, uninterrupted, on the computer. Consider a display-update activity; the behind-the-scenes processing requirement has increased due, for example, to higher-resolution displays and more complex windowing user-interface libraries. This means that a display update requires more CPU cycles in modern systems than in simpler, earlier systems.

For interactive processes, a quantum must be sufficiently large that the processing associated with the user's request can be completed. Otherwise, once the quantum ends, the user's process will have to wait, while other processes take turns, introducing delay to the user's process. In addition, as explained earlier, a smaller quantum size incurs a higher level of system overhead due to scheduling activity. So although CPU cycle speed has increased over time, the typical scheduling quantum size has not.

2.3.1.2 Process States

This section relates primarily to preemptive scheduling schemes, as these are used in the typical systems that are used to build distributed systems.

If we assume that there is only a single processor unit, then only one process can use the processor at any moment. This process is said to be *running*, or in the *run state*. It is the scheduler's job to select which process is *running* at a particular time and, by implication, what to do with the other processes in the system.

Some processes that are not currently *running* will be able to run; this means that all the resources they need are available to them, and if they were placed in the *run state*, they would be able to perform useful work. When a process is able to run, but not actually running, it is placed in the ready queue. It is thus said to be *ready*, or in the *ready state*.

Some processes are not able to run immediately because they are dependent on some resource that is not available to them. For example, consider a simple calculator application that requires user input before it can compute a result. Suppose that the user has entered the sequence of keys 5 x; clearly, this is an incomplete instruction and the calculator application must wait for further input before it can compute 5 times whatever second number the user enters. In this scenario, the resource in question is the keyboard input device, and the scheduler will be aware that the process is unable to proceed because it is waiting for input. If the scheduler were to let this process run, it would be unable to perform useful work immediately; for this reason, the process is moved to the *blocked* state. Once the reason for waiting has cleared (e.g., the IO device has responded), the process will be moved into the *ready* queue. In the example described above, this would be when the user has typed a number on the keyboard.

Taking the Adder program used in Activity P1 as an example; consider the point where the process waits for each user input. Even if the user types immediately, say, perhaps one number each second, it takes 2 s for the two numbers to be entered; and this makes minimal allowance for user thinking time, which tends to be relatively massive compared to the computational time needed to process the data entered.

The CPU works very fast relative to human typing speed; even the slowest microcontroller used in embedded systems executes 1 million or more instructions per second.[2] The top-end mobile phone microprocessor technology (at the time of writing) contains four processing cores, which each operate at 2.3 GHz, while a top-end desktop PC microprocessor operates at 3.6-4.0 GHz, also with four processing cores. These figures provide an indication of the amount of computational power that would be lost if the scheduler allowed the CPU to remain idle for a couple of seconds while a process such as Adder is waiting for input. As discussed earlier, scheduling quanta are typically in the range of 10-200 ms, which given the operating speed of modern CPUs represents a lot of computational power.

The three process states discussed above form the basic set required to describe the overall behavior of a scheduling system generically, although some other states also occur and will be introduced later.

---

[2]This is considered extremely slow relative to other technologies available at present, but embedded systems such as sensor systems tend to have low information-processing requirements. The slower technology gives rise to two advantages: it has very low power consumption and thus sensor nodes can operate on batteries for extended periods; and the devices are very cheap so they can be deployed in large-scale applications.

The three states (*running*, *ready*, and *blocked*) can be described in a state-transition diagram, so-called because the diagram shows the allowable states of the system and the transitions that can occur to move from one state to another. A newly created process will be placed initially in the *ready* state.

Figure 2.10 shows the three-state transition diagram. You should read this diagram from the perspective of a particular process. That is, the diagram applies individually to each process in the system; so, for example, if there are three processes {A, B, C}, we can describe each process as being in a particular state at any given moment. The same transition rules apply to all processes, but the states can be different at any given time.

The transitions shown are the only ones allowable. The transition from *ready* to *running* occurs when the process is selected to run, by the operating system; this is known as dispatching. The various scheduling algorithms select the next process to run based on different criteria, but the general essence is that the process selected either has reached the top of the ready queue because it has been waiting longest or has been elevated to the top because it has a higher priority than others in the queue.

The transition from *running* to *ready* occurs when the process has used up its time quantum. This is called preemption and is done to ensure *fairness* and to prevent *starvation*; this term is used to describe the situation where one process hogs the CPU, while another process is kept waiting, possibly indefinitely.

The transition from *running* to *blocked* occurs when the process has requested an IO operation and must wait for the slower (slow with respect to the CPU) IO subsystem to respond. The IO subsystem could be a storage device such as a hard magnetic disk drive or an optical drive (CD or DVD), or it could be an output device such as a printer or video display. The IO operation could also be a network operation, perhaps waiting for a message to be sent or received. Where the IO device is a user-input device such as a mouse or keyboard, the response time is measured in seconds or perhaps tenths of a second, while the CPU in a modern computer is capable of executing perhaps several thousand million instructions in 1 s (this is an incredible amount). Thus, in the time between a user typing keys, the CPU can perform many millions of instructions, thus highlighting the extent of wastage if the process were allowed to hog the CPU while idle.

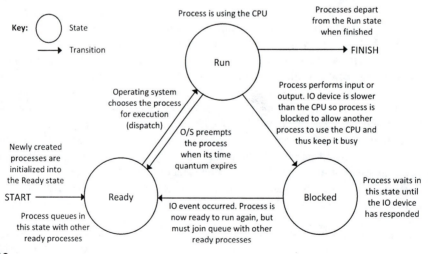

FIGURE 2.10

The three-state state transition diagram.

The transition from *blocked* to *ready* occurs when the IO operation has completed. For example, if the reason for blocking was waiting for a user keystroke, then once the keystroke has been received, it will be decoded and the relevant key-code data provided on the input stream of the process.[3] At this point, the process is able to continue processing, so it is moved to the ready state. Similarly, if the reason for blocking was waiting for a message to arrive over a network connection, then the process will be unblocked once a message has been received[4] and placed into a memory buffer accessible to the process (i.e., the operating system moves the message into the process' memory space).

Note that when a process is unblocked, it does not reenter the *running* state directly. It must go via the *ready* state.

As explained above, blocking and unblocking are linked to actual events in the process' behavior and in the response of IO subsystems, respectively. To illustrate this, consider what takes place when a process writes to a file on a hard disk. A hard disk is a "block device"—this means that data are read from, and written to, the disk in fixed-size blocks. This block-wise access is because a large fraction of the access time is taken up by the read/write head being positioned over the correct track where the data are to be written and waiting for the disk to rotate to the correct sector (portion of a track) where the data are to be written. It would thus be extremely inefficient and require very complex control systems if a single byte were written at a time. Instead a block of data, of perhaps many kilobytes, is read or written sequentially once the head is aligned (the alignment activity is termed "seeking" or "head seek"). Disk rotation speeds and head movement speeds are very slow relative to the processing speeds of modern computers. So, if we imagine a process that is updating a file that is stored on the disk, we can see that there would be a lot of delays associated with the disk access. In addition to the first seek, if the file is fragmented across the disk, as is common, then each new block that is to be written requires a new seek. Even after a seek is complete, there is a further delay (in the context of CPU-speed operations) as the actual speed at which data are written onto the disk or read from it is also relatively very slow. Each time the process were ready to update a next block of data, it would be blocked by the scheduler. Once the disk operation has completed, the scheduler would move the process back into the ready queue. When it enters the running state, it will process the next section of the file, and then, as soon as it is ready to write to the disk again, it is blocked once more. We would describe this as an IO-intensive task and we would expect it to be regularly blocked before using up its full-time slices. This type of task would spend a large fraction of its time in the blocked state, as illustrated in Figure 2.11.

---

[3]Note that a keyboard is an example of a *"character device"*—this means that input from the keyboard is processed on a single key basis. The two main reasons for this are application responsiveness and also to keep the control logic simple. To understand this, consider the possible alternative, that is, making it a *"block device,"* which would return a block of data at a time as, for example, a hard disk does. The problem here is that the process would have to wait for a full "block" of keystrokes before responding (because it would remain blocked until the operating system had counted and forwarded to the process the requisite number of bytes). There are some scenarios where this could operate with some success, such as when typing large numbers of keystrokes as input to a word processor, but in the vast majority of scenarios, it would be unworkable. Modern word processors actually take advantage of the character-by-character basis of the key stream, as they run subcomponents such as the grammar checker and spelling checker and autocomplete, even as the user is typing and the current key sentence is incomplete.

[4]A network interface is effectively a *"block device"* because it sends and receives messages that are groups of data bytes collected together in a memory buffer. The buffer itself is an area of memory reserved to store the message (this is discussed in detail in the Resource view chapter) and has a fixed size. However, for reasons of efficiency, only the actual message will be transmitted over the network, which may be considerably smaller than the buffer can hold. Therefore, messages can vary in size and thus the amount of data passed to/from the process can vary on each send or receive event.

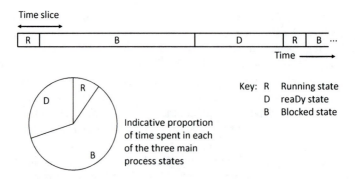

Indicative proportion of time spent in each of the three main process states

IO intense process. Performs IO frequently and rarely uses its full time slice before being blocked. Once it is un-blocked it joins the ready queue before being moved to the running state again

FIGURE 2.11

Run-time behavior illustration for an IO-intensive process.

Figure 2.11 illustrates the process state sequence for a typical IO-intensive process. The actual ratios shown are indicative, because they depend on the specific characteristics of the process and the host system (including the mix of other tasks present, which affects the waiting time).

The above example concerning access to a secondary storage system such as a disk drive raises a key performance issue, which must be considered during design of low-level application behavior, which affects not only its performance but also its robustness. Data held in memory while the program is running are volatile; this means that if the process crashes or the power is lost, the data are also lost. Secondary storage such as a magnetic hard disk is nonvolatile, or "persistent," and thus will preserve the data after the process ends and even after the computer is turned off. Clearly, there is a conflict between ultimate performance and ultimate robustness, because the time-cost overheads of the most robust approach of writing data to disk every time there is a change are generally not tolerable from a performance point of view. This is a good example of a design trade-off to reach an appropriate compromise depending on the specific requirements of the application.

Compute-intensive processes tend to use their full-time slice and are thus preempted by the operating system to allow another process to do some work. The responsiveness of compute-intensive processes is thus primarily related to the total share of the system resources each gets. For example, if a compute-intensive process were the only process present, it would use the full resource of the CPU. However, if three CPU-intensive tasks were competing in a system, the process state behavior of each would resemble that shown in Figure 2.12.

One further example is provided to ensure the behavior is clear. If a compute-intensive process competes with four similar processes, each will account for one-fifth of the total computing resource available, as illustrated in Figure 2.13.

2.3.1.3 Process Behavior
IO-Intensive Processes
Some processes perform IO frequently and thus are often blocked before using up their quantum; these are said to be IO-intensive processes. An IO-intensive program not only could be an interactive program where the IO occurs between a user and the process (via, e.g., the keyboard and display screen)

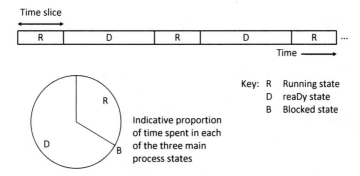

Key: R   Running state
     D   reaDy state
     B   Blocked state

Indicative proportion
of time spent in each
of the three main
process states

Compute-intense process, competing witht woothers. Rarely performs IO and tends to use its full time slice each time it is selected torun, hence in this scenario the process uses one third of the total processing power of the system

FIGURE 2.12

Run-time behavior illustration for a compute-intensive process competing with two similar processes.

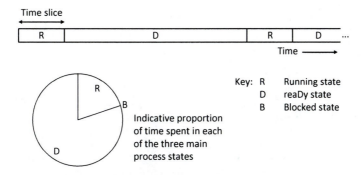

Key: R   Running state
     D   reaDy state
     B   Blocked state

Indicative proportion
of time spent in each
of the three main
process states

Compute intense process, competing with four others. Here the process uses one fifth of the total processing power of the system

FIGURE 2.13

Run-time behavior illustration for a compute-intensive process competing with four similar processes.

ACTIVITY P4 EXAMINING SCHEDULING BEHAVIOR WITH REAL PROCESSES— COMPETITION FOR THE CPU

Prerequisites
The instructions below assume that you have obtained the necessary supplemental resources as explained in Activity P1.

Learning Outcomes
This activity explores the way in which the scheduler shares the CPU resource when several competing processes are CPU-intensive:

ACTIVITY P4 EXAMINING SCHEDULING BEHAVIOR WITH REAL PROCESSES—COMPETITION FOR THE CPU—Cont'd

1. To understand that the CPU resource is finite
2. To understand that the performance of one process can be affected by the other processes in the system (which from its point of view constitute a background workload with which it must compete for resources).

Method

This activity is carried out in four parts and uses a CPU-intensive program, which, when running as a process, performs continual computation without doing any IO and thus never blocks. As such, the process will always fully use its time slice.

Part 1 (Calibration)

1. Start the Task Manager as in Activity P2 and select the "Processes" tab. Sort the display in order of CPU-use intensity, highest at the top. If there are no compute-intensive tasks present, the typical highest CPU usage figure might be about 1%, while many processes that have low activity will show as using 0% of the CPU resource. Leave the Task Manager window open, to the side of the screen.
2. Run the CPU_Hog.exe program in a command window. Navigate to the "ProcessView" subfolder of the SystemsProgramming folder and then execute the CPU_Hog program by typing CPU_Hog.exe followed by the Enter key. The program will now run as a process. Examine the process statistics in the Task Manager window while the CPU_Hog process runs.

   The screenshot below shows that the CPU_Hog takes as much CPU resource as the scheduler gives it, which in this case is 50%.

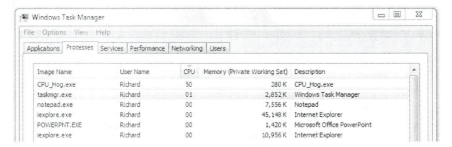

3. Run the CPU_Hog process again, and this time, record how long it takes to run, using a stopwatch. The program performs a loop a large fixed number of times, each time carrying out some computation. The time taken will be approximately the same each time the process is run, on a particular computer, as long as the background workload does not change significantly. It is necessary that you time it on your own computer to get a baseline for the subsequent experiments in this activity and that you do this without any other CPU-intensive processes running. Timing accuracy to the nearest second is adequate. As a reference, it took approximately 39 s on my (not particularly fast) computer.

Part 2 (Prediction)

1. Taking into account the share of CPU resource used by a single instance of the CPU_Hog, what do you think will happen if we run two instances of this program at the same time? How much share of the CPU resource do you think each copy of the program will get?
2. Based on the amount of time that it took for a single instance of the CPU_Hog to run, how long will each copy take to run if two copies are running at the same time?
3. Now, use the batch file named "CPU_Hog_2Starter.bat" to start two copies of CPU_Hog at the same time. Use the Task Manager window to observe the share of CPU resource that each process gets, and don't forget to also measure the run time of the two processes (when they have completed, you will see them disappear from the list of processes).

The screenshot below shows that each CPU_Hog process was given approximately half of the total CPU resource. Is this what you expected?

ACTIVITY P4 EXAMINING SCHEDULING BEHAVIOR WITH REAL PROCESSES—COMPETITION FOR THE CPU—Cont'd

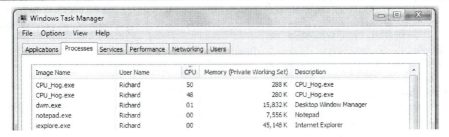

Expected Outcome for Part 2

In my experiment, the processes ran for approximately 40 s, which is what I had expected, on the basis that each process had very slightly less than 50% (on average) of the CPU resource, which was essentially the same as the single process had had in part 1. The fact that the processes took very slightly longer to run than the single process had taken is important. This slight difference arises because the other processes in the system, while relatively inactive, do still use some processing resource and, importantly, the scheduling activity itself incurs overheads each time it switches between the active processes. These overheads were absorbed when the CPU was idle for nearly 50% of the time but show up when the resource is fully utilized.

Part 3 (Stressing the System)

It would not satisfy my inquisitive nature to leave it there. There is an obvious question that we should ask and try to answer: *If a single instance of CPU_Hog takes 50% of the CPU resource when it runs and two copies of CPU_Hog take 50% of the CPU resource each, what happens when three or even more copies are run at the same time?*

1. Make your predictions—for each of the three processes, what will be the share of CPU resource? And what will be the run time?
2. Use the batch file named "CPU_Hog_3Starter.bat" to start three copies of CPU_Hog at the same time. As before, use the Task Manager window to observe the share of CPU resource that each process gets, and also remember to measure the run time of the three processes (this may get trickier, as they might not all finish at the same time, but an average timing value will suffice to get an indication of what is happening).

The screenshot below shows the typical results I get.

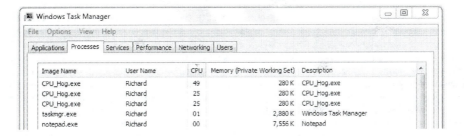

Expected Outcome for Part 3

Interestingly, the first process still gets 50% of the CPU resource and the other two share the remaining 50%. Before the experiment, I had expected that they would get 33% of the resource each. There are almost certainly other schedulers out there for which that would have been the case; but with distributed systems, you won't always know or control which computer your process will run on, or which scheduler will be present, or the exact run-time configuration including workload, so this experiment teaches us to be cautious when predicting run-time performance even in a single system, let alone in heterogeneous distributed systems.

ACTIVITY P4 EXAMINING SCHEDULING BEHAVIOR WITH REAL PROCESSES— COMPETITION FOR THE CPU—Cont'd

Coming back to our experiment, this result means that the first process ends sooner than the other two. Once the first process ends, the remaining two are then given 50% of the CPU resource each, so their processing rate has been speeded up. I recorded the following times: first process, 40 s; second and third processes, approximately 60 s. This makes sense; at the point where the first process ends, the other two have had half as much processing resource each and are therefore about halfway through their task. Once they have 50% of the CPU resource each, it takes them a further 20 s to complete the remaining half of their work—which is consistent.

Part 4 (Exploring Further)

I have provided a further batch file "CPU_Hog_4Starter.bat" to start four copies of CPU_Hog at the same time. You can use this with the same method as in part three to explore further.

The screenshot below shows the behavior on my computer.

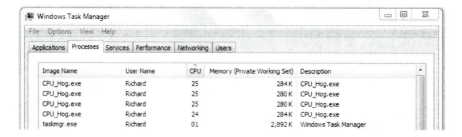

In this case, each process used approximately 25% of the CPU resource and each took approximately 80 s to run—which is consistent with the earlier results.

Reflection

This experiment illustrates some very important aspects of scheduling and of the way in which the behavior of the scheduler and the behavior of the processes interact. This includes the complexities of predicting run times and the extent to which the behavior of schedulers may be sensitive to the mix of processes in the system.

Firstly, we see that the CPU resource is finite and must be shared among the processes in the system. We also see that as some processes complete, the share of resource can be reallocated to the remaining processes. It is also important to realize that a process will take a predictable amount of CPU run time to execute. However, because the process gets typically less than 100% of the CPU resource, its actual execution time (its time in the system, including when it is in the ready queue) is greater than its CPU run time, and the overall execution time is dependent on the load on the system—which in general is continually fluctuating. These experiments have scratched the surface of the complexity of scheduling but provide valuable insight into the issues concerned and equip us with the skills to explore further. You can devise further empirical experiments based on the tools I have provided (e.g., you can edit the batch files to fire off different combinations of programs), or you can use the Operating Systems Workbench scheduling simulations that support flexible experimentation over a wide range of conditions and process combinations and also allow you to decide which scheduler to use. The introductory scheduling simulation provides configurations with three different schedulers and workload mixes of up to five processes of three different types. The advanced scheduling simulation supports an additional scheduling algorithm and facilitates configuration of the size of the CPU scheduling quantum and also the device latency for IO-intensive processes. The workbench will be introduced later in the chapter.

but also may perform its IO to other devices including disk drives and the network—for example, it may be a server process that receives requests from a network connection and sends responses back over the network.

Examples of IO-intensive programs are shown in the pseudocode in Figure 2.14 (user-interactive IO), Figure 2.15 (disk-based IO), and Figure 2.16 (network-based IO).

```
Start
  Set sum = 0
  Repeat 100 times
  {
     Input a number
     Add number to sum
  }
  Display sum
End
```

FIGURE 2.14

The *Summer* IO-intensive (interactive) program (computes the sum of 100 numbers).

Figure 2.14 shows the pseudocode of an interactive IO-intensive process that spends a very large proportion of its time waiting for input. The time to perform the add operation would be much less than a millionth of a second, so if the user enters numbers at a rate of 1 per second, the program could spend greater than 99.9999% of its time waiting for input.

Figure 2.15 shows pseudocode for a disk IO-intensive program that spends most of its time waiting for a response from the hard disk; each loop iteration performs two disk IO operations.

```
Start
   Repeat until end-of-file A reached
   {
       Read next block from file A
       Write block to file B
   }
   End
```

FIGURE 2.15

The *FileCopy* IO-intensive (disk access) program (copy from one file to another).

Figure 2.16 shows pseudocode for a network IO-intensive program that spends most of its time waiting for a message to arrive from the network.

```
Start
  Repeat forever
  {
     Wait for an incoming message
     Identify sender of message from message header
     Send a copy of the message back to sender
  }
  End
```

FIGURE 2.16

NetworkPingService IO-intensive (network communication) program (echo back a received message to the sender).

Figures 2.14–2.16 provide three examples of processes that are IO-driven and the process spends the vast majority of its time waiting (in blocked state). Such processes will be blocked each time they make an IO request, which means that they would not fully use their allocated quanta. The operating system is responsible for selecting another process from the ready queue to run as soon as possible to keep the CPU busy and thus keep the system efficient. If no other process were available to run, then the CPU time would be unused and the system efficiency falls.

Compute-Intensive (or CPU-Intensive) Processes

Compute-intensive processes are ones that perform IO rarely, perhaps to read in some initial data from a file, for example, and then spend long periods processing the data before producing the result at the end, which requires minimal output. Most scientific computing using techniques such as computational fluid dynamics (CFD) and genetic programming in applications such as weather forecasting and computer-based simulations fall into this category. Such applications can run for extended periods, perhaps many hours without necessarily performing any IO activities. Thus, they almost always use up their entire allocated time slices and rarely block.

Figure 2.17 shows pseudocode for a compute-intensive program where IO is performed only at the beginning and end. Once the initial IO has been performed, this process would be expected to use its quanta fully and be preempted by the operating system, thus predominantly moving between the running and ready states.

```
Start
    Load massive dataset from files (IO)

    Perform CFD computation (which involves millions
    of computation iterations, each one updating
    possibly large parts of the dataset)

    Produce output (IO)
End
```

FIGURE 2.17

WeatherForecaster compute-intensive program (perform extensive CFD computation on a massive dataset).

Balanced Processes

The term "balanced" could be used to describe a process that not only uses the CPU moderately intensively but also performs IO at a moderate level. This terminology is used in the Operating Systems Workbench (see the accompanying resources). An example of this category of program could be a word processor that spends much of its time waiting for user input but that also incorporates computationally intense activities such as spell-checking and grammar checking. Such functionality may be activated automatically or on demand by the user and require short bursts of significant amounts of processing resource.

Figure 2.18 shows pseudocode for a "balanced" program the behavior of which is sometimes IO-intensive and sometimes compute-intensive. Such a process would have periods where it spends much of its time in the blocked state, but there would also be periods where it moves predominantly between the run and ready states.

2.3.1.4 Scheduler Behavior, Components, and Mechanisms

The act of moving a process from the ready state to the running state is called "dispatching," and this is performed by a subcomponent of the scheduler called the dispatcher. The dispatcher must ensure the appropriate preparation is carried out so that the process can operate correctly. This involves restoring the process' state (e.g., the stack and also the program counter and other operating system structures) so

```
Start
  Load file (disk-IO)
  Repeat until editing complete
  {
    Wait for user keystroke (interactive-IO)
    Automatically  run   autocomplete  function as
    necessary (compute-intense)
    Automatically  run   spell-checker  function as
    necessary (compute-intense)
    Automatically  run  grammer-checker  function as
    necessary (compute-intense)
  }
  Save file (disk-IO)
End
```

FIGURE 2.18

Word processor "balanced" program (alternates between IO-intensive behavior and bursts of high-intensity computation).

that the process' run-time environment (as seen by the process itself) is exactly the same as it was when the process was last running, immediately before it was preempted or blocked. This changing from the running context of one process to the running context of another is called a context switch. This is the largest component of the scheduling overhead and must be done efficiently because the CPU is not performing useful work until the process is running again. As the program counter is restored to its previous value in the process' instruction sequence, the program will continue running from the exact place it was interrupted previously. Note that this is conceptually similar to the mechanism of returning from a function (subroutine) call. The dispatcher is part of the operating system, and so it runs in what is called "privileged mode"; this means it has full access to the structures maintained by the operating system and the resources of the system. At the end-of-doing its work, the dispatcher must switch the system back into "user mode," which means that the process that is being dispatched will only have access to the subset of resources that it needs for its operation and the rest of the system's resources (including those owned by other user-level processes) are protected from, and effectively hidden from, the process.

2.3.1.5 Additional Process States: Suspended-Blocked and Suspended-Ready

The three-state model of process behavior discussed above is a simplification of actual behavior in most systems; however, it is very useful as a basis on which to explain the main concepts of scheduling. There are a few other process states that are necessary to enable more sophisticated behavior of the scheduler. The run, ready, and blocked set of states are sufficient to manage scheduling from the angle of choosing which process should run (i.e., to manage the CPU resource), but do not provide flexibility with respect to other resources such as memory. In the three-state model, each process, once created, is held in a memory image that includes the program instructions and all of the storage required, such as the variables used to hold input and computed data. There is also additional "state" information created by the operating system in order to manage the execution of the process; this includes, for example, details of which resources and peripherals are being used and details of communication with other processes, either via pipelines as we have seen earlier or via network protocols as will be examined in Chapter 3.

Physical memory is finite and is often a bottleneck resource because it is required for every activity carried out by the computer. Each process uses memory (the actual process image has to be held in physical memory while the process is running; this image contains the actual program instructions, the data it is using held in variables, memory buffers used in network communication, and special structures such as the stack and program counter which are used to control the progress of the process). The operating system also uses considerable amounts of memory to perform its management activities (this includes special structures that keep track of each process). Inevitably, there are times when the amount of memory required to run all of the processes present exceeds the amount of physical memory available.

Secondary storage devices, such as hard disk drives, have much larger capacity than the physical memory in most systems. This is partly because of the cost of physical memory and partly because of limits in the number of physical memory locations that can be addressed by microprocessors. Due to the relatively high availability of secondary storage, operating systems are equipped with mechanisms to move (swap-out) process images from physical memory to secondary storage to make room for further processes and mechanisms to move (swap-in) process images back from the secondary storage to the physical memory. This increases the effective size of the memory beyond the amount of physical memory available. This technique is termed virtual memory and is discussed in more detail in Chapter 4.

To incorporate the concept of virtual memory into scheduling behavior, two additional process states are necessary. The suspended-blocked state is used to take a blocked-state process out of the current active set and thus to free the physical memory that the process was using. The mechanism of this is to store the entire process' memory image onto the hard disk in the form of a special file and to set the state of the process to "suspended-blocked," which signifies that it is not immediately available to enter the ready or run states. The benefit of this approach is that physical memory resource is freed up, but there are costs involved. The act of moving the process' memory image to disk takes up time (specifically, the CPU is required to execute some code within the operating system to achieve this, and this is an IO activity itself—which slows things down) adding to the time aspect of scheduling overheads. The process must have its memory image restored (back into physical memory) before it can run again, thus adding latency to the response time of the process. In addition to regular scheduling latency, a suspended process must endure the latency of the swap to disk and also subsequently back to physical memory.

A swapped-out process can be swapped-in at any time that the operating system chooses. If the process is initially in the suspended-blocked state, it will be moved to the blocked state, as it must still wait for the IO operation that caused it to originally enter the blocked state to complete.

However, while swapped out, the IO operation may complete, and thus, the operating system will move the process to the suspended-ready state; this transition is labeled *event-occurred*. The suspended-ready state signifies that the process is still swapped out but that it can be moved into the ready state when it is eventually swapped-in.

The suspended-ready state can also be used to free up physical memory when there are no blocked processes to swap-out. In such case, the operating system can choose a ready-state process for swapping out to the suspended-ready state.

Figure 2.19 illustrates the five-state process model including the suspended-ready and suspended-blocked states and the additional state transitions of suspend, activate, and event-occurred.

2.3.1.6 Goals of Scheduling Algorithms

As discussed earlier, efficiency in terms of keeping the CPU busy and thus ensuring the system performs useful work is a main goal of general-purpose scheduling. Additional goals of scheduling include the following:

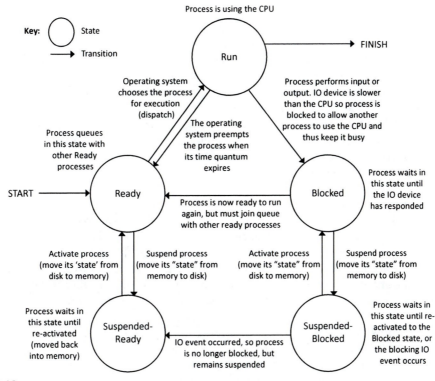

FIGURE 2.19

The extended process state transition model including suspended process states.

- To ensure fairness to all processes

When comparing scheduling algorithms, the concept of "fairness" is usually close behind efficiency in terms of performance metrics. This is in the context of giving the various processes a "fair share" of the processing resource. However, as you shall see later when you carry out experiments with the simulations in the Operating Systems Workbench, the concept of fairness is subjective and difficult to pin down to any single universal meaning. If all processes have the same priority and importance, then it is easy to consider fairness in terms of giving the processes equal processing opportunities. However, things get much more complex when there are different priorities or when some or all processes have real-time constraints. A special case to be avoided is "starvation" in which a process never reaches the front of the ready queue because the scheduling algorithm always favors the other processes.

- To minimize scheduling overheads

Performing a context switch (the act of changing which process is running at any moment) requires that the scheduler component of the operating system temporarily runs in order to select which process will run next and to actually change the state of each of the processes. This activity takes up some processing time and thus it is undesirable to perform context switches too frequently. However, a system can be unresponsive if processes are left to run for long periods without preemption; this can contradict other goals of scheduling, such as fairness.

- To minimize process wait time

Waiting time is problematic in terms of responsiveness, and thus, a general goal of scheduling is to keep it to a minimum for all processes. Waiting time most noticeably impacts interactive processes and processes with real-time constraints, but it is also important to consider waiting time as a ratio of total run time. A process with a very short run-time requirement (in terms of actual CPU usage) will have its performance affected relatively much more than a process with a long run-time requirement, by any given amount of delay. The shortest job first, and shortest remaining job next scheduling algorithms specifically favor shorter run-time processes. This has two important effects: firstly, the shortest processes do the least waiting, and thus, the *mean waiting time ratios* (wait time/run time) of processes are lowered; and secondly, the *mean absolute waiting times* of processes are lowered because a long process waits only a short time for the short process to complete, rather than the short process waiting a long time for the long process to complete.

- To maximize throughput

Throughput is a measure of the total work done by the system. The total processing capacity of the system is limited by the capacity of the CPU, hence the importance placed on keeping the CPU busy. If the CPU is used efficiently, that is, it is kept continuously busy by the scheduler, then the long-term throughput will be maximized. Short-term throughput might be influenced by which processes are chosen to run, such that several short processes could be completed in the same time that one longer one runs for. However, as a measure of performance, throughput over the longer-term is more meaningful.

2.3.1.7 Scheduling Algorithms

First Come, First Served (FCFS)

FCFS is the simplest scheduling algorithm. There is a single rule; schedule the first process to arrive, and let it run to completion. This is a non-preemptive scheduling algorithm, which means that only a single process can run at a time, regardless of whether it uses the resources of the system effectively, and also regardless of whether there is a queue of other processes waiting, and the relative importance of those processes. Due to these limitations, the algorithm is not widely used but is included here as a baseline on which to compare other simple algorithms (see Activity P5).

Shortest Job First (SJF)

SJF is a modification of FCFS, in which the shortest job in the queue is executed next. This algorithm has the effect of reducing average waiting times, since the shortest jobs run first and the longer jobs spend less time waiting to start than if it were the other way around. This is a significant improvement, but this algorithm is also non-preemptive and thus suffers the same general weaknesses with respect to resource use efficiency as FCFS.

Round Robin (RR)

The simplest preemptive scheduling algorithm is round-robin, in which the processes are given turns at running, one after the other in a repeating sequence, and each one is preempted when it has used up its time slice. So, for example, if we have three processes {A, B, C}, then the scheduler may run them in the sequence A, B, C, A, B, C, A, and so on, until they are all finished. Figure 2.20 shows a possible process state sequence for this set of processes, assuming a single processing core system. Notice that the example shown is maximally efficient because the processor is continuously busy; there is always a process running.

Process	Quantum 1	Quantum 2	Quantum 3	Quantum 4	Quantum 5	Quantum 6
A	**Running**	Ready	Ready	**Running**	Ready	Ready
B	Ready	**Running**	Ready	Ready	**Running**	Ready
C	Ready	Ready	**Running**	Ready	Ready	**Running**

FIGURE 2.20

A possible process state sequence for round-robin scheduling with three processes.

ACTIVITY P5 USING THE OPERATING SYSTEMS WORKBENCH TO EXPLORE SCHEDULING BEHAVIOR (INTRODUCTORY): COMPARING FIRST-COME FIRST-SERVED, SHORTEST JOB FIRST, AND ROUND-ROBIN SCHEDULING

Prerequisite
Download the Operating Systems Workbench and the supporting documentation from the book's supplementary materials website. Read the document "Scheduling (Introductory) Activities and Experiments."

Learning Outcomes
1. To gain an understanding of the first-come first-served scheduling algorithm
2. To gain an understanding of the shortest job first scheduling algorithm
3. To gain an understanding of the round-robin scheduling algorithm
4. To gain an understanding of the three-state model of process behavior
5. To reinforce the understanding of general scheduling concepts, discussed in this chapter

This activity uses the "Scheduling Algorithms—Introductory" simulation, which is found on the "Scheduling" tab of the Operating Systems Workbench. We use the same initial configuration of two CPU-intensive processes in each of the three stages below. We compare the behavior using each of three different scheduling algorithms. At the end-of-each simulation, note down the values in the statistics section at the bottom of the simulation window.

This activity is divided into three stages to provide structure.

Activity P5_CPU
Exploring first-come first-served, shortest job first, and round-robin scheduling with CPU-intensive processes

Method
Set process 1 to "CPU-intensive" and set the run time to 60 ms.

Enable process 2, set it to "CPU-intensive," and set the run time to 30 ms.

When you are ready, press the "Free Run" button to start the simulation.

The screenshots below show the initial and final settings, respectively, when running the processes with the FCFS scheduling algorithm.

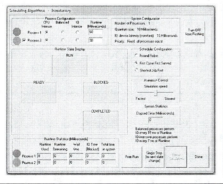
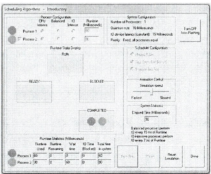

ACTIVITY P5 USING THE OPERATING SYSTEMS WORKBENCH TO EXPLORE SCHEDULING BEHAVIOR (INTRODUCTORY): COMPARING FIRST-COME FIRST-SERVED, SHORTEST JOB FIRST, AND ROUND-ROBIN SCHEDULING—Cont'd

Expected Outcome

The simulation will run through the sequence of state changes for each process, until all processes have completed. You will see the run-time statistics and system statistics updating in real time as the simulation runs. These statistics enable analysis of the low-level behavior of the algorithms and their effects on the processes present.

Activity P5_balanced

Exploring first-come first-served, shortest job first, and round-robin scheduling with "balanced" processes (these are processes that perform moderate amounts of input and output but are also moderately CPU-intensive in between the IO activities)

Method

The same as for Activity P5_CPU above, except set both processes to be "balanced."

Expected Outcome

You will see that processes get blocked when they perform IO and thus accrue time in the blocked state. You should notice a significant difference between behaviors of the three algorithms when a process becomes blocked.

Activity P5_IO

Exploring first-come first-served, shortest job first, and round-robin scheduling with IO-intensive processes (these are processes that perform IO regularly)

Method

The same as for Activity P5_CPU above, except set both processes to be "IO-intensive."

Expected Outcome

You will see that the processes frequently perform IO and get blocked regularly and thus accrue a significant proportion of their time in the system in the blocked state. You should notice that the efficiency of the system overall is impacted if all processes are performing IO frequently, as a temporary situation can arise when there are no processes in the ready state, and thus, none can run.

Reflection

You have examined the behavior of three scheduling algorithms with a variety of differently behaved processes. Based on the run-time statistics you have collected, how do these scheduling algorithms compare to each other? Here are some specific questions to start your investigation:
1. What can be said about the fairness of the algorithms (hint: consider the waiting times for processes)?
2. What can be said about the efficiency of CPU usage (hint: consider the total time in the system for each process and the total system elapsed time)?
3. To what extent does the type of process behavior impact on the effectiveness of the scheduling algorithms? Is there always a clear winner, or do the algorithms have different strengths depending on the types of processes in the system?

Further Exploration

You can perform further experiments with the "Scheduling Algorithms—Introductory" simulation to help gain a deeper understanding. You can use the single step button to run the simulations one step at a time allowing you to work at your own pace.

The three scheduling algorithms discussed up to this point are quite limited in the context of modern general-purpose systems with a very wide variety of types of applications with very different behaviors. These scheduling algorithms lack the sophistication necessary to select processes based on contextual factors relating to dynamics of the system itself and the processes within. Some more-advanced algorithms take into account process priorities, or deadlines, or expected run time, or accumulated run time, or various other factors to improve the performance of individual processes and of the system overall. Round-robin scheduling is however ideally suited for systems in which a number of similar processes have equal importance, and as a result of its simple turn-based approach, it has the advantage of being "starvation-free," which means that one process cannot hog the CPU at the expense of others, which can occur for extended periods, possibly indefinitely in some other schemes.

Shortest Remaining Job Next (SRJN)

SRJN is a preemptive scheduling algorithm that combines the benefits of SJF as discussed above (in which the shortest job in the queue is executed first, thus reducing the average waiting time) with the preemptive behavior of RR (which improves responsiveness by giving processes turns at using the CPU and also improves efficiency by keeping the CPU busy whenever there is a process that is ready to run). The SRJN algorithm gives processes turns at running, similar to the way in which RR does, but with the significant difference that it takes into account the amount of remaining run time (the actual amount of CPU processing time required to complete the process). The process in the ready queue with the shortest remaining run time is selected to run next. In this way, if no processes perform IO (and thus get blocked), the algorithm behaves similar to SJF because although there is preemption the previously shortest job will continue to be shortest if it gets the CPU next. However, once a process becomes blocked, another process gets an opportunity to run, thus keeping the CPU busy. It is also possible for the process ordering (in terms of remaining run time) to alter, as while one process is blocked, another may overtake it in terms of becoming the new process with the lowest remaining run time. The behavior of SRJN is explored, and compared with those of RR and SJF, in Activity P6.

Multilevel Queues

Rather than have a single ready queue, there are several, one for each different category of tasks. So, for example, there could be a queue for system processes (the highest priority), another for interactive processes and another for compute-intensive processes such as scientific computing simulations (the lowest priority). Each queue can have a different scheduling policy applied, so, for example, the compute-intensive processes could be scheduled using FIFO, while the system processes and interactive processes will need a preemptive scheme such as RR. There must also be division of the CPU resource across the different queues, as there can only be one process actually scheduled at any moment (assuming a single core). In a system that has many interactive processes, it might be appropriate to allocate perhaps 80% or more of the processing resource to the interactive processes. Where compute-intensive processes are abundant, it may be necessary to allocate more resource to this category to ensure that users get a reasonable response time while balancing this with the much shorter response times needed by the interactive processes. Note that in the example cited above, the use of FIFO scheduling would only have a localized effect on the compute-intensive process queue and would not affect the finer-grained interleaving of the RR scheduling of interactive processes. The multilevel queues algorithm is illustrated in Figure 2.21.

Multilevel Feedback Queues (MLFQ)

This approach builds on the flexibility introduced with multilevel queues. Here, the processes can be moved between the queues to allow the scheduling to achieve a balance between short-term scheduling to achieve responsiveness of tasks and longer-term scheduling to ensure fairness and system efficiency.

The queues are organized in terms of priority, with the top queue having the highest priority and thus being scheduled first. Within each queue, FIFO scheduling is used. A new process enters at this

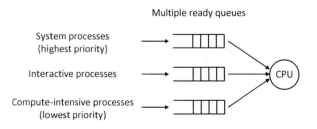

FIGURE 2.21

Multilevel queue scheduling.

level. If the process uses its entire quantum, but does not complete during that quantum, it is down-graded to the next queue level. However, if the process relinquishes control during the first quantum, it remains at the same level. Processes that perform IO and thus become blocked get promoted to the next highest queue. These rules are applied iteratively and at all priority levels such that the priority level of processes is continuously adjusted to reflect their behavior. For example, a compute-intensive process will gradually work its way down to the lowest-priority queue. However, if after a long period of computation the same process began a series of IO operations to deliver its results, or read in further data, it would climb back up some priority levels (because the IO operations cause the process to be blocked before its quantum expires).

This strategy gives priority to short tasks because they will begin at the highest priority and may complete at that level or a few levels down. IO-intensive tasks are also prioritized because they are likely to block before using their time quantum generally, thus ensuring that they are likely to remain at the higher levels of scheduling priority. Compute-intensive tasks do not fare so well in this scheme, as they will work their way down the queue levels and remain at the lowest level, where they are scheduled in RR fashion until they complete. At this level, the tasks only receive processing resource when there are no ready tasks at higher-priority levels.

The interqueue scheduling is performed strictly on a queue-priority basis, so that if there are any processes in the highest queue, they will be scheduled in a locally FIFO manner (i.e., with respect to their position in the particular queue). When the ready queue is temporarily exhausted because processes either complete, are blocked, or demoted, the next level down queue is serviced. If tasks arrive in higher-level ready queues, the scheduler moves back up to the highest populated queue and schedules tasks from there.

The multilevel feedback queue algorithm is illustrated in Figure 2.22.

Figure 2.23 shows the MLFQ algorithm in operation in a system with a mix of interactive and compute-intensive processes. Initially, two processes are in the highest-priority queue (snapshot 1). P1 is a long-running interactive process so this will tend to stay at the top level. P2 however is compute-intensive and gets preempted, thus dropping to priority level 2, while a new process P3 joins the system (snapshot 2). P3 is a short-lived interactive task and thus stays at the highest-priority level, while P2 descends further (snapshot 3). P4, which is a short-lived compute-intensive process, joins (snapshot 4), while P2 descends to the lowest queue level. P4 descends one level in snapshot 5. P4 and P3 complete in snapshots 6 and 7, respectively.

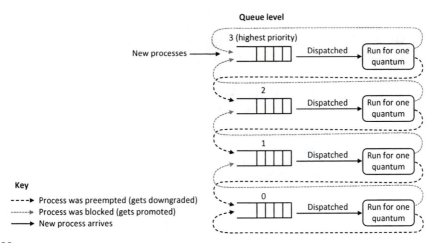

Queue level

FIGURE 2.22

The MLFQ scheduling algorithm.

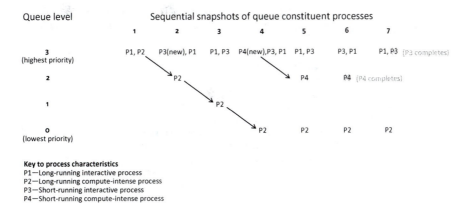

FIGURE 2.23

MLFQ example with two interactive processes and two compute-intensive processes.

ACTIVITY P6 USING THE OPERATING SYSTEMS WORKBENCH TO EXPLORE SCHEDULING BEHAVIOR (ADVANCED): COMPARING THE SHORTEST JOB FIRST, ROUND-ROBIN, AND SHORTEST REMAINING JOB NEXT SCHEDULING ALGORITHMS

Prerequisite

The instructions below assume that you have obtained the Operating Systems Workbench and the supporting documentation as explained in Activity P5.

Read the document "Scheduling (Advanced) Activities and Experiments."

ACTIVITY P6 USING THE OPERATING SYSTEMS WORKBENCH TO EXPLORE SCHEDULING BEHAVIOR (ADVANCED): COMPARING THE SHORTEST JOB FIRST, ROUND-ROBIN, AND SHORTEST REMAINING JOB NEXT SCHEDULING ALGORITHMS—Cont'd

Learning Outcomes

1. To gain an understanding of the shortest remaining job next scheduling algorithm
2. To compare the shortest remaining job next scheduling algorithm with the shortest job first and round-robin scheduling algorithms
3. To discover the features of the Advanced Scheduling simulation of the Operating Systems Workbench, which can be used to support additional exploration
4. To further reinforce the understanding of general scheduling concepts, discussed in this chapter
   This activity is divided into three sections to provide structure.

Activity P6_CPU

Comparing shortest remaining job next with shortest job first and round-robin scheduling with CPU-intensive processes.

Method

This activity uses the "Scheduling Algorithms—Advanced" simulation, which is found on the "Scheduling" tab of the Operating Systems Workbench. The advanced scheduling simulation facilitates deeper investigation into scheduling behavior. It supports an additional scheduling algorithm and up to five processes and allows configuration of the IO device latency and the scheduling quantum size:

1. We use the same initial configuration of five CPU-intensive processes and compare the behavior using each of three different scheduling algorithms. At the end-of-each simulation, note down the values in the statistics section at the bottom of the simulation window.
2. Configuration:
   Set process 1 to "CPU-intensive" and set the run time to 60 ms.
   Enable process 2, set it to "CPU-intensive." and set the run time to 50 ms.
   Enable process 3, set it to "CPU-intensive," and set the run time to 40 ms.
   Enable process 4, set it to "CPU-intensive," and set the run time to 30 ms.
   Enable process 5, set it to "CPU-intensive," and set the run time to 20 ms.
   Set the IO device latency to 10 ms initially (this will not have any effect when all processes are CPU-intensive), and set the quantum size to 10 ms. Set the scheduling algorithm initially to shortest job first.
3. When you are ready, press the "Free Run" button to start the simulation. Repeat the simulation with the same configuration, but using the round-robin and then shortest remaining job next scheduling algorithms. Note the results in the run-time statistics and system statistics windows. These will be used to compare the performance of the different scheduling algorithms.

The screenshots below show the initial and final settings, respectively, when running the processes with the round-robin scheduling algorithm.

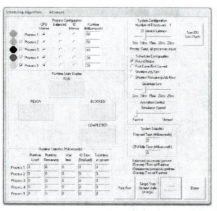
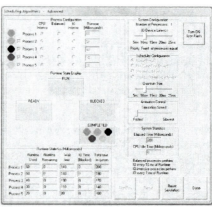

ACTIVITY P6 USING THE OPERATING SYSTEMS WORKBENCH TO EXPLORE SCHEDULING BEHAVIOR (ADVANCED): COMPARING THE SHORTEST JOB FIRST, ROUND-ROBIN, AND SHORTEST REMAINING JOB NEXT SCHEDULING ALGORITHMS—Cont'd

Expected Outcome

The simulation will run through the sequence of state changes for each process, until all processes have completed. You will see the run-time statistics and system statistics updating in real time as the simulation runs, as with the introductory scheduling simulation. These statistics enable analysis of the low-level behavior of the algorithms and their effects on the processes present. It is very important to pay attention to these statistics, when evaluating the relative performance of the algorithms. In the earlier Activity P5, there were only two processes so it was reasonably easy to predict the outcome of the scheduling. With five processes, the run-time system becomes quite complex, and thus, we rely on these automatically generated statistics to compare the behavior of the scheduling algorithms.

Activity P6_balanced

Comparing shortest remaining job next with shortest job first and round-robin scheduling with "balanced" processes

Method

The same as for Activity P6_CPU above, except set all processes to be "balanced." This time, in addition to changing the scheduling algorithm, also investigate the effects of changing the IO device latency and the quantum size.

Expected Outcome

You will see that processes get blocked when they perform IO and thus accrue time in the blocked state. You should notice a significant difference between behaviors of the three algorithms when a process becomes blocked. In particular, pay attention to the wait time and the IO time, and see how these are affected by the various configuration changes.

Activity P6_IO

Comparing shortest remaining job next with shortest job first and round-robin scheduling with "IO-intensive" processes

Method

The same as for Activity P6_balanced above, except set all processes to be "IO-intensive." Once again, be sure to investigate the effects of various configurations of IO device latency and the quantum size.

Expected Outcome

You will see that the processes frequently perform IO and get blocked regularly and thus accrue a significant proportion of their time in the system in the blocked state. You should notice that the efficiency of the system overall is impacted if all processes are performing IO frequently, as a temporary situation can arise when there are no processes in the ready state, and thus, none can run. Look at the automatically generated statistics and try to determine which scheduler is the all-round best performer (good performance being indicated by low wait times and total time in the system for individual processes and by low CPU idle time for the system).

Reflection

You have examined the behavior of three scheduling algorithms with a variety of differently behaved processes and system configurations. By having five processes, the system can exhibit significantly more complex behavior than the earlier two-process introductory simulations. This richer scenario is better in terms of finding the strengths and weaknesses of the various scheduling algorithms. Based on the run-time statistics you have collected, how do these scheduling algorithms compare to each other? Here are some specific questions to start your in vestigation:

1. What can be said about the fairness of the algorithms (hint: consider the waiting times for processes). Do processes ever get "starved," that is, where they have to wait a long time without getting any share of the CPU?
2. What can be said about the efficiency of CPU usage (hint: consider the CPU idle time). Do situations occur where the CPU is unnecessarily idle?
3. To what extent does the type of process behavior impact on the effectiveness of the scheduling algorithms? Is there always a clear winner, or do the algorithms have different strengths depending on the types of processes in the system?
4. To what extent is the SRJN algorithm "the best of both worlds" by taking attributes of SJF and RR. Are there any negative aspects that you can detect from the experiments you have carried out?

Further Exploration

Further experimentation with the "Scheduling Algorithms—Advanced" simulation is strongly encouraged to help gain a deeper understanding. For example, try using a mixture of different process types in the same simulation. You can use the single step button to run the simulations one step at a time allowing you to work at your own pace.

2.4 **SCHEDULING FOR REAL-TIME SYSTEMS**

Real-time scheduling is the term used to describe scheduling algorithms that base their scheduling decisions primarily on the deadlines of tasks, or the periodicity of tasks, tasks being individual activities produced by processes in the system.

Examples of real-time applications include audio and video streaming, monitoring and control (e.g., fly-by-wire systems, factory automation, and robotics), as well as commercial systems such as stock trading, which are highly sensitive to delay.

Real-time processes often have a periodic behavior, in which they must service events at a given rate; for example, a video streaming application that transmits video frames at a rate of 24 frames per second must (as the description suggests) produce 24 frames of video per second. In fact, the constraint is even tighter; it is not adequate to just require 24 frames per second because that could lead to bunching and then gaps; this variation in timing is known as jitter and has a serious impact on the quality of the video stream. What is actually required is an even distribution of the frames in time, so actually, there is a requirement that the frames are spaced 1/24th of a second apart. In such a system, the scheduler needs to be aware of this requirement, so that the video streaming process gets sufficient processing time to produce the frames, at the regular intervals required.

The timing constraints of real-time tasks require careful design of the entire system. In the video example above, there are actually several behavioral constraints arising from the specified frame rate. In addition to the fact that frames must be produced at a constant rate with equal spacing, these must also be delivered across the network to the consumer, maintaining this even spacing. This is a significant challenge for real-time distributed systems. The network technology itself can cause varying delay to the video data stream (and thus introduce jitter, reducing the final quality as perceived by the user). There is also a requirement that each video frame must actually be processed before the next one arrives. So if frames are produced every 1/24th of a second, the maximum processing time available to deal with each frame (e.g., video compression actions) is thus 1/24th of a second; no longer is allowed because that would cause the frame to be delayed, and with each subsequent frame, the delay would increase further. To put this into context, I will briefly describe a system with very tight timing constraints. In the 1980s, I developed a speech recognition system that sampled and digitized the sound input at a rate of 8 kHz. The processor was a Motorola MC68010 running at 10 MHz, which was a typical operating speed at the time, but in the order of one thousand times slower than today's technology. Each sound sample had to be processed within the 125 µs intersample timeslot. The processing included looking for start-of-word, end-of-word, and detecting various characteristics of the energy signature in a word, as well as measuring the duration of silence periods. With a clock speed of 10 MHz, the processor only just had enough clock cycles to finish one sample before starting the next. After painstaking optimization, the worst-case path through my code left just 3 instruction times spare between finishing processing one sample and starting the next.

We can divide real-time systems into "hard," "firm," and "soft" categories. A hard real-time system is one in which a missed deadline has severe consequences (in the context of the application and its users). The most common examples of this type of systems are in control systems such as fly-by-wire systems and robotic control systems. Missing the deadline in these systems is unacceptable, and much emphasis is placed on the design and testing stages to ensure this cannot happen. Systems in the "firm" category require that deadlines are met most of the time, but occasional deadline misses can be tolerated. An example of this could be an automated stock-trading system, which attempts to execute deals at high speed to achieve the current advertised price of a stock when a specific threshold in price has been reached. For these systems, speed is essential and the design will incorporate certain assumptions of transaction response time. A soft real-time system is one where deadline misses have an impact that affects the QoS, but the system can still function and the impact is thus less serious. For example, the responsiveness of an event-driven user interface can be considered to be real time if the application involves some activity where the user needs a time-bounded response. If the user has an expectation of a particular response time, then violation of this could have an impact ranging from dissatisfaction (e.g., if results from database queries are delayed) to considerable financial loss (e.g., in an e-commerce application if an order is placed based on out-of-date information or if the order is placed but lack of responsiveness causes delay in the order being actioned). A large proportion of commercial distributed systems can be classed as soft real-time systems or will at least have some soft real-time processing requirements.

General-purpose schedulers (i.e., non-real-time schedulers) do not prioritize tasks based on their periodicity or deadlines; typically, they are not even aware of deadline as an attribute of processes or tasks generated by processes. These schedulers are however commonly found in use in nonspecialized systems, and therefore, many tasks with soft real-time characteristics (especially business applications) run on systems driven by general-purpose schedulers. There is also a challenge with respect to prioritizing tasks within business and e-commerce applications in the sense that all users consider their own tasks (such as their database queries or their file downloads) to be the most important of all and do not have a business-wide view of what is actually the most important task for the system to perform at any particular moment. Hence, in such scenarios, if users could provide deadline parameters for their tasks, it is possible that all would choose the highest-priority value offered, and of course, this is self-defeating.

2.4.1 LIMITATIONS OF GENERAL-PURPOSE SCHEDULERS FOR REAL-TIME SYSTEMS

Consider the situation we explored in Activity P3 in which the PeriodicOutput processes perform tasks at fixed periods. Imagine that the tasks must occur at a specific rate to ensure a particular QoS, as, for example, in processing video frames in a video streaming application. With a general-purpose scheduler, it may be possible to achieve a specific timing when there is only one active process in the system, but there is no guarantee that timing constraints (deadlines) will be preserved when there are other processes competing for the resources of the system. This is explored in Activity P7, in which three instances of the PeriodicOutput program are used to represent a pseudo real-time application in which regular interleaving of tasks is required. The activity shows how a non-real-time scheduler may be able to achieve this in the absence of compute-intensive background tasks, but when a compute-intensive task is abruptly inserted, the schedule sequence becomes unpredictable, as the compute-intensive task is favored in terms of CPU allocation (it does not block as the IO-intensive ones do).

For hard real-time systems, actually determining the deadline for tasks is usually straightforward because it relates directly to the characteristics of the task itself: the real-world events that are involved, their periodicity, and the processing that needs to be carried out as a result.

ACTIVITY P7 EXAMINING SCHEDULING BEHAVIOR WITH REAL PROCESSES—REAL-TIME CONSIDERATIONS

Prerequisites

The instructions below assume that you have obtained the necessary supplemental resources as explained in Activity P1.

Learning Outcomes

This activity explores the nature of real-time behavior and the limitations of general-purpose schedulers in terms of ensuring deadlines are met:

1. To understand that real-time tasks have timing constraints
2. To understand that general-purpose schedulers do not cater for the timing requirements of real-time tasks
3. To understand how the behavior of real-time tasks can be affected by background workloads

Method

This activity uses the PeriodicOutput program we used in Activity P3 as a pseudo real-time program, and we also use the CPU_Hog CPU-intensive program we used in Activity P4 to create a heavy background workload:

1. Start the Task Manager as in Activity P4 and select the "Processes" tab. Sort the display in order of CPU-use intensity, highest at the top. This will provide a means of inspecting the computer's workload, so leave the Task Manager window open, to the side of the screen. Initially, the computer should be effectively "idle"—this is a term used to describe a computer with no or very little workload (typically CPU utilization will be no more than a few percent).
2. Open two command windows. In each one, navigate to the "ProcessView" subfolder of the SystemsProgramming folder.
3. In one of the command windows, run the PeriodicOutput_Starter.bat batch file. Observe the output; the A's B's, and C's produced by the first, second, and third copies of the program should be reasonably evenly interleaved as we saw in Activity P3. This observation being important, we shall use this interleaving as a pseudo real-time requirement, that is, that the processes produce output alternately. It does not really matter what the processes are actually doing, because the investigation here is concerned with how the background workload of the system can affect the behavior of the scheduling itself.
4. Once the processes running in step 3 have completed, restart them using the same batch file. This time, approximately half-way through their progress, start four copies of the CPU_Hog.exe program using the CPU_Hog_4Starter.bat batch file in the other command window. This creates a significant background workload on the computer, which the scheduler must manage.
5. Observe the effect of the CPU_Hog processes in the Task Manager window. You should also examine the effect of the sharp increase in workload on the interleaving of the output from the PeriodicOutput processes.

   The screenshot below from my computer shows the effect that the CPU_Hog processes had on the interleaving of the output of the PeriodicOutput processes.

**ACTIVITY P7 EXAMINING SCHEDULING BEHAVIOR WITH REAL PROCESSES—
REAL-TIME CONSIDERATIONS—Cont'd**

Expected Outcome

You should see something similar to my screenshot, although the actual behavior is sensitive to exactly which scheduler variant is present. In the screenshot, we can clearly see the behavior before and after the CPU_Hog background workload was started. Initially, the three copies of the PeriodicOutput process were running and their output was interleaved as we would expect. Just after half-way through this experiment, the CPU_hog processes were started in the second command window. You can see that the impact on the PeriodicOutput processes (which regularly perform IO and thus block) was that they received less regular CPU timeslots. The effect of this shows up as a disruption of the interleaving, as the three processes have to wait in the blocked state and then rejoin the ready queue, which always has at least three of the four CPU_Hog processes too, because these processes never block. This is a simple yet very important demonstration of the ways in which the performance of one process can be impacted by the behavior of the other processes that constitute the workload of the host computer. It also demonstrates how the workload intensity can change suddenly and by significant amounts and thus illustrates how difficult it can be to accurately predict process performance or system-wide behavior.

Reflection

This experiment illustrates the limitations of general-purpose schedulers with respect to process ordering and resource sharing. As the scheduler is unaware of any deadline or periodic behavior requirements of its processes, it simply shares the CPU resource based on the process state model. As most real-time tasks are also considerably IO-intensive (consider video streaming, voice and music applications, and reading sensors or making control outputs in machinery), it is likely that they will get blocked regularly, thus having to wait for events and IO hardware mechanisms, before joining the ready queue again. Therefore, these types of task are the most noticeably affected by abrupt changes in system workloads, as we have seen in this activity.

Consider a subsystem in a fly-by-wire[5] system in which a user provides control inputs at a remote command station (e.g., the cockpit of an airplane). The commands must be auctioned within a short time frame such that they take effect on the aircraft as soon as possible after the command has been issued. The user (in this case the pilot) receives feedback through the corresponding change in behavior of the airplane. In some scenarios, there may be a need to apply a control input progressively, using the feedback as an indication of when to ease off. For such a situation, an end-to-end response time of a few tens of milliseconds might be appropriate, that is, the time between the user proving a control input, the system acting upon it, and the user receiving feedback. Thus, for a given input (which becomes a task in the system), a deadline can be determined. A deadline miss in this scenario translates into delayed response and the airplane becomes difficult or impossible to fly. There may be a marginal point at which

---

[5]Fly-by-wire is used to describe remote actuation and control where there is no mechanical linkage. So, for example, in aircraft, the control cables that were used to physically move the ailerons on the wings and tail are replaced by computer systems where the pilot's control inputs are sensed and digitized and then transmitted to remote motors or servos, which actually move the control surface accordingly. These systems have very strict requirements including fail-safety and stability, and perhaps the most obvious realization of the constraints for such systems is in terms of their responsiveness—too long a delay between the pilot making a control input and the system reacting would render the system dangerous. A fixed short delay may be tolerable in some circumstances where the user can adapt, but what would not be acceptable would be a large delay, or fluctuations in delay, which mean that the system is not predictable. Thus, these are hard real-time systems and the deadline for task processing must be very carefully determined.

The concept of fly-by-wire is not limited to aviation systems; various X-by-wire terms are used to describe control in any systems where the traditional mechanical linkage has been replaced by a digital communication system. For example, the term drive-by-wire is used to describe the replacement of mechanical linkages such as the steering column, and similarly brake-by-wire refers to the replacement of brake lines, in road vehicles.

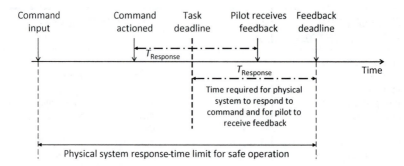

The system behaves correctly (the command is actioned before the task deadline).
The airplane responds, and the pilot receives feedback, in good time

FIGURE 2.24

Simplified illustration of the importance of meeting the deadline in a hard real-time system such as a fly-by-wire vehicle.

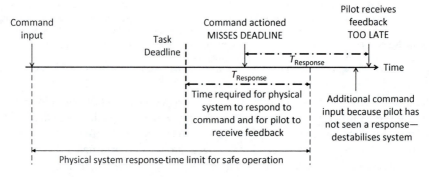

One scenario that could arise because the command misses its task deadline.
The pilot injects a further control signal, causing overshoot and leading to instability

FIGURE 2.25

Simplified illustration of the importance of meeting the deadline in a hard real-time system such as a fly-by-wire vehicle.

the delay causes the airplane to respond in jerky movements as the pilot gets confusing feedback from his actions leading to alternation between overcontrol and compensation inputs. A slight increase in delay beyond this point and the airplane is totally unstable and unflyable. Figures 2.24 and 2.25 provide a simplified illustration of this scenario; $T_{Response}$ is the response time of the control system once the pilot's request has been auctioned; for safe operation, this must be completed by the feedback deadline.

Figures 2.24 and 2.25 provide an example of how a computer task deadline in a real-time system (in this case, a fly-by-wire aircraft control system) maps onto the boundary between safe behavior (Figure 2.24) and unsafe behavior (Figure 2.25). In such systems, it is necessary for the computer system to achieve responsiveness as close to that of systems with a direct mechanical linkage as possible. This is explained in terms of the control systems of two very different aircraft. The Tiger Moth is an iconic biplane developed in the 1930s. Its handling was found to be suitable for use as a pilot trainer and was actually used to train Spitfire pilots during the Second World War. The Moth has direct cable linkages from its central joystick to the ailerons on the wings. You push the stick forward and the plane will dive, pull it back and it climbs, and push it left or right and it performs a banked turn to the left or right, respectively. The pilot receives instant feedback from her actions through the movement of the plane. If, for example, the pilot feels the plane is climbing too steeply, she will ease off on the stick, moving it towards the central position, and the climb will level off. The Moth is very responsive and easy to fly and the control system is very simple—there is no latency added by the control system itself. The pilot's actions in moving the stick translate directly and instantly in the equivalent movement of the ailerons. Now, compare the Moth with modern airliners, which are fly-by-wire with some very sophisticated control systems and in which some of the control surfaces are extremely heavy and large. The pilot demands a system that is as responsive as that of the Moth (having been privileged to have flown a Tiger Moth, I can confirm that the control inputs do indeed have immediate effect and the plane is highly responsive as a result). The modern plane has a vast array of safety systems, sensors, and actuators; to manage these systems, a great many computational processes can be active on its onboard computers at any moment. This is a very good example of a hard real-time system in which various tasks have different deadlines and priorities. There is a need to deal with routine sensor signals on a periodic basis, as well as unpredictable (asynchronous) events such as alarm signals indicating detected faults while ensuring that the control signals to move control surfaces do not miss their deadlines. The various computation and control activities must each be carried out within strict deadlines and the priorities of different tasks may change depending on the flight context, such as whether the plane is taking off, in smooth flight, in turbulent conditions, or landing.

As Figure 2.25 shows, a delay to a control action could lead to additional inputs from the pilot, which leads to overcompensation and ultimately destabilization of the aircraft.

A process that deals with inputs from a joystick could be an example of a periodic process, generating periodic tasks. Instead of detecting joystick movements and reacting to each, a more likely approach is to read the joystick position at a suitably high rate and communicate the value to the control surfaces regardless of whether the stick has been moved or not. In this way, the control surfaces always follow the stick's position with a certain lag, which is the total of the time to read the sensor, process the data to compute the control surface position, transmit the command to the actuator (such as on the wing), and actually move the control surface. The total latency must be small enough that the pilot gets a natural response from the plane; ideally, there should be the illusion of direct cable connection to the stick, pulling the ailerons. In addition to low latency, the actual latency must be consistent so that the pilot gets a predictable and consistent response from the plane; the scheduler must ensure this even when dealing with other urgent actions.

For illustration, consider that the sampling rate could be perhaps 100 Hz (i.e., sample the position of the control stick 100 times a second). The total latency allowed once sampling has occurred might be perhaps 50 ms. This means that the total time delay, between the stick being moved and the aircraft's control surface following it, would be 50 ms plus up to 10 ms due to the sampling interval (i.e., if the stick was moved immediately after sampling, then a further 10 ms would elapse before the new movement would be detected).

Many real-time monitoring and/or control systems include periodic tasks where a sensing activity and a subsequent control activation are performed with a regular time period (as in the aircraft joystick example discussed above). Often, there will be multiple streams of periodic tasks, generated by different processes. For example, playing a movie may involve two different streams of tasks, one for the

$$U = C / P \qquad U = \sum_{i=1}^{n} \frac{C_i}{P_i}$$

FIGURE 2.26

CPU utilization formulas for periodic tasks.

video frames and one for the sound. In this case, the timing relationships not only within the streams but also between the streams must be maintained (so that the sound and vision remain synchronized). Scheduling for such systems has some specific requirements, including the need to maintain the interval between the execution of tasks in a given stream and the need to schedule all tasks from all streams within their time constraints. The CPU processing capacity is a limiting factor in the rate at which tasks can be performed. The utilization of the CPU (for a given stream of tasks) depends on a combination of the period between the tasks and the computation time needed for each task instance.

The formulas to compute CPU utilization for periodic tasks are shown in Figure 2.26. The left-hand formula is for a single periodic task stream (continuous stream of tasks), while the right-hand formula is for a set of n periodic task streams. C is the computation time per task instance (within a stream), P is the intertask period, and U is the resulting CPU utilization as a fraction between 0 and 1. For the right-hand formula, n is the number of periodic task streams in the concurrent set, and i signifies a specific periodic task stream in the set $\{1 \dots n\}$.

The lower the utilization U, the more likely that all tasks can be scheduled correctly. If U exceeds 1.0, then the system is overloaded and some tasks will definitely be delayed. Even at values of U that are below 1.0 where there are multiple streams of tasks, it is possible that some specific task instances will be delayed because of the interleaving requirements of the multiple streams. Table 2.1 illustrates the way the utilization formulas work with some example configurations for a single periodic task stream P_1 $\{P_1T_1, P_1T_2 \dots P_1T_n\}$ and for two periodic task streams P_1 $\{P_1T_1, P_1T_2 \dots P_1T_n\}$ and P_2 $\{P_2T_1, P_2T_2 \dots P_2T_n\}$.

2.4.1.1 The Deadline Scheduling Algorithm

Deadline scheduling orders tasks by their deadlines, the task with the earliest deadline being run first. This has the effect that the task's deadline is its priority. The deadline scheduling approach does not pay attention to the interval between tasks that are generated periodically by a process. Therefore, while deadline scheduling is very good at meeting deadlines (because this is its only criterion when choosing tasks), it is not so good at preserving a regular spacing of tasks, which is necessary in, for example, audiovisual applications where the interframe spacing is an aspect of QoS or, for example, in a highly precise monitoring or control application where the sampling and/or control inputs must be evenly spaced in the time dimension.

2.4.1.2 The Rate Monotonic Scheduling Algorithm

Rate monotonic scheduling assigns a priority value to each process, based on the period of the tasks it generates, the process with the shortest intertask period having the highest priority. This emphasis on the period, rather than the deadline, leads to distinctly different behaviors from that of deadline scheduling under some circumstances. This approach is far better suited for systems that have repetitive streams of tasks generated by processes at regular intervals, where the interval itself is an important aspect of the system's performance. However, in emphasizing the value of preserving the interval, this algorithm is not as good as deadline scheduling at meeting deadlines in some situations.

Activity P8 investigates the behavior of the deadline and rate monotonic real-time scheduling algorithms using a variety of different real-time task mixes.

Table 2.1 CPU Utilization Examples

Period between tasks (ms)	Computation time (ms)	CPU utilization (%)	Illustrative task schedule over a 100 ms interval showing tasks (labeled) and periods when the CPU is unused
10 (single periodic task)	10	100	P_1T_1 P_1T_2 P_1T_3 P_1T_4 P_1T_5 P_1T_6 P_1T_7 P_1T_8 P_1T_9 P_1T_{10}
20 (single periodic task)	10	50	P_1T_1 P_1T_2 P_1T_3 P_1T_4 P_1T_5
50 (single periodic task)	10	20	P_1T_1 P_1T_2
20 and 50 (two periodic tasks)	10 and 20 respectively	50+40=90	P_1T_1 P_1T_2 P_1T_3 P_1T_4 P_1T_5 + P_2T_1 P_2T_2 = P_1T_1 P_2T_1 P_1T_2 P_2T_1 P_1T_3 P_2T_2 P_1T_4 P_2T_2 P_1T_5
20 and 100 (two periodic tasks)	10 and 20 respectively	50+20=70	P_1T_1 P_1T_2 P_1T_3 P_1T_4 P_1T_5 + P_2T_1 = P_1T_1 P_2T_1 P_1T_2 P_2T_1 P_1T_3 P_1T_4 P_1T_5

ACTIVITY P8 USING THE OPERATING SYSTEMS WORKBENCH TO EXPLORE SCHEDULING FOR REAL-TIME SYSTEMS (INTRODUCTORY): COMPARING DEADLINE AND RATE MONOTONIC SCHEDULING ALGORITHMS

Prerequisite

The instructions below assume that you have obtained the Operating Systems Workbench and the supporting documentation as explained in Activity P5.

Read the document "Real-Time Scheduling (Introductory) Activities."

Learning Outcomes

1. To gain an understanding of the nature of real-time processes, especially with respect to deadlines
2. To appreciate the differences between real-time schedulers and general-purpose schedulers
3. To gain an understanding of the rate monotonic scheduling algorithm
4. To gain an understanding of the deadline scheduling algorithm

Method

This activity uses the "Real-Time Scheduling—Introductory" simulation, which is found on the "Scheduling" tab of the Operating Systems Workbench. The simulation supports up to two real-time processes with periodic tasks. For each process, the intertask period and the CPU-time requirement per task can be configured. Two real-time scheduling algorithms are provided: deadline and rate monotonic. The simulation calculates the CPU utilization for the schedule, based on the configuration of the processes. A real-time moving display is provided, showing the current time (the vertical black line), the task's approaching deadlines (the vertical arrows to the right), and a recent history of the scheduled tasks (to the left):

ACTIVITY P8 USING THE OPERATING SYSTEMS WORKBENCH TO EXPLORE SCHEDULING FOR REAL-TIME SYSTEMS (INTRODUCTORY): COMPARING DEADLINE AND RATE MONOTONIC SCHEDULING ALGORITHMS—Cont'd

1. Configuration. For process 1, set the period to 33 ms and computation time to 16 ms. Enable process 2 and set the period to 20 ms and computation time to 10 ms. Select the deadline scheduling algorithm initially.
2. Notice the CPU utilization calculation that is shown. Look at the formula that has been used (this is dynamically updated depending on how many processes are active). Can you see how this formula works? See discussion earlier in the text.
3. When you are ready, press the "Free Run" button to start the simulation; let it run for some time, long enough to appreciate the scheduling behavior. Repeat the simulation with the same configuration, but using the rate monotonic scheduling algorithm instead. Note the results in the run-time statistics and system statistics windows. These will be used to compare the performance of the different scheduling algorithms.
4. Repeat the experiment (for both schedulers), but this time, use the following process configurations:
   * for process 1, period = 30 ms, computation time = 7 ms,
   * for process 2, period = 15 ms, computation time = 10 ms.

   What differences do you notice, in terms of the CPU utilization, the processes' task timing, and the CPU idle time (look at the third horizontal display line with the green bars representing CPU idle time)?
5. Repeat the experiment, for both schedulers again, now using the following process configurations:
   * for process 1, period = 30 ms, computation time = 16 ms,
   * for process 2, period = 20 ms, computation time = 10 ms.

What happens to the CPU utilization, the processes' task timing, and the CPU idle time under these conditions? Note that red bars indicate the task is overdue.

   The screenshot below provides a snapshot of the deadline simulation soon after it was started. The two processes have completed one task each and these tasks have both met their deadlines (the tasks ended before the vertical arrows that signify their deadlines). The second task of process 2 has begun and has had 4 ms of CPU time (see run-time statistics), of the 10 ms in total that this task needs (see the process configuration).

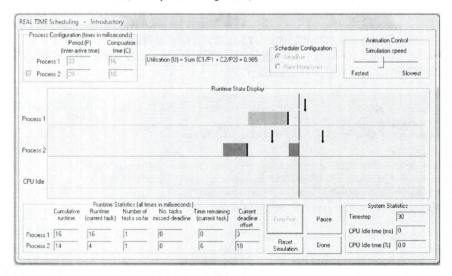

Expected Outcome

The simulations run continuously until stopped by pressing the pause or done buttons. This is because the types of process being simulated have periodic behavior in which tasks, with their own short-term deadlines, are created periodically by each process. As the tasks can be run back to back, a solid black bar marks the last time step of each task for visual clarity. You

---

ACTIVITY P8 USING THE OPERATING SYSTEMS WORKBENCH TO EXPLORE SCHEDULING FOR REAL-TIME SYSTEMS (INTRODUCTORY): COMPARING DEADLINE AND RATE MONOTONIC SCHEDULING ALGORITHMS—Cont'd

---

will see the run-time statistics and system statistics updating in real time as the simulation runs, as with the general-purpose scheduling simulations. These statistics facilitate analysis of the low-level behavior of the algorithms and their effects on the processes present. It is very important to pay attention to these statistics, when evaluating the relative performance of the algorithms. With real-time scheduling, the main goals are to avoid deadline misses and to maintain regular periodic task timing. Therefore, the number of tasks that miss their deadlines is generally the most important statistic to watch.

Reflection
You have examined the behavior of two real-time scheduling algorithms with a variety of process configurations. Based on the run-time statistics you have collected, you should be able to compare their behavior. Here are some questions to guide you:
1. What are the main differences in terms of the way the two algorithms perform scheduling?
2. Which is best at avoiding deadline misses?
3. Which algorithm seems to provide a more regular schedule (i.e., with regular periods between tasks)?
4. Does a CPU utilization level less than 1.0 ensure that no deadlines are ever missed?
Notice that as soon as a process' deadline expires, the scheduler calculates the next deadline for the same process; this is used as the basis for the scheduler's choice of which process to run at each time step. This awareness of deadlines is a major difference between the real-time schedulers and the general-purpose schedulers.

   Make sure you appreciate how the CPU utilization calculation works. You can perform additional experiments with different process configurations to help clarify this, as necessary.

Further Exploration
Carry out additional experiments with the "Real-Time Scheduling—Introductory" simulation using a variety of different process configurations to gain a deeper understanding. In particular, look for evidence of the different task prioritization approaches of the two scheduling algorithms in the patterns of the task schedules produced.

   You may want to use the single step button to run the simulations one step at a time allowing you to work at your own pace.

Introducing Variable, Bursty Workloads

In any open system, the background workload can be variable. This workload can affect the scheduler's effectiveness especially if the CPU utilization is high and all of the tasks present have real-time constraints. It is also important to realize that from the point of view of any specific process p, all other processes constitute the background workload with which it competes for resources, and thus from the point of view of those other processes, p itself is part of the background workload.

   Activity P9 provides an opportunity to investigate the impact of variable workloads on real-time schedules. The advanced version of the Operating Systems Workbench real-time scheduling simulation supports three processes. In part 1 of the activity, we investigate scheduling with three periodic real-time processes. In part 2 of this activity, we use one of the processes to take the role of a bursty background workload (but whose tasks have real-time constraints), which impacts on the scheduler's ability to correctly schedule a pair of periodic real-time processes. The simulation supports configuration of a start-time offset for each process. In the second part of this experiment, we set this for the third process such that it begins in the middle of an established schedule of a pair of periodic processes. This process is configured to generate only a single task, but this has its own deadline and thus the scheduler must try to incorporate the new task into the existing schedule.

ACTIVITY P9 USING THE OPERATING SYSTEMS WORKBENCH TO EXPLORE SCHEDULING FOR REAL-TIME SYSTEMS (ADVANCED): COMPARING DEADLINE AND RATE MONOTONIC SCHEDULING ALGORITHMS

Prerequisites

The instructions below assume that you have obtained the Operating Systems Workbench and the supporting documentation as explained in Activity P5.

You should have carried out Activity P8 prior to this one.

Read the document "Real-Time Scheduling (Advanced) Activities."

Learning Outcomes

1. To gain a more detailed understanding of the nature of real-time scheduling, especially with respect to sensitivity to background workloads
2. To enhance understanding of the rate monotonic scheduling algorithm
3. To enhance understanding of the deadline scheduling algorithm

Method

This activity uses the "Real-Time Scheduling—Advanced" simulation, which is found on the "Scheduling" tab of the Operating Systems Workbench. The simulation supports up to three real-time processes with periodic tasks. For each process, the intertask period, the CPU-time requirement per task, the number of tasks, and the first task start offset can be configured, enabling simulation of a very wide range of circumstances. As with the "Introductory" simulation, two real-time scheduling algorithms are provided: deadline and rate monotonic. The simulation calculates the CPU utilization for the schedule, based on the configuration of the processes. A real-time moving display is provided, showing the current time (the vertical black line), the task's approaching deadlines (the vertical arrows to the right), and a recent history of the scheduled tasks (to the left).

Part 1. Scheduling with Three Processes

1. Configure the processes as follows:

   For process 1, set the period, computation time, first instance start offset, and number of tasks to {35, 16, 0, −1}, respectively (the −1 means an infinite number of tasks, i.e., the process runs endlessly). Enable process 2, and similarly configure with {20, 10, 0, −1}. Enable process 3, and configure with {25, 2, 0, −1}. Select the deadline scheduling algorithm initially.

2. Run the simulation for some time, long enough to appreciate the scheduling behavior. Repeat the simulation with the same configuration, but using the rate monotonic scheduling algorithm instead. Note the results in the run-time statistics and system statistics windows. These will be used to compare the performance of the different scheduling algorithms.

3. What is the fundamental problem with this mix of processes? Examine the behavior until you can clearly see why this schedule will always lead to deadline misses.

4. Increase the period for task 2 until the schedule runs without deadline misses. You may need to try a few different values until you reach and acceptable configuration.

Part 2. Scheduling with a "Bursty" Background Workload

1. Processes 1 and 2 will constitute a regular real-time workload. Process 3 will represent a bursty workload, which starts abruptly, runs for a short time (causing a disturbance to the real-time scheduling), and then stops. Configure the processes as follows:

   For process 1, set the period, computation time, first instance start offset, and number of tasks to {35, 16, 0, −1}, respectively. Enable process 2, and similarly configure with {20, 10, 0, −1}. Enable process 3, and configure with {25, 8, 100, 1}, which means that it will generate one task only, with a processing requirement of 8 ms and with a deadline of 25 ms, and will do this after a 100 ms delay. Select the deadline scheduling algorithm initially.

2. Run the simulation. Note that initially, the scheduler deals with the workload adequately. The additional task then starts and disturbs the scheduling, causing some deadline misses, and then the system settles down again once the third process has completed.

3. Repeat the experiment with the same configuration: except for process 3, which now has {50, 8, 100, 1}.

Observe the behavior—the third process has the same processing requirement as it did in the previous experiment, but this time, the processing is able to be spread over a longer time frame, which means a better opportunity for the scheduler to use any idle CPU time that may occur. Is the overall result any different this time?

ACTIVITY P9 USING THE OPERATING SYSTEMS WORKBENCH TO EXPLORE SCHEDULING FOR REAL-TIME SYSTEMS (ADVANCED): COMPARING DEADLINE AND RATE MONOTONIC SCHEDULING ALGORITHMS—Cont'd

The screenshot below provides a snapshot of the deadline simulation in part 1, with three processes. The CPU utilization has been calculated to be 1.037, which implies that it is not possible to meet all deadlines. We can see that one of the tasks of process 1 has missed its deadline very slightly (red bars signify an overdue task), followed by a more significant overshoot of a task of process 2.

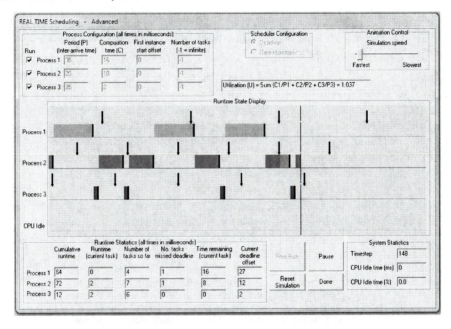

Expected Outcome

This activity has illustrated the added complexity of scheduling three real-time processes with periodic tasks and also the situation that occurs when a finely balanced two-process schedule is disturbed by the introduction of an additional process.

Reflection

As with general-purpose scheduling, CPU utilization is a main concern of real-time scheduling. In the former, an inefficient algorithm or increase in workload will have the effect of a degradation of performance generally, as tasks will take longer to execute; however, since there is no real-time constraint, it does not directly translate into a disaster. In the real-time systems, however, an inefficient algorithm or an overloaded system will lead to deadline misses. The seriousness of this will depend on the type of system. In an automated production line, it could disrupt the necessary synchrony with which the various robots operate. In automated stock trading or e-commerce, it could mean missing out on the best price in a deal. In a fly-by-wire car or aircraft, the delay of control signals reaching the control surfaces could destabilize the vehicle and lead to a crash!

We investigated the impact that background workload and fluctuations in workload can have on time-sensitive tasks. Even with real-time schedulers, a bursty background workload in which system load increases suddenly can impact the scheduling and cause deadline misses. This is an interesting challenge. The additional task could be very unlikely to occur but a very high-priority event such as closing a particular valve in an automated chemical production facility in response to an out-of-range sensor reading. The design of real-time systems thus has to consider all possible timing scenarios, including the most unlikely events, to ensure that the systems can always meet the deadlines of all tasks.

ACTIVITY P9 USING THE OPERATING SYSTEMS WORKBENCH TO EXPLORE SCHEDULING FOR REAL-TIME SYSTEMS (ADVANCED): COMPARING DEADLINE AND RATE MONOTONIC SCHEDULING ALGORITHMS—Cont'd

Further Exploration

Carry out additional experiments with the "Real-Time Scheduling—Advanced" simulation using a variety of different process configurations to gain a deeper understanding.

2.5 SPECIFIC SCHEDULING ALGORITHMS AND VARIANTS, USED IN MODERN OPERATING SYSTEMS

Almost all popular operating systems used in general-purpose computing systems implement variants of MLFQ because of the flexibility it affords when scheduling tasks of different types. Windows NT-based operating systems use MLFQ with 32 priority levels. Priority levels 0-15 are for non-real-time processes and levels 16-31 are for processes with soft real-time scheduling requirements. Linux has used a variety of scheduling algorithms, which include a MLFQ scheduler with a range of priority levels from 0 to 140, of which levels in the range 0-99 were reserved for real-time tasks. In addition to reserving the higher-priority queue levels for real-time tasks, they are also given considerably larger quantum sizes (approximately 200 ms), while the non-real-time tasks get quanta of approximately 10 ms. AIX (a version of Unix) has supported a variety of scheduling algorithms over its various versions, including FIFO and RR. The Mac OS operating system family have used a number of different scheduling algorithms, based on preemptive kernel-level threading. OS X uses MLFQ with four priority levels (normal (lowest priority), system high priority, kernel mode only, and real-time (highest priority)).

2.6 INTERPROCESS COMMUNICATION

Communication between processes in distributed systems is necessary for a wide variety of reasons. Applications may comprise large numbers of different processes, spread across various physical computers. Some communication will be local, between processes on the same computer, and some will be between processes on different computers, perhaps with different processor architectures and/or different operating systems.

Earlier in this chapter, the pipeline was introduced as a means of communication between processes by mapping the output stream of one onto the input stream of another. This can be very useful to construct logic pipes where data flow through a number of processes, being manipulated at each step, as in the Adder | Doubler example used. However, this form of IPC operates in one direction only and the processes are directly coupled by the pipe, that is, they operate as a synchronous unit, and the second process waits on the output of the first. Another significant limitation of the pipe mechanism is that it is mediated by the process-local operating system, and thus, by implication, both processes must be located on the same physical computer.

2.6.1 INTRODUCTION TO SOCKETS

The pipeline is only one of several IPC mechanisms available; sockets are another very important mechanism. Here, we introduce sockets in the context of IPC between local processes. The use of sockets in networking is explored in depth in Chapter 3. However, there are a few important characteristics of sockets that are mentioned briefly at this point so that their importance is recognized as you work through this section. Firstly, sockets have become a standard IPC concept that is implemented on just about every processing platform (both in terms of hardware and in terms of the operating systems that sit on the hardware platforms). Thus, the socket is an ideal basis for IPC in heterogeneous environments as it provides a means of interconnectivity between the different systems and also enhances the portability of applications. Secondly, sockets are supported by just about every programming language; this enables the components of a distributed application to be developed in different languages as appropriate for the functionality of the component. For example, in a client-server application, you might choose C++ for the back-end server processing but favor C# for the client-side graphical user-interface aspects. Finally, sockets operate at the transport layer of the seven-layer network model, and thus, socket-based IPC can be implemented using either of the TCP or UDP communication protocols.

Sockets allow communication though a dedicated channel rather than reusing the input/output streams. We are effectively creating new streams to perform the communication, facilitated by the sockets library.

The socket is a virtual resource (i.e., it is a structure within memory), which serves as an end point for communication between a pair of processes. Each socket is a resource that is associated with a specific process.

Each process can use as many sockets as necessary to permit communication with other processes. Sockets are very flexible in terms of the modes of communication they support. Sockets can be used in unicast or broadcast communication, and the processes involved can be on the same computer, or on different computers.

To set up communication, each process must first create a socket. The socket() system call is used to do this. The operating system actually creates the socket and returns the socket ID to the process, so that it can refer to the appropriate socket when sending and receiving messages. The sockets can be associated together to provide a virtual connection or can be used for discrete send and receive operations, depending on the parameters provided when the socket is created. The mechanism of using sockets to achieve IPC between processes is illustrated in Figure 2.27.

The usage of the socket library primitives is illustrated by means of annotated code segments from the IPC_socket_Sender and IPC_socket_Receiver programs that are used in the Activity P10, which follows. In this particular scenario, the two processes are on the same computer, and unicast communication in one direction only is implemented.

Figure 2.28 presents key-code segments from the IPC_socket_Sender program. Variables are created to hold a reference to the socket and the socket address (the combination of the IP address and

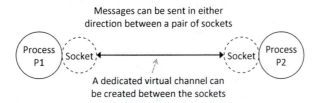

FIGURE 2.27

Sockets are end points for communication between a pair of processes.

```
SOCKET m_SendSOCKET;          // Create a SOCKET variable to hold a reference to the created socket

...

SOCKADDR_IN m_SendSockAddr;   // Create a SOCKADDR_IN variable to hold the recipient's address
                              // i.e. the address we are sending to
...

bool CreateSocket(void)
{
      m_SendSOCKET = socket(AF_INET, SOCK_DGRAM, PF_INET);
      // Create a socket and retain a reference to it. AF_INET indicates that Internet addressing will be used
      // SOCK_DGRAM indicates that discrete messages will be used (as opposed to a data stream)
      // PF_INET indicates that Internet protocols will be used
      if(INVALID_SOCKET == m_SendSOCKET)
      {
          cout << "socket() failed" << endl;          // Report error if socket could not be created
          return false;
      }
      return true;
}

...

void SetUpSendAddressStructFor_LocalLoopback(void)
{   // Initialise a SOCKADDR_IN structure with the recipients socket address details
      m_SendSockAddr.sin_addr.S_un.S_un_b.s_b1 = (unsigned char)127;// Set the four bytes of internet address
      m_SendSockAddr.sin_addr.S_un.S_un_b.s_b2 = (unsigned char) 0; // (this is the address of the recipient).
      m_SendSockAddr.sin_addr.S_un.S_un_b.s_b3 = (unsigned char) 0; // The loopback address is used because both
      m_SendSockAddr.sin_addr.S_un.S_un_b.s_b4 = (unsigned char) 1; // processes will be on the same computer.
      m_SendSockAddr.sin_family = AF_INET;
      m_SendSockAddr.sin_port = htons(8007); // Set the port number. This will be used by the operating system
                                             // to identify the recipient process, once the recipient has bound
                                             // to the port using the bind() primitive
}

...

bool SendMessage(void)
{
      m_iSendLen = m_UserInput.length();
      // Send the user's typed message (which is in the string variable m_UserInput)
      // The sendto() primitive uses the m_SendSOCKET reference to identify the socket in use,
      // and the m_SendSockAddr address structure to identify where to send the message
      int iBytesSent = sendto(m_SendSOCKET, (char FAR *)m_UserInput.c_str(), m_iSendLen, 0,
              (const struct sockaddr FAR *)&m_SendSockAddr, sizeof(m_SendSockAddr));
      if(INVALID_SOCKET == iBytesSent)
      {
          cout << "sendto() Failed!" << endl;          // Report error if send was unsuccessful
          return false;
      }
      return true;
}
```

FIGURE 2.28

Annotated C++ code segments of the IPC_socket_Sender program.

port number) of the recipient process; a special SOCKADDR_IN structure is used for this purpose. The socket is created inside the CreateSocket method, using the socket primitive. The send address structure is then filled out with the IP address and port number that will identify the recipient process. The user's message (preplaced in a string in code not shown here) is then sent, using the sendto primitive, which uses the previously created socket and address structure.

Figure 2.29 presents key-code segments from the IPC_socket_Receiver program. As with the sender program, variables are created to hold a reference to the socket and the socket address (a SOCKADDR_IN structure is used again, but this time, the local address is used, i.e., it is the address on which to receive; it is interpreted as *receive messages, which are sent to this address*). The socket is created inside the CreateSocket method, using the socket primitive. The local address structure is then filled out with the recipients own address details. The bind primitive is used to make an association between the process and the chosen port number. This informs the operating system that any messages addressed to the specified port number should be delivered to this specific process. The recvfrom primitive is then used to retrieve a message (if one has already arrived in the receive buffer), or otherwise, the process will be blocked by the scheduler because it must wait for a message to arrive (which is an IO operation).

```
      SOCKET m_IPC_ReceiveSOCKET;          // Create a SOCKET variable to hold a reference to the created socket

      ...

      SOCKADDR_IN m_LocalSockAddr;         // Create a SOCKADDR_IN variable to hold the local address (for receiving)

      ...

      bool CreateSocket(void)
      {
            m_IPC_ReceiveSOCKET = socket(AF_INET, SOCK_DGRAM, PF_UNSPEC);
            // Create a socket and retain a reference to it. AF_INET indicates that Internet addressing will be used
            // SOCK_DGRAM indicates that discrete messages will be used.
            // PF_INET indicates that Internet protocols will be used.
            if(INVALID_SOCKET == m_IPC_ReceiveSOCKET)
            {
                  cout << "CreateSocket() failed" << endl; // Report error if socket could not be created
                  return false;
            }
            return true;
      }

      ...

      bool SetUpLocalAddressStruct(void)
      {     // Initialise a SOCKADDR_IN structure with the local address (for receiving)
            m_LocalSockAddr.sin_addr.S_un.S_addr = htonl(INADDR_ANY);
                  // INADDR_ANY indicates that a message will be received if it was sent to ANY
                  // of the local computer's IP addresses (it may have one or more)
            m_LocalSockAddr.sin_family = AF_INET;
            m_LocalSockAddr.sin_port = htons(8007); // Set the port number, which will be used to
                                                    // map an incoming message to this process
            return true;
      }

      ...

      bool BindToLocalAddress(void)
      {     // The process associates its socket and thus itself with a port, using the bind() primitive.
            // The operating system makes an association between the process and the port number it binds to.
            // From this point on, the operating system will deliver messages addressed by the selected
            // port number, to this process
            int iError = bind(m_IPC_ReceiveSOCKET,(const SOCKADDR FAR*)&m_LocalSockAddr,
                                                                     sizeof(m_LocalSockAddr));
            if(SOCKET_ERROR == iError)
            {
                  cout << "bind() Failed!"; // Report error if bind failed (port may already be in use)
                  return false;
            }
            return true;
      }

      ...

      void ReadMessageFromReceiveBufferOrWait(void)
      {     // The process uses the receivefrom() to begin waiting for a message. If a message is already in
            // the receive buffer it will be delivered immediately to the process. If a message has not yet
            // arrived, the process will wait (the operating system will move it to 'blocked' state).
            int iBytesRecd = recvfrom(m_IPC_ReceiveSOCKET, (char FAR*)m_szRecvBuf,
                                                           RECEIVE_BUFFER_SIZE, 0, NULL, NULL);
            if(SOCKET_ERROR == iBytesRecd)
            {
                  cout << "Receive failed" << endl; // Report error if receive operation failed
                  CloseSocketAndExit();
            }
            else
            {
                  m_szRecvBuf[iBytesRecd] = 0; // Ensure null termination of the message string in the buffer
            }
      }
```

FIGURE 2.29

Annotated C++ code segments of the IPC_socket_Receiver program.

Activity P10 provides an illustration of socket-based communication between processes, using the two programs discussed above.

The sockets concepts introduced in this section and Activity P10 are very important learning outcomes at the level of the book itself and have been introduced here to link them with other aspects of the process view of systems. However, sockets are revisited and dealt with in greater depth in Chapter 3.

ACTIVITY P10 INTRODUCTION TO SOCKET-BASED INTERPROCESS COMMUNICATION (IPC)

Prerequisites

The instructions below assume that you have obtained the necessary supplemental resources as explained in Activity P1.

Learning Outcomes

This activity introduces sockets as a means of interprocess communication.

1. To understand the concept of a socket as a communication end point
2. To understand that communication can be achieved between a pair of sockets, using the *sendto* and *recvfrom* primitives
3. To understand how the local loopback special IP address can be used to identify the local computer (without having to know its actual unique IP address)
4. To understand how a port number is associated with a particular process, so that a message can be sent to that specific process when there are many processes at the same IP address

Method

This activity uses the IPC_socket_Sender and IPC_socket_Receiver programs to provide an introduction to socket-based IPC:

1. Examine the source code for the IPC_socket_Sender.cpp program. In particular, look at the way the socket primitives are used; in this program, the socket() primitive is used to create a socket, and then, the sendto() primitive is used to send a message from the created socket to another socket in another process. Also examine the socket address structure, which is configured with the IP address of the computer where the destination process is located, and the port number, which identifies the specific process (of the possibly many) on that computer. Notice that in this case, the process is located on the local computer, so the 127.0.0.1 loopback address is used and that the specific port that identifies the destination process is 8007.
2. Examine the source code for the IPC_socket_Receiver.cpp program. Look at the way the socket primitives are used, noticing some similarities with the sender program, especially the fact that a socket is created and an address structure is configured. However, there are also three important differences. Firstly, notice that the same port number is used, but this time, the bind() primitive is used—this makes an association between the receiver process and the specified port number, so that the operating system knows where to deliver the message. Secondly, the IP address used is different, in this case INADDR_ANY—this means that a message will be received by this process not only if it is sent to any address of the computer, so, for example, the special loopback address, which the sender program uses, will suffice, but also if the computer's unique IP address were used (see Chapter 3 for details), then the process would still receive the message. Thirdly, notice that recvfrom() is used to receive the message that has been sent with the sendto() primitive in the other program.
3. Open two command windows. In each one, navigate to the "ProcessView" subfolder of the SystemsProgramming folder.
4. In one of the command windows, run the IPC_socket_Receiver.exe program. This program waits for a message to be sent to it. When a message arrives, it will display it. The program should display *"Waiting for message..."*.
5. In the other command window, run the IPC_socket_Sender.exe program. This program waits for the user to type a message, which it then sends to the other program, via the socket-based IPC. The program should initially display *"Type a message to send..."*.
6. Position the two windows so that you can see both at the same time. Type a message in the IPC_socket_Sender program and press the Enter key. The message will be sent and should be displayed by the IPC_socket_Receiver program. The screenshots below show what you should see.

ACTIVITY P10 INTRODUCTION TO SOCKET-BASED INTERPROCESS COMMUNICATION (IPC)—Cont'd

Expected Outcome

The IPC_socket_Receiver process waits for the message to arrive and then displays it, as in the example shown above. Experiment with this a few times—you are actually sending a message from one process to another, using the sockets library as the mechanism for sending and receiving the message and using the operating system as an intermediary to pass the message.

Reflection

It is important to realize that this communication between processes represents your first step towards developing distributed applications and systems. Sockets are a flexible form of IPC. With sockets, the communication can be bidirectional, the processes can be on different computers, and we can also send a broadcast message to many receivers.

Study the source code for both the sender and receiver programs and make sure that you can reconcile the logic of the two programs with the run-time behavior exhibited, especially in terms of the communication interaction that occurs between the two independent processes.

Consider the opportunities that IPC between processes on different computers opens up for you. Perhaps your interest is in e-commerce or other distributed business applications, in multiplayer games development, or in remote access to computational resources. Think about how communication between processes fits in as a major building block in all of these distributed applications.

2.7 THREADS: AN INTRODUCTION
2.7.1 GENERAL CONCEPTS

A program that has a single list of instructions that run one at a time in the order that the logic of the program dictates can be said to be single-threaded (the program is said to have a single "thread of control"). In contrast, a multithreaded process has two or more threads of control. These threads can all be active at the same time and may operate asynchronously with respect to the other threads (i.e., once started, each thread gets on with its own work until it completes—it does not have to synchronize its activity with the other threads). Alternatively, their behavior may be synchronized; typically, this may involve one thread passing control (yielding) to another thread or one thread pausing until another has completed, depending on the program logic requirements and the actual threading mechanism used.

The thread that initially runs, and creates the other threads, is called the main thread of execution. The other threads are referred to as worker threads. The threads within a process share the process' resources such as memory, open files, and possibly network connections. Once started, these may need to synchronize in order to pass data from one to another or to ensure that accesses to the shared resources are performed in such a way as to prevent inconsistency; for example, if two threads were to update a shared variable independently, it is possible that one overwrites the output of the other. Access to shared resources must therefore be regulated, typically via a synchronization mechanism. Threads in some systems can be blocked (independently of the other threads) by the operating system, which improves responsiveness of the process itself. These characteristics of threads represent significant advantages over their coarser process counterparts, depending on the threading implementation and thread scheduling technique.

One advantage common to all threading schemes is that interthread communication can be achieved using shared memory within the process' address space. This means that the threads communicate by reading and writing to shared variables that they both have direct access to. This requires synchronized access to ensure consistency of the shared data but is very fast because the communication is performed at memory access speed and no context switch is needed to invoke external mechanisms, as with IPC at process level.

2.7.2 THREAD IMPLEMENTATIONS

There are two distinct categories of thread mechanisms: those where the threading is visible to and supported by the operating system scheduler (and are referred to as kernel-level threading) and those that are built in user-space libraries and exist only at the process level (which are referred to as user-level threading).

Kernel-level scheduling is generally the better approach, since each thread is individually scheduled and thus a process comprising multiple threads does not get blocked when a single of its threads performs IO; only the specific thread is blocked, allowing the other threads to continue, and thus, the process can remain responsive and also can get more work done in a given span of time than if it were single-threaded. Kernel-level multithreading also offers improved performance if the threads are scheduled onto different processors or cores within the system, effectively allowing the process to use more resources than the single-threaded equivalent could.

User-level threading is useful where the kernel does not support threading directly. The scheduling of threads must be performed within the process itself. When the process is running (as viewed by the operating system), any one of its internal threads can actually be running. Threads can be preempted using programmable timer mechanisms or can hand over control to other threads when appropriate (this is referred to as yielding).

The operating system schedules the user-level threads collectively—as far as it is concerned, they are a single entity (the process), and it is not aware of the different threads. This impacts on performance in two main ways: Firstly, if one of the threads performs IO, the entire process will be blocked; and secondly, the threads cannot be spread across multiple processor cores to take full advantage of the hardware resources that are available (as kernel-level threads can).

The two approaches are compared in Figure 2.30.

Figure 2.30 shows the different thread-run sequences that arise when the same pair of multithreaded processes are scheduled by user-level and kernel-level threading mechanisms, respectively. Process P_1 comprises three threads: $P_1 = \{P_1T_1, P_1T_2, P_1T_3\}$; process P_2 comprises two threads: $P_2 = \{P_2T_1, P_2T_2\}$. As can be seen on the left-hand side of the figure, the internal threading of the processes in the user-level threading mechanism is invisible to the operating system, and thus, when one of the threads within a process performs IO, the entire process is blocked. In contrast, in the kernel-level threading scheme, the scheduler can run any thread in the ready queue regardless of which process it belongs to (although the selection may be influenced by other factors not discussed here such as process priority). A thread moves through the process states (run, ready, and blocked) independently of its siblings.

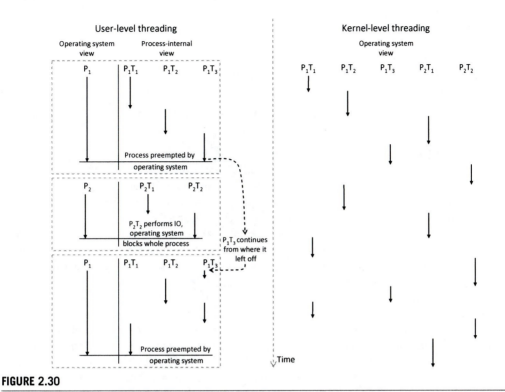

FIGURE 2.30

Comparison of user-level threading and kernel-level threading.

2.7.3 THREAD SCHEDULING APPROACHES

There are two ways in which operating systems perform thread scheduling:

1. The operating system gives a thread a quantum and preempts the thread when the quantum has expired. This is termed preemptive multitasking and is similar to preemptive process scheduling.
2. Threads are started by the operating system and relinquish control when they need to stop processing, for example, when they have completed a task or must wait to synchronize with another thread. This is termed cooperative multithreading.

Preemptive multitasking allows the operating system to determine when context switches (i.e., handing control to a different thread) occur, which can be better for overall system fairness. However, cooperative multithreading allows the individual threads to hand over control at appropriate points within their processing and can therefore be more efficient with respect to the performance of individual processes, whereas operating system-driven preemption can occur at any time irrespective of thread-internal state. Cooperative multithreading requires careful logic design and can be problematic in terms of performance and efficiency if a thread does not relinquish control appropriately; it may temporarily starve other threads of processing resource, or it may hold onto the CPU while waiting for some resource to become available.

Regardless of which of these scheduling approaches are used by the operating system, it is the operating system that chooses the next thread to run, from the set that are available, that is, ready.

2.7.4 SYNCHRONOUS (SEQUENTIAL) VERSUS ASYNCHRONOUS (CONCURRENT) THREAD OPERATION

The thread scheduling approaches discussed above apply at the operating system level and relate to the way in which threads are actually scheduled by the system. Any thread that is able to run can be selected to run next; the developer of the program does not control this aspect.

However, depending on the actual function and logic of applications, there are situations when the developer needs to influence the thread-run ordering as part of the program logic, that is, restricting the set of threads that can be executed at a particular moment by the operating system, based on program logic-specific criteria. One common example is requiring that one particular thread pauses until another specific thread has completed. The developer may need to enforce synchronization in the way in which the threads run to ensure correctness in terms of, for example, the way resources are accessed or the order in which functions are performed.

Synchronous thread operation requires that a particular thread waits for another specific thread to either complete or yield (pass control to another thread) before it continues. Asynchronous thread scheduling enables threads to run concurrently, that is, one does not wait for the other to complete. In this case, the threads run as and when they are given CPU time (scheduled by the operating system) without the process actively controlling the sequence. The extent of synchronicity in the behavior of threads within a process is controlled through the use of thread primitives.

The join primitive can be used to achieve synchronization. The calling thread, the one that calls the join() method, is blocked until the called thread, the thread whose join() method was called, completes. For example, thread A can be made to wait for thread B to complete by thread A calling thread B's join() method. This is illustrated in Figure 2.31, which shows the pseudocode for a scenario in which the thread synchronization is used to ensure action X occurs before action Y.

Thread synchronization with join is explored in more detail in the Threads_Join program (see Figure 2.32).

```
Thread A
{
  ...
  B.join()
  Perform action Y
  ...
}

Thread B
{
  Perform action X
}
```

FIGURE 2.31

Pseudocode example showing the use of join primitive to synchronize threads.

```
void Function1(string sStr)
{
    size_t tThreadID = std::this_thread::get_id().hash();
    thread thread2(Function2 /*function the thread will perform*/,
                   "BBBBBBBBBBBB" /*parameter for thread's function*/);
    thread2.join();     // calling thread (thread1) waits for called thread (thread2) to terminate
    ...
}

void Function2(string sStr)
{
    size_t tThreadID = std::this_thread::get_id().hash();
    thread thread3(Function3 /*function the thread will perform*/,
                   "CCCCCCCCCCCC" /*parameters for thread's function*/);
    thread3.join();     // calling thread (thread2) waits for called thread (thread3) to terminate
    ...
}

void Function3(string sStr)
{
    size_t tThreadID = std::this_thread::get_id().hash();
    ...
}

int main()
{
    ...
    // Create first worker thread (thread 1)
    thread thread1(Function1 /*function the thread will perform*/,
                   "AAAAAAAAAAAA" /*parameters for thread's function*/);
    thread1.join();     // calling thread (main) waits for called thread (thread1) to terminate
    ...
}
```

FIGURE 2.32

Selected code sections—Threads_Join example (C++).

Figure 2.32 shows the threading control parts of the Threads_Join sample program code. The main thread creates the first worker thread (thread1) and then joins the thread to itself. This causes the main thread to pause until thread1 terminates. Thread1 then creates thread2 and joins thread2 to itself, causing thread1 to pause until thread2 terminates. Similarly, thread2 creates thread3 and joins thread3 to itself; thus, thread2 pauses until thread3 terminates. The effect of this chain of joins is that the threads complete their work in the reverse order that they were created, thread 3 finishing first and the main thread finishing last. The synchronous behavior that arises is illustrated in Figure 2.33.

Alternatively, where there is no requirement of synchronized thread behavior, it may be desirable to allow all threads to run concurrently (as far as the process is concerned) and let the operating system schedule them freely, based on its thread scheduling mechanism. The detach primitive can be used to achieve this. detach() has essentially the opposite meaning to join(); it means that the calling thread should not wait for the called thread, but can instead run concurrently with it. This is illustrated in Figure 2.34, which shows the pseudocode for a scenario in which action X and action Y can be performed concurrently.

The use of detach to run threads asynchronously is explored in more detail in the Threads_Detach program (see Figure 2.35).

Figure 2.35 shows the threading control parts of the Threads_Detach sample program code. The main thread creates the three worker threads and then detaches all three of them from itself. This causes the threads to run asynchronously with respect to each other (the creating thread does not wait for the created threads to complete; instead, it is scheduled concurrently with them). This behavior is illustrated in Figure 2.36.

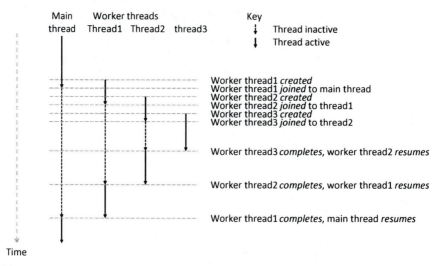

FIGURE 2.33

Synchronous behavior and thread execution order arising from the use of the join primitive in the Threads_ Join sample program.

```
Thread A
{
  ...
  B.detach()
  Perform action Y
  ...
}

Thread B
{
  Perform action X
}
```

FIGURE 2.34

Pseudocode example of use of detach primitive to enable threads to run concurrently.

Threads can relinquish the CPU when they have completed a particular task or when they need to wait for some other activity to be performed before continuing; this is called "yielding" and is performed by the relevant thread using the yield() primitive. However, the thread does not choose which thread runs next; this aspect is a scheduler function and is performed by the operating system based on the subset of other threads that are ready to run.

The use of the join() and detach() primitives to achieve synchronous and asynchronous thread behaviors, respectively, is investigated in Activity P11.

```
void Function1(string sStr)
{
    ...
}

void Function2(string sStr)
{
    ...
}

void Function3(string sStr)
{
    ...
}

int main()
{
    ...
    // Create three threads
    thread thread1(Function1 /*function the thread will perform*/,
                    "AAAAAAAAAAAA" /*parameters for thread's function*/);
    thread thread2(Function2 /*function the thread will perform*/,
                    "BBBBBBBBBBBB" /*parameters for thread's function*/);
    thread thread3(Function3 /*function the thread will perform*/,
                    "CCCCCCCCCCCC" /*parameters for thread's function*/);

    // Detach the threads
    thread1.detach();
    thread2.detach();
    thread3.detach();
    ...
}
```

FIGURE 2.35

Selected code sections—Threads_Detach example (C++).

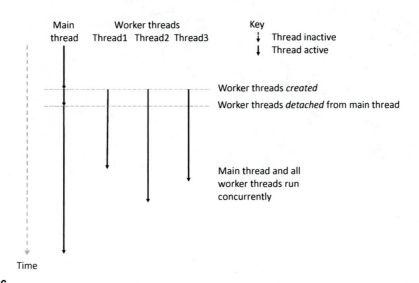

FIGURE 2.36

Asynchronous thread execution behavior arising from the use of the detach primitive in the Threads_Detach sample program.

ACTIVITY P11 EMPIRICAL INVESTIGATION OF THE BEHAVIOR OF THREADS

Prerequisites
The instructions below assume that you have obtained the necessary supplemental resources as explained in Activity P1.

Learning Outcomes
1. To gain an understanding of threads concepts
2. To gain a basic understanding of the ways in which threads are used within programs
3. To gain a basic understanding of synchronous and asynchronous thread execution

Method
This activity uses a pair of programs Threads_Join and Threads_Detach to illustrate how created worker threads can be executed either synchronously or asynchronously. The activity is carried out in two parts.

Part 1. Executing Threads with the join() Operation
1. Examine the source code for the Threads_Join program. Make sure you understand the logic of this program, especially the way in which three threads are created, each inside the previous one (thread1 being created inside the main function, thread2 being created inside thread1, and thread3 being created inside thread2); in each case, the threads are "joined" with their creating thread.
2. Run the Threads_Join program in a command window. Navigate to the "ProcessView" subfolder and then execute the Threads_Join program by typing Threads_Join.exe followed by the Enter key.
3. Observe the behavior of the threads. Try to relate what you see happening to the logic of the source code.

The screenshots below provide examples of the thread execution patterns that occur. The left screen image shows the behavior when join() is used to synchronize the threads behavior—here, the calling thread (the one that uses the join primitive) waits for its called thread to finish before it continues (i.e., the threads run synchronously with respect to each other). The right screen image shows the behavior when detach() is used to start the threads—in this case, the threads run asynchronously.

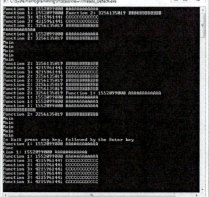

Part 2. Executing Threads with the detach() Operation
1. Use the same method as part 1, but this time using the Threads_Detach program.
2. You should see that the behavior is different each time you run the Threads_Detach program. You will see the outputs from the three threads are interlaced with each other and also with the outputs from main, which indicates they are all running in parallel (i.e., the calling thread does not wait for its called thread to finish before it continues).

ACTIVITY P11 EMPIRICAL INVESTIGATION OF THE BEHAVIOR OF THREADS—Cont'd

Expected Outcome

You should see that the three threads are started as part of the same process, but the threads themselves execute their instructions independently of the other threads. You should see the different effects of using join() and detach() to determine whether the logic in the calling function should synchronize with the termination of the called thread or whether the threads can run concurrently. You should notice that the threads are assigned a unique ID (within the process itself) and that this ID is dynamically allocated and can change each time the program is run. You should also see that with detach(), the actual relative timing of the threads' behavior (and thus the ordering of their output) is not predictable and can differ each time the program is run.

Reflection

Threads are a means of ensuring responsiveness within programs, by having different "threads" of logic running independently, and in parallel with other threads. This not only introduces the potential for efficient operation but also can lead to overall behavior, which is hard to predict, especially with respect to timing, as this activity has shown, and thus emphasizes the need for careful design and testing.

This activity has illustrated the fundamental nature of threads, although it is important to point out that this is a simple example and that multithreaded applications can exhibit significantly more complex behavior than shown here.

2.7.5 ADDITIONAL COMPLEXITY ACCOMPANYING THREADING

A single thread of control is predictable, fundamentally because only one action (such as reading a variable or writing a variable) can occur at any time, and thus, the consistency of its private data space is ensured. However, with multiple threads sharing access to the process' data space, there is the possibility that the timing of different threads' actions will lead to inconsistencies. For example, if one thread writes to a variable and another reads the same variable, the precise timing of these actions becomes critical to ensure updates are performed in the correct order and that data values are not overwritten before they are used. This is an example of what is called "race conditions." Without careful regulation, threaded applications are nondeterministic in the sense that the overall sequence of events and thus the actual behavior and results achieved are sensitive to the actual fine-grained timing behavior in the system, such that if the same process runs twice, it may give different results, even if the actual data values used are the same each time. The necessary regulation to ensure that processes' behavior remains deterministic, at least in terms of data consistency, and ultimately produces the correct result is achieved through the combination of careful program design and the use of run-time control mechanisms such as semaphores and the "mutex," which provides mutually exclusive access to resources so that operations performed by different threads cannot overlap.

Even once the design is correct, the testing required to confirm correctness and consistency is itself complex because it must ensure that under all possible timing and sequencing behaviors, the end result remains correct. Erroneous use of mechanisms such as semaphores and mutexes and the join primitive can lead to deadlock situations in which all threads are blocked, each waiting for another thread to perform some action. The design stage should ensure that such problems cannot occur, but because of the complex timing relationships that can exist between multiple threads at run time, this aspect itself can be challenging. Thus, the design, development, and testing of multithreaded versions of applications can be significantly more complex than for single-threaded versions.

2.7.5.1 Application Scenarios for Multithreading

Multithreading can be used to enable a process to remain responsive despite IO activities. In a single-threaded program, if the single thread performs an IO activity such as reading a large file or waiting for a message from another process, as is a common scenario in distributed applications, the process itself is blocked by the scheduler. This has the undesirable effect that the application "freezes" and does not respond to user commands. If the code is designed such that the tasks that are likely to block are each within separate worker threads that run concurrently with each other, then the application can remain responsive to user input. For example, consider a fast-action networked game that has an event-driven graphical user interface, regularly sends and receives messages across a network, and also requires local access to images and movie clips, which are accessed as files from local secondary storage such as a hard disk. In such an application, a main nonfunctional requirement is high responsiveness to the user commands and the corresponding display updates; in fact, this would likely be a main determining factor as to the usability and user satisfaction rating of the game. Access to the hard drive to retrieve a file or waiting for messages to arrive over the network would interfere with the smooth and fast responsiveness of the user interface that is required. This is a situation where a multithreaded approach would be advantageous, as the user-interface servicing could operate asynchronously to the other IO activities.

However, the simpler game that is used as a case study throughout this book does not require access to the local secondary storage while the game is running. In this case, a multithreaded solution could still be used to perform the network IO on a separate thread to the user interface, but since it is not a fast-action game, with user events occurring on the time frame of several seconds rather than several within a single second, a simpler approach has been taken that involves a single-threaded solution with a nonblocking socket so that the message buffer can be inspected without the process having to wait if there is no message available. This achieves the appropriate level of responsiveness without the added design complexity of a multithreaded solution.

Multithreading is advantageous to maximally leverage the computational resources of a processor. In a parallel application, multiple worker threads will be created that each perform the same computation but work with different subsets of the data. If the application is run on a multicore platform (assuming the kernel-level threading model), its process can use as many cores as it has threads, subject to the operating system's scheduling policy. Even on a single-core platform, multithreading can boost the performance of such applications because individual threads are able to perform IO (causing them to block), while others within the same process continue to run.

2.7.6 A MULTITHREADED IPC EXAMPLE

As discussed earlier, IPC is a form of IO, and thus while waiting for an incoming message, a process will block. Concurrent sending and receiving can be achieved at process level by having separate threads for each of the sending and receiving activities (thus allowing each to be scheduled, and blocked, independently). In this section, we use a multithreaded IPC example to extend the discussion of benefits of multithreading and also to delve a bit deeper into IPC issues.

The Multithreaded_IPC program combines threading and IPC and demonstrates how, by using asynchronous threading, the sending and receiving activities can operate concurrently. Note that in a single-threaded application, these would be serialized and the application would be difficult to use because each of the two activities would block while waiting for IO activities (the send activity waits for user input from the keyboard, while the receive activity waits for IPC messages to arrive on the socket). In contrast, the Multithreaded_IPC process waits for a message while continuing to send typed messages each time the user enters a new line. Send and receive are executed on separate threads, using blocking sockets. Separate sockets are used so that there are no race conditions within the process behavior. The program has two command-line arguments (send port and recv port) so that two instances of it can be configured to communicate together, as explained in Activity P12.

As illustrated in Figures 2.37 and 2.38, the receive function is placed into a worker thread, so when this thread blocks while waiting for an IPC message, it does not block the main thread. In this simple example, the sending activity is run on the main thread, as there is no business logic as such. In a more complex application with specific business logic, it would be possible to place the send activity in a further worker thread so that the business logic can operate while the send thread is blocked waiting for the user to type input; key sections of code concerned with the threading aspect are shown, with annotation, in Figures 2.39 (the main thread) and 2.40 (the receive thread).

Activity P12 uses two process instances of the Multithreaded_IPC program to explore the asynchronous communication behavior achieved by the multithreaded design.

Activity P13 uses the "Threads—Introductory" simulation within the Operating Systems Workbench to explore the behavior of threads and to investigate the differences between synchronous and asynchronous thread execution.

```
Main Thread
Start
   Create sockets
   Configure address structures
   Bind to local address (to facilitate receive)
   Start worker thread (ReceiveThread)
   ReceiveThread.detatch()

   Continue as Send Thread
      Loop (until "Quit" command entered)
        Get message from user
        Send IPC message
      Loop end
End

ReceiveThread
Start
   Loop
      Receive IPC message
      Display message to user
   Loop end
End
```

FIGURE 2.37

Pseudocode of the Multithreaded_IPC program.

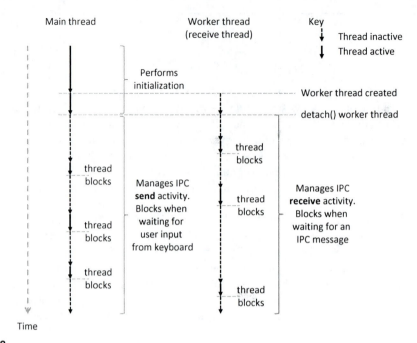

FIGURE 2.38

The main thread and worker thread run concurrently in Multithreaded_IPC.

```
...
bSuccess = CreateSendSocket();

...
bSuccess = CreateReceiveSocket();
...

bSuccess = SetUpLocalAddressStruct();
...
SetUpSendAddressStructFor_LocalLoopback();
...

m_bMainThreadRunning = true;

// Create and start worker thread (performs Receive in loop)
thread ReceiveThread(ReceiveMessages);

// Use detach() to cause the ReceiveThread to run asynchronously with main()
// This means that the 'main' Send thread and the Receive thread run in parallel
ReceiveThread.detach();

// The Send thread simply continues from here (it is the original 'main' thread of execution)
while(1)
{
        for(int iIndex = 0; iIndex < SEND_BUFFER_SIZE; iIndex++)
        {       // Clear the input buffer
                m_szSendBuf[iIndex] = 0;
        }

        cout << endl << "SendThread: Type a message to send (\"Quit\" to quit): ";
        cin >> m_szSendBuf;
        if(     0 == strncmp(m_szSendBuf,"QUIT", 4) ||
                0 == strncmp(m_szSendBuf,"Quit", 4) ||
                0 == strncmp(m_szSendBuf,"quit", 4) )
        {
                m_bMainThreadRunning = false;          // Signal to Receive Thread to stop its operation
                cout << endl << "Quiting" << endl;
                CloseSocketsAndExit();

        }
        iNumberOfBytesSent = SendMessage();
        cout << endl << "SendThread: Sent " << m_szSendBuf << " (" << iNumberOfBytesSent << " bytes)" << endl;

}
```

FIGURE 2.39

Annotated key sections of the *Multithreaded_IPC program, main thread* (C++ code).

```
// ******************************* Beginning of Receive Thread code ********************************
void ReceiveMessages(void) // The Receive Thread body
{
        cout << endl << "ReceiveThread: Waiting for message ...    " << endl;

        while(true == m_bMainThreadRunning)
        {
                ReadMessageFromReceiveBufferOrWait();
        }
}

void ReadMessageFromReceiveBufferOrWait(void)
{
        // The recvfrom call is modified by providing the address and length of a SOCKADDR_IN structure
        // to hold the address of the message sender (so a reply can be sent back).
        int iBytesRecd = recvfrom(m_IPC_ReceiveSOCKET, (char FAR*)m_szRecvBuf, RECEIVE_BUFFER_SIZE,
                                                                  0, NULL, NULL);

        if(true == m_bMainThreadRunning)
        {
                if(SOCKET_ERROR == iBytesRecd)
                {
                        cout << endl << "ReceiveThread: Receive failed" << endl;
                }
                else
                {
                        m_szRecvBuf[iBytesRecd] = 0; // Ensure null termination
                        cout << endl << "ReceiveThread: Message received:       " << m_szRecvBuf << endl;
                }
        }
}
// ******************************* End of Receive Thread code *********************************

int SendMessage(void)  // Called from Main thread
{
        int iLength = strlen(m_szSendBuf);

        // Send a UDP datagram containing the reply message
        int iBytesSent = sendto(m_IPC_SendSOCKET, (char FAR *)&m_szSendBuf, iLength, 0,
                (const struct sockaddr FAR *)&m_SendSockAddr, sizeof(m_SendSockAddr));
        if(INVALID_SOCKET == iBytesSent)
        {
                cout << "SendThread: sendto() Failed!" << endl;
                CloseSocketsAndExit();
        }
        return iBytesSent;
}
```

FIGURE 2.40

Annotated key sections of the *Multithreaded_IPC program, receive thread* (C++ code).

ACTIVITY P12 FURTHER INVESTIGATION OF THREADS AND IPC USING THE *MULTITHREADED IPC* PROGRAM

Prerequisites
The instructions below assume that you have obtained the necessary supplemental resources as explained in Activity P1.

Learning Outcomes
1. To reinforce understanding of threads concepts
2. To reinforce understanding of the use of sockets to achieve IPC
3. To gain an understanding of how asynchronous multithreading facilitates having concurrent blocking activities (in this case, *send* and *receive*), which would otherwise be serialized

ACTIVITY P12 FURTHER INVESTIGATION OF THREADS AND IPC USING THE *MULTITHREADED IPC* PROGRAM—Cont'd

Method

This activity uses two process instances of the program *multithreaded IPC* communicating together to illustrate full-duplex communication in which send and receive operate concurrently in each direction:

1. Examine the source code for the *multithreaded IPC* program. Make sure you understand the logic of this program, especially the way in which the communication activity is separated across the two threads (such that the main thread deals with sending functionality, while a worker thread is created to deal with receive functionality).

2. Run two instances of the program, each in a separate command window, remembering to swap the ports order in the command-line arguments so that the send port of the first instance is the same as the receive port for the second instance, and vice versa. For example,

Multithreaded_IPC 8001 8002   (*send to port 8001, receive on port 8002*)

Multithreaded_IPC 8002 8001   (*send to port 8002, receive on port 8001*)

3. Experiment with the two processes. Try to send and receive in various orders, to confirm that the process itself remains responsive, even when waiting for input from the keyboard or waiting for a message to arrive.

The screenshots below provide examples of the Multithreaded_IPC processes in action during the experiment. Note that the program logic is configured specifically by the port number parameters provided on the command line. Hence, the two processes shown below are communicating with each other using two separate unidirectional communication channels (at thread level) to provide bidirectional communication at the process level.

Expected Outcome

You should see that the two instances of the program work independently because they are separate processes individually scheduled by the operating system. They perform IPC via sockets and this communication works independently in each direction. The processes remain responsive because they use separate threads to perform the sending and receiving actions, and thus, these threads become blocked on an individual basis, as necessary.

Reflection

This activity provides an example of kernel-level threading. The send and receive threads each block when waiting for input. In the case of the receive thread, blocking occurs when it waits for a message to arrive from the other copy of the program. In the case of the main thread (which performs the send function), blocking occurs when waiting for the user to type a message on the keyboard that will be sent to the other copy of the program.

ACTIVITY P13 USING THE OPERATING SYSTEMS WORKBENCH TO EXPLORE THE BEHAVIOR OF THREADS

Prerequisites
The instructions below assume that you have obtained the Operating Systems Workbench and the supporting documentation as explained in Activity P5.

Read the document "Threads (Introductory) Activities."

Learning Outcomes
1. To enhance understanding of threads concepts
2. To enhance understanding of synchronous and asynchronous thread execution

Method
This activity uses the "Threads Introductory" simulation, which is found on the "Threads" tab of the Operating Systems Workbench. The simulation supports up to three threads running concurrently. The threads color randomly chosen pixels on a display area, each thread using a specific color (red, green, or blue) for the three threads, respectively. The progress of the threads can be visually followed by the color density of the screen area—so if the "red" thread receives more computational time than the other two, the "red intensity" will be higher than the green and blue intensities.

Part 1. Asynchronous Thread Scheduling (the Process Does Not Actively Control the Thread Execution Sequence)
1. Create and start a single thread. Notice how the thread gradually paints the (initially black) drawing area with its own color, the intensity of a particular pixel being incremented each time the pixel is randomly chosen. Leave this running for a few minutes or more and you should see near-total coloring.
2. Reset the drawing canvas. Create and start all three threads together with the same priority. Leave this running for a few minutes or more and you should see near-total coloring—which approximates to white—that is, an approximately even mix of red, green, and blue pixels.
3. Reset the drawing canvas. Create and start all three threads together; this time, set the threads to a mixture of highest and lowest priority (the differentiation between the other levels can be quite fine and the effect difficult to see). Leave this running for a few minutes or more and you should see the higher-priority thread(s) dominating with their color coverage.

Part 2. Synchronous Thread Scheduling (the Thread Execution Sequence Is Controlled Within the Process Itself)
1. Select the "Externally impose priority" radio button. Use the "Create and start threads" button to start the simulation with all threads having equal priority. You will notice that each thread runs for a short time in sequence, leading to a color-cycling effect. Experiment with different priorities of the threads (use the highest and lowest priorities to obtain the most visible effects). Notice that in this example, priority is translated into the share of run time that each thread gets, so the average color of the drawing area will be dominated by the colors attributed to the highest-priority thread(s).

The four screenshots below provide snapshots of the threads simulation for part 1 (in the sequence: top left, top right, bottom left, bottom right, respectively): only the red thread is running, the green thread has highest priority, the red and blue threads have highest priority, and, finally, all threads have equal priority.

ACTIVITY P13 USING THE OPERATING SYSTEMS WORKBENCH TO EXPLORE THE BEHAVIOR OF THREADS—Cont'd

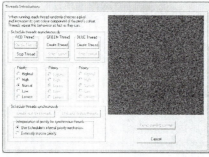

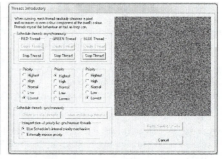

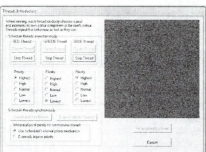

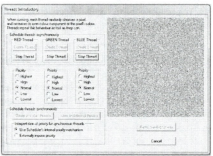

The screenshots below show the transition from red thread to green thread in part 2, on the left when all threads have equal priority and on the right when the red thread has lowest priority, and thus, the display remains mainly blue even after the red thread has run.

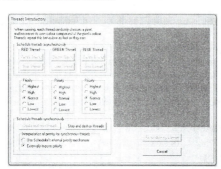

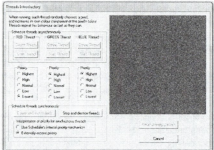

Expected Outcome

By having each thread draw in a different primary color, the simulation provides a means of visualization of the share of run time each thread receives.

In part 1, the threads run concurrently, and because the thread interleaving is very fast, they appear to run in parallel. You can see the resulting interleaving of pixel coloring behavior achieved.

Part 2 shows the effect of synchronous scheduling in which only one thread runs at any instant, leading to a color-cycling effect. It is important to realize that the amount of time for which each thread runs for has been exaggerated to

---

ACTIVITY P13 USING THE OPERATING SYSTEMS WORKBENCH TO EXPLORE THE BEHAVIOR OF THREADS—Cont'd

ensure the effect works visually for the purpose of demonstration. In real systems that schedule threads in sequence, they may typically run for 10s or perhaps 100s of milliseconds at a time.

Reflection

This simulation illustrates the scheduling of threads within a process. There can be many processes in a system, as we have discussed earlier. Within each process, there can be many threads. The individual threads are scheduled entirely by the operating system itself in some systems and are controlled to some extent at the process level (by primitives in the process' code) in other systems.

From an application design viewpoint, try to think of situations where separate threads within a process is an appropriate solution, as opposed to having separate processes.

Further Exploration

Experiment further with the "Threads Introductory" simulation to gain a deeper understanding.

2.8 OTHER ROLES OF THE OPERATING SYSTEM

In addition to process scheduling as discussed in some detail above, operating systems need to perform a variety of related tasks. These arise from the need to manage the resources of the system and make them available to the processes that are running, as they are needed.

Two other roles are briefly identified here as they have impacts on the way that processes operate and the overall efficiency and effectiveness of the platforms on which the processes run. As these activities impact significantly on the use of resources, they are revisited in more detail in Chapter 4.

Memory management. The operating system must ensure that processes have access to a reserved area of memory for the duration of their execution. It must limit the amount of memory used by any single process and ensure that processes are separated from (and protected from) each other, by preventing one process from reading or modifying the part of memory currently in use by another process.

Resource allocation. Processes request access to certain resources dynamically, at times unpredictable (certainly to the operating system). The operating system must ensure that processes are granted resources as needed while maintaining separation of processes and preventing a conflict arising where two processes attempt to use a resource simultaneously. If a request for access to a resource is denied by the operating system, the process may wait (blocked).

2.9 USE OF TIMERS WITHIN PROGRAMS

There are many situations where tasks need to be executed periodically at a certain rate, and possibly, several different types of event or task need to occur at different rates within the same program. Timers provide a means of executing code within a process at a certain period or after a specific interval. These are particularly useful in distributed applications in combination with nonblocking sockets operations, for example, checking to see if a message has arrived, without blocking the application to wait for the message; this is discussed in depth in Chapter 3, and the use of timers is illustrated. Here, the concept of using timers is introduced for completeness as it has some similarities with and can be considered an alternative to using threads in some circumstances.

The expiry of a timer can be considered an event to which the program must respond. The function that is invoked is called the "event handler" for the timer event.

Activity P11 has introduced threads and has shown their main benefit, which is that the threads operate in parallel with each other, but this also reveals a potential weakness—it can be difficult to predict the sequence of operations across multiple threads and can be difficult to ensure that one specific event occurs before, or more frequently, than another. Timers allow blocks of code to execute asynchronously to the main function and can be a useful alternative to threads to ensure responsiveness without the potential complexity overheads that can arise with multithreaded solutions. The fundamental difference is that threads are scheduled by the operating system, and thus, the developer does not have control over their relative ordering or timing. Timers, on the other hand, cause their event handlers to be invoked at developer-decided intervals, and thus, the developer can embed precise timing relationships between events, into the program logic.

A simple example of the use of timer-based activity is an environment monitoring application, which has a temperature sensor and measures the temperature value at a fixed time interval. The Distributed Systems Workbench contains an example of this (the distributed temperature sensor application), which is discussed in Chapter 3.

Figure 2.41 illustrates the run-time sequencing of a program that performs three timer-based functions. The program's logic is initiated in its main function. Three programmable timers are set, and when each of these expire, its related function is invoked automatically. On completion of the function, control is returned to the main function at the point where it previously left off, in the same way that returning from a standard function call works. Annotated sections of the Timers_Demonstration program are provided in Figure 2.42.

Figure 2.43 shows the output produced by the Timers_Demonstration process. The three timers run independently, effectively as separate threads, asynchronously with each other and the main thread. On close inspection of the output, you can see that at the point where 6 s have passed, all three timers expire at the same time, and in such a situation, it is not predictable by looking at the code which one will actually be serviced first. In this case, timer 3 is serviced first, followed by timer 2 and then timer1. Similarly, you can also see that after 2 s has passed, the second timer event handler is serviced before the first timer handler.

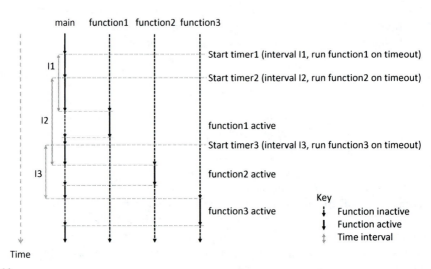

FIGURE 2.41

Timer-driven behavior.

```
...
System.Timers.Timer Timer1 = new System.Timers.Timer(); // Create first timer
Timer1.Elapsed += new System.Timers.ElapsedEventHandler(OnTimedEvent_Timer1); // Set event handler for 1st timer
Timer1.Interval = 1000; // Set time interval to be 1 second (1000 ms)
Timer1.Enabled = false; // Do not start timer running yet

System.Timers.Timer Timer2 = new System.Timers.Timer(); // Create second timer
Timer2.Elapsed += new System.Timers.ElapsedEventHandler(OnTimedEvent_Timer2); // Set event handler for 2nd timer
Timer2.Interval = 2000; // Set time interval to be 2 seconds (2000 ms)
Timer2.Enabled = false; // Do not start timer running yet

System.Timers.Timer Timer3 = new System.Timers.Timer(); // Create third timer
Timer3.Elapsed += new System.Timers.ElapsedEventHandler(OnTimedEvent_Timer3); // Set event handler for 3rd timer
Timer3.Interval = 3000; // Set time interval to be 3 seconds (3000 ms)

// Start all three timers
Timer1.Enabled = true;
Timer2.Enabled = true;
Timer3.Enabled = true;
...

// Event handlers for the three timers
private static void OnTimedEvent_Timer1(Object myObject, EventArgs myEventArgs)
{
    Console.WriteLine("One second");
}

private static void OnTimedEvent_Timer2(Object myObject, EventArgs myEventArgs)
{
    Console.WriteLine("            Two seconds");
}

private static void OnTimedEvent_Timer3(Object myObject, EventArgs myEventArgs)
{
    Console.WriteLine("                        Three seconds");
}
```

FIGURE 2.42

Annotated sections of the Timers_Demonstration c# program.

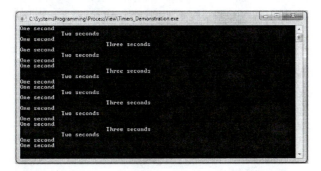

FIGURE 2.43

The Timers_Demonstration process running.

2.9.1 USE OF TIMERS TO SIMULATE THREADLIKE BEHAVIOR

It is possible to achieve threadlike behavior within a process by using timers and their event handlers to achieve multiple "threads" of control. The timer event handlers are similar to threads in the sense that they run independently of the other event handlers and also independently of the main thread of control. However, the main difference is that with timers, the actual timing of when the event handlers run is under the control of the programmer. This approach is better for periodic tasks within a process and can be used to achieve a real-time effect even without the use of a real-time scheduler (although the timing accuracy of the timers is not reliable for small time intervals, typically less than about 100 ms).

The timer countdown is managed by the operating system kernel, and thus, the countdown continues regardless of the whether the process is in the run state or not (i.e., the process is not itself decrementing the timer, this happens automatically as far as the process is concerned and the event handler is invoked automatically when the timer expires—which means its countdown reaches zero).

An example situation where I regularly use timers to achieve a threading-like behavior is in low-end embedded systems where the code runs "on the metal" (i.e., there is no operating system to manage resources). My application has to directly manage the resources it uses and natively runs as a single thread of control, following the various branches in the code based on a combination of the program logic and the contextual inputs from sensors. These systems have various hardware modules that can generate interrupts, including typically several programmable timers. Interrupt handlers have higher priority than the main thread of instruction execution, so I can create a high-priority "thread" by placing its logic in a timer interrupt routine and configuring the timer to interrupt at a suitable rate. For example, consider a sensor node application in which I need to have a general sensor monitoring application running as the foreground thread of control while periodically sampling a particular sensor at a certain rate (using one programmable timer) and also sending a status message to other sensor nodes at regular intervals (using a second programmable timer).

2.10 TRANSPARENCY FROM THE PROCESS VIEWPOINT

Of the various forms of transparency that are required in distributed systems, two forms in particular are important from the process viewpoint. These are briefly introduced here and are treaded in more depth in Chapter 6.

2.10.1 CONCURRENCY TRANSPARENCY

In situations where multiple concurrent processes can access shared resources, the operating system must ensure that the system remains consistent at all times. This requires the use of mechanisms such as locks (discussed in Chapter 4) and transactions (discussed in Chapters 4 and 6) to ensure that processes are kept isolated from each other and do not corrupt each other's results, which would leave the system in an inconsistent state.

2.10.2 MIGRATION TRANSPARENCY

If a resource is moved while in use, any process using the resource must be able to continue to access it without any side effects; this is quite challenging. More commonly, resources are only moved when they are not in use, and then, directory services are updated so that the resources can be found in their new location.

Moving a running process is possible in some systems; it has been done in some load sharing schemes, for example. However, this is far more complex than moving a resource. To move a process, it must first be stopped (frozen), then its process state is captured and transferred to a new location, and the process is restarted running so that it continues from the place it left off. The process must not notice anything different; its state must have been preserved so that its computation will be consistent despite the move. This is analogous to a person being moved between identical hotel rooms while asleep, such that when they wake up, they see the same environment and pick up from where they left off unaware that they have been relocated.

2.11 THE CASE STUDY FROM THE PROCESS PERSPECTIVE

The case study application is a game (tic-tac-toe) that is played across a network. The discussion below focuses on the process perspective, and the other aspects such as the networking and distribution and resource usage are discussed in the relevant other chapters.

The game application comprises two types of component: a client program and a server program. The client will run on each user's (game player's) computer, providing their interface to the game and enabling them to play the game remotely. The server will run on any computer in the network. It can be placed on one of the users' computers or can be on a separate computer. The server provides connectivity between the two clients (who do not communicate directly with each other) and also provides the control and synchronization of the game logic and stores the game state.

Running the game requires that the various components are run on the various computers. Note that there is only one client program, but this will be run on two computers, giving rise to two client process instances. The program logic of each of these is identical, but the actual behavior of these will be different because it is configured by the users inputs (in the game of noughts and crosses, this input includes the selection of which available space to place their token, at each turn).

The client processes will communicate with the server process using sockets as an IPC technique. The server will manage game state, and thus, when two clients are related through a live game, the server will mediate in terms of turn-taking by the users; so the server will enable one of the clients to enter a move while preventing the other.

2.11.1 SCHEDULING REQUIREMENTS

The application has loose timing requirements in the sense that users expect their input to be processed promptly and the response time (in terms of updating both client user interfaces to reflect the latest move) should be low, perhaps within 1 s is acceptable.

The timing requirements are not precise; there are no specific deadlines and the time-bounded aspect is very weak with no real consequences. Some variance (arising, e.g., due to heavy workload at one or more of the host computers) is acceptable without diminishing user satisfaction appreciably; thus, the game is not in the soft real-time category.

Such timing requirements are typical of very many general-purpose user event-driven applications and should be serviced adequately by any of the currently used schedulers in popular operating systems, discussed earlier. There is no requirement for real-time scheduling.

2.11.2 USE OF TIMERS

Programmable timers are required within the game application. A timer is used in both the client and server components to check for incoming messages at regular intervals of 100 ms. Essentially, the timer interrupt handler is used to run the receive functionality asynchronously with respect to the main thread, which handles the user interface and the send functionality (which is driven directly from the user input). By using a nonblocking socket for receive, in combination with the timer, which checks for received messages frequently, a responsive, multithreaded effect is achieved without actually requiring a multithreaded solution.

There are no time-dependent elements in the game logic itself.

2.11.3 NEED FOR THREADS

Client side: Due to the turn-based game play in this particular application, the user interface need not be highly responsive (compare, e.g., with a shoot 'em up-style game where the users are making command inputs and needing display updates at a very high rate). Given the style of game and the relatively low rate of user interaction with the interface, the user-interface aspect of the game client does not need to be multithreaded (whereas, for a fast-action game, this would be needed). A multithreaded solution is not required from the communication point of view because the communication timing requirement is not strict. The combination of a timer and nonblocking sockets lends itself to a simpler solution in this case.

Server side: The game server will support a small number of active games, and the message-load per active game is low; one message is received each time a client move is made, the server then having to compute the new game state and send a message to each of the two clients. Given the low rate of this operation and the low complexity of the game logic itself, the server need not be multithreaded.

However, the game logic could be redesigned as a multithreaded solution if required, for example, if a fast-action aspect with specific timing requirements were added to the game action or if more complex communication timing constraints were added. In such a case, it would be appropriate at the client side to separate send functionality and receive functionality each onto their own threads and have a third thread to handle the user-interface events.

The lack of requirement of multithreading at both client and server sides makes the game very suitable as a case study for the purposes of this book because the program operation is easy to understand, allowing the discussion to focus on the architecture, distribution, and communication aspects.

2.11.4 IPC, PORTS, AND SOCKETS

The IPC between processes in the game will take place across a network. While it is possible to run two clients at the same computer, it does not make sense from a distributed game point of view; it would imply that two players were sat at the same computer. The processes will use sockets as communication end points. The server will bind to a port whose number is known to, or discoverable by, client processes. Chapter 3 will deal with networking aspects in detail.

Figure 2.44 illustrates the structure of the game at various levels. This representation is very useful to help clarify the terminology we should use. It is important to recognize that the game itself is the application, which comprises two different programs: the client and server. These programs cannot really be called applications in their own right, because they do not do anything meaningful on their own; both parts are needed to actually play the game. This particular game is a two-player game, and therefore, the client program will need to run on two computers, one for each player. Note that the client program provides the user interface, which allows the user to interact with the game logic, which in this case actually resides on, and is controlled by, the server. The two players will require the same interface, and thus, both will use the same client program. It is very important to realize that an in-play instance

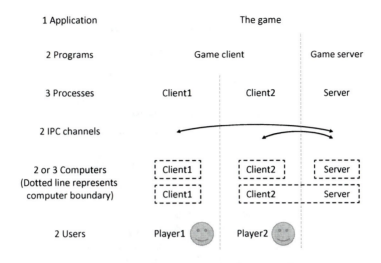

FIGURE 2.44

Structural mapping of the components of the game, at the various levels.

of the game comprises two process instances of the single client program (i.e., not two different client programs). As the figure depicts, the IPC is between each client process and the server process. The IPC channels shown can be considered private communication between each pair of processes. When following the client-server paradigm, it is usual that the clients do not communicate directly. The combination of client-server game architecture and socket-based IPC gives rise to two hardware configurations, that is, two different mappings between the processes and the computers they run on. The first of these is that each process can reside on a separate computer. However, only the location of the clients is important (i.e., their location depends on where the actual players are), but the server can be anywhere in the network and thus can also be on the same computer as one of the clients. Technically, it would be possible to put all three processes on the same computer, and in some applications, this might make sense, but this mapping is not applicable in a two-player game in which each player needs their own keyboard and screen in order to interact with the game.

Figure 2.44 also helps to reinforce the very important concept that a server is a process, and not a computer. A common misconception is that a server is a computer; this arises because often, a dedicated computer is provisioned to run a particular service (i.e., to house a server process) and then the computer itself gets referred to as "the server"; but as illustrated in the figure, the server is very clearly a process and in fact could be moved from one computer to another without affecting the way in which the game works.

2.12 END-OF-CHAPTER EXERCISES

2.12.1 QUESTIONS

1. Consider a single-core processor system with three active processes {A, B, C}. For each of the process state configurations a-f below, identify whether the combination can occur or not. Justify your answers.

Process	Process state combination					
	a	b	c	d	e	f
A	Running	Ready	Running	Blocked	Ready	Blocked
B	Ready	Blocked	Running	Ready	Ready	Blocked
C	Ready	Ready	Ready	Running	Ready	Blocked

2. For a given process, which of the following state sequences (a-e) are possible? Justify your answers.
   (a) Ready → Running → Blocked → Ready → Running → Blocked → Running
   (b) Ready → Running → Ready → Running → Blocked → Ready → Running
   (c) Ready → Running → Blocked → Ready → Blocked → Ready → Running
   (d) Ready → Blocked → Ready → Running → Blocked → Running → Blocked
   (e) Ready → Running → Ready → Running → Blocked → Running → Ready

3. Consider a compute-intensive task that takes 100 s to run when no other compute-intensive tasks are present. Calculate how long four such tasks would take if started at the same time (state any assumptions).

4. A non-real-time compute-intensive task is run three times in a system, at different times of the day. The run times are 60, 61, and 80 s, respectively. Given that the task performs exactly the same computation each time it runs, how do you account for the different run times?

5. Consider the scheduling behavior investigated in Activity P7.
   (a) What can be done to prevent real-time tasks from having their run-time behavior affected by background workloads?
   (b) What does a real-time scheduler need to know about processes that a general-purpose scheduler does not?

2.12.2 EXERCISES WITH THE WORKBENCHES

Use the Operating Systems Workbench to investigate process scheduling behavior.

The following exercises are based on the "*Scheduling Algorithms—Advanced*" simulation within the Operating Systems Workbench.

Exercise 1. Comparison of the SRJN and RR scheduling algorithms. Both SRJN and RR are pre-emptive. The objective of this activity is to compare the efficiency and fairness of the two algorithms

1. Configure the simulation as follows:
   Process 1: Type=CPU Intense, Runtime=40 ms
   Process 2: Type=CPU Intense, Runtime=40 ms
   Process 3: Type=CPU Intense, Runtime=40 ms
   Process 4: Type=IO Intense, Runtime=30 ms
   Process 5: Type=IO Intense, Runtime=30 ms
   IO Device Latency=10 ms
   Quantum Size=10 ms
   Scheduler Configuration=Round Robin

2. Run the simulation and KEEP A RECORD OF ALL THE STATISTICS VALUES.
3. Modify the configuration as follows:
     Scheduler Configuration = Shortest Remaining Job Next
4. Run the simulation and KEEP A RECORD OF ALL THE STATISTICS VALUES.
   Less CPU idle time implies better scheduling efficiency.
   Q1. Which algorithm was more efficient in these simulations? Is this difference due to a carefully chosen set of processes, or will it apply generally?
   A "fair" scheduler will give roughly similar waiting times to all processes.
   Q2. Which algorithm was fairest in these simulations? Is this difference due to a carefully chosen set of processes, or will it apply generally?
   Low waiting time and low "total time in the system" are measures of the responsiveness of processes.
5. Calculate the mean waiting time and mean total time in the system for the set of processes, for each simulation.
   Q3. Which algorithm gave rise to the highest responsiveness of the processes in these simulations? Is this difference due to a carefully chosen set of processes, or will it apply generally?

Exercise 2. Investigation of the effects of changing the size of the Scheduling Quantum

1. Configure the simulation as follows:
     Process 1: Type = CPU Intense, Runtime = 40 ms
     Process 2: Type = Balanced, Runtime = 50 ms
     Process 3: Type = IO Intense, Runtime = 40 ms
     Process 4: Type = Balanced, Runtime = 30 ms
     Process 5: Type = IO Intense, Runtime = 30 ms
     IO Device Latency = 10 ms
     Scheduler Configuration = Round Robin
     Quantum Size = 5 ms
2. Run the simulation and KEEP A RECORD OF ALL THE PROCESS STATISTICS VALUES.
3. Modify the configuration as follows:
     Quantum Size = 10 ms
4. Run the simulation and KEEP A RECORD OF ALL THE PROCESS STATISTICS VALUES.
5. Modify the configuration as follows:
     Quantum Size = 15 ms
6. Run the simulation and KEEP A RECORD OF ALL THE PROCESS STATISTICS VALUES.
7. Modify the configuration as follows:
     Quantum Size = 20 ms
8. Run the simulation and KEEP A RECORD OF ALL THE PROCESS STATISTICS VALUES.
9. Modify the configuration as follows:
     Quantum Size = 25 ms
10. Run the simulation and KEEP A RECORD OF ALL THE PROCESS STATISTICS VALUES.
    Q1. How does the quantum size affect fairness (i.e., which quantum size causes the processes to encounter similar wait times and which quantum size causes the greatest difference in the wait times)? Why is this so?

11. For each set of results, calculate the mean wait time and the mean total time in the system for the processes.

    Q2. How does the quantum size affect the mean wait time? Why is this so?

    Q3. How does the quantum size affect the mean total time in the system? Why is this so?

Exercise 3. Investigation of the effects of changing the IO device latency

1. Configure the simulation as follows:

    Process 1: Type=CPU Intense, Runtime=40 ms

    Process 2: Type=Balanced, Runtime=50 ms

    Process 3: Type=IO Intense, Runtime=40 ms

    Process 4: Type=Balanced, Runtime=30 ms

    Process 5: Type=IO Intense, Runtime=30 ms

    Quantum Size=15 ms

    Scheduler Configuration=Round Robin

    IO Device Latency=5 ms

2. Run the simulation and KEEP A RECORD OF ALL THE PROCESS STATISTICS VALUES.

3. Modify the configuration as follows:

    IO Device Latency=10 ms

4. Run the simulation and KEEP A RECORD OF ALL THE PROCESS STATISTICS VALUES.

5. Modify the configuration as follows:

    IO Device Latency=15 ms

6. Run the simulation and KEEP A RECORD OF ALL THE PROCESS STATISTICS VALUES.

7. Modify the configuration as follows:

    IO Device Latency=20 ms

8. Run the simulation and KEEP A RECORD OF ALL THE PROCESS STATISTICS VALUES.

9. Modify the configuration as follows:

    IO Device Latency=25 ms

10. Run the simulation and KEEP A RECORD OF ALL THE PROCESS STATISTICS VALUES.

    Q1. As IO device latency increases, what happens to the total time in the system (the time it takes to execute to completion) of each process?

    Do any of the processes take longer to execute? If so, why?

    Do any of the processes take less time to execute? If so, why?

11. For each set of results, calculate the mean wait time and the mean total time in the system for the processes.

    Q2. How does the IO device latency affect the mean total time in the system? Why is this so? Is this what you expected?

    Q3. How does the IO device latency affect the mean wait time? Why is this so (think carefully)? Is this what you expected?

Exercise 4. Predict and Analyze the behavior of the SRJN scheduling algorithm (part 1)

1. Configure the simulation as follows:

    Process 1: Type=Balanced, Runtime=40 ms

    Process 2: Type=Balanced, Runtime=50 ms

    Process 3: Type=IO Intense, Runtime=30 ms

    Process 4: Type=Not selected

       Process 5: Type = Not selected
       IO Device Latency = 20 ms
       Quantum Size = 10 ms
       Scheduler Configuration = Shortest Remaining Job Next0
       Q1. Predict which process will finish first.
       Q2. Predict which process will finish last.
       Q3. Predict how much time process 1 will spend in the blocked state.

2. Run the simulation to check your predictions. If you were wrong, make sure that you understand why.

3. Modify the configuration as follows:
       Process 1: Type = CPU Intense, Runtime = 70 ms
       Process 2: Type = Balanced, Runtime = 50 ms
       Process 3: Type = IO Intense, Runtime = 30 ms
       Process 4: Type = Not selected
       Process 5: Type = Not selected
       Q4. Predict which process will finish first.
       Q5. Predict which process will finish last.
       Q6. Predict how much time process 1 will spend in the blocked state.

4. Run the simulation to check your predictions. If you were wrong, make sure that you understand why.

Exercise 5. Predict and Analyze the behavior of the SRJN scheduling algorithm (part 2)

1. Configure the simulation as follows:
       Process 1: Type = IO Intense, Runtime = 40 ms
       Process 2: Type = IO Intense, Runtime = 50 ms
       Process 3: Type = CPU Intense, Runtime = 100 ms
       Process 4: Type = IO Intense, Runtime = 30 ms
       Process 5: Type = IO Intense, Runtime = 40 ms
       Quantum Size = 25 ms
       Scheduler Configuration = Shortest Remaining Job Next
       IO Device Latency = 25 ms
       Q1. Predict which process will start first.
       Q2. Predict which process will finish first.
       Q3. Predict which process will finish last.
       Q4. Predict how much time process 1 will spend in the blocked state.
       Q5. Predict how much time process 4 will spend in the run state.

2. Run the simulation to check your predictions. If you were wrong, make sure that you understand why.

3. Modify the configuration as follows:
       IO Device Latency = 20 ms
       Q6. Predict which process will start first.
       Q7. Predict which process will finish first.
       Q8. Predict which process will finish last.
       Q9. Predict how much time process 2 will spend in the blocked state.
       Q10. Predict how much time process 3 will spend in the run state.

4. Run the simulation to check your predictions. If you were wrong, make sure that you understand why.

The following exercise is based on the "***Real-Time Scheduling Algorithms—Advanced***" simulation within the Operating Systems Workbench.

Exercise 6. In-depth comparison between the RATE MONOTONIC (RM) and DEADLINE (DL) scheduling algorithms

Using each of the following process configurations, experiment with the two scheduling algorithms. Keep detailed notes of behavioral characteristics and any "interesting" observations or problems that occur. The goal is to perform a scientific comparison of the two scheduling algorithms.

Configuration A:
Process 1: Inter-arrival 30, Computation time 12, Start delay 0, and infinite tasks.
Process 2: Inter-arrival 20, Computation time 10, Start delay 0, and infinite tasks.
Process 3: Inter-arrival 25, Computation time 2, Start delay 0, and infinite tasks.
Configuration B:
Process 1: Inter-arrival 33, Computation time 16, Start delay 0, and infinite tasks.
Process 2: Inter-arrival 20, Computation time 10, Start delay 0, and infinite tasks.
Process 3: Inter-arrival 25, Computation time 2, Start delay 0, and infinite tasks.
Configuration C:
Process 1: Inter-arrival 33, Computation time 11, Start delay 0, and infinite tasks.
Process 2: Inter-arrival 33, Computation time 11, Start delay 0, and infinite tasks.
Process 3: Inter-arrival 33, Computation time 11, Start delay 0, and infinite tasks.
Configuration D:
Process 1: Inter-arrival 33, Computation time 6, Start delay 0, and infinite tasks.
Process 2: Inter-arrival 5, Computation time 2, Start delay 0, and infinite tasks.
Process 3: Inter-arrival 5, Computation time 2, Start delay 0, and infinite tasks.
Configuration E:
Process 1: Inter-arrival 30, Computation time 12, Start delay 0, and infinite tasks.
Process 2: Inter-arrival 20, Computation time 10, Start delay 0, and infinite tasks.
Process 3: Inter-arrival 25, Computation time 5, Start delay 50, and 5 tasks.
Configuration F:
Process 1: Inter-arrival 30, Computation time 13, Start delay 0, and infinite tasks.
Process 2: Inter-arrival 20, Computation time 10, Start delay 0, and infinite tasks.
Process 3: Inter-arrival 25, Computation time 5, Start delay 50, and 5 tasks.

When you have performed the comparative simulations, try these questions (in each case, justify your answer based on simulation evidence):

1. Which algorithm is the overall best for meeting task deadlines?
2. Which algorithm is the overall best for achieving high CPU utilization?
3. Do short-lived processes (those that have only a few tasks) interfere with/mess up the scheduling, or do the algorithms cope sufficiently?
4. Which is the overall best algorithm for REAL-TIME scheduling?
5. Are there any circumstances in which the overall-worst algorithm has advantages?
6. Is it possible to state that one algorithm is ALWAYS better than the other?

2.12.3 **PROGRAMMING EXERCISES**

Programming Exercise #P1: Creating a bidirectional socket-based IPC application (extend the provided sample code to send a message and return a reply between a pair of processes).

Step 1: Examine the source code for the *IPC_socket_Sender* and *IPC_socket_Receiver* programs, which comprise the introductory sockets application we used in Activity P10.

Step 2: Rearrange the existing programs to create a new version of the application in which the original message sent to the receiver (which is sent to port 8007) is modified and sent back to the original sender (this time using port 8008). The modification can be something simple such as reversing the order of the characters in the message.

The main modifications you need to perform for the new sender program are the following:

- Create a new socket for receiving the reply message.
- Create a new socket address structure, which contains the address of the local computer and the port number 8008.
- Bind the new receiving socket to the local address structure.
- After the current send statement, add a receive statement, using the new receiving socket, which will wait for the reply message.
- Display the received reply message on the console output.

Note that all of the codes for these steps already exist in the original receiver program. The various sections of code can be copied into the new Sender program, with only minor changes needed.

The main modifications you need to perform for the new Receiver program are the following:

- Create a new socket for sending back the reply message.
- Modify the existing receive method, so that it stores the address of the message sender process.
- Create a new socket address structure, which contains the address of the sender process (so a reply can be sent back to it) and the port number 8008.
- Write a method to reverse the received message (or perform some other simple translation).
- After the current receive statement, add a send statement, using the new sending socket, to send back the reply message to the sender of the first message.

Note that all of the code for these steps already exists in the original Sender program. The various sections of code can be copied into the new Receiver program, with only minor changes needed.

A sample solution to this problem is provided in the programs *IPC_socket_Sender_with_Reply* and *IPC_socket_Receiver_with_Reply*.

Programming Exercise #P2: The *Multithreaded_IPC* program runs the receive activity as a worker thread, while the main thread performs the send activity. Rearrange the code so that both the sending and receiving activities are run on worker threads, and thus, the main thread is left free for other activity (which, in a real application, could be the core business logic).

To achieve this you, will need to refactor the code so that the sending activity is run as a separate thread, using detach() so that the new thread runs asynchronously with the main thread.

An example solution is provided in the application *Multithreaded_IPC_two_worker_threads*.

Programming Exercise #P3: The *Multithreaded_IPC* program shuts down the local process when the command "Quit" is entered. Modify the program so that in addition to this local shutdown, the remote communicating process is also shutdown.

To achieve this, you will need to send the message "Quit" across the network to the other process and then perform the local "quit" action. You also need to modify the receive logic so that the process shuts down if the command "Quit" is received from the socket communication, in the same way that at present it operates if the command is seen from the local user input.

An example solution is provided in the application *Multithreaded_IPC_remote_shutdown*.

2.12.4 ANSWERS TO END-OF-CHAPTER QUESTIONS

Q1. Answer

Assuming a single-core processor system, at most, one process can be in the running state at any time:

Configurations a, d, and f are possible.
Configurations b and e can only exist momentarily because there are processes in the ready state and the CPU is not being used, so the scheduler should immediately dispatch one of the ready-state processes.
Configuration c cannot occur because there is only a single processing core.

Q2. Answer

Sequence a is not possible because a *blocked* to *running* transition is not allowed.
Sequence b is possible.
Sequence c is not possible because a process in the *ready* state cannot become *blocked*.
Sequence d is not possible because a process in the *ready* state cannot become *blocked* and because a *blocked* to *running* transition is not allowed.
Sequence e is not possible because a *blocked* to *running* transition is not allowed.

Q3. Answer

Four times as much CPU processing time is needed. So if the first task had received 100% of the CPU, then we can expect the four tasks to take 400s, as each is now getting 25% of the CPU resource. If however the original task had received a share of the CPU resource less than 100%, then the calculation is more complex—for example, refer back to Activity P4 in which the first task gets 50% but when four run, they get 25% each. In such a case, we would expect the run time to be approximately 200s when all four tasks run at once.

Q4. Answer

Non-real-time tasks are not guaranteed to run in any particular time period. Therefore, variation in actual execution times is the norm, not an exception. The variations arise because of the presence of other processes in the system, which compete for the processing resource. The scheduler makes short-term decisions as to which process to run based on the set of processes present and their individual process states. The state of the system as a whole is in constant flux as processes arrive, perform their work, and then complete; and so it is unlikely that the exact same conditions apply for more than a short sequence of consecutive scheduling decisions.

The minimum execution time can be achieved for a particular process only when it is given exclusive access to the CPU. In this case, the 60s run time could be the minimum execution time, but there is not enough information provided to confirm this.

Q5. Answer

Part (a) A real-time scheduler that takes periodicity or deadlines into consideration is needed.

Part (b) Deadline of processes or either deadline or periodicity of subtasks generated by the process.

2.12.5 LIST OF IN-TEXT ACTIVITIES

Activity number	Section	Description
P1	2.2.2	Exploring simple programs, input and output streams, and pipelines
P2	2.3	Examine list of processes on the computer
P3	2.3.1	Examining scheduling behavior with real processes—Introductory
P4	2.3.1	Examining scheduling behavior with real processes—Competition for the CPU
P5	2.3.1	Using the Operating Systems Workbench to explore scheduling behavior (Introductory): Comparing first-come first-served, shortest job first, and round-robin scheduling
P6	2.3.1	Using the Operating Systems Workbench to explore scheduling behavior (Advanced): Comparing the shortest job first, round-robin, and shortest remaining job next scheduling algorithms
P7	2.4.1	Examining scheduling behavior with real processes—Real-time considerations
P8	2.4.1	Using the Operating Systems Workbench to explore scheduling for real-time systems (Introductory): Comparing deadline and rate monotonic scheduling algorithms
P9	2.4.1	Using the Operating Systems Workbench to explore scheduling for real-time systems (Advanced): Comparing deadline and rate monotonic scheduling algorithms
P10	2.6.1	Introduction to socket-based interprocess communication (IPC)
P11	2.7.4	Empirical investigation of the behavior of threads
P12	2.7.6	Further investigation of threads and IPC using the *multithreaded IPC* program
P13	2.7.6	Using the Operating Systems Workbench to explore the behavior of threads

2.12.6 LIST OF ACCOMPANYING RESOURCES

The following resources are referred to directly in the chapter text, the built-in activities, and/or the end-of-chapter exercises.

- Operating Systems Workbench ("systems programming" edition)
- Source code (including solutions to programming tasks)
- Executable code

Program	Availability	Relevant sections of chapter
Adder.exe	Source code, Executable	Activity P1 (Section 2.2.2)
CPU_Hog.exe	Source code	Activity P4 (Section 2.3.1), Activity P7 (Section 2.4.1)
CPU_Hog_2Starter.bat	Source code	Activity P4 (Section 2.3.1)
CPU_Hog_3Starter.bat	Source code	Activity P4 (Section 2.3.1)
CPU_Hog_4Starter.bat	Source code	Activity P4 (Section 2.3.1), Activity P7 (Section 2.4.1)
Doubler.exe	Source code, Executable	Activity P1 (Section 2.2.2)
IPC_socket_Receiver.exe	Source code, Executable	Activity P10 (Section 2.6.1)
IPC_socket_Receiver_with_Reply. exe	Source code, Executable	End-of-chapter solution to programming exercise 1.
IPC_socket_Sender.exe	Source code, Executable	Activity P10 (Section 2.6.1)
IPC_socket_Sender_With_reply. exe	Source code, Executable	End-of-chapter solution to programming exercise 1
Multithreaded_IPC.exe	Source code, Executable	Activity P12 (Section 2.7.6)
Multithreaded_IPC_remote_ shutdown.exe	Source code, Executable	End-of-chapter solution to programming exercise 3
Multithreaded_IPC_two_worker_ threads.exe	Source code, Executable	End-of-chapter solution to programming exercise 2.
PeriodicOutput.exe	Source code, Executable	Activity P3 (Section 2.3.1), Activity P7 (Section 2.4.1)
PeriodicOutput_Starter.bat	Source code, Executable	Activity P3 (Section 2.3.1), Activity P7 (Section 2.4.1)
Threads_Detach.exe	Source code, Executable	Activity P11 (Section 2.7.4)
Threads_Join.exe	Source code, Executable	Activity P11 (Section 2.7.4)
Timers_Demonstration.exe	Source code, Executable	Section 2.9

THE COMMUNICATION VIEW

CHAPTER CONTENTS

3.1 RATIONALE AND OVERVIEW

A key goal of distributed systems design is the achievement of transparency. At a high level, this is usually interpreted as hiding the underlying architecture, functional division into components, and communication between those components. Essentially, the goal is to make the distributed components of the system appear to the user as a single coherent whole. However, for the developer, the functional split and the communication between components are critically important aspects that impact overall quality and performance of the system and thus must be studied in detail.

This section looks at distributed systems from the communication viewpoint. This aspect of systems is important not only in terms of the reliability and quality of service achieved by applications but also in terms of the efficiency with which the finite communication bandwidth that must be shared by all applications in the system is used. Thus, it is vital that designers of systems have a clear understanding of communication concepts and of the features and limitations of the communications mechanisms that underpin the higher-level systems and are able to use communication protocols efficiently and effectively. The chapter starts with the configuration of the most basic form of communication between a pair of processes and progresses through to more complex derived forms including Remote Procedure Call and Remote Method Invocation.

3.2 THE COMMUNICATION VIEW
3.2.1 COMMUNICATION BASICS

Communication in distributed applications takes place between a pair of processes, which can be located on the same or different computers.

We start by identifying the minimum requirements for communication to take place between a pair of processes, which we shall refer to as the sender and receiver, respectively.

A. The receiver process must be able to receive a message.
B. The sender process must be able to send a message; it also must have the actual message data stored in a buffer (this is a reserved block of memory).
C. The sender must also know (or be able to discover) the address of the receiver.
D. There must be a transmission system that both sender and receiver are connected to.

Consider the analogy of sending a letter to a friend.

As illustrated in Figure 3.1, for requirement (A), the receiver must have the means to receive the message; that is, there must be a fixed address that the postal service will be able to find and must have an actual letter box into which the letter can be placed by the postman. For requirement (B), the sender must write the content of the message. For requirement (C), the sender must know the address of the recipient and write this on the envelope. For requirement (D), in this scenario, the postal service is the network that connects the sender and recipient. Is the recipient guaranteed to receive the letter? This depends on the quality of the postal service; most postal services loose at least some letters.

The postal service may be viewed as a discrete block, as in Figure 3.1, or can be expanded to reveal its internal detail, as in Figure 3.2.

Figure 3.2 provides a simplified illustration of the internal details of the postal service. Letters are sorted by the hierarchical components of the address (country, region, town, local area) until they are in finely grained delivery-zone groups, which are then delivered to the recipients. The postal system

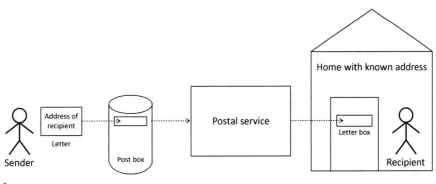

FIGURE 3.1

Sending a letter; user (external) view of communication system.

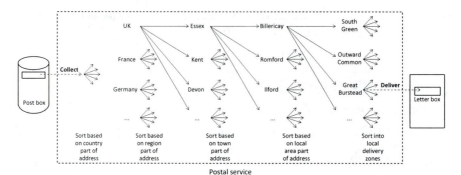

FIGURE 3.2

Sending a letter; network (internal) view of communication system.

requires a carefully designed internal structure to provide a large-scale yet efficient service. It is important to realize that the user of the system does not need to understand the precise nature of the internal structure, but should be aware of the basic principle on which it works and hence write the address clearly on the envelope. This is analogous to the operation of a communication protocol such as the Internet Protocol (IP). Its routing function is hierarchical for efficiency (based on patterns within the IP address), and its internal operation is transparent to the end user.

There are a wide variety of communication techniques that are used within distributed systems; the choice depends on a wide variety of factors, which include the application requirements in terms of time constraints and reliability, the nature of the data to be transmitted, and the scale of the system. The rest of this chapter discusses the various techniques and the relative suitability for each. This is placed in the context of specific application examples, and the discussion and examples are linked to the popular protocols and technologies in current use.

3.3 COMMUNICATION TECHNIQUES

3.3.1 ONE-WAY COMMUNICATION

One-way communication has limited applicability, but there are situations where it is adequate. In such cases, it is advantageous due to its simplicity both in terms of design and behavior; this is illustrated with an example. Consider an automated factory system, in which the production chain has a number of chemical processes that must be monitored to ensure that the temperatures of various parts of the system are kept within safe limits.

One component within this system is a temperature sensor unit that is connected to a part of the machinery. This unit has the following equipment:

- A temperature sensor
- A process that controls the reading of sensor values (sampling) and converts the analogue reading from the sensor into a digital value (which will be the message content)
- A network connection, so that the process is able to transmit the message

We might require that the sensor unit reads the sensor and sends a message containing the temperature once every 10 s.

Another component in this system is the monitoring unit that collects the data from the temperature sensor and determines if the system is within the safe limits; if not, it sounds an alarm. In all cases, the temperature value is displayed. This unit has the following equipment:

- A display.
- An audible alarm.
- A process that receives the message, extracts the temperature data from the message, compares the temperature data with a threshold level, sounds the alarm if the temperature has exceeded the temperature threshold, and in all cases displays the temperature value. Sound the alarm if there is a loss of signal from the temperature sensor unit.
- A network connection, so that the process is able to receive the message.

The system is illustrated in Figure 3.3.

Figure 3.3 shows the communication (the solid arrow) between the two processes in the remote temperature monitoring system. The sensing process is responsible for sampling the temperature sensor on a periodic basis and sending the digitized temperature data in a message to the monitoring process. The diagram does not show physical computer boundaries, and it is important to note that the two processes are each part of different software components but are not necessarily running on physically different computers; they could be running on the same machine.

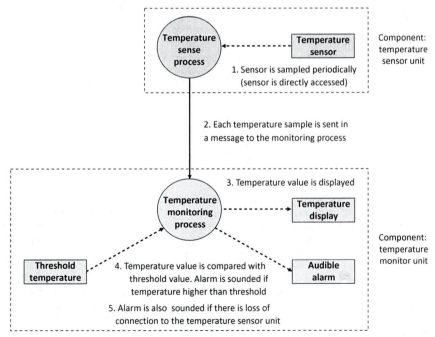

FIGURE 3.3

One-way communication between two processes in the temperature monitoring system.

The two processes can be fully decoupled; this means that they operate independently, having the communication as the only common link. In this simple scenario, we can assume that the temperature sense process transmits its periodic messages to a predecided address whenever it is running, that is, regardless of whether there is a monitoring process present. This approach is robust in the sense that the monitoring process can be shut down, or may fail, without affecting the behavior of the sensing process. Similarly, the monitoring process, when it is running, simply waits for the periodic messages from the sensing process. The lack of messages does not cause the monitoring process to fail; it simply continues to wait. As far as the monitoring process is concerned in this case, the communication is asynchronous; that is, even though the messages are sent on a periodic basis, the monitoring process does not need to be aware of this in either its design or its behavior. If the monitoring process were a critical part of a larger system, this decoupling could offer the significant benefit that if the sensing component would fail, the monitoring component would continue to function and could generate an alarm to signal loss of connection to the sensor. This approach is also flexible because each component can be upgraded independently, the only invariant being the communication mechanism, including the format of the communication messages. The approach is also flexible with respect to the process lifetimes. It is feasible that in some implementations, the sensing activity would run continuously, while the monitoring process might only operate at certain times; the decoupling allows independent process lifetimes.

Activity C1 explores one-way communication, independent process lifetimes, and the decoupling aspect.

ACTIVITY C1 USING THE DISTRIBUTED SYSTEMS WORKBENCH TO EXPLORE ONE-WAY COMMUNICATION, DECOUPLING, AND PROCESS LIFETIMES

Prerequisites

The instructions below assume that you have previously performed activity I1 in Chapter 1. This activity places the necessary supplemental resources on your default disk drive (usually C:) in the directory "SystemsProgramming." Alternatively, you can manually copy the resources and locate them in a convenient place on your computer and amend the instructions below according to the installation path name used.

Learning Outcomes

1. To gain an initial understanding of process-to-process communication
2. To gain an understanding of one-way communications
3. To gain an appreciation of the decoupling of components (loose synchrony through message passing)
4. To gain an appreciation of independent lifetimes and behaviors of components

Method

This activity uses the "Temperature Sensor" application, which is found on the "One-way Comms" tab of the Distributed Systems Workbench. The actual temperature sensor itself is mocked up with a random value generator to avoid the need for a physical temperature sensor. The Temperature Sensor sender process sends the generated temperature values at 10 s intervals. The communication aspect is implemented as it would be in a real application; this is the aspect we are interested in.

Start two copies of the Distributed Systems Workbench. These can be either on the same computer or on different computers. From one of the copies of the workbench, start the Temperature Sensor sender program (from the "One-Way Communication" tab at the top level), and from the other copy of the workbench, start the Temperature Sensor receiver (user console) program.

The Temperature Sensor sender program requires that the IP address of the computer hosting the user console process is entered in the GUI. It autodetects its own IP address and populates the input field with this by default, so if both processes are on the same computer, there is no need to change the IP address; otherwise, you need to enter the IP address of the computer where the receiver is running into the sender's GUI. If you do not know the IP address of

ACTIVITY C1 USING THE DISTRIBUTED SYSTEMS WORKBENCH TO EXPLORE ONE-WAY COMMUNICATION, DECOUPLING, AND PROCESS LIFETIMES—Cont'd

the receiver, you can use broadcast communication instead, so long as both processes are running within the same local network. Ensure that the sender's port number is set to the same value as the user console's "receive" port.

The communication behavior is evaluated under various scenarios to demonstrate the decoupling, separate lifetimes, and robustness aspect of the design.

1. Normal operation. Click the "START Temperature Sender" button on the sender and click the "START receiving" button on the user console. The temperature sensor values are generated periodically and sent to the user console for display. Observe the behavior. The screenshots below show the two processes running normally. Notice that because I started the sender slightly before the user console, the first sent message was not received; this is the correct behavior when using the UDP (which has no reliability or delivery guarantee mechanisms) and should be noted.

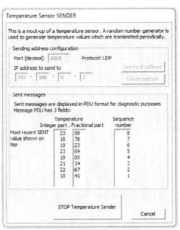 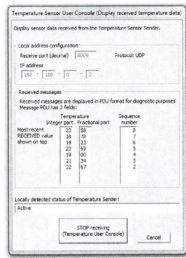

2. Receiver not present. Have both processes running initially. Close down the receiver process (you can either shutdown just the program or the entire parent workbench). Notice that the sender process is unaffected. The two components are said to be decoupled in this design, and the sender is robust to failures in the receiver. Restart the receiver. Note that it picks up transmissions from the sender automatically.

3. Receiver stopped. Have both processes running initially. Stop the **receiver** process by pressing the button that was labeled "START…" initially but is now labeled "STOP…," but **do not shutdown the process**. Wait while the sender generates at least three temperature values and sends them, and then, restart the receiver. Observe that the receiver has not actually missed any of the intervening messages and they have been held in a buffer and are now displayed on the user console. Message buffering will be explored in more depth in subsequent activities.

4. Sender stopped. Have both processes running initially. Stop the **sender** process by pressing the button that was labeled "START…" initially but is now labeled "STOP…," but do not shutdown the process. The receiver will notice after some time that the messages are not arriving and will signal an alarm to indicate possible failure of the sender component. However, note that the receiver component is not adversely affected by the failure of the sender in the sense that it continues to operate and provides important diagnostic information. Restart the sender process by pressing the "START…" button. Notice that the receiver resumes its normal display mode. This is an illustration of purposefully designed robust behavior in which the receiver handles the lack of communication from the sender in a predictable way. The screenshots below show the situation where the receiver has detected the absence of expected periodic messages from the sender (whose transmission has been stopped purposefully in the experiment but equally could have crashed from the viewpoint of the receiver).

ACTIVITY C1 USING THE DISTRIBUTED SYSTEMS WORKBENCH TO EXPLORE ONE-WAY COMMUNICATION, DECOUPLING, AND PROCESS LIFETIMES—Cont'd

Expected Outcomes

You have explored one-way communication in an example application scenario that demonstrates its value, although it should be noted that most distributed systems communication is bidirectional between components. You have seen an example of decoupled components where each component's lifetime is independent of the other and where each can operate correctly in the absence of the other. Robustness stems from this decoupling; in this case, one component is able to detect the failure of the other.

Reflection

The ability to stop and start components independently without causing their communication partners to fail is a highly desirable characteristic for distributed applications. A robust design should support this where feasible because it is not possible to predict when one software component in a system or the hardware platform it is hosted on will crash or be purposefully shutdown.

The rules for a particular communication system are collectively called the protocol. The temperature sensing application described above is just about the simplest possible protocol scenario, as it is limited to one-way message transmission between a single sender and a single receiver (which the example assumes is at a preknown location).

Almost all communication is more complex, due to one or more of the following factors:

- Processes are not at preknown locations.
- Some processes perform services only when requested (rather than the continuous-send example discussed above).
- Multiple processes can be involved (possibly, more than one process may request service).
- Communication is bidirectional, where in the simplest scenario, the requestor initiates communication by making a request and supplies their address details to the server so that the server is able to direct resultant data messages back to the requester. Considerably, more complex scenarios are possible.

- Application-specific aspects, such as the mean interval between message transmission and the mean size of messages.
- Systems are dynamic. The location and availability of services and components can change. Load, and hence delay, is continuously varying.
- Network infrastructure and message transmission is intrinsically unreliable. Messages can be lost, and if these are important, then some means to detect their loss and retransmit them are needed.

These factors lead to potentially highly complex communication scenarios in distributed systems, in terms of the component to component connectivity, the number of components involved, the size and frequency of transmission of messages, and the need for components to locate and identify each other. In addition, distributed applications have specific communication requirements and are impacted differently by the various aspects of interaction complexity and the resulting intensity of communication, depending on the specific application functionality. Due to the diverse communication requirements of distributed applications, a wide variety of communications protocols have been developed.

The communication protocol defines the rules of communication. The protocol governs aspects such as the quantity and format of information that is transmitted; the sequence of interactions between two parties and which party initiates the sequence; and whether a reply or an acknowledgment that the message has been received is sent back. Some protocols also incorporate features such as sequence numbers to ensure that messages are differentiable and that ordering of message delivery can be guaranteed. Automatic retransmission of sent messages that have not been acknowledged within a certain time frame is a popular way to add reliability.

The communication protocol is in many systems the only invariant between components that are moved or upgraded and thus is a vital aspect of reliable distributed systems. In addition, the communication protocol and the underlying support mechanisms such as network sockets facilitate connectivity in otherwise heterogeneous systems, thereby facilitating network transparency. For example, using TCP as the communication protocol, a client written in C# operating on a Microsoft Windows-based personal computer can interface to a server process written in C++ and operating on a rack-mounted processor unit running the Linux operating system. So long as both of the software components use the communication protocol correctly and both the platforms implement the underlying communication mechanisms correctly, the two components will be able to interact and exchange application data.

3.3.2 REQUEST-REPLY COMMUNICATION

The request-reply communication mechanism is the basis of a popular yet simple group of protocols in which simple two-way communication occurs between a specific pair of processes.

A generic description of request-reply communication is as follows: Interaction begins with a request for service message, which is sent from a service requestor process to a service provider process. The service provider then performs the necessary computation and returns the result in a single message to the requestor; see Figure 3.4.

Figure 3.4 shows the request-reply protocol concept. The essence of this strategy is that control flows to the service provider, that is, a request message, and data (the result of the request) flow back to the requestor.

A popular and easy to understand example of a request-reply protocol is the Network Time Protocol (NTP) service, which is one of several time services that constitute the Internet Time Service (ITS) provided by the National Institute of Standards and Technology (NIST), based in the United States.

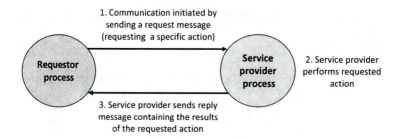

FIGURE 3.4

The request-reply protocol.

Synchronizing the time value of the clock on a computer to the correct real-world time is a vital pre-requisite action in order that many applications function correctly. NTP provides a means of getting an accurate time value from one of a pool of specially designated NTP time servers. The synchronization among the various time servers within the ITS service itself is performed separately with its own internal hierarchical structure comprising several stratum's (layers) of clocks, with highly accurate clocks, such as atomic clocks, in stratum 0. It is a very important point to note that external users of the NTP service do not need to know any details of this internal configuration; they simply send a request message to any one of the NTP time servers and receive a response containing the current time value. The ITS NTP service operation is illustrated in Figure 3.5.

Figure 3.5 shows how the NTP service is accessed to retrieve a current time stamp value. In step 1, a request message formatted to comply with the NTP protocol is sent to one of the pool of NTP servers. In step 2, the specific NTP server responds with a reply message, which is sent back to the original

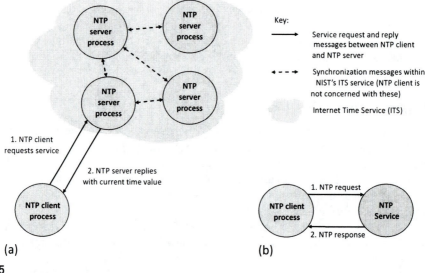

FIGURE 3.5

Overview of the operation of the NTP service.

```
Start
  Prepare request message
  Send request message to a specific NTP server
  Wait for reply from NTP server
  Update local clock
End
```

FIGURE 3.6

The NTP client pseudocode.

requester (who is identified by examining the source address details in the request message). Part A of the figure provides an overview of the actual system, while part B shows the user's simplified view of the system. This example provides some important early insights into transparency requirements for distributed systems services: the NTP client does not need to know the details of the way in which the ITS service operates internally (in terms of the number of participating NTP servers and the way in which updates and synchronization are performed among the servers) in order to use the service. In terms of behavior, the NTP time service should provide a low-latency response, further reinforcing the transparency as seen by the user. In this respect, the NTP server instance should return the instantaneously available time value from its local clock, which has been presynchronized by the NTP service itself, rather than requesting a fresh synchronization activity within the service. Figure 3.6 provides pseudocode for an NTP client.

Activity C2 explores request-reply protocols and the behavior of the Network Time Protocol (NTP) using the NTP client provided within the Distributed Systems Workbench.

ACTIVITY C2 USING THE NETWORK TIME PROTOCOL (NTP) CLIENT WITHIN THE DISTRIBUTED SYSTEMS WORKBENCH TO EXPLORE REQUEST-REPLY PROTOCOLS AND THE BEHAVIOR OF NTP

The US National Institute of Standards and Technology (NIST) maintains the Internet Time Service (ITS), which provides a number of well-known standard time services, one of which is the Network Time Protocol service.

Learning Outcomes
- To examine the use of a request-reply protocol
- To gain an initial understanding of time services
- To gain an initial understanding of the Network Time Protocol
- To gain an appreciation of the importance of standardization of well-known services
- To gain an appreciation of the importance of a clear separation of concerns between components of a distributed application
- To gain an appreciation of the importance of transparency in distributed applications

Method
Start the NTP client from the NTP tab in the Distributed Systems Workbench.

Part 1. The NTP client provides a partial list of NTP server URLs. Select each one in turn and see if they all respond with time values, and if so, do they all give the SAME time? NIST maintains a webpage at http://tf.nist.gov/tf-cgi/servers.cgi, which reports the current status of some of the NIST servers: it is not uncommon to find that one or more are unavailable at any time. This reinforces the reason why there are multiple NTP time servers available.

ACTIVITY C2 USING THE NETWORK TIME PROTOCOL (NTP) CLIENT WITHIN THE DISTRIBUTED SYSTEMS WORKBENCH TO EXPLORE REQUEST-REPLY PROTOCOLS AND THE BEHAVIOR OF NTP—Cont'd

Part 2. NIST provides a global address: time.nist.gov, which is automatically resolved to different NIST time server addresses in a round-robin sequence to equalize the service-request load across the servers. Try selecting this URL and see what IP address it resolves to. If you make several attempts within a short time frame, then you will likely be directed to the same time server instance each time. However, if you wait several minutes between attempts, you will see that it does sequence through the available servers. Try this for yourself. Think about the importance of using this global address (especially if hard-coded into an application) rather than individual server domain names.

Expected Outcome

The first screenshot below shows the NTP client in operation, using the wolfnisttime.com NIST time server. The URL wolfnisttime.com has been resolved to IP address 207.223.123.18 and a series of NTP time requests have been sent, and responses received.

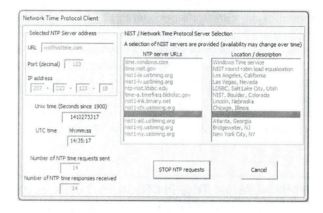

The screenshot below illustrates the use of NIST's global address time.nist.gov. In this instance, it resolved to the server at IP address 128.138.141.172. This screenshot also reveals the unreliability of UDP; NTP requests are carried over the UDP, and you can see that while 86 requests were sent, only 84 responses were received.

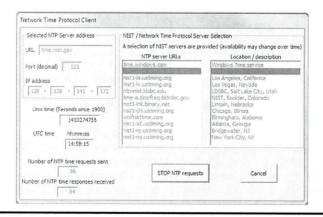

ACTIVITY C2 USING THE NETWORK TIME PROTOCOL (NTP) CLIENT WITHIN THE DISTRIBUTED SYSTEMS WORKBENCH TO EXPLORE REQUEST-REPLY PROTOCOLS AND THE BEHAVIOR OF NTP—Cont'd

The screenshot below shows how NIST's global address time.nist.gov resolves to different NIST time server addresses at different times. In this instance, it resolved to the server at IP address 24.56.178.140.

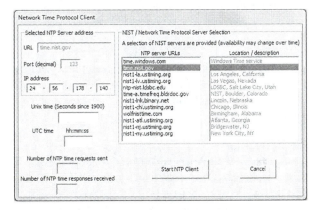

Reflection

This activity provides some insight into the importance of a clear separation of concerns in a distributed application. In this example, the client is a bespoke program, which requests and uses the up-to-date time value from the NTP time service, which is a well-known service with publicly documented behavior and a standard interface. The client in this application has very little business logic; it is limited to resolving the URLs of the NTP service domain names into IP addresses and actually making the NTP protocol request. The rest of the client's functionality is related to the user interface. All of the time service-related business logic is held at the NTP server side. The request-reply protocol is very well suited to this software architecture; the client sends a request and the server sends back the appropriate reply in a stateless way (i.e., the server does not need to keep track of the particular client or keep any specific context about the client's request). This stateless approach leads to a highly scalable service, and the combination of the simple protocol and the high degree of separation of concerns means that it is very easy to develop NTP clients or to embed NTP client functionality into other applications.

The activity also illustrates some important aspects of transparency; the user does not need to know the internal structure of the ITS time services, the number of NTP server replicas or the way in which they are updated, in order to use the service. The NTP service appears to the client as a single server entity.

Further Study

The design and operation of the NTP client is explored in detail in the form of a case study in Chapter 7.

3.3.3 TWO-WAY DATA TRANSFER

As explained above, the request-reply protocol is very common in services in which a command or request is passed in one direction and the reply (data) is passed in the other. There are also a very large number of applications in which data and control messages are passed in both directions (and not necessarily in such a structured sequence as with request-reply), for example, eCommerce, online banking, online shopping, and multiplayer games.

The various approaches to communication can be described in terms of the addressing methodology used and also in terms of the actual design of higher-level protocols and mechanisms built on top of the simpler transport layer protocols. These are discussed in the following sections.

3.3.4 ADDRESSING METHODOLOGIES

There are four main addressing methodologies, that is, ways in which the recipient of a message is identified.

3.3.4.1 Unicast Communication

A message is delivered to a single destination process, which is uniquely addressed by the sender. That is, the message contains the address of the destination process. Other processes do not see the message.

Figure 3.7 illustrates unicast communication in which a message is sent to a single, specifically addressed destination process.

3.3.4.2 Broadcast Communication

A single message (as transmitted by the sender) is delivered to all processes. The most common way to achieve this is to use a special broadcast address, which indicates to the communication mechanism that the message should be delivered to all computers.

Figure 3.8 illustrates broadcast communication in which the sender sends a single message that is delivered to all processes. When considering the Internet specifically, the model of broadcast communication depicted in Figure 3.8 is termed "local broadcast," in which the set of recipients are the processes on computers in the same IP subnet as the sender. The special IPv4 broadcast address to achieve this is 255.255.255.255.

It is also possible to perform a directed broadcast with the IP. In this case, a single packet is sent to a specific remote IP subnet and is then broadcast within that subnet. In transit, the packet is forwarded

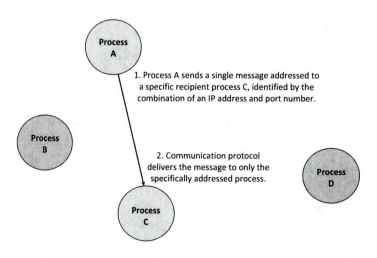

FIGURE 3.7

Unicast communication.

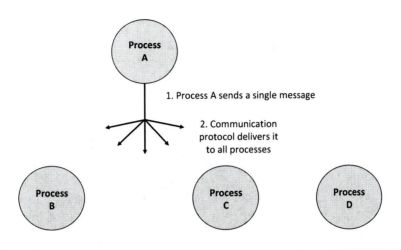

FIGURE 3.8

Broadcast communication.

in a unicast fashion. On reaching the destination subnet, it is the responsibility of the router on the entry border of the subnet to perform the last step as a broadcast. To achieve a directed broadcast, the network component of the original address must be the target subnet address, and all bytes of the host part of the address are set to the value 255. On reaching the final router in the delivery path, the address is converted to the IP broadcast address (i.e., 255.255.255.255) and thus delivered to all computers in the subnet. As an example, consider that the subnet address is 193.65.72.0, which may contain computers addressed from 193.65.72.1 to 193.65.72.254. The address used to send a directed broadcast to this subnet would be 193.65.72.255. The concept of directed broadcast is illustrated in Figure 3.9.

When broadcasting using a special broadcast address, the sender does not need to know, and may not be able to know, the number of receivers or their identities. The number of recipients of messages can range from none to the entire population of the system.

A broadcast effect can also be achieved by sending a series of identical unicast messages to each other process known by the sending process. Where the communication protocol does not directly support broadcast (e.g., with TCP), this is the only way to achieve the broadcast effect. The advantage is greater security as the sender identifies each recipient separately, but the disadvantages are greater overheads for the sender in terms of the processing associated with sending and greater overheads on the network (in terms of bandwidth used, as each individual message must now appear on the medium).

There is also the consideration of synchronization. With broadcast address-based communication in a local area network, the transmission time is the same (there is only one message sent), the propagation times will be similar (short distances), and thus, although the actual delivery to specific processes at each node may differ because of local workloads on host computers, the reception is reasonably synchronized; certainly more so than when a series of unicast messages are sent, when one receiver will possibly get the message before the other messages are even sent. This could have an impact in some services where voting is used or where the order of response is intended to be used to influence system behavior. For example, in a load balancing mechanism, a message to solicit availability may be sent and the speed of response might be a factor in determining suitability (on the basis that a host that responds quickly is likely to be a good candidate for sending additional work to), and thus, the use of

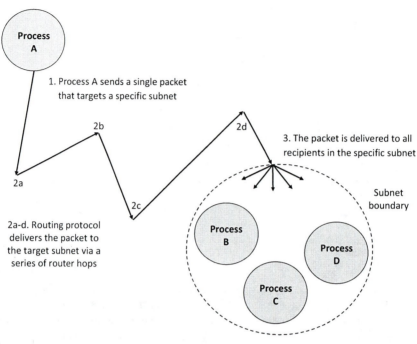

FIGURE 3.9

IP-directed broadcast communication.

the unicast approach of achieving a multicast or broadcast effect may require further synchronization mechanisms to be used (because the sender has implicitly preordered the responses in the ordering of the sending of requests).

Broadcast communication is less secure than unicast because any process listening on the appropriate port can hear the message and also because the sender does not know the actual identities of the set of recipient processes. IP broadcast communication can also be inefficient in the sense that all computers receive the packet at the network (IP) layer (effectively an interrupt requiring that the packet be processed and passed up to the transport layer) even if it turns out that none of the processes present are interested in the packet.

3.3.4.3 Multicast Communication

A single message (as transmitted by the sender) is delivered to a group of processes. One way to achieve this is to use a special multicast address.

Figure 3.10 illustrates multicast communication in which a group (a prechosen subset) of processes receive a message sent to the group. The light-shaded processes are members of the target group, so each will receive the message sent by process A; the dark-shaded processes are not members of the group and so ignore the message. The multicast address can be considered to be a filter; either processes listen for messages on that address (conceptually they are part of the group) or they do not.

The sender may not know how many processes receive the message or their identities; this depends on the implementation of the multicast mechanism.

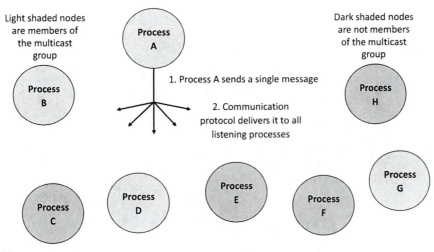

FIGURE 3.10

Multicast communication.

Multicast communication can be achieved using a broadcast mechanism. UDP is an example of a protocol that supports broadcast directly, but not multicast. In this case, transport layer ports can be used as a means of group message filtering by arranging that only the subset of processes that are members of the group listen on the particular port. The group membership action *join group* can be implemented locally by the process binding to the appropriate port and issuing a receive-from call.

In both types of multicast communication, that is, directly supported by the communication protocol or fabricated by using a broadcast mechanism, there can be multiple groups, and each individual process can be a member of several different groups. This provides a useful way to impose some control and structure on the communication at the higher level of the system or application. For example, the processes concerned with a particular functionality or service within the system can join a specific group related to that activity.

3.3.4.4 Anycast Communication

The requirement of an anycast mechanism is to ensure that the message is delivered to one member of the group. Some definitions are stricter, that is, that it must be delivered to exactly one member. Anycast is sometimes described as "delivery to the nearest of a group of potential recipients"; however, this is dependent on the definition of "nearest."

Figure 3.11 illustrates the concept of anycast communication, in which a message is delivered to one member of a group of potential recipients. Whereas broadcast and multicast deliver a message to 0 or more recipients (depending on system size and group size, respectively), the goal of anycast is to deliver a message to 1 (or possibly more) recipients.

Neither TCP nor UDP directly supports anycast communication, although it could be achieved using UDP with a list of group members, sending a unicast message to each one in turn and waiting for a response before moving on to the next. As soon as a reply is received from one of the group, the sequence stops.

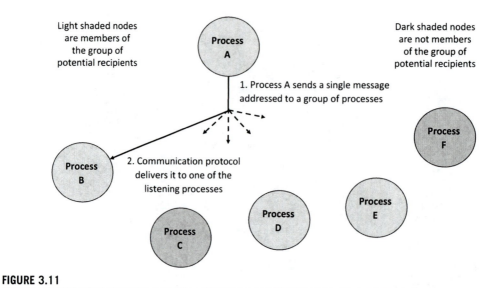

FIGURE 3.11

Anycast communication.

The Arrows application within the Networking Workbench provides an interesting case example for exploring addressing modes; see Section 3.15.

3.3.5 REMOTE PROCEDURE CALL

Remote Procedure Call (RPC) is an example of a higher-level mechanism built on top of the TCP. RPC involves making a call to a procedure that is in a different process space to that of the calling procedure. All programmers will understand the normal procedure call concept (which to avoid confusion we shall now call local procedure call) in which a call from one procedure to another occurs, all within the same program, and thus, at run time, the entire activity occurs within a single process. Both the calling procedure and the called procedure are within the same code project and are compiled together. The local call, if successfully compiled, is guaranteed to work because both procedures are in the same process image, which either is running or is not, and there is no network communication required to make the call.

Remote Procedure Call is an extension of local procedure call in which the called procedure is part of a different program to the calling procedure, and thus, at run time, the two procedures are in two different process spaces. Perhaps, the main benefit of RPC is that from the programmer's viewpoint, the procedure call works the same regardless of whether it is a local or remote call. Thus, RPC provides location and access transparency and removes the need for the programmer to manually implement the communication aspects.

This is a very powerful facilitator for developing modular component-based applications. The developer is able to focus on the business logic of the application and to distribute the application logic across multiple software components and also to potentially distribute those software components over several physical computers, without significant effort spent on the networking aspects.

However, it would be misleading to suggest that the transparency provided by RPC removes all of the design challenges of distribution or that it removes all of the complications that networking introduces. In order to produce high-quality, robust, and scalable applications and systems, a developer needs to pay attention to the overall architecture of systems and the configurations of specific components and also the communication that occurs between pairs of components. The frequency of procedure calls and the amount of data transferred in each of the request and reply arms of the call and the relative processing effort required in the called procedure compared with the time costs of making the call itself and the underlying network latency when the call takes place should be considered. Programmers who have not yet implemented distributed systems will not immediately realize the potential pitfalls associated with inappropriate use of communications mechanisms such as RPC, so here are two example scenarios to put this into context.

RPC example 1. The called (remote) procedure is a helper procedure that performs some substeps in a large computation and has been separated off from the calling procedure as a result of a refactoring activity to improve code structure. A large amount of data must be passed into the called procedure, which performs a few straightforward computational steps requiring very limited processing time. It then returns the results to the calling procedure. Even with local code refactoring, it is important to understand the costs involved in performing the call, relative to the advantages of having the improved code structure. It may be that the call is invoked by several different callers and thus the improvement in structure is highly valuable, avoiding duplication of code. Where the called procedure is remote, there are additional costs of the network bandwidth used and the latency of the network communication. As RPC works on top of TCP, a connection has to be established at the beginning of an RPC call and has to be shut down at the end; thus, the additional latency can be significant for fast-operating applications. In addition, there are also the latency and processing costs associated with causing a system-level software interrupt in the host computer of the called procedure. For this particular example, RPC would appear to be inappropriate in the general case.

RPC example 2. An application is structured such that user-interface functionality is separated from the business logic, the latter needing access to data that are shared by many running instances of the application. This could be part of a banking system, for example. The Remote Procedure Call is used as a means of having the calling procedure based in the user-interface component, while the called procedure is in a back-end system close to where the data are located and also much more secure because this component only runs on the bank's own computers, behind their firewalls. Here, the use of RPC is for the purpose of implementing a scalable and secure system. The amount of data passed in banking transactions is usually quite low and is not the significant factor, neither is the typical amount of processing performed in the procedure particularly high. Rather, it is the need for secure and shared access to the database while retaining transparency to the developer of the user-interface (client) component of the system that is the critical factor. RPC is highly appropriate in this type of scenario.

Figure 3.12 illustrates the mechanism of RPC. A local procedure call is shown for comparison. From the view point of the main thread of execution, both the local procedure call and the Remote Procedure Call appear the same. This is very important from the programmer viewpoint. The abstraction is that all procedure calls are local, and this removes from the developer of the application component the burden of implementing the network communication. The underlying communication is based on a TCP connection, which is set up and maintained automatically by the stubs (also referred to as proxies). This enables the developer of the calling application to write code as if calling a local procedure, while it also allows the developer of the remote procedure to write the code as a normal

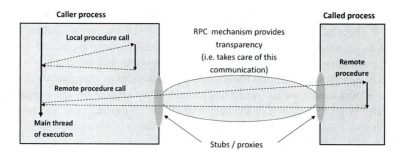

FIGURE 3.12

The Remote Procedure Call mechanism.

procedure and to not be concerned with the fact that it is actually called from a nonlocal procedure (i.e., from a different process).

The best known RPC implementation is Open Network Computing (ONC) RPC, which was developed by Sun Microsystems and is thus also known as Sun RPC. This originally supported C and C++ on Unix systems but is now available on Linux and Windows platforms. Heterogeneity is supported by using a special language and platform-independent data format called eXternal Data Representation (XDR).

XDR is one solution to the problem of facilitating communication between heterogeneous components when using mechanisms such as RPC. Another common approach is to use an intermediary language to define the component interfaces in a programming language-independent and platform-independent way. These are generically called Interface Definition Languages (IDLs). IDL is revisited in Chapter 6.

3.3.6 REMOTE METHOD INVOCATION

Remote Method Invocation (RMI) is the object-oriented equivalent of RPC. Instead of remotely calling a procedure, a remote method is invoked. RMI was first introduced in the Java language, and this specific implementation is sometimes referred to as Java RMI. However, the mechanism of RMI is also supported in other languages such as C#, in which case it is properly referred to as C# remoting. Figure 3.13 provides an overview of the operation of Java RMI.

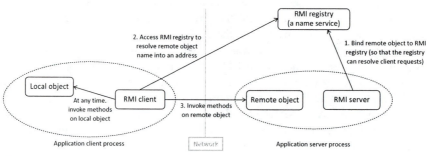

FIGURE 3.13

The Remote Method Invocation mechanism.

Figure 3.13 shows the basic operation of RMI. There needs to be some way by which the RMI client (within the calling process) can locate the required object; this is facilitated through the use of a specialized name service called the RMI registry. Step 1 in the figure shows the RMI server registering with the RMI registry the object that will be made accessible for remote access. The RMI registry can subsequently resolve requests for this object, as shown in step 2 where the calling process provides the name of the object it requires and is returned the address details. The calling process can now invoke method calls on the remote object, as shown in step 3 in the figure.

3.3.6.1 Java Interfaces

An interface defines the methods that are exposed on a remote interface, without providing any implementation detail (i.e., it contains method names and parameter types, but does not include the program code within those methods).

The interface is necessary because the client-side code needs to be compiled independently of the server side. The compiler needs to be able to check that the remote methods are being used correctly in the client (in terms of the types and numbers of parameters passed in to the method and the type of return parameter expected). However, the compiler does not need to know details of the way in which the methods are actually implemented by the server, in order to perform these checks, and thus, the interface provides sufficient details. Note that the Java interface performs a similar role to header files in C or C++ and the Interface Definition Language (IDL), which is used in middleware.

To illustrate, an example interface for an Event Notification Service (ENS) is provided (see Figure 3.14). A non-RMI-based ENS is the subject of one of the case studies in Chapter 7. The example here is based loosely on that case study; the interface is essentially the same except that in the case of an RMI implementation, the functionality of the ENS is provided through remote method calls, instead of through the use of discrete application messages sent over a TCP connection, as in the case study version.

Figure 3.14 shows the Java RMI interface for an ENS. There are three server-side methods that are made available to be invoked remotely (SubscribeToEvent, UnSubscribeToEvent, PublishEvent) each described in terms of their parameter lists and types, but without revealing implementation detail. The use of the interface allows the application developer to incorporate calls to these methods in the client-side code, as if they were local methods; in this way, RMI achieves distribution transparency from the perspective of the client-side application developer. Notice that the interface extends the interface java.rmi.remote. This is mandatory and causes the lower-level communication infrastructure to be automatically put in place so that the stated methods can be invoked remotely, without the program developer having to be concerned with the mechanistic aspects of the communication. As with RPC, RMI performs its communication over a TCP connection, which is set up and managed silently from the programmer's perspective.

```
import java.rmi.Remote;
import java.rmi.RemoteException;

public interface EventNotificationService extends Remote
{
    public void SubscribeToEvent (String sEventType) throws RemoteException;
    public void UnSubscribeToEvent (String sEventType) throws RemoteException;
    public void PublishEvent (String sEventType, String sEventValue) throws RemoteException;
}
```

FIGURE 3.14

Java RMI interface example.

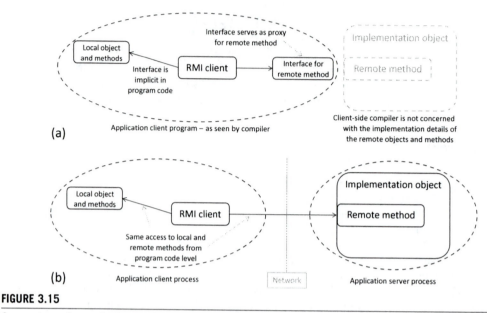

FIGURE 3.15

Comparison of compile-time and run time views of Remote Method Invocation, showing the role of the Java interface.

A wide variety of run time problems can occur when invoking remote methods; these include problems associated with the server side of the application, the RMI registry, and the network connection. It is necessary to detect and handle these problems appropriately in order to achieve robust operation. For this reason, each method declared in a remote interface must specify java.rmi.RemoteException in its throws clause.

The Java interface contributes to implementation transparency, since the client-side object can invoke methods without knowledge of their implementation. This approach also contributes to component decoupling and thus flexibility with respect to deployment and maintenance. For example, after the client has been compiled, it is possible for the server-side implementation to be changed (e.g., a more efficient technique to achieve the same functionality may have been discovered); so long as the interface details are not changed, the application will still function correctly. Figure 3.15 illustrates the role of the Java interface.

Figure 3.15 shows the way in which a Java interface serves as a proxy for a remote method and therefore facilitates a compile-time view of remote methods, which are not actually present in the software component being compiled. At run time, the real remote methods are invoked.

3.4 LAYERED MODELS OF COMMUNICATION

The examples provided in the early part of this chapter have served to introduce the general concepts of communication and have also provided some insight into the key requirements and challenges of communication mechanisms for distributed systems.

Due to the many different types of technical challenge involved, communication systems are structured as a set of layers, each layer providing a specific set of functionalities. The layers are connected by well-defined interfaces that are called service-access-points (SAPs), because these are the means by which the components in one-layer access services provided by components in an adjacent layer.

The division of network services into a set of well-defined layers has a number of benefits that include the following:

- Limiting the complexity of any particular layer: Each layer performs a well-defined subset of the network functionality.
- Simplifying further development of specific protocols without the need to modify adjacent layers: Well-defined interfaces between layers ensure that the communication between the layers is consistent and independent of the internal behavior of any specific layer. This allows replacement or upgrade of a particular layer within the stack without disturbing other layers, so long as the interface specifications are strictly adhered to.
- Facilitating standards and stable documentation: The interfaces between layers, and the functionality of each layer, are well defined and documented as standards.
- Interchangeability of technologies within the protocol stack: Technologies can be exchanged at a specific layer without affecting the layers' either side because the interfaces to these layers are standardized. For example, changing the data-link layer technology from a wired LAN technology such as Fast Ethernet to a wireless LAN technology such as IEEE 802.11 does not disturb the higher-level functionality of the network layer and above. The network layer has a logical view of the network connectivity and is not concerned with the actual technology of the links available to it.
- Application independence from the characteristics and behavior of the lower protocol layers: Applications need to operate independently of the underlying network technology. The layered model allows the communication technologies to change over time without affecting the behavior of the higher-level applications that use the network. This is important for the stability and robustness of applications.
- Separation of logical concerns: The upper layers of the network stack are concerned with issues such as logical connections, communication semantics, and the presentation of data. The lower layers are focused on the actual transmission of messages from point to point. Therefore, it is important to separate high-level concepts such as the sending and receiving of messages from the lower-level physical concerns related to, for example, the communication medium, frame formats, timing, signaling, and bit errors that occur.

There are two very important layered models for network communication. The Open Systems Interconnection (OSI) model (ISO/IEC 7498-1), produced and supported by the International Organization for Standardization (ISO), divides the network communication functionality into seven clearly defined and standardized layers. This model is mostly viewed as being conceptual, since there are a relatively small proportion of popular protocols that adhere closely to this model. The model is however very useful as a structure guide and an aid to understanding and describing behavior in networks. The TCP/IP model on the other hand directly maps onto the TCP/IP suite, which is by far the most popular set of protocols in use and is the basis for the majority of Internet communication.

Protocol Data Units: The correct term for a network message format is protocol data unit (PDU). PDUs are defined for each protocol, at each level of the network-layered model. The normal format for a communication protocol PDU is a header part with predefined fields and a payload part that contains the PDU of the layer above. This concept is called encapsulation.

Encapsulation: Encapsulation is the term given to embedding the PDU of one protocol as the payload of another. In this way, the lower protocol carries the higher-layer protocol's data. This process repeats all the way down the protocol stack. This is illustrated in Figure 3.16.

Figure 3.16 illustrates the concept of encapsulation using a common real example scenario in which a file transfer using the File Transfer Protocol (FTP) is passed across an Ethernet network link. Encapsulation serves to keep separate the concerns of the different layer protocols as the application data is passed across the network.

In the example scenario, the application layer protocol is FTP. The FTP protocol is concerned with information such as the file name and the type of data encoding used. FTP is not concerned with the type of network technology used or whether individual packets arrive successfully or have to be retransmitted. The overall concern of the FTP protocol is to ensure that the entire file is sent from one specific location to another.

The transport layer protocol is concerned with the identity of the process the message must be delivered to when it reaches the final destination computer. The process is indicated indirectly by the port number held in the transport layer header. A process on the destination computer will have to have associated itself with this port number in advance, so that the message can be delivered correctly. In the specific example, the transport layer protocol would be TCP because FTP requires a reliable transport protocol and so rules out UDP. The overall concern of TCP in this example is to ensure that each separately transmitted chunk of the file is delivered to the destination process (which is either the FTP client or FTP server at the destination computer) in such a way that the entire file can be reconstructed from the chunks.

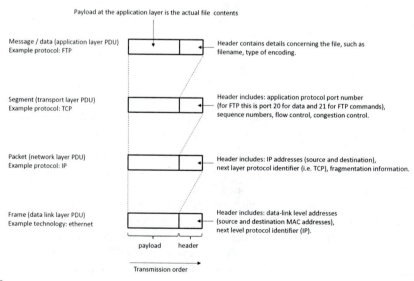

FIGURE 3.16

Encapsulation of higher-layer protocols into the payload of the protocol in the layer below.

The network layer protocol is IP. The overall concern of the IP in this example is to get the TCP segments containing the file data to the destination computer. The routing protocol in the system will use the IP address information in the IP packet header to select the path the packet takes through the network.

The concern of the data-link layer technology, in this example Ethernet, is to pass the packet across a single data link to the correct destination (at the link level), which for all but the final link will be the next router in the chain. If the next link the message must pass through is a different type of technology, such as wireless IEEE 802.11, then the Ethernet frame will be discarded and a new link technology-dependent frame will be used to carry the data. In such case, the higher-layer data are not changed; they are re-encapsulated into the new frame.

3.4.1 THE OSI MODEL

The ISO-OSI seven-layer model provides a conceptual reference for communication systems. The model supports a modularized approach in which each layer is isolated from the concerns of the layers above and below it; this enforces clear demarcation of responsibilities, avoids duplication of functionality, and promotes better understanding.

Figure 3.17 shows the OSI model network layers and their main functions. The model serves as a standard reference for network protocol design. Communication systems are vastly complex dealing with a very wide range of challenges that range from higher-level concerns such as the way in which applications interface to the network system and the way in which data are represented such that heterogeneous systems can communicate, to concerns relating to how devices are addressed, the ways in which information is routed to the correct destination, to lower-level issues such as how to accommodate different network link technologies, the type of signaling used, and very many more. The OSI

OSI layer #	OSI layer name	Main concerns
7	Application	Protocols to support specific application communication needs, such as file transfer, remote login, hypertext transfer.
6	Presentation	Data representation, conversion of data between platform dependent and platform independent formats, data encryption and decryption.
5	Session	Managing communication flows / conversations (sessions).
4	Transport	Reliable process to process communication.
3	Network	Computer to computer communication: addressing, routing and delivery of packets.
2	Data link	Reliable direct communication link between devices which may be routers or computers.
1	Physical	Transmission of bits over a communication link (concerned with signalling, timing, voltages, noise suppression).

FIGURE 3.17

The ISO OSI seven-layer reference model.

model therefore plays a vital role as a standard reference and framework for the division of concerns and functionalities.

The TCP/IP model was already well established when the OSI standard was introduced. In particular, the popularity of TCP/IP is driven by the fact that the Internet is based on the TCP/IP suite. As a result, the TCPs/IPs are far more commonly used than the OSI-specific technologies. The OSI model is however extremely useful as a discussion and modeling framework. It serves to describe network systems in a common language that is independent of any particular implementation and is thus used in teaching and also in research, with the TCP/IP model being mapped onto it so that specific protocols in the TCP/IP suite can be discussed in terms of their position within the seven-layer reference model.

3.4.2 THE TCP/IP MODEL

The TCP/IP model comprises four layers. The lowest of these generically represents the network interface and physical network aspects. The upper three layers represent logical communication (i.e., they are concerned with communication based on logical addresses and are not concerned with the physical technologies and characteristics of networks such as host adapters, cables, frame formats, bandwidth, and bitrates). The protocols of the TCP/IP suite reside in the three upper layers.

Figure 3.18 shows the TCP/IP network layers aligned against the OSI equivalent layers and also shows the protocol data units used at each layer and some popular example protocols found at each layer.

The link layer is not of concern to application developers in general. This layer deals with the technical and operational characteristics of the underlying technology of the network links. The use of layers provides decoupling of the application concerns (at the upper levels) from the technology at the lower levels, and thus, applications can be developed without having to know details of the network itself. This is very important because apart from the technical complexity that would otherwise be involved each time an application were built, the decoupling allows for the technology to change over time without affecting the behavior and operation of the applications.

The Internet layer is of limited interest to application developers. This is because the IP (IPv4 or IPv6) operates at the level of the host; that is, it is concerned with the delivery of messages between computers and is not concerned with specific applications and their processes. Obviously, the way

TCP/IP layer #	TCP/IP layer name	OSI layer equivalents	Protocol Data Unit	Example protocols
4	Application	Application	Message / data	FTP, Telnet, SMTP, NTP,
		Presentation		HTTP, RPC, RMI, DNS,
		Session		NFS, SNMP, SMTP, SSH
3	Transport	Transport	Segment	TCP, UDP
2	Internet	Network	Packet	IP, ICMP
1	Link	Data link	Frame	Ethernet, IEEE 802.11
		Physical	Bits transmitted on medium	100BASE-TX, OC-48, OC-192

FIGURE 3.18

The TCP/IP network model.

that IP delivers messages (its datagram basis and the way it uses addressing) needs to be understood by application developers, but they will not find themselves directly sending messages at the IP level.

The transport layer, on the other hand, is concerned with communication between specific processes. This is the lowest level that the application programmer can work. The main protocols in this layer are the Transport Control Protocol (TCP) and the User Datagram Protocol (UDP), which will be discussed in detail later.

The application layer is also very important to applications developers. This layer contains a wide range of application protocols that perform specific commonly required functions such as transferring files or web pages. A developer needs to be aware of what protocols are supported in this layer and the functionality they provide and any limitations. This is very important when determining whether the needs of a particular system can be met with the generic protocols or otherwise whether bespoke communication schemes based on top of the transport layer protocols need to be developed. The case study game used throughout this book follows the latter approach; that is, the communication is designed for the specific needs of the game and is based directly on the transport layer protocols; it does not use any of the protocols in the application layer.

3.5 THE TCP/IP SUITE

The notation TCP/IP can be ambiguous; it can imply the specific use of the TCP carried over an IP-based network (in this text, this will be written as "TCP over IP"), but more correctly, it is used to refer to the protocol family itself (this is the meaning ascribed here). This means that when a system is described as using TCP/IP, it could actually be using any combination of the protocols in the TCP/IP suite, so long as the layer ordering is respected. The following protocol combinations provide common examples: UDP over IP, TCP over IP, SNMP over UDP over IP, and FTP over TCP over IP.

You may be familiar with many of the protocols that occupy the application layer. These include FTP (File Transfer Protocol) and HTTP (HyperText Transfer Protocol), which are used very frequently. Protocols in this layer provide well-defined fixed functionality.

Figure 3.19 shows a subset of application layer protocols and their mapping onto the transport layer protocol that carries them. The mapping is significant because the TCP and UDP have distinctly different characteristics. The Simple Mail Transfer Protocol (SMTP), the HyperText Transfer Protocol (HTTP), the File Transfer Protocol (FTP), and the Telnet Protocol are all examples of protocols that are transported via TCP because of its advantage of ensuring reliable data transfer. The Simple Network Management

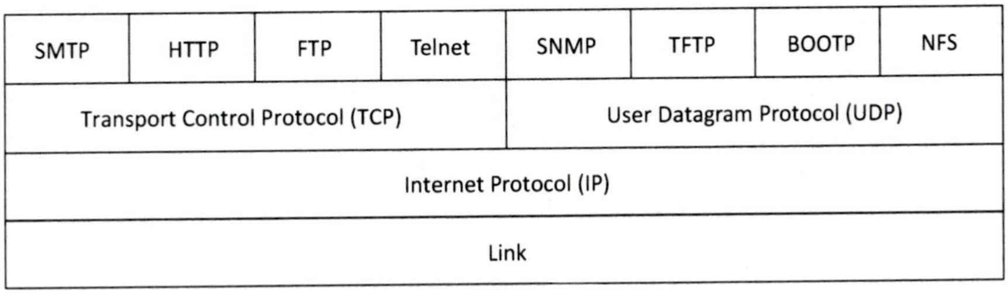

SMTP	HTTP	FTP	Telnet	SNMP	TFTP	BOOTP	NFS
Transport Control Protocol (TCP)				User Datagram Protocol (UDP)			
Internet Protocol (IP)							
Link							

FIGURE 3.19

The TCP/IP suite showing a subset of application layer protocols.

Protocol (SNMP), the Trivial File Transfer Protocol (TFTP), the Bootstrap Protocol (BOOTP), and the Network File System (NFS) are each transported via UDP because of one or more relative benefits of UDP (which are lower overheads, lower latency, and the ability to use broadcast addressing).

However, many applications have specific communication requirements that need greater flexibility than are provided by the well-defined generic functionality of the application layer protocols. This can be achieved by directly using sockets programming at the transport layer. The transport layer operates at a lower level than the application layer and supports flexible communication based on the passing of messages (called segments) between software components in whatever pattern or sequence is necessary. There are two main protocols in the TCP/IP transport layer: the Transmission Control Protocol (TCP) and the User Datagram Protocol (UDP). Applications that directly transmit data over the network use either or both of these.

TCP and UDP implement process-to-process communication and use ports to identify a particular process within a computer. Both TCP and UDP operate over the Internet Protocol (IP), which works in the network layer. IP will deliver a packet to a destination computer, but does not know about processes. Therefore, the transport layer protocols make use of the IP's ability to deliver a message to a computer and extend the addressing with a port number to determine which process the message will be delivered to. Note that it is the combination of IP address and port number that constitutes a unique identifier of a particular process in a network. To use the TCP or UDP, an application developer uses the "socket API" to make calls into the protocol software stack.

3.5.1 **THE IP**

The IP is the main protocol of the network layer. The IP is at the very heart of Internet operation. Network traffic is carried across the Internet from computer to computer in the form of IP packets. Routing in the Internet is based on the IP destination address carried in the IP's header. In short, without the IP, there would be no Internet.

Two versions of IP are currently in use: IPv4 and IPv6. IPv4 was introduced in the early 1980s and has worked very well for many years. However, there is a limit to the IPv4 address range, which led to the development of IPv6 that has a far greater IP address range and several other important improvements over IPv4, for example, in terms of better quality of service provision.

IPv6 was defined during the mid-1990s and was due to run concurrently with IPv4 for a number of years and then replace IPv4 completely. The take-up of IPv6 has been much slower than expected, and IPv4 is still in common use. However, the current severe shortage of IPv4 addresses is likely to cause an accelerated rate of take-up of IPv6 (during 2011-2014, the availability of new addresses officially ran out in several geographic regions).

Figure 3.20 shows the IPv4 header. The first field is a 4-bit version number, which will always be set to the value 4 in an IPv4 packet. The second field is the header length measured in units of 4 bytes. For example, in the default case where no options are added at the end of the header, the header will be 20 bytes long and the value in the header length field will thus be 5. The type of service field has been used for various purposes related to quality of service, priority, and congestion notification. In addition to knowing the header length, it is necessary to know the length of the whole packet because the data portion, which follows the header, can have variable length. The Total Length field is 16 bits wide and thus can hold a value up to $(2^{16}) - 1$, which is 65,535; this therefore limits the size of an IP packet. The IP supports fragmentation, such that packets can be broken into smaller "fragments" to pass over link

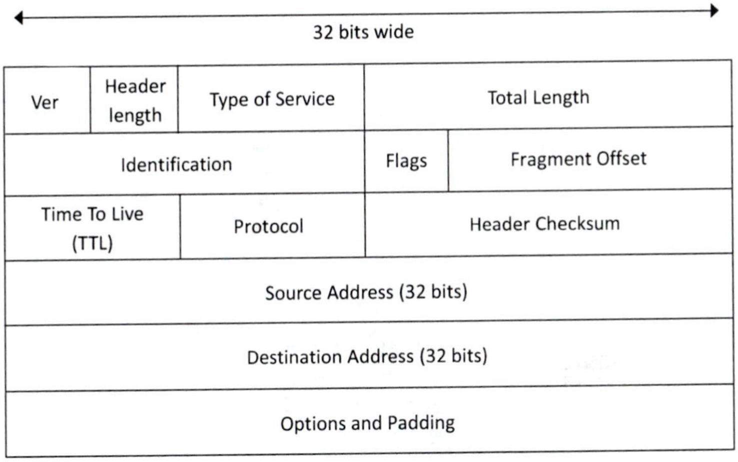

Ver	Header length	Type of Service	Total Length	
Identification			Flags	Fragment Offset
Time To Live (TTL)		Protocol	Header Checksum	
Source Address (32 bits)				
Destination Address (32 bits)				
Options and Padding				

FIGURE 3.20

The IPv4 header format.

technologies with different size frame limits (this limit is called the Maximum Transmission Unit—MTU). The Identification field thus identifies each IP packet and all fragments thereof, which retain the original ID, so the packet can be subsequently defragmented at the receiving computer. There are three flag bits but only two are used. The More Fragment flag, if set, signifies that the packet has been fragmented and that there are more fragments to follow this current fragment. If not set, the flag signifies either that the packet was not fragmented or that this is the last of several fragments. The Don't Fragment flag, if set, prevents the packet from being fragmented; this means that if the packet exceeds the MTU for a particular link, it will be dropped. The fragment offset field signifies the position of the fragment within the original packet. If this is the first fragment or the packet has not been fragmented, then the offset will be zero. The fragment offset field is only 13 bits long, so in order that it can represent the same overall packet length as the Total Length field, the offset values increment at 8-byte intervals. Thus, a fragment offset of 1000 actually means that the data carried in that fragment start at position 8000 in the original packet. The 8-bit TTL field is used to prevent routing loops. Each time a packet passes through a router, the TTL value is decremented, and if the TTL value reaches zero, the packet is dropped. TTL values are usually initialized to a value such as 64, which should be adequate to get to all destinations without issue so long as routers are configured and operating correctly. The Protocol field identifies the next layer protocol and thus identifies how the packet's payload should be handled. If, for example, the packet contains a TCP segment as its payload, then the value in the Protocol field will be the code 6. The code 17 is used to signify UDP. The header checksum provides a means of verifying that the header has not been corrupted in transit. IPv4 does not check the correctness of the data it carries, which are left for higher-layer protocols to deal with. The IP source address and destination address are each 32-bit values discussed in a subsequent section.

Figure 3.21 shows the IPv6 header. As with IPv4, the first field is a 4-bit version field, which will always be set to the value 6 in an IPv6 packet. IPv6 has a fixed-length main header, replacing the header options of IPv4 with extension headers and thus not needing a header length field. The Traffic Class

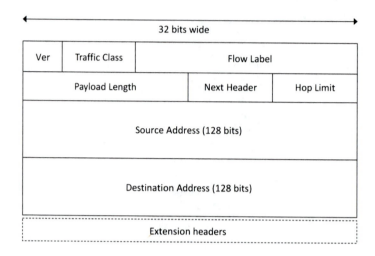

FIGURE 3.21

The IPv6 header format.

field serves two purposes: classification of packets for quality of service purposes and explicit congestion notification and control. The Flow Label field is used by routers to keep packets of related flows
on the same path. The Payload Length field contains the length of the payload, including any extension
headers. The Next Header field indicates which extension header, if any, follows the current header.
The Next Header field is also used to signify payload; for example, a TCP header or UDP header can
follow the IPv6 extension headers. The Hop Limit field serves the same purpose as the TTL field in
IPv4. The IPv6 source address and destination address are each 128-bit values. Extension headers are
only used when needed, avoiding a huge inefficient single-header format, which would be necessary
to support all of the features of the sophisticated IPv6 protocol. Extension headers deal with additional
functionality including hop-by-hop options, fragmentation, and authentication.

3.5.2 THE TCP

TCP is a connection-oriented protocol. This means that a logical connection must be established before
messages (termed segments in transport layer parlance) can be sent and received over the connection.
Because a connection is necessary, all TCP communication is unicast; that is, a connection can only be
between a pair of processes and thus each process can only communicate with one other, via a particular connection. Processes can however have multiple connections, if they need to communicate with
more than one other process.

　TCP divides the application data to be transmitted into segments (the TCP message type). Each segment begins with a TCP header of the format shown in Figure 3.22. The TCP header contains various
fields, which are necessary to support its quality and reliability features. The source and destination
ports provide the process-level addressing capability and thus facilitate process-to-process communication. The sequence and acknowledgment numbers support segment ordering and also facilitate detection of lost segments. When a segment is sent, a timer is started on the sender side. When the segment
is received by the connected process, an acknowledgment is sent back to the original sender. When

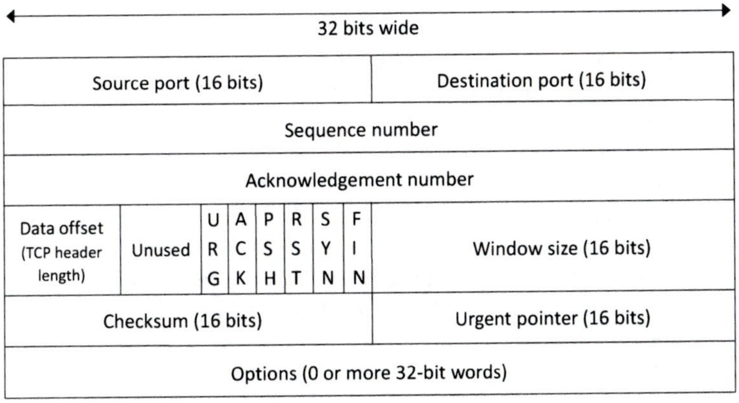

FIGURE 3.22

The TCP header format.

the acknowledgment is received, it cancels the timer. If, however, the acknowledgment is not received before the timer expires, the segment is assumed to have been lost, and so, the original segment is retransmitted.

An application data stream may have to be broken down into many TCP segments for transmission across the network. The 32-bit sequence number is used in each segment to provide a unique identifier (this represents the numerical offset of the data in the segment, measured from the beginning of the stream). The acknowledgment number indicates which byte in the stream is expected next and thus which bytes have been received. This enables the original sender to determine which of its sent segments have been received and which ones need retransmitting. The use of sequence numbers thus also provides the benefit of ensuring that received segments are ordered correctly when reconstituting the data stream as it is passed up to the higher-layer protocol or application.

There are six flags that support the setup (SYN), closing down (FIN), and reset (RST) of connections, as well as the ACK flag that indicates when the value in the acknowledgment field is valid (i.e., the message contains an acknowledgment), the URG flag that signals that urgent data have been placed in the message at the offset indicated by the urgent pointer and must be processed before other data, and the PSH flag that causes TCP to send a message before a full buffer is available (this "push" function is used, e.g., in Telnet, which requires that a TCP message is sent for each character that is typed).

The TCP also includes two transmission-management mechanisms: flow control and congestion control. TCP flow control uses a sliding window technique to prevent a sending process from overwhelming a receiving process; this is important in heterogeneous systems in which the different host computers may have different processing speeds, different workloads, or different buffer sizes. To implement this, the receiver process advertises the amount of buffer space it has to the sender (via the window size field); this is a dynamic quantity as the buffer may be partially filled with data. TCP congestion control helps prevent congestion buildup by controlling the rate at which data enter the network. TCP detects congestion indirectly by the fact that when routers' queues are full, they drop any newly arriving packets; this triggers TCP's congestion control activity. Each side of a TCP connection maintains a congestion window variable, which limits the total number of unacknowledged packets that may be in transit at the same time. In response to the detection of congestion, the congestion window is reduced in size. TCP uses a "slow-start" technique in which the congestion window is increased with each successful transmission. In this way, the congestion control mechanism is continuously adaptive, which is necessary because congestion levels in networks are dynamic and can change abruptly.

As a result of the reliability and quality mechanisms outlined above, TCP incurs significant overheads when compared with simpler protocols such as UDP. Additional network bandwidth is used because of the larger header size necessary to contain the additional control information and also because of the need for additional handshaking messages used in the setup and teardown of network connections, as well as acknowledgment messages. There is also additional communication latency because there is additional processing that must be carried out in both the sender and receiver processes; there are also the initial delay while a connection is set up and the delays that occur while waiting for segments to be acknowledged.

3.5.3 **THE TCP CONNECTION**

A TCP connection is set up using three primitives (listen, connect, and accept) in sequence. Each component must initially create a socket. A connection is then established as follows. First, the passive side (usually the server in a client server application) executes the listen primitive, which has the effect of making it receptive to connection requests from other processes. The active side (usually the client in a client server application) then executes the connect primitive, which initiates the special sequence of three messages necessary to set up a connection, thus called the TCP three-way handshake; see Figure 3.23.

Figure 3.23 illustrates the three-way handshake and the sequence of primitive calls and related actions, which occur to establish a TCP connection between two processes. The so-called three-way handshake requires that each side sends a synchronization request message (SYN), which must be

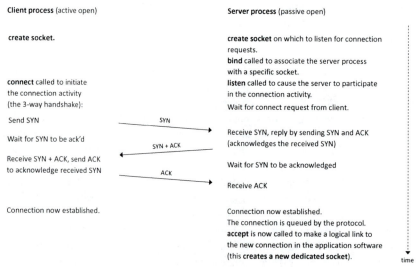

FIGURE 3.23

The TCP three-way handshake.

acknowledged by the other process (by replying with an ACK message). The first ACK is piggybacked onto the second SYN, so there are only three messages sent to achieve the four components of the handshake.

At this point, the connection is established, and the active side already has a socket associated with the connection so is ready to proceed with communication. The passive side must now execute the accept primitive, which makes a logical link between the application and the new connection (specifically, a new socket is created on the passive side for dedicated use with the new connection). The additional accept stage is necessary to allow the passive (server) side to continue to listen for additional connection requests, using the original socket that was created specifically for this purpose.

In many applications, a server will support many connections simultaneously; consider, for example, a web-server application. In this case, the server will still only need to execute the listen primitive once. However, the accept primitive will have to be executed each time a different client makes a connect request. To achieve this, it is usual to place the accept primitive call in a loop or in a timer event handler that is invoked periodically, perhaps every 100 ms. As the accept primitive creates a new socket each time it successfully accepts a connection request, the server ends up with multiple sockets: the original listen socket and one new socket for each connected client. Recall that the endpoint for communication is actually a socket, so this model of the server having one socket per client is ideal in terms of reflecting the communication configuration of the components and also in terms of code structure.

Figure 3.24 illustrates the way in which the accept primitive creates a new socket for each client, leaving the original "listen" socket to await additional connection requests. The server process accumulates an additional socket for each connected client; this simplifies application logic as the socket provides a representative identity at the server side for its specific connected client and keeps the state for each connection separate from other connections.

3.5.3.1 Higher-Layer Protocols That Use TCP as a Transport Protocol

- File Transfer Protocol (FTP). This is because files must be transferred verbatim and the received version must be an identical replica of the original, thus requiring a reliable transport protocol.

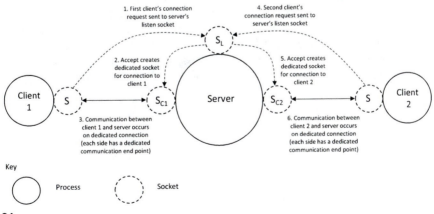

FIGURE 3.24

accept primitive creates dedicated sockets for each connection.

- Telnet. Telnet facilitates remotely logging in to a computer and executing commands. The characters typed at the keyboard form a continuous stream that must be replicated, in the exact order at the remote computer. It is vital that no parts of the character sequence are lost or duplicated. It is also not desirable that Telnet data be buffered and delivered in discrete chunks as would be the case if UDP were used (single character datagrams would have to be used).
- HyperText Transfer Protocol (HTTP). Web pages contain mixed media content, which must be delivered and rendered exactly as designed and therefore warrant the use of TCP.
- Simple Mail Transfer Protocol (SMTP). Email content is fundamentally data and thus has similar correctness requirements to file transfers. Hence, TCP is used as the transport protocol.

3.5.4 THE UDP

UDP is a connectionless protocol; it does not establish logical connections. A process can send a segment to another process without any prior handshaking. As there is no connection, UDP communication need not be unicast (although this is the default mode of addressing used); it is also possible to broadcast a UDP segment. UDP segments are also called datagrams.

Figure 3.25 shows the UDP header format; this is significantly shorter than the TCP header and reflects the fact that the UDP has less functionality than TCP. UDP is a transport layer protocol, so (as with TCP) it uses ports to achieve process-to-process communication. The length field holds the length of the UDP datagram (header and data), and the checksum field is used to detect transmission errors in both header and data.

UDP is a simple protocol, lacking the reliability and quality mechanisms provided by TCP. There are no sequence numbers, acknowledgments, or automatic retransmission. There is also no congestion control or flow control. As a result, UDP is said to be unreliable. In fact, the chances of any single UDP segment being lost in isolation are basically the same as the chances of an isolated loss of a TCP segment. However, the big difference is that while TCP has mechanisms to discover the loss and automatically retransmit the segment, UDP does not have such mechanisms, so a lost segment stays lost unless this is resolved by a higher-layer protocol or at the level of the application. For this reason, UDP is often described as having "send and prey" reliability.

The order in which UDP datagrams are received is not guaranteed to be the same as the order in which they were sent because of the lack of sequence numbers. Without sequence numbers, it is also not possible for the receiver to know if a datagram has been duplicated during transmission across the network and thus received twice or more; as far as UDP is concerned, these are all different datagrams. Thus, if an application is sensitive to the receipt of duplicate data, then additional support to detect

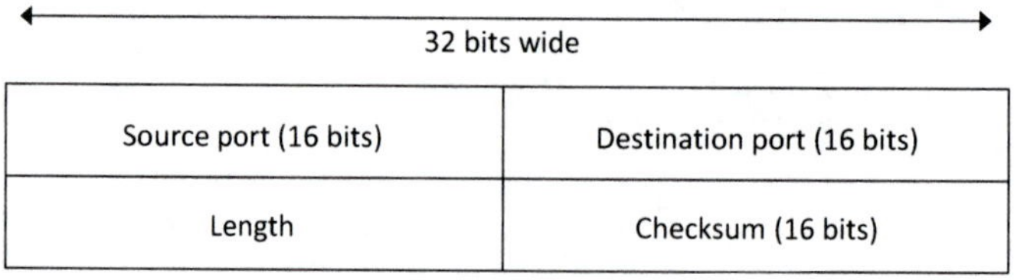

FIGURE 3.25

The UDP header.

this must be designed in to the application itself. If UDP datagrams carry commands in the application information flow, then it is highly recommended that the commands are designed to be idempotent; that is, they are designed to be repeatable without having side effects. The concept of idempotent commands is discussed in Chapter 6, but to give a simple example, the command "add ten pounds to account number 123" is not idempotent, while the command "set the balance of account number 123 to thirty pounds" is.

UDP incurs significantly lower overheads than its transport layer counterpart TCP does. UDP uses less network bandwidth because it has a smaller header (8 bytes compared with TCP's 20 bytes) as it does not have to carry the additional control information that TCP needs. UDP does not send any hand-shaking messages, further reducing bandwidth usage when compared with TCP. UDP is a low-latency protocol as it does not require that a connection be set up and does not wait for acknowledgments.

3.5.4.1 Higher-Layer Protocols That Use UDP as a Transport Protocol

- Trivial File Transfer Protocol (TFTP). TFTP was designed as a lightweight file transfer mechanism primarily used for transferring short configuration files to routers and other devices, typically over a short dedicated link or at least within a LAN environment. TFTP is a cut-down version of FTP, designed so that a TFTP server can be hosted within a device such as a router without requiring excessive processing and memory resources. Many text files that are used to configure routers will fit into a single typical segment, so the issues of ordering are greatly reduced. Therefore, for TFTP, the use of UDP at the transport layer is desirable because the low overheads and latency outweigh any reliability concerns. TFTP uses simple checksum techniques to detect if a file is actually corrupted in which case it is rejected.
- Domain Name System (DNS). DNS uses UDP as its transport protocol (by default) for lookup queries sent to DNS servers and for responses returned from DNS servers. The fundamental reason for this is to keep the latency of DNS lookups as low as possible; using TCP would incur significantly higher latency because of the need to set up and shut down a TCP connection. However, DNS uses TCP to perform zone transfers between DNS servers, as these are effectively the equivalent of a file transfer, and it is vitally important that the data are not corrupted.
- Simple Network Management Protocol (SNMP). SNMP uses UDP as its transport protocol fundamentally because of the need for low latency and also to keep network usage overheads low so that the network management system does not itself become a source of excessive network load.

3.5.5 TCP AND UDP COMPARED

The main distinguishing characteristics of the TCPs and UDPs are compared in Table 3.1.

3.5.6 CHOOSING BETWEEN TCP AND UDP

The choice as to which transport protocol is used depends entirely on the communication needs of the particular application or on the higher-layer protocols that the application uses. As discussed above, the TCPs and UDPs are significantly different in almost all aspects of their operation, to the extent that they are almost complete opposites. Therefore, when the communication needs of any particular application are scrutinized, it will usually become clear which transport protocol is most appropriate. Where there are conflicts (e.g., one part of the application requires reliable transport and another part

Table 3.1 Comparison of TCPs and UDPs

Characteristic	TCP	UDP
Protocol data unit	Segment (stream-oriented)	Segment (discrete datagram-oriented)
Connections and handshaking	Connection-oriented. A connection is set up before data are exchanged. Messages form part of an ordered stream of data. Handshaking is required during the setup and teardown of connections, as well as to maintain existing connections, for example, in the form of "keep alive" messages during times when no data are being transmitted, to prevent automatic shutdown on timeout	Connectionless. Datagrams are sent individually, on demand. There is no additional handshaking
Reliability	High. Each segment is acknowledged and any lost segments are automatically retransmitted	Unreliable on the basis that there are no detection of datagram loss and no recovery mechanism. If reliability is needed, it must be designed in at a higher layer
Flow control	Supported. Prevents a sender from overwhelming a receiver, by only allowing data to be transmitted for which the receiver has buffer space. Improves efficiency because it reduces the occurrence of segments being dropped at the receiver side and having to be retransmitted	No support
Congestion control	Supported. Dynamically adjusts TCP's transmission rate to suit the level of congestion in the network and thus contributes to overall network efficiency	No support
Support for one/one communication	This is the only mode of communication supported	This is the default mode of communication supported
Support for broadcast	No. Communication is always one/one within a connection	Broadcast is supported by changing the socket configuration and sending datagrams to a broadcast address
Sequence numbers	Sequence numbers are added to all segments and are used in acknowledgments to relate them to specific segments	Sequence numbers are not built into UDP but can be added at the application level if need be
Message ordering and duplicates	Segments can arrive at the destination's transport layer entity out of order but are reordered correctly using the sequence numbers before being passed up to the higher layers. Duplicate segments are detected and automatically ignored thanks to the use of sequence numbers	Datagrams are transmitted and received as independent entities (from both the sender and receiver viewpoints). The lack of sequence numbers means that if datagrams arrive in a different order than they were sent, the receiver will be unaware of this and also that if duplicates are generated in the network, they are not detected as such by UDP. If ordering or duplicate suppression is important for the application, then it must be provided either in a higher-layer protocol or in the application logic itself

Table 3.1   Comparison of TCPs and UDPs—Cont'd

Characteristic	TCP	UDP
Handling lost messages	A timeout will occur if an acknowledgment is not received within a designated time frame. The original segment is retransmitted; this can lead to the creation of duplicates (in cases where the original segment was delayed but not lost), but these are detected at the receiver by their sequence numbers	No support
Buffering	Data are treated as a continuous stream, and therefore, the original segment boundaries are not maintained once data arrive in a buffer. A receive request will potentially retrieve the entire contents of the buffer	Data are transmitted in discrete units called datagrams. The boundaries between datagrams are retained in the receiving process' buffer, and a receive request will retrieve only the next datagram in the buffer
Overheads and efficiency	Due to the various reliability and quality mechanisms, the overheads are relatively high, both in terms of network bandwidth usage and also in terms of latency	Low overheads and thus more efficient than TCP

requires the use of broadcast), it may be necessary to use a mixture of both TCP and UDP, each for the specific parts of the communication they are suited to. An example of the combined use of both TCP and UDP is provided by DNS (as explained above). There are also applications that use connection-oriented communication to transmit data between processes but use the broadcast capability of UDP to implement server advertising and thus allow the processes to initially locate each other automatically (see the programming exercise at the end of this chapter for an opportunity to practice this).

Some general guidelines for choosing between the two transport protocols are provided:

- If reliable transport is required, choose TCP.
- If ongoing dialogues between components are necessary or otherwise one component needs to keep track of the number of and state of its communication partners, TCP is likely to be the best choice.
- If broadcast communication is needed, choose UDP.
- If latency and network bandwidth usage are the main considerations, choose UDP.
- If the higher-layer protocols or the application itself provides reliability, the case for using TCP is reduced, and in some cases, UDP would be acceptable.
- UDP datagrams are the simplest units of communication at the transport layer and thus are suitable as building blocks on which to build other protocols. A hybrid transport protocol (developed on top of UDP datagrams) may have a subset of the features of TCP, with some other features not supported by TCP; for example, a broadcast mechanism might be needed, but with acknowledgments from recipients.
- UDP is ideal for real-time data streaming applications in which it is better to permanently loose a dropped packet rather than to suffer the retransmit latency that would occur if TCP were used.
- If the communication is unidirectional, such as service advertisement, heartbeat messages, and some synchronization messages such as clock synchronization, the UDP is likely to be the most

suitable transport protocol. If the messages are transmitted periodically, such that occasional loss has no overall effect on the application's behavior, then the case for UDP is even stronger.

TCP is more complex than UDP from the developer viewpoint. However, in situations where the additional reliability or other features of TCP are warranted, it is a false economy to save on development effort and end up with an inferior application.

3.6 ADDRESSES

An address is a description of where to, or perhaps how to, find something. Everyone will be immediately familiar with this concept, because everyone has an "address" where they live. If you want your friend to come round to your house, you must first give them your address. However, rather than one address, most people have many addresses, perhaps as many as ten or even more! What am I talking about? Well, the address where you live could be more specifically described as your postal address, the address I would use to post a letter to you. However, if I wish to phone you, I need to know your phone number. Assuming that the full number including international code and regional code is used, then your phone number is a worldwide unique address; if I use this number, it will connect me to you. You may even have several phone numbers (home, mobile, and work). Similarly, if I wish to send you an email, I need to know your email address. If I wish to contact you through social media, I will need to know your Facebook name, or to connect via Skype, I need your Skype name. If you have a website, it has a unique address that I would use to view the site. So, you can see that there can be a wide variety of types of address, with various different formats, but all of the examples above have one thing in common; they are unique to you (i.e., they identify you).

Resources in a computer system must also have addresses, so that we can access them. Some of the examples above are relevant to this point, especially website addresses and email addresses. These are actually special cases of a class of addresses called Universal Resource Locators (URLs).

Network addresses are long numeric values that are not human-friendly (to illustrate this point, consider how many of your friends' phone numbers you can remember). In contrast, URLs are a textual form of address that is much easier for humans to remember and communicate; this largely due to their pattern-based nature, so that reciting, for example, a website address becomes relatively easy compared to trying to remember the numerical IP address.

The Domain Name System (DNS) provides a special translator service to translate the textual URL addresses into their numeric format when necessary. URLs are discussed in Chapter 4, and DNS is discussed in Chapter 6.

3.6.1 FLAT VERSUS HIERARCHICAL ADDRESSING

Addresses can be flat (which means that there is no pattern or structure within the addresses that can be used to aid locating resources) or hierarchical (which means that the address values contain a structure and that addresses can be allocated in such a way that the value of the address identifies the resource's position in the network).

Phone numbers provide a useful analogy. A phone number has a three- or four-level structure; it comprises an international code, an area code, and a subscriber number. Some subscriber numbers are followed by an extension number, which extends the single subscriber number to represent the different users within an organization (this is analogous to the way a port number extends an IP address; see later). The subscriber number is unique within the set of phone numbers that share the same combined international code and area code values. Of course, it is possible to duplicate each subscriber number in the other international code and area code combinations. The hierarchical structure of a phone number is used to efficiently route the call. The international code is used to route the call to the correct country's phone system. Only once in the correct country does it make sense to apply the area code. Once routed to the correct area, the subscriber number is used to connect to a specific user. If phone numbers used a flat scheme, that is, if a phone number was just a long number with no pattern to it, then the routing would be very difficult. At each routing node in the network, there would need to be access to a full database of all the phone numbers and how to route calls to them from any position in the network.

The Phillips Inter Integrated Circuit system (I²C) is a short-range serial bus communication system designed to facilitate interconnecting microprocessors and peripherals. The I²C address scheme provides a useful example of a flat addressing system. The 7-bit address range limits the number of addressable devices to 127, as address 0 is used to make a general call (broadcast). Applications are usually closed systems of embedded components, for example, a factory automation system with several microcontrollers controlling machines, conveyor belts, and robots and providing control, synchronization, and monitoring. Another example of its use is within a complex piece of office machinery such as a multifunction printer/photocopier or a paper-folding machine in which several microcontrollers are connected via a short bus. The scale of such systems is limited, and thus, the flat addressing is not usually a problem.

3.6.2 ADDRESSES IN THE LINK LAYER

The link layer provides connectivity between devices on a single data link. This can include an entire LAN, for example, Ethernet, up to the point where it is bounded by a router. The link layer needs to uniquely identify physical devices and ensure that no two devices have the same physical address. Therefore, the MAC address is fixed for the specific hardware network interface and must be globally unique.

There are many different manufacturers of network hardware devices (network adapter cards, routers, switches, etc.), which all need MAC addresses. The problem of ensuring global uniqueness is solved by having the first three bytes of the MAC address assigned centrally to the device manufacturer. The value of these three bytes is referred to as the Organizationally Unique Identifier (OUI). The device manufacturer is then responsible for ensuring that the second group of three bytes is unique for each OUI. Figure 3.26 shows some typical MAC addresses. Note that several of the MAC addresses have the same OUI, indicating the same hardware manufacturer, but that there is no pattern to the MAC addresses overall and that each one is unique.

The OUI is purely used to ensure global uniqueness across the different manufacturers. Thus, even though MAC addresses do in some sense have two components, they are a flat addressing scheme as the OUI plays no role in terms of locating devices.

3.6.3 ADDRESSES IN THE NETWORK LAYER

The network layer provides logical computer to computer communication. By logical, it is meant that the network is divided into groups of devices (called subnets), with each group having a set of related addresses and the groups of addresses having patterns such that it is easy to find a specific computer.

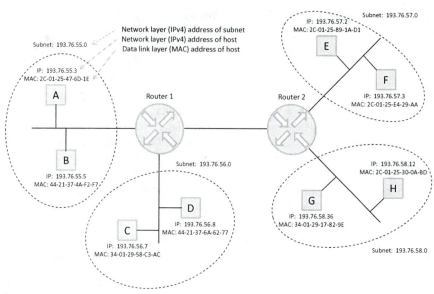

FIGURE 3.26

Link layer addresses and network layer addresses.

This is facilitated by the hierarchical nature of IP addresses; all computers in a particular subnet will have the same network component of their address, but a different host part, making their overall address unique. Therefore, the computer's network layer address is based on its position within a network and not on the identity of its physical network adapter; see Figure 3.26.

Figure 3.26 illustrates the differences between link layer addresses and network layer addresses and the roles they play. The diagram shows the way in which the hierarchical network layer (IPv4) addresses contain patterns in their network part (the first three bytes in the case of the IPv4 addresses shown) based on the subnet to which they belong, thus relating to their logical position within the network. The subnet addresses are used by routing protocols to deliver packets to the appropriate subnet. The host part of the address (the fourth byte in the case of the addresses shown), which is unique within each subnet, is then used to deliver the packet the last step of its journey, that is, to the specifically addressed computer. In order to achieve this last step, it is important that each computer has a unique address at the link technology level, to which a frame must be addressed, hence the requirement that MAC addresses are globally unique, because regardless of what device is placed in a particular subnet, it must not be possible for it to have the same MAC address as any other device in that subnet.

The MAC addresses contain an OUI (the first three of the six bytes; see earlier), which can be common among devices produced by the same manufacturer. Figure 3.26 depicts an example where several of the MAC addresses share the same OUI, while others don't; this is done to make the point that this partial pattern plays no role in terms of locating devices.

Note that if we were to replace one computer with another, in the same network, we could assign the same IP address to the replacement as the original had, but the physical address (the MAC address) will be different. If we move a computer to a new location, its IP address will change to reflect its new location, but its physical address will remain the same (because it has the same network adapter).

3.6.3.1 IP Addresses

There are two versions of the IP in current use: IPv4 and IPv6. One of the main reasons that IPv6 was introduced was because the address range provided by IPv4 is insufficient to meet the growing demand for Internet addresses. Thus, IPv6 supports a much wider range of address values.

3.6.3.2 IPv4 Addresses

IPv4 addresses are 32 bits long (4 bytes). An IPv4 address is written in the format of 4 decimal numbers each separated by a single dot, hence called dotted decimal notation. This is generically represented as d.d.d.d where each d represents a decimal number in the range 0-255. An example is 193.65.72.27.

IPv4 addresses are hierarchical in the sense that they contain a network component that is used by routing protocols to deliver packets to the appropriate subnet (as discussed above) and a host part that is used to deliver a packet to a specific computer within the subnet. IPv4 addresses are divided into classes A, B, and C based on the way the 32 bits are split across the network and host parts of the address. Class D is reserved for multicast addressing, used, for example, within some routing protocols so that the routers can communicate among themselves. The division into classes is illustrated in Figure 3.27.

Figure 3.27 shows the three main address classes used in IPv4 and the multicast address class D. The address class can be determined by inspecting the first few bits of the highest-order byte; the critical bits for this purpose are shown in the figure; for example, if the address begins with "10," then it is class B.

A subnet mask is a bit pattern that is used to separate the network part of an address from the host part. It is particularly important that routers can determine which part of an address is the network part; this is determined by the part of the subnet mask that is set to binary "1s" (where 255 decimal is the pattern "11111111" in binary). The default subnet masks for address classes A, B, and C are shown in the right-hand side of Figure 3.27.

Some computers have multiple network adapters (each with their own IP address) and can receive packets on any of them. The developers of distributed applications are usually not interested in which physical interface is used to receive a particular packet. However, in such cases where there are multiple adapters and thus the computer has multiple IP addresses, problems can arise if the socket address structure is set up to contain the specific IP address of one of the adapters. The special IP address INADDR_ANY can be used when binding a socket, indicating to the TCP or UDP that the socket can receive any of the IP addresses the computer has. Note that if a socket bound with INADDR_ANY is used for sending, the actual address used (the source address in the packet sent) will be the computer's default IP address, which is the lowest numbered of the addresses it has.

Address class					Address range			Default subnet mask
A	0 N	H	H	H	1.0.0.0	to	127.255.255.255	255.0.0.0
B	10 N	N	H	H	128.0.0.0	to	191.255.255.255	255.255.0.0
C	110 N	N	N	H	192.0.0.0	to	223.255.255.255	255.255.255.0
D	1110	multicast address			224.0.0.0	to	239.255.255.255	

Key: N = network address byte   H = host address byte

FIGURE 3.27

IPv4 address classes.

If a message is to be sent to a destination process, which is on the same computer (it is said to be "local"), the special loopback address 127.0.0.1 can be used. This causes the outgoing message to be turned around (looped back) by the network adapter and thus is not actually transmitted externally on the network. The most common usage of the loopback address is for testing and diagnostics.

3.6.3.3 IPv6 Addresses

IPv6 addresses are 128 bits (16 bytes). An IPv6 address is written in the format of 8 hexadecimal numbers each separated by a single colon. This is generically represented as x:x:x:x:x:x:x:x where each x represents a 16-bit hexadecimal number, that is, in the range 0H-FFFFH. An example is FF36:0:0:0:11CE:0:E245:4BC7. The address range represented by an IPv6 address is so vast that parts of the number range may be effectively unused for some time to come, leading to several "0s" in the address; in such cases, a compressed form can be used to replace one string of "0s" (the longest such string) with the symbol "::." The example given above thus becomes FF36::11CE:0:E245:4BC7, and because only one continuous series of "0s" was changed, it can be unambiguously converted back to the original 8 hexadecimal number representation.

3.6.3.4 Translation Between IP Addresses and MAC Addresses

The Address Resolution Protocol (ARP) translates an IP address into a MAC address. It is used when a sending device (computer or router) needs to create a frame (which is a link layer message) to carry a packet (a network layer message) to another device for which the sender only knows the IP address and therefore needs to find out the destination device's MAC address.

3.6.4 ADDRESSES IN THE TRANSPORT LAYER (PORTS)

A distributed application comprises two or more processes. Each process must have a unique address so that messages can be directed to it. The transport layer provides process-to-process communication and thus is perhaps the most significant layer from the viewpoint of distributed application developers.

An IP address refers to a particular computer. Thus, the IP address is sufficient to get a packet to the correct computer, and all messages with a particular IP address will be delivered to the same computer. However, modern computers support many processes concurrently, and it is always a process that is the final recipient of a message. Hence, a further level of address detail is needed to provide a unique address to each process within the computer, to facilitate communication, that is, to ensure that the message can be passed to the appropriate process. The additional part of the address is called the port; that is, a port is an extension of the IP address that specifies which process to deliver a message to, once the packet that carries the message has reached the destination computer.

A useful analogy here (which extends the postal address scenario provided earlier) is that of a shared house in which several people live, each having a room numbered from 1 to 4. The sender of a letter addressed to one of these people will write the room number as an additional line of address. The postal system (analogous to the IP) will ignore the room number detail; it is meaningless to the postman; his job is to post the letter to the right building based on the street address, but he has no knowledge of the internal allocation of rooms inside the house. Once the letter has been received at the property, the occupants can examine the room number detail (analogous with port) to determine which person (analogous with process) should receive the message.

Figure 3.28 illustrates a scenario where there are several processes spread across two computers, and the requirement is to send a message (which is encapsulated within a packet) to one specific

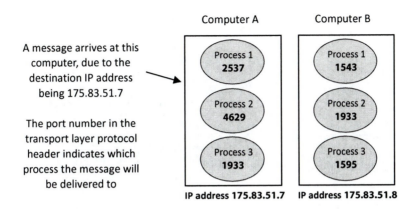

A message arrives at this computer, due to the destination IP address being 175.83.51.7

The port number in the transport layer protocol header indicates which process the message will be delivered to

FIGURE 3.28

Ports identify specific processes located at a particular computer.

process. As the two computers have different IP addresses, the IP address (which will be included in the IP header of the packet) is sufficient to get the message delivered to the correct computer. The port number is included in the transport layer protocol (e.g., TCP or UDP) as this layer is concerned with process-to-process communication. Once the packet has reached the destination computer, the transport layer header is inspected and the operating system will extract and deliver the message to the appropriate process based on the port number. Notice that while IP addresses must be globally unique, it is only necessary that port numbers be locally unique (i.e., there cannot be any two the same at a single computer). In the figure, there is a process using the port number 1933 on each computer. Note that even in this case, the combination of an IP address and a port number is still globally unique.

The port number can be written as an extension of the IPv4 address, using a colon to separate the address and port:

Notation   IPv4 address:port   An example is   193.65.72.27:23

The port number is expressed in decimal and in the example above signifies Telnet.

This is unambiguous because the separator character used between the address components is a dot. However, IPv6 uses the colon as its address component separator character, and thus, the use of a colon to indicate port number is confusing. There are several ways in which an IPv6 address and port number combination can be written, but the preferred technique is to place the IPv6 address within square brackets, followed by a colon, and then the port number:

Notation   [IPv6 address]:port   An example is   [FF36:0:0:0:11CE:0:E245:4BC7]:80

The port number is expressed in decimal and in the example above signifies HTTP.

3.6.5 WELL-KNOWN PORTS

Port numbers (in TCP and UDP) are 16-bit values, which means that approximately 65 thousand are available on each computer. Bespoke applications are free to use the majority of the port numbers, but some parts of the number range are reserved for the common protocols and services, so that particular

Port	Service	Port	Service
5	Remote Job Entry	118	Structured Query Language (SQL) services
7	Echo	123	Network Time Protocol (NTP)
20	File Transfer Protocol (FTP) data	264	Border Gateway Multicast Protocol (BGMP), routing
21	File Transfer Protocol (FTP) command	389	Lightweight Directory Access Protocol (LDAP)
23	Telnet	513	Rlogin (remote access)
25	Simple Mail Transfer Protocol (SMTP)	520	Routing Information Protocol (RIP)
53	Domain Name System (DNS)	521	Routing Information Protocol Next Generation (RIPng)
69	Trivial File Transfer Protocol (TFTP)	530	Remote Procedure Call (RPC)
80	HyperText Transfer Protocol (HTTP)	546	Dynamic Host Configuration Protocol v6 Client (DHCPv6)
88	Kerberos (authentication system)	547	Dynamic Host Configuration Protocol v6 Server (DHCPv6)
110	Post Office Protocol version 3 (POP3)	944	Network File Service (NFS)
111	ONC Remote Procedure Call (SUN RPC)	976	Network File Service (NFS) over IPv6
115	Simple File Transfer Protocol (SFTP)		

FIGURE 3.29

A selection of well-known port allocations.

values can be mapped to specific services. This greatly simplifies the development of distributed systems and the components thereof, as the port numbers that the server side will bind to (and the client side will connect to), are preknown and fixed for a wide variety of services and thus can be designed into software, reducing the amount of run time discovery and configuration needed.

The well-known port numbers are of the range 1-1023. Some examples are shown in Figure 3.29

Figure 3.29 illustrates the great diversity of services that have been allocated well-known port numbers to facilitate service location and client-service binding. The well-known port numbers can be considered the premier set reserved for the most popular services. There is also a secondary set called the registered ports, which are reserved for a larger group of less common services. These occupy the numerical range of port numbers from 1024 to 49,151. A sample of the registered ports is shown in Figure 3.30.

Port numbers greater than 49,151 are called dynamic ports and can be used by any application or service. If you are developing an experimental system or a service for one specific company, then it should use ports in the dynamic range.

Port	Service
2483	Oracle database service
3306	MySQL database system
3690	Subversion (SVN) version control system
3702	Web Services Dynamic Discovery (WS-Discovery)
5353	Multicast DNS (mDNS)
8080	HTTP (alternate), e.g. when running a webserver as a non-root user
8332	Bitcoin JSON-RPC server

FIGURE 3.30

A selection of the registered port allocations.

3.7 **SOCKETS**

A socket is a structure in memory that represents the endpoint for communication (i.e., sockets are the means by which processes are identified by the communication system). The central concept is that sockets belonging to each communicating process are connected together, to create communication channels between the processes.

TCP and UDP operate in the transport layer; thus, the sockets are virtual. A socket exists only in the form of a data structure and is a means of making a logical association between processes. Do not confuse virtual sockets with physical sockets; that is, a virtual socket is not a physical portal such as an Ethernet socket.

Figure 3.31 illustrates the concept of virtual sockets. A socket represents the process in terms of identifying it for communication purposes; this means that the socket is effectively the process' interface to the communication system. A socket is associated with the address of the process, which includes both its IP address (identifying the host computer) and the port number, which is unique on each computer and thus identifies the specific process. Each process creates as many sockets as necessary, depending on its communication requirements. The figure shows the way in which processes can communicate via sockets with other processes, which are on the same, or different, physical computer. This aspect is important in fully appreciating the "virtual" nature of the communication. The transport layer protocols send and receive messages on behalf of processes in an access-transparent way; that is, the mechanism is exactly the same from the process' point of view regardless of whether its communication partner is local or remote.

Blocking Versus Nonblocking IO Modes of Sockets: *A Brief Introduction*: Network communication is a form of IO. Writing a message to a network adapter for transmission over the network is similar to writing a file to a disk in the sense that both cases involve slow external devices requiring specific handling via a device driver. Waiting for a network message to arrive is similar to reading a file from a disk in the sense that in both cases, there is significant delay because the device involved operates slowly relative to the speed of the processor.

Sockets can be configured to operate in one of two IO modes, blocking or nonblocking. The choice between these modes impacts on the scheduler's treatment of the owner process. If the socket is in

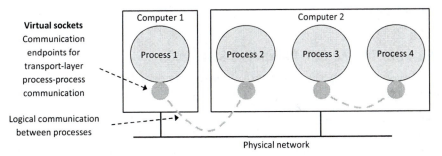

FIGURE 3.31

Virtual sockets provide process-to-process connections.

blocking mode, then the process will be moved into the blocked process state whenever it has to wait for an event such as receiving a message, whereas if the socket is in nonblocking mode, the process can carry on with other activities while the event is pending.

The behavior of the communication protocol itself, either TCP or UDP, is unaffected by the socket's IO mode. The socket IO mode is discussed in more detail later.

3.7.1 THE SOCKET API: AN OVERVIEW

The socket Application Programmer Interface (API) is a set of library routines (called socket primitives) that a programmer uses to configure and use the TCP and UDP communication protocols from within an application.

Versions of the socket API are available on almost every platform and supported by almost every high-level programming language, making the TCPs and UDPs near-universally available to applications developers.

The main advantages of developing at the transport level are flexibility and control. At this level, the communication is broken down to the level of individual messages, which can be combined together as building blocks to create any protocol necessary. For example, higher-level communication mechanisms such as RPC, RMI, and middleware are all built on top of the TCP and thus developed using the socket primitives. Some applications require specific communication patterns and behaviors that are not provided by the existing application layer communication protocols. Using the socket API, it is possible to embed the custom communication protocol required for a particular application directly into the program code of each component. The case study game provides an interesting example of this approach.

However, building communication logic at the transport level is challenging as the developer needs to understand the low-level characteristics of communication and especially the types of error that can occur and the run time behaviors that these will cause and ultimately the impact these have on the reliability and correctness of the application itself. The developer must ensure that faults and failures are handled robustly, taking care to use the resources of the system efficiently, especially in terms of network bandwidth.

The socket API primitives are explained individually in Appendix. Annotated code examples are provided for each primitive.

3.7.2 THE SOCKET API: UDP PRIMITIVE SEQUENCE

This section describes the typical use sequence of the socket primitives when implementing communication based on the UDP.

1. The socket primitive is used to create a socket. All of the other primitives require the identity of this socket when performing actions such as connect, send, and receive.

The socket's configuration is important; it can be set to operate as a TCP stream-based socket or as a UDP datagram-based socket. It can be configured to operate in either the blocking or nonblocking IO mode, using the ioctlsocket utility.

2. The bind primitive is used to map a process to a port (binding is discussed in detail later in this chapter).

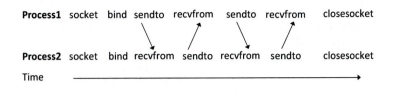

FIGURE 3.32

Sequence of primitive calls in a typical exchange between a pair of processes using UDP.

3. The sendto primitive is used to send data to another process.
4. The recvfrom primitive is used to retrieve data from the receive buffer.
5. The closesocket primitive is used to close the socket.
A typical sequence for UDP communication is illustrated in Figure 3.32.

Figure 3.32 shows a possible sequence of primitive calls involved in a typical exchange between two processes using the UDP. Prior to communication, each process creates a socket that is necessary as the logical endpoint for the communication that will take place. Each process then binds its socket to its local address (which comprises the computer's IP address and the port that the specific process will use to receive messages). This is necessary because when the process subsequently issues a recvfrom primitive request, the local operating system must have a mapping between the process and the port the process uses, so that the operating system can direct arriving messages to the appropriate process. The two processes now issue sendto and recvfrom requests in whatever sequence necessary to achieve the application's communication needs. For example, if transferring a large file in a series of fragments, process 1 could send the first fragment and process 2 could send back an acknowledgment (there are no in-built acknowledgments provided by the UDP); this could be repeated several times until the file transfer is complete. Each process then closes its socket, using the closesocket primitive.

Note that in Figure 3.32 (and all similar figures in which arrows are used to depict communication events against a time line), the arrows are sloped in the time direction. This is to reinforce that all communication has some latency and thus the actual sending of a message always occurs a short time before the message arrives at its destination.

Activity C3 provides an introduction to the UDP and datagram buffering.

3.7.3 THE SOCKET API: TCP PRIMITIVES SEQUENCE

This section describes the typical use sequence of the socket primitives when implementing communication based on the TCP.

1. The socket primitive is used to create a socket.
2. The bind primitive is used to map a process to a port.
3. The listen, connect, and accept primitives are used to set up a connection.
4. The send primitive is used to send data to another process.
5. The recv primitive is used to retrieve data from the receive buffer.
6. The shutdown primitive is used to close the connection.
7. The closesocket primitive is used to close the socket.

ACTIVITY C3 USING THE NETWORKING WORKBENCH TO EXPLORE THE UDP AND DATAGRAM BUFFERING

Prerequisite

Download the Networking Workbench and the supporting documentation from the book's supplementary materials website. Read the document "Networking Workbench Activities and Experiments."

Learning Outcomes

1. To gain an initial understanding of the UDP
2. To understand the concept of datagrams and the sending and receiving of messages without having to set up a connection
3. To gain an initial understanding of message buffering and how it applies to UDP datagrams
4. To gain basic familiarity with the Networking Workbench

Method

This activity is carried out in three steps:

1. Experimentation with UDP

Use two copies of the "UDP Workbench" application, within the Networking Workbench (on the UDP Tab), to investigate the basic communication functionality of UDP. Ideally, use two computers (but you can run both instances of the workbench on the same computer if need be). Set up a simple two-way communication in which each user can send and receive messages to/from the other.

Ensure that the unicast radio button is selected. You will need to configure the send IP address (Address 1) in each instance of the UDP Workbench to hold the address of the computer where the other copy is located. You will also need to set the send and receive ports appropriately. If running the two copies on separate computers, start with all the port numbers being the same; otherwise, set the ports as shown in the screenshot below. After you have set the receive port number, you need to click on the "Enable Receiver" button. The screenshot shows the configuration of two copies of the UDP Workbench on a single computer. A single message has been sent in each direction.

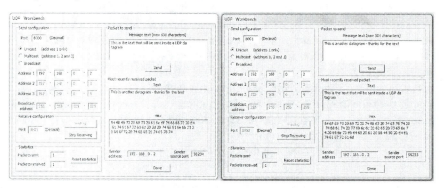

2. Buffering (Part 1)

For this part, you will need to use one copy of the UDP Workbench (this will be used to send messages) and one copy of the Non-Blocking Receive, which is also available on the UDP tab of the Networking Workbench (this will be used to receive messages).

The two applications can be on the same or different computers, but ensure that address and port settings are appropriate before continuing (make sure that the sending IP address of the UDP Workbench is that of the computer where the Non-Blocking Receive resides and that the send port on the UDP Workbench is the same as the receive port on the Non-Blocking Receive).

Take care to follow the EXACT sequence of the steps set out below.

Start the Non-Blocking Receiver, but do not press any buttons.

1. Using the unicast addressing mode, use the UDP Workbench to send a message containing "A" to the receiver (the send port should be 8000).
2. Ensure that the receive port on the Non-Blocking Receiver is set to 8000, and click "Bind."

ACTIVITY C3 USING THE NETWORKING WORKBENCH TO EXPLORE THE UDP AND DATAGRAM BUFFERING—Cont'd

3. Click "Receive" on the Non-Blocking Receiver—did it receive the "A"? If not, why not?
4. Send a message containing "B" to the receiver.
5. Did anything happen at the receiver?
6. Click "Receive"—what happens?

The result is different from that of step 3 above. Why?

7. Send a message containing "C" to the receiver.
8. Send a message containing "D" to the receiver.
9. Click "Receive"—what happens?
10. Click "Receive" again—what happens?

The screenshot below shows the configuration of the two applications on the same computer (after step 6).

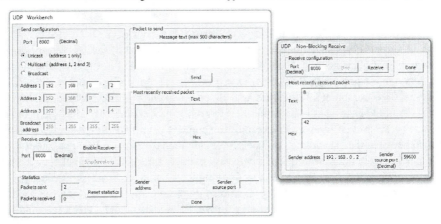

3. **Buffering (Part 2)**

Use the same configuration as for the experiment: Buffering part 1.

1. Start the Non-Blocking Receiver, and press "Bind."
2. Use the UDP Workbench to send a message many times to the receiver in quick succession.
3. Now press "Receive"—what happens? And again?
4. Describe what is happening here in terms of packet queuing and buffering.
5. Where do you think the buffer is held, at the sender or receiver end?
   a. Devise a simple experiment to confirm your hypothesis? (Hint: what happens if the sender is shut down after it sends a message but before the message has been displayed by the receiver?)
6. Are the UDP segment boundaries maintained throughout the entire transmission process (including any buffering that might occur), or can they be further divided or concatenated? In other words, are the messages kept separate, or are they merged when retrieved from the buffer? Try to confirm your answer through empirical investigation (i.e., carry out some more experiments to find out).

Expected Outcome

Through these experiments, you should have gained an initial understanding of how the UDP works and how datagrams are sent and received. The second and third parts of the activity focus specifically on the buffering behavior; you should have found that the datagrams are buffered on the receiver side and that they are kept separate in the buffer, so that each datagram must be retrieved one by one.

Reflection

As a result of doing this activity, you should be able to list, in correct sequence, the different actions that need to be performed in order to set up and use UDP communication between a pair of processes. Try to identify the steps required, starting from "each process creates a socket." You may wish to rerun the activity to enable further exploration.

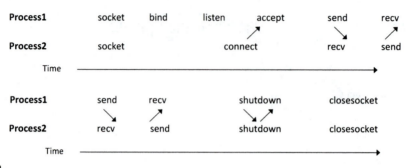

FIGURE 3.33

A typical TCP exchange.

A typical sequence for TCP communication is illustrated in Figure 3.33.

Figure 3.33 shows a typical sequence of primitive calls involved in the setting up, using of, and shutting down of a TCP connection. Each process first creates a socket as the logical endpoint for the connection between the processes. The server side (process 1) then binds its socket to its local address (which comprises the computer's IP address and the port that the specific process will use to receive messages). If the bind primitive is successful, the server-side process then executes the listen primitive. The client side (process 2) subsequently executes the connect primitive, which causes a connection to be established between the two processes. The server side then executes the accept primitive to handle the specific newly created connection; this involves creating a new dedicated socket at the server side for use with the connection. The processes now communicate using send and recv requests in whatever sequence is necessary depending on the application's communication needs. The connection is then shutdown by each side invoking the shutdown primitive. Each process then closes its socket, using the closesocket primitive.

Activity C4 provides an introduction to the TCP and stream buffering.

ACTIVITY C4 USING THE NETWORKING WORKBENCH TO EXPLORE THE TCP, THE TCP CONNECTION, AND STREAM BUFFERING

Prerequisite

Download the Networking Workbench and the supporting documentation from the book's supplementary materials website. Read the document "Networking Workbench Activities and Experiments."

Learning Outcomes

1. To gain an initial understanding of the TCP
2. To understand the concept of the TCP connection
3. To understand sending and receiving of messages using a connection
4. To gain an initial understanding of message buffering and how it applies to TCP data streams

Method

This activity explores the TCP and thus uses the TCP:Active Open and TCP:Passive Open applications (each found on the TCP tab of the Networking Workbench). The TCP:Active Open application initiates connection establishment; this is typically the client side of a client server application. The TCP:Passive Open application waits for connection requests; this would typically be the server side.

The activity is carried out in three steps.

1. Understand the behavior of the TCP primitives and the sequences in which these are used

ACTIVITY C4 USING THE NETWORKING WORKBENCH TO EXPLORE THE TCP, THE TCP CONNECTION, AND STREAM BUFFERING—Cont'd

The TCP API is implemented as a set of primitives (simple functions). These primitives (such as *bind*, *listen*, *accept*, *connect*, *send*, and *recv*) must occur in a valid sequence between the two endpoint processes, in order to establish and use a connection. For example, the Passive Open end must create a socket and then *bind* that socket to a port before certain other steps can occur.

This experiment is designed to enable students to investigate the effects of using the primitives in various sequences. It is intended that students identify the correct sequence through logical deduction.

1. Start two copies of the Networking Workbench, preferably at different computers (one for TCP:Active Open and one for TCP:Passive Open).
2. Use the applications to create connections, send and receive packets, and close connections.
3. Investigate the event sequences that lead to successful communication. Perform sufficient experiments to confirm your understanding.

The screenshot below shows the two processes once a connection has been set up and a single message has been sent in each direction.

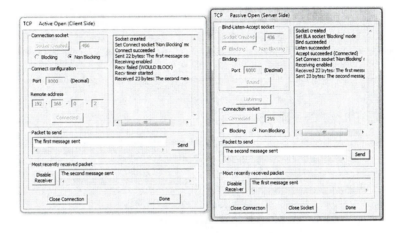

2. Understand the behavior of streams and stream communication
    1. Start two copies of the Networking Workbench, preferably at different computers (one for TCP:Active Open and one for TCP:Passive Open).
    2. Establish connection.
    3. Set the active open end's socket to nonblocking.
    4. Enable receive at the Active Open end, and send a packet to it.
    5. Note that the packet is delivered as it was sent.
    6. Disable receive at the Active Open end and then send two packets to it.
    7. Enable receive.
    Q1. What happens (what exactly is delivered to the application)?
    Q2. What does this tell you about the nature of stream communication?
3. Understand connections and the relationship between listen and accept
    1. Start two copies of the Networking Workbench, preferably at different computers (one for TCP:Active Open and one for TCP:Passive Open).
    2. Create sockets at both the Active and Passive ends.
    3. At the Active end, try to Connect—what happens and why?
    4. Bind at the Passive end.
    5. At the Active end, try to Connect—what happens and why?
    6. Listen and Accept at the Passive end.

ACTIVITY C4 USING THE NETWORKING WORKBENCH TO EXPLORE THE TCP, THE TCP CONNECTION, AND STREAM BUFFERING—Cont'd

7. At the Active end, try to Connect—what happens and why?
8. Close connections and sockets at both ends.
9. Repeat steps 2 and 4, and then, listen at the passive end.
10. At the Active end, try to Connect—what happens and why?
11. Accept at the Passive end—what happens and why?

You should now have a better idea of the relationship between Listen and Accept.

Q1. State the role of each.
Q2. Why might it be important to separate these two steps of connection establishment (hint: think of typical process behavior and lifetimes in client server applications).

Expected Outcome

Through these experiments, you should have gained an initial understanding of how the TCP works, the nature of the TCP connection, and the steps required to create a connection. You should also have found that the stream segments become concatenated together when buffered on the receiver side so that the entire buffer contents can be retrieved in one go.

Reflection

As a result of doing this activity, you should be able to list, in correct sequence, the different actions that need to be performed in order to use the TCP. In particular, the sequence for creating a connection is important. Continue exploration until the concepts and event sequences are clear to you.

3.7.4 BINDING (PROCESS TO PORT)

Binding is the term used to describe the making of an association between a process and a port and is performed by the local operating system (i.e., the operating system of the computer where the particular process resides). The port is particularly important in the mechanism of receiving a message, as the operating system must know which process to pass a particular arriving message to. This is done by inspecting the port number in the received message's transport layer header (e.g., TCP and UDP both have a destination port number in their header). The operating system then looks at its port table to find a match. There will be an entry in the port table for each process-port relationship, so if a process is associated with the particular port number, the operating system will be able to get the process' PID and thus deliver the message to the process.

The bind primitive (discussed in outline earlier; see also Appendix) is the means by which a process makes a request to its operating system to request use of a port. There are a few restrictions that the operating system must check before granting the request. Firstly, the operating system must ensure that the port is not already in use by another process; each port must be mapped to only one process because otherwise the operating system will not know how to deliver a message. Allowing two processes to use the same port at the same time would be analogous to having two houses in the same street with the same door number: how would the postman know how to deliver letters? Another analogy would be giving two people the same telephone number; it would be ok when they make calls, but what would happen when someone tries to call one of them?

You might at this point be asking why are ports needed? Why not send messages addressed using the process' ID (the PID), which is created when the process is created (and thus is also known by the operating system), is guaranteed unique, and cannot change throughout the process' lifetime? It is on the face of it a very good question. The answer is that because the operating system allocates a process

ID automatically when a process is created, in a simple round-robin fashion, it is not possible to know in advance what the PID will be for any particular process. In fact, if you think back to the discussion of programs and processes in the Process View chapter, you will recall that a single program can be executed several times simultaneously, even at the same computer, giving rise to several processes (each having a different PID). Even if the program is only executed once at a time, the process ID allocated to the process is far more likely to be different each time it is executed, than it is likely to be the same. A further consideration is that if we execute the same program on a number of different computers at the same time, each process will likely have a different PID. Although in all cases, the PID is guaranteed to be locally unique to its process, a sending process located on a different computer cannot know what the PID is. If the PID were used as the delivery address, a lot of additional work would have to be done in order that the sender process could find out the appropriate PID number of a particular remotely running process. In contrast, because the port number is supplied by the process itself when making a bind request to the operating system, it can be known in advance; in particular, it can be known when the application is written and thus can be embedded in the logic of both the sending and receiving programs. This is the reason why certain port numbers are "well known" and reserved for a particular application (see earlier discussion). As an example, an FTP server uses the well-known port numbers 20 (for data transfer) and 21 (for control and commands). An FTP client does not need to perform any complex lookups to find out the PID of the remote file server process; it simply has to send its messages to the appropriate port number. A new FTP client can be developed without any knowledge of the internal operation of the FTP service itself. As long as the FTP communication protocol is used and ports 20 and 21 are used appropriately to address the server, the client will be able to connect to the FTP server and have its FTP commands actioned.

Arriving messages are filtered based on their destination IP address (this is performed by the IP device driver), and for those that match the local machine's address, the operating system takes responsibility to deliver the message to the appropriate process. The operating system looks up the destination port number identified in the transport layer header within the message, in its port table. If there is an entry for the particular port number, then the message will be passed to the appropriate process (identified by its PID in the port table). If the port number is not found in the port table, then the message is dropped. This basic mechanism is illustrated in Figure 3.34.

Figure 3.34 illustrates the mechanism of binding a process to a port. In step 1, the process identified by its PID (17) issues a bind request, asking to use port number 1234. In step 2, the operating system

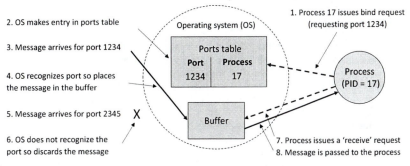

FIGURE 3.34

Binding a process to a port.

checks to see if the port is already in use, and as it is not in use, it creates an entry in the ports table and returns "success" when the bind call completes (so that the process knows the port has been allocated to it). Subsequently, a message arrives, addressed to port 1234 (step 3). The operating system searches the port table and finds that process 17 is using this port number, so the message is held in a buffer for the process. If a message arrives for a port that does not have an entry in the port table (as in step 5), it is discarded (step 6). Storing the message would tie up precious space in the buffer and would be pointless because there is no process interested in the message. When process 17 issues a receive request (step 7), the message is passed to the process (step 8).

Although discussed in other sections, it is worth mentioning here that the illustration of the operation of bind (as shown in Figure 3.34) reinforces the important point that the operating system's buffering of arriving messages decouples the target process from the actual mechanism of receiving the message from the network. As long as the process has issued a successful bind request, the operating system will receive messages from the network on behalf of the process. This is important for two main reasons: (1) that individual processes do not directly access or control the network adapter and the IP driver and (2) that the process may not be in the "run" state at the time the message actually arrives and in such case would not be able to move the message into a buffer as it arrived.

Activity C5 explores binding.

ACTIVITY C5 USING THE NETWORKING WORKBENCH TO EXPLORE BINDING

Prerequisite
You should have completed Activity C3 and have gained a reasonable understanding of the UDP before attempting this activity.

Learning Outcomes
1. To gain an understanding of the need for binding processes to ports
2. To gain an initial understanding of the operation of bind
3. To use bind to establish a link between a process and a port
4. To understand why incoming messages are ignored before bind has been executed
5. To understand common reasons why bind may fail
6. To understand that the same port number can be reused on different computers, that is, it is the port and IP address combined that must be unique

Method
This activity is carried out in two parts:
1. The fundamental purpose of binding
Use two copies of the "UDP Workbench" application, both running on the same computer.
   Set up the IP addresses and port numbers appropriately. Both IP addresses should be set to the address of the local computer. Set the send port of the first copy of the UDP Workbench to 8000 and its receive port to 8001. Set the send port of the second copy of the UDP Workbench to 8001 and its receive port to 8000.
   1. BEFORE enabling the receiver at either copy, send a message from the first copy to the second copy.
   Q1. What happens (does the message arrive)?
   2. Now, enable the receiver at the second copy of the UDP Workbench.
   Q2. Does the message arrive if you now enable the receiver (i.e., has it been buffered)?
   3. Send a second message from the first copy to the second copy.
   Q3. What happens (does the message arrive)?
   Q4. What does this behavior tell you about the significance of binding?

ACTIVITY C5 USING THE NETWORKING WORKBENCH TO EXPLORE BINDING—Cont'd

2. Exclusive Use of Ports

Use two copies of the "Non-Blocking Receiver" (found on the UDP tab of the Networking Workbench), both running on the same computer.

　1. Start a copy of the Non-Blocking Receiver and leave its receive port at the default value.

　2. Press "Bind."

　3. Start a second copy of the Non-Blocking Receiver at the same computer. Ensure that its receive port value is the same as for the first copy.

　4. Press "Bind."

　Q1. What happens? Why is this behavior not only correct but also necessary?

　Q2. What do you think would have happened if the second receiver had been at a different computer?

　Q3. Confirm your hypothesis empirically (check your answer by trying it out). What happens?

　The screenshot below shows the situation after the second attempt to bind to the same port.

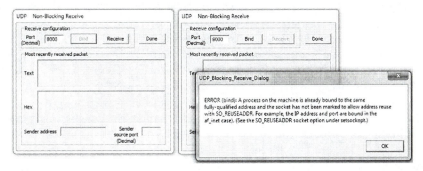

Expected Outcome

From part 1, you should have discovered that messages sent to a port before the bind has occurred are ignored; that is, they are not placed in the buffer. This is because the operating system is not aware that the receiver process is expecting them, until it has bound to the particular port.

　From part 2, you should have discovered that you can only bind one process per computer to any particular port. If two processes try to bind to the same port, the second attempt is refused. This is important because the operating system needs to know which process to pass a received message to, and it does this based on the port number in the message. If two processes were to be allowed to bind to the same port then the operating system would not know which one to pass an arriving message to.

　From part 2, you should have also discovered that the same port number can be reused on different computers. For example, two processes on different computers can both bind to the same port number. It is the port and IP address combined that must be unique.

Reflection

It is very important to understand the way in which the operating system identifies the recipient processes by the port number contained in each message and the role that bind plays in making the association between the process and the port.

3.8 BLOCKING AND NONBLOCKING SOCKET BEHAVIORS

The discussion above provides an explanation of the basic mechanism of receiving a message and passing it to a process (see Figure 3.34). However, the way in which the message is passed to the process is affected by additional factors, thus leading to several variations in behavior, as discussed here.

Sockets can be configured to operate in two IO modes: blocking and nonblocking. This affects the way in which the operating system treats the socket's owner process if it attempts an operation that uses the socket and that cannot complete immediately. For example, the process may issue a recv request and have to wait for a message to arrive. The process must be in the run state when it actually issues the recv request (because it can only execute instructions when using the CPU). This means that the process must either be able to do something else useful while waiting for the message to arrive or must be moved into the blocked process state until the message arrives. The programmer chooses between these two approaches when deciding which socket IO mode to use.

A socket in blocking mode will cause its process to be moved to the blocked state, by the operating system, whenever a request cannot be completed immediately. This means that the process will be held at the point where the primitive request (e.g., accept, recv, or recvfrom) was made until the awaited event occurs. Put another way, think of the primitive request as being effectively a subroutine call; the call will not return until the event (such as receiving a message) has completed. There is no limit as to how long a process may have to wait.

A socket in nonblocking mode will cause an error message (type="WOULD_BLOCK") to be returned by the operating system, to the process whenever a request cannot be completed immediately. The important point here is that the process does not encounter any delay (it does not wait for the event to occur). Instead, the process must examine the error message received and determine its action accordingly.

Figure 3.35 shows the sequence and behavior of socket primitives when a message is sent by one process to another process that is using a blocking socket. In order that communication can take place, each process first creates a socket. This must be accompanied by a socket address structure populated with the appropriate address details; for the UDP example illustrated, the sending side must be configured with the IP address and port number of the process it is sending to. For the receiving side, the address structure must contain its own IP address and the port number on which the message will be received.

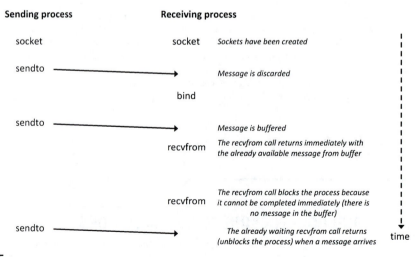

FIGURE 3.35

Behavior of socket primitives, in a UDP context, when the socket is set to blocking mode.

As the UDP is datagram-based, there is no need to establish a virtual connection (as there would be with TCP). As soon as the sender has created its socket, it can use it as the basis to make a sendto primitive call.

The receiving side must use the bind primitive call to take ownership of the required port (thus identifying the receiving process to the operating system and enabling the operating system to associate the process ID and the port number together in its port table). The figure shows the scenario where a message arrives at the receiving side before the bind has occurred; in this case, the operating system rejects the message as it has no entry in its port table and thus cannot identify the recipient process. Messages arriving after the bind has been completed are buffered and forwarded to the receiving process. Exactly how this occurs depends on the timing, with respect to the issuance of recvfrom calls. If the message arrives before a recvfrom has been issued, it is buffered and delivered upon issuance of the recvfrom call (as with the second message sent in Figure 3.35). If a recvfrom call has already been issued, the process will be in blocked state, and in this case, a message will be delivered to the process as soon as it arrives in the operating system's buffer. This has the effect of moving the process into the ready state.

Figure 3.36 shows the same sequence of primitive calls and with the same relative timing as in Figure 3.35; however, in this case, the socket is set to nonblocking mode. The important difference in behavior arises when the second recvfrom primitive call is made. In the nonblocking socket case, the call returns immediately and the process can continue in the running state, whereas in the blocking socket mode, the process was blocked until a message arrived.

Figure 3.37 shows an overview of the behavior of, and sequence of use of, the main socket primitives in a TCP context. As with UDP, the exact behavior depends on whether the socket is configured for either blocking or nonblocking operation, and this leads to the same two types of behavior in cases when the process would have to wait for an event to occur; either the process is moved into the blocked state by the operating system, or an error message is returned to the primitive call that would have otherwise blocked. However, the TCP is more complex than UDP, especially in terms of the need to set up a connection prior to communication taking place and the need to close (teardown) the connection

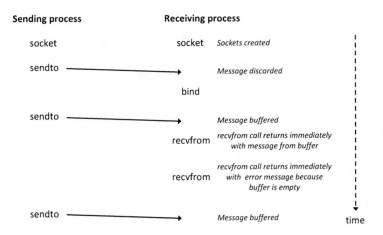

FIGURE 3.36

Behavior of socket primitives, in a UDP context, when the socket is set to nonblocking mode.

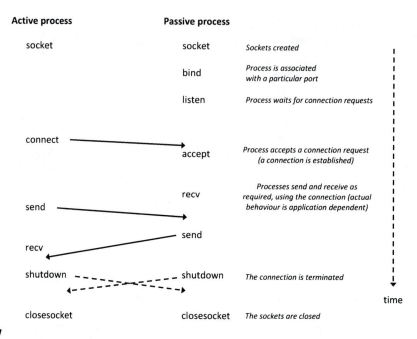

FIGURE 3.37

Behavior of socket primitives, in TCP context.

when communication is complete. Thus, it is not possible to clearly represent all of the possible timing sequences and resulting behaviors in a single diagram.

The TCP primitives that are of most interest in terms of the socket IO mode are recv and accept. recv is analogous to and exhibits the same respective behavior as UDP's recvfrom in each of the two socket modes. This is for the same underlying reason that it is not possible to know at the receiving side exactly when a message will be sent to it and thus when it will arrive (so there is always a likelihood that it will have to wait for it). Similarly, it is not known in advance when the accept primitive is issued whether a connection request is pending or when in the future such a connection request will arrive. Note however that the listen primitive only has to be issued once and its waiting behavior is handled at a lower level, within the TCP software.

3.8.1 HANDLING NONBLOCKING SOCKET BEHAVIOR

When a nonblocking primitive call cannot complete immediately, it returns with an error code. In most cases, this does not represent a real error in the sense that something has gone wrong, merely that the requested action could not be performed yet. Thus, a common requirement is for the application logic to wait a while and then try the action again. Perhaps, the easiest way to achieve this is to use a timer that generates a software interrupt after a programmable time interval. This can be implemented as follows: When a primitive call such as recv returns with the "WOULD_BLOCK" error code, start a

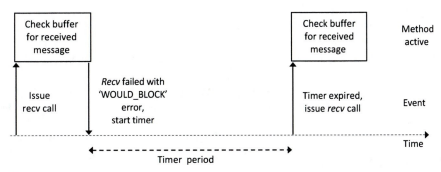

FIGURE 3.38

Using a timer to facilitate autoretry for failed nonblocking primitive calls.

timer (configured for the appropriate time interval), so that the action can be tried again after the given time span. In the meantime (while the timer is counting down), continue with other processing, which is entirely application-dependent. When the timer expires, retry the primitive again. This approach is illustrated in Figure 3.38.

Figure 3.38 shows how a timer can be used to enable a process to repeat its failed actions after a set time period. My preferred extension of this approach is to assume that due to the asynchronous nature of network message receipt, in general, there will not be a message waiting when the process requests it. Therefore, to make the attempt to receive a message periodic by design and to effectively treat the timer and event handler mechanism as a separate thread of control that operates continuously in the background. By shortening the time period, I can make the process more responsive to message arrival (by checking for messages more frequently), but with the trade-off of increased processing overheads. This trade-off can be tuned so that the rate of checking for messages matches the typical rate of actual message arrival in a particular application. This approach is illustrated in Figure 3.39 and has been used in both the client and server components of the case study game; see later.

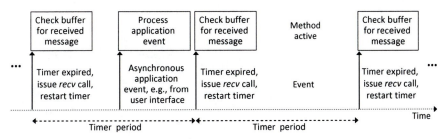

FIGURE 3.39

Periodic handling of nonblocking primitive events using a programmable timer.

3.8.2 **COMMUNICATION DEADLOCK**

A deadlock occurs in a system when a group of two or more processes each wait for resources that are held by other processes in the group, such that none can make progress and hence the resources are never released for the waiting processes to use them. This is explored in detail in Chapter 4.

Distributed deadlock is an extension of the deadlock problem that occurs in distributed systems, where the processes and resources involved in the deadlock are spread across more than one of the computers in the system.

Communication deadlock is a special case of distributed deadlock, in which the resources that the group of blocked processes are waiting for are messages from other processes in the group. See Figure 3.40.

Figure 3.40 illustrates the problem of communication deadlock in which a pair of processes are each blocked while waiting for a message to arrive from the other one. Since each process is blocked, it will not be able to send a message, and thus, the messages that each process is waiting for will never arrive.

Fortunately, the situation can only arise when certain communication configurations are used and thus can be avoided by design. The requirements for communication deadlock to be possible are that the receive sockets are both configured in the blocking IO mode and that the send operations are on the same threads as the receive operations in both processes. In addition, both processes have to be waiting to receive at the same time for the deadlock to actually occur.

The easiest way to prevent communication deadlock by design is to ensure that at least one of the processes uses the nonblocking socket IO mode. Alternatively, use separate threads to handle sending and receiving actions such that the send thread can continue to operate while the receive thread is blocked.

Activity C6 investigates blocking and nonblocking socket behavior.

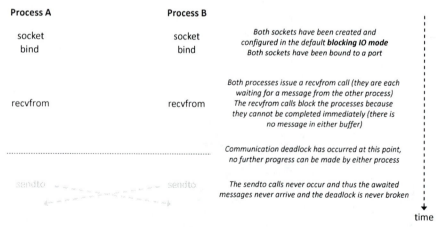

FIGURE 3.40

Communication deadlock.

ACTIVITY C6 PRACTICAL INVESTIGATION OF BLOCKING AND NONBLOCKING SOCKET BEHAVIORS AND COMMUNICATION DEADLOCK, USING THE NETWORKING WORKBENCH

Prerequisite

You should have completed Activity C4 and have gained a clear understanding of the TCP and how to establish a connection, before attempting this activity.

Learning Outcomes

1. To gain a basic understanding of the differences between blocking and nonblocking socket behavior
2. To understand what is meant by communication deadlock and how it can occur

Method

This activity is carried out in two parts:

1. Understand the Implications of Blocking Versus Nonblocking Communication
    1. Start two copies of the Networking Workbench, preferably at different computers (one for TCP:Active Open and one for TCP:Passive Open).
    2. Establish a connection between the Active and Passive ends.
    3. Set BOTH connection sockets to nonblocking mode.
    4. Enable both receivers.
    5. Send and receive several messages in each direction between the two ends.
    6. Set ONE of the connection sockets to blocking mode.
    7. Send and receive several messages in each direction between the two ends. Do you notice any change in behavior from that in step 5 above? How do you account for this behavior?
2. Understand how deadlock can occur within communicating applications when both ends use blocking sockets
    1. Start two copies of the Networking Workbench, preferably at different computers (one for TCP:Active Open and one for TCP:Passive Open).
    2. Establish connection between Active and Passive ends.
    3. Set BOTH connection sockets to blocking mode.
    4. Enable both receivers.
    5. Attempt to send and receive several messages in each direction between the two ends. What happens? How do you account for this behavior?

Expected Outcome

From part 1, you should have discovered the fundamental difference between blocking and nonblocking socket IO modes. When both sockets were set to nonblocking mode, you should see that both processes can send and receive in any order that the user chooses. However, when the socket is set to blocking mode, the process is unresponsive while waiting to receive a message (i.e., the process has been blocked by the operating system because it is waiting for an IO operation to complete).

From part 2, you should have encountered communication deadlock. When both processes have blocking sockets and are waiting to receive a message from the other one, they are each in blocked state; this means that neither one is able to send a message, and thus, they are both doomed to keep waiting indefinitely for a message that can never be sent and thus will never arrive.

Reflection

The IO mode is one of the more complex aspects of sockets. However, from this activity, you should appreciate how the choice of mode can have significant effect on the behavior of processes, and thus, it is an aspect well worth mastering early on. You need to understand the different behaviors arising from each of the two modes and also be able to determine when each mode is appropriate to use.

You can also explore the socket IO modes with the UDP, within the workbench. Use the UDP Workbench as the sending process and experiment with each of the Blocking Receiver and the Non-Blocking Receiver applications (all available on the UDP tab).

3.9 ERROR DETECTION AND ERROR CORRECTION

Communication protocols in general are designed to detect errors that occur in transmission so that they can reject corrupted messages. The actual detection of corruption is usually based on a checksum-based technique in which a low-cost numerical representation of the data is generated at the sending side and included in the header of the communication protocol. On arrival at the receiver, the checksum is again generated from the received data and compared with the value that was included in the message. If there is any difference, the message is considered corrupted and is discarded. Reliable protocols go a step further by signaling that a retransmission is needed. Forward Error Correction (FEC) codes, in contrast, carry additional information to enable reconstruction of the data at the receiver side, without the need for retransmission.

There is a clear trade-off between the two techniques. Error detection incurs additional latency while a message retransmission is requested, and the original message is resent. This is generally suitable for use where errors occur infrequently and the occasional added latency can be tolerated. Error correction incurs additional overhead in every message, so it is costly to use in systems where errors occur rarely but is ideal where errors occur very frequently (such as over very unreliable links) because in such situations, even if there is a retransmission mechanism in place, there is no guarantee that the resent message will not also be corrupted. Error correction avoids the additional latency incurred by retransmission, and this could be very important in high-speed services but is perhaps even more important where there are high propagation delays due to long-distance connections. A very good example of this is space exploration. Messages sent to spacecraft or robot missions to other planets take a very long time to propagate due to the large distances involved, making retransmissions highly undesirable.

Error-correcting codes are also important where the messages have very high value, for example, control signals used in fly-by-wire systems, or when sensing dangerous environments such as the internal state of a nuclear reactor. In such scenarios, it is important to ensure that a message can be understood despite a limited number of bit errors, thus being able to deal with the information promptly, avoiding the delay of having to resend the message.

3.9.1 A BRIEF INTRODUCTION TO ERROR DETECTION AND ERROR CORRECTION CODES

When designing an FEC code, a main consideration is the number of bit errors that the code will be able to correct. In other words, the number of bit transitions (0-to-1 or 1-to-0) that can occur within a given-length stream of bits transmitted and yet the original data value can still be determined.

Consider the 8-bit data value 11001100. A single bit error could give rise to, for example, 10001100, 11011100, or 11001110. Two bit errors could give rise to, for example, 00001100, 11101110, or 01001101.

The number of bits that are different in the data (from the original to the modified versions) is called the Hamming distance (d); the single-bit error examples shown above have a Hamming distance of 1 (i.e., $d = 1$), while the two-bit error examples have a Hamming distance of 2 (i.e., $d = 2$).

If all bit combinations in a particular code are possible correct values, then the value of d for the data code is 1 and there is no redundancy; that is, a single bit change shifts the code from one legal value to another and therefore cannot be detected as an error. Consider a 4-bit code that holds a Customer ID (CID) and that CIDs can range from 0 to 15 (decimal). The following binary values are all acceptable:

0000, 0001, 0010, 0011, ..., 1111. If, during transmission, a single bit error occurs in any of these values, the resulting code (which is wrong) has the value of another acceptable code and is thus undetectable as an error. For example, 0010 can become 0011, which are both valid codes, and thus, the receiver of the value 0011 cannot tell if this is the value that was actually sent or if an error has occurred turning a different value into 0011.

To perform error detection or correction on an original data message, additional information must be added at the point of transmission. The additional information is a form of overhead (also referred to as "redundant bits") since it must be transmitted as part of the new larger message but does not carry any application-level information.

The simplest way to detect a single bit error in the 4-bit code is to use parity checking, in which case one additional bit must be added (the parity bit). In this case, for every four data bits transmitted, a fifth parity bit must be transmitted, so the overhead is 20%; or alternatively, you can consider that the efficiency is 80%; since 80% of the bits transmitted carry application data, the remaining 20% are redundant from the application viewpoint.

Consider "even parity" in which the number of "1" bits must be even in the 5-bit code that is transmitted. CID values 0000, 0011, and 1001 are examples where the number of "1" bits is already even; thus, a parity bit of "0" will be added, turning these values into 00000, 00110, and 10010, respectively. CID values 0001, 0010, and 1101 are examples where the number of "1" bits is odd; thus, a parity bit of "1" will be added, turning these values into 00011, 00101, and 11011, respectively.

If a single bit error occurs now, for example, 00110 becomes 00100 during transmission, the error will be detected by the receiver, because the parity check will fail (there are not an even number of "1s"). Notice that although the error is detected, it cannot be corrected because there are many possible valid codes that could have been translated into the received value 00100 by a single bit translation, including 00101, 10100, and 01100.

To achieve error correction, additional redundant bits must be added such that there is only one valid data code that could be translated into any particular received value, as long as the number of bit errors does not exceed the number supported by the error correction code. The theory aspect of error correcting codes is a complex subject, so the discussion will be limited to a simple example based on the triple modular redundancy technique to provide an introduction.

In a triple modular redundancy code, each bit is repeated three times, that is, transmitted as 3 bits, so each "0" becomes "000" and each "1" becomes "111." There are only two valid code patterns per three-bit sequence that can be transmitted, and it is not possible for a single bit error to convert one valid code into another. A single bit error turns 000 into one of 001, 010, or 100, all of which are closer to 000 than 111, and thus, all are interpreted as a 0 and not a 1 data value. Similarly, a single bit error turns 111 into one of 110, 101, or 011 all of which are closer to 111 than 000, and thus, all are interpreted as a 1 data value. Thus, a single bit error can be automatically corrected, but at the cost of a significantly increased message size. For the triple modular redundancy technique, the overhead is 67%; in other words, the code efficiency is 33%; since 33% of the bits transmitted carry useful data, the remaining 67% are redundant. Fortunately, more efficient error-correcting codes do exist.

If triple modular redundancy were applied to the earlier customer ID example, each 4-bit CID value would be transmitted as a 12-bit message. For example, 0001 would be transmitted as 000000000111, and 0010 would be transmitted as 000000111000.

3.10 APPLICATION-SPECIFIC PROTOCOLS

An application-specific protocol describes the structure, sequence, and semantics of the communication between the components of a distributed application. This is necessary when applications communicate directly at the transport layer or otherwise have communication requirements beyond the functionality provided by the standard protocols in the application layer.

An application-specific protocol is designed for a particular application and represents the sequence of messages and the contents of those messages, necessary to achieve the communication requirements of the application.

The application-specific protocol is not the same as an application-layer protocol. This is a very important distinction. The application-layer protocols are a set of standard protocols to provide clearly defined communication services, such as transfer a file (FTP), retrieve a WWW page (HTTP), facilitate remote login (Rlogin), and many others (some of which were discussed earlier). These all reside in the application layer of the network stack. However, a specific application may require a unique mix of different types of communication. For example, it may require that an initial connection is made using TCP to exchange credentials and check security and access rights and establishing the actual communication requirements for a specific data exchange. An eCommerce application may involve access to some web services, transfer of a specific file, and/or retrieval of data from one or more databases. It may use a time service such as NTP to provide trusted timestamps for transactions (i.e., not trusting the local computer's clock). A multimedia service may use HTTP as its main interface but, depending on user selections, may require access to various databases or may need to transfer files or stream some real-time data; this may require use of FTP, Rlogin, and others. A networked game may use TCP or UDP directly to achieve the main login and in-play game-data transfers but may also require other protocols, for example, to stream some content or to provide players with an in-built text-chat or email facility. Thus, the application itself must be considered to be "above" the application layer and not "within" this layer because it uses the resources of the application layer.

The application-specific protocol will build on the facilities provided by the underlying communication protocol. So, for example, when using TCP, the application-specific protocol can rely on the transport protocol (i.e., TCP) to deliver the messages in the correct sequence, because TCP has in-built acknowledgment-based recovery and sequence number-based message ordering. However, if the same application were redesigned to use UDP instead as the transport layer protocol (e.g., because of UDP's broadcast capability), then the application would have to take care of message recovery and sequencing itself because UDP does not provide these functions. This would require that the application implements its own sequence numbers and also sends and monitors acknowledgments for packet arrival.

3.11 INTEGRATING COMMUNICATION WITH BUSINESS LOGIC

When developing distributed applications, it is necessary to integrate the communication events (send and receive) with the application's business logic. The way in which the application functionality is split across the various components will be a major factor in determining the nature of the communication between the components. Handling communication aspects brings a new dimension to application development and can introduce significant additional complexity, which must be managed without compromising the quality by which the business logic is designed and implemented.

Developers may prefer to build the two aspects of systems separately and then combine once each part has reached a certain level of maturity (e.g., initially invoking business logic functions from local "stub" interfaces rather than making calls from remote components and/or testing communication mechanisms in skeletal code that does not contain the business logic).

A mapping is required for each component, detailing the way in which internal events cause messages to be sent to other components and also detailing the way messages received from other components are handled and the way such messages drive local behavior. For the purposes of a simple illustration, consider a distributed application in which a user-local client component provides a user interface and depending on the user's actions causes contextual processing to occur remotely (at a server component). In this scenario, a user clicking a certain button on the client interface might cause a particular message to be sent to the server. Figure 3.41 shows one way to represent the addition of communication between a pair of components.

Figure 3.41 illustrates a scenario in which an application operates as a pair of processes distributed across two computers. The two application processes operate independently, loosely synchronized by the passing of messages. The figure provides an example of how application logic can be divided across two components, coupled together by message transmission. In this case, a GUI-based client provides the user interface to the application whose business logic is mostly located at the server side. User requests arising from interface interaction are passed in network messages to the server process, which provides the business logic to deal with the requests. Each message contains a "type" field that signals to the server the meaning of the message, and thus, the server is able to divide the messages based on

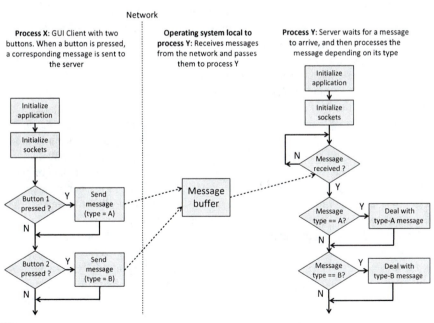

FIGURE 3.41

Representation of application-level logic showing the client and server components, loosely synchronized by the passing of messages across the network.

this application-specific type value, for contextualized processing. The figure emphasizes the lack of direct coupling between the processes. Messages sent by one process are initially buffered by the host operating system of the other process, this being a requirement due to the multiprocessing scheduling in use and the fact that the server process may not be running at the instant the message arrives. The server process pulls messages from the receive buffer using one of the receive primitives: recv (if using TCP) or recvfrom (if using UDP). Despite the loose synchrony between the processes, it is important to realize that they remain independent entities.

3.12 **TECHNIQUES TO FACILITATE COMPONENTS LOCATING EACH OTHER**

One of the main challenges in the operation of distributed applications is to enable components to locate each other.[1] Ideally, this should be automatic and transparent to users. Applications and their subcomponents generally need to operate in the same manner regardless of their relative locations, and it is not realistic to design-in location details such as the IP address as these will change whenever a component is relocated or if the network itself is restructured. This implies that the mechanism of locating communication partners needs to be dynamic, to reflect the state of the system at the moment when the connection needs to be established. Typically, the active component (the client in a client server application) will contact the passive component (the server). In order to set up a TCP connection or to send a UDP datagram, the sender must first know the IP address of the server. Several techniques by which that can be achieved, each having specific strengths and weaknesses, are described:

- Service advertising: A broadcast message with the meaning "I am here" is sent periodically by the server. The message contains the IP address and port number and possibly other information such as a description of services offered. This technique is highly effective in local environments but does not work beyond the first router that blocks the broadcast. It is efficient in the sense that the one message may be heard by many recipients, but inefficient in the sense that the transmission continues indefinitely even when there are no curious clients present.
- Use of local broadcast to find a server: A client, upon startup, broadcasts a message with the meaning "where are you." The server responds with a unicast message containing its IP address and port number, and on receipt of this, the client has the necessary information to bind to the server. As with service advertising, the "where are you" technique is highly effective in local environments, but limited by the local range of the broadcast. However, this technique can be more efficient than service advertising because the request is only sent when needed and can be more responsive because the client does not have to wait for a periodic broadcast from the server; with the "where are you" approach, the server should respond promptly.
- Hard coding: Embedding an IP address is only suitable for prototyping and testing communication aspects of systems. It is the most secure but least scalable approach, as the client application requires recompilation if the server address changes. Hard coding should be avoided in general.
- Asking the user: Requiring that the user provide the address details of the server, via the user interface of the client has very limited applications as it assumes that the user knows what an

---

[1]This is sometimes referred to as binding. In this particular context, it refers to one component locating and associating with another. Take care not to confuse this use of the term "binding" with the process to port binding facilitated by the sockets API bind primitive (discussed earlier in this chapter).

IP address is and how to find it for the computer hosting the server. It is useful in development environments when developer needs to focus on the business logic of the application and/or, for example, when there are multiple prototype servers to choose from, as part of a testing regime.

- Lookup file: Upon startup, the client reads a locally held file to find the address or domain name details of the server. Storing configuration details in a client-local file offers security and should be considered for use with very sensitive applications in which accidental connection to a spoof service represents a significant threat. This approach can also be used as a simple form of access control, as the configuration file is only given to users with the appropriate rights to use the service, such as having security clearance or having paid a license fee. This approach is far superior to hard coding, because only the configuration file needs to be updated when the server address changes; the client application does not need recompilation. However, the lookup file approach is not very scalable due to the need to update and propagate the configuration files.
- Name service: A name service maintains a database of services and their locations. When component A needs to find the address of component B, it sends a request to the name service, supplying the name of component B as a parameter. The name service replies with the address details of component B. This is a superior and location-transparent approach because the location-finding aspect is handled externally to the user applications and is kept updated by techniques such as service registration. For example, upon startup, a server sends a message to the name service informing it of its location and the services it offers; these details are then added to the name service's database. The most common and important example of a name service is the Domain Name System (DNS), which is discussed in Chapter 6.
- Middleware: Middleware is a collection of services, which sit between software components and the platforms they run on, to provide various forms of transparency to applications. Middleware usually provides location transparency by means of an in-built name service or subscription to an external service such as DNS. Middleware is discussed in detail in Chapter 6.

The use of well-known ports (as discussed earlier) contributes to transparency, as for many popular services the client will know the (fixed) port number of the service, and in such cases, the port number can often be hard-coded since these values are standardized.

3.13 TRANSPARENCY REQUIREMENTS FROM THE COMMUNICATION VIEWPOINT

Several forms of transparency are particularly relevant from the communication viewpoint, as discussed below.

Access transparency. Network-to-device boundaries should not be visible to applications and the communications mechanisms they use. Requests to services should have the same format and should not require any different actions at the application level, regardless of whether the communication partner is local or remote.

Location transparency. Network resources, especially communication partners, should be automatically locatable. A location-transparent system enables connecting to and sending a message to a process without prior knowledge of its physical location.

Network transparency. This involves hiding the physical network characteristics, such as the actual technology and its configuration, and faults that occur at the physical network level, such as bit errors and frame corruption. Ideally, the presence of the network itself is hidden, such that the separation of components and the heterogeneity of the underlying platforms are hidden.

Distribution transparency. This concerns hiding the separation between components, such that the entire application appears to be running on a single computer. All communication should appear to be local, that is, between pairs of processes that are local to each other.

Failure transparency. Some applications require reliable transmission of data and thus need a protocol that ensures that data are received at the intended destination or otherwise are automatically retransmitted, without involvement by the application itself.

Scaling transparency. Communication mechanisms and protocols need to be efficient in terms of network resource usage to maximize the scalability of communications aspects of systems. This in turn impacts on the number of communicating components that can be supported with appropriate quality of service before the system performance degrades noticeably.

3.13.1 LOGICAL AND PHYSICAL VIEWS OF SYSTEMS

A physical view of a system is based on actual physical details such as the location and configuration of devices and is related to concepts at the lower layers of the network model. In contrast, a logical view is based on concepts in the higher layers.

The goals of transparency in distributed systems require that physical details are hidden from the user. It is perhaps more accurate to say that users of the system (including the developers of applications) need to be shielded from the underlying complexity of systems, thus the need to provide an abstract or logical view. From a communication viewpoint, it is very important to be able to separate out logical and physical views of the system and to use each where appropriate.

For distributed systems, perhaps, the most important topic in the context of logical and physical views is connections. There is a need to achieve connectivity at the software component level without having to know the actual physical locations, details of underlying platforms, network technologies, and topologies. A developer needs to ensure that a particular group of components can interact, through the use of higher-level mechanisms provided in systems, without having to take into consideration all of the possible network technologies and configurations that could occur. This is quite significant because some of the network technologies that the application will eventually operate over may not even have been invented at the time the application is developed.

Therefore, when developing distributed systems, it is necessary to use a combination of logical and physical representations of systems and to be able to translate between them as necessary. Most or all of the application-level design, especially communication- and component-level connectivity, is necessarily done on a logical basis to abstract away the physical aspects, which are specific to a particular computer, network technology, or system.

3.14 THE CASE STUDY FROM THE COMMUNICATION PERSPECTIVE

A main consideration is the choice of transport layer communication protocol for the game application. The relative advantages and disadvantages of TCP and UDP need to be considered in the context of the specific communication requirements of the game. The choice of transport layer protocol in turn impacts other aspects of design and implementation.

In the case of the game, all messages are valuable. Any loss would result in incorrect game status or play sequence, thus indicating that a reliable protocol such as TCP should be used, or otherwise, if UDP is chosen, additional mechanisms must be implemented at the application level to take care of message sequence and acknowledgment and recovery if a message is lost. TCP is the better choice in this scenario and has been used in the implementation.

Socket IO modes. It was decided that both components should use nonblocking sockets. For the client (user-interface) component, this solves the issue of responsiveness without the need to make it multithreaded. For the server, this approach makes it responsive to many connected clients simultaneously, again without the need for multithreading. For this particular application, multithreading was considered to be unnecessary, and the avoidance of multithreading makes it a simpler and more suitable example to illustrate the communication aspects. The fact that at least one side of the communication is nonblocking means that the game is not susceptible to communication deadlock.

Having chosen the transport layer protocol, it is necessary to define the application-specific protocol for the game. This is a particular set of allowable message sequences, unique to the game, which facilitates the operation of the game.

The specific game application requires the following activity sequence:

- The server is started and runs continuously as a service.
- A user starts an instance of the client when they wish to join in.
- The client connects to the server.
- The user chooses an alias name, which is sent to the server and propagated to other clients as part of a list of all available players.
- The user selects an opponent from the advertised list of available players.
- The game is played, each user taking turns. The server mediates by determining whose turn it is and keeps track of the game state to determine if the game has ended and, if so, what the outcome is. The server propagates a user's gameplay moves to the user's opponent, so their interface can be updated.
- Users are notified of the game result by the server.
- The client's connection to the server is closed.

Each of these activities involves sending messages between the game components to update state and synchronize behavior. The actual message sequence that arises from the activity sequence is illustrated in Figure 3.42.

Figure 3.42 shows a typical message sequence that occurs in a scenario in which three clients connect to the server, and then, a game is created between two of the clients. The server can support up to ten connected clients. It does this by having an array of structures each of which represents a single connected client (or is unused). The structure contains the client socket and its related socket address structure and the user's chosen alias name and a flag to signify whether each instance of the structure is in use or otherwise available for use when the next client connect request is received. The in-use flag also enables functionality such as iterating through the array of the structures and sending player list messages to all connected clients.

Figure 3.43 shows some of the game state information maintained by the server. The connection structure (which is discussed above) is shown and is central to the operation of the server. The server has an array of these connection structures so that it can support up to 10 client connections simultaneously. A logical game object is used to keep track of game instances that exist between pairs of clients. This is represented in the code by the game structure; an array of 5 of these is maintained because each

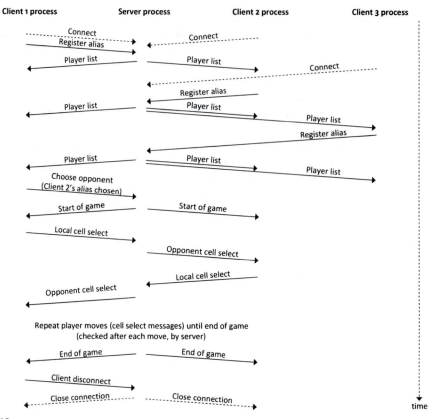

FIGURE 3.42

The game application-specific protocol, showing interaction between three clients and the server.

```
#define  MAX_GAMES  5
#define  MAX_CONNECTIONS  MAX_GAMES * 2

struct Connection {
      SOCKET m_iConnectSock;
      SOCKADDR_IN m_ConnectSockAddr;
      CString csAlias;
      bool bInUse;
};

struct Game {
      int iConnection[2];
      bool bInUse;
      int iGrid[3][3];
};

Connection m_ConnectionArray[MAX_CONNECTIONS];
Game m_GameArray[MAX_GAMES];
```

FIGURE 3.43

The connection and game structures.

game is shared between 2 clients. The game structure holds the connection array index positions of the two involved clients and the gameplay state in terms of the actual tic-tac-toe grid.

The message sequence shown in Figure 3.42 describes the communication behavior of the application but is not a full description of the application logic. The application comprises two programs: a server and a client. And an in-progress game comprises three processes: a server process and two client processes (it is important to realize that the two client processes are instances of the same client program and thus have the same logic, although their run time state will be different as they represent two different players in the game). Flowcharts for each program are provided in Figures 3.46 (client) and 3.47 (server).

The choice of TCP as the transport layer protocol has another advantage, in addition to the earlier discussion, in that only the server needs to bind to a specific port; that is, one that is known in advance by the clients so they can issue connect requests. The fact that the clients don't need to use any particular port means that they can be coresident with the server and with each other on the same computer. This is ideal for this particular application because its fundamental purpose is the demonstration of process-to-process communication and the fact that applications should operate in the same way regardless of the physical location of components. The game can be configured with all three components on a single computer, with two components on one computer and the other component on a separate computer, or with all three components on separate computers. Obviously, for a real distributed game, the normal configuration would be that each user sits in front of their own computer (hence each one running the client process locally), and the server can be hosted on any computer in the network.

As TCP is used, all messages are sent in unicast mode. PLAYER_LIST messages are sent to each connected client in rapid succession, creating the effect of a broadcast.

Figure 3.44 shows the receive logic for the game client and shows how careful selection of message content and structure facilitates well-structured receive-handler code. The outer-level switch statement deals with the message type, while where relevant inner switch statements deal with actual message data contextually.

The first step after the call to the recv primitive is to check for errors that may have occurred. Since a nonblocking socket has been used, the WSAEWOULDBLOCK error is not a true error in the sense that it signals that there was no message in the buffer and thus the call would have otherwise blocked (instead, it returns this error code). This is thus a normal occurrence, and the response in the code is to restart the interval timer and exit this instance of the handler (after 100 ms, the timer will expire, and the receive handler will be entered again). If however another error has occurred, the StopTimerIfConnectionLost() method is called to check if the error code is one of several that indicate that the TCP connection has been lost (e.g., because the server has been shut down), and if so, the client is shut down gracefully. A further check on the received message length is performed; receipt of a zero-byte message (as opposed to no message) is also taken to imply that the connection has been lost in the context of the communication logic of this game.

Next, the message type field is checked, and the message processing is performed contextually based on the specific message type code; this is performed with a switch statement, which ensures good code structure. For each message type that can be received by a client, the specific actions followed are discussed:

• PLAYER_LIST: Display the list of available players, sent by the server, in the player list box on the user interface.

```
void CNoughtsCrossesCLIENT::DoReceive()                              case END_OF_GAME:
{                                                                        switch(Message.iCode)
    StopTimer();                                                         {
                                                                             case END_OF_GAME_DRAW:
    int iBytesRecd;                                                              MessageBox("The game was a draw","Game Over");
    Message_PDU Message;                                                         break;
                                                                             case END_OF_GAME_WIN:
    iBytesRecd = recv(m_iConnectSocket, (char *) &Message, sizeof(Message_PDU), 0);    MessageBox("Well done! You won","Game Over");
    if(SOCKET_ERROR == iBytesRecd)                                                  break;
    {                                                                            case END_OF_GAME_LOOSE:
        int iError = WSAGetLastError();                                             MessageBox("Unlucky - You lost","Game Over");
        if(WSAEWOULDBLOCK == iError)        // Non-blocking socket used                break;
        {                                                                        }
            InitiateTimer();                // 100ms interval              OnBnClickedTcpAoDone();    // Exit
        }                                                                  break;
        else                                                          case OPPONENT_CELL_SELECTION:
        {                                                                  switch (Message.iCell)
            StopTimerIfConnectionLost(iError);                             {
        }                                                                      case 0:
        return;                                                                    m_Cell0.SetWindowText(m_csOpponentToken.GetString());
    }                                                                              m_Cell0.EnableWindow(false);
    else                                    // A message was received               break;
    {                                                                          case 1:
        if(iBytesRecd == 0)                                                         m_Cell1.SetWindowText(m_csOpponentToken.GetString());
        {                                                                          m_Cell1.EnableWindow(false);
            ConnectionLost();                                                       break;
            return;                                                            case 2:
        }                                                                          m_Cell2.SetWindowText(m_csOpponentToken.GetString());
                                                                                   m_Cell2.EnableWindow(false);
        switch(Message.iMessageType)                                               break;
        {                                                                      case 3:
            case PLAYER_LIST:                                                      m_Cell3.SetWindowText(m_csOpponentToken.GetString());
                DisplayPlayerList(Message);                                         m_Cell3.EnableWindow(false);
                break;                                                             break;
            case START_OF_GAME:                                                case 4:
                m_SelectPlayer.EnableWindow(false);   // Disable Select Opponent control    m_Cell4.SetWindowText(m_csOpponentToken.GetString());
                m_OpponentAlias.SetWindowText(Message.cAlias); // Set and display opponent alias    m_Cell4.EnableWindow(false);
                if(Message.iToken == 0)                // Set and display our token              break;
                {                                                                  case 5:
                    m_csToken = "0";                                                   m_Cell5.SetWindowText(m_csOpponentToken.GetString());
                    m_csOpponentToken = "X";                                           m_Cell5.EnableWindow(false);
                }                                                                      break;
                else                                                               case 6:
                {                                                                      m_Cell6.SetWindowText(m_csOpponentToken.GetString());
                    m_csToken = "X";                                                   m_Cell6.EnableWindow(false);
                    m_csOpponentToken = "0";                                           break;
                }                                                                  case 7:
                m_Token.SetWindowText(m_csToken.GetString());                          m_Cell7.SetWindowText(m_csOpponentToken.GetString());
                                                                                       m_Cell7.EnableWindow(false);
                if(Message.bFirstMove == true)         // Configure first-move logic        break;
                {                                                                  case 8:
                    m_Status.SetWindowText("Your Move");                               m_Cell8.SetWindowText(m_csOpponentToken.GetString());
                    EnableEmptyCells();                                                m_Cell8.EnableWindow(false);
                }                                                                      break;
                else                                                               }
                {                                                                  m_Status.SetWindowText("Your Move");
                    m_Status.SetWindowText("Opponent's Move");                      EnableEmptyCells();
                    DisableEmptyCells();                                            break;
                }                                                          }
                m_GameStatus.SetWindowText("Game In Progress");  // Display game status    }
                break;                                                   InitiateTimer();
```

FIGURE 3.44

The receive logic of the client (C++), showing nested switch statements to provide contextual handling of the message based on message type and content.

- START_OF_GAME: If the server has signaled that a game has started, a number of things must be done at the client, driven by the message content: the opponent's alias is displayed on the user interface; the game tokens for the user and the opponent are set, for display as the game progresses; the user is told either that it is their move or that it is the opponent's move (this game sequencing is controlled by the server); and the game status displayed value is set to "Game In Progress."
- END_OF_GAME: A second-level switch statement is used to provide a contextual end-of-game on-screen notification depending on the message's end-of-game code, which can indicate that the user has won or lost or that the game was a draw.
- OPPONENT_CELL_SELECTION: This signals that the opponent has made a move. This also uses a second-level switch statement to update the user's display by drawing the opponent's token in the cell of the game grid identified by the iCell field of the message. This signaling by the server that the opponent has made a move is also used as a trigger to enable the user interface to accept a move, through a call to the method EnableEmptyCells(), and the user is told it is their move.

Figure 3.45 shows the server-side receive logic for the game. The DoReceive method is called periodically from within a timer handler routine, once per connected client, at a rate of ten times per second to ensure that the server is highly responsive to received messages. As with the client logic, the first step after the call to the recv primitive is to check for errors that may have occurred. The server also

```cpp
void CNoughtsCrossesSERVER::DoReceive(int iConnection)
{
    Message_PDU Message;
    int iBytesRecd = recv(m_ConnectionArray[iConnection].m_iConnectSock, (char *) &Message, sizeof(Message_PDU), 0);
    if(SOCKET_ERROR == iBytesRecd)
    {
        int iError = WSAGetLastError();
        // Non-blocking sockets used
        // If no packet is queued for the socket the operation would block.
        if(iError != WSAEWOULDBLOCK)
        {
            MessageBox("Receive failed","CNoughtsCrossesSERVER");
            ConnectionLost(iConnection, iError);
            return;
        }
    }
    else
    {
        if(iBytesRecd == 0)
        {
            return;
        }

        CString csStr;
        switch(Message.iMessageType)
        {
            case REGISTER_ALIAS:
                csStr.Format("Alias '%s' Registered", Message.cAlias);
                WriteStatusLine(csStr);
                m_ConnectionArray[iConnection].csAlias.Format("%s", Message.cAlias);
                SendPlayerList();
                break;
            case CHOOSE_OPPONENT:
                if(CreateGame(iConnection, Message) == false)
                {
                    csStr.Format("ChoseOpponent '%s' FAILED", Message.cAlias);
                }
                WriteStatusLine(csStr);
                break;
            case LOCAL_CELL_SELECTION:
                SendOpponentCellSelectionMessage(iConnection, Message.iCell);
                SetCellInGame(iConnection, Message.iCell);
                if(!CheckForWin(iConnection))
                {
                    EndOfGame(iConnection);              // Check for end of game (all cells full)
                }
                break;
            case CLIENT_DISCONNECT:
                csStr.Format("Client %s Disconnected", m_ConnectionArray[iConnection].csAlias.GetString());
                WriteStatusLine(csStr);
                CloseGameAndConnection(iConnection);
                break;
        }
    }
}
```

FIGURE 3.45

Server-side receive logic (C++), showing use of switch statement to provide contextual handling of the message based on message type.

uses nonblocking sockets; but here, an array of sockets is used, one for each connected client. If the WSAEWOULDBLOCK error has occurred, the remainder of the method is skipped. If another error has occurred, the ConnectionLost() method is called to check if the error code is one of several that indicate that the TCP connection has been lost (e.g., because the specific client has been shut down), and if so, the server closes its socket related to the particular client and also closes the connection to the opponent of the disconnected client. If the recv has been successful, a check on the received message length is performed; any zero-byte messages are ignored.

Next, the message type field is checked, and the message processing is performed contextually based on the specific message type code, following the same approach as in the client. This is performed with a switch statement. The specific actions followed for each message type that can be received by the server are discussed:

- REGISTER_ALIAS: The client identified by its index position in the connection array has sent the alias name the user wishes to use for identification in the game. The server updates its diagnostic display and also writes the alias name into the client's connection array entry. The server then updates all connected clients by sending a PLAYER_LIST message containing a list of all connected users' aliases.
- CHOOSE_OPPONENT: The client identified by its index position in the connection array has made a selection from the available players list. In response, the server creates a game (this is a server-internal logical game entity that represents the game and its state and is the basis on which the server relates the two clients together, synchronizes their moves, and determines the outcome of the game). As a substep of creating the game, the server sends a START_OF_GAME message both to the client that has chosen an opponent and to the opponent. These messages inform each client of the token that it is to use ("o" or "x") and whether it has the next move or must wait for the other player to move. The server updates its diagnostic display accordingly.
- LOCAL_CELL_SELECTION: The client identified by its index position in the connection array has made a move (the user has selected a cell in which to place their token). The server sends the client's opponent an OPPONENT_CELL_SELECTION message so that the user interface can be updated and the opponent user is thus informed. The server updates the game status and then checks to see if the new move has led to a win (any straight line of three tokens in any orientation). If so, the winner's client is sent an END_OF_GAME message with the message iCode field containing END_OF_GAME_WIN, and the opponent client is sent an END_OF_GAME message with the message iCode field containing END_OF_GAME_LOSE. If the game has not been won, a draw is checked for; this situation arises when all cells have been filled and there has been no winner. If a draw has occurred, both clients are sent an END_OF_GAME message with the message iCode field containing END_OF_GAME_DRAW.
- CLIENT_DISCONNECT: This message type supports graceful disconnect of a client and causes the corresponding game to be closed in the server. Upon receipt of this message type, the server updates its diagnostic display, closes the socket it uses to communicate with the specific client, and clears the relevant connection array entry. It also closes the opponent client's connection. The list of available players is updated, and a PLAYER_LIST message containing a list of remaining players is sent to all connected clients.

Figure 3.46 shows the behavior of the client process. The client is event-driven, and each event is modeled as a separate activity, which starts and stops independently of other events. In addition to the timer-based activity (which deals with message receiving on the nonblocking socket), there are a number of user activity events, which start when a specific user-interface event occurs, such as when the user selects an opponent to play against or makes a move in the gameplay.

Figure 3.47 shows the behavior of the server process. The server is event-driven; each event is modeled as a separate activity, which is initiated when the relevant event is detected. Nonblocking sockets are used in combination with a timer to implement periodic listening and receiving activities. The server maintains one socket for listening for connection requests and one socket per connected client, on which messages are received. The per client sockets are held in an array and can thus be tested for message receipt in a loop, each time the timer handler is invoked. The timer operates at 10 Hz to ensure that the server is responsive to connection requests and incoming messages from game clients.

3.15 END-OF-CHAPTER EXERCISES
3.15.1 QUESTIONS

1. Determine which transport layer protocol is most appropriate for the following applications, justify your answers.
   (A) Real-time streaming
   (B) File transfer that is only used in a local area network
   (C) File transfer that is used across the Internet
   (D) A clock synchronizing service for all computers in a local network
   (E) An eCommerce application
   (F) A local file-sharing application in which clients need to automatically locate the server and cannot rely on a name service being present
2. Determine which sequences of socket primitives are valid to achieve communication, and also, state whether the communication implied is based on UDP or TCP.
   (A) create socket (client side), sendto (client side), create socket (server side), recvfrom (server side), close (server side), close (client side)
   (B) create socket (client side), create socket (server side), bind (server side), listen (client side), connect (client side), accept (server side), send (client side), recv(server side), shutdown (server side), shutdown (client side), close (server side), close (client side)
   (C) create socket (client side), create socket (server side), bind (server side), sendto (client side), recvfrom (server side), close (server side), close (client side)
   (D) create socket (client side), create socket (server side), bind (server side), listen (server side), connect (client side), accept (server side), send (server side), recv(client side), shutdown (server side), shutdown (client side), close (server side), close (client side)
   (E) create socket (client side), create socket (server side), bind (server side), listen (server side), connect (server side), accept (client side), send (server side), recv(client side), shutdown (server side), shutdown (client side), close (server side), close (client side)
   (F) create socket (client side), create socket (server side), sendto (client side), bind (server side), recvfrom (server side), close (server side), close (client side)

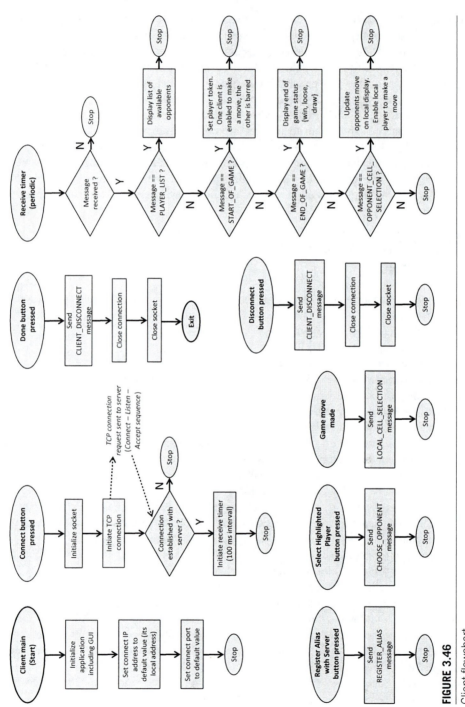

FIGURE 3.46

Client flowchart.

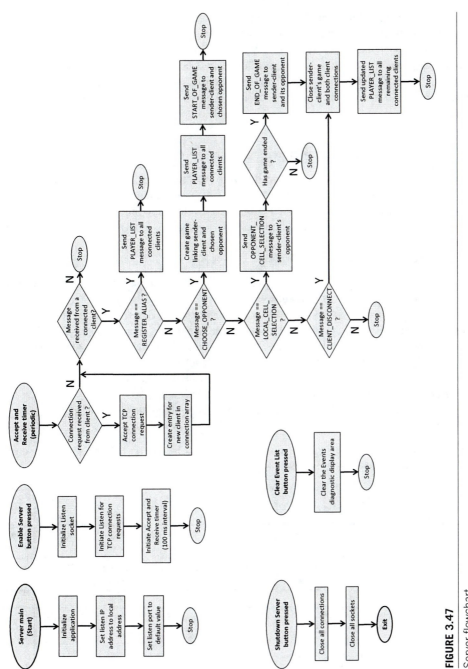

FIGURE 3.47

Server flowchart.

3. Explain the fundamental difference between RPC and RMI.
4. Explain the main differences between constructed forms of communication such as RPC or RMI and lower-level communication based on the socket API over TCP or UDP.
5. Identify a way in which communication deadlock can occur when using the socket API primitives to achieve process-to-process communication, and explain a simple way to avoid it.
6. Identify one benefit and one drawback for each of the two socket IO modes (blocking and nonblocking).

3.15.2 EXERCISES WITH THE WORKBENCHES

The exercises below use the Networking Workbench to investigate various aspects of the behavior of the UDP and TCP, ports and binding, buffering, addressing, multicasting, and broadcasting.

Most of the exercises are best performed using two networked computers, although they can be partially completed (in some cases, fully completed) by running two or more copies of the Networking Workbench on a single computer.

Exercise 1. Understanding the Use of Ports

1. Start one copy of the UDP Workbench (found under the UDP tab on the Networking Workbench) on computer A and one copy on computer B.
2. Set the correct (destination) IP addresses for each workbench so that the address shown in the "Address 1" field is the address of the other computer. Select the "unicast" mode for this exercise.
3. The **send port** corresponds to the port that the packet will be sent to; that is, it is the value that is written into the **destination port** number in the UDP packet header.
4. The **receive port** number is the port number that the receiving UDP software module listens on.
5. You must click the "Enable Receiver" button to enable receiving.
6. To change a receive port number, you must click the "Stop Receiving" button, then change the port number, and then re-enable receiving.

Try each of the port number configurations shown below. In each case, try holding a two-way conversation between the two workbench instances.

A	Computer A	Computer B
Send port	8000	8001
Receive port	8002	8003

B	Computer A	Computer B
Send port	8001	8001
Receive port	8002	8002

C	Computer A	Computer B
Send port	8001	8002
Receive port	8001	8002

D	Computer A	Computer B
Send port	8001	8001
Receive port	8001	8001

E	Computer A	Computer B
Send port	8001	8002
Receive port	8002	8001

F	Computer A	Computer B
Send port	8000	8002
Receive port	8001	8003

Q1. Which of these send and receive port configurations work (i.e., allow 2-way communication)?

Q2. What then is the underlying requirement for port-based communication?

Q3. Which of the above configurations work if both copies of the UDP Workbench are running on the same computer?

Q4. What is the reason for the difference in outcome?

Exercise 2. Achieving a Multicasting Effect with UDP

There are several ways to achieve multicast addressing over UDP in the higher software layers (as it is not directly provided by UDP; UDP directly supports only unicast and broadcast modes of addressing).

Q1. Suggest one method by which multicast could be achieved.

1. Start the UDP Workbench. Select multicast communication.
2. Set the three addresses ("Address 1," "Address 2," and "Address 3") to point at three different, existing computers.
3. Set up additional copies of the UDP Workbench, one on each target computer, and enable the receivers.
4. Make sure the port configurations are correct (refer to exercise 1 above if you have any doubt).

Q2. What happens when you send a message, in terms of the number of messages actually sent by the sending process and the numbers of messages received by each of the receiving process?

5. Now, set the three addresses to all point at the *same* computer.

Q3. Now, what happens when you send a message (hint: look at the statistics windows)?

Q4. Can you now determine which method has been used (in the UDP Workbench) to achieve the multicast effect?

Exercise 3. Broadcasting with UDP

Devise a simple experiment using several copies of the UDP Workbench to determine how broadcasting is achieved in UDP.

Q1. How does the sender know the addresses of the receiver(s)? Does it need to?

Q2. When a message is broadcast to a network of 5 computers, how many messages are sent? How many messages are received (hint: look at the statistics windows)? Explain how this can be.

Exercises 4, 5, and 6 use the **"Arrows"** application within the Networking Workbench (on the UDP tab). The Arrows application consists of the **Arrows Server** (which is simply a display server) and the **Arrows Controller** (which tells one or more Arrows Servers what to display).

The Arrows application requires that each Arrows Server be given a different port number (whether on the same computer or not). The port numbers used by the Arrows Servers must be sequential (e.g., you might use 8000, 8001, 8002, etc). The Arrows Controller must be told the lowest port number used (i.e., 8000 in this example and the number of Arrows Servers in use).

Each Arrows Server must bind to its port (click "listen" to achieve this) before it can start to receive UDP messages from the Arrows Controller.

The rest of the controls on the Arrows Controller are intuitive and should become familiar after a few minutes' experimentation.

Figure 3.48 shows the configuration of an Arrows Controller and three Arrows Servers on the same computer, before clicking on the "listen" buttons. Note that the port numbers allocated to the servers are in sequence.

Figure 3.49 shows the Arrows application in operation; the arrow "moves across" the server windows in sequence.

FIGURE 3.48

Initial state of the Arrows application components.

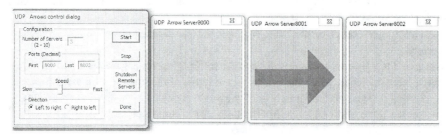

FIGURE 3.49

The Arrows application in operation.

Exercise 4. Bind Constraints

Q1. Can 2 or more Arrows Servers reside at the same computer?

Q2. If so, are there any specific conditions (with respect to Binding) that must be met?

Try to predict the answer and then try binding two Arrows Servers (by clicking "listen") at the same computer with various port combinations.

Exercise 5. Addressing (Identifying Servers)

Q1. How does the Arrows Controller identify its Arrows Servers?

* IP address only
* Port only
* IP address and port

Q2. Is this approach appropriate for applications in general?

Q3. Is this approach appropriate for the Arrows application?

Q4. Can you think of any alternative addressing scheme that would be suitable (remember that there can be more than one Arrows Server per computer)?

Exercise 6. Buffering

Configure two copies of the Arrows Controller to control at least two Arrows Servers (both controllers are to attempt to control the SAME pair of Arrows Servers, so the settings at the two controllers will be identical).

1. Assign the port values to the Arrows Servers, and click "listen" on each one.
2. Configure and start both Arrows Controllers.

3. Move the speed slider control to maximum on both controllers and leave the system running for about a minute.

4. Now, click stop on each Arrows Controller and close the Arrows Controller windows. The Arrows Servers keep running—apparently still receiving messages.

Q1. Explain what is actually happening.

3.15.3 PROGRAMMING EXERCISES

Programming Exercise #C1: The case study game currently requires that the user enters the IP address of the server into the client user interface so that the client can establish communication with the server.

Modify the game so that when both the client and server are in the same local network, the client can automatically locate the server, based on server advertisement broadcasts. To do this, you will need to implement UDP broadcast. The server should broadcast a message containing its IP address and the port it is listening on, at regular time intervals such as every second. The client, during initialization, should listen for the server's broadcast message, and once it has received it, the client should use the address contained in the message to automatically send a connection request to the server. This means that the client may appear unresponsive for a short while until the server's message is received, which is the reason why the interval between the server's advertisement messages should not be too long.

An example solution is provided in the programs: CaseStudyGame_Client_withServerAdvertising and CaseStudyGame_Server_withServerAdvertising.

Programming Exercise #C2: The case study game server currently detects client disconnection, which can occur by explicit disconnection of the client (using the "Disconnect" button), by closing the client process (using the "Done" button), or by the client's host computer crashing or by network connectivity problems between the client and server. The current response of the server, on detecting a client disconnect, is to close its socket related to the particular client and also to close the connection to the opponent of the disconnected client, which causes the opponent client to close abruptly.

Modify the game server code such that when a client disconnect is detected, it sends a new message type such as "opponent connection lost" to the disconnected client's opponent. Alternatively, you could send an existing "END_OF_GAME" message type, but with a new message code which means "opponent connection lost." You will also need to modify the client code such that on receipt of this new message, the opponent client returns to its initial connected state, so that the user can select another player from the available players list and does not automatically shut down, as it does now.

An example solution is provided in the programs:
CaseStudyGame_Client_withServerAdvertising_AND_ClientDisconnectManagement   and CaseStudyGame_Server_withServerAdvertising_AND_ClientDisconnectManagement.

3.15.4 ANSWERS TO END-OF-CHAPTER QUESTIONS

Q1. Answer
  (A) UDP is preferable due to its lower latency.
  (B) Either TCP or UDP is possible. FTP uses TCP as its transport layer protocol, but TFTP uses UDP and works well on local networks and especially where short files are transferred.
  (C) TCP is needed because of its error-handling and message-ordering capabilities.

(D) UDP is needed because of its broadcast capability.

(E) TCP is needed because of its robustness and message ordering.

(F) Use UDP broadcast to locate the server (server advertisement), and then, use TCP for file sharing/file transfers.

Q2. Answer

(A) The set of primitives is consistent with the UDP. However, the client sends a datagram to the server before the server has created a socket, and thus, the datagram will not be delivered. Also, the server side does not bind to a port.

(B) The set of primitives is consistent with the TCP. However, the client listens where in fact, the server should listen, so a connection will not be established.

(C) The set of primitives is consistent with the UDP. The sequence of primitive calls is correct; a single datagram will be sent from the client to the server.

(D) The set of primitives is consistent with the TCP. The sequence of primitive calls is correct; a single datagram will be sent from the server to the client.

(E) The set of primitives is consistent with the TCP. However, the connect primitive occurs at the server side and the accept primitive occurs at the client side (these have been reversed), so a connection will not be established.

(F) The set of primitives is consistent with the UDP. However, the client sends a datagram to the server before the server binds to a port, and thus, the datagram will not be delivered.

Q3. Answer

RPC is a means of remotely calling procedures. It is used with procedural languages such as C and also supported by C++.

RMI is a means of remotely invoking methods on remote objects. It is used in Java, and also, a similar mechanism called remoting is supported in C#.

RMI can be considered the object-oriented version of RPC.

Q4. Answer

Constructed forms of communication such as RPC or RMI provide structured communication within a particular framework (i.e., calling remote procedures or invoking remote methods). An abstraction is provided to developers such that remote objects can be accessed in program code as local ones are. Lower-level communication details are handled automatically, such as the setup of the underlying TCP connection and dealing with certain types of error. This approach achieves a high degree of transparency in several of its forms.

On the other hand, lower-level communication based on the socket API over TCP or UDP is less structured and more flexible. Developers can construct their own protocols and higher-layer communication mechanisms (e.g., it is possible to construct an RMI or RPC system in this way). However, the developer must deal with many more aspects of the communication in this case, such as establishing and maintaining connections, controlling the sequence of messages, and dealing with errors that arise. Most significantly, the low-level communication does not provide transparency; the developer is faced with the complexity of the transport layer and the separation of processes.

Q5. Answer

Communication deadlock can occur when two processes communicate with blocking sockets (and are single-threaded). If a situation arises where both processes are waiting for a message from the other process, communication deadlock has occurred.

There are several ways to prevent communication deadlock. The use of nonblocking sockets ensures that a process does not wait indefinitely for a message to arrive. Alternatively, placing send and receive activities in different threads can resolve the problem as long as the operating system schedules at the thread level (and thus blocks at this level) and not at the process level.

Q6. Answer

Blocking socket IO is efficient in terms of the use of system resources. A process will be blocked while waiting for an event such as message receipt or for a client connection request to occur. Blocking IO is the simplest operation mode of sockets from a programmer viewpoint. However, blocking sockets can lead to unresponsive applications and possibly communication deadlock.

Nonblocking socket IO is more flexible than blocking socket IO and can be used to achieve responsive processes that are able to perform other processing while waiting for communication events. However, nonblocking IO mode requires more complex program logic, as there is a requirement for the use of timers, the need to retry failed actions, and handling the pseudo-error code returned when an event could not complete immediately.

3.15.5 ANSWERS/OUTCOMES OF THE WORKBENCH EXERCISES

Exercise 1. Ports

Q1. Combinations D and E work.

Q2. The send port (the port to which the message is sent) at the sender must be the same as the receive port (the port that is listened on) at the receiver.

Q3. Only configuration E works.

Q4. When the two processes are hosted on the same computer, they cannot bind to the same port. So, while they can both send to the same port, they cannot both receive on the same port. The second one to request the same port (using bind) will have its attempt refused.

Exercise 2. Multicasting

Q1. There are two easy ways to achieve a multicast effect with UDP. One is to actually use broadcast, but to arrange that only a subset of the potential recipient processes are actually listening on the appropriate port. The other way is to use unicast addressing and to send the same message to each of a set of specific computers, using a loop at the sending process.

Q2. In the experiment, you should see that the sender actually sends three messages and that each recipient process receives one message.

Q3. When all three addresses are the same, you should see that the sender actually sends three messages and that the addressed recipient process receives three messages.

Q4. The UDP Workbench is using unicast addressing, in a loop to send one copy of the message to each of the three specified addresses.

Exercise 3. Broadcasting

Q1. The sender does not need to know the addresses of receivers when using broadcast. A special broadcast address is used.

Q2. The delivery of a broadcast message is implemented by the communication protocol and underlying network mechanisms. This means that the sender only has to send a single message, which is delivered to each recipient (they each receive one message).

Exercise 4. Experimentation with the Arrows Application: Exploring Bind Constraints

Q1. Yes, many Arrows Servers can reside at the same computer.

Q2. Each Arrows Server must be bound to a different port.

Exercise 5. Experimentation with the Arrows application: Exploring Addressing

Q1. The Arrows Servers are identified by port only. All messages are broadcast by the Arrows Controller, so the servers can be anywhere in the local network (within the broadcast domain of the controller).

Q2. This is a quite specific means of addressing. It is not appropriate for most applications in general fundamentally because it is so reliant on broadcasting, which should be used sparingly.

Q3. This means of addressing is ideal for the Arrows application because it allows the servers to be placed on the same or different computers, and the port number sequence is used as the means to order the servers logically; this is necessary to get the "traveling arrow" effect across a number of Arrows Server instances.

Q4. An alternative is unicasting to each process specifically. This would require a combination of IP address and port number.

Exercise 6. Experimentation with the Arrows application: Exploring buffering

Q1. The Arrows Servers do not recognize any particular instance of the Arrows Controller; they simply receive command messages and perform the appropriate display action. Hence, when multiple Arrows Controllers are present (and because both controllers are using broadcast communication), all Arrows Servers receive the (possibly conflicting) commands from all controllers. Hence, the display behavior may appear erratic as the servers perform the display actions as soon as they get commands from each controller.

3.15.6 LIST OF IN-TEXT ACTIVITIES

Activity Number	Section	Description
C1	3.3.1	One-way communication with a temperature sensor application
C2	3.3.2	Request-reply communication and an NTP application example
C3	3.7.2	Introduction to UDP and datagram buffering
C4	3.7.3	Introduction to TCP and stream buffering
C5	3.7.4	Exploration of binding
C6	3.8.2	Investigation of blocking and nonblocking socket IO modes and communication deadlock

3.15.7 LIST OF ACCOMPANYING RESOURCES

The following resources are referred to directly in the chapter text, the in-text activities, and/or the end-of-chapter exercises.

- Distributed Systems Workbench ("Systems programming" edition)
- Networking Workbench ("Systems programming" edition)

Note that in addition to the actual exercises supported by the workbenches, the Networking Workbench in can be used as a powerful diagnostic tool when developing networking applications. In particular, for UDP, the UDP Workbench, the blocking receive programs, and nonblocking receive programs and, for TCP, the TCP:Active Open and TCP:Passive Open programs are useful for testing connectivity of applications you are developing, for example, if you are developing an application with client and server components and need to test the client in the absence of the server, or vice versa.

- Source code
- Executable code

Program	Availability	Relevant sections of chapter
Use-case game application: client	Source code, Executable	3.14
Use-case game application: server	Source code, Executable	3.14
CaseStudyGame_Client_withServerAdvertising (Solution to end-of-chapter programming task #1 client side)	Source code, Executable	3.15
CaseStudyGame_Server_withServerAdvertising (Solution to end-of-chapter programming task #1 server side)	Source code, Executable	3.15
CaseStudyGame_Client_withServerAdvertising_AND_ ClientDisconnectManagement (Solution to end-of-chapter programming task #2 client side)	Source code, Executable	3.15
CaseStudyGame_Server_withServerAdvertising_AND_ ClientDisconnectManagement (Solution to end-of-chapter programming task #2 server side)	Source code, Executable	3.15

APPENDIX SOCKET API REFERENCE

This section presents the socket API primitives individually with the method prototypes and annotated code examples in C++, C#, and Java. Supporting information concerning socket options and the socket address structure is also provided.

Important note. To avoid repetition, examples of exception/error handling are shown only for some API calls. However, all socket API calls can fail for a variety of reasons relating to the state of the connected-to or intended-to-be-connected-to process and the sequence in which the primitive calls are used, so robust exception/error handling is necessary in all cases.

A1. SOCKET

C++ prototype: SOCKET **socket**(int *AddressFamily*, int *Type*, int *Protocol*)

Types: SOCK_DGRAM (for UDP), SOCK_STREAM (for TCP)
Return parameter: SOCKET is derived from an integer type and identifies the socket

Example:
```
SOCKET ClientSock = socket(AF_INET, SOCK_DGRAM, PF_UNSPEC);
if(INVALID_SOCKET == ClientSock)
{
    // Display error message "Could not create socket"
}
```

C#
Example:

```
Socket ClientSock;
try
{
    ClientSock=new Socket(AddressFamily.InterNetwork, SocketType.Stream, ProtocolType.Tcp);
}
catch (SocketException se)
{
    // If an exception occurs, handle it and display an error message
}
```

Java. A variety of Socket classes are available, including for client-side TCP use, for server-side TCP use, and for use with UDP.

Client-side TCP: uses the Socket class. There are various overloads of the Socket constructor, which automatically perform the connect action; one use example is shown below:

```
InetAddress IAddress; // An object which represents the IP address to connect to
int iPort;
    ... assign application-specific values to IAddress and iPort to identify remote socket to connect to ...
```

```
Socket ClientSock;
    try
    {
        ClientSock=new Socket(IAddress, iPort);
        // Create socket and connect it to the socket identified by the InetAddress object and port number.
    }
    catch (IOException e)
    {
        System.out.println(e);
    }
```

There is also a socket constructor that creates an unconnected socket:

```
Socket ClientSock=Socket(); // Create an unconnected socket, which requires subsequent use of
Connect().
```

Server-side TCP uses the ServerSocket class, which automatically performs the bind and listen actions.

```
int iPort=8000; // Assign server-side port number, for binding
ServerSocket ServerSock=new ServerSocket(iPort); // Create a socket and bind to the local port
specified.
```

```
// A timeout can be set, which allows the socket to be used in a nonblocking fashion.
ServerSock.setSoTimeout(50); // wait 50 milliseconds.
// For example, when attempting to receive data from the socket, the process will wait (block) for a
specified
// time (rather than permanently), before returning control to the process.
```

UDP: uses the DatagramSocket class, which automatically binds the socket to a port.
Example:
ClientSock=new **DatagramSocket**(5027); // Create a UDP socket and bind to the port specified.

A2. SOCKET OPTIONS

Options that can be selected for use with a particular socket include the following:

- SO_DEBUG   Debugging info
- SO_KEEPALIVE   Keep connection alive (reset timer on timeout)
- SO_DONTROUTE   Routing bypass
- SO_BROADCAST   Allow broadcasts
- SO_USELOOPBACK   Bypass H/W if possible
- SO_LINGER   Linger on CLOSE if data are present
- SO_TYPE   (get only) socket type
- SO_SNDBUF   (set only) output buffer size
- SO_RCVBUF   (set only) input buffer size

C++. To get or set socket options, calls to getsockopt() or setsockopt() are made.
Prototype: int **setsockopt**(SOCKET *s*, int *level*, int *optname*, const char* *optval*, int *optlen*);
Prototype: int **getsockopt**(SOCKET *s*, int *level*, int *optname*, char* *optval*, int* *optlen*);
If no error occurs, setsockopt and getsockopt return zero, otherwise they return an error code.
level is the level at which the option applies (usually SOL_SOCKET).
optname is the name of the option to set.
optval is the buffer containing the option value to set or in which to place the option value (set or not set).
optlen is the length of the *optval* buffer.

Example (turn on broadcasting):
```
char cOpt[2];
cOpt[0] = 1; // true
cOpt[1]=0; // null terminate the option array
int iError=setsockopt(ClientSock, SOL_SOCKET, SO_BROADCAST, cOpt, sizeof(cOpt));
if(SOCKET_ERROR == iError)
{
    // Display error message "setsockopt() Failed"
}
```

Example (test if broadcasting mode is set):
```
char cOpt[2];
int iError=getsockopt(ClientSock, SOL_SOCKET, SO_BROADCAST, cOpt, sizeof(cOpt));
if(SOCKET_ERROR == iError)
{
    // Display error message "getsockopt() Failed!"
}
```

C# uses the **GetSocketOption**() and **SetSocketOption**() methods, some examples are given:

// Set option to allow socket to close gracefully without lingering
ClientSock.**SetSocketOption**(SocketOptionLevel.Socket, SocketOptionName.DontLinger, true);

// Set option to allow broadcasts on the socket
ClientSock.**SetSocketOption**((SocketOptionLevel.Socket, SocketOptionName.Broadcast, true);

// Test whether the linger option is set on the ServerSock
byte[] SockOptResult=new byte[1024]; // byte array to hold the result of the GetSocketOption() call
SockOptResult=(byte[])ServerSock.**GetSocketOption**(SocketOptionLevel.Socket,SocketOptionName.
Linger);

Java uses a variety of methods on the socket object; some examples are given:

boolean getKeepAlive()	// Determines whether the SO_KEEPALIVE socket option is enabled
int getSoLinger()	// Returns the setting for the SO_LINGER property
int getSoTimeout()	// Returns the setting for the SO_TIMEOUT property
void setSoTimeout(int timeout)	// Sets the SO_TIMEOUT property value, in milliseconds, for the socket
int getReceiveBufferSize()	// Returns the value of SO_RCVBUF, i.e. the receive buffer size
void setReceiveBufferSize(int size)	// Sets the value of SO_RCVBUF, i.e. set the receive buffer size
int getSendBufferSize()	// Returns the value of SO_ SNDBUF, i.e. the send buffer size
void setSendBufferSize(int size)	// Sets the value of SO_ SNDBUF, i.e. set the send buffer size
boolean isBound()	// Determines whether the socket has been bound to a port
boolean isClosed()	// Determines whether the socket is closed
boolean isConnected()	// Determines whether the socket is connected
boolean isInputShutdown()	// Determines whether the connection is shutdown in the read direction
boolean isOutputShutdown()	// Determines whether the connection is shutdown in the write direction

A3. SOCKET ADDRESS FORMATS

A socket address comprises an IP address and a port number. A socket address can represent the local socket to which other sockets connect or can represent a remote socket to connect to, depending on the context of its use.

C++ uses a socket address structure.
```
struct sockaddr {
    unsigned short int   sa_family;   // address family (fixed size of 2 bytes)
    char   sa_data[14];   // up to 14 bytes of address
};
```

A special version of the Socket Address Structure is used with IP addresses:
```
struct sockaddr_in {
    short int   sin_family;   // Address family (AF_INET signifies IPv4 address)
    unsigned short int   sin_port;   // Port number (fixed size of 2 bytes)
    struct in_addr   sin_addr;   // Internet address (fixed size of 4 bytes for IPv4)
};
```

C#
System.Net.IPEndPoint represents a socket address (the equivalent of the *sockaddr_in* structure in C++).
System.Net.IPAddress represents an IP address.

Example:
// Combine an IP address and a port to create an endpoint
IPAddress DestinationIPAddress = **IPAddress**.Parse("192.168.100.5");
int iPort = 9099;
IPEndPoint localIPEndPoint = new **IPEndPoint**(DestinationIPAddress, iPort);

ServerSock.Bind(localIPEndPoint); // bind the socket to the IPEndPoint
Java
The **SocketAddress** class represents a socket address (the equivalent of the *sockaddr_in* structure in C++).
The **InetAddress** class represents an IP address.

Prototype:
InetSocketAddress(InetAddress address, int port) // Creates a socket address using the supplied parameters.

Related methods on the socket object which determine address-related settings include:
int **getPort()** // Returns the remote port number the socket is connected to.
int **getLocalPort()** // Returns the local port number the socket is bound to.
SocketAddress **getRemoteSocketAddress()** // Returns the remote endpoint address the socket is connected to.
SocketAddress **getLocalSocketAddress()** // Returns the local endpoint address the socket is bound to.

A4. SETTING A SOCKET TO OPERATE IN BLOCKING OR NONBLOCKING IO MODE

A socket operates in blocking mode by default. It can be changed between the two modes, to suit application requirements.

C++ uses a utility, **ioctlsocket** to control the IO mode of a socket.
Example:

```
unsigned long lArg=1; // 1=NON_BLOCKING, 0=BLOCKING
int iError=ioctlsocket(ServerSock, FIONBIO, &lArg);  // FIONBIO signifies that Blocking or Non-blocking IO
                                               // is selected, based on the value of the lArg parameter
```

C# uses a property **Blocking** on the socket object to set IO mode.

Example:
ServerSock.**Blocking**=true; // or false to set to Non-blocking IO mode

Java uses a timeout value to determine how long a socket will block for. This is a flexible approach that combines the benefits of blocking initially for a period during which an event (such as message receipt) is expected and preventing the socket from waiting indefinitely.

Example:

```
ClientSock=new DatagramSocket(8000);    // Create a UDP socket and bind to port 8000
ClientSock.setSoTimeout(50);            // Set timeout to 50 milliseconds
ClientSock.receive(receivePacket);      // This call blocks for up to 50 milliseconds. The call returns when
                                        // either a message is received or when the timer expires.
```

A5. BIND

Binding associates a socket with a local socket address (which comprises a local port and IP address). The side that will be connected to (usually the server side in client server applications) must issue this call, so that clients can "locate" the server by its port number.

C++ uses the **bind()** function.
Prototype: int **bind**(SOCKET *s*, const struct sockaddr* *name*, int *namelen*);
// name is a sockaddr structure that holds the address to bind to (comprises IP address and port number).
// namelen is the size of the sockaddr structure.

Example:
int iError=**bind**(ServerSock, (const SOCKADDR FAR*)&m_LocalSockAddr, sizeof(m_LocalSockAddr));

C# uses the **Bind()** method of the Socket class.
Example:
int iPort=8000;
IPEndPoint localIPEndPoint=new IPEndPoint(IPAddress.Any, iPort); // Create an Endpoint
// IPAddress.Any signifies that the binding will apply to all IP addresses of the computer, such that
// a message arriving on any network interface, addressed to the appropriate port, will be received
ServerSock.**Bind**(localIPEndPoint); // Bind to the local IP Address and selected port

Java uses the **bind()** method of the Socket class, but note that bind is performed automatically when creating a ServerSocket (in which case a separate bind action is not performed).

// Create a socket address object using the local host's IP address and port 8000.
InetAddress Address=InetAddress.getLocalHost(); // Get local host's IP address
InetSocketAddress localSocketAddress = new InetSocketAddress(Address, 8000)
ServerSock.**bind**(localSocketAddress); // Bind to the local IP Address and selected port

A6. LISTEN

Listen is used on the passive side (usually the server side in client server applications), after bind. This sets the socket into listening-for-connection state. This is only used with TCP sockets.

C++
Prototype: int listen(SOCKET *s*, int *backlog*);
backlog is the maximum length of the queue of pending connections.

Example:
int iError=**listen**(ServerSock, 5); // Listen for connections, with a backlog queue maximum of 5

C#
Example:
ServerSock.**Listen**(4); // Listen for connections, with a backlog queue maximum of 4

Java. The listen action is integrated with binding. This is performed automatically when creating a ServerSocket, or can be performed separately using the bind() method of the Socket class.

A7. CONNECT

Connect is used on the active side of a connection (usually the client side in client server applications), to establish a new TCP connection with another process. This is not required when using UDP.

C++
Prototype: int connect(SOCKET *s*, const struct sockaddr* *name*, int *namelen*);
name is the socket address structure containing the address and port details of the other socket to connect to.
namelen is the size of the sockaddr structure.

Example:
int iError = **connect**(ClientSock, (const SOCKADDR FAR*)& ConnectSockAddr, sizeof(ConnectSockAddr));

C#
Example:
String szIPAddress = IP_Address_textBox.Text; // Get a user-specified IP address from a text box
IPAddress DestinationIPAddress = IPAddress.Parse(szIPAddress); // Create an IPAddress object

String szPort = SendPort_textBox.Text; // Get a user-specified port number from a text box
int iPort = System.Convert.ToInt16(szPort, 10);

IPEndPoint remoteEndPoint = new IPEndPoint(DestinationIPAddress, iPort); // Create an IPEndPoint
m_SendSocket.**Connect**(remoteEndPoint); // Connect to the remote socket identified by the endpoint

Java
Connect is performed automatically with several of the Socket() method constructors (those with address arguments so that the remote-side address and port details can be supplied).
If the no-argument constructor was used, connect is necessary and serves as a means of supplying the remote-side address and port details (in the form of a SocketAddress object).

Example:
ClientSock.**connect**(new InetSocketAddress(hostname, 8000));

A8. ACCEPT

Accept is used on the passive side of a connection (usually the server side in client server applications). It services a connection request from a client. Accept automatically creates and returns a new socket for the server side to use with this specific connection (i.e., to communicate with the specific connected client). This is only required when using TCP.

C++

Prototype: SOCKET accept(SOCKET *s*, struct sockaddr* *addr*, int* *addrlen*);

addr is the socket address structure containing the address and port details of the connecting process.

addrlen is the size of the sockaddr structure

Example:

SOCKET   ConnectedCliSocket=**accept**(ServSock,   (SOCKADDR   FAR*)&   ConnectSockAddr, &iRemoteAddrLen);

C#

Example:

Socket ConnectedClientSock = ServerSock.**Accept**();

Java

Example:

Socket ConnectedClientSock = ServerSock.**accept**();

A9. SEND (OVER A TCP CONNECTION)

C++

Prototype: int send(SOCKET *s*, const char* *buf*, int *len*, int *flags*);

If no error occurs, send returns the number of bytes sent. Otherwise, it returns an error code.

buf is the area of memory containing the message to send.

len is the size of the message in the buffer.

flags can be used to specify some control options.

Example:

int iBytesSent;

iBytesSent=**send**(ClientSock, (char *) &Message, sizeof(Message_PDU), 0);

C#

Example

int iBytesSent;

byte[] bData=System.Text.Encoding.ASCII.GetBytes(szData); // Assumes message to send is in string szData

iBytesSent=ClientSock.**Send**(bData, SocketFlags.None);

Java. Sending is performed using IO streams. First, the stream objects need to be obtained, and then, IO operations can be performed.

Example:

OutputStream out_stream=ClientSock.getOutputStream(); // Obtain OutputStream object

DataOutputStream out_data=new DataOutputStream(out_stream); // Obtain DataOutputStream object

out_data.writeUTF("Message from client"); // Write data to stream

A10. RECV (OVER A TCP CONNECTION)

The receiving action checks the local buffer to see if any messages have been received and placed there (used with a TCP connection). If there is a message in the buffer, it is passed to the application.

C++

Prototype: int **recv**(SOCKET *s*, char* *buf*, int *len*, int *flags*);

If no error occurs, recv returns the number of bytes received. If the connection has been closed, the return value is zero. Otherwise, it returns an error code.

buf is the area of memory that will contain the message.

len is the size of the buffer (i.e., the maximum amount of data that can be retrieved in one go).

flags can be used to specify some control options.

Example:

int iBytesRecd = **recv**(ConnectedClientSock, (char *) &Message, sizeof(Message_PDU), 0);

C#

Example:

byte[] ReceiveBuffer = new byte[1024]; // Create a byte array (buffer) to hold the received message
int iReceiveByteCount;
iReceiveByteCount = ConnectedClientSock.**Receive**(ReceiveBuffer, SocketFlags.None);

Java. Receiving is performed using IO streams. First, the stream objects need to be obtained, and then, IO operations can be performed.

Example:

InputStream in_stream = ClientSock.getInputStream(); // Obtain InputStream object
DataInputStream in_data = new DataInputStream(in_stream); // Obtain DataInputStream object
System.out.println("Message from server: " + in_data.readUTF()); // Read data from stream

A11. SENDTO (SEND A UDP DATAGRAM)

C++

Prototype: int **sendto**(SOCKET *s*, const char* *buf*, int *len*, int *flags*, const struct sockaddr* *to*, int *tolen*);

If no error occurs, sendto returns the number of bytes sent. Otherwise, it returns an error code.

buf is the area of memory containing the message to send.

len is the size of the message in the buffer.

flags can be used to specify some control options.

to is the sockaddr structure holding the address of the recipient socket.

tolen is the size of the address structure.

Example:

int iBytesSent = **sendto**(UDP_SendSock, (char FAR *) szSendBuf, iSendLen, 0,
(const struct sockaddr FAR *)& SendSockAddr, sizeof(SendSockAddr));

C#

Example:

byte[] bData = System.Text.Encoding.ASCII.GetBytes(szData);
UDP_SendSock.**SendTo**(bData, remoteEndPoint);

Java

UDP is datagram-based, so sending over UDP sockets cannot use stream-based IO. Instead, a DatagramPacket object is used to encapsulate the message data and the IP address and port number of the destination socket. This is then sent as a discrete datagram.

Example:
datagram = new DatagramPacket(buf, buf.length, address, port); // Create the datagram object
UDP_SendSock.**send**(datagram); // Send the datagram to its specified destination

A12. RECVFROM (RECEIVE A UDP DATAGRAM)

C++

Prototype: int **recvfrom**(SOCKET *s*, char* *buf*, int *len*, int *flags*, struct sockaddr* *from*, int* *fromlen*);
If no error occurs, recvfrom returns the number of bytes received. If the connection has been closed, the return value is zero. Otherwise, it returns an error code.
buf is the area of memory that will contain the message.
len is buffer size (i.e., max amount of data that can be retrieved in one go).
flags can be used to specify some control options.
from is a sockaddr structure containing the sending socket's address (optional).
fromlen is the length of the address structure.

Example:
int iBytesRecd = **recvfrom**(UDP_ReceiveSock, (char FAR*) szRecvBuf, 1024, 0, NULL, NULL);

C#

Example:
IPEndPoint SenderIPEndPoint = new IPEndPoint(IPAddress.Any, 0);
EndPoint SenderEndPoint = (EndPoint) SenderIPEndPoint; // Create endpoint to hold sender's address
UDP_ReceiveSock.Bind(endPoint);
byte[] ReceiveBuffer = new byte[1024]; // Create buffer to hold received message
int iReceiveByteCount;
iReceiveByteCount = UDP_ReceiveSock.**ReceiveFrom**(ReceiveBuffer, ref SenderEndPoint);

Java

UDP is datagram-based, so receiving over UDP sockets cannot use stream-based IO. Instead, a DatagramPacket object is created to hold received message data and the IP address and port number of the sending socket. The receive method is used to receive a message and place it into the datagram object.

Example:
byte[] buf = new byte[1024];
DatagramPacket datagram = new DatagramPacket(buf, buf.length); // Create an empty datagram object
UDP_ReceiveSock.**receive**(datagram); // Receive a message and place it into the datagram object

A13. SHUTDOWN

Shutdown closes a connection and is used only with TCP.

C++

Prototype: int **shutdown**(SOCKET *s*, int *how*);
how is a flag that indicates which actions are no longer allowed. Values are {SD_RECEIVE (subsequent calls to recv are disallowed), SD_SEND (subsequent calls to send are disallowed), SD_BOTH (disables sends and receives)}.

Example:
int iError = **shutdown**(ClientSock, SD_BOTH);

C#
Example:
ClientSock.**Shutdown**(SocketShutdown.Both);

Java uses two methods on the socket object:

    void shutdownInput()   // Close the input stream.
    void shutdownOutput()   // Close the output stream.

A14. CLOSESOCKET

Close or Closesocket closes a socket. Used with TCP and UDP.

C++
Example:
int iError = **closesocket**(ClientSock);

C#
Example:
ClientSock.**Close**();

Java
Example:
ClientSock.**close**();

THE RESOURCE VIEW

CHAPTER CONTENTS

4.1 RATIONALE AND OVERVIEW

A computer system has many different types of resource to support its operation; these include the central processing unit (CPU) (which has a finite processing rate), memory, and network bandwidth. Different activities use different combinations and amounts of resources. All resources are finite, and for any activity, there will often be one particular resource that is more limited than the others in terms of availability and thus acts as a bottleneck in terms of performance. Resource management therefore is a key part of ensuring system efficiency, and it is thus necessary for the developers to understand the distributed applications they build in terms of the resources they use. It is also very important from a programming viewpoint to understand the way resources such as message buffers are created and accessed. This chapter presents a resource-oriented view of communication between processes, with a focus on how the resources are used by applications and the way the resources are managed, either by the operating system or implicitly through the way applications use them.

4.2 THE CPU AS A RESOURCE

The CPU is a very important resource in any computer system, because no work can be done without it. A process can only make progress when it is in the running state, that is, when it is given access to the CPU. The other main resources (memory and network) get used as a result of process executing instructions.

Even when there are several processing cores available in a system, they are still a precious resource that must be used very efficiently. As we investigated in Chapter 2, there can be very many processes active in a modern multiprocessing system, and thus, the allocation of processing resource to processes is a key aspect that determines the overall efficiency of the system.

The Chapter 2 has focused mainly on the CPU in terms of resources. In particular, we looked at the way in which the processing power of the CPU has to be shared among the processes in the system by the scheduler. We also investigated the different types of process behavior and how competition for the CPU can affect the performance of processes. This chapter therefore focuses mainly on the memory and network resources.

However, the use of the various resources is intertwined; their use is not orthogonal. A process within a distributed system that sends a message to another process actually uses many resource types simultaneously. Almost all actions in a distributed system involve the main resource types (CPU, memory, and network) and virtual resources such as sockets and ports to facilitate communication.

For example, when dealing with memory as a resource, it is important to realize that the CPU can only directly access the contents of its own registers and the contents of random-access memory (RAM). Other possibly more abundant memory types, such as hard disk drives and USB memory sticks, are accessed with significantly higher latency as the data must be moved into RAM before being accessed. This illustrates the importance of understanding how the resources are used and the interaction between resources that occurs, which in turn is necessary in order to be able to make good design decisions for distributed applications and to be able to understand the consequences of those design decisions.

Poor design leading to inefficient resource usage can impact the entire system, beyond a single application or process. Negative impacts could arise, for example, in the form of network congestion, wasted CPU cycles, or thrashing in virtual memory (VM) systems.

4.3 MEMORY AS A RESOURCE FOR COMMUNICATION

Consider the very simple communication scenario between a pair of processes in which a single message is to be sent from one process to the other. Several types of resource are needed to achieve this, so let us first look at the use of memory.

In order to be able to send a message, the sending process must have access to the message; that is, it must have been defined and stored in memory accessible to the process. The normal way to arrange this is to reserve a block of memory specially for holding a message prior to sending; we call this the *send buffer* or *transmission buffer*. A message can then be placed into this buffer for subsequent transmission across the network to the other processes.

A buffer is a contiguous block of memory, accessible by the process that will read and write data to/from it. The process may be part of a user application or may be part of the operating system. By contiguous, we mean that the memory must be a single unbroken block. For example, there must not be a variable stored in the same block of memory. In fact, we say that the block of memory is "reserved" for use as the buffer (of course, this requires sensible and informed behavior on the part of the programmer).

There are three significant attributes of a buffer (start address, length, and end address), as illustrated in Figure 4.1.

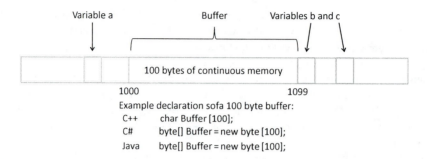

FIGURE 4.1

Illustration of a buffer; the one illustrated is 100 bytes long starting at address 1000 and ending at address 1099. Suitable declaration statements for some popular languages are also shown.

A buffer can be described precisely by providing any two of its three attributes, and the most common way to describe a buffer is by using start address and length. As each address in memory has a unique address and the memory used by the buffer must be in a contiguous block as discussed above, this description precisely and uniquely describes a particular block of memory. For the example shown in Figure 4.1, this is 1000 and 100. This information can be passed to the communication part of the application process; in the case of the sender, this indicates where the message that must be sent is stored, or in the case of the receiver, this indicates where to place the arriving message. Figure 4.1 also illustrates the requirement that the buffer's memory must be reserved such that no other variables overlap the allocated space. It is very important to ensure that accesses to the buffer remain within bounds. In the example shown, if a message of more than 100 bytes were written into the buffer, the 101st character would actually overwrite variable b.

The first resource-related issue we come across here is that the size of the buffer must be large enough to hold the message. The second issue is how to inform the code that performs the sending where the buffer is located and the actual size of the message to send (because it would be very inefficient to send the entire buffer contents if the message itself were considerably smaller than the buffer size, which would waste network bandwidth).

Figure 4.2 illustrates the situation where a message of 21 bytes is stored into a buffer of 40 bytes in size. From this figure, we can see several important things. Firstly, each byte in the buffer has an index that is its numerical offset from the start of the buffer, so the first byte has an index of 0, the second byte an index of 1, and so on, and perhaps, the most important thing to remember when writing code that uses this buffer is that the last byte has an offset of 39 (not 40). We can also see that each character of the message, including spaces, occupies one byte in the buffer (we assume simple ASCII encoding

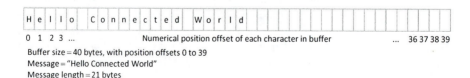

FIGURE 4.2

Buffer and message size.

in which each character code will always fit into a single byte of memory). We can also see that the message is stored starting from the beginning of the buffer. Finally, we can see that the message in this case is considerably shorter than the buffer, so it is more efficient to send across the network only the exact number of bytes in the message, rather than the whole buffer contents.

A single process may have several buffers; for example, it is usual to have separate buffers for sending and receiving to permit simultaneous send and receive operations without conflict.

For many years, memory size was a limiting factor for performance in most systems due to the cost and the physical size of memory devices. Over the last couple of decades, memory technology has advanced significantly such that modern multiprocessing systems have very large memories, large enough to accommodate many processes simultaneously. The operating system maintains a memory map that keeps track of the regions of memory that have been allocated to each process and must isolate the various processes present in the system from each other. In particular, each process must only have access to its allocated memory space and must not be able to access memory that is owned by another process.

Each process is allocated its own private memory area at a specific location in the system memory map. Processes are unaware of the true system map and thus are unaware of the presence of other processes and the memory they use. To keep the programming model simple, each process works with a private address range, which starts from address 0 as it sees it (i.e., the beginning of its own address space), although this will not be located at the true address 0 at the system level. The true starting address of a process' memory area is used as an offset so that the operating system can map the process' address spaces onto the real locations in the system memory. Using the private address space, two different processes can both store a variable at address 1000 (as they see it). This address is actually address 1000 relative to the offset of where the process' memory begins; thus, its true address is 1000 plus the process' memory offset in the system memory address space; see Figure 4.3.

Figure 4.3 illustrates the way in which different processes are allocated private memory areas with offsets in the true address range of the system and the way in which relative addressing is used by processes within their allocated memory space. This permits two process instances of the same program to run on the same computer, each storing a variable X at relative address 1000. The operating system stores the offsets for the two memory spaces (in this example, 10,000 and 20,000), thus using the true memory address offsets for each of the processes; the true locations of the two variables are known to the operating system (in this example, 11,000 and 21,000). This is a very important mechanism because it means that the relative addresses used within a program are independent of where the process is loaded into the true physical memory address range; which is something that cannot be known when the program is compiled.

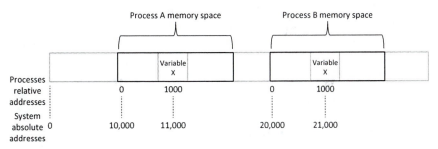

FIGURE 4.3

Process memory offsets and relative addressing.

Position offset of the buffer in the process memory space (not to scale)

Process memory space = 10,000 bytes
Buffer size = 40 bytes, starting at address 2000

FIGURE 4.4

A buffer allocated within a process' address space.

Next, let us consider what information is needed to represent the size and location of a buffer within the address space of a particular process and thus the size and location of the message within it.

Figure 4.4 shows how the buffer is located within the process' memory space. Note here that the memory address offsets of the 10,000 bytes are numbered 0 through 9999 and that address 10,000 is not actually part of this process' memory space.

The message starts at the beginning of the buffer (i.e., it has an offset of 0 within the buffer space) and has a length of 21 bytes. Therefore, by combining our knowledge of the message position in the buffer and our knowledge of the buffer position in the process' memory space, we can uniquely identify the location of the message within the process' memory space. In this case, the message starts at address 2000 and has a length of 21 bytes. These two values will have to be passed as parameters to the send procedure in our code, so that it can transmit the correct message.

We now consider the role of memory buffers in the complete activity of sending a message from one process (we shall call the sender) to another process (we shall call the receiver). The sender process must have the message stored in a buffer, as explained above, before it can send the message. Similarly, the receiver process must reserve a memory buffer in which to place the message when it arrives. Figure 4.5 provides a simplified view of this concept.

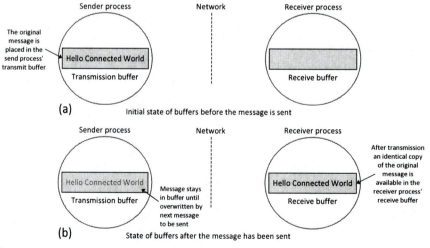

FIGURE 4.5

Simplified view of sender and receiver use of buffers.

Figure 4.5 shows the role of memory buffers in communication, in a simplified way. Part (a) of the figure shows the situation before the message is sent. The message is stored in a buffer in the memory space of the sending process, and the buffer in the receiving process is empty. Part (b) of the figure shows the situation after the message has been sent. The essential point this figure conveys is that the sending of a message between processes has the effect of transferring the message from a block of memory in the sender process to a block of memory in the receiver process. After the transfer is complete, the receiver can read the message from its memory buffer, and it will be an exact replica of the message the sender had previously placed in its own send buffer.

As stated above, this is a simplified view of the actual mechanism for the purpose of establishing the basic concept of passing a message between processes. The message is not automatically deleted from the send buffer through the action of sending; this is logical because it is possible that the sender may wish to send the same message to several recipients. A new message can be written over the previous message when necessary, without first removing the earlier message. The most significant difference between Figure 4.5 and the actual mechanism used is that the operating system is usually responsible for receiving the message from the network and holding it in its own buffer until the recipient process is ready for it, at which point the message is transferred to the recipient process' receive buffer.

The receive mechanism is implemented as a *system call* that means that the code for actually performing the receive action is part of the system software (specifically the TCP/IP protocol stack). This is important for two main reasons: Firstly, the system call mechanism can operate when the process is not running, which is vital because it is not known in advance exactly when a message will arrive. The receiver process is only actually running when it is scheduled by the operating system, and thus, it may not be in the running state at the moment when the message arrives (in which case, it would not be able to execute instructions to store the message in its own buffer). This is certain to be the case when the socket is configured in "blocking" mode that means that as soon as the process issues the receive instruction, it will be moved from the running state to the blocked state and stays there until the message has been received from the network. Secondly, the process cannot directly interact with the network interface because it is a shared resource needed by all processes that perform communication. The operating system must manage sending and receiving at the level of the computer itself (this corresponds to the network layer). The operating system uses port numbers, contained in the message's transport layer protocol header to determine which process the message belongs to. This aspect is discussed in depth in Chapter 3, but the essence of what occurs in the context of the resource view is shown in Figure 4.6.

The most important aspect of Figure 4.6 is that it shows how the operating system at the receiving node decouples the actual sending and receiving processes. If the receiving process were guaranteed to be always running (in the running state), then this decoupling may be unnecessary, but as we have seen in Chapter 2, the receiving process may actually only be in the running state for a small fraction of the total time. The sending process cannot possibly synchronize its actions such that the message arrives at exactly the moment the recipient process is running, because, among other things, the scheduling at the receiving node is a dynamic activity (and thus, the actual state sequences are not knowable in advance) and also the network itself is a dynamic environment (and thus, the end-to-end delay is continuously varying). If the operating system did not provide this decoupling network, communication would be unreliable and inefficient as the two communicating processes would have to be tightly synchronized in order that a message could be passed between them.

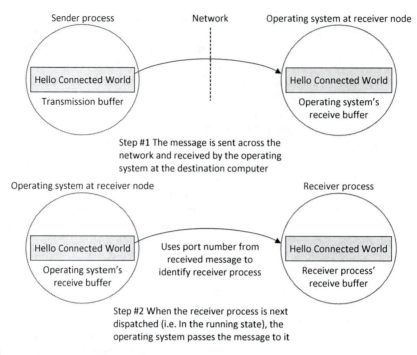

FIGURE 4.6

A message is initially received by the operating system at the destination computer and then passed to the appropriate process.

4.3.1 MEMORY HIERARCHY

There are many types of memory available in a distributed system, the various types having different characteristics and thus being used in different ways. The memory types can be divided into two main categories: primary memory and secondary storage.

Primary memory is the memory that the CPU can access directly; that is, data values can be read from and written to primary memory using a unique address for each memory location. Primary memory is volatile (it will lose its contents if power is turned off) and comprises the CPU's registers and cache memory and RAM.

Secondary storage is persistent (nonvolatile) memory in the form of magnetic hard disks, optical disks such as CDs and DVDs, and flash memory (which includes USB memory devices and also solid-state hard disks and memory cards as used, e.g., in digital cameras). Secondary storage devices tend to have very large capacities relative to primary memory, and many secondary storage devices use replaceable media, so the drive itself can be used to access endless amounts of storage, but this requires manual replacement of the media. The contents of secondary storage cannot be directly addressed by the CPU, and thus, the data must be read from the secondary storage device into primary storage prior to its use by a process. As the secondary storage is nonvolatile (and primary memory is volatile), it is the ultimate destination of all persistent data generated in a system.

Let us consider the memory-use aspect of creating and running a process. The program is initially held in secondary storage as a file that contains the list of instructions. Historically, this will have been held on a magnetic hard disk or an optical disk such as a CD or DVD. In addition, more recently, flash memory technologies have become popular, such that large storage sizes of up to several gigabytes can be achieved on a physically very small memory card or USB memory stick. When the program is executed, the program instructions are read from the file on secondary storage and loaded into primary memory RAM. As the program is running, the various instructions are read from the RAM in sequence depending on the program logic flow.

The CPU has general purpose registers in which it stores data values on a temporary basis while performing computations. Registers are the fastest access type of memory, being integrated directly with the processor itself and operating at the same speed. However, there are a very limited number of registers; this varies across different processor technologies but is usually in the range of about eight to about sixty-four registers, each one holding a single value. Some processor architectures have just a handful of registers, so registers alone are not sufficient to execute programs; other forms of memory and storage are needed.

The data values used in the program are temporarily held in CPU registers for purposes of efficiency during instruction execution but are written back to RAM storage at the end of computations; in high-level languages, this happens automatically when a variable is updated, because variables are created in RAM (and not registers). This is an important point; using high-level languages, the programmer cannot address registers, only RAM locations (which are actually chosen by the compiler and not the programmer). Assembly language can directly access registers, but this is a more complex and error-prone way of programming and in modern systems is only used in special situations (such as for achieving maximum efficiency on low-resourced embedded systems or for achieving maximum speed in some timing critical real-time applications).

The memory hierarchy shown in Figure 4.7 is a popular way of representing the different types of memory organized in terms of their access speed (registers being the fastest) and access latency (increasing down the layers) and the capacity (which tends to also increase down the layers) and cost, which if normalized to a per byte value increases as you move up the layers. The figure is a generalized mapping and needs to be interpreted in an informed way and not taken literally in all cases. For example, not all flash USB memory drives have larger capacity than the amount of RAM in every system, although the trend is heading that way. Network-accessible storage has the additional latency of the network communication, on top of the actual device access latency. Network-accessible drives are not necessarily individually any larger than the local one, but an important point to note, especially with the distributed systems theme of this book, is that once you consider network access, you can potentially access a vast number of different hard drives spread across a large number of remote computers. Cartridge disk drives and removable media systems such as CD and DVD drives are shown as being slower to access than network drives. This is certainly the case if you take into account the time required for manual replacement of media. The capacity of replaceable media systems is effectively infinite, although each instance of the media (each CD or DVD) has well-defined limits.

RAM is so named because its data locations can be accessed individually, in any order (i.e., we can access memory locations in whatever sequence is necessary as the process runs), and the access order does not affect access time, which is the same for all locations. However, the name can be misleading; there is usually a pattern to the accesses that tends to exhibit spatial or temporal locality. The locations accessed are done so purposefully in a particular sequence and not "randomly." Spatial locality arises for a number of reasons. Most programs contain loops or even loops within loops, which cycle through

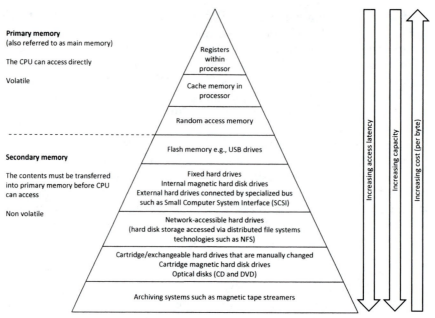

FIGURE 4.7

The memory hierarchy.

relatively small regions of the instruction list and thus repeatedly access the same memory locations. In addition, data are often held in arrays, which are held in a set of contiguous memory locations. Iteration through an array will result in a series of accesses to different, but adjacent, memory locations, which will be in the same memory page (except when a boundary is reached). An event handler will always reference the same portion of memory (where its instructions are located) each time an instance of the event occurs; this is an example of spatial locality, and if the event occurs frequently or with a regular timing pattern, then this is also an example of temporal locality.

The characteristics of secondary storage need to be understood in order to design efficient applications. For example, a hard disk is a block device; therefore, it is important to consider the latency of disk IO in terms of overall process efficiency. It may be more efficient, for example, to read in a whole data file into memory in one go (or at least a batch of records) and access the records as necessary from the cache, rather than reading each one from disk when needed. This is very application-dependent and is an important design consideration.

4.4 MEMORY MANAGEMENT

In Chapter 2, we looked closely at how the operating system manages processes in the system; in particular, the focus was on scheduling. In this chapter, we examine memory management, which is another very important role of the operating system. There are two main aspects of memory management: dynamic memory allocation to processes (which is covered in depth in a later section) and VM (which is discussed in this section).

As we have seen above, processes use memory to store data, and this includes the contents of messages received from the network or to be sent across the network. Upon creation of a process, the operating system allocates sufficient memory to hold all the statically declared variables; the operating system can determine these requirements as it loads and reads the program. In addition, processes often request allocation of additional memory dynamically; that is, they ask the operating system for more memory as their execution progresses, depending on the actual requirements. Thus, it is not generally possible to know the memory requirements of processes precisely at the time of process creation.

As discussed in the section above, there are several different types of storage in a computer system, and the most common form of primary memory is RAM, which is addressable from the processor directly. A process can access data stored in RAM with low latency, much faster than accessing secondary storage. The optimal situation is therefore to hold all data used by active processes in RAM. However, in all systems, the amount of RAM is physically limited, and very often, the total amount of memory demanded by all the processes in the system exceeds the amount of RAM available.

Deciding how much memory to allocate to each process, actually performing the allocation, and keeping track of which process is using which blocks of memory and which blocks are free to allocate are all part of the memory management role of the operating system. In the earliest systems, once the physical RAM was all allocated, then no more processes could be accommodated. VM was developed to overcome this serious limitation. The simplest way to describe VM is a means of making more memory available to processes than what actually exists in the form of RAM, by using space on the hard disk as temporary storage. The concept of VM was touched upon in Chapter 2 when the suspended process states were discussed. In that chapter, the focus was on the management of processes and the use of the CPU, so we did not get embroiled in the details of what happens when a process' memory image was actually moved from RAM to disk (this is termed being "swapped out").

Activity R1 explores memory availability and the way this changes dynamically as new memory-hungry processes are created. The activity has been designed to illustrate the need for a VM system in which secondary storage (the hard disk) is used to increase the effective size of primary memory (specifically the RAM).

"Thrashing" is the term used to describe the situation in which the various processes access different memory pages at a high rate, such that the paging system spends almost all of its time swapping pages in and out, instead of actually running processes, and thus, almost no useful work can be performed.

ACTIVITY R1 EXAMINE MEMORY AVAILABILITY AND USE. OBSERVE BEHAVIOR OF SYSTEM WHEN MEMORY DEMAND SUDDENLY AND SIGNIFICANTLY INCREASES BEYOND PHYSICAL AVAILABILITY

Learning Outcomes
1. Understand memory requirements of processes.
2. Understand physical memory as a finite resource.
3. Understand how the operating system uses VM to increase the effective memory availability beyond the amount of physical memory in the system.

This activity is performed in two parts. The first of these involves observing memory usage under normal conditions. The second part is designed to stress-test the VM mechanics of the operating system by suddenly and significantly increasing the amount of memory demanded by processes, beyond the amount of physical RAM available.

ACTIVITY R1 EXAMINE MEMORY AVAILABILITY AND USE. OBSERVE BEHAVIOR OF SYSTEM WHEN MEMORY DEMAND SUDDENLY AND SIGNIFICANTLY INCREASES BEYOND PHYSICAL AVAILABILITY—Cont'd

Part 1: Investigate memory availability and usage under normal conditions.

Method

(Assume a Windows operating system; the required commands and actions may vary across different versions of the operating system. The experiments were carried out on a computer with Windows 7 Professional installed.)

1. Examine memory availability. Open the Control Panel and select "System and Security," and from there, select "System." My computer has 4 GB RAM installed, 3.24 GB usable (available for processes).
2. Use the Task Manager utility to examine processes' memory usage. Start the Task Manager by pressing the Control, Alt, and Delete keys simultaneously and select "Start Task Manager" from the options presented. Select the "Applications" tab to see what applications are running in the system.
3. Select the "Processes" tab, which provides more details than the Applications tab; in particular, it provides memory usage per process. Look at the range of memory allocations for the processes present. These can range from about 50 kB up to hundreds of megabytes. Observe the memory usage of processes associated with applications you are familiar with, such as Windows (File) Explorer and Internet Explorer and perhaps a word processor; are these memory usage values in the ranges that you would have expected? Can you imagine what all that memory is being used for?
4. With the Task Manager "Processes" tab still open for diagnostic purposes, start the Notepad application but do not enter any characters into the form. How much memory is needed for the application itself? We could call this the memory overhead, as this much memory is needed for this application without including any user data (in my system, this was 876 kB). I typed a single character and the memory usage went up to 884 kB; does that tell us anything useful? I don't have access to the source code for this application, but it seems as if a single memory page of 8 kB was dynamically allocated to hold the user data. If I am right, then typing a few more characters will not further increase the memory usage; try it. After some experimentation, I found that Notepad allocates a further 8 kB of memory for approximately each 2000 characters typed into the form. This is approximately what I would expect and is quite efficient; using 4 bytes of memory to hold all the information, it needs about each character of data. You should experiment further with this simple application as it is an accessible way to observe dynamic memory allocation in operation in a real application.

Part 2: Investigate system behavior when memory demand increases beyond the size of physical RAM available in the system.

Caution! This part of the activity can potentially crash your computer or cause data loss. I recommend that you follow this part of the activity as a "pseudo activity," since I have performed the activity and reported the results so you can observe safely without actually risking your system. The source code for the Memory_Hog program is provided so that you can understand its behavior. If you choose to compile and run the code, make sure you first save all work, close all files, and shut down any applications, which may corrupt data.

Method

(Part 2A uses the system default page file size, which is 3317 MB; this is approximately the same size as the amount of physical RAM installed; the VM size is the sum of the usable RAM plus the page file size and was 6632 MB for this experiment.)

5. Keep the Task Manager "Processes" tab open for diagnostic purposes, while completing the following steps. You can also use the "Performance" tab to inspect the total memory in use and available in the system.
6. Execute a single copy of Memory_Hog within a command window to determine the maximum amount of memory that the operating system will allocate to a single process. The Memory_Hog requests increasing memory amounts, starting with 1 megabyte (MB). Each time it is successful, it frees the memory, doubles the request size, and requests again. This is repeated until the request is refused by the operating system, so the maximum it gets allocated might not be the exact maximum that can be allocated, but it is in the approximate ballpark, and certainly, the system will not allocate twice this much. The screenshot below shows the output of the Memory_Hog on my computer. The maximum size that was successfully allocated was 1024 MB.

ACTIVITY R1 EXAMINE MEMORY AVAILABILITY AND USE. OBSERVE BEHAVIOR OF SYSTEM WHEN MEMORY DEMAND SUDDENLY AND SIGNIFICANTLY INCREASES BEYOND PHYSICAL AVAILABILITY—Cont'd

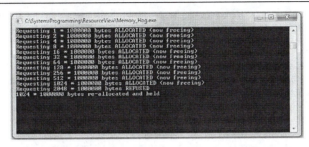

7. Execute multiple copies of the Memory_Hog each in a separate command window. Do this progressively, starting one copy at a time and observing the amount of memory allocated to each copy, both in terms of the output reported by the Memory_Hog program and also by looking at the Task Manager "Processes" tab. I used the Task Manager "Performance" tab to inspect the amount of memory committed, as a proportion of the total VM available. The results are presented in the table below.

Instance of Memory_Hog	Memory allocated (specific process)	Memory committed (system-wide)	Adverse effects on system performance
1	1024 MB	2267/6632	None
2	1024 MB	3202/6632	None
3	1024 MB	4157/6632	Severe short-term disruption. Recovered once the majority of page swap-outs were completed (after about 1 min)
4	1024 MB	5142/6632	Severe short-term disruption. Recovered once the majority of page swap-outs were completed (after about 1 min)
5	1024 MB	6145/6632	Severe short-term disruption. Recovered once the majority of page swap-outs were completed (after about 1 min)
6	256 MB	6392/6632	Minimal disruption noticed
7	128 MB	6536/6632	Minimal disruption noticed

The first and second instances of the Memory_Hog process were allocated the process maximum amount of memory (1024 MB, as discovered in step 6 above). This was allocated without exceeding the amount of physical RAM available, so there was no requirement for the VM system to perform paging.

The third, fourth, and fifth instances of the Memory_Hog process were also allocated the process maximum amount of memory (1024 MB). However, the memory requirement exceeded the physical memory availability, so the VM system had to swap currently used pages out to disk to make room for the new memory allocation. This caused significant disk activity for a limited duration, which translated into system disruption; processes became unresponsive and the media player stopped and started the sound in a jerky fashion (I was playing a music CD at the time). Eventually, the system performance recovered once the majority of the disk activity was completed. No data were lost and no applications crashed, although I had taken the precaution of closing down almost all applications before the experiment.

The sixth instance of the Memory_Hog process was allocated 256 MB of memory. The VM system had to perform further swap-outs, but this was a much smaller proportion of total memory and had a much lower, almost unnoticeable effect on system performance.

ACTIVITY R1 EXAMINE MEMORY AVAILABILITY AND USE. OBSERVE BEHAVIOR OF SYSTEM WHEN MEMORY DEMAND SUDDENLY AND SIGNIFICANTLY INCREASES BEYOND PHYSICAL AVAILABILITY—Cont'd

The seventh instance of the Memory_Hog process was allocated 128 MB of memory. As with the sixth instance, the VM system performed further page swap-outs, but this had an almost unnoticeable effect on system performance.

When evaluating the system disruption effect of the Memory-Hog processes, it is important to consider the memory-use intensity of the large amounts of memory it requests. If you inspect the source code for the Memory_Hog program, you will see that once it has allocated the memory, it does not access it again; it sits in an infinite loop after the allocation activity, doing nothing. This makes it easy for a paging mechanism based on Least Frequently Used or Least Recently Used memory pages to be able to identify these pages for swapping out. This indeed is the effect witnessed in the experiments and explains why the system disruption is short-lived. If the processes accessed all of their allocated memory aggressively, then the system disruption would be continual, as the paging would be ongoing, for each process. If multiple processes are making such continuous access, then the VM system may begin to "thrash." This means that the VM system is continually moving pages between memory and disk and that processes perform very little useful work because they spend most of the time in the blocked state waiting for a specific memory page to become available for access.

Method

(Part 2B uses an increased page-file size of 5000 MB, which exceeds the physical memory size significantly. The VM size in this case was 8315 MB.)

8. Execute multiple copies of the Memory_Hog each in a separate command window, progressively as in step 7. The results are presented in the table below.

Instance of Memory_Hog	Memory allocated (specific process)	Memory committed (system-wide)	Adverse effects on system performance
1	1024 MB	2244/8315	None
2	1024 MB	3199/8315	None
3	1024 MB	4176/8315	Minor disruption as the allocated memory amount exceeded the physical memory limit and the paging activity began
4	1024 MB	5185/8315	Severe short-term disruption. Recovered once the majority of page swap-outs were completed (after about 1 min)
5	1024 MB	6162/8315	Minor disruption
6	1024 MB	7147/8315	Sporadic disruption during the memory allocation activity
7	1024 MB	8134/8315	Severe short-term disruption; processes became unresponsive. Recovered after about 1 min
8	128 MB	8265/8315	Minimal disruption noticed

A similar pattern of disruption was observed as with the experiment in part 2A. When the total memory requirement can be satisfied with physical memory, there is no system performance degradation. Once the VM system starts performing page swaps, the performance of all processes is potentially affected. This is due to the latency of the associated disk accesses and the fact that a queue of disk access requests can build up. Once the majority of page swaps necessary to free the required amount of memory for allocation have been completed, the responsiveness of the other processes in the system returns to normal.

Reflection

This activity has looked at several aspects of memory availability, allocation, and usage. The VM system has been investigated in terms of its basic operation and the way in which it extends the amount of memory available beyond the size of physical memory in the system.

> **ACTIVITY R1 EXAMINE MEMORY AVAILABILITY AND USE. OBSERVE BEHAVIOR OF SYSTEM WHEN MEMORY DEMAND SUDDENLY AND SIGNIFICANTLY INCREASES BEYOND PHYSICAL AVAILABILITY—Cont'd**
>
> When interpreting the results of parts 2A and 2B, it is important to realize that the exact behavior of the VM system will vary each time the experiment is carried out. This is because the sequence of disk accesses will be different each time. The actual set of pages that are allocated to each process will differ as will the exact location of each page at any particular instant (i.e., whether each specific page is held on disk or in physical RAM). Therefore, the results will not be perfectly repeatable, but can be expected to exhibit the same general behavior each time. This is an example of nondeterministic behavior that can arise in systems: It is possible to describe the behavior of a system in general terms, but it is not possible to exactly predict the precise system state or low-level sequence of events.

4.4.1 VIRTUAL MEMORY

This section provides an overview of the mechanism and operation of VM.

Figure 4.8 illustrates the mapping of process' memory space into the VM system and then into actual locations on storage media. From the process' viewpoint, its memory is a contiguous block, which is accessible on demand. This requires that the VM mechanism is entirely transparent; the process accesses whichever of its pages it needs to, in the required sequence. It will incur delays when a swapped out page is requested, leading to a page fault which the VM mechanism handles, but the process will be moved to the blocked state while this takes place and is unaware of the VM system activity. The process does not need to do anything differently to access the swapped out page, so effectively, the VM

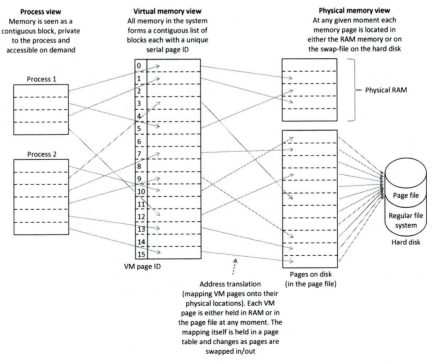

FIGURE 4.8

VM overview.

mechanism is providing access transparency. The VM system however is aware of the true location of each memory page (which it keeps track of in a special page table), the set of pages that are in use by each process and the reference counts or other statistics for each page (depending on the page replacement algorithm in use). The VM system is responsible for keeping the most needed memory pages in physical memory and swapping in any other accessed pages on demand. The physical memory view reflects the true location of memory pages, which is either the RAM or a special file called the page file on the secondary storage (usually a magnetic hard disk).

4.4.1.1 VM Operation

Memory is divided into a number of pages, which can be located either in physical memory or on the hard disk in the page file. Each memory page has a unique VM page number. Memory pages retain their VM page number but can be placed into any numbered physical memory page or disk page slot as necessary.

A process will use one or more memory pages. The memory pages contain the actual program itself (the instructions) and the data used by the program.

The CPU is directly connected to the physical memory via its address and data buses. This means that it can directly access memory contents that are contained in pages that are held in physical memory. All memory pages have a VM page ID, which is permanent and thus can be used to track a page as it is moved between physical memory and the page file on disk.

Memory pages that are not currently held in physical memory cannot be immediately accessed. These have to be moved into the physical memory first and then accessed. Running processes can thus access their in-memory pages with no additional latency but will incur a delay if they need to access a page currently held on disk.

Some key terms are defined:

Swap-out: A VM page is transferred from physical memory to disk.

Swap-in: A VM page is transferred from disk to physical memory.

Page fault: Processes can only access VM memory pages that are held in physical memory. A page fault is the name given to the error that occurs when an attempt is made to access a memory page that is not currently in physical memory. To resolve a page fault, the relevant page must be swapped in. If there are no physical memory pages available to permit the swap-in, then another page must be swapped out first to free space in physical memory.

Allocation error: If the VM system cannot allocate sufficient memory to satisfy a memory allocation request from a process, an allocation error will occur.

Thrashing: When processes allocate a lot of memory, such that a significant amount of the swap file is used and also makes frequent access to the majority of their allocated pages, the VM system will be kept busy swapping out pages to make room for required pages and then swapping in those required pages. This situation is worse when there is low spatial locality in the memory accesses. In extreme cases, the VM system is continuously moving pages between memory and disk, and processes are almost always blocked, waiting for their memory page to become available. The system becomes very inefficient, as it spends almost all of its effort moving pages around and the processes present perform very little useful work.

As is reflected in the results of Activity R1, the overall performance of the VM system depends in part on the size of the swap file allocated on the disk. The swap file size is usually chosen to be in the range of 1-2 times the primary memory size, with 1.5 times being a common choice. It is difficult to find an optimum value for all systems, as the amount of paging activity that occurs is dependent on the actual memory-use behavior of the processes present.

4.4.1.2 Page Replacement Algorithms

When a page in memory needs to be swapped out to free up some physical memory, a page replacement algorithm is used to select which currently in-memory page should be moved to disk.

There are a variety of different page replacement algorithms that can be used. The general goal of these is the same: to remove a page from memory that is not expected to be used soon and store it on the disk (i.e., swap out this page) so that a needed page can be retrieved from disk and placed into the physical memory (i.e., the needed page is swapped in).

4.4.1.3 General Mechanism

As processes execute, they access the various memory pages as necessary, which depends on the actual locations where the used variables are held. Access to a memory location is performed either to read the value or to update the value. If even a single location within a page is accessed, it is said to have been referenced, and this is tracked by setting a special "referenced bit" for the specific page. Similarly, modification of one or more locations in a page is tracked by setting a special "modified bit" for the specific page. The referenced and/or modified bits are used by the various page replacement algorithms to select which page to swap out.

4.4.1.4 Specific Algorithms

The *Least Recently Used* (LRU) algorithm is designed to keep pages in physical memory that have been recently used. This works on the basis that most processes exhibit spatial locality in their memory refer-encing behavior (i.e., the same subset of locations tend to be accessed many times over during specific functions, loops, etc.), and thus, it is efficient to keep the pages that have been recently referenced in physical memory. Referenced bits are periodically cleared so that old reference events are forgotten. When a page needs to be swapped out, it is chosen from those that have not been recently referenced.

The *Least Frequently Used* (LFU) algorithm keeps track of the number of times a VM page in physical memory is referenced. This can be achieved by having a counter (per page) to keep track of the number of references to that page. The algorithm selects the page with the lowest reference count to swap out. A significant issue with LFU is that it does not take into account how the accesses are spread over time. Therefore, a page that was accessed many times, for example, in a loop, a while ago may show up as being more important than a page that is in current use but is not used so repetitively. Because of this issue, the LFU algorithm is not often used in its pure form, but the basic concept of LFU is sometimes used in combination with other techniques.

The *First-In, First-Out (FIFO)* algorithm maintains a list of the VM pages in physical memory, ordered in terms of when they were placed into the memory. Using a round-robin cycle through the circular list, the algorithm selects the VM page that has been in physical memory the longest, when a swap-out is needed. FIFO is simple and has low overheads but generally performs poorly as its basis for selection of pages does not relate to their usage since they were swapped in.

The *clock variant of FIFO* works fundamentally in the same round-robin manner as FIFO, but on the first selection of a page for potential swapping out, if the referenced bit is set, the page is given a "second chance" (because at least one access to the page has occurred). The referenced bit is cleared and the round robin continues from the next page in the list until one is found to swap out.

The *Random algorithm* selects a VM page randomly from those that are resident in physical memory for swapping out. This algorithm is simpler to implement than LRU and LFU because it does not need to track page references. It tends to perform better than FIFO, but less well than LRU, although this is dependent on the actual patterns of memory accesses that occur.

The performance of a page replacement algorithm is dependent on the general memory-access behavior of the mix of processes in the system. There is no single algorithm that works best in all circumstances, in terms of it being able to correctly predict which pages will be needed again soon and thus keep these in physical memory. The various algorithms discussed above have relative strengths and weaknesses, which are highlighted with the aid of some specific scenarios below:

- LRU and LFU are well suited to applications that allocate a large amount of memory and iterate through it or otherwise access it in a predictable way in which there is a pattern to references, for example, a scientific data processing application or a simulation that uses techniques such as computational fluid dynamics (as used, e.g., in weather prediction). In such scenarios, the working set of pages at any moment tends to be a limited subset of the process' entire memory space, so pages that have not been used recently are not particularly likely to be needed in the short term. Depending on the relative size of the working set of pages and the total allocated memory, the clock variant of FIFO may work well.
- An application that has a very large allocated memory and uses the contents very sparsely and with low repetition will have a much less regular patterns in terms of the pages used. In this case, it is very difficult to predict which pages will be needed next and which ones are thus likely to be good candidates to swap out. In such a case, the Random algorithm may perform relatively better than it would with programs that display greater temporal or spatial locality, since no algorithm is able to predict very well, but the Random algorithm at least has very low overheads.

Memory management behavior can be investigated using the Operating Systems Workbench. The VM simulation demonstrates the need for VM and facilitates experimentation with swapping pages between RAM and the hard disk as necessary to meet the applications' memory needs. Activity R2 examines the basics of the VM mechanism and its operation and does not focus on any particular algorithm although the simulation can support evaluation of specific page replacement algorithms, which can be investigated subsequently (see Section 4.11).

ACTIVITY R2 USING THE OPERATING SYSTEMS WORKBENCH TO EXPLORE THE BASICS OF MEMORY MANAGEMENT AND VM

Prerequisite: Download the Operating Systems Workbench and the supporting documentation from the book's supplementary materials website. Read the document "Virtual Memory—Activities and Experiments."

Learning Outcomes
1. To gain an understanding of the need for memory management
2. To gain an understanding of the operation of VM
3. To gain an understanding of the meaning of "page fault," "swap-out," and "swap-in"
4. To explore the basics of page replacement algorithms

This activity uses the "virtual memory" simulation provided by the Operating Systems Workbench on the Memory Management tab. The simulation provides an environment in which there are four pages of physical memory and a further eight pages of storage on the disk. Each page holds 16 characters. Either one or two simple text-editing type applications (which are built in to the simulation) can be used to access the memory, for the purpose of investigating the memory management behavior.

ACTIVITY R2 USING THE OPERATING SYSTEMS WORKBENCH TO EXPLORE THE BASICS OF MEMORY MANAGEMENT AND VM—Cont'd

Part 1: Simple illustration of the need for, and basic concept of, VM.

Method

1. Enable the first application.
2. Carefully type the letters of the alphabet (from A to Z) in uppercase initially and then repeat in lower case and watch how the characters are stored in the memory as you type. This initial block of text comprises 52 characters. The memory is organized into 16-character pages, so this text spans 4 pages. At this point, all of the text you have typed is held in VM pages currently in physical memory—this is an important observation.
3. Now, type the characters "11223344556677889900"; this adds another 20 characters, totaling 72, but the four physical memory pages can only hold only 64, so what happens? We get a page allocation error.

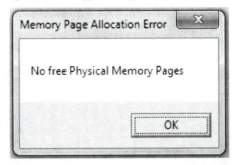

4. You have exhausted the physical memory when you get to the first "7" character. The solution is to select one of the four VM pages in use, to be swapped out (i.e., stored in one of the disk pages), thus freeing up a physical memory page so that you can finish typing your data. Select VM page 0 and press the adjacent "Swap OUT (to Disk)" button. Notice that VM page 0 is moved onto the disk and that the "7" character is now placed into the new page (VM page 4), at the physical page 0 address. Now, you can continue typing the sequence.

The screenshot below shows what you should see after step 4 has been completed.

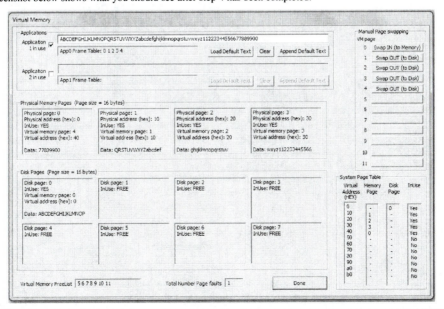

ACTIVITY R2 USING THE OPERATING SYSTEMS WORKBENCH TO EXPLORE THE BASICS OF MEMORY MANAGEMENT AND VM—Cont'd

Expected Outcome for Part 1

You can see how your application is using five pages of memory, but the system only has four physical pages. This is the fundamental basis of VM; it allows you to use more memory than you actually have. It does this by temporarily storing the extra pages of memory on the disk, as you can see in the simulation.

Part 2: An example of a page fault; we shall now try to access the memory page that is held on the disk. This part of the activity continues from where part 1 above left off.

5. Try to change the first character you typed, the "A," into an "@" by editing the application data in the same text box where you originally typed it. You will get a "page fault" because this character is in the page that we swapped out to disk; that is, at present, the process cannot access this page.

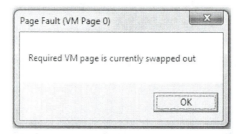

6. We need to swap in VM page 0 so we can access it—press the button labeled "Swap IN (to Memory)" for VM page 0 at the top of the right-hand pane. What happens? We get a page allocation error, because there are no free pages of physical memory that can be used for the swap-in.

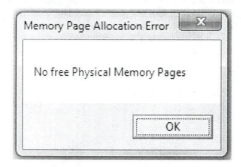

7. We need to select a page to swap out so as to create space to swap in VM page 0. Ideally, we will choose a page that we won't need for a long time, but this can be difficult to predict. In this case, we shall choose VM page 1. Press the button labeled "Swap OUT (to Disk)" for VM page 1 at the top of the right-hand pane. Notice that VM page 1 is indeed swapped out and appears in the disk pages section of the display.

8. Now, we try to swap in VM page 0 again. Press the button labeled "Swap IN (to Memory)" for VM page 0 at the top of the right-hand pane again. This time, it works and the page appears back in physical memory—but not in its original place—the contents are still for page 0, but this time, the page is mapped as physical page 1. This is a very important point to note: The system needs to keep a mapping of the ordering of the pages and this is done by the fact that the page is still numbered as VM page 0. The frame table for application 1 confirms that it is using page 0 (as well as pages 1, 2, 3, and 4). Note also that as soon as the page reappears in physical memory, the application is able to access it and the "A" is finally changed to the "@" you typed.

The screenshot below shows what you should see after step 8 has been completed.

ACTIVITY R2 USING THE OPERATING SYSTEMS WORKBENCH TO EXPLORE THE BASICS OF MEMORY MANAGEMENT AND VM—Cont'd

Expected Outcome for Part 2

You should be able to see how the VM pages have been moved between physical memory and disk as necessary to make more storage available than the actual amount of physical memory in the system and to enable the application to access any of the pages when necessary. Note that steps 6-8 were separated for the purpose of exploration of the VM system behavior, but in actual systems, these are carried out automatically by the VM component of the operating system.

Reflection

It is important to realize that in this activity, we have played the role of the operating system by choosing which page to swap out on two occasions: first, to create additional space in the physical memory and, second, to reload a specific swapped out page that we needed to access. In real systems, the operating system must automatically decide which page to swap out. This is achieved using page replacement algorithms that are based on keeping track of page accesses and selecting a page that is not expected to be needed in the short term, on a basis such as it being either the Least Recently Used or Least Frequently Used page.

Further Exploration

VM is one of the more complex functions of operating systems and can be quite difficult to appreciate from a purely theoretical approach. Make sure you understand what has happened in this activity, the VM mechanism by which it was achieved, and the specific challenges that such a mechanism must deal with. Carry out further experiments with the simulation model as necessary to ensure that the concept is clear to you.

Figure 4.9 shows the VM manager behavior as the process makes various memory page requests during Activity R2. Part (a) depicts the first four memory page allocation requests, which are all granted. Part (b) shows that the fifth memory page request causes an allocation error (all RAM is in use). Part (c) shows how VM page 0 is swapped out to free RAM page 0, which is then allocated to the requesting process (as VM page 4); this coincides with the end of part 1 of Activity R2. Part (d) shows

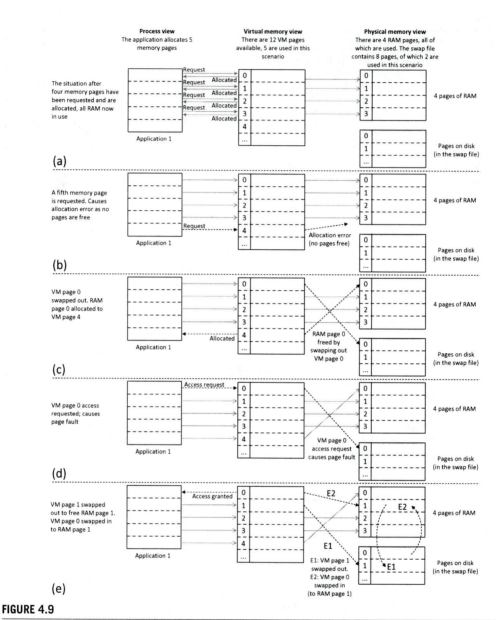

FIGURE 4.9

Illustration of VM manager behavior during Activity R2.

that when VM page 0 is subsequently requested by the process, it causes a page fault (the page is not currently in RAM). Part (e) shows the steps required to swap in VM page 0 so that the process can access it. E1: VM page 1 was swapped out (from RAM page 1) to disk page 1 (because initially, VM page 0 occupied disk page 0 so disk page 1 was the next available). This frees RAM page 1. E2: VM page 0 was then swapped in to RAM page 1, so it is accessible by the process. This reflects the state of the system at the end of part 2 of Activity R2.

4.5 RESOURCE MANAGEMENT

4.5.1 STATIC VERSUS DYNAMIC ALLOCATION OF PRIVATE MEMORY RESOURCES

Memory can be allocated to a process in two ways. Static memory allocation is performed when a process is created, based directly on the declarations of variables in the code. For example, if an array of 20 characters is declared in the code, then a block of 20 bytes will be reserved in the process' memory image and all references to that array will be directed to that 20-byte block. Static memory allocation is inherently safe because by definition, the amount of memory needed does not change as the process is running.

However, there are situations where the developer (i.e., at design time) cannot know precisely how much memory will be needed when a program runs. This typically arises because of the run-time context of the program, which can lead to different behaviors on each execution instance. For example, consider a game application in which the server stores a list of active players' details. Data stored about each player may comprise name, high score, ratio of games lost to games won, etc.; perhaps a total of 200 bytes per player, held in the form of a structure. The designer of this game might wish to allow the server to handle any number of players, without having a fixed limit, so how is the memory allocation performed?

There are two approaches that can be used. One is to imagine the largest possible number of players that could exist, to add a few extra for luck, and then to statically allocate an array to hold this number of player details structures. This approach is unattractive for two reasons: Firstly, a large amount of memory is allocated always, even if only a fraction of it is actually used, and secondly, ultimately, there is still a limit to the number of players that can be supported.

The other approach that is generally more appropriate in this situation is to use dynamic memory allocation. This approach enables an application to request additional memory while the program is running. Most languages have a dynamic memory allocation mechanism, often invoked with an allocation method such as malloc() in C or by using a special operator such as "new" to request that enough memory for a particular object is allocated. Using this approach, it is possible to request exactly the right amount of memory as and when needed. When a specific object that has been allocated memory is no longer needed, the memory can be released back to the available pool. C uses the free() function, while C++ has a "delete" operator for this purpose. In some languages such as C# and Java, the freeing of dynamically allocated memory is performed automatically when the associated object is no longer needed; this is generically termed "garbage collection" (Figure 4.10)

This approach works very well in applications in which it is easy to identify all of the places in the code and the logical flows through that code, where the objects are created and where the objects need to be destroyed.

However, in programs with complex logic or in which the behavior is dependent on contextual factors leading to many different possible paths through the code, it can be difficult to determine where in the code to allocate and release memory for objects. This can lead to several types of problem, which include the following:

- An object is destroyed prematurely, and subsequently, an access to the object is attempted causing a memory-access violation.
- Objects are dynamically created in a loop that does not terminate properly, thus causing spiraling memory allocation that will ultimately reach the limit that the operating system will allow, leading to an out-of-memory error.

Dynamic memory allocation of a 100 byte character buffer

Common to all languages illustrated
         int iSize = 100;   *// Required size of the buffer, value can be set dynamically as necessary*

C   char * MyBuffer;   *// A pointer of type char*
          MyBuffer = (char *)malloc(iSize);   *// Allocate 100 bytes of memory and set the MyBuffer pointer to point to it*

C++   char * MyBuffer;   *// A pointer of type char*
          MyBuffer = new char[iSize];   *// Allocate 100 bytes of memory and set the MyBuffer pointer to point to it*

C#   char[] MyBuffer;   *// An array of type char*
          MyBuffer = new char[iSize];   *// Allocate 100 bytes of memory to the MyBuffer array*

Java   char[] MyBuffer;   *// An array of type char*
          MyBuffer = new char[iSize];   *// Allocate 100 bytes of memory to the MyBuffer array*

Releasing dynamically allocated memory
C   free(MyBuffer);
C++   delete[]MyBuffer;
C#
Java   ⎱─Automatically performed by the garbage collector when the object is no longer in use

FIGURE 4.10

Dynamic memory allocation of a character array (compare with the static allocation code shown in Figure 4.1).

- Objects are created over time, but due to varying paths through the code, some do not get deleted; this leads to an increasing memory usage over time. This is called a "memory leak" as the system gradually "loses" available memory.

These types of problem can be particularly difficult to locate in the code, as they can arise from the run-time sequence of calls to parts of the code which are individually correct; it is the actual sequence of calls to the object creation and object deletion code that is erroneous, and this can be difficult to find with design-time test approaches. These types of problem can ultimately lead to the program crashing after it has been running for some period of time, and the actual behavior at the point of crashing can be different each time, therefore making detection of the cause even harder.

For these reasons, the use of dynamic memory allocation should be treated with utmost respect and care by developers and is perhaps the most important aspect of program design from a memory-resource viewpoint. Figure 4.11 illustrates some common dynamic memory allocation patterns.

Common dynamic memory allocation and deallocation sequences are illustrated in Figure 4.11. The scenarios are kept simple for the purpose of clarity and are intended to show general common patterns that arise rather than specific detailed instances. It is clear that if the common mistakes shown can occur in simple cases, there is considerable scope for these problems in larger, complex code with many contextual branches and loops and many function call levels and thus very large numbers of possible logical paths. Therefore, these problems can be very difficult to locate, and it is better to prevent them through high vigilance and rigor in the design and testing stages of development. For the specific patterns shown: (a) is the simplest correct case; (b) illustrates a more complex yet correct scenario; (c) causes a memory leak, but the program logic itself will work; (d) can cause an access violation as it is possible to attempt to access unallocated memory, depending on which branch is followed; (e) causes an access violation because there is an attempt to access memory after it has been de-allocated; (f) causes a behavior to arise that is highly dependent on the loop characteristics—it causes a memory leak, and if the loop runs a large number of times, the program may crash due to memory allocation failure, having exhausted the memory availability limits; (g) is representative of a wide variety of situations with complex

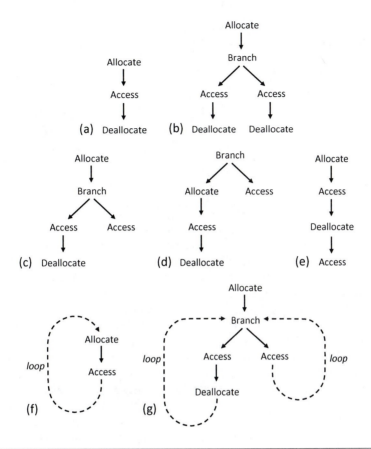

FIGURE 4.11

Dynamic memory allocation and deallocation. Examples of correct sequences and some simplified illustrations of common mistakes.

logical paths, where some paths follow the allocation and access rules of dynamic memory allocation correctly and some do not. In this specific scenario, one branch through the code de-allocates memory that could be subsequently accessed in another branch. In large software systems, this sort of problem can be very complex to track down, as it can be difficult to replicate a particular fault that may only arise if a certain sequence of branches, function calls, loop iterations, etc. occurs.

4.5.2 SHARED RESOURCES

Shared resources must be managed in such a way that the system remains consistent despite several processes reading and updating the resource value. This means that while one process (or thread) is accessing the resource, there must be some restriction on access by other processes (or threads). Note that if all accesses are reads, then there is no problem with consistency because the resource value cannot change. However, even if only some accesses involve writes (i.e., changing the value), then care must be taken to control accesses to maintain consistency.

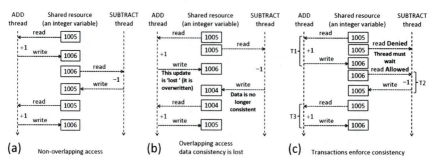

FIGURE 4.12

The problem of lost updates.

One way in which a system can become inconsistent is when a process uses an out-of-date value of a variable as the basis of a computation and subsequently writes back a new (but now erroneous) value. The lost update problem describes a way in which this can occur.

Figure 4.12 illustrates the problem of lost updates. The three parts to the figure all represent a scenario in which two threads update a single shared variable. To keep the example simple, one thread just increments the variable's value, and the other thread just decrements the variable's value. Thus, if equal numbers of events occur in each thread, the resulting value should be the same as its starting value. Part (a) shows an ideal situation (that cannot be guaranteed) where two or more processes access a shared resource in an unregulated way without an overlap ever occurring in their access pattern; in such a scenario, the system remains consistent. Part (b) shows how it is possible for the accesses to overlap. In such a case, it is possible that one process overwrites the updates performed by the other process, hence the term "lost update." In this example, the ADD thread reads the value and adds one to it, but while this is happening, the SUBTRACT thread reads the original value and subtracts one from it. Whichever thread writes its update last overwrites the other thread's update, and the data become inconsistent. In this specific case, one thread adds 1 and one thread subtracts 1, so the value after these two events should be back to where it started. However, you can see that the resulting value is actually one less than it should be. The third event, on the ADD thread, does not actually overlap any other accesses, but the data are already inconsistent before this event starts.

To put this "lost update" concept into the context of a distributed application, consider a banking system in which the in-branch computer systems and automatic teller machines (ATM) are all part of a large complex distributed system. The ADD thread could represent someone making a deposit in a branch to a joint account, while at the same time, the SUBTRACT thread represents the other account holder making a withdrawal from an ATM. In an unregulated-access scheme, the two events could overlap as in part (b) of Figure 4.12 depending on the exact timing of the events and the various delays in the system; one of the events could overwrite the effect of the other. This means that either the bank or the account holders lose money!

4.5.3 TRANSACTIONS

The lost update problem illustrates the need to use special mechanisms to ensure that system resources remain consistent. Transactions are a popular way of achieving this by protecting a group of related accesses to a resource by a particular process from interference arising from accesses by other processes.

The transaction is a mechanism that provides structure to resource access. In overview, it works as follows: When a process requests access to a resource, a check is performed to make sure that the resource is not already engaged in an on-going transaction. If so, the new request must wait. Otherwise, a new transaction is started (preventing access to the resource by other processes). The requesting process then makes one or more accesses that can be read or written in any order, until it is finished with the resource, and the transaction is then terminated and the resource is released.

To ensure that transactions are implemented robustly and provide the appropriate level of protection, there are four criteria that must be met:

Atomicity. The term atomic is used here to imply that transactions must be indivisible. A transaction must be carried out in its entirety, or if any single part of it cannot be completed or fails, then none of it must be completed. If a transaction is in progress and then a situation arises that prevents it from completing, all changes that have been made must be rolled back so that the system is left in the same consistent state as it was originally, before the transaction began.

Consistency. Before a transaction begins, the system is in a certain stable state. The transaction moves the system from one stable state to another. For example, if an amount of money is transferred from one bank account to another, then both the deduction of the sum from one account and the addition of the sum to the other account must be carried out, or if either fails, then neither must be carried out. In this way, money cannot be "created" by the transaction (such as if the addition took place but the deduction did not) or "lost" (such as if the deduction took place but not the addition). In all cases, the total amount of money in the system remains constant.

Isolation. Internally, a transaction may have several stages of computation and may write temporary results (also called "partial" results). For example, consider a "calculate net interest" function in a banking application. The first step might be to add interest at the gross rate (say 5%), so the new balance increases by 5% (this is a partial result, as the transaction is not yet complete). The second step might be to take off the tax due on the interest (say at 20%). The net gain on the account in this particular case should be 4%. Only the final value should be accessible. The partial result, if visible, would lead to errors and inconsistencies in the system. Isolation is the requirement that the partial results are not visible outside of the transaction, so that transactions cannot interfere with one another.

Durability. Once a transaction has completed, the results should be made permanent. This means that the result must be written to nonvolatile secondary storage, such as a file on a hard disk.

These four criteria are collectively referred to as the ACID properties of transactions.

Transactions are revisited in greater depth in Chapter 6 (Section 6.2.4); here, the emphasis is on the need to protect the resource itself rather than the detailed operation of transactions.

Part (c) of Figure 4.12 illustrates how the use of transactions can prevent lost updates and thus ensure consistency. The important difference between part (b) and part (c) of the figure is that (in part (c)) when the ADD thread's activity is wrapped in a transaction T1, the SUBTRACT thread's transaction T2 is forced to wait until T1 has completed. Thus, T2 cannot begin until the shared resource is stable and consistent.

4.5.4 LOCKS

Fundamentally, a lock is the simple idea of marking a resource as being in-use and thus not available to other processes. Locks are used within transactions but can also be used as a mechanism in their own right. A transaction mechanism places lock activities into a structured scheme that ensures that the resource is first locked, then one or more accesses occur, and then the resource is released.

Locks can apply to read operations, write operations, or read and write operations. Locks must be used carefully as they have the effect of serializing accesses to resources; that is, they inhibit concurrency. A performance problem arises if processes that hold locks on resources do not release them promptly after they finish using the resource. If all accesses are read-only, then the lock is an encumbrance that does not actually have any benefit.

Some applications lock resources at a finer granularity than others. For example, some databases lock an entire table during access by a process, while others lock only the rows of the table being accessed, which enhances concurrency transparency because other processes can access the remainder of the table while the original access activity is ongoing.

Activity R3 explores the need for and behavior of locks and the timing within transactions of when locks are applied and released.

ACTIVITY R3 USING THE OPERATING SYSTEMS WORKBENCH TO EXPLORE THE NEED FOR LOCKS AND THE TIMING WITHIN TRANSACTIONS OF WHEN LOCKS ARE APPLIED AND RELEASED

Prerequisite
Download the Operating Systems Workbench and the supporting documentation from the book's supplementary materials website.

Read the document "Threads (Threads and Locks) Activities and Experiments."

Learning Outcomes
1. To gain an understanding of the concept of a transaction
2. To understand the meaning of "lost update"
3. To explore the need for and effect of locking
4. To explore how an appropriate locking regime prevents lost updates

This activity uses the "Threads and Locks" simulation provided by the Operating Systems Workbench. Two threads execute transactions that access a shared memory location.

Part 1: Run threads without locking to see the effect of lost updates.

Method
1. Press the "Reset data field" button and check that the value of the data field is initialized to 1000. Run the ADD thread by clicking the "Start ADD Thread" button. This will carry out 1000 transactions each time adding the value 1. Check if the end result is correct.
2. Now, run the SUBTRACT thread by clicking the "Start SUBTRACT Thread" button. This will carry out 1000 transactions each time subtracting the value 1. Check if the end result is correct (it should be back to the original value prior to step 1).
3. Press the "Reset data field" button again; check that the value of the data field is initialized to 1000. Without setting any locking (leave the selection as "No Locking"), run both threads concurrently by clicking the "Start both threads" button. This will carry out 1000 transactions of each thread. The threads run asynchronously (this concept has been discussed in Chapter 2). Each thread runs as fast as it is allowed, carrying out its particular action (so either adding or subtracting the value 1 from the data value). Check the end result—is it correct?

ACTIVITY R3 USING THE OPERATING SYSTEMS WORKBENCH TO EXPLORE THE NEED FOR LOCKS AND THE TIMING WITHIN TRANSACTIONS OF WHEN LOCKS ARE APPLIED AND RELEASED—Cont'd

The screenshot below provides an example of the behavior that occurs when the two threads are run concurrently without locking.

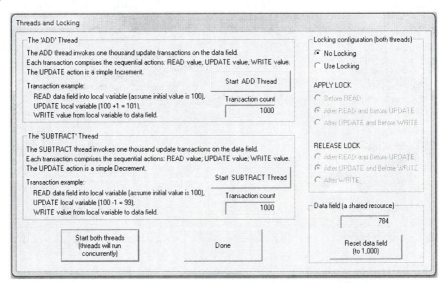

Expected Outcome

Overlapped (unprotected) access to the memory resource has led to lost updates, so that although each thread has carried out the same number of operations (which in this simulation are designed to cancel out), the end result is incorrect (it should be 1000).

Part 2: Using locks to prevent lost updates

Method

Experiment with different lock and release combinations to determine at which stage in the transaction the lock should be applied and at which stage it should be released to achieve correct isolation between transactions and thus prevent lost updates.

1. On the right-hand pane, select "Use Locking."
2. The transactions in the two threads each have three stages, during which they access the shared data field (Read, Update, and Write). The APPLY LOCK and RELEASE LOCK options refer to the point in the transaction at which the lock is applied and released, respectively. You should experiment with the APPLY and RELEASE options to determine which combination(s) prevents lost updates.

The second screenshot shows a combination of lock timing that results in complete isolation of the two threads' access to the memory resource, thus preventing lost updates.

ACTIVITY R3 USING THE OPERATING SYSTEMS WORKBENCH TO EXPLORE THE NEED FOR LOCKS AND THE TIMING WITHIN TRANSACTIONS OF WHEN LOCKS ARE APPLIED AND ELEASED—Cont'd

Threads and Locking

The 'ADD' Thread

The ADD thread invokes one thousand update transactions on the data field.
Each transaction comprises the sequential actions: READ value; UPDATE value; WRITE value.
The UPDATE action is a simple Increment.

Transaction example:

READ data field into local variable (assume initial value is 100).
UPDATE local variable (100 +1 = 101).
WRITE value from local variable to data field.

| Start ADD Thread |
| Transaction count |
| 1000 |

The 'SUBTRACT' Thread

The SUBTRACT thread invokes one thousand update transactions on the data field.
Each transaction comprises the sequential actions: READ value; UPDATE value; WRITE value.
The UPDATE action is a simple Decrement.

Transaction example:

READ data field into local variable (assume initial value is 100).
UPDATE local variable (100 -1 = 99).
WRITE value from local variable to data field.

| Start SUBTRACT Thread |
| Transaction count |
| 1000 |

Locking configuration (both threads)

○ No Locking
● Use Locking

APPLY LOCK

● Before READ
○ After READ and Before UPDATE
○ After UPDATE and Before WRITE

RELEASE LOCK

○ After READ and Before UPDATE
○ After UPDATE and Before WRITE
● After WRITE

Data field (a shared resource)

| 1000 |

| Start both threads (threads will run concurrently) | Done | Reset data field (to 1,000) |

Expected Outcome

Through experimentation with the various lock timing combinations, you should determine that the isolation requirements of transactions are only guaranteed when all accesses to the shared resource are protected by the lock. Even just allowing one thread to read the data variable before the lock is applied is problematic if the second thread then changes the value before releasing the lock so that the first thread can write its change (which is based on the previously read value). See the main text for full discussion of lost updates.

Reflection

This activity has illustrated the need for protection when multiple processes (or threads) access a shared resource. To ensure data consistency, the four ACID properties of transactions must be enforced (see main text for details).

4.5.5 DEADLOCK

Depending on the way in which resources are allocated and on which resources are already held by other processes, a specific problem called deadlock can arise in which a set of two or more processes are each waiting to use resources held by other processes in the set, and thus, none can proceed. Consider the situation where two processes P1 and P2 each require to use resources R1 and R2 in order to perform a particular computation. Suppose that P1 already holds R1 and requests R2 and that P2 already holds R2 and requests R1. If P1 continues to hold R1 while it waits for R2 and P2 continues to hold R2 while waiting for R1, then a deadlock occurs—that is, neither process can make progress because each requires a resource that the other is holding, and each will continue to hold the resource until it has made progress (i.e., used the resource in its awaited computation). The situation is permanent until one of the processes is removed from the system. Figure 4.13 illustrates this scenario.

For the system shown in Figure 4.13, a deadlock is possible. This is indicated by the fact that the arrows can be followed in a complete cycle. However, this does not mean that a deadlock will actually

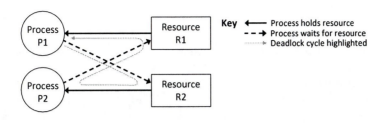

FIGURE 4.13

A deadlock cycle.

occur; it depends on the timing and ordering of the various resource requests. Specifically, there are four conditions that must hold simultaneously in order for a deadlock to occur; these are the following:

1. Mutual exclusion. Resources already held by processes are nonshareable; that is, the holding process has exclusive access to them. A process may hold one or more resources in this way.
2. Hold and wait. While holding at least one resource, a process waits for another resource (i.e., it does not release already held resources while waiting).
3. No preemption. Processes cannot be forced to release resources that they are holding; they can be held indefinitely.
4. Circular wait. A cycle is formed of two or more processes, each holding resources needed by the next one in the cycle. For example, Figure 4.13 shows a cycle where process P1 holds a resource R1 needed by process P2, which in turn holds a resource R2 needed by P1; hence, the cycle is complete.

If these four conditions hold, a deadlock occurs. The only way to resolve the situation is to stop (kill) one of the processes, which causes the resources it was holding to be released. Deadlock detection and resolution are additional roles within the resource allocation umbrella that the operating system should ideally perform. It is however the responsibility of application developers to understand the nature of deadlock and thus identify and avoid (to the extent possible) circumstances where it may occur.

Deadlock is explored in Activity R4, using the Deadlock simulation within the Operating Systems Workbench.

The occurrence of deadlock is sensitive to the relative timing of events, and there is usually a limited window of opportunity where a deadlock will actually occur, as the resource acquisition stages of transactions have to relate to the same set of resources and overlap in time. Identifying that a deadlock may occur does not actually mean that a deadlock will occur. The theoretical technique of cycle drawing is used to determine if a deadlock is possible, but this does not indicate actual probability of deadlock. The deadlock simulation allows exploration of the factors that affect the likelihood of a deadlock.

The deadlock simulation characteristics are described below. Note that the simulation user interface refers to threads, so the discussion below does for consistency. However, the deadlock simulation equally applies at the level of processes within a system, as it does at the level of threads within a process.

- The number of resources per transaction is one or more and chosen randomly up to the limit number that each thread is permitted to use (but also within the limit number of resources enabled in the simulation).
- The actual resources to be used in a particular transaction are chosen randomly from the set that is enabled.
- The resources are considered shared, so each thread makes its decision to use a resource independently of what the other thread is doing and what resources it is using.

- Threads acquire resources individually and lock them while waiting to acquire others (the **hold and wait** condition).
- Once all resources needed are held, the transaction begins. There is **no preemption**; held resources are only released at the end of the transaction.
- A resource is **used exclusively** by the thread that holds it.
- A **circular wait** develops if a thread is waiting for a resource held by another thread, which is itself waiting for a resource held by another thread in the same chain, such that a complete cycle forms. This is easy to see in the simulation because only two threads will be involved. In real systems, it is possible for cycles to involve more than two threads, and these of course can be complex in nature and difficult to detect.

ACTIVITY R4 USING THE OPERATING SYSTEMS WORKBENCH TO EXPLORE DEADLOCK DURING RESOURCE ALLOCATION

Prerequisite: Download the Operating Systems Workbench and the supporting documentation from the book's supplementary materials website.

Read the document "Deadlock—Activities and Experiments."

Learning Outcomes
1. To gain an understanding of the nature of deadlock
2. To explore the circumstances required for deadlock to occur
3. To explore factors that affect the likelihood of a deadlock

This activity uses the "Deadlock" simulation provided by the Operating Systems Workbench. Up to two threads are supported (the simulation applies conceptually to either threads or processes), which compete for up to 5 resources.

Part 1: Exploration of the nature of deadlock and the conditions under which it can occur

Method
1. Run the simulation with a single thread by clicking the top leftmost button entitled "Start Thread." Experiment with different numbers of resources, by enabling or disabling them with the column of buttons to the right of center. Using the radio buttons at top right, set the maximum number of resources each thread is permitted to use to 2. Does deadlock occur? Do your observations indicate that a deadlock can occur in these circumstances?
2. Repeat step 1 but this time using both threads and only a single resource. Does deadlock occur in this case?
3. Repeat step 1 again, now using both threads and two resources. Does deadlock occur in this case?

The screenshot below from step 3 of part 1 shows the situation when a deadlock has occurred.

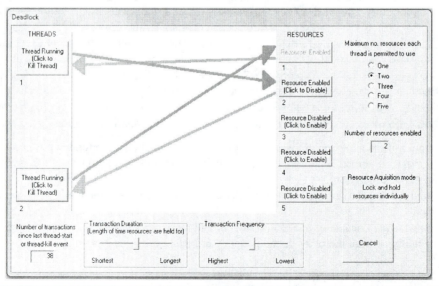

ACTIVITY R4 USING THE OPERATING SYSTEMS WORKBENCH TO EXPLORE DEADLOCK DURING RESOURCE ALLOCATION—Contd

Expected Outcome
A deadlock is detected by having a cycle in the resource allocation pattern. This is seen in the screenshot. You can see that thread 1 has acquired resource 1 (blue arrow) and is waiting for resource 2 (red arrow). At the same time, thread 2 has acquired resource 2 and is waiting for resource 1. The arrows form a directed cycle (i.e., the arrows all point in the same direction around the cycle). The only way to break this cycle is to kill one of the threads; this will cause the held resource to be released and thus the remaining thread will be granted access to it and can continue with its transaction.

Part 2: Exploration of factors that affect the likelihood of deadlock

In this part of the activity, you should explore different configurations of the simulation and observe how this affects the likelihood of deadlock. Use both threads for this part of the experiment. Initially change only one parameter at a time, as set out in the four steps below. Once you think you understand the circumstances that make deadlocks more or less likely, then try changing several parameters at the same time to confirm or reinforce your understanding.

1. Experiment with different numbers of resources available (enabled) for the two threads to use.
2. Experiment with different limits on the number of resources each thread is permitted to use simultaneously.
3. Experiment with different values of the transaction duration.
4. Experiment with different values of transaction frequency.

The screenshot below relates to part 2. It shows a scenario with five resources active but each process only using a maximum of two.

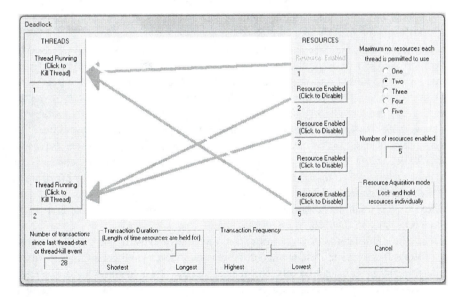

Expected Outcome
In part 2 of the activity, you should see that deadlock likelihood is affected by certain factors. For example, the longer a resource is held while acquiring others (use the "transaction duration" control to adjust this), the greater the window of opportunity for deadlock. The more resources a thread uses, the greater the opportunity for deadlock, while having more resources available for use dilutes the probability that the threads will each use the same set of resources (see the screenshot above as an example where two threads simultaneously use two resources each without conflict).

Reflection
Deadlock prevents threads continuing with their work and thus impacts on the performance of specific tasks and also on the robustness of systems themselves because deadlock resolution involves killing one of the threads that may then have

---

ACTIVITY R4 USING THE OPERATING SYSTEMS WORKBENCH TO EXPLORE DEADLOCK DURING RESOURCE ALLOCATION—Contd

to be restarted, depending on circumstances. Realization of the way in which deadlock can occur and the factors that affect its likelihood is important for the design of robust and efficient distributed systems.

Further exploration

Carry out further experiments with the deadlock simulation until you have a clear appreciation of the cause of deadlock and the factors, which increase its likelihood of occurrence.

4.5.6 REPLICATION OF RESOURCES

This section introduces the concept of replication of resources as it is important as part of the resource view of systems. Chapter 5 discusses replication in greater detail, including the semantics of replication, and provides an activity in which an example implementation of replication is explored. In addition, replication transparency is discussed in Chapter 6.

Having only a single copy of each resource in a distributed system is limiting in several ways. A key issue is the possibility of permanent loss of data. There is a risk that the resource will be lost; for example, if stored on a single hard disk, it is susceptible to a disk crash or physical damage to the host computer caused by fire or flood, for example, or even theft of the computer. If the only up-to-date copy of a resource is held temporarily in volatile memory such as RAM, it is susceptible to the computer being switched off or a momentary interruption to the power supply.

There is also a risk that shared access to a specific resource will become a performance bottleneck and may limit the usability or scalability of the system. For example, if the resource in question is a highly visited web page hosted on a single server, then the accessibility of the web page is limited by the processing throughput of the computer on which the server sits and also limited by the throughput of the network and of the connection to the computer. These limitations translate into a cap on the number of simultaneous users who can access the resource with an acceptable response time.

A further risk arises in terms of availability. If there is only a single copy of a specific resource, then its availability is dependent on every component in the chain of access working correctly simultaneously. If the computer on which the resource is hosted has an uptime of 98% (i.e., 2% of the time, it is unavailable because of system maintenance or failures) and the network connection to that computer has a reliability of 99%, then the resource is available for 97.02% of the time. That is, the entire chain of access has a reliability of $0.98 \times 0.99 = 0.9702$.

To overcome these limitations, it is common to replicate resources in distributed systems. This essentially means that there are multiple copies of the resource stored in different places within the system, thus enhancing robustness, availability, and access latency. The actual number of replicas and their dispersal within a system are system-specific issues that are highly dependent on the particular applications that use the resources. Managers of large commercial distributed applications such as banking, stock trading, and ecommerce will likely choose to ensure that the replicas are spread across multiple geographically spread sites to ensure disaster resilience (protection against such things as natural disasters, civil disturbance, and terrorism). Smaller-scale applications or applications owned by smaller organizations may hold replicas at the same site; but the system architecture should be designed to ensure that they are not on the same physical disk or host computer. The number of replicas should take account of the expected access rate, which in turn is related to the number of concurrent users expected.

The provision of replicas introduces two new main challenges. The first of these is consistency. Each copy of the resource must hold the same value. When one copy is updated, so too must all the other copies be. An application reading one copy of the resource should get the same value as if it were to read any other copy. Data consistency is in itself a major challenge in large-scale distributed systems, especially if multiple replicas can be write-accessed by applications and have their values changed simultaneously. To limit the extent of this challenge, it is possible to arrange that only one replica at any time can be written to, and all other copies support only read-only access. In this case, the problem is reduced to the need for timely propagation of value updates, from the read-write copy to the read-only copies.

The second main challenge introduced by replication is a special case of transparency requirements. Applications should be designed such that they access a (from their viewpoint) nonreplicated resource, for example, opening a file or updating a database. That is, the host system must provide the illusion of a single instance of the resource, regardless of whether it is replicated or not. The application behavior and its interface to the underlying system must not change because of the replication of one of the resources it uses. Instead, the replication must be managed within the (distributed) system. This form of transparency is termed replication transparency. Lack of this transparency would imply that the application had to be aware of the number of and location of replicas and to update each one directly.

The application developer should not need to be aware of replication; there should be no special actions required because a resource is replicated and no new primitives to use. The application developer should not know (or need to know) that a resource is replicated, how many replica instances exist, where they are located, or what the consistency management mechanism is.

Similarly, users of applications should not be aware of resource replication. A user should have the illusion that there is a single copy of each resource that is robustly maintained and always up-to-date. All details of how this is achieved should be completely hidden.

Consider, for example, your bank account value, which you quite likely access through an Internet online facility. You see a single value of your account balance, which should always be consistent, reflecting accurately the various financial transactions that have been carried out. The fact that in reality, the bank stores your bank account balance value on several computers, likely spread geographically, possibly even internationally, should be of no concern to you. The bank will have in place mechanisms to propagate updates so that replicas remain consistent and to manage recovery if one copy becomes corrupted or inaccessible, using the values of the other copies.

The need for timely propagation of updates to all replicas can be illustrated using the documents that contain the text for this book as a simple example. As I write, I keep copies of the document files on two different hard disks to avoid problems arising from a hardware fault on my computer and from accidental deletion by myself. There are always two copies of the work. In order for this to be effective, I use the copies on one specific drive as the working set and back up the files to the other disk on a regular basis, typically at the end of each couple-of-hour period that I have been working on the book. There are thus moments when the two copies are actually different and there is a risk of losing some work. In this situation, the update rate is chosen to reflect the risk involved. I can accept the risk of losing at most a couple of hours of work. Notice that the lost update problem also applies here. During moments when the copies are unsynchronized, if I accidentally open the older copy, add new material, and then save as the latest version, I will have overwritten some changes I had previously made.

4.6 **THE NETWORK AS A RESOURCE**
4.6.1 **NETWORK BANDWIDTH**

Bandwidth is the theoretical maximum transmission rate for a specific network technology and thus applies separately to each link in the network depending on which technology is involved. For example, Fast Ethernet has a bandwidth of 100 megabits per second. Bit time is the time taken to transmit a single bit. For any given technology, this value is a constant and is derived as the reciprocal of bandwidth. The bit time for Fast Ethernet is thus 10 ns (or 10^{-8} s). Throughput is the term used to describe the actual amount of data transmitted.

Network bandwidth will always be finite in a given system. Advances in technology means that over time, bit rates are increasing (so newer technologies support transmitting more data in a given amount of time) and infrastructure is becoming more reliable. However, improvements in network technology can barely keep up with the increasing demands from users to transmit ever more data.

Developments in other technologies also can lead to large increases in network traffic volumes; consider, for example, the improvements in digital camera technology in recent years. Image fidelity has improved from typically 1 megapixel (one million pixels per image) to cameras that produce images of 20 megapixels and more. The actual size of image files produced depends on the image coding and the data compression techniques used. The "True Color" encoding scheme uses 24 bits per pixel; 8 bits are used to represent each of the red, green, and blue components, providing 256 intensity values for each. Thus, before compression, some systems encode 3 bytes of data per pixel in the image. For a 20-megapixel image, this would give rise to a precompression file size of 60 MB. A very popular example of digital image compression is the Joint Photographic Experts Group (JPEG) scheme, which can achieve a compression factor of about 10:1 without noticeable degradation of image quality. Using JPEG, our 20-megapixel image is now reduced to 6 MB, which is still a significant amount of data to be transmitted across a network.

These devices are also increasingly abundant, a high-resolution digital camera is now cheap enough for many people to buy, and of course, other devices such as mobile phones and tablets contain cameras. The situation is further exacerbated by the fact that social networking has become extremely popular in the last couple of years and many people are continually uploading not only large amounts of data in the form of pictures but also other digital media such as sound and video that can represent much larger transfers than still images.[1] On top of all this, the total number of users and the proportion of their daily activities that involve "online" behavior of some sort or another are also increasing rapidly.

We can conclude from the trends in device technology to generate ever-larger data volumes and the trends in society to be ever more dependent on data communication that bandwidth will always be a precious resource that must be used efficiently. A large proportion of network performance problems are related to network bandwidth limitations. Bandwidth is typically shared among many traffic flows, so when we compute the time taken to transfer a certain amount of data over a particular network, based on the bandwidth of a specific link, we must keep in mind that we are calculating the best-case time. For example, if we wish to transmit a file of 100 MB over a 100 megabit per second link, we do the following sum:

---

[1] Video frame rates in digital cinema and TV are typically in the range 24-30 frames per second (FPS). Faster standards are emerging in line with advances in camera and display technology; these include 60 FPS for high-definition TV. Action video games use frame rates typically between 30 and 60 FPS, but some games exceed 100 FPS. Therefore, it is very important to consider the actual network bandwidth requirements of applications that transmit even short bursts of video. Compression of such data is vital.

$$100\text{million }(\text{bytes})\times 8(\text{convert to bits})/100\text{million bits per second}=8\text{s}.$$

So 8 s is the time required to transmit the file at the maximum possible rate, which assumes dedicated access to the link. The actual time to transfer the file depends on the actual share of the link that our application flow uses. In a busy network, the link the file may take considerably longer to transmit over the same link.

The situation is more complex when traversing a path through a network, which comprises several links that may have different bandwidths. In this case, the highest theoretical throughput end-to-end is limited by the slowest link bandwidth on the path.

Designers of distributed applications can never afford to be complacent with respect to the way they use bandwidth. For the reasons explained above, it is not realistic to assume that technological improvements over time (e.g., link speeds will be higher or routers will have faster forwarding rates) will lead to overall better performance as perceived by the users of any particular application.

There are several ways in which an application developer can ensure that their application is efficient with respect to network bandwidth, these fall into two categories: Firstly, minimize what is sent such that only essential communication takes place and, secondly, minimize the overheads of communication through careful selection and tuning of communication protocols.

4.6.1.1 Minimal Transmissions

In order to use network bandwidth effectively and to ensure that individual applications are efficient in their communication behavior, it is important that messages are kept as short as possible. Care should be taken when designing distributed applications to avoid transmission of redundant or unnecessary information. Only the minimum data fields necessary for correct operation should be transmitted; this may require having a number of different message structures for different scenarios within an application, especially where the range of message sizes varies greatly in the same application. The data fields themselves should be as small as possible to contain the necessary information. Messages should only be transmitted when needed and where periodic transmission is necessary; the rate of message transmission should be carefully optimized as a trade-off between timeliness of information update and communication efficiency. In some applications, it might be possible to perform aggregation of several messages at the sending side and transmit the resulting information at a significantly reduced rate. This is particularly relevant for sensor systems where data from sensors are often transmitted periodically. The rate of transmission needs to be aligned to the rate at which the actual sensed attribute changes. For example, the temperature in a residential room or office does not change significantly over a one second period but might do over a 1 min period. Thus, it might be appropriate to send update messages at 1 min intervals, especially if the data are used to control an air conditioning system. If, however, the purpose of measuring temperature is only for historical logging purposes, then it may be better to collect temperature samples every 1 min and aggregate the values of perhaps ten samples together into a single message that is sent every 10 min. The aggregation could be in the form of taking a single average value or by collecting the ten samples into a data array and sending them in a single message (note that in this latter case, the same amount of data is sent, but the amount of communication overhead is reduced). In contrast, if temperature is being sensed within a stage of a chemical process in a production facility, it may be necessary to sample temperate at high rates, perhaps at intervals of 100 ms. In such a scenario, the data may be safety related; it may indicate that a particular valve needs to be closed to prevent a dangerous situation developing. If this is the case, it is necessary to transmit each message immediately in its raw form.

4.6.1.2 Frame Size (Layer 2 Transmission)

Transmission errors (caused by electromagnetic interference, voltage glitches, and cross talk between conductors) impact at the level of individual bits. The probability of a single bit being corrupted by such errors is considered the same for all bits transmitted on a particular link, although some sources of interference occur in bursts and may affect several bits transmitted in a short time frame.

Short frames are less likely to be impacted by bit errors[2] than longer frames. This is because for a given bit error rate on a link, the probability of the error affecting a particular frame is directly proportional to the size of the frame.

For example, if the bit error rate is 10^{-6}, one bit error occurs, on average, every 1 million bits transmitted. For a frame of size 10^3 bits, the probability of suffering a bit error is $10^3/10^6 = 10^{-3}$, so there is a 1 in 1000 chance that a specific frame will be corrupted. The problem of a corrupted frame is resolved by retransmitting the entire frame; thus, the cost of each bit error is actually 1000 bits of transmission, and so, the overall cost of bit errors for this configuration is 1/1000th of the total resource. However, if the frame size is 10 times larger, fewer frames are sent per second, but the total number of bits transmitted is the same. In this case, the probability of a frame suffering a bit error is $10^4/10^6 = 10^{-2}$, so there is a 1 in 100 chance that a specific frame will be corrupted. Retransmitting the frame in this case costs 10,000 bits of transmission. The overall cost of bit errors for this configuration is thus 1/100th of the total resource.

The way in which a particular packet is divided into frames for transmission over a link carries an efficiency trade-off because each frame has a transmission overhead. Using fewer, larger frames translates into lower total overheads (in the absence of errors); however, smaller frames are cheaper to retransmit if affected by a bit error. Figure 4.14 illustrates this efficiency trade-off with an example based on Ethernet.

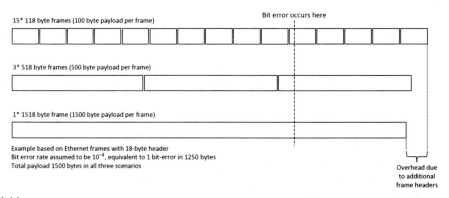

FIGURE 4.14

Frame size relationship with bit error rates.

---

[2] A bit error is where a single bit is transmitted as a "1" and is corrupted, for example, by electrical noise to appear at the receiver as a "0" (or vice versa). A single corrupted bit in a frame renders the entire frame unusable, and the network will "drop" (discard) it. Thus, either the frame must be transmitted again, which uses additional bandwidth and also adds delay to the overall message transmission time, or if it is a real-time data stream, the loss may be ignored (to avoid the delay imposed by its recovery), in which case its omission reduces the fidelity of the received data.

Figure 4.14 shows three scenarios for transmitting a 1500-byte (12,000 bit) payload over an Ethernet network in terms of the way it is divided into frames. The payload is the maximum size for a single Ethernet frame, and hence, one of the scenarios uses a single, maximum length frame. The other scenarios shown arise from dividing the payload into three and fifteen parts. The frame overhead (the Ethernet header) is 18 bytes. The figure shows the effect of the additional overhead when transmitting the same payload distributed over a higher number of smaller frames. Bit errors operate at the physical level and do not respect frame boundaries; that is, a bit error corrupts the current bit in transmission, regardless of which frame it belongs to. In the example, the bit error rate for the link is assumed to be 10^{-4}, which means that one bit error occurs on average for every 10,000 bits transmitted (this bit error rate value is used for the purpose of illustration; it would typically be much lower). The payload in this case is greater than 10,000 bits, so there is a high probability that a bit error will occur during its transmission. For the purpose of the example, a bit error is assumed to occur at the same bit position measured from the start of the first transmission, in all three scenarios. The frame that is in transmission when the bit error occurs becomes corrupted and must be retransmitted. Assuming that the retransmissions succeed with no further bit errors, then the true cost of the single bit error is an overhead of 100%, 33%, and 6.7% for the 1518-byte, 518-byte, and 118-byte frame size scenarios, respectively.

The susceptibility of larger frames to bit errors is one of the reasons why link technologies have upper limits on frame sizes; this tends to be in the region of a few hundred to a few thousand bytes. Shorter frames also have advantages in terms of achieving finer-grained multiplexing, thus enhancing the illusion of a dedicated circuit on shared links.

4.6.1.3 Packet Size (Layer 3 Transmission)

From a message transmission viewpoint, packets can be considered as an intermediary format mapping the content of an application-level message into frames. This is because during the encapsulation down, the protocol stack a message is divided into one or more packets, which are each then divided into one or more frames.

Each link in a network has a fixed maximum frame size and thus a maximum payload size within those frames. For a given specific link, the maximum transmission unit (MTU) determines the maximum size of packet that can be carried within a frame. This may be configured at routers up to the maximum frame payload size for the relevant link technology. For example, for Ethernet, the maximum MTU size is 1500 bytes.

With IPv4, packets are fragmented as necessary to fit within the MTU for each link and may get further fragmented by routers as they travel across the network. In IPv6, the sending node is required to determine the MTU for the entire end-to-end journey and to perform the fragmentation based on the determined MTU, such that no further fragmentation is necessary by intermediate routers.

Fragmentation is generally undesirable. Each packet has its own network-layer header, which contains, among other things, the IP address of the destination node that routers use to make packet-forwarding decisions. Each fragment of a packet must contain a modified copy of the original packet header, which indicates the original packet ID to which the fragment belongs and the offset of the fragment within the original packet (for reassembly purposes). Therefore, packet fragmentation and the subsequent reassembly introduce computational overhead at the involved devices. The reassembly process must wait for all fragments to arrive and thus can add latency to the delivery of the packet to the application. A set of smaller packets that avoid fragmentation is potentially more efficient than the equivalent number of fragments derived from a single larger packet.

4.6.1.4 Message Size (Upper Layers Transmission)

Careful design of distributed applications needs to include resource efficiency in terms of network bandwidth, which in turn improves scalability and performance transparency. This of course must be done such that the application's business logic requirements, and any timing constraints, are not affected.

A golden rule for network message design is "only send what is necessary." The communication design should in general aim to minimize message size. This ensures that the message is transmitted in less time, uses less resource, and contributes less to congestion. Large messages are divided into multiple packets, which are themselves spread across multiple frames, depending on their size. Each frame introduces additional overhead because it must have its own header containing MAC addresses and identification of the next higher-layer protocol. Similarly, each packet introduces additional overhead in terms of its header, which contains IP addresses and identification of the transport layer protocol.

It is important to realize that the effect of reducing message size is not linear in terms of the reduction in number of bits transmitted. Frames have a certain minimum size and some fixed overheads. A message that is increased in size by a single byte could lead to an additional frame being transmitted, while reduction by a single byte could actually save an entire frame. The Ethernet family of technologies is the most popular wired access-network technology and will be used to illustrate this point. To recap, Ethernet has a minimum frame size of 64 bytes, comprising an 18-byte header and a payload of 46 bytes. It also has a maximum frame size of 1518 bytes, in which case the payload is 1500 bytes.

If the message to be sent leads to a frame size of less than the 64-byte minimum, the additional bytes are padded. If we send a TCP protocol message (which typically has a 20-byte header), encapsulated in an IPv4 packet (typically a 20-byte header), then there is room for 6 bytes of data while still keeping within the minimum frame size. There are a few scenarios where this could be achieved, for example, where the message contains data from a single sensor, for example, a 16-bit temperature value, or is an acknowledgment of a previous message that contains no actual data. However, this accounts for a small fraction of all messages within distributed applications; in most cases, the minimum frame size will be exceeded. However, due to the variable payload size up to 1500 bytes, there are a large number of application scenarios where the message would fit into a single Ethernet frame.

The ideal situation would be where the application-level message is divided into a number of packets that each fit within the minimum frame MTU for the entire end-to-end route to their destination, thus avoiding packet fragmentation.

A developer cannot at design time know the link technologies that will be in place when the program actually runs. Therefore, the designer of a distributed application should always try to minimize the size of messages, with the general goal of making the network transmission more efficient but without certainty or precise control of this outcome.

In some applications, there may be choice as to whether to send a series of smaller messages or to aggregate and send a single longer message. There are trade-offs: shorter individual messages are better for responsiveness as they can be sent as soon as they are available, without additional latency. Combining the contents of smaller messages into a single larger message can translate into fewer actual frames, and thus, less bytes are actually transmitted.

Minimizing message size requires careful analysis of what data items are included in the message and how they are encoded. A specific scenario is used to illustrate this: consider an eCommerce application that includes in a query "Customer Age" represented as an integer value. When this is marshaled into the message buffer, it will take up 4 bytes (typically, this aspect depends somewhat on the actual

Type of data	Representation of data	Storage requirements	Efficiency saving compared to verbose form (bits,%)
Age	integer	4 bytes, 32 bits	none
	byte or char	1 byte, 8 bits	24 bits, 75%
	Optimized minimum	7-bits (range 0 –127)	25 bits, 78% (only if the 8th bit carries data)
Sex **(male / female)**	string, values {"male","female"} char, values {'m','f'}	6 byte array to hold 6 characters 1 byte	none 40 bits, 83%
	Optimized minimum	1-bit (range 0 –1) where 0 = male, 1 = female	47 bits, 98% (only if the other 7 bits carry data)
Age and Sex combined	Optimized minimum	1 byte 7-bits for Age, 1 bit for Sex	72 bits, 90%

Representation of Age and Sex data as a single byte. Example shown: a 51 year-old female

$$1\;0\;1\;1\;0\;0\;1\;1$$

Sex   Age

Efficient algorithm to perform encoding:

```
Start
    Move Age data to a single byte variable
    And with value 0x7F              // Ensure most significant bit is initialised as a '0'
    If Sex equals "female",
        Add the value 128 (0x80)      // Set the most significant bit
End
```

FIGURE 4.15

Examples of simple techniques to minimize data transmission length.

language and platform involved). However, some simple analysis is warranted here. Customer age will be never higher than 255, and thus, the field could be encoded as a single byte or character (char) data type, thus saving 3 bytes. If "Sex" is encoded as a string, it will require 6 characters so that it can hold the values "Male" or Female"; this could be reduced to a single byte if a Boolean value or a character field containing just M or F is used. I would suggest that we can go one step further here, if we consider that customer age cannot for all intents and purposes exceed 127; we can encode it as a 7-bit value and use the single remaining bit of the byte to signify male or female. This is just a simple illustration of how careful design of message content can reduce message sizes, without incurring noticeable computational overheads or complex compression algorithms. Of course, these can be used as well; however, if the data format has already been (near) optimized to maximize information efficiency, the compression algorithms will have a greatly reduced benefit (because they actually work by removing redundancy, which is already reduced by the simple techniques mentioned above). Figure 4.15 illustrates some simple techniques to minimize the size of the message to be transmitted across the network including, for the example given above, a simple and efficient algorithm to perform the encoding.

4.6.2 DATA COMPRESSION TECHNIQUES

To minimize network traffic generation by distributed applications, data compression should be considered where appropriate. This is only useful where there is sufficient redundancy in the transmitted data such that the saving in bandwidth is worth the additional processing cost associated with running the data compression and decompression algorithms and where the computer systems have sufficient processing power to perform the data compression suitably quickly.

The technique described in the section above compresses data on a context-aware basis and thus is highly application-specific and is performed as part of the designed-in behavior of the application itself. This is a very useful technique where opportunities present themselves to designers without making the design overcomplex.

There are also data compression techniques that are algorithmic and are applied to the data stream itself. Such algorithms target inefficiencies in coding schemes, reducing the transmitted data size by removing redundancy. The advantage of these techniques is that they do not require additional work on the part of the designer, although they do incur run-time overheads in terms of processing time. However, for most modern computer systems, the processing speed is significantly faster than network transmission speeds, and thus, compression has a net performance benefit as a result of the trade-off between processing time expended and the network latency saved. It is also important to minimize data transmissions to reduce network congestion.

4.6.2.1 Lossy Versus Lossless Compression

There are two fundamental classes of data compression technique: those that lose data and those that do not.

Lossy data compression removes some actual data but leaves enough remaining data for the compressed format to be still usable; however, it is not reversible. A classic example is the reduction of the resolution of an image. The lower-resolution image is still recognizable as the same picture, and thus, the data loss is a useful trade-off between image quality and file size.

An important example of where picture quality reduction is desirable is where they are displayed on web pages. The time taken to download images is directly related to the size of the image file. If the purpose of the transfer is only to display on the screen, then there is no point in transmitting an image that has greater resolution than the display screen itself. In general, a 12-megapixel image will not look any different to a 1-megapixel image when displayed on a screen with a resolution of 1 million pixels (which is equivalent to a grid of, e.g., 1000 pixels by 1000 pixels). However, the 12-megapixel version of the file would take a lot longer to download and contribute much more to the level of traffic on the network.

Actual data, such as financial data or text in a document, cannot be subjected to lossy data compression. It would be meaningless to just remove a few characters from each page of a document to reduce the file size, for example. Instead, lossless techniques must be used. The application-specific example in the section above is a simple form of lossless compression, as the information content is squeezed into a more efficient form of encoding, but with no loss of precision or accuracy.

4.6.2.2 Lossless Data Compression

Huffman coding provides an easy to understand example of lossless data compression. This technique uses a variable length code to represent the symbols contained in the data. It is necessary to perform a frequency analysis on the data to order the symbols in terms of their frequency of occurrence. The shorter code words are assigned to the symbols that occur more frequently in the data stream, and the longer code words are assigned to rarely occurring symbols. This could be performed for a single document or more generally for all documents written in a particular language.

For example, let us consider the English language. The most commonly occurring letters are E, T, A, and O, followed by I, N, S, R, and H, and then D, L, U, C, M, W, F, P, G, Y, and B. The infrequent letters are V, K, and J, and the rarest are X, Q, and Z. Based on this frequency analysis, we can expect that there will be more "E's," "T's," "A's" and "O's" (and thus, these should be allocated shorter codes) and few "Q's" and "Z's" (so these should be allocated longer code words).

The code words themselves must be carefully chosen. Since they are of variable length, once a string of code words has been compiled, there must be a way to decode the string back to its original symbols unambiguously. This requires that the receiving process knows the boundaries between the code words in the stream. Sending additional information to demark the boundaries between the code words would defeat the object of compression to minimize the amount of data transmitted, so the code words must be self-delimiting in terms of the boundaries.

To satisfy this requirement, the set of code words used in Huffman coding must have a special prefix property, which means that no word in the code is a prefix of any other word in the code. Without this requirement, when reading a particular code word, it would not be possible to know where the word ended; you could just keep reading into the next word without knowing. For example, if the word 101 was part of the code, then 1011 or in fact any other word beginning with 101 is not allowed. In the example given, the prefix rule would be broken because the code 101 would be a prefix of the code 1011.

A valid code set that exhibits the prefix property can be generated by using a binary tree, in which only leaf nodes are used as codes and nonleaf nodes are used to generate deeper layers of the tree. The tree is extensible to generate additional codes so long as some leafs remain unused for codes at each level. To limit the size of the tree for illustration purposes, imagine that we only need to represent the 26 letters of the alphabet plus the space character and a full stop; that is, we need a total of 28 codes. One way to achieve this is to use the binary tree shown in Figure 4.16 (this particular tree is not necessarily optimal; it is used only to illustrate the generation of a valid code set).

The binary tree shown in Figure 4.16 has been arranged to generate 28 codes in which none of the codes are the prefix of any other codes in the set. This is achieved by only using leaf nodes as code values and allowing specific branches to continue down the tree until sufficient codes have been generated. This tree is extensible because four nodes have been left unused at the lowest level.

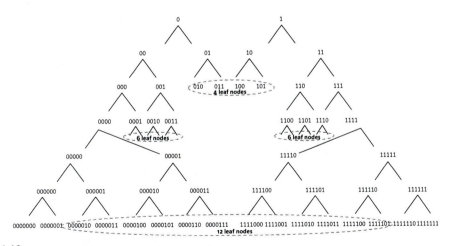

FIGURE 4.16

Binary tree to generate a 28-code set, which exhibits the prefix property.

Symbol	Code	Symbol	Code	Symbol	Code	Symbol	Code
Space	010	S	00101	C	11100	B	0000111
E	011	R	00110	M	11101	V	1111000
T	100	H	00111	W	0000010	K	1111001
A	101	Full-stop	11000	F	0000011	J	1111010
O	00010	D	11001	P	0000100	X	1111011
I	00011	L	11010	G	0000101	Q	1111100
N	00100	U	11011	Y	0000110	Z	1111101

FIGURE 4.17

The codes assigned to symbols in occurrence-frequency order.

The next step is to place the letters of the alphabet and the space and full stop into a table in occurrence-frequency order and to assign the codes to the letters such that the shortest codes are allocated to the most frequently occurring symbols, as shown in Figure 4.17.

Notice that the code assignment in Figure 4.17 gives 3-bit codes to the most frequent symbols and 7-bit codes to the least frequent symbols. If a fixed length code were used, it would need to be 5 bit in order to generate 28 codes (it would actually generate 32 codes). Based on the code assignment shown in Figure 4.17, you should be able to decode the following message without ambiguity:

1000011101101000001000011001100000110001111110110100000100001100001000001000110011000010

10000000110010111011011111001011001010100001110001001110100101000011011000

4.6.2.3 Lossy Data Compression

JPEG (a standard created by the JPEG, from which it takes its name) provides a well-known example of lossy compression, specifically for digital images. JPEG supports adjustment of the compression ratio, which translates into a trade-off between reducing the size of the image file and maintaining the quality of the image. A compression factor of about ten can be achieved without significant reduction in image quality. Once compressed, some of the original data are permanently lost. As with all lossy compression, it is not possible, starting with the compressed image, to recreate the original full quality image.

4.6.3 MESSAGE FORMAT

It is very important that the message is encoded by the sender in such a way that it can be decoded unambiguously by the receiver. For each field of data within the message, the receiver must know or be able to calculate the length and must know the data type.

Protocol data units (PDU) have been introduced in Chapter 3. To recap, a PDU is a message format definition that describes the content of a message in terms of a series of fields each with a name, an offset from the start of the message, and a length. This is important to facilitate the sender and receiver of a message synchronizing on the meaning and value of each field in a message. Protocol-level PDUs have specific names depending on the level of the protocol in the stack. Data link-layer PDUs are called frames, while network-layer PDUs are called packets, for example.

4.6.3.1 Fixed Versus Variable-Length Fields

The fields within a network message can have fixed or variable length. Fixed length is preferable generally because the boundaries between fields are determined at design time, simplifying aspects of the program logic that deal with messages, especially at the receiving side. Fixed-length fields also reduce the range of errors that can occur when populating fields with data and thus simplify testing. One further benefit of having the length of each field fixed is that the message itself has a fixed length, and thus, buffer memory allocation is simplified. In contrast, variable-length fields introduce the challenge (in the message receiver) of determining where one field ends and the next begins. If one or more fields have variable length, then the message itself has variable length making buffer memory allocation complex, especially at the receiver side as the buffer must be large enough to hold any message that arrives.

Variable-length fields are useful where there can be large variations in the actual length of message contents. However, because the data have a variable length, there needs to be an unambiguous means of determining the length of the field, at the receiving side. This is necessary both in interpreting the data in the field and in order to know where the next field begins. This can be achieved by either adding an additional field-length field or using an end-of-field termination character. Of these, the separate length field can be easier to implement but may require more bytes in the message. The end-of-field terminator must be a character or sequence of characters that cannot occur in the data part. The numerical value 0 (the ASCII NULL character) is often used (not to be confused with the character "0," which has the ASCII code value 48). If data are ASCII-encoded, then the NULL character should not occur in normal text. In the specific case where an ASCII-encoded string is terminated with a numerical zero, the string is termed an ASCIIZ string.

The termination character approach requires additional processing to check through the field data until the end character or sequence is found. For variable-length fields where the field-data length has low variability, the additional design complexity combined with the processing overheads may outweigh the benefits.

Figure 4.18 shows three possible ways of representing the same three data fields. Each has some relative advantages and disadvantages. For example, the fixed-length field has the advantage of a simple fixed structure requiring no additional information or associated processing to describe the data. However, the field must be large enough to contain all possible values of the data, which can be very inefficient in highly variable data. Providing a separate length indicator solves the problem of having variable-length fields, but if the number is an integer, it adds two bytes (for an INT_16) and four bytes (for an INT_32) of overhead for each field and requires additional processing at both sender and

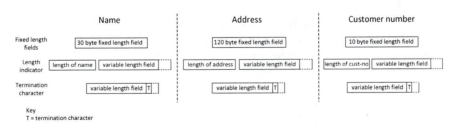

FIGURE 4.18

Comparison of different data representations: fixed-length fields, variable-length data with separate length indicator field, and variable-length data with termination character.

receiver. The ASCIIZ representation is a well-known format that uses a termination character. It is an efficient way of representing variable-length data within a process but is far less convenient when used in a message because in addition to the individual fields being variable, the message length itself is variable, and the only way to determine the length is to read each field until the terminator is reached, to count the bytes, and to repeat until all the fields have been accounted.

In summary, there is no single approach that will be *ideal* for all circumstances, but in a network-message context, fixed-length fields and thus fixed length messages are far easier to serialize and de-serialize (see next section). As such, in any application where message field sizes tend to be generally short, I prefer to use fixed-length fields exclusively, thus trading some efficiency to achieve greater simplicity both in terms of code development and more significantly in terms of testing effort (because the size of all messages sent is preknown and thus the buffers can be allocated such that a message is guaranteed to fit within).

Fixed-length fields can be achieved using a single char array or byte array for the whole message and indexing into this as required, with specific index positions having specific meanings. A more flexible way to implement fixed-length fields is to define a structure to contain the message, which itself has a set of fixed-length data items. This predefined message format must be identified at both sender and receiver.

From a practical perspective, when developing in C or C++, it is ideal to place the message structure definition in a header file shared across both client and server projects; an example of this is provided in Figure 4.37 in a later section.

4.6.3.2 Application-Level PDUs

An application that sits above the network protocols, that is, uses the protocols in the stack to communicate application-specific messages across the network, will need to have one or more defined message formats. These message formats can be called application-level PDUs (this signifies that they are PDUs specific to the particular application and not defined universally in standards documents as are the protocol PDUs). Consider the case study application, the networked game of Tic-Tac-Toe; there will be a number of different messages, each sent either by a client to the server or by the server to one of the clients. Whichever part of the application receives the message must be able to interpret the message and extract the various fields of data back into the exact same form as they were held in at the sender prior to transmission.

4.6.4 SERIALIZATION

In the context of communication in distributed systems, serialization is the process of converting a structure or object into a linear byte format suitable for storing in a buffer and subsequently transmitting across a network. On receipt, the receiver will store the serialized data temporarily in a buffer and then deserialize it back into its native format. Serialization is also known as flattening, marshaling, and pickling.

In keeping with the game case study theme, consider the format of a message a game server could send to a game client to inform it of the current player scores; this is illustrated in Figure 4.19.

Figure 4.19 shows a group of data variables relating to current game state, comprising the name and score of each of the players, to be transmitted by the game server as a single message. We can represent this data in the form of a structure, which can simplify the program logic and thus the coding. The C++-equivalent structure is shown in Figure 4.20.

Variable name	Data type	Data field length
PlayerName	Characters	20 characters (20 bytes)
iPlayerScore	Integer	Single integer (4 bytes)
cOpponentName	Characters	20 characters (20 bytes)
iOpponentScore	Integer	Single integer (4 bytes)

(a) The intended message content, held as a structure or discrete data variables

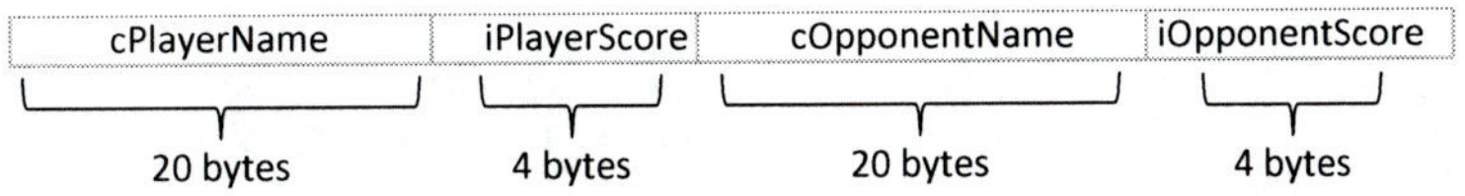

cPlayerName	iPlayerScore	cOpponentName	iOpponentScore
20 bytes	4 bytes	20 bytes	4 bytes

(b)   The serialised equivalent message held in a sequential buffer

FIGURE 4.19

The concept of serialization, mapping data variables onto a sequential memory buffer.

```
struct Score_message {
        char   cPlayerName[20];
        int    iPlayerScore;
        char   cOpponentName[20];
        int    iOpponentScore;
};
```

FIGURE 4.20

C++ structure holding game state information.

The C++ structure shown in Figure 4.20 contains only fixed-length fields, and thus, the structure itself has a fixed size. It will also be held in contiguous memory. These characteristics greatly simplify the serialization process. In C++, it is possible to use the structure memory directly as the buffer itself; a pointer to the start of the structure can be cast as a character array, and thus, the buffer is simply an overlay over the same memory that the structure occupies, without actually moving any data or changing any data types. The pointer and the size of the data structure (which is also the length of the buffer) are passed to the send primitive, and the message contents are transmitted as a stream of bytes, without the sending mechanism having to know the format or meaning of the individual bytes (see Figure 4.21).

In some languages, serialization is not so straightforward, requiring the use of special keywords and/or methods that invoke mechanisms to perform the serialization, for example, in C# where the memory allocation is usually automatically managed and not under direct control of the programmer. In this regard, C# requires that the structure fields are allocated sequentially in memory (hence the use of "StructLayout(LayoutKind.Sequential)" in the example in Figure 4.22). The Marshal class provides methods for allocating and copying unmanaged memory blocks and converting between managed and unmanaged memory types. Python has "marshal," which is a bare-bones serialization module, and "pickle," which is a smarter alternative. Java requires that any class that is to be serialized "implements" java.io.Serializable. The ObjectOutputStream class is used to perform the actual serialization of the object.

C# automatically manages memory and uses dynamic memory allocation when creating certain data objects, including strings. This means that a programmer is not by default in complete control of the size of such objects. Also, because of the automatic memory management and the fact that strings may be extended dynamically, the various fields of a structure are not held in a contiguous block of

```
// Create a new instance of the data structure
struct Score_message Message;

// Populate the structure fields with data values
strcpy(Message.cPlayerName, LocalPlayerName);
Message.iPlayerScore = LocalPlayerScore;
strcpy(Message.cOpponentName, OpponentPlayerName);
Message.iOpponentScore = OpponentScore;

// Send the message (the structure IS the message data that is sent)
int iBytesSent = send( iSocket, (char*) &Message, sizeof(Message), 0 );
if(SOCKET_ERROR == iBytesSent)
{
        MessageBox("Send failed","Game Client");
}
```

FIGURE 4.21

Serialization of a structure in C++ using a pointer and type cast (shown bold).

```
[StructLayout(LayoutKind.Sequential)]           // Enforce sequential layout of the structure's fields, in the order
                                                // stated in the code (necessary for subsequent serialisation)
public struct Score_message
{
    // In preparation for when the structure is serialised it is necessary to enforce
    // the size and type of non-fixed length variables using MarshalAs()
    [MarshalAs(UnmanagedType.ByValTStr, SizeConst = 20)]
    public string sPlayerName;                  // Set the field size to 20 bytes

    public int iPlayerScore;                    // This field is already fixed length, no change needed

    [MarshalAs(UnmanagedType.ByValTStr, SizeConst = 20)]
    public string sOpponentName;                // Set the field size to 20 bytes

    public int iOpponentScore;                  // Fixed length (see above)
};
```

FIGURE 4.22

C# serializable structure holding game state information (compare with the C++ version in Figure 4.20).

memory. Thus, special mechanisms are needed to perform serialization. Firstly, a special mechanism (MarshalAs) is used to fix the size of strings within the structure; see Figure 4.22. Secondly, a serialization method is needed (Figure 4.23), which collects the various data fields into a continuous buffer format (a byte array) necessary for sending as a network message.

Serialization is performed in the sending process, prior to the message being sent across the network. Upon receipt, the message will be placed into a message buffer, which is a flat byte array, prior to deserialization to recreate the original data structure so that the various fields of the message can be accessed. In C++, a similar technique of pointer casting (as was used for serialization) can be used to achieve this without actually moving the memory contents. For C#, deserialization is more complex due to the use of managed memory (as with serialization discussed above). An example C# deserialize method is provided in Figure 4.24.

In summary of this section, Figures 4.21 and 4.23 provide two quite different ways of performing serialization in order to show the variety of techniques used. The C++ technique shown is very simple

```
private byte[] Serialize(Object myObject)
{
    // Converts any object into a byte array which is sequential and contiguous

    int iObjectSize = Marshal.SizeOf(myObject);           // Determine the size of the object

    IntPtr ptr = Marshal.AllocHGlobal(iObjectSize);       //Allocate the required amount of unmanaged memory to hold the object

    Marshal.StructureToPtr(myObject, ptr, false);          //Copy the object's bytes into the allocated unmanaged memory

    byte[] MessageBuffer = new byte[iObjectSize];          //Create the message buffer byte array (this will be the returned parameter)

    Marshal.Copy(ptr, MessageBuffer, 0, iObjectSize);     //Copy the content of the allocated unmanaged memory into the byte array

    Marshal.FreeHGlobal(ptr);                              //Free the unmanaged memory

    return MessageBuffer;                                  //Return the byte array (will be subsequently passed to the send primitive)
}
```

FIGURE 4.23

A C# method to serialize an object into a byte array.

```
public Score_message DeSerialize(byte[] ReceivedBuffer)
{
        //Converts a byte array (e.g. a received message) to a Score_message structure

        IntPtr ptr = Marshal.AllocHGlobal(ReceivedBuffer.Length);        //Allocate unmanaged memory

         //Copy the received message to the unmanaged memory
        Marshal.Copy(ReceivedBuffer, 0, ptr, ReceivedBuffer.Length);

        //DeSerialize the unmanaged memory contents to recreate the Score_message structure
        Score_message MyScoreMessage = (Score_message) Marshal.PtrToStructure(ptr, typeof(Score_message));

        Marshal.FreeHGlobal(ptr);                                        //Free the unmanaged memory

        return MyScoreMessage;
}
```

FIGURE 4.24

A C# method to deserialize (recreate) an object from a byte array.

fundamentally because the original data structure contains only fixed-length fields and thus it itself is a held in a fixed-length block of memory. In this case, the serialization is simply performed by treating the structure as a buffer, identified by its starting address and length. In contrast, in C#, special methods are required to perform serialization and deserialization principally because of the automatic management of memory allocation.

4.6.5 THE NETWORK AS A SERIES OF LINKS

First, we very briefly define the terms used to describe the various components of a network. A physical connection between two points in a system is called a link. A collection of such links is called a network. A particular path from one point in the network to another, possibly traversing several links, is called a route. The devices that are placed within the network, at the interconnection points, and responsible for finding routes are called routers.

Of particular interest to this discussion are the lower layers, especially the data link layer and the network layer. As their names suggest, these deal with passing data across links and networks,

Layer	Devices	PDU	Address type
Application		Data	URL
Presentation		Data	
Session		Data	
Transport		Segment	Port
Network	Router	Packet	IP (logical)
Data link	Switch, bridge, network adapter	Frame	Media access control (physical)
Physical	hub, repeater, network adapter, line driver, wireless access point	Bit stream	

FIGURE 4.25

Network devices, PDUs, and address types related to the layers of the OSI network model.

respectively. The data link layer operates on a single-link basis, transmitting data in a format called a frame to the point at the other end of the link. The data link-layer behavior and the frame format used are technology-specific, so they, for example, are different in Fast Ethernet and the IEEE 802.11 wireless LAN technologies. The network layer on the other hand is concerned with finding a route through the network comprising a series of links. This layer works independently of the actual link technologies; it is concerned with the link options that are available to it to enable data to be transmitted (in a format called a packet) from one part of the network to another.

The structure of networks is reflected in the ISO OSI seven-layer network model, which has been discussed in Chapter 3. Figure 4.25 relates the network devices discussed later in this section to the lower layers of this model and shows the PDUs, addressing schemes used at the various layers.

The path between source node and destination node may comprise many devices including hubs, switches, and routers, but hubs and switches do not make routing decisions, so from a routing point of view, such devices are transparent. Another way to think of this is that routing decisions are made based on the addresses carried in IP packet headers (IP being a network-Layer protocol), and thus, routing is associated with the network layer. Hubs essentially boost signals but do not understand any type of address; hence, they operate at the physical layer only. Switches use media access control (MAC) addresses to select paths at the data link level and so are described as layer 2 devices.

The PDUs at the network layer are called packets, while at the data link layer, they are called frames. These have the same basic structure, comprising a header that contains information required by the network to transmit the PDU through the network and for the recipient node to understand the meaning and content of the PDU and a payload. The payload of the frame will be a packet (as illustrated in Figure 4.26). This is the concept of encapsulation, which has been discussed in more detail in Chapter 3.

To transmit a packet across a network path comprising several links, a series of frames are used, one per link. The frame is used to carry the packet across a single link. On reception of a frame at a router, the packet is extracted from the frame, and the frame is discarded (as it was addressed to the specific router and thus has served its purpose). The router creates a new frame, addressed to the next router in the chosen route, and the original packet is re-encapsulated into the new frame, which is then transmitted onto the outgoing link.

Switches do not understand IP addresses, and thus, a switch that lies in the path between a pair of routers will forward frames from one router to another at the link level based on the MAC-level

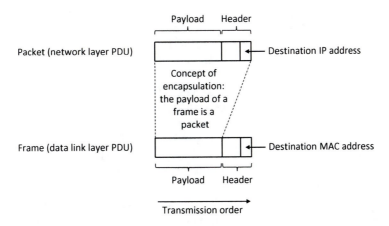

FIGURE 4.26

Encapsulation of a packet into a frame.

addresses of the routers and does not influence the higher-level routing activity. This is illustrated in Figure 4.27.

Figure 4.27 illustrates how the entire system of links between the two routers appears as a single link to the network layer. This is because a packet is transmitted across this system of links unchanged. The routers cannot tell if there are zero, one, or more switches in the path; thus, the switches are said to be transparent to packets and the network layer.

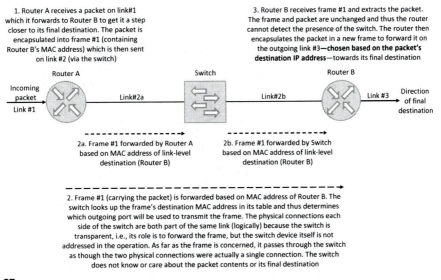

FIGURE 4.27

Combined use of MAC addresses within frames and IP addresses within packets to transmit a packet over a series of links.

4.6.6 **ROUTERS AND ROUTING**

Routers are specialized computers that direct network traffic and thus have a large influence on the effectiveness of message transmission. Therefore, it is important for developers of distributed applications to understand the basic concept of their operation.

Networks are highly dynamic environments. Dynamic behavior arises primarily from changes in the types and volumes of traffic flowing, which is driven by the different types of applications being used, by different numbers of uses at different times. In addition, links and routers and other devices can fail and be repaired unpredictably, changing the availability of routes and the total capacity of parts of the network from time to time. New devices and links are added, computers and services are upgraded, and so forth. The router has to choose the "best" route (see below) for a given packet, very quickly, despite the high level of dynamism.

The router keeps track of its knowledge of available routes and current network conditions in a routing table, which is updated frequently to reflect the dynamic characteristics of the network. When a packet arrives at a router, the router will inspect the destination IP address in the packet header. Based on the destination address and the current state of the routing table, the router will select an output link on which to pass the packet, with the goal of moving the packet one step (one "hop") closer to its destination.

This is illustrated in Figure 4.28. Part (a) of the figure shows a core network of seven routers (i.e., it does not show the various devices such as switches and computers that are connected to routers at the periphery of the network). Part (b) of the figure shows the routing table for Router B. The routing table forms a link between three pieces of information that the router uses to route packets: the destination network address of the particular packet (which it reads from the packet's header and uses as an index into the table); the outgoing link that represents the best known route (in this example, it is based on the number of hops to the destination); and the actual distance of the current best known route (this is necessary so that if a new possible route for a particular destination is discovered, the router can determine if it is better than the current one held).

The router's use of the routing table is illustrated with a couple of examples: (1) A packet arrives from Router A, with a destination network address of 12.13.0.0. The router looks up the destination address 12.13.0.0 and finds that the current best known route is via link 2. This means that the packet

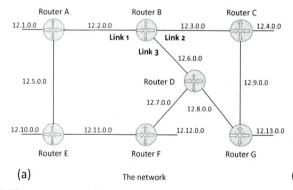

Destination network	Outgoing link	Distance (hops)
12.1.0.0	1	1
12.2.0.0	1	0
12.3.0.0	2	0
12.4.0.0	2	1
12.5.0.0	1	1
12.6.0.0	3	0
12.7.0.0	3	1
12.8.0.0	3	1
12.9.0.0	2	1
12.10.0.0	1	2
12.11.0.0	1	2
12.12.0.0	3	2
12.13.0.0	2	2

(a) The network

(b) Routing table for Router B (assumes distance vector routing)

FIGURE 4.28

A core network of seven routers and the routing table for Router B.

will be passed to Router C. 2. A packet arrives from Router D, with a destination network address of 12.1.0.0. The router looks up the destination address and finds that the current best known route is via link 1, so the packet is passed to Router A.

In distance vector routing (which is the basis of the example shown in Figure 4.28), each router only has partial knowledge of the entire network topology and does not have to know the full configuration of all routers and links. In this case, Router B does not need to know the actual connectivity beyond its immediate neighbors, but through the exchange of routing protocol messages with its neighbors, it will learn the best routes (in terms of the outgoing links to use) to the destinations.

The actual way in which the router chooses the output link is determined by the actual routing protocol in use and the actual metrics used by that protocol, which define what is meant by "best" route (e.g., the least number of hops, least loaded, and most reliable). In some cases, there will only be one output link that can move the packet on its way in the right direction, so regardless of the routing protocol, this link will be chosen. Things are more complex when there are many possible routes to choose from and where the network traffic conditions are highly dynamic, leading to fluctuations in link utilization and queue lengths in the routers themselves. Under such circumstances, it can be difficult to predict which link the router will select for any specific packet and two consecutive packets sent by the same source node and heading to the same destination node may actually be passed along different links by a given router; see Figure 4.29.

Figure 4.29 illustrates dynamic routing in which packets with the same source and destination addresses are passed along different routes. This can lead to different delays to the packets as they encounter different congestion on each route. It is also possible that the arrival order of the packets will be changed by each taking different routes. Referring to the example in the figure, the second packet sent (labeled 2) may arrive at the destination before the first packet that was sent (labeled 1).

As discussed earlier, layer 1 and 2 devices are transparent to routing, that is, they do not affect the route taken, and thus can be ignored for the purpose of packet routing. From the perspective of a packet moving from source to destination, its path can be described in terms of the routers it passes through, as it is only at these points that its path can change. Each time a packet is passed from one router to another, it is deemed to have traveled one "hop." Essentially, each router represents a queue. This is because the outgoing link can only transmit packets at the fixed rate, which is determined by the link

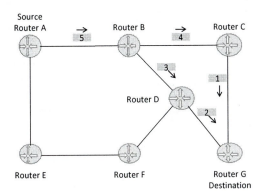

Dynamic routing scenario:
• A series of 5 packets are sent from Router A to Router G
• The routing metric is delay, which is sensitive to fluctuating traffic levels in the network
• The router dynamically adjusts its choice of route to reach the destination node, each time choosing the route with lowest expected delay

FIGURE 4.29

Dynamic route determination based on network conditions.

technology (so, e.g., if the link technology is Fast Ethernet, the router will transmit onto the link at a rate of 100 Mb/S, and thus, a packet of 1000 bits will take 1000 bit times to transmit. In this case, a bit time is 10^{-8} s. The transmission time is thus $10^{-8} \times 10^3 = 10^{-5}$ s $= 10\,\mu S$). If packets destined for a particular outgoing link arrive at the router faster than the rate at which the router can transmit them, then a queue forms. It is important to realize that the time taken to process the queue depends on both the bit rate of the outgoing link and also the length (number of bits) of each packet. If the buffer is empty when the packet arrives, it will start to be transmitted straight away. However, if there are other packets in buffer already, the new packet has to wait.

The end-to-end route is effectively a series of queues the packet must move through, and the total queuing delay is the sum of the delays in each of these queues; see Figure 4.30.

As shown in Figure 4.30, a packet moves through each queue in sequence until it reaches the destination. The length of the queues is resultant of the amount of traffic flowing on the various links, and when there is more traffic, the mean queue lengths increase; this is commonly described as congestion.

Figure 4.31 illustrates the way in which congestion builds up as the result of many different traffic flows, which combine (share links) at different points in the network, and thus, the congestion is both dynamic and nonsymmetric. In the example shown, traffic flows 1 and 3 share part of the same route as the application flow (shown as the darker, fine-dotted line) between the source and destination nodes highlighted and thus impact on the lengths of the queues on router output links that the application flow uses.

It is very important that as designers of protocols and applications, we understand the nature of this congestion and the way it builds up and the way it affects the delay and packet loss levels encountered by messages sent within our applications. The simplest observation is that a buildup of queues in the path of a packet means that the packet will take longer to travel through the system. The router is itself a specialized computer, and it has to process each packet in turn and transmit it onto the appropriate outgoing line. The router operates at a finite speed, and the outgoing line has a finite bit rate. For a specific packet, the transmission time onto the outgoing line is directly proportional to the length of

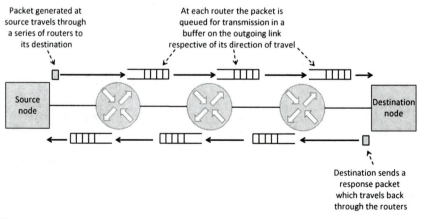

FIGURE 4.30

Resource view of a network route; a series of queues.

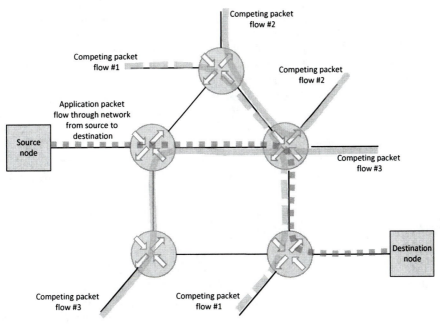

FIGURE 4.31

The combined effect of many traffic flows gives rise to complex traffic patterns.

the packet. However, the time spent in the queue is dependent on the number of packets already in the queue, which must be processed ahead of our specific one.

The router also has a finite amount of memory, in which it can store packets. This is organized as buffer space, and there may be a separate buffer designated for each output link. The finite aspect of the buffer leads to another important observation; the buffer will eventually fill up if packets arrive quickly to the router, faster than they can leave. This is analogous to vehicles arriving at a road junction at a busy time of the day. If the vehicles join the end of the queue faster than they leave the front of the queue, then the queue will get longer and longer. This fact is well known to everyone who drives in a city during the rush hour. Once the rush hour is over, the queues reduce quickly, because there are far less vehicles joining the queue per unit time, but the number of vehicles that are able to leave the queue per unit time (i.e., by entering the junction) does not change.

Each packet that arrives at a router must be held in memory while it is processed. If the buffer is full (the queue is full), the router has to ignore the packet; that is, it cannot store the packet because there is nowhere to put it, so the packet ceases to exist. This is termed "dropping" the packet and is a main cause of packet loss in networks. The term packet loss can lead to some misunderstanding; people sometimes talk about packets being (or getting) "lost," which might imply that the router was careless and mislaid them somehow or that it directed them to the wrong destination, implying that the cause of the loss was linked to the packet address and the processing thereof. It is very important to realize that in fact, most loss is linked to congestion and finite buffers in routers; this motivates us to find appropriate ways to minimize this loss or design protocols or applications to be less sensitive to it and/or to be more efficient in transmission so that less traffic is generated.

Note that it is the finite characteristic of memory buffers in routers that is the fundamental problem we have to address. Put another way, no matter how large the buffer is, it will always fill up given enough congestion. I have heard many arguments for making buffers larger, in the hope that this will solve the problem of packet loss. However, larger buffers allow the queue to build up longer before packets are dropped, which translates into more delay for the packets that are in the queue and longer time required for the queues to clear after a period of congestion. This last point is significant because much network traffic has a "bursty" nature[3], and enabling longer queues to build up can cause the effect of a sudden burst of traffic to impact on the network performance for longer after the event. Optimization of router queue lengths is itself a complex subject due to the number of dynamic factors involved, but it is important to realize that facilitating longer queues does not necessarily translate into better performance; the salient point is that it all depends on which performance metric is used; packet loss is traded against packet delay.

4.6.7 OVERHEADS OF COMMUNICATION

The transport layer provides a good example of the way in which trade-offs can arise in the design of protocols. Two very well-known protocols are provided in the transport layer, namely, TCP and UDP as discussed in Chapter 3.

The choice of transport protocol is of interest from a resource viewpoint because it can have a significant impact on communication overheads. TCP is described as a reliable protocol. This is warranted because TCP has a number of mechanisms, which ensure that segment loss is detected and the affected segments are retransmitted. In addition, duplicate segments are filtered out at the receiver node, using the in-built sequence numbers. TCP also implements flow control and congestion control mechanisms, which further enhance robustness. Each of these features adds overhead, in terms of additional fields in the TCP header, transmission of acknowledgments, and additional processing at both sender and receiver nodes. UDP in contrast is a basic transport protocol without any mechanisms to enhance reliability and is thus described appropriately as unreliable.

In addition to the overheads, TCP also introduces additional latency because of the need to establish a connection prior to transmitting data. UDP can send a datagram immediately without the need for a connection to be established or any other handshaking.

There are many categories of distributed application for which reliable transport is mandatory, that is, where no message loss can be afforded. For these applications, TCP must be used. However, there are some applications where some message loss is acceptable, especially if this is accompanied by lower communication overheads and lower latency. The benefits of TCP's reliability are reduced when the communicating nodes are within the same local area network as there is less likelihood of packet loss, especially where there is no router between the nodes, so no possibility of being dropped from a queue. UDP has the advantage of being able to perform broadcasts, although these are blocked at the edge of the local broadcast domain by routers. UDP is thus popular for local communication scenarios such as service discovery.

---

[3]A large proportion of network traffic is generated in bursts as opposed to a smooth continuous flow. This arises because of the underlying nature of the activities in applications and ultimately on the behavior of users. Consider, for example, downloading a web page, spending some time reading it, and then downloading another page.

4.6.8 RECOVERY MECHANISMS AND THEIR INTERPLAY WITH NETWORK CONGESTION

Reliable protocols, such as TCP, have in-built recovery mechanisms, whereas unreliable protocols such as UDP do not. This is a main criterion when selecting the most appropriate protocol for a particular application.

There is a complex interaction between recovery mechanisms and congestion. Firstly, congestion leads to queues building up, and eventually when buffers are full, packets are dropped, as discussed earlier. A recovery mechanism will detect the loss of a packet, by the fact that the packet does not arrive at the destination and subsequently that the sender does not receive an acknowledgment. The recovery mechanism then retransmits the packet, which adds to the traffic in the network. In some situations, this could lead to perpetuation of the congestion conditions.

Figure 4.32 illustrates the communication mechanism view of end-to-end transmission of TCP segments (carried in IP packets) and the resulting return of acknowledgments. Solid arrows show the network-layer path determined by the IP forwarding actions of the routers. Dotted arrows show the logical view, at the transport layer, between socket end points in processes at the source and destination computers.

Figure 4.33 illustrates the timing behavior view of end-to-end TCP transmission and the resulting return of acknowledgments. The timer is used as a means of detecting a lost packet; it is configured to allow enough time for a packet to reach the destination and for an acknowledgment to propagate back (this is the Round Trip Time (RTT)), plus a safety margin. The timer is canceled on receipt of the expected acknowledgment. If the transmission has not been acknowledged at the point when the timer expires, then the packet is considered lost and it is retransmitted. Under normal circumstances (when packets are not lost), the timer gets canceled and no retransmission occurs. However, networks are highly dynamic generally, and thus, the end-to-end delay can vary significantly, even over short timeframes. This makes setting any fixed timeout period problematic and so TCP automatically adjusts its timeout based on recent RTT values in an attempt to compensate for the variations in delay.

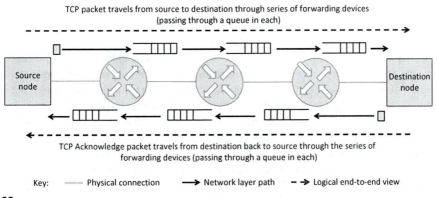

FIGURE 4.32

End-to-end acknowledgment as implemented in TCP (communication mechanism view); the situation without congestion.

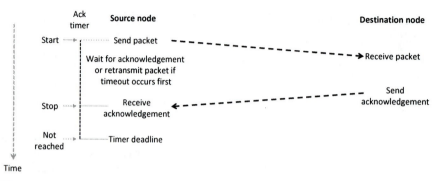

FIGURE 4.33

End-to-end acknowledgment as implemented in TCP (timing behavior view); the situation without congestion.

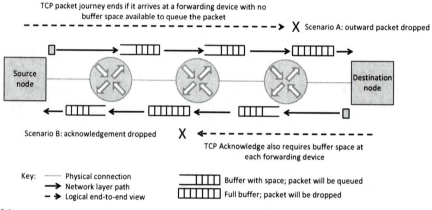

FIGURE 4.34

End-to-end acknowledgment as implemented in TCP (communication mechanism view); the situation with congestion.

Figure 4.34 illustrates the effect of congestion on packet transit. Queues operate independently at each router, thus the congestion can occur in one direction or both directions. This leads to two different failure modes: An outward packet could be dropped, in which case the destination node will not generate an acknowledgment (scenario A in Figures 4.34 and 4.35), or the outward packet may be delivered and the acknowledgment that is sent back could be dropped because of a full buffer (scenario B in Figures 4.34 and 4.35). In each case, the source node will retransmit the packet when its timer expires, and in the scenario A, the new packet is the only one to arrive at the destination. However, in scenario B in which it was only the acknowledgment that was lost, the new packet arrives at the destination as a duplicate. TCP resolves this further issue by placing sequence numbers in each packet. Such aspects of protocol behavior are discussed in depth in Chapter 3; here, the focus is on resource issues.

The timing diagram in Figure 4.35 assumes that congestion is short-lived and that the retransmitted packet is successfully delivered and acknowledged. However, in heavily congested networks, a

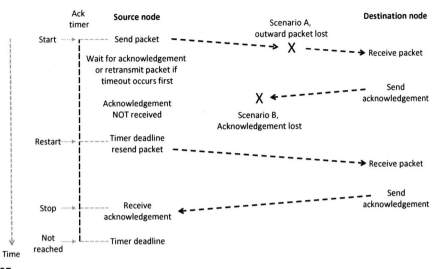

FIGURE 4.35

End-to-end acknowledgment as implemented in TCP (timing behavior view); the situation with congestion.

whole series of retransmissions may be lost due to full buffers, and in such case, the retransmission mechanism is adding to the problem; it is adding packets to the queues upstream of the congestion and consuming processing resources of the forwarding devices, as well as wasting network bandwidth. The further along the round-trip the congestion is from the source node; the more resources are wasted. To prevent an infinite perpetuation of traffic in such circumstances, protocols such as TCP have a configurable maximum retransmission count, and when this is reached, the protocol signals the layer above reporting that the transmission has failed.

Recovery of lost packets has resource implications and, as with almost every aspect of protocol design, involves trade-offs. The application designer needs to bear in mind the functional and nonfunctional requirements of applications when choosing the appropriate approach and be aware of the network overhead incurred by retransmission. The most general trade-off is between communication robustness and efficient use of bandwidth and queue buffers within the transmission path. The recovery of lost messages also increases end-to-end delay at the application level. This represents a trade-off between responsiveness and data completeness. For data applications such as file transfer or online transactions, the data completeness is paramount, so recovery using a reliable transport protocol is vital. In contrast, recovery is not usually beneficial in real-time applications such as live audio or video streaming. The retransmitted data may arrive too late to be useful and potentially increase jitter and delay.

There are some applications that send low-value periodic messages, the loss of some of which can be tolerated without recovery. For example, many services send heartbeat messages, which serve to inform the rest of the system that the particular sending component is still healthy. If there is a period where none of these messages are received by other components, one of the others will instigate an application-level recovery, for example, by starting another instance of the missing service. Such mechanisms are typically designed such that a heartbeat is sent every few seconds and that perhaps five such messages in sequence must be omitted before action is taken. Thus, each message is individually dispensable without recovery. Another example would be a periodic clock synchronization message, which could, for example, be transmitted once per minute. Even with the lowest-accuracy local clock technology currently available, the clock drift over several minutes would be very small, and thus, one of more of these messages could be lost without having any discernible quality impact on the service provided.

In situations where some message loss is acceptable or where the latency associated with recovery is undesirable, it may be appropriate to choose a simpler transport protocol such as UDP rather than a more complex protocol such as TCP, which has a significant management overhead.

4.7 VIRTUAL RESOURCES

This section describes a number of resources that are necessary to facilitate communication and thus on which the operation of distributed systems and applications is dependent. These resources can be considered to be virtual in the sense that they are not tangible; for example, a port number is a numerical value and a specific port can only be bound by a single process at a particular computer.

4.7.1 SOCKETS

Sockets are the end point of communication. A process needs at least one socket to communicate; however, it can use as many as necessary to manage the communication effectively. The program logic is generally clearer if there is one socket dedicated for communication with each of its communication partners. An important example of this is when a server process accepts many connections from clients, using TCP. "Listen" need to only occur once (at the server), and thereafter, clients can attempt to "connect" to the server. The "accept" primitive can be placed in a loop on the server side such that each time a client connection request is accepted, a new socket is created for the server's communication with that particular client. This can greatly simplify the communication logic, as the socket itself is a means of identifying which client is being communicated with; a socket has a numerical value and is created and managed by the operating system.

4.7.2 PORTS

Ports are an extension of addressing in the transport layer of the TCP/IP protocol stack. Specifically, a port number identifies a particular process at a particular computer (identified by its IP address) or can be used to address a set of processes that are using the same port but with different IP addresses (i.e., on different computers). This latter usage is ideal with broadcast communication, which can be facilitated, for example, with UDP.

The port number identifies which process the message carried by either a TCP or UDP segment should be delivered to. Recall that the IP address carried in the network-layer header identifies the computer that the message should be delivered to. The combined IP and port number addresses are written in the form IP address:port, for example, 192.56.64.3:80.

Processes are already uniquely identified at each computer by their process ID (PID). However, this value can be different each time the process runs, because they are allocated dynamically by the operating system, usually in round-robin sequence. This means that they are not predictable and cannot be used by another process as a means of addressing the target process. In contrast, port numbers are preknown values independent of the PID. The operating system has to maintain a mapping between the two types of identifier, in a dynamic table, so it knows which process a particular message (addressed by port number) should be passed to.

A port number is a 16-bit value. The port number may be chosen by the developer, taking care to avoid the reserved ranges of values for well-known services, unless the application is such a service. So, for example, if a Telnet service is being developed, the port 23 should be used. Notice that this only applies to the service (server) side of the communication. This is so that the client will be able to find the service.

A process requests to use a particular port number via the "bind" system call. If the operating system permits the process to use the requested port, it adds an entry into a table, which is subsequently used to match an incoming message to the appropriate process. There are two main reasons why the use of a requested port may be refused. Firstly, a process may not be authorized to use the port if it is in the reserved (well-known) range; secondly, the port may already be in use by another process located at the same computer.

4.7.3 NETWORK ADDRESSES

This section briefly discusses network addresses from the resource viewpoint.

IP addresses are described as logical addresses because they are chosen so as to collect computers into logical groupings based on connectivity and the structure of networks. The IP address has a hierarchical format comprising network part and host part. This is vital so that routing algorithms can make packet-forwarding decisions without having to know the actual physical location of individual computers or the full topology of networks. IPv4 addresses are 4 bytes long each, which means that every IPv4 packet contains 8 bytes of IP address (destination address and source address). This is a relatively small overhead when compared with IPv6 addresses, which are 16 bytes each, and thus, addresses take up 32 bytes of every IPv6 packet. A computer can have multiple IP addresses. Routers in particular have a logical presence in each network they are directly connected to, so they need to have an IP address for each of these networks.

Media control access (MAC) addresses are described as being physical addresses because they provide a globally unique identification of a specific network adapter and thus of the host computer. The address remains the same regardless of where the computer is located. A computer can have multiple network adapters; for example, it may have an Ethernet adapter and a wireless network adapter, in which case it would have two MAC addresses. MAC addresses are ideal for local link communication between devices. They are unsuitable as a basis for routing because routers would need massive memories to hold the routing table; essentially, the router would have to know explicitly how to reach each specific computer. In addition to the memory size problem, there would be the associated time required to search through the memory and also the serious overhead of keeping the table up-to-date, which would be effectively impossible now that mobile computing is so popular and devices change physical locations regularly. MAC addresses are typically 6 bytes (48 bits) although this is dependent on the actual link-layer technology. MAC addresses thus account for 12 bytes of every frame transmitted (destination MAC address and source MAC address).

4.7.4 RESOURCE NAMES

Resources such as files and objects that are located within a distributed system need to have names, which are independent of their location. This means that the resource can be accessed by only knowing its system-wide unique name and without the need to know its physical location.

http://www.bbc.co.uk/weather/
Access the weather page on the web server at computer www.bbc.co.uk, using the http protocol

mailto:Richard@BillericayDicky.net
Send an email to the inbox of the email account named Richard associated with the address *BillericayDicky.net*

telnet://193.76.56.14:23
Establish a Telnet connection with the computer whose IP address is 193.76.56.14, using port 23

FIGURE 4.36

A selection of URL format examples.

The uniform resource identifier (URI) provides a globally unique identification of a resource, and the uniform resource locator (URL) describes how to find (locate) the resource. The difference between these is often overlooked, and the terms are often used interchangeably, but strictly URLs are a subset of URIs.

URLs often contain a host name, which is mapped into the name space of the domain name system (DNS), which means that they can be looked up and translated into an IP address by the underlying access mechanisms wherever needed in the system. DNS is discussed in Chapter 6.

There are several forms of URL used with different classes of resource such as email inboxes (so an email can be sent to your inbox without knowledge of the IP address of the host computer) and similarly for files, hosts, and web pages. A URL has the generic form:

protocol://host-name/path/resource-name

where protocol identifies the type of service used to access the resource, such as ftp or http; the host-name field can contain an IP address and an optional port number or a DNS name space entry—in either case, it uniquely identifies the host that holds the resource; path is the location of the resource on the host computer; and the resource name is the actual name of the resource, such as a filename.

Some examples of URLs are provided in Figure 4.36.

4.8 DISTRIBUTED APPLICATION DESIGN INFLUENCES ON NETWORK EFFICIENCY

Designers of distributed applications need to be well informed with respect to the way in which design choices affect the use of resources and the efficiency with which the resources are used. They need to be aware of the ways in which the performance and behavior of applications are impacted by the design of the underlying networks and the dynamic traffic characteristics of those networks and also to be aware of any specific sensitivities of their applications to issues such as congestion and resource shortages.

Designers need to keep in mind the finite nature of critical resources in systems and that typically there is competition for key resources from other applications present. The design of distributed applications should take into consideration the fact that applications share these resources and that the behavior of their application adds to the level of congestion in networks (and thus impacts indirectly on the performance of other applications in the system).

A main challenge is that at design time, it is not possible to know the various configurations of run-time systems in terms of architecture, resource availability, and the loading on those resources. The safest approach is to build distributed applications that are lean and efficient in terms of resource usage. This enhances their own performance and scalability as they are better able to operate when resource availability is restricted or fluctuates, as is common in networks when traffic levels change continuously, causing changes in delay and packet loss levels. Resource-hungry applications fare worse in busy systems and also impact more severely (through competition for resources) on other applications.

This chapter has identified a number of resource-related challenges and techniques for ensuring applications are efficient with respect to resource use. Communication design aspects should be first-class concerns when designing robust and efficient distributed systems. Aspects to consider include the choice of transport protocol (because of the trade-offs between reliability, overheads, and latency), cautious use of local broadcasts, data compression prior to transmission, careful design of message format and size, and the frequency and pattern of sending messages, taking into account the possibility of data aggregation where appropriate.

4.9 TRANSPARENCY FROM THE RESOURCE VIEWPOINT

The forms of transparency that are particularly important from the resource viewpoint are briefly identified here and are examined in more depth in Chapter 6.

4.9.1 ACCESS TRANSPARENCY

Resources that are remote to a process must be accessible by the same mechanisms as local resources. If this form of transparency is not provided, application developers must build specific mechanisms, and this can restrict flexibility, portability, and robustness.

4.9.2 LOCATION TRANSPARENCY

Developers should not need to know the location of resources. Naming schemes such as URLs, in combination with name services such as DNS, enable the use of logical addresses and remove the need to know the physical location.

4.9.3 REPLICATION TRANSPARENCY

Resources are often replicated in distributed systems to improve access, availability, and robustness. Where this is done, the resources must be accessible without having to know the number of or location of the actual copies of the resource. For example, updating a single resource instance should cause mechanisms in the system to automatically update all other copies. Techniques to achieve replication transparency are presented in Chapter 6.

4.9.4 CONCURRENCY TRANSPARENCY

Where resources are shared by concurrently executing threads or processes, it is vital that the values of the resources remain consistent. Problems arising from unregulated interleaved access to resources can corrupt data and render a system useless, so must be prevented using mechanisms such as locks and transactions.

4.9.5 SCALING TRANSPARENCY AND PERFORMANCE TRANSPARENCY

The network is a fundamentally key resource for distributed systems. The network is a shared resource and the bandwidth is finite. Careful design of communication aspects of distributed applications is an important contribution both towards high scalability and also towards maintaining high performance as scale increases.

4.10 THE CASE STUDY FROM THE RESOURCE PERSPECTIVE

The case study game is not particularly resource-intense. It does not require a lot of processing power and also does not send very much data across the network. Nevertheless, it must be designed to be efficient and therefore to be scalable, to have low impact on the availability of the resources in the system, and also to be minimally impacted by the demands on resources made by other processes.

It was decided to implement the game directly on top of the TCP protocol and not use UDP. The primary reason for this decision was the fact that every message sent is critical to the operation of the game, so if TCP were not used, then application-level message-arrival checking would have to be implemented in any case and this would incur significant additional design and testing cost. Additional reasons include that the game does not have any real-time performance requirements and so would not benefit from the end-to-end latency improvements that UDP may be able to achieve. The communication within the game occurs at a low rate (see discussion below) such that the additional overheads incurred by using TCP are negligible. Finally, the game has no requirement for broadcasting, further confirming the case for avoiding UDP.

A number of message types have been identified, used to indicate the meaning of messages passed at the various stages within the game. Message types include the client registering a player's chosen alias name with the server (REGISTER_ALIAS), the server sending and updating to clients a list of connected players (PLAYER_LIST), a client selecting an opponent to play against from the advertised list (CHOOSE_OPPONENT), the server signaling the state of a game to clients (START_OF_GAME), the server signaling game moves from one client to the server and then from the server to the opponent client (LOCAL_CELL_SELECTION, OPPONENT_CELL_SELECTION), the server informing clients of the outcome of a game (END_OF_GAME), and a message to enable clients to disconnect gracefully (CLIENT_DISCONNECT).

Enumerations are used in the definitions of message type and also message code type (which is used when signaling the end-of-game status). This is a much better alternative to defining constants as it collects the related definitions together and improves the readability and maintainability of code.

The message PDU is defined as a structure and contains the message type enumerator (which is essentially an integer value) that is set appropriately prior to sending the message. This greatly simplifies the message receiving logic, as a switch statement can be used to process the message type value and thus handle the message accordingly. The enumerations and message PDU structure are required when compiling both the client and server application codes. As the game was written in C++, it is ideal to place these commonly needed definitions into a header file, which is then included into both the client and server code projects. The contents of the header file are shown in Figure 4.37.

Figure 4.37 shows the single PDU format used for all messages in the game. It contains a number of fixed-length fields, and thus, the message itself always has a fixed length. This approach simplifies design and implementation and testing. It ensures that both sides of the communication (client and

```
#define PORT 8000
#define MAX_ALIAS_LEN 15

enum MessageType { REGISTER_ALIAS, PLAYER_LIST, CHOOSE_OPPONENT,
                   LOCAL_CELL_SELECTION, OPPONENT_CELL_SELECTION,
                   START_OF_GAME, END_OF_GAME, CLIENT_DISCONNECT };

enum CodeType { END_OF_GAME_DRAW, END_OF_GAME_WIN, END_OF_GAME_LOOSE };

struct Message_PDU {
       MessageType iMessageType;                  // The MessageType enumerated value
       char cAlias[MAX_ALIAS_LEN +1];             // The sending client identified by its player alias
       char cPlayerList[(MAX_ALIAS_LEN +1) *10];  // Comma-separated list of player aliases
       int iCell;                                 // Signals the latest move
       CodeType iCode;                            // Signals the result at the end of a game
       int iToken;                                // Indicates the token the client should use (a 'o' or an 'x')
       bool bFirstMove;                           // Indicates whether the recipient client should move first
};
```

FIGURE 4.37

C++ header file, which defines the message types and PDU format for the game.

server) have predefined message structures and statically allocated message buffers, and there is no need for additional processing to calculate message sizes or field boundaries within messages. Testing is simplified because the fixed-length approach prevents certain failure modes, for example, the message size is too large for the receive buffer, or another common mistake is that a termination character was overwritten or omitted.

The single PDU contains all of the data fields each time it is sent, but each of the various message types only uses a subset of these as necessary. This can be justified in terms of the trade-off between a more complex multi-PDU design that reduces the individual message sizes and the simpler more robust design achieved here. The game logic is quite simple and the game play is not communication-intense, the rate of sending messages being determined mainly by the user's thinking time to make their move selection. Typically, one move might be completed every 5 s or so, causing one message to be sent to the server from the player's client and a corresponding update message being forwarded to the opponent's client, which also serves as a means of informing the opponent that it is their turn (and allowing the user interface to accept a move). This represents a form of message aggregation as two logical messages are combined into a single transmitted message. The application-level communication load is thus two messages per user action (the one sent to the server and one sent by the server to update the other client).

A single PDU format has a size of 196 bytes. If PDUs were repeatedly sent at a rapid rate, such as in a high-action game, then there would be a strong argument for separation into a number of message type-specific PDUs, which are smaller, especially removing the single largest field of cPlayerList (160 bytes) from the messages where it is not needed.

TCP/IP encapsulation adds overheads of the TCP segment header, which is typically 20 bytes, and the IP packet header, which is also typically 20 bytes, and if connected over an Ethernet network, the 18 byte Ethernet frame header must also be added. Thus, the actual size of each transmitted message taking into account encapsulation through the layers is $196 + 20 + 20 + 18 = 254$ bytes, which is equivalent to 2032 bits, and the total for the two messages sent at each activity is thus 4064 bits.

However, with messages being transmitted only every 5 s or slower, the total bandwidth requirement of this game is a maximum of 813 bits per second which is very low. To place this in context with typical bandwidth availability, it represents approximately 8 millionths of the total bandwidth of a Fast Ethernet link. In this case, the simplifications of having a single PDU format were deemed to outweigh the benefits of optimizing the message size further.

As with all distributed applications, there is a need to ensure data consistency. The game has been designed such that the server maintains all game state information. Clients only have indirect access to the game state through defined interactions on the communication interface with the server, so they cannot directly update it. Thus, so long as the server code is designed carefully, there should be no consistency issues, especially as it is single-threaded. If the server were multithreaded, where each thread handled a single client (which is a common design in many server systems), then maintaining consistency across the threads would need consideration. Also, if the server were replicated and shared its state across multiple server instances, then consistency issues could arise.

Nonblocking sockets have been used in both client and server. When a game is in progress, the server will have at least two connected clients, each using a different socket on the server side. The use of nonblocking sockets removes any issues that could arise from specific sequences of messages, for example, if the server process was blocked on one socket and a message arrived on the other. In the client side, the use of a nonblocking socket ensures that the user interface remains responsive while waiting for messages to arrive. The application logic is sufficiently simple in this case that a single-threaded approach in combination with nonblocking sockets achieves the necessary responsiveness without the additional complexity of designing and testing a multithreaded solution.

Port numbers. It was decided to design the game in such a way that all three run-time components in a minimum single-game scenario (the server process and two client processes) could coexist on the same computer to simplify some aspects of testing and also for some demonstration purposes. Obviously, to play the game in the distributed form as intended, each user (and thus each client process) would be located on a different computer. Even in this case, it is still desirable that the server and one of the clients can be colocated. To support two or all three components being colocated on the same computer, it is necessary to ensure that they do not all attempt to bind to the same port number. By using TCP as the transport protocol, it is only necessary for the server to bind to a specific port known to the clients so that they can issue TCP connect requests. The client processes do not need to explicitly bind to any ports because they only receive messages within established TCP connections.

4.11 END-OF-CHAPTER EXERCISES
4.11.1 QUESTIONS

1. PDUs and serialization
    (**1a**) Create a suitable PDU format to hold the following data:
        Customer name = Jacob Jones
        Customer age = 35
        Customer address = 47 Main Road, Small Town, New County, UK
    (**1b**) Provide an illustration of the serialized form of your PDU; state any assumptions that you make.
    (**1c**) Based on your PDU design and means of serialization, describe how the receiver will perform deserialization. Is there enough information for the received data to be extracted to reconstruct the original data format? If not, revisit part (1a) and modify your scheme.

2. PDUs and message types

Consider a PDU containing the following fields:

　　char Customer ID [8];
　　char Customer name [100];
　　char Customer address [200];
　　char Customer Phone number [15];

This single PDU format is used in two different message types:

* *Retrieve full customer details*
* *Retrieve customer phone number*

(2a) Identify the two issues arising from this single PDU design: one relating to efficiency and one relating to message identification.

(2b) Design new PDU formats to resolve the issues identified in part (2a).

(2c) Now that there are multiple PDUs, is it possible for the receiver of a message know in advance how much memory to reserve as a buffer?

3. Dynamic memory allocation

Consider the three dynamic memory allocation scenarios shown in Figure 4.38.

(3a) Assuming that there is no automatic garbage collection (as, e.g., in C and C++), evaluate the consequences of the three scenarios given.

(3b) If automatic garbage collection is present (as, e.g., with Java and C#), how does this affect the situation?

4.11.2 **EXERCISES WITH THE WORKBENCHES**

Exercise 1: Understanding the "lost update" problem (part 1: the fundamental problem)

The exercises below use the *"Threads—Threads and Locks"* application within the Operating Systems Workbench to investigate the **lost update problem**.

1. Inspect the initial value of the data field.

　　Q1. If one thousand increment updates are performed, what value should it end up at?

2. Click the "Start ADD Thread" button to run the ADD thread in isolation.

　　Q2. Was the result as expected?

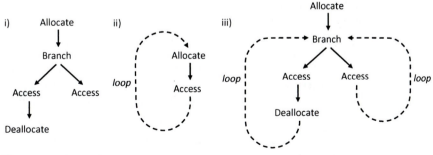

FIGURE 4.38

Dynamic memory allocation scenarios.

3. Note the value of the data field now.

   Q3. If one thousand decrement updates are performed, what value should it end up at?

4. Click the "Start SUBTRACT Thread" button to run the SUBTRACT thread in isolation.

   Q4. Was the result as expected?

   Q5. If the threads are run sequentially (as above), are there any issues concerning access to the shared variable that can lead to its corruption?

5. Click the "Reset data field" button to reset the value of the data variable to 1000.

   Q6. Given a starting value of 1000, if one thousand increment updates are performed and one thousand decrements are performed, what should the final value be?

6. Click the "Start both threads" button to run the two threads concurrently.

7. When both threads have finished, check their transaction counts to ensure both executed 1000 transactions; hence, determine the correct value of the data variable.

   Q7. Is the actual data variable value correct? If not, what could have caused the discrepancy?

Exercise 2: Understanding the "lost update" problem (part 2: exploring the nature of the problem)

The *lost update part 1* activity exposed the lost update problem. We saw that a discrepancy occurred between the expected value and the actual final value of a shared variable. Some of the updates were lost. This is because one thread was allowed to access the variable, while the other had already started a transaction based on the value of the variable.

Q1. How does this problem relate to transactions in database applications?

Q2. How many of the ACID properties of transactions have been violated?

Q3. How could this problem affect applications such as

   an online flight-booking system?

   a warehouse stock-management system?

Q4. Think of at least one other real-world application that could be affected by the lost update problem?

Investigate the nature of the problem. Repeat the following steps three times:

A. Ensure that the value of the data variable is 1000 (click the "Reset data field" button if necessary).

B. Click the "Start both threads" button to run the two threads concurrently.

C. When both threads have finished, check their transaction counts to ensure both executed 1000 transactions; hence, determine the correct value of the data variable.

D. Make a note of the extent of the discrepancy.

Q5. Compare the three discrepancies. Is the actual discrepancy predictable or does it seem to have a random element?

Q6. If there is a random element, where does it come from (think carefully about the mechanism at play here—two threads are executing concurrently but without synchronization—what could go wrong)?

Q7. Is the problem more serious if the discrepancy is predictable? Or is it more serious if the discrepancy is not predictable?

Exercise 3: Understanding the "lost update" problem (part 3: the need for locks)

The *lost update parts* 1 and 2 activities exposed the lost update problem and showed us that the extent of the problem is unpredictable. Therefore, we must find a mechanism to prevent the problem from occurring.

Q1. Could a locking mechanism be the answer? If so, how would it work?

Q2. Would it be adequate to apply the lock to only one of the threads or does it have to apply to both?

Q3. Is it necessary to use a read-lock and a write-lock, or is it important to prevent both reading and writing while the lock is applied to ensure that no lost updates occur (think about the properties of transactions)?

The transactions are a sequence of three stages:

> Read the current value into thread-local storage.
> Increment (or decrement) the value locally.
> Write the new value to the shared variable.

Q4. At what point in this sequence should the lock be applied to the transaction?

Q5. At what point should the lock be released?

Investigate the various combinations of locking strategies:

1. Click the "Use Locking" button.
2. Repeat the following steps until all combinations of lock apply and release have been tried:
   A. Ensure that the value of the data variable is 1000 (click the "Reset data field" button if necessary).
   B. Select an option from the APPLY LOCK choices.
   C. Select an option from the RELEASE LOCK choices.
   D. Click the "Start both threads" button to run the two threads concurrently.
   E. When both threads have finished, check their transaction counts to ensure both executed 1000 transactions; hence, determine the correct value of the data variable.
   F. Make a note of the extent of the discrepancy.

Q6. Have you found a combination of applying and releasing locks that always ensures that there is *no* discrepancy? Repeat the emulation with these settings a few times to ensure that it always works?

Q7. Could you explain clearly to a friend what the statement below means? Try it.

The use of the lock forces mutually exclusive access to the variable.

Q8. Could you explain clearly to a friend what the statement below means? Try it.

Mutual exclusion prevents the lost update problem.

Exercise 4: Exploring the deadlock problem

The exercise below uses the "***Deadlock—Introductory***" application within the Operating Systems Workbench.

1. Ensure that all the default settings are used (the safest way to ensure this is to press the cancel button if the application is already open and then reopen the application from the top-level menu).
2. Start thread#1.
3. Now, start thread#2.
   > Q1. Observe the behavior for about 30 s. What is happening in terms of the drawing of arrows? What does this mean in terms of the transactions that are taking place?
4. Now, incrementally enable resources #2-#5 (so that eventually all resources are enabled for use).

Follow the steps below *each time* you enable one extra resource:

4.1. Experiment with different transaction duration settings.

4.2. Experiment with different transaction frequency settings.

4.3. Experiment with different "maximum number of resources each thread is permitted to use" settings.

Q2. From your observations, what characteristics of resource usage increase the probability of deadlock?

Q3. How could deadlock affect applications such as

    a. a distributed database application with one user?

    b. a distributed database application with two users accessing records randomly?

    c. a distributed database application with two users accessing details of separate customer records in a single table?

    d. a stock-price-information application in which the prices of stocks are read by many clients simultaneously?

Exercise 5: Exploring VM and the basics of page replacement algorithms

The exercise below uses the "**Virtual Memory**" simulation provided by the Operating Systems Workbench.

1. Using both of the applications within the VM simulation, fill up the physical memory and swap pages out as necessary to make more room in the physical memory. Do this until each application is using four pages of memory (so eight are in use in total).

2. Continue to access the allocated pages, to edit the text, without allocating additional pages. As you edit the text, you will encounter page faults. Try to use one of the standard page replacement algorithms when selecting the page to be swapped out to make space. Start with Least Recently Used.

3. Repeat step 2, trying to repeat basically the same editing pattern, but this time, try to select pages for swapping out on the basis of Least Frequently Used.

4. Repeat step 2 again, trying to repeat basically the same editing pattern but this time try to select pages for swapping out on the basis of First-In, First-Out.

Q1. How would you measure the performance of the page replacement algorithms (i.e., what performance metric would you use)?

Q2. Did you notice any difference in the performance of the different algorithms in your experiments?

Note: There are of course limits to the extent that this simple experiment can reveal the real performance of the page replacement algorithms; however, it is very useful as an exercise to understand how they operate.

4.11.3 PROGRAMMING EXERCISES

Programming Exercise #R1: Write a command line program that allocates memory in 100-kB blocks each time the user presses a key.

Test the program works as expected using the Task Manager to monitor the actual memory usage of the process.

Use any language of your choice.

An example solution is provided in the program DynamicMemoryAllocation.

Programming Exercise #R2: Based on the structure sample code examples in Figures 4.20 and 4.21, modify the *IPC_socket_Sender* and *IPC_socket_Receiver* programs to use the following structure as the message PDU (they currently use a string to contain the message to be sent):

```
struct MyDetailsMessage {
        char cName [20];
        int iAge;
        char cAddress[50];
};
```

Note that the code in Figures 4.20 and 4.21 is presented in C++, but the task can easily be modified such that the solution is built in other languages such as C# and Java.

The task requires that you serialize the structure prior to sending it. You will also need to deserialize the received message.

An example solution is provided in the programs IPC_Receiver_MessageSerialisation and IPC_Sender_MessageSerialisation.

4.11.4 ANSWERS TO END-OF-CHAPTER QUESTIONS

Q1. (PDUs and serialization) answer

(1a) One possible example is (in C++)

```
struct CustomerDetails_PDU
{
        char CustomerName[50];
        int CustomerAge;
        char CustomerAddress[100];
}
```

(1b) The fields of the structure map onto a sequential buffer of 154 characters in this case: Some possible assumptions include:
- that the sample data is a fair reflection of the generic case, when estimating the sizes of character arrays,
- that there is a means of determining the field length (either fixed size or with a separate field-length field or with a known termination character). The example answer to part (1a) used fixed-length fields.

(1c) Deserialization should be a direct reversal of serialization. There must be enough information in the serialized form to unambiguously reconstruct the original data.

Q2. (PDUs and message types) answer

(2a) Efficiency; the second message type only uses $8+15=23$ bytes of the 323 in the PDU; this is very inefficient and should be addressed by creating a second PDU containing just customer ID and phone number.

Missing information; the PDU needs a message type field {full_ details, phone_only} to signal which data are valid on receipt of the entire PDU.

(2b) First, PDU for full sending customer details:

```
    int MessageType;    // For example this could be message type 1
(full_ details)
    char Customer ID [8];
    char Customer name [100];
    char Customer address [200];
    char Customer Phone number [15];
```

Second PDU for sending just phone number (still need to identify the customer):

```
    int MessageType;    // For example this could be message type 2
(phone_only)
    char Customer ID [8];
    char Customer Phone number [15];
```

Note that the MessageType field must be in the same place in all PDUs. As they have different fields MessageType must be the first field.

(2c) In the general case, it is not possible for the receiver of a message to know in advance how much memory to reserve as a buffer, because generally, it does not know which PDU will be sent at any time.

The receiver *must* always allocate a buffer large enough to hold the largest PDU that could arrive.

Once the message has arrived, the MessageType field will be examined to determine which actual PDU is present.

Q3. (Dynamic memory allocation) answer

(3a) Scenario (i) causes a memory leak but will otherwise function correctly; scenario (ii) will eventually cause a crash because memory will be depleted; and scenario (iii) causes a crash if either loop is followed after the left one has been taken.

(3b) For scenario (i), the memory leak is still a problem over the shorter term. Eventually, the garbage collection may detect and free the unreachable memory, but in some mechanisms, this will only happen if the size of the block is sufficient to make it worthwhile. Scenario 2 is not changed. Scenario 3 is only changed if the programmer omits the manual deallocation because of the presence of automatic garbage collection, in which case the scenario becomes correct.

4.11.5 ANSWERS/OUTCOMES OF THE WORKBENCHES EXERCISES

Exercise 1: Understanding the lost update problem (part 1: the fundamental problem)

Q1. The value should start at 1000 and end up at 2000.

Q2. When a single thread runs in isolation the result is always correct.

Q3. The value should now be 2000 and end up at 1000.

Q4. When a single thread runs in isolation, the result is always correct.

Q5. No corruption can occur because there are no overlapping accesses to the data value.

Q6. The final value should be 1000.

Q7. Unregulated overlapping accesses to the data variable lead to lost updates and the system becomes inconsistent.

Exercise 2: Understanding the "lost update" problem (part 2: exploring the nature of the problem)

Q1. Transactions in database applications need to be isolated from one another. Partial results must be hidden from processes outside of the transaction to prevent the system becoming inconsistent.

Q2. The atomicity, consistency, and isolation properties of transactions have been violated.

Q3. An online flight-booking system could be affected by overbooking seats or by leaving seats empty when the number remaining appears in the computer system to be zero.

A warehouse stock-management system could be affected by having more, or less, items actually in stock than what the computer system shows.

Q4. Example systems susceptible to the lost update problem include online banking, stock trading, online shopping, and eCommerce.

Q5. The discrepancy is random.

Q6. The discrepancy arises because the threads execution timing is highly sensitive to sequences of low-level scheduler decisions, which differ from run to run based on precise system conditions.

Q7. The discrepancy is not predictable and therefore potentially more serious.

Exercise 3: Understanding the "lost update" problem (part 3: the need for locks)

Q1. A locking mechanism prevents overlapping access to a resource.

Q2. Locks must apply to both of the threads.

Q3. Both reading and writing by outside processes must be prevented while the lock is applied.

Q4. The lock should be applied before the read stage of the transaction.

Q5. The lock should be released after the write stage of the transaction.

Q6. The experiments should confirm the answers to Q4 and 5 above.

Q7. The statement means that the locks ensure that only one process can access the resource at a time.

Q8. The statement means that by allowing only one process to access the resource at a time, the lost update problem cannot occur.

Exercise 4: Exploring the deadlock problem

Q1. The threads request a resource needed for the transaction (red arrow). Once the resource is free, the thread is granted access to the resource and holds it while the transaction executes (blue arrow).

Q2. Deadlock is more likely when a greater number of resources are used within each transaction, when transactions lock the resources for longer, and when transactions occur more frequently.

a. Deadlock should not be possible.

b. Deadlock is possible if at least two resources are used in each transaction (e.g., if transactions each access two or more records in the database).

c. If locking is performed at the table level and no other resources are used, then deadlock will not occur, but one process will have to wait for the other to finish with the resource. If row-level locking is used and each process accesses a separate set of records, then deadlock should not be possible.

d. If the access mode is entirely read-only, then locking is not needed, in which case deadlock cannot occur.

Exercise 5: Exploring VM and the basics of page replacement algorithms

Q1. A suitable performance metric is the number of page faults occurring when each page replacement algorithm is used.

Q2. This is dependent on the actual scenario in which memory accesses occurred. If you simulate an application with good spatial locality that repeatedly accesses a small subset of memory pages, then the LFU or LRU page replacement algorithms should perform better than random or FIFO.

4.11.6 **LIST OF IN-TEXT ACTIVITIES**

Activity number	Section	Description
R1	4.4	Examine memory availability and use. Observe behavior of system when memory demand suddenly and significantly increases beyond physical availability
R2	4.4.1	Using the Operating Systems Workbench to explore the basics of memory management and VM
R3	4.5.4	Using the Operating Systems Workbench to explore the need for locks and the timing within transactions of when locks are applied and released
R4	4.5.5	Using the Operating Systems Workbench to explore deadlock during resource allocation

4.11.7 **LIST OF ACCOMPANYING RESOURCES**

The following resources are referred to directly in the chapter text, the in-text activities, and/or the end-of-chapter exercises.

- Operating Systems Workbench ("Systems Programming" edition)
- Source code
- Executable code

Program	Availability	Relevant sections of chapter
Memory_Hog	Source code	Activity R1 (Section 4.4)
IPC_socket_Receiver	Source code, executable	Programming exercises (Section 4.11.3)
IPC_socket_Sender	Source code, executable	Programming exercises (Section 4.11.3)
DynamicMemoryAllocation (Solution to end-of-chapter programming task #1 dynamic memory allocation)	Source code, executable	Programming exercises (Section 4.11.3)
IPC_Receiver_MessageSerialisation and IPC_Sender_MessageSerialisation (Solution to end-of-chapter programming task #2 message serialization)	Source code, executable	Programming exercises (Section 4.11.3)

THE ARCHITECTURE VIEW

5

CHAPTER CONTENTS

5.1 RATIONALE AND OVERVIEW

A distributed system by definition comprises at least two components, but some systems comprise many components and exhibit very complex behavior as a result. Architecture describes the way in which systems are structured and how the constituent components are interconnected and the relationships between the components; this includes the organization of communication and control channels between pairs or groups of components. The choice of architecture for a given system will impact on its scalability, robustness, and performance, as well as the efficiency with which the resources of the system are used; in fact, it potentially impacts all aspects of the system's effectiveness.

There are many reasons why systems are designed as a number of components, some relating to functionality, some relating to access to resources, and some relating to scale of systems, among others. The reasons why systems are built as a collection of components, and also the wide variety of system architectures that arise as a result, are discussed. There are a number of commonly occurring structures and patterns and also many application-specific structures. In addition, some structures are static, that is, the connectivity between components is decided at design time, while other systems have dynamic structures and connectivity, which arises due to the operating context and the state of the wider system itself in which the application runs. Mechanisms to support dynamic component discovery and connectivity are explored, as well as techniques to automatically configure services and allocate roles to server instances.

The effects of heterogeneity in systems are examined, as well as ways in which the heterogeneity challenge can be overcome with services such as middleware and techniques such as hardware virtualization. Structure at the component level is examined with the aid of practical examples of refactoring and the creation of a software library. The use of replication as an architectural design technique to meet nonfunctional requirements including robustness, availability, and responsiveness is explored in an extensive practical activity.

5.2 THE ARCHITECTURE VIEW

The architecture of a system is its structure. Distributed applications comprise several components that have communication relationships and control relationships with other components. These components may be organized into a hierarchical structure where components occupy different layers depending on their role.

Perhaps, the single largest influence on the overall quality and effectiveness of a distributed application is its architecture. The way in which an application is divided into components, and the way these components are subsequently organized into a suitable structure, supporting communication and control has a very strong impact on the performance achieved. Performance characteristics influenced by architecture include scalability (e.g., in terms of the way in which the performance is affected by increases in the number of components in the system or by increases in throughput measured as the number of transactions per unit time), flexibility (e.g., in terms of the coupling between components and the extent that dynamic (re)configuration is possible), and efficiency (e.g., in terms of the communication intensity between components measured by the number of messages sent and the overall communication overhead incurred).

There is an important difference between a physical architecture and a logical architecture. Physical architecture describes the configuration of computers and their interconnectivity. Developers of distributed applications and systems are primarily concerned with the logical architecture in which the logical connectivity of components is important, but the physical location of these components (i.e., their mapping to actual computers) is not a concern. The application logic is considered distributed even if all the processes that carry out the work reside on the same physical computer. It is common that processes are actually spread across multiple computers, and this introduces not only several special considerations, most obviously the communication aspect, but also timing and synchronization issues.

5.2.1 SEPARATION OF CONCERNS

An application is defined and distinguished by its functionality, that is, what it actually does. In achieving this functionality, there are a number of different concerns at the business logic level. These concerns may include specific aspects of functionality, meeting nonfunctional requirements such as robustness or scalability, as well as other issues such as accessibility and security. These various requirements and behaviors are mapped onto the actual components in ways that are highly application-dependent, taking into account not only the functionalities themselves but the specific prioritization among the functionalities that is itself application-dependent.

It should be possible to identify the specific software component(s) that provides a particular functionality. This is because a functional requirement is something the system must actually do, or perform, and thus can usually be explicitly expressed in design documentation and eventually translated into code. For example, encryption of a message prior to sending may be performed in a code function called *EncryptMessage*(), which is contained within a specific component of the application. However, it is not generally possible to implement nonfunctional requirements directly in code (by implication of their "nonfunctional" nature). Take a couple of very common requirements such as scalability and efficiency; almost all distributed applications have these among their nonfunctional requirements, but even the most experienced software developers will be unable to write functions *Scalability*() or *Efficiency*() to provide these characteristics. This is because scalability and efficiency are *not* functions as such they are qualities. Instead of providing a clearly demarked function, the entire application (or certain key parts of it) must be designed to ensure that the overall resulting structure and behavior are scalable and efficient. There may however be functions that directly or indirectly contribute to the achievement of nonfunctional requirements. For example, a method such as *CompressMessageBeforeSending*() may contribute to scalability as well as efficiency. However, the achievement of scalability and efficiency additionally depend on the higher-level structure such as the way in which the components are themselves coupled together, as well as specific aspects of behavior.

One of the key steps in defining the architecture of an application is the separation of the concerns, that is, deciding how to split the application logic so that it can be spread across the various components. This must be done very carefully. Architectures where the functional separation of the business logic across the components is quite clear with well-defined boundaries tend to be easier to implement and are potentially more scalable. Situations where there are many components but the functionality is not clearly split across them are more likely to suffer performance or efficiency problems (due to additional communication requirements) and also are likely to be less robust because of complex dependencies between components and ongoing updates through the system's life cycle; this is because when components are tightly coupled with one another, it is very difficult to upgrade one component without the possibility of destabilizing several others.

Often, services such as name services and broker services are employed specifically to decouple components to ensure the components themselves remain as simple and independent as possible; this promotes flexibility in terms of run-time configuration and agility in terms of through lifetime maintenance and upgrade.

5.2.2 NETWORKING AND DISTRIBUTION

Not all applications that use the network to communicate are classified as distributed applications.

A network application is one in which the network conveys messages between components but where the application logic is not spread across the components, for example, situations where one of the components is simply a user interface as with a terminal emulator, such as a Telnet client. The user runs a local application that provides an interface to another computer so that commands can be executed remotely and the results presented on the user's display. The user's application in this case is only an access portal or interface that allows the user to execute commands on the remote computer. It does not actually contain any application logic; rather, it connects to the remote computer and sends and receives messages in predefined ways. The application(s) that is used remains remote to the user.

In a network application, the two or more components are usually explicitly visible to users; for example, they may have to identify each component and connect to them (as in the Telnet example above, where the user is aware that they are logging into a remote site). A further example is when using a web browser to connect to a specific web page, the user is aware that the resource being accessed is remote to them (usually, the user has explicitly provided the web page URL or clicked on a hyperlink).

In contrast with network applications, the terms "distributed application" and "distributed system" imply that the logic and structure of an application are somehow distributed over multiple components, ideally in such a way that the users of the application are unaware of the distribution itself.

The main difference is thus transparency (in addition to the differentiation as to whether the business logic is distributed); the goal of good distributed system design is to create the illusion of a single entity and to hide the separation of components and the boundaries between physical computers. The extent of transparency is a main metric for measuring the quality of a distributed application or system. This issue is discussed in more detail later in the chapter.

5.2.3 COMPLEXITY IN DISTRIBUTED SYSTEMS

Managing complexity is a main concern in the design and development of distributed applications and systems. Systems can be highly complex in terms of their structure, their functionality, and/or their behavior.

There are a wide variety of sources of complexity; common categories include the following:

- The overall size of the system. This includes the number of computers, the number of software components, the amount of data, and the number of users.
- The extent of functionality. This includes the complexity of specific functions and also the variety and breadth of functionality across the system.
- The extent of interaction. This includes interaction between different features/functions, as well as communication between software components, the nature and extent of communication between users and the system, and possibly indirect interaction between users as a result of using the system (e.g., in applications such as banking with shared accounts and games).
- The speed at which the system operates. This includes the rate at which user requests arrive at the system, the throughput of the system in terms of the number of transactions completed in a given amount of time, and the amount of internal communication that occurs when processing transactions.
- Concurrency. This includes users submitting requests for service concurrently and also the effects arising from having many software components and also many processing elements operating in parallel within most systems.
- Reconfigurations. This includes forced reconfiguration caused by failure of various components, as well as purposeful reconfiguration (automatic or manual) to upgrade functionality or to improve efficiency.
- External or environmental conditions. This broad category of factors includes power failures that affect host computers and dynamic load levels in the communication network.

From this list, it is apparent that there are very many causes of complexity. A certain level of complexity is inevitable to achieve the necessary richness of behavior required for the applications to meet their design goals. It is not possible to entirely eliminate complexity.

Complexity is undesirable because it makes it difficult to understand all aspects of systems and their possible behaviors completely, and thus, it is more likely that weaknesses in terms of poor design or configuration can occur in more complex systems. Many systems are so complex that no individual person can understand the entire system. With such systems, it is very difficult to predict specific behavior in certain circumstances or to identify causes of faults or inefficiencies, and it is also very time-consuming to configure these systems for optimal behavior, if even possible in a realistic time frame.

Given that it is not possible to eliminate complexity from distributed applications, best practice is to reduce complexity where opportunities arise and to avoid introducing unnecessary complexity. This requires that designers consider the available options very carefully and make a special effort to understand the consequences of the various strategies and mechanisms they employ. The architecture of a system potentially has a large impact on its overall complexity because it describes the way in which components are connected together and the way that communication and control occur between these components.

5.2.4 **LAYERED ARCHITECTURES**

A flat architecture is where all of the components operate at the same level; there is no central coordination or control; instead, these systems can be described as collaborative or self-organizing. Such architectures occur in some natural systems in which large numbers of very simple organizations such as insects or cells in substances such as molds interact to achieve structures and/or behaviors beyond those capable of an individual element. This concept is called emergence and has been used effectively in some software systems such as agent-based systems.

However, such approaches rely on system characteristics that include having large numbers of similar entities as well as randomly occurring interactions between only neighboring entities, and these systems tend to work best when the entities themselves are simple in terms of the knowledge they hold and the functions they perform. Scalability is a serious challenge when the communication between components extends beyond immediate neighbors or where interactions occur at such a rate as to exceed the communication bandwidth available.

Most distributed computing systems contain much smaller numbers of components than occur in emergent systems (although there can still be large numbers running into the thousands). However, the various components are typically not identical across the system. There may be groups of identical components such as where a particular service comprises a number of replica server components to achieve robustness and/or performance, but such groups will be subsystems and effectively cogs in a larger machine. The communication and control requirements between components of distributed systems are not usually uniform; it is likely that some components coordinate or control the operation of others and also that some components interact intensely with some specific other components and much less, or not at all with others.

Layered software architectures comprise multiple layers of components that are placed into logical groupings based on the type of functionality they provide or based on their interactions with other components, such that interlayer communication occurs between adjacent layers. Applications and their subcomponents that interface directly with users occupy the upper layer of the architecture, services are lower down, the operating system then comes next, while components such as device drivers that interface with the system hardware are located at the bottom layers of the architecture. Layers can also be used to organize the components within a specific application or service; see Figure 5.1.

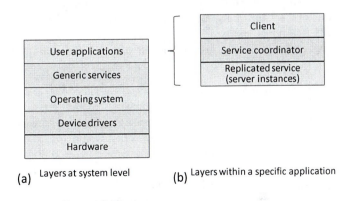

(a) Layers at system level   (b) Layers within a specific application

FIGURE 5.1

Generalization of the use of layers to provide structure.

Figure 5.1 illustrates in a generalized way how systems can be organized into layers to provide structure and thus manage complexity. Modern systems are too complex for users to be able to understand in their entirety, and therefore, it is difficult and cumbersome to make configuration choices across the full range of functionality in order to use the system. Separation into layers limits the scope of each layer and allows relevant configuration to occur while abstracting away details that are the concern of other layers. Part (a) of the figure shows how layers can be used to separate the concerns of applications from those of systems software and hardware. To put this into context, when using a particular application, the user should only have to interface with the application itself. It is undesirable from a usability viewpoint for the user to have to configure support services or make adjustments to operating settings in order to use the application. A simple example of this in practice is the use of a word processing application to write this paragraph. The application is one of many on my computer that can use the keyboard. The application indicates to the operating system that it requires input from the keyboard and the operating system performs the input stream mapping from the keyboard device driver to the word processing process without the user having to get involved or even being aware of this taking place. The operating system automatically maps the keyboard device to other processes if the user switches between different applications (e.g., once I get to the end of this paragraph, I might check my e-mail before continuing with the book). There is also the issue of hardware updates; if I replace my keyboard with a different one (perhaps one with additional function keys or an integrated roller ball), it is likely that a new device driver will be needed for the new keyboard. I do not want to have to reconfigure my word processing application to accommodate the new keyboard; the operating system should remap the input stream of my application process to the new device driver in a way that is transparent to the process itself and thus to the user.

Part (b) of the figure illustrates how applications can themselves be internally structured into several layers (this ability to subdivide also applies to the other parts of the system shown in part (a)). An important example is shown in which an application is divided into several components, of which the user is only exposed to the client part (hence, it is shown as the topmost component; conceptually, the user is looking down from above). This theme is explored in detail in Section 5.5 of this chapter.

The beneficial use of layers in network protocol stacks has been discussed in Chapter 3 and provides further justification of the value of layered structures to ensure maintainability and manageability of complex systems with rich functionality.

Layered architectures are very popular for distributed systems. The reasons for this include the following:

- Within a distributed system, there may be many distributed applications. These applications may each share some services; a good example of this is an authentication service that thus ensures that specific users have consistent access rights to services across the entire system and thus the security of the system is less likely to suffer weaknesses that would arise if some points of entry are less well protected than others. It can be useful to logically separate out the distributed end applications (the ones that provide service to users), from the service applications (which may themselves be distributed but provide services to other applications rather than directly to users). Figure 5.2 illustrates the situation where multiple end applications interact with multiple services; the use of layers maintains structure.

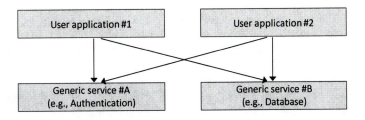

FIGURE 5.2

Layers facilitate logical separation of types of components and provide structure for interaction between components of systems.

- In addition to distributed applications and services, there is the system software that includes operating systems and various specialized components such as device drivers. The system software itself can be very complex in terms of the number of components it comprises and the range of functionalities it provides.
- The layers provide a structure, in which components occupy the same layer as similar components; sit in higher layers than the components they control or coordinate or use the services of; and sit below components that coordinate them or that they provide service to.
- There is a natural coupling between adjacent layers. There is also a decoupling of nonadjacent layers that contributes to flexibility and adaptability; this encourages clear division of roles and functionality between categories of components and also encourages the use of standardized and well-documented interfaces between components (especially at the boundaries between layers).

5.2.5 HIERARCHICAL ARCHITECTURES

A hierarchical architecture comprises multiple levels of components connected in such a way as to reflect the control and communication relationships between them. The higher node in a particular relationship is referred to as the parent, while the lower node in the relationship is referred to as the child. A node that has no nodes below it is termed a leaf node. Hierarchal organization has the potential to achieve scalability, control, configuration, and structure simultaneously.

The hierarchy illustrates the relative significance of the components, those being higher in the structure typically having more central or key roles. This maps onto the way most businesses are organized, with senior central managers higher in the structure, then department leaders, while workers with very specific well-defined areas of responsibility (functionality) occupying the leaf nodes. In hierarchically organized businesses, the normal communication is between workers and their manager (who is at the next level up in the structure). If something has to be passed up to a higher level, it is normally relayed via the managers at each level and not passed directly between nonadjacent layers. This has the effect of maintaining a clear control and communication regime that is appropriate for many large organizations that would otherwise struggle with scalability issues (e.g., imagine the complexity and confusion that could result if all workers in a large company contacted the senior management on a daily basis). Another example of the use of hierarchy is in the organization of large groups of people, such as armies, police forces, and governments. In such cases, it is important to have central decision making for the highest-level strategies, while more localized decisions are made lower in the structure. The result is hopefully a balance between a uniform centrally managed system with respect to major policy while allowing local autonomy for issues that do not need the attention of the senior leadership.

However, rigid hierarchical structures can work against flexibility and dynamism; for example, the need to pass messages up through several layers causes overheads and delays. Reorganizations can be prohibitively complex especially where components are heavily interconnected.

Figure 5.3 illustrates common variations of hierarchical structures. Broad (or flat) trees are characterized by having few levels and a large number of components connected at the same level to a single parent node; this can affect scalability because the parent node must manage and communicate with each of the child nodes. Deep trees have many layers with relatively few nodes at each layer. This can be useful where such a detailed functional separation is justified, but in general, the additional layers are problematic because they add complexity. The main specific problems are increases in the communication costs and the latency of communication and control, as on average messages have to be passed up and down more levels of the tree. In general, a balanced tree (i.e., a balance is achieved between the breadth and the depth of the tree) is close to optimal in terms of the compromise between short average path lengths for communication and also the need to limit the number of subordinates at any point in the tree for manageability. A binary tree is a special case in which each node has (at most)

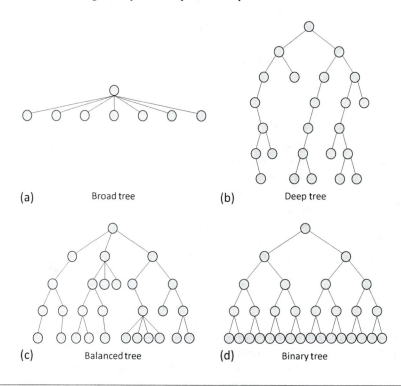

(a)   Broad tree   (b)   Deep tree

(c)   Balanced tree   (d)   Binary tree

FIGURE 5.3

Hierarchical structures.

two subordinates. These are more likely to be found within data structures than in system component architectures but are included here for completeness.

5.3 HETEROGENEITY

Homogeneous systems are those in which all computers are the same, in terms of their hardware and configuration, resources, and operating system. These systems exist when, for example, a company or university equips an office or a laboratory with identical computers or a bespoke sensor system with identical sensor nodes is deployed. However, in the general case, processing systems are not identical and the various differences between them can impact on the configuration and management effort and can cause problems for interoperability, of varying complexity.

Heterogeneity is a very important concept for distributed systems, both in terms of a purposeful architectural feature to achieve a certain performance or behavior and in terms of it being one of the main challenges for interoperability and code portability.

5.3.1 DEFINITIONS AND SOURCES OF HETEROGENEITY

There are three main causes of heterogeneity, these being technological, intended, and accidental. Technological advances lead to new platforms or better resourced upgrades of earlier platforms. Other technological factors include advances in operating systems and programming languages as well as the occasional introduction of new network protocols. Heterogeneity is often intentionally introduced through design or configuration. For example, when more powerful platforms are used to host services, while users have less powerful workstations to access the services. A second example is where an operating system such as Microsoft Windows is chosen for the access workstation because of the popular user interface it provides, while Unix is chosen for the service-hosting platforms due to it having better configurability. A third example is where a service is hosted on a conventional static computer, while mobile computing devices, with completely different platforms and resource levels, are used to access the service. Heterogeneity is accidentally introduced, for example, when there are staged upgrades across hardware systems or when individual machines are enhanced or when different versions of the same base operating system are installed on different computers. Even an automated online update of the operating system that occurs on one computer but not on another potentially introduces heterogeneity if the behavior of one is changed in a way that the behavior of the other is not.

There are three main categories of heterogeneity: performance, platform, and operating system.

Performance heterogeneity arises from differences in resource provision leading to different performance of computing units. Common resource characteristics that lead to performance heterogeneity include memory size, memory access speed, disk size, disk access speed, processor speed, and network bandwidth at the computer-to-access network interface. In general, it is unlikely that any two computers will have identical resource configuration, and thus, there will usually be some element of different performances. There are many ways in which performance heterogeneity arises through normal system acquisition, upgrade, and configuration of hosted services such as file systems. Even buying computers in two batches a few months apart can lead to differences in the actual processor speed, memory size, or disk size supplied.

Platform heterogeneity (also termed architecture heterogeneity) arises from differences in the underlying platform, hardware facilities, instruction set, storage and transmission byte ordering, the number of actual processors within each machine's core, etc.

Operating system heterogeneity arises from differences that occur between different operating systems or different versions of operating systems. These include differences in the process interface, different types of thread provision, different levels of security, different services offered, and the extent to which interfaces are standard or open (published) versus proprietary designs. These differences affect the compatibility of, and challenges involved with porting of, software between the systems.

5.3.2 PERFORMANCE HETEROGENEITY

Figure 5.4 shows three computers, all having the same hardware platform and operating system. Computers A and B have the same level of resource and are thus performance homogeneous. Computer C has different levels of resource, having a slower CPU processing speed, more primary memory, and a smaller hard disk. All three computers will run the same applications, with the same operating system interface and support and the same executable files (as the hardware instruction set is the same in all cases). However, applications will perform differently on computer C than on A or B. Applications requiring a lot of file storage space are more likely to exceed capacity on computer C, and compute-intense applications will take longer to run. However, applications requiring a lot of primary memory may perform better on computer C. This is a simplified example that only considers the main resource types.

The example illustrated in Figure 5.4 represents the very common scenario that arises from piecemeal upgrade and replacement of systems, resulting in situations where you have a pair of computers configured with the same CPU and operating system, but, for example, one has had a memory expansion or been fitted with a larger or faster access time hard disk.

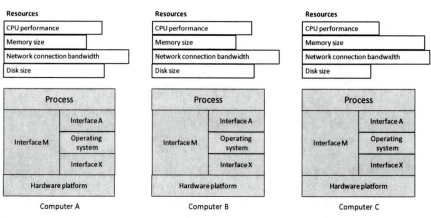

FIGURE 5.4

Performance heterogeneity.

5.3.3 PLATFORM HETEROGENEITY

Figure 5.5 illustrates a platform heterogeneous system. Each of the three computers D, E, and F has a different hardware platform, but all three run compatible variants of the same operating system.

Different platforms imply that the computers have different types of processor architecture, although different versions of the same processor family also represent a form of platform heterogeneity in cases where the run-time interface is different and thus the application code must be recompiled to run (e.g., one version of the processor family may support additional hardware instructions not available in the others). To some extent, performance heterogeneity (as a side effect) is inevitable in such cases because the CPUs may operate at different processing speeds (the number of instructions executed per second) or have different levels of internal optimization (such as branch prediction techniques to allow additional machine code instructions to be prefetched into cache ahead of execution). The interface between the platform and the operating system is different in each case; note the different interfaces X, Y, and Z, which means that different versions of the operating system are needed for each platform. If the operating system is the same, as in the three scenarios shown, the process interface to the operating system will remain the same; that is, it will have the same system calls to interface with devices, files, programmable timers, threads, the network, etc. Linux provides a very good example of this scenario in which the same operating system runs on many different platforms but provides the same process interface in each case. However, even though the source code for the applications could be the same in the three scenarios shown in Figure 5.5, the code will have to be compiled specifically for each platform, as the process-to-machine interface is different in each case (see interfaces M, N, and P). The differences, at this "machine code" level, may include a different instruction set, a different register set, and a different memory map.

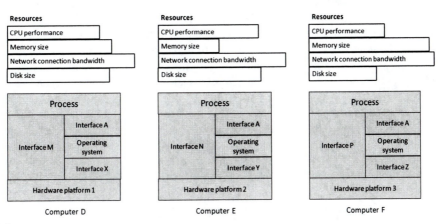

FIGURE 5.5

Platform heterogeneity.

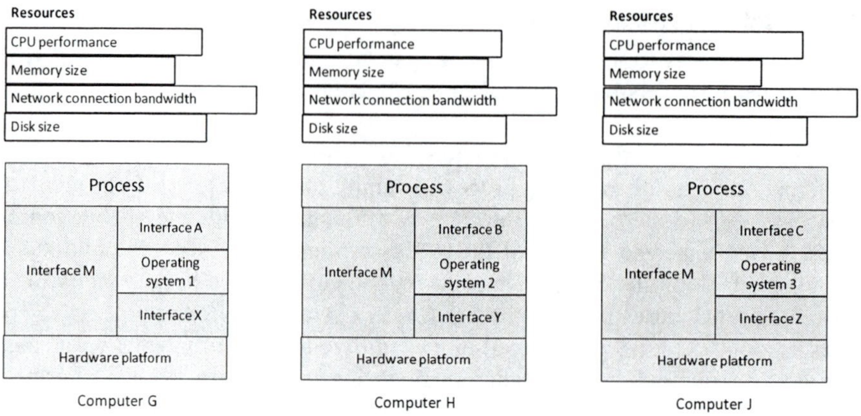

FIGURE 5.6

Operating system heterogeneity.

5.3.4 OPERATING SYSTEM HETEROGENEITY

Figure 5.6 illustrates operating system heterogeneity. In the scenario shown, all three computers G, H, and J have different operating systems but the same hardware platform. The three different operating systems will each have to use the facilities of the same platform type, so there will be differences in the interface between the operating system and the hardware, that is, interfaces X, Y, and Z, although the differences are in the ways the different operating systems use the resources of the hardware, rather than the interface provided by the hardware per se (which is actually constant in the three configurations shown). Although the application process has the same business-level behavior in all three systems, the way this is achieved at the code level will differ slightly as the different operating systems will have different interfaces (fundamentally the set of system calls and the syntax and semantics of their use). For example, there may be different versions of the file handling commands available, with differences in the parameters passed to them. This is reflected in the figure by the different process-to-operating system interfaces A, B, and C. Transferring applications from one of these computers to another is called porting and would require modification of those parts of the code that are sensitive to the differences in the operating system calls supported. As the hardware platforms are the same in each case, the same machine code interface is provided in each case. Changing the operating system may affect the effective resource provision of the computer and so impacts on performance. The most notable way in which this tends to occur is in terms of the amount of memory taken up by the operating system and thus the amount of memory remaining for user processes to use. This is reflected in the figure by the different amount of memory resource shown for each computer (i.e., it is based on the effective resource availability after the operating system has taken its share of the resource).

5.3.5 IMPACT OF HETEROGENEITY

All forms of heterogeneity potentially impact on interoperability. Applications that operate in platform heterogeneous or operating systems heterogeneous systems thus rely on standardized communications between the platforms. This requires standard interfaces and protocols to ensure that the contents of messages and the semantics of communication itself are preserved when a message is passed between two dissimilar computer systems. The sockets API that operates at the transport layer and has been discussed in detail in the communication view chapter provides a good example of a standard interface at the process level. The sockets API is supported by almost all operating systems and programming languages and across almost all platforms.

The TCP and UDP protocols (of the TCP/IP protocol suite) are very good examples of standard protocols that facilitate interoperability between almost any combinations of platforms, using the sockets interface to a process as the end point for communication. These two protocols are extremely important for the Internet; they are not only used directly to provide bespoke process-to-process communication (as, e.g., in the case study game) but also used to construct most of the higher-layer communication mechanisms such as RPC, RMI, middleware, and web services.

These protocols are examples of the few invariants in distributed systems that have stood the test of time. The extent that they are embedded into such a wide range of essential services and higher-layer communication mechanisms reinforces their value as standards. It is relatively safe to assume that support for these protocols will remain for many years to come: future-proofing communications based on these protocols.

Performance heterogeneity is very common, to the extent that it is sometimes difficult to find computers with identical performance. However, if this is the only type of heterogeneity present, then applications will generally operate correctly on any of the host computers; but the overall speed and responsiveness will vary depending on the actual resource provision. Ideally, the functional split across software components and the subsequent deployment of these components onto processing nodes should match resource provision to ensure that the intended performance is achieved (but this is subject to the limitations of the design-time knowledge of the eventual run-time systems).

Platform heterogeneity is increasingly common, especially with the recent explosion of popularity of mobile devices including smart phones and tablets. Users demand applications that operate the same on their personal computer (PC), their phone, and their tablet, fundamentally because there is a desire to be "always connected" to favorite applications whether at home, in the office, or traveling between. It is not always possible to make applications identical on the different platforms, for example, the user interface on a smartphone with a touch screen cannot be identical to the user interface on a PC using a keyboard and mouse. The different platforms have different levels of resource, and this is sometimes evident in the way the software responds, for example, a fast-action game running on a smartphone with a small screen cannot in general be as impressive and responsive as the same game running on a PC that has been optimized for gaming with a very fast processor, expanded memory, and graphics accelerator processor.

Support for platform heterogeneity can add significant cost to software projects. Firstly, there will need to be a design approach that separates out the core functionality, which is device-independent, from the device or platform-specific functionality (typically mostly related to the user interface), which must be developed separately for each platform (see Section 5.13). The more platforms that are supported and the greater diversity between these, the greater the additional costs will be. Secondly, there are the additional testing costs. Each time the software is upgraded, it must be tested on all supported platforms; this in itself can be problematic in terms of the man power needed and the availability of a test facility in which the various platforms are all available. Some difficult to track down faults may occur on one platform only, requiring specific fixes that must then be tested to ensure they don't destabilize the product when on the other platforms. In some software projects, the testing team may be larger than the software development team.

Porting of code from one platform to another is less costly than ongoing maintenance and support for code across multiple platforms simultaneously, although it can still be challenging and potentially very expensive. In the simplest case where the operating system on each target platform is the same and the platforms themselves are similar, porting may only require that the source code (unchanged) must be recompiled to run on the new platform. However, if the operating system is also different, or where the platforms have significant differences, porting can require partial redesign.

Operating system heterogeneity introduces two main types of differences that affect processes: the first type being at the process-to-operating system interface and the second type being differences in the internal design and behavior of the operating systems. For the former, redesign of the sections of application code that make system calls (such as exec, read, write, and exit) and subsequent recompilation of the code may be sufficient. If the implementation of system calls is similar in the two operating systems, there may be no noticeable change in the application's behavior. However, for the latter, there potential problems in that the two operating systems may have different levels of robustness or one may have security weaknesses that the other may not have. For example, one operating system may be vulnerable to certain viruses and other threats that the other is immune to. There could also be effects on performance of applications due to differences in operating system behaviors including scheduling and resource allocation.

5.3.6 PORTING OF SOFTWARE

Porting applications from one system to another can be very complex because the two host systems can be very different in the various ways discussed above. The end result may be applications that are functionally similar, but some aspects such as the user interface or the response time may be noticeably different due to resource availability. Browsers provide a good example where essentially, the same functionality is available but with different look and feel on the various different platforms they run on. Browser technology was initially established on the general-purpose PCs (laptop and desktop computers) for many years but has now been adapted to operate in the same well-understood ways on mobile devices, which have different processors and operating systems and generally fewer resources in terms of memory, processing speed, smaller displays, and often lower bandwidth network connections than their PC counterparts.

A virtual machine (VM) is a software program that sits between application processes and the underlying computer. As far as the computer's scheduler is concerned, the VM is the running process. The VM actually provides a run-time environment for applications that emulates the real underlying computer; we can say that the applications run in, or on, the VM. Because the application processes interact with the VM instead of the physical computer, the VM can mask the true nature of the physical computer and can enable programs compiled on different platforms to run. By providing a mock-up of the environment the application needs to run on, the VM approach avoids the need for porting per se. The VM approach is key to the way in which Java programs are executed. An application is compiled to a special format called Java bytecode; this is an intermediate format that is computer platform-neutral. A Java-specific VM (JVM) interprets the bytecode (i.e., it runs the instructions from the bytecode) the same regardless of the physical environment; therefore, portability is much less of an issue for Java programs generally than it is for programs written in other languages. The VM (or JVM) approach does of course require that a VM (or JVM) is available for each of the platforms that you wish to run the applications on. The VMs (or JVMs) themselves are platform-specific; they are compiled and run as a regular, native, process on whichever platform they are designed for. VMs and the JVM are discussed in more detail later in this chapter.

Middleware provides various services to applications that decouple some aspects of their operation from the underlying physical machine, especially with respect to access to resources that may be either local (on the same computer) or remote. In this way, middleware enables processes to execute in the same logical way regardless of their physical location. For example, the middleware may automatically locate resources the process needs or may automatically pass messages from one process to another without them having to have a direct connection or to even know the location of each other (refer to Section 5.5.1 in this chapter). The middleware may be implemented across different hardware platforms so that a process running on one platform type may transparently use resources located at a computer with a different platform type. Middleware does not however actually execute applications' instructions in the way that a VM does, and thus, it does not solve the portability problem directly. However, because middleware can enable the remote use of resources that are on different platforms, as well as communication between processes on different types of platforms, it offers an indirect solution to portability, that of transparent remote access, without the process actually moving to the other platform. An overview of middleware is provided later in this chapter and a more detailed discussion is provided in Chapter 6.

5.4 HARDWARE AND SYSTEM-LEVEL ARCHITECTURES

Distributed applications comprise software components that are dispersed across the various computers in the system. In order for these components to operate as a coherent single application, as opposed to isolated components doing their own thing, there need to be some means for the components to communicate. For this to be possible, there must be some form of connection between the underlying processors, on which the communication support software runs.

There are two fundamentally different approaches to connecting the processors together. Tightly coupled architectures are those in which the processors are part of a single physical system, and thus, the communication can be implemented by direct dedicated connections. In such systems, the processors may be equipped with special communication interfaces (or channels) designed for direct interconnection to other processors, without the need for a computer network. The processors share the resources of the computer, including the clock, memory, and IO devices.

Stand-alone computer architectures are those in which each processor is the core of a complete computer with its own dedicated set of resources. The PC, smartphone, tablet, and laptop computers are all examples of this class of computer. Stand-alone devices need an external network to communicate. There needs to be a network interface connecting each computer to the network as well as special communication software on each computer to send and receive messages over the network. This form of connecting the computers together yields a less tight and more flexible coupling; hence, it is termed loose coupling.

5.4.1 TIGHTLY COUPLED (HARDWARE) SYSTEMS

The main characteristic of tightly coupled systems is that they comprise a number of processor units integrated together in the same physical computer. This means that several threads of program code can run at the same time, that is, in parallel, since each processor can execute one instruction in each timestep. In these architectures, the communication channels between processor units are very short and can be implemented using similar technology to that of the processor units, meaning that communication can take place at similar speeds to memory accesses. In fact, since the processors usually have shared access to at least part of the system memory, it is possible for the program threads to actually communicate using the memory. For example, if one process writes a new value to a particular variable stored in a shared memory location, all of the other processes can read the variable, without the need to specifically send a message to each process. The main advantages of this form of communication are that it has the same near-perfect reliability as memory accesses and that it does not become a bottleneck in terms of performance; writing to memory is effectively the same operation as sending a data value to another processor. This means that parallel applications can be developed to solve algorithms in which there is high communication intensity (a high rate of communication between the processors). In contrast, such applications do not perform so well on loosely coupled architectures due to the presence of an external network technology that operates at lower speeds than memory accesses, has higher latency due to greater physical distances, and is also less reliable. In tightly coupled architectures, there is usually a single shared clock, and thus, it is possible to synchronize processes accurately in terms of the application-level events and resulting actions carried out. Each processor executes instructions at exactly the same rate; there can be no relative clock drift when there is only a single clock.

5.4.2 LOOSELY COUPLED (HARDWARE) SYSTEMS

This book focuses on distributed applications that run on loosely coupled systems. These systems consist of a number of self-contained computers able to function independently of any others. A perfect example of this is the PC I'm using to write the book. The computer has its own power supply, processor, clock, memory, hard disk storage, operating system, and IO devices. However, the fact that the computer is self-contained does not necessarily mean that the computer can do what I require of it in isolation. Most of the applications that are used in modern business, as well as in hobbies and entertainment and social media, require access to data held at other computers and also require a means to communicate with other users, via the computers that they are using. Therefore, almost every computer has a network connection to support the communication requirements of distributed applications and data. This form of coupling is termed "loose" because the network is external to the computer itself. The communication over networks is slower and less reliable than in tightly coupled systems. However, the communication in loosely coupled systems can be flexibly reconfigured so that a particular computer can be logically connected to any other that is reachable in the network.

Each computer has its own set of resources, which is beneficial in general, because the local scheduler has control of the way the resources (such as memory and the processor's computing cycles) are shared across the local processes. However, the fact that each computer also has its own clock that governs the precise rate at which instructions are executed and is also used to keep track of wall clock time (the actual real-world notion of time) introduces some challenges of synchronization when running distributed applications. For example, it is difficult to determine the global sequence with which a particular set of detected events occur (such as stock-trading transactions or deposits and withdrawals on a particular bank account) or to ensure the correct sequence of a set of critical actions is maintained (such as opening and closing control valves in an automated chemical production factory) if the actual processes associated with the events and actions are executing on different computers with imperfectly

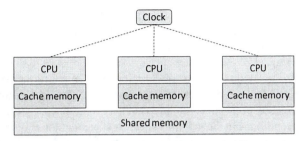

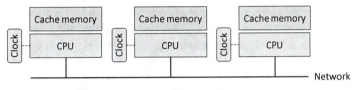

(a) Tightly-coupled processors with private cache memories and shared main memory

(b) Loosely-coupled processors use the network to communicate

FIGURE 5.7

Tightly and loosely coupled hardware architectures.

synchronized clocks. The challenges of clock synchronization and some techniques to overcome these challenges are discussed in Chapter 6.

A further challenge arising for the use of interconnected but self-contained computers is that they can fail independently. Failures that occur when applications are quiescent do not corrupt data and thus are relatively easy to deal with. However, consider the failure of a computer during a data transfer. Whether or not the data become corrupted depends on a number of factors that include the exact timing with which the failure occurs and the extent to which the communication mechanism in use was designed to be robust with regard to maintaining data integrity.

Figure 5.7 illustrates the main concepts of tightly and loosely coupled hardware architectures. There are actually many variations of tightly coupled architectures—the main differences concerning access to memory and the way in which the processors communicate. In some designs, all of the memory is shared, while in others, there is also some private cache per processor (as shown), and some designs have dedicated communication channels between the processors.

5.4.3 PARALLEL PROCESSING

Parallel processing is a special class of distributed application, which is briefly described here for completeness.

A parallel application generally comprises a number of processes all doing the same calculations but with different data and on different processors such that the total amount of computing performed per unit time is significantly higher than if only a single processor is used.

The amount of communication that occurs between the processes is highly dependent on the nature of the application itself. In most parallel applications, the data at each processing node are not processed in isolation; there is generally a need to interact with the computation of data values in other nodes, representing bordering regions of the application data space.

A classic example of a parallel processing application that most of us benefit from daily is weather forecasting, which uses specialized techniques such as computational fluid dynamics (CFD). The geographic area to be studied is divided up into small regions, which are further subdivided into smaller and smaller cells. The actual forecast of the weather at a particular time in the future, in a particular cell, is based not only on the history of weather conditions in the cell at times leading up to the forecast time but also on the weather conditions in the neighboring cells at each of those times, which influences the weather in our cell of interest. The weather conditions in the direct neighbor cells of our cell of interest are also affected by the conditions in the neighbors of neighbors cells at each timestep, and so it goes on. CFD works in iterations such that the state of each of the cells at a particular time point t_1 is computed based on the state of the cell at time t_0 and also the state of the neighboring cells at time t_0. Once the new state of the cells at time t_1 is computed, it becomes the starting point for the next iteration to compute the state of the cells at time t_2. The total amount of computation is determined by the complexity of the actual algorithm and the number of cells in the model and the number of timesteps (e.g., the actual weather forecast for a region the size of the United Kingdom may work with a geographic data cell size of perhaps $1.5 \, km^2$). The amount of communication depends on the extent of the dependency between the cells during the iteration steps of the algorithm.

A parallel application that has a high ratio of computation to communication (i.e., it does a lot of computation in between each communication episode) may be suited to operation on loosely coupled systems. However, an application where the communication occurs at a high rate with a low amount of computation in between the communication is only suitable for execution on specialized tightly coupled architectures. If executed on a loosely coupled system, such applications tend to progress slower, possibly even slower than an equivalent nonparallel version on a single processor. This is because of the communication latency and that the total communication requirement can exceed the communication bandwidth available, so more time is spent waiting for the communication medium to become free and for messages to be transmitted than actually performing useful processing.

5.5 SOFTWARE ARCHITECTURES

In distributed applications, the business logic is split across two or more components. A good design will ensure that this is done to achieve a "separation of concerns" to the greatest extent possible. By this, it is meant that it is ideal to split the logical boundary of components on a functional basis rather than on a more abstract basis. If the logic is divided into components on an arbitrary basis (e.g., perhaps to try to keep all components the same size), then there will likely be more communication and interdependence between the resulting components. This can lead to a more complex and fragile structure because problems affecting one component also affect directly coupled components and can be propagated through a chain of components.

A design in which component boundaries are aligned with the natural functional behavior boundaries can result in a much less coupled structure in which individual functionalities can be replaced or upgraded without destabilizing the entire architecture, and whereby faults can be contained, such that a failed component does not lead to a domino-effect collapse. Dividing the business logic along functional lines also makes it possible to target robustness and recovery mechanisms (such as replication of services) to specific areas of the system that either are more critical to system operation or perhaps are more sensitive to external events and thus more likely to fail.

The way in which the business logic is functionally divided across the components is in many cases the single most significant factor that influences the performance, robustness, and efficiency of distributed applications. This is because it affects the way in which binding between components takes place and the extent of, and complexity of, communication. If done badly, the intensity of communication may be several times higher than the optimal level.

Some functionality however needs to be implemented across several components, due to the way the application is structured or operates. For example, the business logic of a client-server (CS) application may distribute the management and storage of state information across the two types of component. State that is needed only on the client side may be managed within the client component (improving scalability because the server's workload per client is reduced), while shared state needs to be managed and stored at the server side because it is accessed by transactions involving several clients.

5.5.1 COUPLING BETWEEN SOFTWARE COMPONENTS

There are a variety of ways in which multiple software components (running as processes) can be connected together in order to achieve a certain configuration or structure. The application-level business logic and behavior are thus defined by the collective logic of the components and communication between them. The term "coupling" is used to describe the ways in which the various processes are connected together in order to achieve the higher business-level (logical) connectivity. The nature of this coupling is a critical aspect of successful design of distributed systems.

As discussed above, excessive connections and direct dependencies between components are generally problematic in terms of scalability and robustness. Direct dependencies also inhibit dynamic reconfiguration, which is increasingly important in highly complex feature-rich applications and in application domains in which the operating environment is itself highly dynamic.

There are several forms of coupling as explained below. Whether the coupling is tight or loose is determined by the extent of run-time flexibility built in at design time.

Tight (or fixed) coupling is characterized by design time-decided connections between specific components. Explicit references to other components introduce direct dependencies between the components, which means that the application can only function if all of the required components (as per its fixed design-time architecture) are available. If one component fails, the other components that depend on it either fail or at least cannot provide the functionalities that the failed component contributes to. Thus, tightly coupled design tends to increase sensitivity to failure, reduce flexibility, reduce scalability, increase the difficultly of maintenance, and inhibit run-time reconfigurability.

Loosely coupled (decoupled) components do not have connections with specific other components decided at design time. This form of coupling is characterized by intermediary services, which provide communication between components (such as middleware), and/or by the use of dynamic component discovery mechanisms (such as service advertisement). The components are coupled with indirect references. This is a run-time flexible approach as it is possible for the intermediary service to modify the references to other components based on the at-the-time availability of other components; thus, components are not directly dependent on specific instances of other components or processes. For example, a client could be mapped to one of many instances of a service, depending on availability at the time the service request is made, thus making the application robust with respect to the failure of individual service components. Intercomponent mapping can also be based on a description of required functionality rather than based on a specific component ID, thus, at run time, the intermediary (such as middleware) can connect components based on a matching of what one needs and what the other provides.

As loose coupling uses external services or mechanisms to provide the mapping between pairs of components, it has the potential to make applications access and location transparent. Loosely coupled applications are easier to maintain as upgrades can be supported by changing the run-time mapping to swap the new version of a component into the position held by the old version. Loosely coupled applications are also extensible as new components with new functionality can be added without redesigning the other components or recompiling the system. See Figure 5.8.

Figure 5.8 illustrates the advantages of loose coupling. The dynamic mapping facilitates location transparency as the client does not need to know the location of the service component. This enables automatic remapping to a different service instance if the currently used one fails (as between times t_1 and t_3 when server instance A of the service fails and the client requests are remapped to instance B of the same service) and also remapping to an upgraded version of a service (as between times t_3 and t_5 when the service is upgraded and subsequent client requests are mapped to a new version 2 server instance). Access transparency is also provided in some cases where the connectivity service handles differences in the application service interfaces (arising, e.g., during a service upgrade) so that the client components remain unchanged. This is very important where there are high numbers of clients deployed and upgrading them all in step with each server upgrade would be expensive in terms of logistics, time, and effort and risks the situation where different versions of the client could be in use in the system at the same time.

Logical connections can be direct between communicating components or can be facilitated indirectly by intermediate components:

Direct coupling is characterized by the fact that the process-to-process-level connections correspond with the application's business-level communication. The transport layer logical connections map directly onto the higher-level connectivity. For example, there may be a direct TCP or UDP connection between the business-level components.

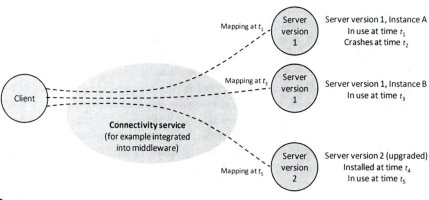

FIGURE 5.8

Dynamic mapping in loosely coupled systems.

Indirect coupling describes the situation where components interact through an intermediary. A stock-trading system provides an example where clients have private connections but see the effects of other clients' trades (in the form of changes in the stock price), which may lead to further transactions. Another example is provided by a multiplayer game hosted on a central server, where the game clients are each aware of the other's presence at the application level (they are logically connected by the fact that they are opponents in the same game) but are not directly connected together as components. Each client is connected only to the server and any communication between the clients is passed to the server and forwarded to the other client. The use-case game application provides a useful example of this form of coupling. A further example is e-mail, in which people use their e-mail clients to send e-mail messages to each other (the logical connection is in terms of the e-mail conversation). The e-mail clients each connect to the users' respective e-mail server, which holds their mail inbox and also sends outgoing mail; see Figure 5.9.

Figure 5.9 uses e-mail to illustrate indirect coupling. The users (actually the e-mail client processes they use) have a logical connection in the passing of e-mail messages at the application level. The e-mail clients are not connected directly, not even if both users have the same e-mail server. In the figure, there are two intermediaries between the e-mail clients. Each client is directly coupled to its respective e-mail server, and the two servers are directly coupled to each other. Notice that this does not affect whether the directly coupled components are tightly or loosely coupled; this depends on how the association between the components is made (e.g., there could be an intermediary service such as middleware that provides dynamic connectivity).

Isolated coupling describes the situation where components are not coupled together and do not communicate with each other although they are part of the same system. For example, a pair of clients each connected to the same server do not need to communicate directly or even be aware that the other exists. Consider, for example, two users of an online banking system. Their client processes each access the banking server, but there is no logical association between the two clients; they each have independent logical connections with the bank. The e-mail example shown in Figure 5.9 provides the framework for another example: consider two users who do not know each

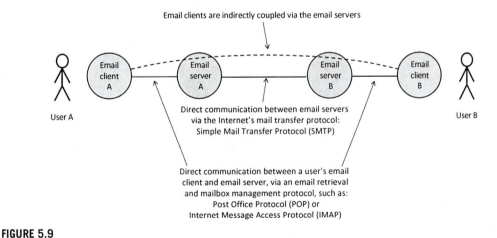

FIGURE 5.9

Sending e-mail involves several components. E-mail clients are indirectly coupled.

other and never send e-mails to each other. The respective e-mail client processes are each part of the same system but have no logical association in this case, and thus, the processes are not coupled together.

Figure 5.10 illustrates the coupling variations possible, based on a CS application as an example. Part (a) shows direct coupling in which the business-level connectivity is reflected directly by the process-to-process connection. This is a very common configuration in small-scale applications. Part (b) shows indirect coupling using a specific component as an intermediary that forwards communication between the connected processes. The central component is part of the application and participates in, and possibly manages, the business-level connectivity; this is reflected in the figure by the business logic connection being shown to pass through the server component. The use-case game provides an example of this, as the server needs to observe game-state changes, update its own representation of the game state, and forward the moves made by one client to the other. The server also has to check for game-end conditions, that is, one client has won or it was a draw and also needs to regulate the turn-based activity of the clients. Part (c) comprises parts (a) and (b) to illustrate

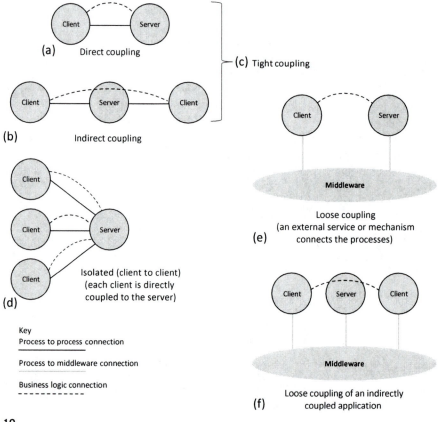

FIGURE 5.10

Coupling variations, illustrated in the context of a client-server application.

tight coupling between components, that is, where the components connect directly to specific other components with which they have a business logic relationship. The application-level architecture is "designed into" these components such that they connect to other components in a predecided way. Part (d) shows that clients using a common service, where each client interaction with the service is private to that specific client, are isolated (i.e., the clients are not coupled to each another) at the business level. Each client obtains service from the server without interaction with, or knowledge of the presence of, the other clients. Part (e) shows how an external connectivity mechanism or service, such as middleware, can be used to provide connectivity between processes without them having to actually form or manage the connectivity directly between themselves. The connectivity mechanism is not part of the application and does not participate in the business-level connectivity; its role is to transparently pass messages between the two components without knowledge of their meaning or content. This is a much more flexible means of connecting processes and is very important for large-scale or dynamically reconfigurable applications. Each of the direct and indirect coupling modes can be achieved in loosely coupled ways, as confirmed by part (f) of the figure, where the messages are passed through the middleware instead of directly between components, but the component relationships at the business logic level are unchanged.

Scalability is in general inversely related to the extent of coupling between components due to the communication and synchronization overheads that coupling introduces. Therefore, excessive coupling can be seen as a cost and should be avoided by design where possible. Thus, for large systems, scalable design will tend to require that most of the components are isolated with respect to each other and that each component is only coupled with the minimum necessary set of other components.

Figure 5.11 shows two different possible couplings between components in the same system. Part (a) shows a tree configuration that tends to be efficient so long as the natural communication channels are not impeded by having to forward messages through several components. This requires good design so that the case where a message is passed from a leaf node up to the root of the tree and down a different branch to another leaf is a rare occurrence and that most communication occurs between pairs of components that are adjacent in the tree. Part (b) shows a significantly more complex mapping, which introduces a higher degree of intercomponent dependency. It may be that the complexity of the connectivity is inherent in the application logic and cannot be further simplified, although such a mapping should be carefully scrutinized.

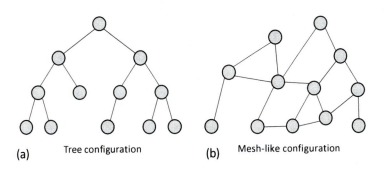

(a) Tree configuration   (b) Mesh-like configuration

FIGURE 5.11

Different complexities of component coupling.

5.6 TAXONOMY OF SOFTWARE ARCHITECTURE CLASSES

The various activities performed by an application can be generically divided into three main strands of functionality: The first strand is related to the user interface, the second strand is the business logic of the application, and the third strand is functionality related to storage of and access to data. These are three areas of functionality that are usually present in all applications to some extent, and if their descriptions are kept general enough, they tend to cover all common activities. This broad categorization is very useful as a means of describing and comparing the distribution of functionalities over the various components of a system. Note that the description in terms of these strands is purposely kept at a high level and is thus more useful to describe and classify the approach taken in the distribution (i.e., in terms of the overall design and behavioral effect of the design) rather than to describe specific features of a design in any detail.

5.6.1 SINGLE-TIER APPLICATIONS

A single-tier application is one in which the three main strands of functionality are all combined within a single component, that is, there is no distribution. Such applications tend to be local utilities that have restricted functionality. In terms of business applications, single-tier design is becoming quite rare as it lacks the connectivity and data-sharing qualities necessary to achieve the more advanced behaviors needed in many applications.

Figure 5.12 illustrates the mapping of the three main strands of functionality onto a single application component. Such applications are sometimes referred to as stand-alone applications.

5.6.2 TWO-TIER APPLICATIONS

Two-tier applications split the main strands of functionality across two types of component. The most common example of a two-tier application is the CS architecture (discussed in detail later).

Figure 5.13 shows some of the possible variations of functionality distribution for CS applications. Note that the figure is illustrative only and is not intended to provide an accurate indication as to the proportion of processing effort dedicated to each of the functional strands.

Peer-to-peer applications (also discussed later in detail) can be considered a hybrid between the single-tier and two-tier approaches. This is because each peer instance is essentially self-contained and thus has elements of all of the three functionality strands. However, to cooperate as peers, there must

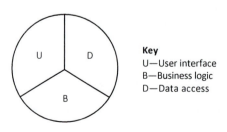

FIGURE 5.12

Single-tier design places all of the main strands of functionality in a single-component type.

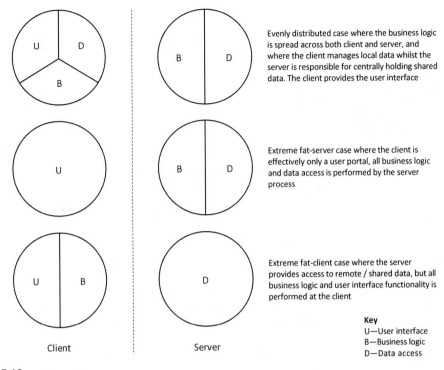

Evenly distributed case where the business logic is spread across both client and server, and where the client manages local data whilst the server is responsible for centrally holding shared data. The client provides the user interface

Extreme fat-server case where the client is effectively only a user portal, all business logic and data access is performed by the server process

Extreme fat-client case where the server provides access to remote / shared data, but all business logic and user interface functionality is performed at the client

Key
U—User interface
B—Business logic
D—Data access

Client   Server

FIGURE 5.13

Two-tier design distributes the main strands of functionality across two-component types.

be some communication between instances, for example, it is common for peer-to-peer applications to facilitate data sharing, where each peer holds a subset of data and makes it available to other peers on demand (see Figure 5.14).

As Figure 5.14 implies, each peer contains elements of each functional strand and therefore can operate independently to some extent. For example, a music-sharing peer can provide its locally held files to the local user without connection to any other peers. Once peers are connected, they can each share the data held by the others.

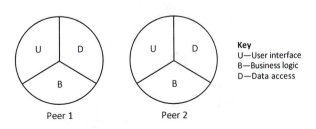

Key
U—User interface
B—Business logic
D—Data access

Peer 1   Peer 2

FIGURE 5.14

Peer-to-peer applications represented as a hybrid of single-tier and two-tier architecture.

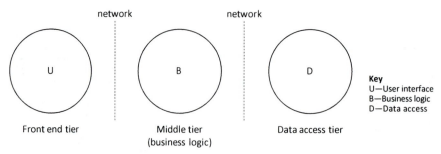

FIGURE 5.15

An idealized three-tier application.

5.6.3 **THREE-TIER APPLICATIONS**

Three-tier applications split the main strands of functionality across three component types. A general aim of this architecture is to separate each main strand of functionality into its own tier; see Figure 5.15. The potential advantages of splitting into three tiers include performance and scalability (because the workload can be spread across different platforms and replication can be introduced at the middle tier and/or the data access tier as necessary) as well as improved maintainability and extensibility (because, if the interfaces between tiers are well designed, functionality can be added at one tier without having to reengineer the other tiers).

Figure 5.15 illustrates an idealized three-tier application in which each of the three functional strands is implemented in a separate component to enhance scalability and performance. In reality, the separation of the functional strands is rarely this clean, and there will be some spread of the functional strands across the components. For example, there may be some data access logic and/or data storage in the middle tier, or there may be some aspect of business logic that is implemented in either the front-end or data access tiers because it may be more efficient or effective, depending on the actual application requirements.

5.6.4 **MULTITIER APPLICATIONS**

Many applications have extensive functionality and require the use of various additional services beyond performing the underlying business role. For example, a banking application may need functionality associated with security and authentication (of users as well as connected systems), interest rates, currency exchange rates, funds transfers between in-house accounts and to/from externally held accounts, calculation of fees and charges, and many others, in addition to the basic operations of managing funds within a bank account. Such functionally diverse systems cannot be built effectively using two-tier or three-tier approaches. In order to manage the complexity of the system itself and to ensure its extensibility, as well as to ensure the maintainability of the subcomponents, these systems need potentially very many component types, and the distribution of functional strands across the components is highly dependent on the needs of each specific business system.

Figure 5.16 illustrates the concept of multitier design. The same basic ideas of three-tier design apply, but the functionality is spread over more component types to give a modular and thus more scalable and extensible design. A main motivation for this approach is to manage (limit) the complexity of

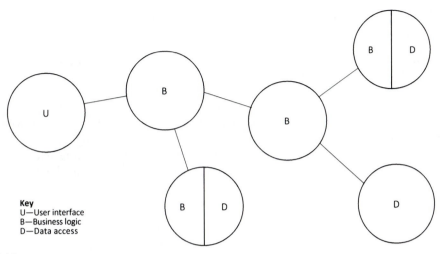

Key
U—User interface
B—Business logic
D—Data access

FIGURE 5.16

An example of functional distribution in a multitier application.

each component type and to achieve flexibility in the way the components are used and connected. For example, there may be some specific functions that are not required in all installations of the software; if the mapping of functionality onto components is done appropriately, then the relevant components can be omitted from some deployments. The modular approach also facilitates upgrade of individual components without disrupting others.

5.7 CLIENT-SERVER

CS is perhaps the most well-known model of distributed computing. This is a two-tier model in which the three main strands of functionality are divided across two types of component.

A running instantiation of a CS application comprises at least two components: at least one client and at least one server. The application's business logic is divided across these components that have defined roles and interact in a prechoreographed way to various extents in different applications. The interaction is defined by the application-level protocol, so for a very simple example, the client may request a connection, send a request (for service) message, receive a reply from the server, and then close the connection. Application-level protocols are discussed in Chapter 3.

5.7.1 LIFETIMES OF CLIENT AND SERVER

In most CS applications, the server runs continually and the client connects when necessary. This arrangement reflects the typical underlying business need: that the server should be always available because it is not possible to know when human users will need service and hence run the client. Essentially, the user expects an on-demand service. However, the user has no control over the server, and clients cannot cause the server to be started on demand. The client is usually shutdown once the user session is ended.

It is not desirable to leave the client components running continuously for several reasons that include the following:

1. It would use resources while active even when no requests are made, and there is no certainty that any further requests will ever be made.
2. Keeping clients running requires that their host computers are also kept running, even when they are not actually needed by their owners.
3. Many business-related applications involve clients handling user-private or company-secret information and generally require some form of user authentication (examples include banking, e-commerce, and e-mail applications); so even if the client component itself remains running, the user session has to be ended (and typically that also ends the connection with the server). A new user would have to be authenticated and a new connection established with the server, hence still incurring a large fraction of the total latency incurred when restarting the component from scratch.

5.7.2 ACTIVE AND PASSIVE SIDES OF THE CONNECTION

The component that initiates a connection is described as the active side, and the component that waits for connection requests is described as the passive side. (Think of actively striking up a conversation with someone, as opposed to being approached by someone else who starts up a conversation with you. You don't have to do anything initially except to be there; hence, your behavior is passive.)

Client on-demand connection to services is supported by two main features of the way servers usually operate: firstly, the fact that servers tend to be continually available (as discussed above) and, secondly, because they tend to be bound to well-known ports and can be addressed by fixed URLs (i.e., they can be located using a service such as DNS; see the detailed discussion in Chapter 6).

5.7.3 THE CS ARCHITECTURAL MODEL

CS is a logical architecture; it does not specify the relative physical locations of components, so they can be both on the same computer and on different computers. Each component runs as a process; therefore, the communication between them is at the transport layer (and above) and can be based on the use of sockets, the TCP or UDP protocols, and higher-level communication.

Figure 5.17 illustrates the general CS architecture, in a situation where two client processes are each connected to a single server. It is quite common that a server will allow many clients to be connected

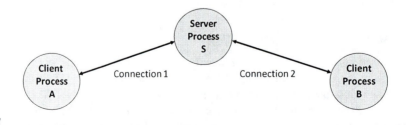

FIGURE 5.17

Client-server generalized representation.

at one time, depending on the nature of the application, but the communication is private between the server and each client.

CS is so named because normally, the server provides some sort of service to the clients. The communication is usually initiated by the client as the server cannot predict when a client will require service. Clients typically do not interact with each other directly as part of the CS application, and any communication that does occur between them is via the server. In many applications, the individual clients are unaware of each other's presence; in fact, this is a key design requirement for a wide variety of applications such as online banking, stock-trading, and media-steaming services.

In such applications, the business model is based on a private client-to-server relationship, which operates a request reply protocol in which the server responds to the requests of the client. The fact that there may be many clients simultaneously connected to the server should be completely hidden from the clients themselves; this is the requirement of concurrency transparency at the higher architecture level. However, a performance effect of other clients could become felt if the workload on the server is high enough that the clients queue for service on a timescale noticeable to the users (this is highly application-dependent). Techniques to ensure services remain responsive as load and scale increases include replication of servers, which is discussed in depth in this chapter and is also discussed from a transparency perspective in Chapter 6.

The clients in such applications can be said to be isolated from each other with respect to coupling, and they are independent of each other in terms of their business logic and function. The clients are each coupled with the server, either loosely or tightly depending on the design of the application-level protocol and the way that components are mapped to each other.

In contrast, a CS multiplayer game is a good example of an application where clients are logically connected via the game (their business logic) and thus are necessarily aware of each other and do interact but indirectly via the server (i.e., the clients are indirectly coupled to each other as discussed previously). In such an application, it is likely that the server will manage shared resources such as the game state and will control game flow, especially in turn-based games. In this case, the architecture fits the fat-server variant of CS; see the next section.

For interactive applications, the client is usually associated with human users (it acts as their agent). For example, an e-mail client connects to a remote e-mail service. The client provides an interface through which the user can request e-mail messages to be retrieved from the server or can send messages to the server to be sent as e-mails to other users.

Figure 5.18 illustrates a typical e-mail configuration and usage scenario. By holding the e-mail inbox centrally at a well-known location (which is identified by the domain part of the user's e-mail address URL), a user can access their e-mail from anywhere that they have a network connection. The user can access the server using one of several e-mail client programs running on different devices. The user interface and data presentation may be different in each case, but the actual data will be the same. Recipients of e-mail will not be able to determine which device, or e-mail client, was used to create the e-mail as all e-mails are actually sent out by the e-mail server.

Application servers are often hosted on dedicated computers that are configured specially for the purpose (e.g., it might have larger memory and faster CPU to ensure it can handle requests at a high speed and with low delay). In such cases, the computer itself is sometimes referred to as being the server, but in fact, it is the process that is running on the computer, which is actually the server.

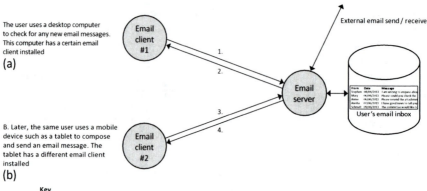

FIGURE 5.18

An e-mail application example of client-server configuration.

5.7.4 VARIANTS OF THE CS MODEL

As discussed earlier, there are three main strands of functionality in distributed applications, related with the user interface, the business logic, and access to and maintenance of data, respectively. Several architectural variants of CS arise, based on different distributions of these functional strands over the client and server components.

As the names suggest, fat server (also known as thin client) describes a configuration in which most of the work is performed at the server, while in fat client (also known as thin server), most of the work is performed in the client. Balanced variants are those where the work is more evenly shared between the components (these variations were illustrated in Figure 5.13). Even within these broad categories, there are various ways the actual strands of functionality are distributed, for example, the client may hold some local state information, the remainder being managed at the server. In such a case, this should be designed such that the clients hold only the subset of state that is specific to individual clients and the server holds shared state.

Fat server configurations have advantages in terms of shared data accessibility (all the data access logic and data are held at a central location), security (business logic is concentrated on the server side and is thus protected from unauthorized modification, and all data accesses can be filtered based on authorization), and upgradeability (updates to the business logic only have to be applied to the small number of server components, and are thus potentially much simpler than when large numbers of deployed clients have to be upgraded).

Fat client configurations are appropriate when much of the data are local to the individual users and do not require sharing with other clients. Fat client design is also ideal in situations where the business logic is somehow customized for individual users (this could be relevant, e.g., in some games and business applications such as stock trading). An important advantage of the fat client approach is scalability. The client does much of the work, such that the server is by implication "thin" (does less work per client) and thus can support more clients as the incremental cost of adding clients is relatively low.

CS applications that distribute the business logic and the data access functions across both client and server components can be described as balanced configurations. In such applications, there are two categories of data: that which is used only by individual clients, such as personal data, historical usage data, preferences, and configuration settings and that which is shared across all or many of the clients and thus needs to be held centrally. The business logic may also be divided across the two-component types such that processing that is local to the client and does not require access to the shared data is performed on the client's host (e.g., to allow behavior customization or to add specialized options related to the preferences or needs of the particular client or the related user). This also has the benefit of reducing the burden on the server's host, making the service more responsive and improving scalability. However, the core business logic that manipulates shared data and/or is expected to be subject to future change runs at the server side for efficiency and to facilitate maintenance and updates. The balanced configuration represents a compromise between the flexibility advantages of the fat client approach and the advantages of centralized data storage and management (for security and consistency) of the fat server.

5.7.5 STATEFUL VERSUS STATELESS SERVICES

In some cases, the client may hold all the application state information, and the server holds none; it simply responds to each client request without keeping any details of the transaction history. This class of service is thus referred to as stateless; see Figure 5.19.

Figure 5.19 provides a comparison of stateful services, in which the server process keeps track of the state of the application, with stateless services, in which the server treats each new client request independently of all others and does not keep state information concerning the current application activity. The stateless approach is very powerful for achieving robustness, especially in high-scale systems. This is primarily because the failure of a stateful server disrupts the activities of all connected clients and requires the state be recovered to ensure ongoing consistency when the server is restarted, whereas the failure of a stateless server does not lose any state information. When a stateless server fails, its clients can be connected to a new instance of the server without the need for any state recovery (because each client maintains the state for its own application session, locally). Another way in which robustness is enhanced with the stateless server approach is that it leads to lower complexity in server components, making them easier to develop and test. The use-case multiplayer game provides an example of a stateful server design; the server stores the game state such as which player's turn it is to make a move.

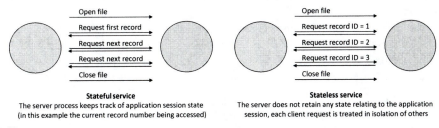

FIGURE 5.19

Stateful versus stateless services.

5.7.6 MODULAR AND HIERARCHICAL CS SYSTEMS

Having only two-component types may be limiting in some situations. There may be a need to divide the functionality of a service across several subcomponents to ensure an effective design and to limit the complexity of any single component. Such distribution also tends to improve robustness, maintainability, and scalability. Consider the situation where a company has its own in-house authentication system, which is intended to validate all service requests in several different applications. There are three different CS applications used to provide the services necessary for the company's business, and each user has a single set of access credentials to use all three services.

One option would be to integrate the authentication system into each of the business services, so that when any client request arrives (at any of the servers), the same authentication activity would occur. This approach is undesirable because it requires that all three applications are reengineered and that the server components grow in terms of complexity, actual code size, and run-time resource requirement. The authentication logic has to be duplicated across the three services and this costs greater design, development, and testing effort. This approach also means that any future upgrade of the authentication system must be performed on all three copies; otherwise, there will be differences in behavior and the authentication strength may become inconsistent.

A better option from an architectural viewpoint would be to develop the authentication system as a separate service (let us assume that the CS model is appropriate for the purpose of the example). The server side of the authentication system will actually perform the authentication checks, which will involve comparing the credentials provided by clients against data held by the service to determine who has the rights to perform various actions or access data resources. The client side of the authentication service can be "thin" (see discussion above), such that it is suitable for integration into other services without adding much complexity. The authentication client can thus be built into the three business services the company uses, such that the authentication is consistent regardless of which business service is used and so that the authentication service can be maintained and upgraded independently of the business services.

To illustrate this hierarchical service scenario, a specific application example is presented: consider an application comprising two levels of service (database access and authentication service). The system is built with three types of component: the database server (which consists of the database itself and the business logic needed to access and update the data), the database client (which provides the user-local interface to access the database), and an authentication server (which holds information necessary to authenticate users of the database). Note that the database server needs to play the role of a client of the authentication service as it makes requests to have its users authenticated. This provides an example where a single component changes between client and server roles dynamically or plays both roles simultaneously,[1] depending on the finer details of the behavioral design. This example is illustrated in Figure 5.20.

Figure 5.20 illustrates a modular approach to services in which a database server makes service requests to a separate authentication service. Both of these services are implemented using the CS model, and the authentication client-side functionality is embedded into the database server component. In this way, the database server effectively becomes a client of the authentication service. This approach has

---

[1] A human behavior analogy of the changing of component's role is provided by the relationship between a salesperson in a shop and the customer. The salesperson (the server) serves the customer (who is the client). However, the salesperson may need to order some special goods for the customer, from another distributor. Thus, the salesperson's role changes to customer for the purposes of the second transaction when the salesperson requests goods from the external supplier.

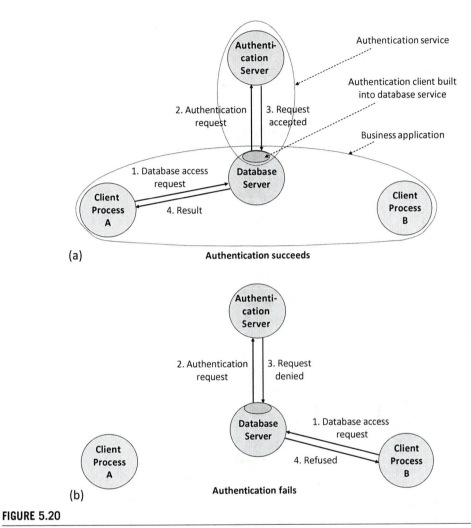

FIGURE 5.20

Modular services; the database service uses the authentication service.

further advantages in terms of transparency and security. The users do not need to access the authentication service directly; all accesses are performed indirectly via the other applications. This means that the user is not aware of the internal configuration and communications that occur. In part A of the figure, client A is authenticated to access the database, while in part B, client B is refused access; in both cases, it appears to the clients that the database server has performed the authentication check itself.

CS architectures can extend to situations in which a client needs access to more than one server, especially where an application component needs to access multiple remote or shared resources. An example of this is where the data required is spread across multiple databases or where a single database is itself distributed throughout a system. The scenario where a single component needs to access two separate databases is explored with the aid of Figure 5.21 in the next section.

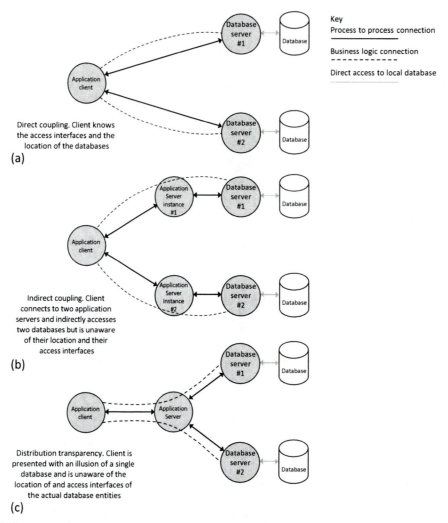

FIGURE 5.21

Two-tier direct coupling versus three-tier indirect coupling to services.

5.8 THREE-TIER AND MULTITIER ARCHITECTURES

CS is a form of two-tier architecture, its main architectural strength being its simplicity. However, it is not particularly scalable for several reasons, which include (1) the application logic concentrated in the single server component type (and thus the complexity of the component increases approximately linearly with functionality); (2) the flexibility limitations and robustness limitations that arise from the direct communication relationships between the service user and the service provider; and (3) the performance bottleneck that arises because all clients connect to a specific service, which may comprise a single process instance.

The introduction of additional tiers, that is, splitting the application logic into smaller modules and distributing it over more types of component, provides greater flexibility and scalability and can also have other benefits such as robustness and security. These architectures have three or more tiers and are commonly referred to as three-tier architectures, but the term multitier is also used. Note that neither usage is strictly adhered to in terms of the actual number of tiers implemented.

The benefits of the three-tier architecture are illustrated using an example for which it is well suited: online banking. Consider some of the main design requirements for such an application:

- The service must be secure. There must be no unauthorized access to data.
- The service must be robust. There must be no data corruption and the system must remain consistent at all times. Individual component failures should not lead to overall system failure, and users should not be able to detect such component failures.
- The service must be highly scalable. There should be a straightforward way to expand capacity as the bank's customer base, or the set of services offered, grows.
- The service must be flexible. The bank needs to be able to change or add functionality. The operation of the system itself needs to comply with legislation such as data protection and privacy laws, which can be changed from time to time.
- The service must be highly available. Customers should be able to gain access to the service at any time of the day or night (the target is a 24/7/365 service).

Although these requirements have been stated specifically in the context of an online banking scenario, it turns out that they are actually generally representative of the requirements of a large proportion of corporate distributed applications. They are listed in a possible order of priority for a banking application, and this order will not necessarily be the same for other applications. In essence, the requirements are security, robustness, scalability, flexibility, and availability. Keeping the example quite high level, let us now consider the ways in which the three-tier architecture satisfies or contributes to each of these requirements.

Security. The client is decoupled from the data access tier by the middle business logic tier. This allows for robust user validation to occur before user requests are passed to the security-sensitive components. It also obscures the internal architecture of the system; an attacker may be able to send a fake request to the middle tier, but the system can be set up such that the third tier only accepts requests from the middle tier and that, when viewed externally from the bank's network, the third tier is not detectable.

Robustness. The three-tier architecture enables replication to be implemented at all tiers except the first tier. This is because each user must have exactly one client process to access the system; there can be many clients active at once, but this is not replication as each client is unique and is controlled independently by its user. The business logic tier and the data access tier can each be replicated, to different extents as necessary, to ensure that the service is robust. It is the design of the replication mechanism at the data access tier that contributes most significantly to ensuring data consistency despite individual component failures.

Scalability. Replication at both the business logic and the data access tiers also contributes to scalability. Additional instances of the components can be added to meet growing service demand. The second and third tiers can be scaled up asymmetrically depending on where the bottlenecks occur. For example, if user validation becomes a choke point as the load on the validation mechanisms is increased, then the business logic layer can be expanded with a higher replication factor than the data access layer, which may continue to perform satisfactorily with its current level of resource.

Flexibility. Recall that three-tier architectures are also sometimes called multitier. This is because there does not have to be exactly three layers and the use of terminology is not always precise. Consider what would happen if not only the user validation mechanism were to become a serious bottleneck due to increased load (as described in the paragraph above) but also the legislation governing the way that banks perform user validation was tightened up requiring significantly stronger checks are put in place (which are correspondingly more resource-intensive). In such a case, if the validation remains part of the business logic, this component type will become very complex and heavyweight. A better approach could be to introduce a new layer into the system and to separate out the user validation logic from the other business logic. The multitier approach allows for changes like this to occur in one layer without affecting the other components, so, for example, the user-client component and the data access component can ideally remain unchanged. This limits the cost of change and perhaps more significantly reduces the risks of instability that arise if too many things are changed at once.

Availability. Once again, it is the flexibility of being able to replicate at multiple layers that provides the basis for a highly available service. If some of the replicas are located at different physical sites, then the service can even continue to operate despite site-local disasters such as floods and power cuts. As long as at least one component of each type is operating, then it is possible that the overall service will be fully functional. Note however that this must be subject to meeting all other requirements; for example, the data consistency aspect of the robustness requirement may enforce that a minimum of, for example, three data access components are running at any time.

Three-tier architectures have further advantages over two-tier designs, the most important of these being the greater extent of transparency they provide and the additional benefits associated with this.

A generic database-oriented application that accesses two different databases is used to exemplify the transparency benefits arising through progression from a two-tier design to a three-tier design; this is explained with the aid of Figure 5.21.

Figure 5.21 illustrates the benefits of using additional tiers. The figure shows three possible ways to connect an application component to a pair of databases. Part (a) of the figure shows a two-tier configuration in which the component is connected directly to the database services. In this situation, all business logic is implemented in the single application component (which is shown as a client in the figure, because it makes service requests to the database service). This configuration is an example of direct coupling and has the advantage of low initial development cost and operational simplicity.

However, this configuration lacks transparency in several important ways. This configuration requires that the client-side application developer deals with the distribution of the components directly; we can say it is not distribution-transparent. The developer has to take account of which data are located at each database when developing the application code that accesses the data. Complex scenarios such as what should happen when only one of the databases is available, or if one fails to perform a transaction but the other succeeds (which can be especially complex in terms of data consistency), must be decided and the scenarios automatically detected and supported in the application logic.

In terms of location and access transparency, the client component must know or find the location of the database servers in order to connect and, because the connection is direct, must know the native format of the database interface. If the database type were changed, then the client component may have to be updated to account for changes in the interface to the databases, such as the message formats used, and the way in which logical connectivity with the database server is achieved (e.g., the way in which the client authenticates itself may change or be different for each of the two databases).

Part (b) of Figure 5.21 shows a more sophisticated alternative architecture in which a third tier is introduced. Part of the business logic is moved into application-level server components that handle the connectivity to and communication with the database services.

The application-level servers can perform additional functions such as security and access control, providing access and location transparency to the client: the former in the sense that the databases may have their own native formats, which the application server deals with, thus hiding these differences from the client, and the latter because the application server can deal with locating the database service without the client needing to know its location or having the required mechanism to locate it.

This approach is superior in several ways. Firstly, it hides the possible heterogeneity of the databases from the client making the client logic simpler. Secondly, it decouples the client component from the database components potentially improving security and robustness since authentication and filtering of requests can be added into the new tier if necessary, and thus, the client cannot directly manipulate the data. Thirdly, many clients can potentially use the same application server component. This centralizes the application business logic making the application generally easier to maintain and simplifying business logic upgrades.

Part (c) of Figure 5.21 shows a further developed architecture in which an application-level server deals with all aspects of database connectivity, such that the client is presented with the illusion that there is only a single database entity. This is achieved because the client only connects to a single application server, which takes care of the connection to the multiple databases, providing the client with a single-system abstraction. In this configuration, the server provides distribution transparency in addition to the other forms of transparency achieved by configuration (b).

Notice that configuration (c) is an example of a three-tier application: The application client is the first tier (the user interface), the application server is the second tier (the business logic), and the database server is the third tier (managing the data access). However, this arrangement of components could also be considered to be effectively two levels of CS in which the application logic is developed as a CS application, and the database is itself developed as a self-contained CS application and the two then merged together. In fact, this might be a helpful way to reason about the required functionality of the various components during the design phase. In the resulting three-tier architecture, the middle component (the application server) takes the role of client in one CS system and has the role of server in the other; see part (b) of Figure 5.22.

Figure 5.22 illustrates some mechanistic aspects of the three-tier architecture. Part (a) of the figure shows a possible communication configuration using sockets. In the configuration shown, the middle tier connects to the data tier (the data tier is the passive side and the middle tier is the active side that initiates the connection). The application client connects to the middle tier whenever service is needed (the application client is the active side and the middle tier is the passive side in this case). Part (b) of the figure shows a possible way to construct a three-tier architecture as two CS stages. This way of visualizing three-tier systems is particularly useful when considering the extension of existing two-tier applications or during the design phase of a three-tier application because it facilitates a modular approach to the design, and in particular, it can help with the elicitation of clear design requirements for the various components. The mechanistic detail shown in Figure 5.22 is applicable to both architectures (b) and (c) depicted in Figure 5.21.

The multiple database scenarios described above have been developed as a series of three application versions, which each map directly onto the configurations illustrated in Figure 5.21. Activity A1 explores the behavior of the three versions, to facilitate understanding of aspects such as the transparency differences between the configurations, the relative strengths and weaknesses of the different configurations, and the different coupling approaches represented.

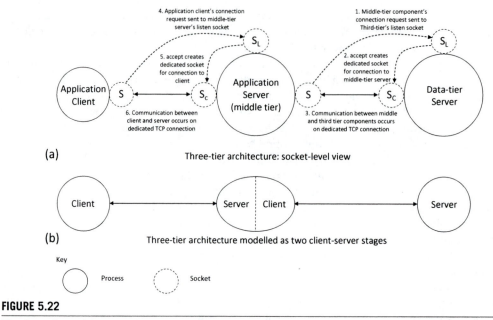

(a)   Three-tier architecture: socket-level view

(b)   Three-tier architecture modelled as two client-server stages

Key

Process   Socket

FIGURE 5.22

The three-tier architecture; some mechanistic aspects.

The components in the three applications communicate over TCP connections, configured in the same manner as shown in part (a) of Figure 5.22.

There can be many reasons why data are distributed within a system. Data may be held in a variety of places based on, for example, the type of data or the ownership of the data or the security sensitivity of the data. It may be purposefully split across different servers to reduce the load on each server, thus improving performance. It may also be replicated, such that there are multiple copies of the same data available in the system. The distribution of data using different physical databases may also be a design preference to ensure maintainability and to manage complexity. For example, a retail company will very likely have an information structure that separates out the customer details into a customer database, the stock details into a stock database and the staff, and payroll details into a further database.

For any large system, the data are much more likely to be distributed than not. It would be generally undesirable for a large organization to collect all of its data about customers, suppliers, products, etc., into a single database, which would be complex and unwieldy, possibly require a very large amount of localized storage, and likely be a performance bottleneck because all data queries would be passed to the same server. In addition, many e-commerce applications operate across multiple organizations, and they are very unlikely to allow their data to be stored remotely, at the other organization's site. More likely, each organization will split their data into two categories: that that they are happy to allow remote organizations to access via a distributed e-commerce application and that that they wish to keep private.

The designers of distributed applications are thus faced with the challenge of accessing multiple databases (and other resources) from within a specific application such that the users of the system are unaware of the true locations of the data (or other resources) and do not have to be concerned with the complexity of the physical configuration of the underlying systems. This is a very useful

ACTIVITY A1 EXPLORING TWO-TIER AND THREE-TIER ARCHITECTURES

Three differently structured versions of the same application are used to explore a number of important aspects of software architectures.

The applications each access two different remote database servers. To simplify the configuration of the software and to ensure that the focus of the experimentation is on the architectural aspects (and not the installation and configuration of databases), the database server programs used in the activity actually hold their data in the form of in-memory data tables instead of real databases. This does not affect the architectural, communication, and connectivity aspects of their behavior.

Prerequisites
Copy the support materials required by this activity onto your computer; see Activity I1 in Chapter 1.

Learning Outcomes
To gain an understanding of different configurations of CS
To gain an appreciation of the distributed nature of resources in most systems
To understand robust design in which some services may be absent, but the remainder of the system still provides partial functionality
To understand the differences between two-tier and three-tier architectures
To gain an appreciation of different coupling approaches
To explore access transparency in a practical application setting
To explore location transparency in a practical application setting
To explore distribution transparency in a practical application setting
The activity is performed in three main stages.

Method Part A: Understanding the Concept of Distributed Data
The first part uses a two-tier implementation comprising the following software components: DB_Arch_DBServer_DB1_Direct (this is the implementation of the first of the two database servers and is used throughout the entire activity), DB_Arch_DBServer_DB2_Direct (this is the implementation of the second database server and is also used throughout the entire activity), and DB_Arch_AppClient (this version of the client connects directly to each of the two database servers). This configuration corresponds to part (a) of Figure 5.21.

The data needed by the client are split across the two database servers, such that each can provide a specific part of it independently of the other. One database server holds customer name details; the other holds customer account balance details. The single client thus needs to connect to both servers to retrieve all the relevant data for a particular customer but can retrieve partial data if only one of the servers is available.

This part of the activity demonstrates direct connection between the application client and the database servers. The location (address and port) of the database servers has to be known by the client. In the demonstration application, the port numbers have been hard-coded, and the server IP address of each server is assumed to be the same as that of the client; the user must enter the correct IP address if the server is located on a different computer.

The connectivity and behavior can be explored in three substeps.

Part A1. Run the client with a single database server.

Start by running the client (DB_Arch_AppClient) and the first of the two database servers (DB_Arch_DBServer_DB1_Direct) on the same computer. Attempt to connect the client to each server. This should succeed for the first database server and fail for the second. Since each connection is managed separately by the client in this particular design, the absence of one server does not interfere with the connectivity to the other.

Now request some data. Provide a customer ID number from the set supported {101, 102, 103} and click the "request data" button. You should see that the partial data held by the particular server that is running are retrieved. The application is designed to send the same request (i.e., the key is the customer ID) to all connected database servers, so the fact that one of the servers is unavailable does not prevent the other from returning its result, that is, only the customer name is returned to the client.

Part A2. Run the client with the other database server.

Confirm that that behavior is the symmetrical with regard to whichever of the databases is unavailable. This time, run the client (DB_Arch_AppClient) and the second of the two database servers (DB_Arch_DBServer_DB2_Direct) on the same computer. Follow the same steps as before. Once connected and a customer data request has been submitted,

ACTIVITY A1 EXPLORING TWO-TIER AND THREE-TIER ARCHITECTURES—Cont'd

the database should return the appropriate customer account data, even though database #1 is not available to supply the customer name.

Part A3. Run the client with both database servers.

Now run the client and both database servers on the same computer. Connect the client to each database server, and then, submit a data request. Notice that the request in this case is sent to both database servers and that both respond with the data they hold, based on the customer ID key in the request message.

You may be able to just about notice the delay between the two data fields being updated in the client, which arises because the data arrive in two messages, from the two different database servers.

Expected Outcome for Part A

You should see that the distributed application functions correctly and that its behavior corresponds to what is expected based on the procedure described above.

You should see how the client sets up and manages the connections to the two databases separately.

Use the diagnostic event logs provided in the database server components to see details of the connections being established and messages being passed between the client and the servers. Make sure that you understand the behavior that occurs.

The screenshots below show the resulting behavior when all three components interact successfully, for part A3 of the activity.

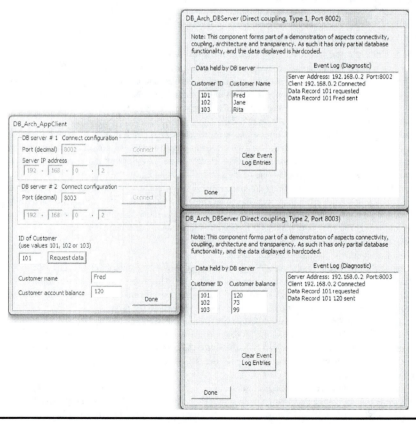

ACTIVITY A1 EXPLORING TWO-TIER AND THREE-TIER ARCHITECTURES—Cont'd

Method Part B: Extending to Three Tiers

This part of the activity is concerned with the introduction of a middle tier to decouple the application client from the database servers (which were directly connected to the client in the configuration used in part A).

This second part of the activity introduces a pair of application servers that each deal with the connection to one of the database servers. This configuration comprises the following five software components: DB_Arch_ DBServer_DB1_Direct (the implementation of the first of the two database servers), DB_Arch_DBServer_DB2_ Direct (the implementation of the second of the two database servers), DB_Arch_AppServer_for_DB1 (the middle tier that connects to the first database type), DB_Arch_AppServer_for_DB2 (the middle tier that connects to the second database type), and DB_Arch_AppClient_for_AppServer1and2 (a modified client component that connects to the new middle-tier application servers instead of directly connecting to the database servers). This configuration corresponds to part (b) of Figure 5.21.

The important difference from the configuration in part A is that now, the client only knows its application servers. It still has to connect to two other components, but it is now indirectly coupled to the data access tier and does not need to know how that tier is organized (in the configuration used in part A, it was directly coupled).

The connectivity and behavior are explored in three substeps.

Part B1. Run the client, the application server that connects to DB1 and the DB1 database server. Request data for one of the customer IDs and observe the result. Notice that the client still manages its connections separately, and thus, data can be received from DB1 in the absence of the other database.

Part B2. Now, run the client with the other application server (which connects to DB2) and the DB2 database server. Confirm that the client's behavior is symmetrical with regard to the unavailable components and that data can be received from DB2 in the absence of DB1.

Part B3. Run all five components such that the complete three-tier system is operating. Connect each application server to its respective database server, connect the client to the application servers, and then submit a data request. Notice that the request is sent separately to each application server, which then forwards it to its database server. Note also that the responses from the database servers are forwarded on the client, which displays the resulting data.

As with part A3, you may also be able to just about notice the delay between the two data fields being updated in the client. It may be slightly more obvious in this case, as the two sets of messages have to pass through longer chains of components, increasing latency.

Expected Outcome for Part B

By experimenting with this configuration, you should be able to see some of the differences that arise as a result of this being a three-tier application, in which the application client is the first tier (user interface), the application server is the second tier (business logic), and the database server is the third tier (data access).

Use the diagnostic event logs provided in the application server components and the database server components to see details of the connections being established and messages being passed between the three tiers. Make sure that you understand the behavior that occurs.

The application servers break the direct coupling that was used in the two-tier architecture. The application servers provide location and access transparency. Location transparency is achieved because the application servers connect to the database servers such that the client does not need to know the location details of them and does not even need to know that the database servers are external components. Access transparency is achieved because the application servers hide the heterogeneity of the two databases, making all communication with the client homogeneous, using a consistent application-specific communication protocol.

It is also important to note that the demonstration has limited scope and that in a real application, the middle tier could additionally provide services as authentication of clients and of the requests they make, before passing them on to the database service.

The screenshots below show the resulting behavior when all five components interact correctly, for part B3 of the activity.

ACTIVITY A1 EXPLORING TWO-TIER AND THREE-TIER ARCHITECTURES—Cont'd

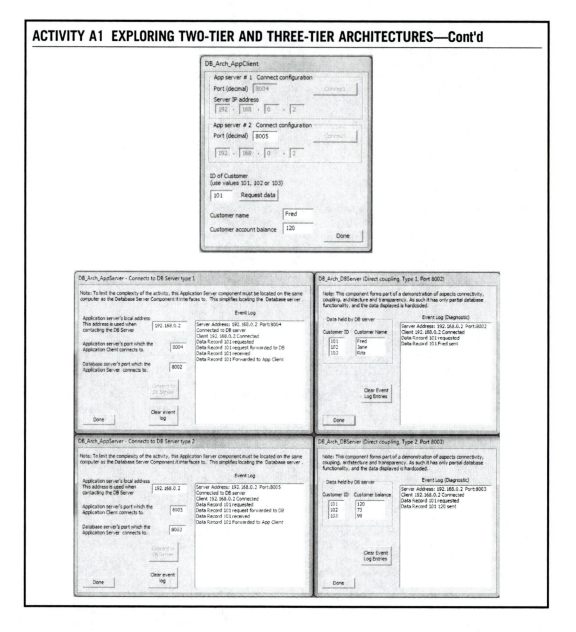

ACTIVITY A1 EXPLORING TWO-TIER AND THREE-TIER ARCHITECTURES—Cont'd

Method Part C: Achieving Distribution Transparency

The third part of this activity is concerned with achieving the transparency goals of distributed systems; in this particular case, we focus on hiding the details of the database services and connectivity such that the client is provided with the illusion that there is a single, locally connected database. This is achieved by refining the middle tier such that the client only has to connect to a single application server that takes care of the connection to the separate databases.

The third configuration uses a modification of the three-tier implementation used in part B. This comprises the following four software components:

DB_Arch_DBServer_DB1_Direct (the implementation of the first of the two database servers), DB_Arch_DBServer_DB2_Direct (the implementation of the second of the two database servers), DB_Arch_AppServer_for_DB1andDB2 (the middle tier that connects to the both of the databases, transparently from the viewpoint of the client), and DB_Arch_AppClient_for_SingleAppServer_DB1andDB2 (a modified client component that connects to the single new middle-tier application server). This configuration corresponds to part (c) of Figure 5.21.

The important difference from the configuration in part B is that now, the client only knows its single application server. It has no knowledge of the way in which the data are organized and cannot tell that the data are retrieved from two different databases. The client is indirectly coupled to the database servers.

The connectivity and behavior are explored in three substeps.

Part C1. Run the client, the application server and the DB1 database server. Request data for one of the customer IDs and observe the result. Notice that the client sends a single request to the application server (the client is unaware of the database configuration). This time, it is the application server that manages the connections to the two database servers, and for robustness, it handles them independently. Therefore, the application server is able to return partial data to the client when only one of the databases is connected.

Part C2. Repeat part C1, this time with only the other database server available.

Part C3. Run the system with all components connected correctly. Request data for one of the customer IDs and observe the result. The single request sent by the client is used by the application server to create a pair of tailored requests, one to each specific database. Responses returned by the two databases are forwarded on by the application server as two separate responses to the client.

Expected Outcome for Part C

Through the experiments in this part of the activity, you should be able to understand the way in which distribution transparency has been added, where it was absent in part B. The client is unaware of the presence of the two different databases and their interfaces. The client is presented with a single-system view in the sense that it connects to the single application server component that provides it all the resources it needs; the design of the client is not concerned with the configuration of the rest of the system.

As with the other parts of the activity, use the diagnostic event logs provided in the application server and the database server components to inspect the behavior in detail.

The screenshots below show the resulting behavior when all four components interact successfully, for part C3 of the activity.

ACTIVITY A1 EXPLORING TWO-TIER AND THREE-TIER ARCHITECTURES—Cont'd

DB_Arch_AppClient for Single AppServer (DB1 and DB2)

App server Connect configuration

Port (decimal) 8004 — Connect

Server IP address

192 . 168 . 0 . 2

ID of Customer
(use values 101, 102 or 103)

101 — Request data

Customer name — Fred

Customer account balance — 120

Done

DB_Arch_DBServer (Direct coupling, Type 1, Port 8002)

Note: This component forms part of a demonstration of aspects connectivity, coupling, architecture and transparency. As such it has only partial database functionality, and the data displayed is hardcoded.

Data held by DB server

Customer ID	Customer Name
101	Fred
102	Jane
103	Rita

Event Log (Diagnostic)

Server Address: 192.168.0.2 Port:8002
Client 192.168.0.2 Connected
Data Record 101 requested
Data Record 101 Fred sent

Clear Event Log Entries

Done

DB_Arch_AppServer - Connects to both DB server type 1 and DB server type 2

Note: To limit the complexity of the activity, this Application Server component must be located on the same computer as the Database Server Component it interfaces to. This simplifies locating the Database server.

Application server's local address
This address is used when
contacting the DB Server — 192.168.0.2

Application server's port which the
Application Client connects to. — 8004

Database DB1 server's port which
the Application Server connects to. — 8002

Database DB2 server's port which
the Application Server connects to. — 8003

Connect to DB Server #1 — Connect to DB server #2

Done — Clear event log

Event Log

Server Address: 192.168.0.2 Port:8004
Connected to DB1 server
Connected to DB2 server
Client 192.168.0.2 Connected
Data Record 101 requested
Data Record 101 request forwarded to DB
Data Record 101 request forwarded to DB
Data Record 101 received from DB1
Data Record 101 Forwarded to App Client
Data Record 101 received from DB2
Data Record 101 Forwarded to App Client

DB_Arch_DBServer (Direct coupling, Type 2, Port 8003)

Note: This component forms part of a demonstration of aspects connectivity, coupling, architecture and transparency. As such it has only partial database functionality, and the data displayed is hardcoded.

Data held by DB server

Customer ID	Customer balance
101	120
102	73
103	99

Event Log (Diagnostic)

Server Address: 192.168.0.2 Port:8003
Client 192.168.0.2 Connected
Data Record 101 requested
Data Record 101 120 sent

Clear Event Log Entries

Done

Reflection

This activity provides some insight into the design and operation of two-tier and three-tier applications.

The two-tier configuration used in part A lacks transparency because the client directly connects with the two database servers. The second configuration introduces the third tier, but in such a way as to limit the extent of transparency achieved (access and location transparency are provided). The third configuration reorganizes the middle tier to add distribution transparency such that the client process is shielded from the details of the database organization and is not even aware that there are multiple databases present.

A good exercise to reinforce your understanding of the concepts shown in this activity is to choose any distributed application (some examples are banking, online shopping, and e-commerce) and to sketch outline designs for it, using both the two-tier and the three-tier architectures. Evaluate the designs in terms of their expected transparency, scalability, and flexibility.

---

example of the importance of transparency. Care has been taken to ensure that the applications developed to support Activity A1 capture both the challenge of accessing multiple distributed resources and the resulting transparency that can be achieved through appropriate design. Note that the actual database functionality that has been implemented in the applications explored in Activity A1 is minimal; it is just sufficient for the examples to be understandable, as the learning outcomes of the activity are focused around the communications and architectural aspects rather than the database itself.

5.9 **PEER-TO-PEER**

The term peer means "with equal standing"; it is often used to describe the relative status of people, so, for example, if you are a student in a particular class, then your classmates are your peers. In software, peers are components that are the same in terms of functionality. The description peer-to-peer suggests that for such an application to reach full functionality, there need to be multiple peer components interacting, although this is dependent on the design of the actual application and the peer components. To place this in context, if the purpose of the application is to facilitate file sharing, then each peer component may have some locally held files that it can share with other peers when connected. If a user runs one instance of the application in the absence of other peers, then only the locally held files will be available; this may still be useful to the user. In contrast to this, consider a peer-to-peer travel information service in which users share local travel information such as news of train delays or traffic jams with other users of the application. The locally held information is already known to the local user (because they create it), so this particular application is only useful when multiple peer components are connected.

5.9.1 **CHARACTERISTICS OF PEER-TO-PEER APPLICATIONS**

The essence of a peer-to-peer application is that two or more peers connect together to provide a service to the users. Some peer-to-peer applications are designed to work well with just a small number of users (such as media sharing), while for some applications, the utility increases in line with the number of peers connected; for example, some games become increasingly interesting when the number of players reaches a critical mass.

Mechanistically, if peers are symmetrical, then any instance can offer services to the others. This means that in a typical peer-to-peer application, any component can be a service provider or a service requester, at different times depending on circumstances. This is a significant difference from the CS and three-tier models, in which the various components have predetermined roles that are not reversible, for example, a client and server cannot swap roles because the specific behaviors are embedded into the different logic of each component type.

From an interaction viewpoint, peer-to-peer applications tend to rely on automatic discovery and connection among peers. Interactions are sometimes "by chance" due to coexistence of users with related needs. For example, peer-to-peer is popular with mobile devices for game playing and file/media sharing, using wireless links such as Bluetooth for connection. If such applications are enabled on devices, then a connection will be automatically established when the devices are in close proximity to one another. Since it is not generally predictable when peers will come into contact and establish relationships, peer-to-peer applications are often described as having ad hoc interaction behavior. This is in contrast with the CS model, in which the interaction is quite structured and in some senses choreographed at design time (in the sense that a particular client is designed to connect to a particular server, either automatically upon start-up or when the user explicitly requests).

The general characteristics of peer-to-peer applications can be summarized as follows:

- Peers communicate with others to achieve their function (e.g., games, messaging, and file sharing).
- The applications often have limited scope (typically with a single main function) and the requirement for connection to remote "others" on a simple and flexible basis.
- Connectivity is ad hoc (i.e., it can be spontaneous, unplanned, and unstructured).
- Peers can interact with others in any order, at any time. Figure 5.23 captures the essence of this.
- Peer-to-peer is well suited to mobile applications on mobile devices.

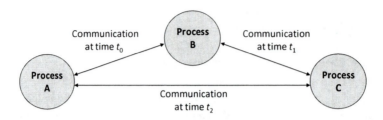

FIGURE 5.23

Peers communicate with different neighbors at different times depending on the application requirements and peer availability.

Figure 5.23 illustrates the dynamic nature of peer-to-peer applications, in which peers may join or leave independently at various times. Therefore, a group of peers may not all be present or connect to each other at the same time; the connections may occur opportunistically as different peers become available.

5.9.2 COMPLEXITY OF PEER-TO-PEER CONNECTIVITY

The complexity of peer-to-peer connectivity is potentially much higher than in other architectures, which are more structured. In CS, the number of connections to a given server is one per client, so if there are n clients, there are n connections to the server; thus, we say the interaction complexity is "order n" stated $O(n)$. This is a linear relationship. With this in mind, consider a peer-to-peer scenario where five peers are present and there are multiple connections established in an ad hoc manner among them.[2] A possible outcome is shown in Figure 5.24.

Figure 5.24 shows a configuration of five peers with a total of seven connections between the peers. The maximum number of connections that would occur if all peers connected to each other peer would be ten, in which case each peer would have four connections to other peers. There is a calculation that can be used to determine the maximum number of connections that can occur between a certain number of peers, given in formula (5.1):

$$C = \frac{P(P-1)}{2} \tag{5.1}$$

where P is the number of peers present and C is the resulting maximum number of connections. Let's insert some values: for four peers, we get $C=(4*3)/2=6$; for five peers, we get $C=(5*4)/2=10$; while for six peers, we get $C=(6*5)/2=15$, and if we consider ten peers, we get $C=(10*9)/2=45$. This is clearly increasing in a steeper-than-linear fashion. Such a pattern of increase is generally described

---

[2]The phrase "connections established in an ad hoc manner" essentially means that there will be various connections established between a particular peer and its neighbors, depending on perhaps the sequence with which specific peers joined the group (because some applications may limit the number of peers that an individual connects to), and the actual range between each pair of individuals (so different subsets are visible to each individual). Therefore, the exact mapping of connections might not be predictable and may be different even in similar (slightly different) situations.

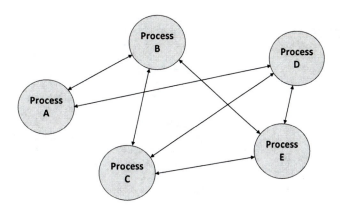

FIGURE 5.24

Ad hoc connectivity in peer-to-peer architectures.

as exponential, and in this particular case, it has order $O((n(n-1))/2)$, which is derived from formula (5.1). With such a steeply increasing pattern of communication intensity, at some point, the number of connections and the associated communication overheads will impact on the performance of the application, thus limiting scalability. In other words, there is a limit to the scale at which the system can grow to and still operate correctly and responsively.

However, some peer-to-peer systems are designed such that peers connect only to a subset of neighbors (i.e., those other peers that are in communication range). For example, some applications (including some sensor network applications) rely on peer connectivity to form a chain to pass information across a system.

5.9.3 EXPLORING PEER-TO-PEER BEHAVIOR

As mentioned above, a popular application for peer-to-peer architectures is media sharing (such as photos and songs) and is especially popular with mobile platforms such as phones and tablets.

A media-sharing peer-to-peer application MediaShare_Peer has been developed to facilitate practical exploration of a peer-to-peer application and is used in Activity A2. The exploration includes aspects of the way in which peer-to-peer systems work, their benefits in terms of flexibility and ad hoc connectivity, and the way in which automatic configuration can be achieved.

ACTIVITY A2 EXPLORATION OF THE PEER-TO-PEER ARCHITECTURE

A media-sharing application is used to explore a number of important aspects of the peer-to-peer architecture.

The application is based on the concept that each user has some music files that they are prepared to share with other users, on a like-for-like basis. The user runs a single peer instance. When there are no other peers available, the user can play only the songs that are held by the local instance. When another peer is detected, the two peers automatically discover each other (in terms of their addresses) and thus form an association (the term connection is

ACTIVITY A2 EXPLORATION OF THE PEER-TO-PEER ARCHITECTURE—Cont'd

avoided because it could imply the use of a connection-oriented transport protocol, such as TCP, when in fact this application uses UDP, partly because of the ability of UDP to broadcast, which is necessary for the automatic peer discovery). The peers then exchange details of the media files they each hold. At this point, the user display is updated to reflect the wider set of resources available to the user (the user can now play any of the music files held on either of the peers).

The demonstration application displays various diagnostic information including an event log, which indicates what is happening behind the scenes, such as the discovery of other peers, and also indicates which specific peer has supplied each music file. This information is included specifically to enhance the learning outcomes of the activity; in a real application, there is no need for the user to see such information.

To avoid unnecessary complexity in the demonstration application, only the resource file names are transferred (i.e., a list of music file filenames) and not the actual music files themselves. In a real implementation, when a user wishes to play a song, the actual song data file would need to be transferred if not already held locally. This simplification does not affect the value of the activity since it is focused on demonstrating the peer discovery and transparency aspects.

Prerequisites
Copy the support materials required by this activity onto your computer; see Activity I1 in Chapter 1.

Learning Outcomes
To gain an understanding of the peer-to-peer architecture
To become familiar with a specific example peer-to-peer application
To appreciate the need for dynamic and automatic peer discovery
To understand one technique for achieving automatic peer discovery
To appreciate the need for transparency in distributed applications
To explore the transparency provision in the demonstration application
The activity is performed in three main stages.

Method Part A: Running a Peer in Isolation
This part of the activity involves running a single instance of the MediaShare_Peer program on a single computer. Note the peer ID number, the list of songs and artists displayed, and the diagnostic event log entries. Close the peer instance and start it again, several times, each time noting the data displayed. You will see that the demonstration application has been designed to generate a unique ID randomly and also to select its local music files randomly, so that the single program can be used to simulate numerous peers with different configurations, without the user having to manually configure it.

Expected Outcome for Part A
This step provides an opportunity to familiarize yourself with the application in the simplest scenario. It also demonstrates two important concepts: Firstly, a single peer operates correctly in isolation (i.e., it does not fail or behave strangely when no other peers are available, but instead operates correctly as a peer-to-peer application that just happens to have only one peer). Secondly, a user sees a list of resources (song files in this case) available for use. Depending on the actual application requirements, it will be generally desired that locally held resources are always available to the local user regardless of the wider configuration of the other peers.

The screenshot below shows a single peer operating in isolation. The media files listed as available are the locally held resources, and thus, a user can access these (i.e., play the soundtracks) without needing any additional components.

ACTIVITY A2 EXPLORATION OF THE PEER-TO-PEER ARCHITECTURE—Cont'd

Peer - Peer demonstration (Media sharing example)

Media data is hardcoded. Ten different pre-determined configurations are provided to allow simulation of a realistic Peer-Peer scenario in which peers have different resouces that they can share with other peers

Random media configuration (represents different peer instances, 0 - 9) 1

Peer ID (Diagnostic) 15680

Event Log (Diagnostic)

Peer Address (recv discovery broadcasts): 192.168.0.2 Port:8004
Peer Address (recv application messages): 192.168.0.2 Port:8005

Media Files Available

Song	Artist	Provider Peer ID (Diagnostic)
Undercover Of The Night	The Rolling Stones	15680
Dancing In The Moonlight	Thin Lizzy	15680
Get Back	The Beatles	15680

Done

Clear Event Log Entries

Method Part B: Automatic Peer Discovery

Leaving the local peer instance running (from part A), start another instance on another computer in the same local network (this is important because broadcast communication is used, which is blocked by routers). You can also confirm empirically that only one peer instance can be operated on each computer (try running two copies on one computer). This restriction arises because each peer has to bind to both of the application ports that are used (one for receiving peer self-advertisement messages for automatic peer discovery and one for receiving the peer-to-peer application messages).

Discovery is achieved by each peer sending a self-advertisement message (PEER_SELF_ADVERTISEMENT message type) containing the unique ID of the sending peer, as well as the IP address and port number details that should be used when application messages are sent to that peer. On receipt of these messages, a peer stores the details in its own, locally held known_peers array. This enables the recipient of future self-advertisement messages to distinguish between peers already known to it and new peers.

Discovery of a new peer automatically triggers sending a request message to that peer (REQUEST_MEDIA_LIST message type) causing the peer to respond with a series of data messages (SEND_MEDIA_RECORD message type), each one containing details of one media data item. Note that in the demonstration application, only the song title and artist name are transferred, but in a real media-sharing application, the actual music file would be able to be transferred on demand.

Expected Outcome for Part B

You should see the automatic peer discovery activity in progress, followed by the transfer of available media resources information between the peers. The diagnostic information would not be shown in a real application, since users do not need to know which peers provide which resources, or even be aware of the existence of the remote peers, or see any other information concerning the structure or connectivity of the application itself. Each user would only see the media resources available to them and would be able to access them in the same manner regardless of location, that is, the application provides access and location transparency.

The screenshots below show the two peer instances on two separate computers after they have each discovered the other peer. The first image is of the same peer as shown in part A above (it was left running) and the second image is of the second peer that was started on a different computer during part B of this activity.

ACTIVITY A2 EXPLORATION OF THE PEER-TO-PEER ARCHITECTURE—Cont'd

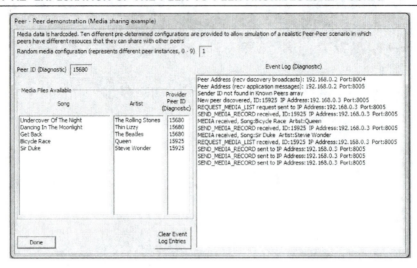

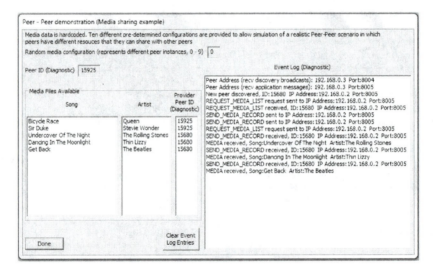

Method Part C: Understanding the Application-Level Protocol

This step involves further investigation to reinforce understanding. In particular, the focus is on the application-level protocol, that is, the sequence of messages passed between the components, the message types, and the message contents.

Part C1. Run the application several times with two peers each time. Look closely at the entries displayed in the activity log. From this, try to map out the application-level protocol (i.e., the message sequence) that is used in the mutual discovery and subsequent mutual exchange of media data between the peers.

ACTIVITY A2 EXPLORATION OF THE PEER-TO-PEER ARCHITECTURE—Cont'd

Hints: Each peer has the same program logic. The peer discovery and media exchange operate independently in each direction, due to the purposeful symmetrical design that was possible in this case and that makes the application simpler to design, develop, and test. Therefore, it is only necessary to map out the messages necessary for one peer (peer A) to discover another peer (peer B), to request peer B to send its media data, and for peer B to respond to that request by actually sending its data. The same sequence occurs when peer B discovers peer A.

Part C2. Run the application with at least three peers. Check that your mapping of the application-level protocol is still correct in these more complex scenarios.

In addition to empirical evaluation by running the application, you can also examine the application source code, which is provided, to confirm your findings and also to inspect the actual contents of the various message types.

A diagram showing the application-level protocol message sequence is provided in an Appendix at the end of the chapter so that you can check your findings.

Reflection

This activity has supported empirical exploration of two important aspects of peer-to-peer applications: firstly, a demonstration of automatic discovery between components, in which each peer keeps appropriate information in a table so that it can differentiate newly discovered peers from previously known peers and, secondly, an investigation of transparency requirements and transparency provision in distributed applications. The aspects of transparency that are most pertinent in this particular application are that the user does not need to know which other peers are present, where they are located, or the mapping of which music files are held at each peer. In a fully transparent application, the user will see only a list of available resources; if the diagnostic information were removed from the demonstration application's user interface, then this requirement would be satisfied.

These aspects of mechanism and behavior are of fundamental importance to the design of a wide variety of distributed applications. Repeat the experiments and observe the behavior a few more times if necessary until you understand clearly what is happening and how the behavior is achieved.

5.10 DISTRIBUTED OBJECTS

The distinguishing characteristic of the distributed objects approach is that it divides the functionality of an application into many small components (based on the objects in the code), thus allowing them to be distributed in very flexible ways across the available computers.

From the perspective of the number of components created, the distributed objects approach might show some resemblance to the multitier architectures discussed earlier. However, there are important differences in terms of the granularity and the functional basis on which the separation is performed. Object-oriented code separates program logic into functionally related and/or specific data-related sections (the objects). In most applications, components are deployed at a coarser grain than the object level. For example, a client (in a CS or multitier application) may comprise program code that is internally broken down into multiple objects at the code level, but these objects run together as a coherent single process at the client component level and similarly for the server component(s). In contrast, distributed objects target a fine-grained division of functionality when creating the software components, based on partitioning the actual code-level objects into separate components. Therefore, when comparing the distributed objects and multitier approaches, we should generally expect to see the distributed objects implementation comprises a larger number of smaller (or simpler) objects, perhaps each performing only a specific single function.

The component-location emphasis of the two approaches is also different. Multitier architectures are primarily concerned with the software structure and the division of the business logic over the various components, which is fundamentally a design-time concern. The distributed objects approach better supports run-time decisions for the placement of instances of components, as it operates on the level of individual objects and can take into account their specific resource requirements at run time.

However, a main challenge of such fine division of functionality is the number of connections between the components and the amount of communication that occurs. There may be opportunities to improve performance by ensuring that pairs of components that interact intensively are kept located on the same physical computer.

Figure 5.25 provides an illustrative distribution of seven objects across five computers, as part of a distributed banking application. The object location may be dynamic based on resource availability, and the communication relationships between components may change over time; hence, the caption describes the configuration as a snapshot (it may be different at other times). Notice that there can be multiple objects of the same type (such as "Customer account" in the example) as well as objects of different types spread across the system. The figure also shows how the services of one particular object (such as "Authentication" in the example) may be used by several other objects on demand. The objects communicate by making method calls to one another, for example, in order to execute a foreign currency transaction, the "Foreign currency transaction manager" component may need to call methods in the "Exchange rates converter" object.

Figure 5.25 also illustrates some of the differential benefits of the distributed objects architecture compared with multitier. In the example shown, the functionality of an application has been divided across many software components. The benefit of this is the flexibility with which the components can be distributed, for example, to be located based on proximity to specific resources. The location of

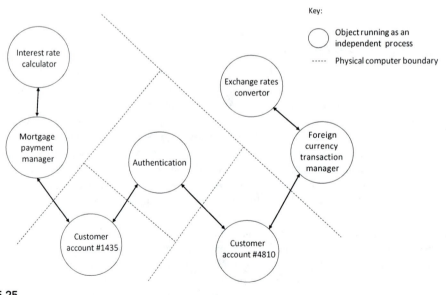

FIGURE 5.25

A distributed objects application; a run-time snapshot.

objects can also be performed on a load balancing basis. For example, if there are several objects (of the same type) in the system that each require a lot of processing resource, the distributed objects approach allows these objects to be executed at different physical sites (processors). Whereas, with the multitier architecture, if all these objects require the same type of processing, they would all have to queue to be processed by a particular server component that provides the requisite function.

Some infrastructure is necessary to support a distributed objects environment. Specific support requirements include a means for objects to be identified uniquely in the system, a means for objects to locate each other, and a means for objects to communicate (make remote method calls to each other). Middleware is commonly used to provide this support; see the next section.

5.11 MIDDLEWARE: SUPPORT FOR SOFTWARE ARCHITECTURES

This section deals with the way in which middleware supports software architectures. A more detailed discussion of the operation of middleware and the ways in which it provides transparency to applications is provided in Chapter 6.

Middleware is essentially a software layer that conceptually sits between processes and the network of computers. It provides to applications the abstraction of a single coherent processing platform, hiding details of the actual physical system including the number of processors and the distribution and location of specific resources.

Middleware provides a number of services to applications, to support component-based software architectures in which many software components are distributed within the system, and need assistance, for example, to locate each other and pass messages. Middleware is very important for dynamic software systems, such as distributed objects, because the location of the actual software components may not be fixed or at least not design time-decided.

5.11.1 MIDDLEWARE OPERATION, AN OVERVIEW

The following discussion of how middleware works focuses on the general principles of operation because there are actually many specific middleware technologies with various differences and special features for particular types of systems (examples include support for mobile computing applications and support for real-time processing).

Middleware provides a unique identifier for each application object that is supported in the system. When these objects are instantiated as running processes, the middleware keeps track of their physical location (i.e., what actual processor they are running on) in a database that itself may be distributed across the various computers in the system (as are the processes that constitute the middleware itself). The middleware may also keep track of the physical location of certain types of resource that the application uses.

Based on its stored information of which objects (running as processes) and resources are present, and where they are located, the middleware provides transparent connectivity services, essential to the operation of the applications in the system. A process can send a message to another process based only on the unique ID of the target process. The middleware uses the process ID to locate the process and deliver the message to it, and it then passes any reply message back to the sender process. This is achieved without either process having to know the actual physical location of the other process, and it operates in the same manner whether the processes are local to each other (on the same processor) or remote. This transparent and dynamic location of objects (processes) also enables movement of objects within the system or for objects to be closed down in one location and subsequently to be run at another location; the middleware will always know the ID of the object and its current location.

It is important to recognize that the middleware plays the role of a communication facilitator. The middleware is not part of any of the applications it supports, but an external service. As such, the middleware does not participate in the business-level connectivity within the application; it does not understand the meaning or content of messages or indeed the specific roles of the various application objects present.

By using the middleware to facilitate connectivity, the objects do not need to have any built-in information concerning the address or location of the other components that they communicate with, and the applications do not need to support their own component discovery mechanisms (an example of such is found in the MediaShare_Peer example discussed earlier). Hence, by using the middleware services, applications can take advantage of run-time dynamic and automated connectivity. This is a form of loose coupling in which the middleware is the intermediary service. This has the benefits of flexibility (because components can be placed on processors based on dynamic resource availability) and robustness (because the application is not dependent on a rigid mapping of components to physical locations). A further important benefit is that the design of the application software is simplified by not having to manage connectivity directly; the value of this benefit increases dramatically for larger applications with many interacting objects.

Figure 5.26 depicts how the presence of the middleware as a virtual layer hides details of the true location of processes and makes them equally accessible regardless of actual location. This means that a process need not know where other processes that it communicates with are physically situated in the system. A process is decoupled from the underlying platform even if it is physically hosted on it. From a logical viewpoint, all processes are equally visible from any platform and all platform resources are equally accessible to all processes.

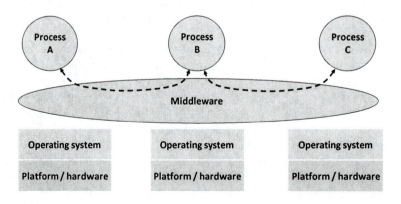

FIGURE 5.26

Overview of middleware.

5.12 SYSTEM MODELS OF COLLECTIVE RESOURCES AND COMPUTATION RESOURCE PROVISION

There are ongoing evolving trends in the ways that computing resources are provided. This section deals with the various models of computing provision that are important to the developers of distributed applications.

To implement successful distributed applications, in addition to the design of the software architectures of the applications themselves (which is the main concern of this book), there is also a need to consider carefully the design of the systems of computers upon which these applications run. The software developer will probably not be directly involved in the selection of processing hardware and the network technologies that link them together. However, it is nevertheless important for software developers to understand the nature of the various common system models and the impacts these may have on the level of resource available to applications, as well as issues such as robustness and communication latency that may have impacts on the overall run-time behavior.

To fully understand the various models of computation resource provision in the modern context, it is helpful to briefly consider some aspects of the history of computer systems.

Starting with the advent of the PC in the early 1980s, the cost of computing power was suddenly in the reach of most businesses where previously it had been prohibitively expensive. Initially, most applications were stand-alone and were used for the automation of mundane yet important tasks such as managing accounts and stock levels, as well as electronic office activities such as word processing. Local area networks became commonplace within organizations a few years later (towards the end of the 1980s), and this revolutionized the types of applications that were used. Now, it was possible to access resources such as databases and physical devices such as printers that were located at other computers within the system. This initial remote access to resources progressed to distributed computing in which the actual business logic of the applications was spread across multiple components, enabling better use of processing power throughout the system, better efficiency by performing the processing locally to the necessary data resources, and also the ability to share access to centrally held data among many users in scalable ways.

The next step was the widespread availability of connections to the Internet. This allowed high-speed data transfer between sites within organizations and between organizations themselves. Applications such as e-mail and e-commerce and online access to data and services revolutionized the role of the computer in the workplace (and elsewhere).

During this sequence of events, the actual number of computers owned by organizations was growing dramatically, to the point where we are today with almost every employee across a very wide range of job roles having a dedicated computer and relying on the use of that computer to carry out a significant proportion of their job tasks.

In addition to the front-end or access computers, there are also the service provision computers to consider. In the days of stand-alone computing, the resources were all in the one machine. In the days of remote access to resources, via local networks, the computers that hosted resources were essentially the same in terms of hardware configuration and levels of resource as the access computers. In fact, one office user could have remote access to a printer connected to a colleague's computer with exactly the same hardware specification as their own. However, once distributed computing became popular, the platforms that hosted the services needed to be more powerful: they needed more storage space on the hard disks, more memory, faster processors, and faster network links. Organizations became increasingly dependent on these systems, such that they could not tolerate downtime, and thus, expert teams of systems engineers were employed. The service-hosting resources and their support infrastructure, including personnel, became a major cost center for large organizations, requiring specialist management.

In addition, most organizations involved in business, finance, retail, manufacturing, and service provision (such as hospitals and local government), in fact just about all organizations, have complex computer processing needs, requiring many different applications running and using a wide variety of different data resources. Prioritizing among these computing activities to ensure efficient usage of resources can be very complex, and thus, the simple resource provision model of just buying more and more expensive server hosting platform computers becomes inadequate, and a more structured resource base is needed.

As a result of these challenges, several categories of resource provision systems have evolved in which resources are pooled and managed collectively to provide a computing service. The various approaches differently emphasize a number of goals that include increased total computing power available to applications (especially the cluster systems); private application-specific logical grouping of resources to improve the management and efficiency of computing (especially the grid systems); the provision of computing as a service to reduce the cost of ownership of processing and storage (especially the data centers); and large-scale, robust, virtual environments where computing and storage are managed (especially the cloud systems).

5.12.1 CLUSTERS

Cluster computing is based on the use of a dedicated pool of processing units, typically owned by a single organization, and often reserved to run specific applications. The processors are usually loosely connected (i.e., connected by a network; see Section 5.4) and managed with special software so that they are used collectively and are seen by the clients of the cluster as a single system.

5.12.2 GRIDS

Grid computing is based on physically distributed computer resources used cooperatively to run one or more applications. The resources may be owned by several organizations and the main goal is the efficient processing of specific applications that need access to specific resources, for example, there may be data resources held at various locations that must all be accessed by a particular application. To ensure the performance and efficiency of the applications' execution, these resources can be brought together within a structure with common management and dedicated processors (a grid).

Typically, grids are differentiated from cluster computing in that the former tend to have geographically distributed resources, which are also often heterogeneous and are not limited to physical computing resources but may include application-specific resources such as files and databases, whereas the cluster resources are fundamentally the physical processors themselves and are more localized and likely to be homogeneous to provide a high-performance computing platform.

5.12.3 DATA CENTERS

Data centers are characterized by very large collections of processing and storage resources owned by a service provision company. Processing capacity is offered as a service to organizations that need large pools of computing resource. Typical data centers have thousands of processing units, so an organization can in effect rent as many as needed to run parallel or distributed applications.

The use of data centers reduces the cost of ownership of processing and storage resources because organizations can use what they need, when they need it, instead of having to own and manage their own systems. A particular advantage arises when an organization needs an additional large pool of resource for a short time, and the data center can rent it to them immediately without the time lag and cost of having to set up the resource in-house. The longer-term costs associated with leasing resources rather than owning them may be further compensated by the fact that the user organizations do not need to dedicate large areas of air-conditioned space to locally host services and also do not have to be concerned with expanding systems over time or continually upgrading hardware platforms and performing operating software updates. In addition, they also do not suffer the indirect costs such as workplace disruption and technical staff retraining associated with the hardware and software updates.

5.12.4 CLOUDS

Cloud computing can be thought of as a set of computing services, including processing and storage, which is provided in a virtualized way by a service provider. The actual processing resources are usually provided by an underlying data center, but the cloud concept provides transparency such that the infrastructure and its configuration are invisible to users.

In addition to the use of cloud facilities for processing, there is currently a lot of emphasis on the storage of bulk data, and this is increasingly popular for use with mobile devices and mobile computing applications. Collections of media files such as videos, songs, and images can be massive in terms of storage requirements and easily exceed the storage available on users' local devices such as tablets and smartphones. The cloud facilities let users upload their files into very large storage spaces (which are relatively huge compared with the capacities of their physical devices) and also offer the advantage of the users being able to access their files from anywhere and also to share them with other users.

The emphasis of cloud computing is towards an extension of personal computing resource (but shifted into a centralized, managed form) in which the cloud storage is allocated permanently to specific users. In contrast, the emphasis of the data center approach is more towards a rentable on-demand computing service. In some respects, a cloud system can be thought of as a set of services hosted on a data center infrastructure.

5.13 SOFTWARE LIBRARIES

Simple programs with limited functionality may be developed as a single source file containing the program code. Such programs are becoming increasingly rare as the extent of functionality and complexity of applications rises. Additional complexities arise from aspects that include multiple platform support, connectivity with other components, and user customization. There is also a growing trend for software components to have increasing inbuilt intelligence or smartness to deal with situations dynamically. Such applications can be very complex, and it is not feasible to write them as single programs. Some highly functional software, such as electronic office applications, as well as the operating systems themselves can reach hundreds of thousands of lines of code; and it is very likely in such cases that they are developed by large teams of developers. There are many applications for which it is unlikely that any single developer fully understands every single line of code and its purpose within the application itself.

A library is a collection of program functions that are related in some way. This could be a specific type of software functionality (such as a mathematics library, which will contain pretested methods for a variety of mathematical functions including trigonometry, computation of square roots, matrix calculations, and many more) or relating to interfacing to a specific hardware device, such as a security camera (in which case the library would have methods to support pan, tilt, and zoom actions on the camera). As a further example, a data encryption library will contain functions to perform encryption and also to perform decryption of data.

Libraries are a key requirement to manage the complexity of software development and also to manage the development costs, especially in terms of the time requirement. Developing all functionality from scratch simply is not a realistic option in most projects. As an example of how important and commonplace libraries are, consider the very simple C++ program "Adder" that was first seen in Chapter 2; the code for this program is shown in Figure 5.27.

Figure 5.27 illustrates the point that even the simplest of programs rely on libraries. I have written the code to input two numbers; add them together and output the result; this was very easy. However, if I had to write a program that did exactly as I have described, from scratch without using any library code, then it would a more complex task. Look closely at the program code listing, and you will see evidence of the use of a library. There are two specific clues here. Firstly, the statement "#include<iostream>"

```cpp
#include "stdafx.h"
#include <iostream>

using namespace std;

int _tmain(int argc, _TCHAR* argv[])
{
  // Input two numbers from the input stream
  int iFirstNumber;
  int iSecondNumber;
  cin >> iFirstNumber;
  cin >> iSecondNumber;

  // Add the numbers
  int iTotal = iFirstNumber + iSecondNumber;

  // Output the result onto the output stream
  cout << iTotal;
  return 0;
}
```

FIGURE 5.27

A very simple program that uses a library.

indicates that I have included a C++ header file, which contains the declarations of some methods; in this case, they are specifically related to the use of the input and output streams (the way these operate was discussed in Chapter 2). The second clue is the statement "using namespace std" that indicates to the compiler that the set of functionalities provided within the namespace (effectively library) called std can be used, without having to place "std::" in front of each call. If this statement is removed, the compiler complains about the use of the cin and cout methods. What is happening here is that the iostream header file contains the definitions of the cin and cout methods, and the actual implementation of these is provided in the std library. Instead of incorporating the namespace at the program level, I could state the namespace explicitly in the code statements in the form std::cin and std::cout, as in the alternative version of the program shown in Figure 5.28.

Figure 5.28 provides a code listing that is exactly equivalent in logic and function to the one shown in Figure 5.27, but it has been modified to emphasize the use of the std namespace. The use of this library is significant because the seemingly innocuous cin and cout methods hide a lot of complexity that I do not have time to study and replicate (and test, in all sorts of input and output data combinations) when developing my applications. The use of the library has saved me time and made my code more robust.

Libraries are a generic concept supported in almost all languages. Java provides a comprehensive set of standard class libraries, the Java class library (JCL), which is organized in the form of packages (each having a specific functional theme, e.g., sockets programming or input/output functions). "Import" statements are used to signal which specific library packages are to be used within a particular program. The .NET Framework class library is part of the Microsoft .NET Framework Software Development Kit (SDK). This library is supported for a number of popular languages including Visual Basic, C#, and C++/CLI (C++ with the Common Language Infrastructure). To incorporate a particular library into a specific program, Visual Basic uses the "Imports [library name]" clause, C# has the "using [library name]" clause, and C++ has "using namespace [library name]."

```cpp
#include "stdafx.h"
#include <iostream>

int _tmain(int argc, _TCHAR* argv[])
{
  // Input two numbers from the input stream
  int iFirstNumber;
  int iSecondNumber;
  std::cin >> iFirstNumber;
  std::cin >> iSecondNumber;

  // Add the numbers
  int iTotal = iFirstNumber + iSecondNumber;

  // Output the result onto the output stream
  std::cout << iTotal;
  return 0;
}
```

FIGURE 5.28

Emphasis of the use of library methods.

Libraries can evolve alongside an application. In particular, when some parts of one application are needed for use in another application, the common parts can be separated off into a library. This not only greatly speeds up the development of the second application but also ensures consistency between the common functionalities of all the applications that use the newly created library.

The main motivations for the use of libraries can be summarized as follows:

- The need to divide code into modules for development and testing purposes.
- The need to reuse code to reduce development time and increase the robustness of applications.
- The need to reuse code to achieve standardized behavior. For example, the use of a method from a standard mathematics library is safer from a correctness viewpoint than a home-grown method. For a second example, using the same user interface libraries across a suite of applications enables maintaining a consistent look and feel to the applications.
- The need to be able to support variants of applications. For example, to achieve the same business logic functionality across several versions of an application that use different IO devices, just the IO-related libraries can be swapped, minimizing the disruption to the application-level code.

The need for refactoring. It is typical that the first working version of a program is not optimal in terms of clear structure and code brevity. Good requirements analysis and design stages of the life cycle help define a good basic structure, but there is usually room for refinement. Common reasons for refactoring are to group together related methods (those that perform related functions or manipulate the same set of data) into new classes and also to subdivide large methods into smaller ones, making the code more modular and readable and thus easier to maintain.

Duplication of code is undesirable because it increases the bulk of a program, not only making it more difficult to verify and test but also reducing readability. In addition, if a particular piece of functionality is repeated several times in the same program and a change to that functionality is needed, the change must be performed the same in all of the duplicate sections; this is costly and error-prone. Refactoring is often performed to remove duplicate sections of code. For example, suppose there is a small section of three lines of code that performs a particular calculation within an application. This calculation is needed in three different parts of the program logic, so the original developer had copied the already tested three-line section to the additional two places in the code. If the nature of the calculation changes (consider an accounting application, being kept up-to-date in line with changing government legislation and tax rules), then it is necessary to change the code. Difficult-to-detect errors will creep in unless all three copies of the function are updated identically. Refactoring resolves this problem by placing the critical three-line section of code into a new method with a meaningful name that succinctly describes what the method does. The new method is then called from the three places in the program where the three copies of the code were located. In this way, the duplication is removed.

5.13.1 SOFTWARE LIBRARY CASE EXAMPLE

The peer-to-peer media-sharing application will be used as a case example for the creation of a software library. This case example will approach the task of creating a software library using a real application that readers will be familiar with and going through the same typical sequence of steps that a software developer would follow.

A seasoned software developer will see application code in a different way to how a novice sees it. The original sample code for the peer-to-peer media-sharing application provides a good example. A novice might look at the code and be content with the fact that the various methods and variables are meaningfully named so as to make the code easy to understand (such features are termed "self-documenting features" and should be part of everyday practice). Where more explanation is needed, comments have been added into the code source. These contain enough detail to explain any complex functionality or to give the reader a hint as to why a particular section of code was designed in a certain way or perhaps why a sequence of steps are carried out in a particular order. However, it is also important to not have too many comments; otherwise, the important ones don't stand out and the readability of the code goes down instead of up. When they run the code, it works as they expect (from having studied the code) and so the novice developer is satisfied.

However, a seasoned software developer would look at the code and think that it needs "refactoring," which basically means that there are opportunities to improve the structure of the code by further dividing into additional methods and possibly even creating additional classes. To put this into context, part of the application code is shown in Figure 5.29.

Figure 5.29 shows a sample of the original source code for the MediaShare_Peer application. Three sections of code have been selected (in each case separated by a line of three dots) to illustrate the way the functionality related to managing peer discovery data was merged into the main application class in the original version of the MediaShare_Peer application.

5.13.1.1 A Brief Description of the Original Code

The first section of code shown in Figure 5.29 shows the format of the data structure used to hold details of each discovered peer. Peers are identified by their IP address and port number (the SOCKADDR_IN structure), combined with a randomly chosen ID, which is generated upon the process' start-up. The InUse flag is necessary because a list of these structures is maintained dynamically and it is important that details of a newly discovered peer do not overwrite a currently used instance of the array (consider the behavior of the peer discovery function when there are many peers joining and leaving the application dynamically). The MediaDataReceived flag is used so that each known peer is only asked for details of its media resources until it has provided them.

The next section of code shows five methods that are all related to the maintenance of and access to the data concerning the list of known peers. This is a very important subarea of functionality of the application; data concerned with known peers are used not only in the peer discovery behavior but also in the logic controlling the sending of messages and the processing of received messages.

The third section of code shown in Figure 5.29 shows an example of the way the data concerning known peers are used in the sending of one of the message types: REQUEST_MEDIA_LIST. Firstly, the index of the data entry for the particular target peer is retrieved from the array of structures via one of the methods GetIndexOf_KnownPeer_InPeersList (shown in the earlier code section) using the peer's ID as a search term. The address of the target peer is then retrieved from the array of structures, accessed directly using the peer's index position in the list. Later in the same code section, data from the array are accessed directly when providing diagnostic output indicating the address and port number the message was sent to.

The full program code for the MediaShare_Peer application is available as part of the book's accompanying resources.

```
struct Known_Peer_details {
    int iPeer_ID;
    SOCKADDR_IN Peer_sockaddr_in;
    bool bInUse;
    bool bMediaDataReceived;
};
...
void CMediaShare_PeerDlg::Initialise_KnownPeers_Array()
{
    for(int iIndex = 0; iIndex < MAX_KNOWN_PEERS; iIndex++)
    {
        m_Known_Peers_List[iIndex].bInUse = false;
        m_Known_Peers_List[iIndex].bMediaDataReceived = false;
    }
    m_iNumberOfKnownPeers = 0;
}

int CMediaShare_PeerDlg::GetIndexOf_Available_KnownPeersList_Entry()
{
    int iNextAvailableEntryIndex = -1;  // Signals array full
    for(int iIndex = 0; iIndex < MAX_KNOWN_PEERS; iIndex++)
    {
        if(false == m_Known_Peers_List[iIndex].bInUse)
        {
            iNextAvailableEntryIndex = iIndex;
            break;
        }
    }
    return iNextAvailableEntryIndex;
}

int CMediaShare_PeerDlg::GetIndexOf_KnownPeer_InPeersList(int iPeerID)
{
    for(int iIndex = 0; iIndex < MAX_KNOWN_PEERS; iIndex++)
    {
        if(true == m_Known_Peers_List[iIndex].bInUse)
        {
            if(iPeerID == m_Known_Peers_List[iIndex].iPeer_ID)
            { //Matched by Peer ID
                return iIndex;
            }
        }
    }
    return -1;
}

bool CMediaShare_PeerDlg::CheckIfPeerExistsIn_KnownPeersList(int iPeerID, SOCKADDR_IN Sockaddr_in)
{
    for(int iIndex = 0; iIndex < MAX_KNOWN_PEERS; iIndex++)
    {
        if(true == m_Known_Peers_List[iIndex].bInUse)
        {
            if(iPeerID == m_Known_Peers_List[iIndex].iPeer_ID &&
                Sockaddr_in.sin_addr.S_un.S_addr ==
                m_Known_Peers_List[iIndex].Peer_sockaddr_in.sin_addr.S_un.S_addr)
            { // Matched by combination of ID and IP address
                return true;
            }
        }
    }
    return false;
}

bool CMediaShare_PeerDlg::Add_NewlyDiscoveredPeerTo_KnownPeersList(int iPeer_ID, SOCKADDR_IN Sockaddr_in)
{
    int iIndex = GetIndexOf_Available_KnownPeersList_Entry();
    if(-1 == iIndex)
    {
        return false;       // No space in array
    }
    m_Known_Peers_List[iIndex].bInUse = true;
    m_Known_Peers_List[iIndex].iPeer_ID = iPeer_ID;
    m_Known_Peers_List[iIndex].Peer_sockaddr_in = Sockaddr_in;
    return true;
}
...

void CMediaShare_PeerDlg::DoSend_REQUEST_MEDIA_LIST_To_NewlyDiscoveredPeer(int iNewlyDiscoveredPeerID)
{
    CString csStr;
    KillTimer(m_nTimer_Send_REQUEST_MEDIA_LIST); // Stop timer - this method is only invoked once per discovered peer

    int iIndex = GetIndexOf_KnownPeer_InPeersList(iNewlyDiscoveredPeerID);
    if(-1 == iIndex)
    {
        csStr.Format("Target peer ID not found in Known Peers array");
        WriteStatusLine(csStr);
        return;
    }

    Message_PDU Message;
    Message.iMessageType = REQUEST_MEDIA_LIST;
    Message.bDataValid = false;
    Message.iSender_Random_ID = m_iPeer_Random_ID;
    Send_ApplicationMessage(Message,m_Known_Peers_List[iIndex].Peer_sockaddr_in);

    csStr.Format("REQUEST_MEDIA_LIST request sent to IP Address:%d.%d.%d.%d  Port:%d",
        m_Known_Peers_List[iIndex].Peer_sockaddr_in.sin_addr.S_un.S_un_b.s_b1,
        m_Known_Peers_List[iIndex].Peer_sockaddr_in.sin_addr.S_un.S_un_b.s_b2,
        m_Known_Peers_List[iIndex].Peer_sockaddr_in.sin_addr.S_un.S_un_b.s_b3,
        m_Known_Peers_List[iIndex].Peer_sockaddr_in.sin_addr.S_un.S_un_b.s_b4,
        htons((u_short) m_Known_Peers_List[iIndex].Peer_sockaddr_in.sin_port));
    WriteStatusLine(csStr);
}
```

FIGURE 5.29

Sections of the original peer-to-peer media-sharing application source code.

5.13.1.2 Refactoring Example for the MediaShare_Peer Application

A partial refactoring of the MediaShare_Peer application is performed to illustrate some of the refactoring concepts in practice. The refactoring focuses on the functionality associated with dealing with managing peer discovery data as was shown in Figure 5.29. The refactoring also serves as a precursor step to separating the code into an application-specific part and a software library that can be reused by other applications that have similar requirements with regard to dynamic peer discovery.

The steps taken for this particular refactoring exercise were the following:

1. Identify a group of methods that are related in terms of the functionality they perform and also in terms of the data items they manipulate.
2. Create a new class called CKnownPeers.
3. Move the identified methods into the new class. Move the class-specific data item (the array of KnownPeers structures) into the new class, as a member variable.
4. Map the new CKnownPeers class into the remaining application logic, by placing calls to the new class' constructor and methods to replace the previously direct access to the data items.
5. Test carefully; the pre- and postrefactoring versions of the application should have identical behavior at the application level. Note that refactoring is not intended to change behavior or to fix errors, so even though the internal architecture of the code has changed, the business functionality should not. If there are any resultant differences in behavior, then the refactoring is incorrect.

Figure 5.30 contains two sections of the code of the new class created in the refactoring process, and the sections are separated by the row of three dots. The first section of code is the class definition from the C header file KnownPeers.h. This defines the class in terms of its member functions and data items. Zcore to the operation of this class. The second section of code shows part of the implementation of the class. The class header file is included, followed by definitions of two of the class methods, the first of these being the constructor.

Figure 5.31 shows some aspects of the mapping between the two classes. The main application class still contains the application-specific logic. This class contains a member variable m_pKnown-Peers, which is actually an object instance of the new CKnownPeers class (see the first section of code in the figure). The m_pKnownPeers is initialized by calling the class constructor within the outer class' constructor (the second section of code in the figure). From this point onward, the methods of the m_pKnownPeers object can be called.

The third section of code in Figure 5.31 shows the new version of the DoSend_REQUEST_MEDIA_LIST_To_NewlyDiscoveredPeer method, which uses the methods of the new class to indirectly access the KnowPeers data; the occurrences of the m_pKnownPeers variable have been highlighted (compare with the version shown in Figure 5.29).

5.13.1.3 Library Example for the MediaShare_Peer Application

Common code (which is used by multiple applications) or code with some specific bounded functionality can be extracted from application code into a library. It is very important that the separation between the application-specific code and the library code is performed along a clear boundary and should not cut across classes, for example.

```
class CKnownPeers
{
public:
    CKnownPeers(void);
    int GetIndexOf_Available_KnownPeersList_Entry();
    int GetIndexOf_KnownPeer_InPeersList(int iPeerID);
    bool CheckIfPeerExistsIn_KnownPeersList(int iPeerID, SOCKADDR_IN sockaddr_in);
    bool Add_NewlyDiscoveredPeerTo_KnownPeersList(int iPeer_ID, SOCKADDR_IN Sockaddr_in);

    // Use of these 'getter' and 'setter' methods replace any direct access to the data
    // that occurred in the original version
    // The data is 'private' to this class, enforcing object oriented design principles
    struct Known_Peer_details get_Known_Peers_List_entry_byIndex(int iIndex);
    void set_Known_Peers_List_entry_bMediaDataReceived_flag_byIndex(int iIndex);

private:
    void Initialise_KnownPeers_Array();

    Known_Peer_details m_Known_Peers_List[MAX_KNOWN_PEERS];
};

...

#include "KnownPeers.h"

CKnownPeers::CKnownPeers(void)
{
    Initialise_KnownPeers_Array();
}

void CKnownPeers::Initialise_KnownPeers_Array()
{
    for(int iIndex = 0; iIndex < MAX_KNOWN_PEERS; iIndex++)
    {
        m_Known_Peers_List[iIndex].bInUse = false;
        m_Known_Peers_List[iIndex].bMediaDataReceived = false;
    }
}
```

FIGURE 5.30

The new CKnownPeers class extracted by refactoring.

The refactoring described above has created an additional class with specialized functionality associated with the management of peer discovery data. This functionality is quite clearly differentiated from the application-specific functionality remaining in the main application class and is potentially useful to many applications so it is an ideal candidate for separation into a software library to promote reuse.

From this starting point, the creation of a software library is straightforward. First of all, a new software project is created, and the new class is moved across from the original project into the new one. The compiler must be configured to create a library rather than an executable application. This is important because of the way in which the resulting library file will be used. It does not have its own entry point, for example, so it cannot be run as a separate process. Instead, the library will be linked in to applications after their own code has been compiled.

```
// Declaration of a member variable of type class CKnownPeers in the header of the
// MediaShare_PeerDlg class
class CKnownPeers* m_pKnownPeers;


// Initialisation of the pKnownPeers object in the constructor of the
// MediaShare_PeerDlg class
m_pKnownPeers = new CKnownPeers();


// Example use of the pKnownPeers member variable to call methods on the newly
// created CKnownPeers class from within the MediaShare_PeerDlg class
void CMediaShare_PeerDlg::DoSend_REQUEST_MEDIA_LIST_To_NewlyDiscoveredPeer(int iNewlyDiscoveredPeerID)
{
    CString csStr;
    KillTimer(m_nTimer_Send_REQUEST_MEDIA_LIST);
    // Stop the timer - this method is only invoked once per discovered peer

    int iIndex = m_pKnownPeers->GetIndexOf_KnownPeer_InPeersList(iNewlyDiscoveredPeerID);
    if(-1 == iIndex)
    {
        csStr.Format("Target peer ID not found in Known Peers array"); //Should not be able to happen
        WriteStatusLine(csStr);
        return;
    }
    struct Known_Peer_details KPD = m_pKnownPeers->get_Known_Peers_List_entry_byIndex(iIndex);

    Message_PDU Message;
    Message.iMessageType = REQUEST_MEDIA_LIST;
    Message.bDataValid = false;
    Message.iSender_Random_ID = m_iPeer_Random_ID;
    Send_ApplicationMessage(Message,KPD.Peer_sockaddr_in);

    csStr.Format("REQUEST_MEDIA_LIST request sent to IP Address:%d.%d.%d.%d  Port:%d",
                  KPD.Peer_sockaddr_in.sin_addr.S_un.S_un_b.s_b1,
                  KPD.Peer_sockaddr_in.sin_addr.S_un.S_un_b.s_b2,
                  KPD.Peer_sockaddr_in.sin_addr.S_un.S_un_b.s_b3,
                  KPD.Peer_sockaddr_in.sin_addr.S_un.S_un_b.s_b4,
                  htons((u_short) KPD.Peer_sockaddr_in.sin_port));
    WriteStatusLine(csStr);
}
```

FIGURE 5.31

Mapping between the main application class and the KnownPeers class.

The library is compiled, creating a file with a .lib extension. For the specific example described here, the file name is DemonstrationLibrary_for_MediaShare_Peer.lib (the project and source codes are available as part of the resources that accompany the book).

The application project no longer contains the CKnownPeers class functionality that was moved across into the library. Thus, the application project needs to link in the library; this is achieved by setting the library as an input file (dependency) of the project in the linker settings.

Figure 5.32 provides a summary representation of the sequence of stages described above, resulting in a software library component that can be linked into one or more applications.

It is important to reinforce the message that all three versions of the application have the same external behavior. The application logic has been redistributed across software classes and components, but the behavior is identical in each case. To confirm this, the versions were tested for interoperability, simultaneously running peers from the different versions. You can repeat this version cross testing yourself, as all the versions of the code are available in the accompanying resources.

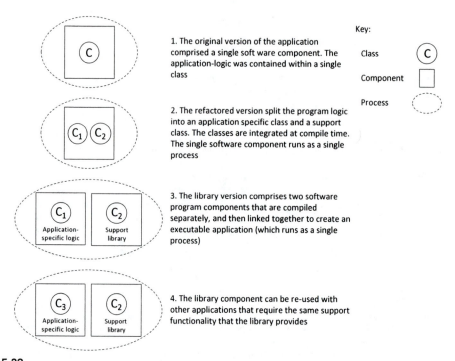

1. The original version of the application comprised a single soft ware component. The application-logic was contained within a single class

2. The refactored version split the program logic into an application specific class and a support class. The classes are integrated at compile time. The single software component runs as a single process

3. The library version comprises two software program components that are compiled separately, and then linked together to create an executable application (which runs as a single process)

4. The library component can be re-used with other applications that require the same support functionality that the library provides

Key:

Class

Component

Process

FIGURE 5.32

Diagrammatic representation of the stages of library creation and use.

5.13.2 STATIC LINKING AND DYNAMIC LINKING

Libraries are linked to application source code in two main ways: statically, where the linking is performed at the component build stage (typically, this is immediately after compilation) and a self-contained executable is created and, dynamically, where the linking is postponed to run time (the linking is performed when the component is run as a process).

5.13.2.1 Static Linking

Static linking is performed when a software component is built (i.e., when the executable file is created). The compiler checks the syntax of the code and creates an intermediate code representation of the program. The linker then includes all necessary library code into the binary image (the executable file). This can increase the size of the resulting executable file significantly, although many optimized linkers only add in the actually used fragments of code from the library (only the implementations of the methods actually referenced in the application source code).

5.13.2.2 Dynamic Linking

Dynamic linking is performed at run time and uses a special variation of a library format called dynamic link library (DLL). This approach is very popular with Microsoft operating systems and came about to limit the size of application executable files and also their run-time images. The approach is advantageous when multiple applications run in the same system and require the same library, because the operating system reads the DLL file into memory and holds its image, separately to the images of the two or more application processes, such that each can call sections of code from the library as necessary. The more applications using the same DLL, the more memory savings that are made. However, if only a single application is using the DLL, there are no space savings because the combined size of the application executable file and the DLL file will take up approximately the same space on the secondary storage (such as hard disk) as the single application with the static library prelinked in. Also, since both parts need to be held in memory at run time, they will require approximately the same combined memory as the equivalent statically linked process would.

5.13.2.3 Trade-Offs Between Static and Dynamic Libraries

The executable file is larger when static linking is used than with dynamic linking. The size difference can be significant for large applications and impacts the storage space requirements, the time taken to transmit the file over a network, and also the amount of time required to load the file as the first step in execution.

The memory image size is larger for processes where the libraries have been statically linked; however, a process that uses dynamic linking still needs access to the library code. Therefore, the DLL must also be loaded into memory, evening out the gains when it is used by only a single process, but potentially saving a lot of memory space when many applications are sharing the same DLL image.

Dynamic linking can be used to achieve deployment-time configurability, in which there are different versions of the same DLL but with different functionality. The method names in the library will be the same, such that the application code can be linked with either version and operate correctly. This then allows some control over the way the application operates by changing which version of the DLL is present and without changing the application code or the executable image. However, DLL versioning can be problematic. Most applications are released as particular build versions, which have been carefully tested and are found to be stable, for example, a new release may be issued after some upgrades have been done. Similarly, DLLs can undergo upgrades and also have version numbers. Having two interdependent component types (one application and one DLL) that are each versioned separately over time can lead to complex run-time mismatches. If a method name in one of the components has changed, or the set of passed parameters is different, then the application either will not run or may crash when the problem call is made. If the changes concern only logic within a library method, then the application may appear to work correctly but return the wrong result. To put the problem into context, consider an application that has an initial release version 1.1, which works perfectly with its DLL version 1.1. After some months, there have been three more versions of the application (versions 1.2, 1.3, and 2.0) and five more versions of the DLL (versions 1.2, 1.3a, 1.3b, 2.0, and 2.1). It is quite likely that there are numerous combinations that work fine, some that have not occurred yet so the outcome is unknown (but considered unsafe), and some that definitely do not work. If you add into the scenario the existence of hundreds of customer sites each with their own technical teams performing system updates, you can start to see some aspects of the versioning challenges that can occur with multicomponent software projects. The possibility of such problems increases the testing burden, to ensure that deployed system images contain only valid combinations of the components. An undesirable situation that could arise is the need to keep multiple backdated DLL versions available to ensure that whatever version of a particular application is installed, it can be run correctly.

The DLL may be omitted from a target computer. Similarly to the problem above, the external DLL requirements of applications must be taken into account when installing the applications. A frustrating situation arises when the application runs perfectly on the development computer (which obviously has the DLL present) but then does not run when ported to another computer because the DLL is not present at that site. This situation is usually easy to fix on a small scale but adds to the overall cost of systems maintenance.

Statically linked applications are self-contained; the library code has been merged in to create a single executable file with no external dependencies. This is robust because it avoids the issues of DLL omission or DLL version mismatch.

5.13.3 LANGUAGE-DEPENDENT FEATURE: THE C/C++ HEADER FILE

The C and C++ languages have a header file type as well as the source code file type. The use of the header file type can improve the internal code architecture of individual components and help ensure consistency across multiple components of a distributed application; hence, it is included in this chapter.

The header file is used to hold definitions of things, as opposed to implementation details. Well-structured C++ code will be divided into a number of classes, each class having one source file (with a .cpp filename extension) and one header file (with a .h filename extension). The class header file will contain the definition of the class and its methods and will declare any class-level member variables. The class header file may also contain the definitions of constants, structures, enumerations, and other constructs used in the class. There can also be additional header files, that is, ones that are not related to any specific class. These can be part of the language itself (e.g., related to the use of libraries, as with the afxsock.h header depicted in Figure 5.34, necessary because the application uses the sockets library) or can contain application-wide definitions that are used across several components. Figure 5.33 illustrates the way in which header files may be used for multiple purposes in an application.

Figure 5.33 illustrates some common uses of header files to provide structure to the source code of a distributed application. Language library header files relate to the inclusion of library routines (e.g., the sockets API library); they contain the declarations of the routines, which are needed by the compiler at compile time in order that the syntax can be checked. For example, even though the actual libraries are not linked by the compiler, it needs to ensure that the various methods that have been used from a particular library have been used correctly, with the appropriate syntax, the requisite number of and types of parameters, etc. Component-specific header files provide the definitions for the implementation classes (the application-specific functionality). Application-wide headers can be used to provide global definitions that are compiled into each of the components and thus are very important for ensuring consistency in the ways that certain related components behave. A good example of this is in the

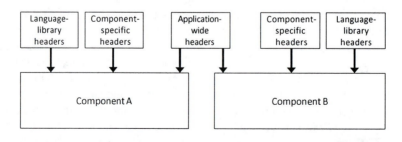

FIGURE 5.33

Use of header files when building distributed applications.

definition of message types and message formats (PDUs; see Chapter 4) that must be the same for each component so that messages are interpreted correctly. In the application shown in Figure 5.33, each of the components A and B will be compiled separately, but the same application-wide header files will be used in both compilations.

Figure 5.34 puts the use of header files into a specific use-case scenario, using the three-tier database application discussed and used in Activity A1 earlier. For each component, only the main class name is shown to avoid unnecessary complexity, but otherwise, this figure accurately reflects the software architecture at the component level. The application comprises three different software components (application client, application server, and database server), which are each compiled to a separate executable file and each run as a separate process. Since the three components are part of the same application, they need to have unambiguous definitions of message formats, message-type identifiers, and the predefined application port numbers. This is achieved by placing these definitions in the file DB_Arch_General.h and including it into all three compilations. The contents of this header file are shown in Figure 5.35.

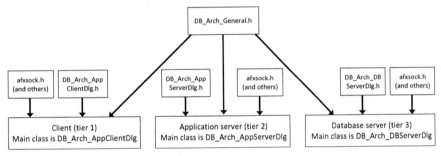

FIGURE 5.34

Header file usage example, a three-tier database application.

```
#pragma once

#define DB_TYPE1_PORT 8002 // Decimal
#define DB_TYPE2_PORT 8003 // Decimal

#define MAX_CUST_NAME_LEN 20

enum MessageType {REQUEST_RECORD, SEND_RECORD, CLIENT_DISCONNECT};

struct Message_PDU {
  MessageType iMessageType;
  int iCust_ID;
  bool bCustNameValid;
  char cCustName[MAX_CUST_NAME_LEN +1];
  bool bCustBalanceValid;
  int cCustBalance;
};
```

FIGURE 5.35

The contents of the header file DB_Arch_General.h from Figure 5.34.

The contents of the application-wide header file DB_Arch_General.h are shown in Figure 5.35. This file provides important definitions that must be consistent for all of the application components. If a new message type were to be added to the application to extend functionality, then adding it into the enumeration provided in this one header file would ensure that it is defined the same for all of the components. Similarly, if the new message type also required an additional field be added to the message PDU, adding it in the structure defined here will have an application-wide effect.

5.14 HARDWARE VIRTUALIZATION

In order to explain hardware virtualization in a clear and accessible way, it is first necessary to briefly revisit the concepts of nonvirtualized (some may say "traditional") computing.

The nonvirtualized model of computing is that each computer has an operating system installed and the operating system has a scheduler component that runs processes, so that the processes can use the resources of the computer (this aspect was discussed in depth in Chapter 2). The operating system hides some aspects of the hardware platform's configuration. One very important aspect of this is resource management that is done to ensure that resources are used efficiently (e.g., each process may only be given access to a particular fraction of the entire system memory space, thus allowing multiple processes to run concurrently without interference). The operating system also isolates application processes from physical devices, a particular example discussed in Chapter 2 was the way in which input and output streams are managed by the operating system so that the processes do not actually directly manipulate the IO devices. This operating system management of devices has two important benefits, one being that the various IO devices can be used by multiple processes without conflict and the other being that the specific interface details of individual IO devices are abstracted away at the program level. So, for example, a programmer can write an input or output statement without knowing the type or size of screen, the type of keyboard, etc., that is present and also the program once written will work correctly even if the IO devices are changed in the future.

Hardware virtualization is the term used to describe the addition of a software layer, which sits on the real hardware platform and acts as though it is actually the platform itself. The software layer is called a virtual machine. The VM is able to execute processes in the same way as the operating system would in the traditional (nonvirtualized) model of computing described above.

In some ways, hardware virtualization can be considered an extension of the isolation and transparency aspects provided to processes by operating systems. However, hardware virtualization is motivated by the need to support flexible retasking and reconfiguration of computers, which can involve replacing the entire software image on the computer, including the operating system (or running two different operating systems on the same computer) and performing these changes in a short time frame.

In order to appreciate the significance of the additional flexibility represented by the VM approach, over the nonvirtualized approach, it is necessary to consider the high degrees of heterogeneity that occur in modern distributed systems. Heterogeneity manifests in many forms, as was discussed earlier in this chapter. The existence of so many different hardware platforms, operating systems, and resource configurations adds a lot of complexity to the management of computer systems. Users need to run a variety of applications that may require different configuration of resources or even different operating systems, yet it is not feasible to reinstall the operating system in order to run a particular application or to provide each user with several differently configured computers in order to allow them to run the various different applications they need throughout the working day. The problem is more significant for the owners of large-scale computing resources due to the cost of purchasing equipment and the potentially even greater ongoing management costs associated with the man power needed to support users with such requirements. Data centers in particular need a way to automatically deal with issues of heterogeneity, because they rent out their computing resources to numerous different customers, hence multiplying the numbers of different resource configurations likely to be needed. Clearly, data centers cannot meet this demand in a cost-effective and timely manner with specifically configured physical platforms because they would have to have a much larger total number of computers and a very large technical support team.

5.14.1 VIRTUAL MACHINES

VMs have become an essential tool to overcome the challenge of frequent reconfiguration of platforms to meet users' diverse needs, which arise in part from the various forms of heterogeneity in modern systems and also because of the very wide variety of applications of computing with ever-increasing extent of functionality and the inevitable accompanying complexity.

A VM is a process that runs on the physical computer and presents an interface to application process, which mimics that of the real computer. The VM thus isolates the application processes from the physical machine. For example, a computer that is running one particular operating system (such as Microsoft Windows) may host a VM that emulates a computer running a different operating system such as Linux, in which case Linux applications will run on the VM and will behave the same as if on a real computer with the genuine Linux operating system installed. The VM is the process that the Windows scheduler deals with; see Figure 5.36.

Figure 5.36 shows how a VM can be run on top of a conventional operating system such as Microsoft Windows, to enable nonnative applications to run. In other words, the VM provides an emulation of a different operating system (Linux in this case) and thus allows applications designed for that operating system to run.

For environments where computers need to be configured with different VMs, a VM manager or hypervisor can be used. The hypervisor creates and runs VMs as needed. The need for automated VM management can be understood by considering a data center scenario: each particular customer wishes to run their specific application, which requires a certain run-time system (i.e., the operating system and various needed services). Instead of having to provision the computer for each customer by

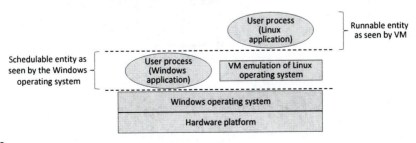

FIGURE 5.36

Using a VM to emulate additional operating systems on a single computer.

installing the appropriate operating system and then each of the required services and then the various components of the customer's specific application, which involves many separate stages and is thus time-consuming and subject to failure of individual steps, the hypervisor can generate the appropriate VM image in a single step.

Type 1 hypervisors run directly on the computer hardware (i.e., they replace the operating system), whereas type 2 hypervisors are hosted by an operating system (i.e., they run on top of the operating system in the same way that the VM runs on top of the operating system in Figure 5.36).

5.14.2 JAVA VIRTUAL MACHINE

Java implements a specific VM, the JVM, which offers a consistent interface to Java programs regardless of the actual operating system and architecture. Java programs actually run in the JVM and not directly on the underlying platform; this means that Java programs are inherently portable. This concept is illustrated with the aid of Figures 5.37 and 5.38.

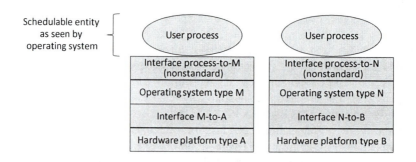

FIGURE 5.37

The conventional process-to-operating system interface is operating system-dependent.

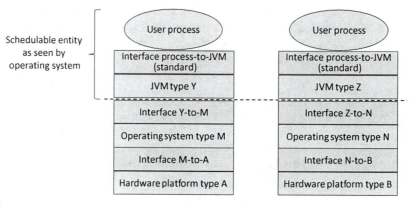

FIGURE 5.38

The JVM standard interface to processes.

Figure 5.37 shows that the conventional process run-time environment (the process-to-operating system interface) is provided differently by each operating system (as explained in detail in Section 5.3 earlier). This means that applications must be built specifically for their target operating system, and therefore, executables are not transferrable across operating systems.

Figure 5.38 shows that the JVM provides a standard interface to application processes, regardless of the underlying system comprising any combination of operating system and hardware platform. This is achieved by using a special universal code format called the Java bytecode, which is a simple and standardized representation of the program logic with a low-level format that is similar to assembly language in some respects. The end result is that the user process in left part of Figure 5.38 will run correctly in the system shown in the right of Figure 5.38 without any modification or recompilation.

The JVM itself does have to be built specifically for the platform on which it runs, hence the differences in the JVM type, and the operating system interface to the JVM (the layer below the JVM), in Figure 5.38. The operating system sees the JVM as the schedulable entity; in other words, the JVM itself is the process that runs directly on top of the operating system and not the Java application.

5.15 STATIC AND DYNAMIC CONFIGURATIONS

The issue of static versus dynamic software configurations has been touched upon in several earlier sections, including Section 5.5.1 and also in Section 5.9 where ad hoc application configurations were discussed and explored in an activity. Later in this chapter, Section 5.16.1 also examines dynamic configuration of a service to mask failure of an individual server instance.

This section brings together the various issues associated with the choice between static and dynamic configurations of distributed applications. The main aspects that need to be considered are the way in which components locate each other, the way in which components form connections or at least communicate with each other, and the way in which roles are allocated to individual components in a group (e.g., when there are several instances of a service and a single coordinator is needed).

5.15.1 STATIC CONFIGURATION

Static configuration is achieved by default when building multicomponent applications. If a design fixes the roles of components and the ways in which the components relate to each other, connect to each other, and perform processing as part of the wider application, then you will end up with a static configuration. In such situations, there is no need for any additional services to dynamically map the components together; the one configuration is deemed to suit all situations. If you run the application a number of times, you will always arrive at the same component-to-component mapping.

The identity of software components can be represented in several different ways. Components need unique IDs that can be based, for example, on their IP address or on a URL, the URL being more flexible because it allows for relocation of services while still identifying the service components uniquely. Component IDs can also be system-wide unique identifiers allocated by services such as middleware, specifically for the purpose of mapping components together when messages need to be passed between them.

The essence of static configuration is that components connect to one another based on design time-decided mappings. This is most obvious if a direct reference to the identity of one component is built into another and used as the basis of forming connections or at least sending messages.

Statically configured applications are generally simpler to develop and test than their dynamically configured counterparts. However, they rely on complete design-time knowledge of their run-time behavior and also the environment in which they run. This is very difficult to confirm unless the application has very limited functional scope and comprises a small number of components. This also means that statically configured systems may need more frequent version updates to deal with any changes in the run-time environment, because each specific configuration is fixed for a particular setting. Perhaps, the most significant limitation of static configuration is that it is inflexible with respect to dynamic events such as component failures or failure of the specifically addressed platform where a resource is located.

5.15.2 DYNAMIC CONFIGURATION

Dynamic configuration of distributed applications increases run-time flexibility and potentially improves efficiency and robustness. In the case of efficiency, this is because components can be moved between physical locations to better map onto resource availability, or component requests can be dynamically diverted to different instances of server processes (e.g., to balance the load on a group of processors). Robustness is improved because component-to-component mappings can be adjusted to account for events such as the failure of a specific component; so, for example, if a client is mapped to a particular instance of a service and that instance fails, then the client can be remapped to another instance of the same service. There are mechanisms that can be used to do this automatically.

The essence of dynamic configuration is that components discover one another based on roles rather than component-unique IDs. That is, components know what types of services they require and request connections to components that provide those services without knowing the IDs of those components in advance. Typically, additional services are required to facilitate this, specifically to advertise the services provided by components, or otherwise to find services based on a role description, and to facilitate connectivity between the two processes. Examples of external services that facilitate dynamic discovery and connectivity include name services and middleware.

Some services perform dynamic configuration internally, for example, to balance load or to overcome or mask failures of individual subcomponents of the service. Mechanisms such as election algorithms are often used to automatically select a coordinator of a dynamic group of processes whose membership can change over time, as different nodes join and leave the service cluster. An election algorithm follows several steps: firstly to detect that a particular component has failed, secondly to carry out an election or negotiation among the remaining components to choose a new coordinator, and finally to inform all components of the identity of the new coordinator to suppress additional unnecessary elections. Election algorithms are discussed in detail in Chapter 6. Other mechanisms for dynamic configuration discussed elsewhere in the current chapter include the use of heartbeat messages by which one component informs others of its ongoing presence and health status and service advertisement messages that facilitate automatic discovery of components or the services they offer.

Dynamic configuration mechanisms also facilitate context-aware behavior in systems (see next section).

5.15.3 CONTEXT AWARENESS

Context awareness implies that an application's behavior or configuration takes the operating context into account, that is, it dynamically adjusts its behavior or configuration to suit environmental or operating conditions. This is a complex aspect of systems behavior, which is out of scope for the book generally, but is very briefly introduced here for completeness.

Context is information that enables a system to provide a specific, rather than generic response. To give a very simple example, you ask me the weather forecast for tomorrow and I respond "it will rain." This is only of use to you if we have previously communicated the location we are referring to (which contextualizes both the question and the answer in this case). One example relating to distributed services concerns the failure of a server instance. The number of remaining servers is a very important context information because if there are still one hundred servers operating, the failure of one is relatively insignificant, but if there are only one, or none remaining, then it is serious and new servers need to be instantiated.

Dynamic configuration mechanisms and context information provide a powerful combination to enable sophisticated and automated reconfiguration responses to events such as sudden load increases or failure of components.

5.16 NONFUNCTIONAL REQUIREMENTS OF DISTRIBUTED APPLICATIONS

There are a number of common nonfunctional requirements of distributed applications, most of which have already been mentioned several times in various contexts in the book. Here, they are related and differentiated.

Robustness. This is a fundamental requirement of almost all distributed applications, although it can be interpreted in different ways. Robustness in the sense that there are no failures at the component level is unrealistic because no matter how well designed your software is, there are always external factors that can interrupt the operation of a distributed application. Examples include excessive network traffic causing delay or a time-out, a network failure isolating a server from its clients, and a power failure of the computer hosting the server. Therefore, a key approach to robustness is to build in redundancy, that is, to have multiple instances of critical components such that there is no single point of failure (i.e., there is no single component that, if it fails, causes the system itself to fail).

Availability. This requirement is concerned with the proportion of time that the application or service is available for use. Some business- or finance-related services can cost their owners very large sums of money for each hour that they are unavailable; consider stock-trading systems, for example. Some systems such as remote monitoring of dangerous environments such as power stations and factory production systems are safety critical, and thus, availability needs to be as near to 100% as possible. You may come across the term "five nines" availability, which means that the goal is for the system to be available 99.999% of the time. Availability and robustness are sometimes confused, but technically, they are different; an example is scheduled maintenance time in which a system is not available, but has not failed. Another example is where a system can support a certain number of users (say, 100). The 101th user connects to the system and is denied service, so the service is not available to him specifically, but it has not failed.

Consistency. This is the most important of all of the nonfunctional requirements. If the data in the system do not remain consistent, the system cannot be trusted and so has failed at the highest level. To put this into context with a very simple example, consider a banking application in which customers can transfer money between several of their own accounts online (over the Internet). Suppose a customer has £200 in her current account and £300 in her savings account. She moves £100 from the current account into the savings account. This requires multiple separate updates within the bank's system, possibly involving two different databases and several software components. Suppose the first step (to remove £100 from the current account) succeeds, but the second step (to place it in the savings account) fails; the system has become temporarily inconsistent because the customer's credit has gone from £500 to £400 when the total should have remained at £500. If the system has been designed well, it should automatically detect that this inconsistency has arisen and "roll back" the state of the system to the previous consistent state (in this case the initial balance values).

Performance (or Responsiveness). This is the requirement that a transaction is handled by the system within a certain time frame. For user-driven queries, the reply should be timely in the context of the use of the information. For example, if the application is stock trading, then a response within a second or so is perhaps acceptable, whereas if it is an e-commerce system in which one company is ordering wholesale batches of products from another, a longer delay of several seconds is adequate as the transactions are not so time-critical. See also the discussion on Scheduling for Real-Time systems in Chapter 2.

Consistent performance is also important for user confidence in the system. Variation in response times impacts some aspects of usability, since long delays can frustrate users or lead to input errors (e.g., where a user is uncertain that the system has detected a keystroke and so enters it again, this can lead to duplicate orders, duplicate payments, and so forth).

Scalability. This is the requirement that it should be possible to increase the scale of a system without changing the design. The increase could be in terms of the number of concurrent users supported or throughput (the number of queries or transactions handled per unit of time). Scaling up a system to meet the new demand could involve adding additional instances of components (see Section 5.16.1), placing performance-critical components on more powerful hardware platforms, or redesigning specific bottleneck components in isolation, but should not require a redesign of the overall system architecture or operation.

It is important not to confuse scalability and responsiveness; a lack of scalability as load increases may be the underlying cause of reduced responsiveness, but they are different concerns.

Extensibility. It should be possible to extend the functionality of a system without needing to redesign the system itself and without impact on the other nonfunctional requirements, the only permissible exception being that there may be an acceptable trade-off between the addition of new features and a corresponding reduction in scalability as the new features may lead to an increase in communication intensity.

Transparency. This is the requirement that the internal complexities of systems are hidden from users such that they are presented with a simple to use, consistent, and coherent system. This is often cited as the fundamental quality metric for distributed systems.

A general transparency goal is the single-system abstraction such that a user, or a running process that needs access to resources, is presented with a well-designed interface to the system that hides the distribution itself. All resources should appear to be available locally and should be accessed with the same actions regardless if they are truly local or remote. As mentioned in numerous other sections, there are many different flavors of transparency and a wide variety of ways to facilitate it.

Transparency provision is potentially impacted by the design of every component and the way they interact. It should be a main theme of concern during the requirements analysis phase because it is not generally possible to post-fit transparency mechanisms to an inherently nontransparent design.

Usability. This is a general label for a broad set of concerns that overlap several of the other non-functional requirements, especially responsiveness and transparency. Usability is also related to some specific technical aspects, such as the quality of user interfaces and consistency in the way information is presented, especially if there are several different user interfaces provided by different components.

In general, the more transparency that is provided, the more usable a system is. This is because users are shielded from having to know technical details of the system in order to use the system. Usability in turn improves overall correctness because with clear, easy to use systems, in which users do not have to follow complex procedures and are not asked to make decisions based on unclear situations, there are fewer mistakes made by users or technical managers.

5.16.1 REPLICATION

Replication is a commonly used technique in distributed systems, not only having the potential to contribute to several of the nonfunctional requirements identified above, most notably robustness, availability, and responsiveness, but also having the potential to disrupt consistency if not implemented appropriately.

This section focuses on the relationships between replication and the nonfunctional requirements of distributed systems. Transparency and mechanistic aspects of replication are discussed further in Chapter 6.

The simplest form of replication is service provision replication where there are multiple server instances, but each supports its own set of clients, so there is no data sharing across the servers. This approach is used to improve availability and responsiveness but does not improve robustness as there is still only one copy of the state of each client session and only one copy of the data used by each client. There is no requirement for data update propagation, but instead, there is a need to direct the clients to servers so as to balance the load across them, since if all clients connect to one server, then the service provision replication has no effect on performance.

Consider the use-case game. Multiple copies of the server could be started at different locations to achieve a simple form of replication without the need for any modification to the current design. This replicates function, but not data or state. Each client would still connect to a specific server instance (identified by its IP address) and thus would only see the other players connected to the same server instance, advertised in the available players list. More users in total could be supported, that is, availability is enhanced, and because users could connect to the geographically nearest server, the network latency may be reduced, increasing responsiveness. However, the clients are associated, via their server, in isolated groups. There is no mechanism to move games between servers or to back up game state at other servers; each client is still dependent on a particular server to hold the game state, so robustness is not improved in regard to active games.

Where replication of data occurs, the extent of performance benefits and the extent of the challenge to manage data and ensure data consistency are related to the data access mode supported, specifically whether data can be modified or is read-only, during transactions. If the replication is of active application state, or of updateable resources, then the additional complexity can be very high due to the need to propagate updates to all copies. This is relatively simpler if only one copy of the shared data is writable by the user application, but even so, there is still a significant challenge of ensuring that copies that go off-line are brought up-to-date correctly when they reappear. There are three common scenarios that occur:

1. The data are read-only at all of the replicas. This could apply to information-provision applications such as an online train timetable system, in which multiple servers could be used to support a great many clients retrieving train journey details simultaneously. However, the data itself can only be modified by a separate system (a management portal not available to the public users). There are no user queries that can cause any data updates. In such cases where the replication is across multiple server instances of read-only resources, then the additional complexity arising from the replication itself is relatively low and the scheme can scale very well.
2. The replication is implemented such that only a single copy of the data is writable and the other copies are readable. The challenges here are ensuring that only one copy of the data really is ever writable at any specific time and also ensuring that all updates to the writable copy are copied promptly and reliably to the other copies. This can work well in applications in which read accesses significantly outnumber write accesses.
3. The replication is implemented such that all copies of the data are writable. This can lead to various issues, including the specific problem of a lost update, where two copies of a particular data value are both modified in parallel. When each of the changes is then propagated across the system, the one that is applied last will overwrite the one that was applied first, that is, the first update has been lost. The lost update problem is significant because it occurs even when all components are functioning correctly, that is, it is not caused by a failure, but rather is an artifact of the system usage and the specific timing of events.

This approach can be very complex to manage and is generally undesirable because in addition to the lost update problem, there a number of ways the system can become inconsistent.

The primary objective when adding replication is to ensure that the system remains consistent under all circumstances and use scenarios. This must always be the case, to ensure the correctness of systems even when the original motivation and purpose for implementing replication are to improve availability, responsiveness, or robustness.[3]

Figure 5.39 illustrates a simple form of replication in which a single instance of the service (and thus data) is available to users at any given time. This is because all service requests are directed to the master instance of the service, so the backup instance is effectively invisible to users. When a user request causes data held by the server to change, the master instance updates its local copy of the data and also propagates any updates to the backup instance. The backup instance monitors the presence of the master instance. This could, for example, be facilitated by the master instance sending a status massage to the backup instance periodically, in which case if these messages cease, the backup instance becomes aware that the master instance has failed. Figure 5.39 shows the situation when both instances of the service are healthy and updates are performed on both replicas of the data. The mechanics of step 1 (parts a and b) in Figure 5.39 could be based on multicast or directed broadcast or by using a group communication mechanism, which is discussed in Chapter 6.

---

[3] Replication mechanisms provide a very good example of the general rule that whenever a new feature is added to an application or system, for whatever reason, it potentially introduces additional challenges or new failure modes. Circumventing the new challenges or protecting against these new failure modes can be costly in terms of design and development effort and especially testing (which must cover a wide state space of possible scenarios). Ultimately, we can find ourselves doing what the author terms "complexity tail chasing" in which we add increasing layers of complexity to deal with the issues arising from the complexity of earlier layers. Therefore, before adding any additional mechanisms such as replication, it is vital that a detailed requirements analysis has been carried out and that the consequences of adding the mechanism are considered and a balanced decision is made through in-depth understanding of the effective costs and benefits.

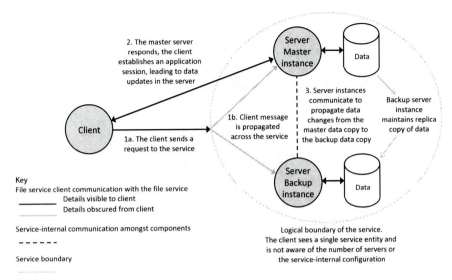

FIGURE 5.39

Master-backup data replication of active application state and data.

Figure 5.40 illustrates the adaptation of the configuration of the replicated service that occurs when the master server instance has failed. Initially, there will be a period in which the service is unavailable, because the backup instance has not yet detected the previous master's failure, so has not taken over the master role. Once the backup server instance detects that the master has failed, it takes over as master (this is also described as being promoted to master state). From this point onward, service requests are dealt with by this server instance.

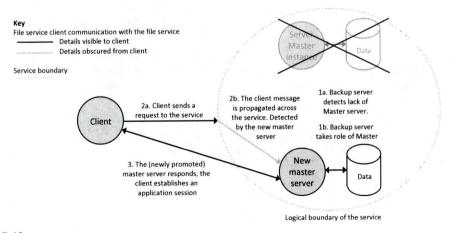

FIGURE 5.40

Backup-promotion scenario in master-backup data replication.

The mechanism by which the failure of the master instance is detected must itself be reliable. The detection is usually based on some form of heartbeat mechanism such that the healthy master server sends a periodic massage to inform the backup that it is still healthy. This may be omitted when updates are occurring regularly (because the update messages also serve the purpose of informing the backup that the master is still healthy, without adding any additional communication) and only switched on if the interval between updates exceeds some threshold. Thus, the backup copy should not wait more than a specified period without a message from the master. However, messages can be lost or delayed by the network itself, and thus, it is not safe to trigger the backup copy switching over on the omission of a single heartbeat message; perhaps, three omitted messages in sequence are appropriate in some systems. The configuration of the heartbeat scheme (which includes the interval between messages and the number of messages that must be missed in sequence to serve as confirmation that the master has failed) must be tuned for the specific application as it represents a three-way trade-off between the responsiveness of the backup system, the message overheads to maintain the backup system, and also the risk of a false alarm, which introduces a further risk of data inconsistency if both copies become writable simultaneously.

5.16.2 SEMANTICS OF REPLICATION

When implementing mechanisms such as replication, it is important to consider carefully the merits of the various alternative ways of achieving the required functionality. For replication, semantics are concerned with the actual way the replication mechanisms behave in terms of the way they manipulate the system data. Issues that need to be considered include the following:

- What should happen when the master copy becomes unavailable, should the backup copy become available for access, or is it maintained only to establish the system consistency once the master server has been repaired?
- If the backup copy is made available (upon master failure), there is the issue as to whether it should be made read-only or read-write; the main concern is that the two copies could get out of sync. This could happen if updates occur at the backup copy, and then, it also fails; when the previous master copy comes back on line, it has no knowledge of the intervening transactions.
- Are the roles of master and backup preassigned or do they arise dynamically from the system behavior (e.g., the most accessed instance may be automatically assigned to be the master instance)? If the roles were preassigned, then what should happen after a master that had failed (and hence the initial backup instance is now acting as master) recovers? Does the original master reclaim its master role, or does it assume backup status?
- Some implementations of replication employ an odd number of server instances (at least three) so that in the event that the copies become out of sync, then a vote can be taken, that is, the correct value is taken to be the majority value. However, there are no absolute guarantees that the majority are correct (it is less likely, but possible that two out of the three missed a particular update). There is also no guarantee that there will even be a majority subset (consider a group of five server instances, in which one has failed and the four remaining are split with two having a particular data value and the other two having a different value).

Figure 5.40 illustrates one of the possible fallback scenarios when the master copy fails. In the approach illustrated, upon detection of master failure, the backup instance promotes itself to master status (i.e., it takes over the role of master). Data consistency is preserved so long as the previous master instance had propagated all data updates to the (then) backup copy, which it should do if it is operating correctly.

5.16.3 AN IMPLEMENTATION OF REPLICATION

A demonstration application is provided to illustrate the implementation and operation of replication in the context of a simple database application. The same database theme as used in Activity A1 is continued, but in this case, there is a single database that is replicated, instead of two different databases, as used in the earlier activity. In this specific example, the replication has been used to ensure the service is robust against server-process failure. A single master status instance of the service deals with client service requests. The master instance also broadcasts periodic heartbeat messages to signal its presence to other instances of the service. An additional instance can exist, having the status of backup; its role is to monitor the status of the master instance by receiving heartbeat messages. If the absence of three successive heartbeat messages is detected, then the backup instance promotes itself to master status. The master instance of the service propagates any data updates made by the client, to the backup instance, therefore keeping the data held at the backup instance synchronized with the master instance and thus keeping the service consistent. If the backup copy has to take over from the master instance then, the data will be up-to-date and reflect any changes made before the master instance crashed.

In order to show the variety of design choices available, the implementation uses an alternative means of clients locating the service to that shown in Figures 5.39 and 5.40. The technique shown in those examples is based on the client sending a service discovery broadcast message and the master instance of the service responding. Instead, the implementation of the demonstration replicated service uses service advertising in which the master instance of the service sends broadcast messages at regular short intervals of a few seconds. A newly started client must wait to receive a service advertisement message that contains the IP address and port details needed to connect to the service. If the backup server instance elevates itself to master status, it takes over sending the service advertisement broadcasts, so that clients always detect the current master instance of the service. In this implementation, a failed master instance that recovers will take on the status of backup (assuming that another instance now has master status, such as the previous backup instance).

Figure 5.41 shows the service-internal behavior that determines the state of each instance of the replicated database application. The diagram shows the behavior of a single process; each process maintains its own copy of the state transition logic and represents its state internally as a pair of variables. In this case, the state variables that govern the state transition behavior are as follows:

m_ServerState {Backup, Master}	An enumerated type
m_iHeartbeatMissedCount ≥ 0	An integer

Each time a heartbeat is detected within the expected time frame, the m_iHeartbeatMissedCount variable is reset to 0. When a time-out occurs (the heartbeat was not detected in the expected time frame), the variable is incremented. If the variable reaches the value 3, the backup instance elevates itself to master status. There are two ways in which a master status instance can cease to exist; firstly, if it crashes or is purposely removed from the system and, secondly, if it detects any heartbeat messages from another master instance (in which case it demotes itself to backup status). This is a fail-safe mechanism to prevent the coexistence of multiple master instances.

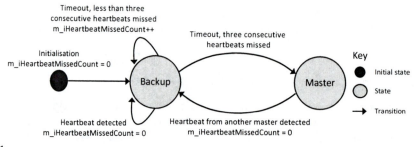

FIGURE 5.41

The state transition diagram of the replicated database demonstration application.

There are two types of communication within the replication demonstration application: communication within the service itself (between the server instances) and communication between the application client and the master instance of the service. Figure 5.42 shows the socket-level connectivity between the various components.

Figure 5.42 shows the socket-level communication within the replication demonstration application. The communication between the application client and the master instance of the service is shown to the left. It comprises the server sending service advertisements, which are broadcast over UDP and used by the client to gain the server's address details and thus connect using TCP. The TCP connection is used for all application requests and replies between the client and the server. The communication between the master instance of the service and the backup instance is shown to the right. Both processes have the same sockets, but the broadcast sockets and the TCP sockets used to connect to clients are inactive on whichever instance is in backup state. Only the master instance broadcasts heartbeat messages, which the backup instance receives. When the client has caused an update of the data held by the master instance, the master sends an update propagation message to the backup instance.

The behavior of the replication demonstration application is explored in Activity A3. The full source code is available as part of the book's accompanying resources.

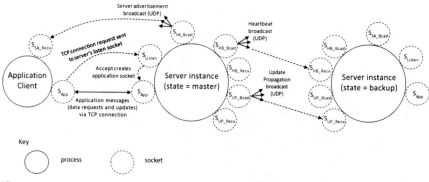

FIGURE 5.42

The socket-level connectivity between the components of the replication service.

ACTIVITY A3 EXPLORING THE MASTER-BACKUP DATA REPLICATION MECHANISM

A replicated database application is used to investigate the behavior of a data replication mechanism, as well as aspects of dynamic service configuration and component role allocation through the use of heartbeat messages, data update propagation between server instances, and service advertisement broadcasts to enable clients to locate the master service instance.

This activity uses the Replication_Client and Replication_Server programs. To simplify the configuration of the software and to ensure that the focus of the experimentation is on the architectural aspects of replication, the database servers actually hold their data in the form of in-memory data tables. The values are initially hard-coded, but can be updated through client requests. Any updates that occur at the master server instance are then propagated to the backup server instance.

During the experiments, observe the diagnostic event information displayed in each component, which provides details of internal behavior.

Prerequisites
Two networked computers are needed because each instance of the service needs to bind to the same set of ports; therefore, they cannot be coresident on the same computer. Since broadcast communication is used, the computers need to be in the same local network.

Learning Outcomes
- To understand the concept of data replication
- To become familiar with a specific replication mechanism
- To explore the behavior of a simple replicated database application
- To explore automatic service configuration and component role allocation
- To explore dynamic service discovery with service advertisement broadcasts
- To explore update propagation
- To gain an appreciation of failure transparency in a practical application setting

The activity is performed in five stages.

Method Part A: Component Self-Configuration and Self-Advertisement (One Server)
This part of the activity is concerned with the self-configuration that occurs when a single server instance of the replicated database service is started.

Start a single copy of the client program Replication_Client and the server program Replication_Server on different computers. The server process initializes itself to backup state. It listens for heartbeat messages, and because it does not detect any (it counts three consecutively missed heartbeats), it elevates itself to master state. Once in master state, it begins to broadcast periodic service advertisements. This is to enable any clients to locate the server.

Initially, the client process does not know the address of the server, so it cannot send a connection request. Notice how it receives a service advertisement message (containing the server's address details), updates its record of the server's address, and then uses this information to automatically connect to the service.

Expected Outcome for Part A
You should see the server initializes itself to backup state, then waits for heartbeat messages and on receiving none, and elevates to master status. At this point, you see it starts to send service advertisement and heartbeat messages.

The client process receives the server advertisement.

The screenshot below shows the server instance initializing to backup state and then elevating to master state, at which point it begins sending heartbeat messages and server advertisement messages.

ACTIVITY A3 EXPLORING THE MASTER-BACKUP DATA REPLICATION MECHANISM—Cont'd

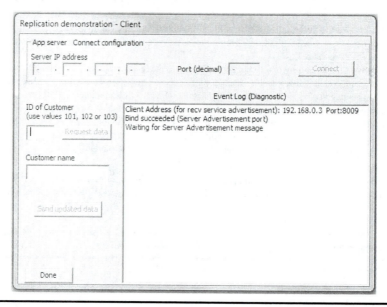

The following screenshots show the client component waiting for the service advertisement message and then receiving it and updating the server address details it holds.

ACTIVITY A3 EXPLORING THE MASTER-BACKUP DATA REPLICATION MECHANISM—Cont'd

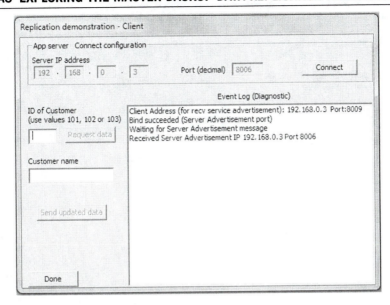

Method Part B: Using the Database Service

The application can now be used. Experiment with connecting the client to the server and requesting data items from the server. Data values held at the server can also be updated; try a few requests and a few updates.

Expected Outcome for Part B

The client should connect to the server (it establishes a TCP connection). You should be able to perform data requests and updates at the client and see the effect of these at the server.

The screenshot below shows the server state after the client has connected, and the customer number 101 name has been changed by the client from "Fred" to "Frederick."

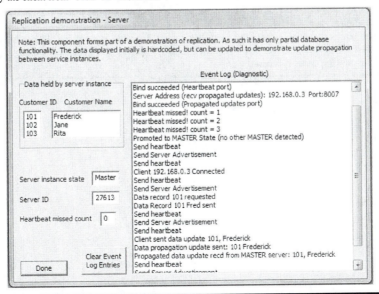

ACTIVITY A3 EXPLORING THE MASTER-BACKUP DATA REPLICATION MECHANISM—Cont'd

The screenshot below shows the corresponding state of the client interface after the data value was updated and sent to the server.

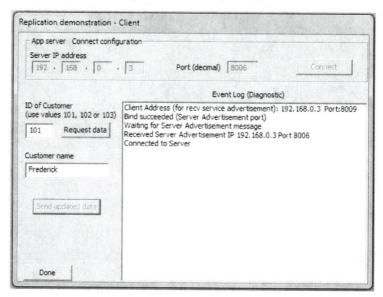

Method Part C: Component Self-Configuration (Two Servers)

This stage explores the self-configuration that occurs when there are two server instances present.

Start two instances of the service on different computers. One process should promote itself to master status (the same event sequence as explored in part A); the second instance then detects the heartbeat messages from the master process, causing it to remain in the backup state.

Expected Outcome for Part C

You should see that, by using the heartbeat mechanism, the service autoconfigures itself so that there is one master instance and one backup instance.

This screenshot shows the service instance that elevates to master. Typically, it is the one that is started first, because each instance waits the same time period to detect heartbeat messages, and the first one to start waiting is the first one to get to the end of the waiting period and elevate.

ACTIVITY A3 EXPLORING THE MASTER-BACKUP DATA REPLICATION MECHANISM—Cont'd

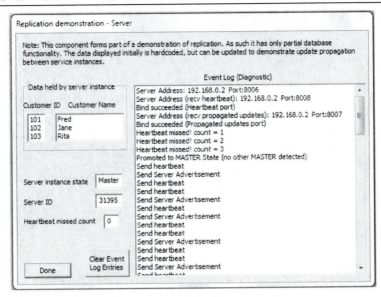

This screenshot (below) shows the server instance that remains in backup state because it is receiving the heartbeat messages from the master instance.

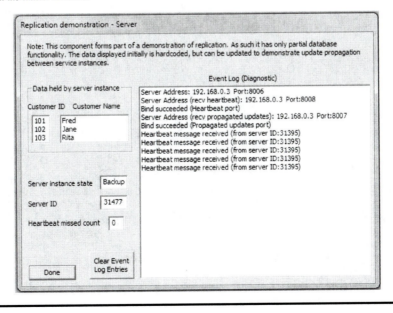

ACTIVITY A3 EXPLORING THE MASTER-BACKUP DATA REPLICATION MECHANISM—Cont'd

Method Part D: Update Propagation in Operation

Start two instances of the service on different computers (or continue on from part C).

Start a client on the same computer as one of the server instances, or use a third computer. The client will receive service advertisement messages from the master instance, and therefore, always connect to master; confirm this experimentally.

Notice that the customer with ID 102 initially has the name "Jane." Use the client to change this to "John" (request the data, then manually edit the data in the client user interface, and then use the "Send updated data" button to send the new value back to the master server instance).

Expected Outcome for Part D

You should see that the update is performed successfully by the client, using the request-change-send sequence described above. The client interface is shown in the following screenshot.

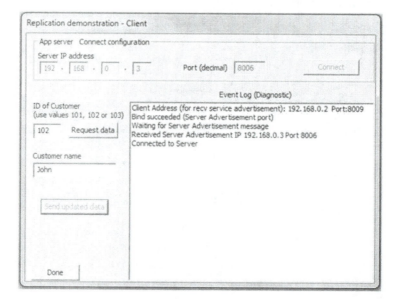

The master server instance receives the update request message from the client, performs the update on its own copy of the data, and also propagates the update to the backup server instance (as shown in the screenshot below) to maintain data consistency.

ACTIVITY A3 EXPLORING THE MASTER-BACKUP DATA REPLICATION MECHANISM—Cont'd

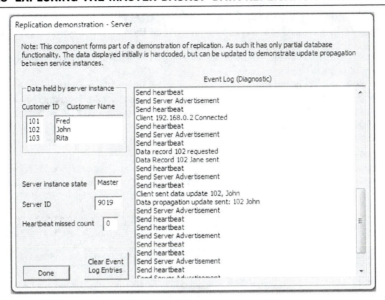

The backup server instance receives the propagated update from the master instance and updates its copy of the data accordingly; see the screenshot below.

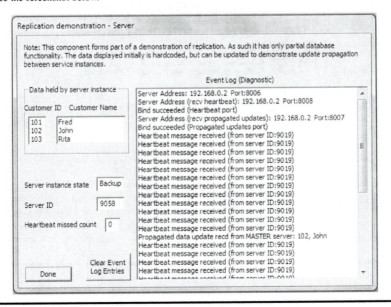

ACTIVITY A3 EXPLORING THE MASTER-BACKUP DATA REPLICATION MECHANISM—Cont'd

Method Part E: Automatic Reconfiguration and Failure Transparency

This stage explores the behavior when the master instance fails, and the backup server detects the lack of heartbeat messages.

Start one instance of the service on each of two different computers. Watch while the service self-organizes (i.e., one of the servers becomes the master instance, and the other remains in backup state).

Now, close the master instance (simulating a crash). Observe the behavior of the backup instance. It should detect that the master is no longer present (there are no heartbeat messages) and thus promote itself to master status.

Once the new master has established itself, restart the other server (which was originally the master). Upon starting up, it should detect the heartbeat messages being sent by the current master instance, and thus, the restarted server should remain in the backup state.

Expected Outcome for Part E

The screenshot below shows the backup service instance detecting the absence of the master: when three consecutive heartbeats have been missed, it promotes itself to master status and begins to broadcast heartbeat messages and server advertisements.

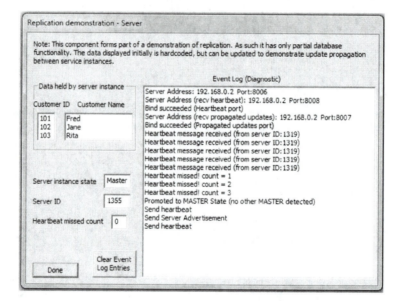

When the other instance of the service (which was previously the master and then crashed) is restarted, it detects the heartbeat messages from the current master and thus assumes backup status, as shown in the screenshot below. Note the new server ID of the restarted instance (1884), instead of its original ID (1319) when it was running previously (evidenced in the screenshot above when it was sending heartbeat messages). This is because the ID is randomly generated when the server process starts. Note also the ID of the other (now master) instance remains unchanged (1355).

ACTIVITY A3 EXPLORING THE MASTER-BACKUP DATA REPLICATION MECHANISM—Cont'd

Replication demonstration - Server

Note: This component forms part of a demonstration of replication. As such it has only partial database functionality. The data displayed initially is hardcoded, but can be updated to demonstrate update propagation between service instances.

Data held by server instance

Customer ID   Customer Name

101	Fred
102	Jane
103	Rita

Event Log (Diagnostic)

Server Address: 192.168.0.3 Port:8006
Server Address (recv heartbeat): 192.168.0.3 Port:8008
Bind succeeded (Heartbeat port)
Server Address (recv propagated updates): 192.168.0.3 Port:8007
Bind succeeded (Propagated updates port)
Heartbeat message received (from server ID:1355)
Heartbeat message received (from server ID:1355)
Heartbeat message received (from server ID:1355)
Heartbeat message received (from server ID:1355)
Heartbeat message received (from server ID:1355)

Server instance state   Backup

Server ID   1884

Heartbeat missed count   0

Done   Clear Event Log Entries

Reflection

This activity facilitates exploration of data replication in a realistic application setting. Through practical experimentation, you can see how several important mechanisms operate (service advertisement, heartbeat messages, and data update propagation). These are used to achieve automatic component discovery and service self-configuration, as well as the higher-level achievement of active data replication to achieve a robust, failure transparent database service.

It is recommended that you experiment further with the replication demonstration application to gain an in-depth understanding of its various behaviors. You should also inspect the source code and try to marry up the behavior witnessed to the underlying program logic.

5.17 THE RELATIONSHIP BETWEEN DISTRIBUTED APPLICATIONS AND NETWORKS

Distributed systems add management, structure, and most significantly transparency on top of the functionality provided by the underlying networks to achieve their connectivity and communication. Therefore, distributed applications should be considered as being in a layer conceptually above the top of the network protocol stack and not as part of the application layer.

To put this into context, consider the File Transfer Protocol (FTP). This commonly used application-layer protocol can be realized in an application form, that is, a file transfer utility, and also can be embedded into applications that may integrate a file transfer function within their general operation (such as system configuration and management utilities and automated software installers). See Figure 5.43.

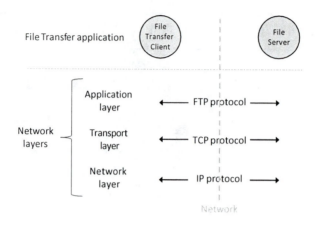

FIGURE 5.43

Distributed applications sit above the application layer.

Figure 5.43 shows the distinction between FTP, which is part of the network protocol stack, and a file transfer application. A file transfer application wraps the FTP functionality within an application form; it is software built on top of the FTP protocol and possibly integrates the functionality of transferring files with other functionality such as security and a bespoke user interface suitable for the intended use scenario. In the case of a file transfer utility, the client component is fundamentally a user interface enabling the user to submit commands to the server. The business logic is contained within the server component. The user must identify the file server by address when connecting, so this application provides limited transparency, and as such, it could be described as a network application rather than a distributed application.

Distributed applications use the connectivity provided by the network protocols as building blocks to achieve more sophisticated communication scenarios, especially by incorporating services and mechanisms such as name services and replication to achieve higher usability and especially transparency such that the user need not be aware of the distributed nature of the applications. For example, a file service that automatically mirrors changes in your local file system to a backup service in the cloud would have greater functionality than a file transfer utility and significantly would be far more transparent. See Figure 5.44.

Figure 5.44 illustrates a distributed file service application. The extent of transparency provided enables the client to make service requests without being aware of the configuration of the service itself. The client does not need to know the actual number of server entities, their location, or the way they communicate within the service, achieve a logical structure, and maintain data consistency. So long as the client's service requests are met, then all is well from the client's point of view.

Network printing provides a further example for discussion. The print-client component can be embedded into, or invoked by, various applications from which the user may need to print a document (such as word processors and web browsers). The print server is a process that runs on the remote computer, which is connected to the printer, or the server may be embedded into the printer itself if it is a stand-alone network printer with its own network identity. The client performs the role of sending documents to the printer. This is essentially a file transfer, but with added control information, which includes the portion of the document to print, the print quality to use, and the number of copies

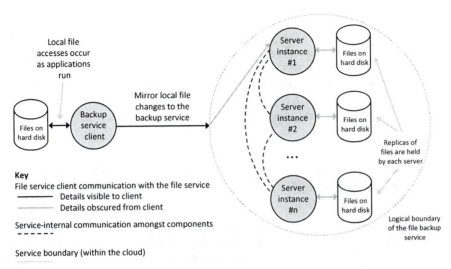

FIGURE 5.44

A file service as an example of a distributed application.

required. The main business logic (such as checking access rights, queue management, and logging print jobs) and the actual printing are managed within the print server component. As with a file transfer utility, a network printing facility has limited transparency and thus could be described as a network application rather than a distributed application.

5.18 TRANSPARENCY FROM THE ARCHITECTURE VIEWPOINT

The forms of transparency that are particularly important from the architecture viewpoint are briefly identified here and are treaded in more depth in Chapter 6.

Access transparency. The mechanisms to access resources should not be affected or modified by the software architecture of the application or by the type of coupling between components. The use of services to facilitate connectivity, such as name services and middleware, should not negatively impact access transparency.

Location transparency. Software architectures should be designed to support location transparency, especially where dynamic configuration and/or loose coupling is used. Location transparency should be maintained when components are relocated or when component roles change dynamically due to internal service reconfiguration.

Replication transparency. Replication of components is a key architectural technique to enhance robustness, availability, and responsiveness. This must be implemented such that the internal configuration and behavior within the replicated services (including details of server cardinality, server failures, and update propagation) are hidden from the external components that communicate with the services, such that they are presented with a single-instance view of the service.

Failure transparency. Failure transparency at the component level should be supported within the architectural design, using techniques such as loose coupling, dynamic configuration, and replication.

Scaling transparency. Software architectures should avoid unnecessarily complex or intense coupling between components. Tight coupling should be replaced with loose coupling using intermediate connectivity services where possible. The extent of interdependency and rigid structure between components impacts on maintainability and flexibility aspects of scalability.

Performance transparency. The intensity of communication between components should be considered carefully in the architectural design, because it can impact severely on performance. In general, the number of other components that each component communicates with should be kept to a minimum.

5.19 THE CASE STUDY FROM THE ARCHITECTURAL PERSPECTIVE

The game has a CS architecture. The game server has limited functional scope since it is intended primarily for demonstration and exploration; it only provides the business logic for a simple game, as well as the management of a list of up to ten connected users and a list of up to five simultaneously active games. The CS design is well suited to the game in its current form, simplicity being its main advantage in this case. There are only two-component types; the client provides the user interface and the server provides the business logic. At the small scale of this application, there are no issues with performance.

If the application were to be extended to support features such as user registration and authentication or multiple different games or if it needed to be scaled up to support large numbers of users, then a three-tier design may be more suitable because of its flexibility and better transparency provision.

5.19.1 STATEFUL SERVER DESIGN

The game is based on a stateful server design; the server stores the game state including which players are associated by a particular game and which of the players has the next turn to make a move. The server sends messages to each client containing details of the moves made by the opponent so that both clients display an up-to-date representation of the game-board positions. When designing the game application, it was necessary to weigh up the relative advantages and disadvantages of the stateful and stateless approaches, in the specific context of the game. The stateful server approach is the more natural choice for this particular application because the server provides a connection between pairs of clients playing a game and needs access to the game state to mediate between the clients in terms of controlling the game action; if the server did not store the state locally, then the messages passed through the server between the clients would need to additionally contain the state information. The negative aspect of stateful design in this case is that if the server were to crash, the game will be destroyed.

The stateless server alternative requires spreading the state across the two clients such that they each hold details of their own and their opponent's move positions. This approach would increase the complexity of both the client and the server components. The client becomes more complex as it has to manage the state locally, and the server becomes more complex because it is much harder to govern the game, in terms of preventing clients from making multiple moves at one turn, not taking a turn, or reversing previous moves. This is because the server would only see snapshots of the game from step to step, instead of following it/enforcing it on an alternating move-by-move basis, which it controls (as in the case of the stateful design). In addition, the stateless server approach causes there to be separate copies of the state at each client, and therefore, it is possible for inconsistency to arise through the two sets of state becoming out of sync, such as if both clients think it is their turn to move at the same time (in which case the game is effectively destroyed anyway). The additional design and testing that would be required to ensure the game state remains consistent in all scenarios that could occur would far outweigh the single negative aspect of the stateful design in this case, and bear in mind that the stateless server approach is still sensitive to the failure of either client.[4]

5.19.2 SEPARATION OF CONCERNS FOR THE GAME COMPONENTS

The game comprises two-component types with clearly defined roles. The server keeps the application state organized in a two-level hierarchy. The lower level holds information concerning the connected clients (representing players), which is held within an array of connection structures (one structure per client). The higher level relates players to games in play using an array of game structures (one structure per game). The game structure also holds the game-grid state, which is updated as the server receives gameplay move messages from each client and forwards them to the client's opponent. A logical game is created when one player selects another from the "available players" list, which is updated and transmitted to each connected client when a new client joins, leaves, or becomes tied up in a game. The demonstration application supports up to five simultaneous games, by holding an array of five game structures. The connection and game structures have been presented in Chapter 3.

5.19.2.1 CS Variant

The game is an example of the fat-server variant of the CS architecture, in which the client provides the user interface logic, while the server provides the game logic as well as the data and state management. In this case, the processing demands on the server, per game (and thus per client), are quite low. The message arrival frequency is low, with game move messages arriving at typical intervals of at least two seconds or so, per game.

5.19.2.2 Client and Server Lifetimes

As with most CS applications, the game has been designed such that the client is the active component that connects to the server on demand of the user (i.e., when the user wishes to play a game, they will run the client process). To support on-demand connectivity, the server is required to run continuously, whereas the client has a short lifetime (the duration of a game session). The individual client lifetimes are independent of those of other clients, but of course, a client can only be linked in a game with another client that is present at the time of game initiation. To ensure meaningful game management, and to avoid wasting system resources, one of the roles of the server is to detect the loss of connection with one of the client processes and to close the game.

---

[4]For this particular application (in which games are played between pairs of clients), a peer-to-peer design could also be considered and would have similar merits to the stateless server design, except that there would be no server, so there would need to be a mechanism to facilitate clients discovering and associating with one another to establish games. The peer-to-peer design would encounter the same challenges of duplication of game state and the need to ensure consistency as the stateless server approach does.

5.19.3 **PHYSICAL AND LOGICAL ARCHITECTURES OF THE GAME APPLICATION**

Physical architecture is concerned with the relative distribution of components, the specific location of each and the way in which they are connected and communicate. In contrast, logical architecture is concerned with the identity of components and the communication mappings between components without knowledge of actual physical system configuration. This difference gives rise to two different architectural views of the game.

Figure 5.45 shows the physical view of the game application when a game between two users is in play. The two users (players) each have a computer on which they run the game client program (which causes an instance of the game client process to run on each computer). The game server program is running on a third computer (the running instance of this program is the server process). The computers are connected via the physical network and communicate using the IP protocol at the network layer. The processes communicate the game-application messages at the transport layer and thus could use either the TCP or the UDP protocols, each of which is encapsulated and carried across the network by the IP protocol. TCP was chosen for the game due to its reliability. The processes are identified for the purposes of the TCP communication by a combination of their host computer's IP address and the port number they are using, because this is the way in which the sockets (the communication end points) are differentiated. Figure 5.46 provides a logical view of this situation.

Figure 5.46 shows the logical view of the physical system that was shown in Figure 5.45. This can be mapped onto the transport layer of the network model, in which the communicating processes are identified by the ports they are mapped to. The separation between the processes is indicated by the dotted lines; this indicates that the processes are independent entities in the system. This could, but does not have to, designate the presence of the physical network. In other words, the logical view is only concerned with which processes communicate with which other processes and is not concerned with the actual locations of processes. The communication used in the game has been configured such that

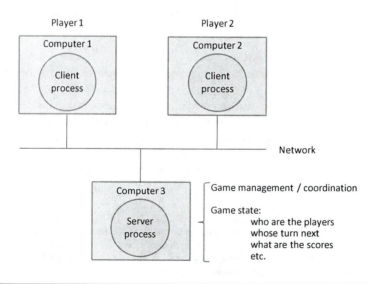

FIGURE 5.45

The physical architecture of the game.

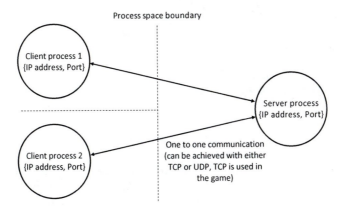

FIGURE 5.46

Logical view of the game connectivity.

processes can be located on the same or different computers because only the server process binds to the port that is used. At the transport layer, the network can be abstracted as a logical concept (because it facilitates process-to-process connectivity without concern for details of how it is achieved, such as which technologies are used or how many routers there are in the path). Both the TCP and the UDP transport layer protocols will deliver messages from process to process in an access transparent manner (this means that the mechanism to perform the send and receive actions is identical regardless of whether the two processes are on the same computer or different computers). See also the discussion of logical and physical views of systems in Chapter 3.

Server replication can be used to increase the robustness of an application such as the game, and it can also improve scalability and availability in large systems. However, replication also increases complexity, especially if state has to be propagated between the server instances. The example game does not need to scale up to large numbers of players and the service provided is not considered sufficiently important to justify the additional design, build, and test expense of adding server replication. However, if the game were to be part of an online casino, with paying customers expecting a highly robust and available service, then the decision would be different.

5.19.4 TRANSPARENCY ASPECTS OF THE GAME

Ideally, users of distributed applications are provided with an abstraction, which hides the presence of the network and the boundaries between physical computers such that the user is presented with a single-machine view of the system. Obviously, in a multiplayer game, the user is aware that there is at least one other user who is located at a different computer and that they are connected by a network; this is an example where full network transparency is not necessary or achievable. However, the user does not need to know any of the details concerning the connectivity, distribution, or internal architecture of the game application.

Locating the server: In the case study game, the user manually enters the IP address of the server. This is an issue from a transparency point of view because it reveals the distributed nature of the game and also requires the user to know, or find out, the address of the server. Techniques to automatically locate the server, such as the server advertisement used in the replication demonstration earlier in the chapter, could be used. Adding server advertisement to the use-case game is one of the programming challenges at the end of Chapter 3.

5.20 END-OF-CHAPTER EXERCISES

5.20.1 QUESTIONS

Q1. Design-specific transparency implications. This question refers to the Activity A1, specifically the three-tier single application server configuration (configuration C).

A single data request message is sent by the client to the single application server. The application server uses the content of this message to create a pair of request messages, one for each specific database. Responses to these messages are returned from the two databases to the application server and are forwarded on by the application server as two separate responses to the client.

(a) Explain the transparency implications of this design decision.
(b) What would be the consequences of combining the two responses (one from each database) into a single reply to the client?

Q2. Software architectures. Identify the main benefits and drawbacks of the following architectures:

(a) Client-server
(b) Peer-to-peer
(c) Three-tier
(d) Multitier
(e) Distributed objects

Q3. Component coupling. Identify the type(s) of coupling occurring in each of the following scenarios:

(a) A CS application operating over middleware
(b) A prototype three-tier system that uses hard-coded addresses to identify the locations of components
(c) A multitier application in which components use a directory service to find the addresses of other components
(d) A peer-to-peer application in which components connect to one another when discovered in the local network (the discovery process is automatic, based on the use of broadcast messages)
(e) A social-media application in which clients connect to an online service to exchange information
(f) A CS application that uses server advertising broadcasts to enable the client to locate the server and establish a connection.

Q4. Identifying heterogeneity. Identify the classes of heterogeneity that may occur in each of the following scenarios:

(a) A computer laboratory with computers purchased in batches over a two-year period, installed with the Windows operating system and the same suite of application software on all computers.

(b) A small company network system comprising a couple of different desktop computers running various versions of the Windows operating system and a couple of laptops also running the Windows operating system.

(c) A system that supports a CS business application. A powerful computer running the Linux operating system is used to host the server process. Users access the service through lower-cost desktop computers running the Windows operating system.

(d) An ad hoc network created between a group of friends playing a multiplayer game over wireless links on a collection of mobile devices including smartphones and tablets.

(e) A home network system comprising a desktop computer running the Linux operating system and a laptop running the Windows operating system and a laptop running the Mac OS X operating system.

5.20.2 PROGRAMMING EXERCISES

Programming Exercise #A1: This programming challenge relates to the demonstration distributed database application used in Activity A1. Base your solution on configuration C of the database application architecture (see the details in the activity).

Implement autoconfiguration so that the application server component can detect and automatically connect to the database servers. The recommended way to achieve this is for a service advertisement mechanism to be added to the database servers (see the replication demonstration application source code for an example mechanism).

Programming Exercise #A2: This programming challenge relates to the demonstration distributed database application used in Activity A1. Base your solution on configuration C of the database application architecture (see the details in the activity).

Implement autoconfiguration so that the application client component can detect and automatically connect to the application server. The recommended way to achieve this is for a service advertisement mechanism to be added to the application server (see the replication demonstration application source code for an example mechanism).

Programming Exercise #A3: This programming challenge relates to the demonstration peer-to-peer application used in Activity A2. The peer-to-peer media-sharing application automatically discovers peers and displays the additional resources they have. This allows the user to play soundtracks regardless of which peer holds them. However, the demonstration application does not detect peer disconnection, so the actual music track availability list could be stale. This programming task is to extend the functionality of the peer-to-peer application to correct this situation.

Starting with the provided project and source code (for the application used in Activity A2), add a simple heartbeat detection mechanism so that each peer can monitor the continuing presence of those other peers that it has already detected. Hint: the peers already generate periodic self-advertisement messages, but currently, a receiver ignores these from a particular sender once it has discovered that sender. Modification of the receive logic would allow these to be used to check that the peer is still present. If a peer is not detected for a certain period, then it is assumed to be no longer present and the local peer must stop advertising the resources that the lost peer held. In terms of how long to wait before determining that a peer has gone, perhaps, three missed self-advertisement messages in sequence are appropriate (as was done with the master presence detection in the replication demonstration; see Activity A3) although you can experiment with other configurations.

Implementation note: After being used in Activity A2, the peer-to-peer application was refactored and developed as a library version, in Section 5.13. Hence, there are three versions of the sample code available. You can use any of these versions of the peer-to-peer application as your starting point (the original version, the refactored version, or the library version, but note that the sample solution is based on the refactored version).

An example solution is provided in the program MediaShare_Peer_Disconnect.

Programming Exercise #A4: This programming challenge relates to the demonstration replicated database application used in Activity A3.

Implement a full-database transfer mechanism. The replicated database example application currently only supports incremental update propagation. What this means is that each update that happens at the master instance is propagated, on an individual basis, to the backup instance. This has the potential weakness that if the backup server was unavailable for some time (it has a crash or is shutdown) and then restarted, it may have missed several updates. This task requires you to develop a mechanism whereby the backup server instance (upon start-up) requests a full-database transfer from the master server instance. You will need to add a new message type REQUEST_FULL_DATABASE_TRANSFER to enable the backup instance to make the request. You may be able to use the existing update propagation mechanism (but within a loop) to transfer the database rows one by one.

An example solution is provided in the program Replication_Server_DB_Transfer.

5.20.3 ANSWERS TO END-OF-CHAPTER QUESTIONS

Q1. Answer

(a) The transparency implications of the design include the following:
  * Sending back two replies, arising as the result of a single query sent by the client, requires the client logic to be able to receive and process the messages without confusion.
  * The approach reveals clues as to the internal architecture of the service, specifically in this case that there are multiple database servers (breaking the single-system view).
  * In the specific way it has been implemented, this approach is robust and to some extent provides failure transparency in the sense that it allows the client to receive data from one database when the other is unavailable.
  * The approach is not universally suitable, since in many database applications, it is not desirable to receive incomplete responses from queries.

(b) The consequences of combining the two responses (one from each database) into a single reply to the client include the following:
  * Additional complexity in the application server. The two replies from the database servers arrive asynchronously at the application server, so there would need to be a means of waiting until both responses were available before passing a single reply message back to the client.
  * The timing aspects could be difficult, specifically how long should the application server wait for the pair of responses. If it waits indefinitely, the service will be unreliable in the event that

one of the database servers has crashed. If it waits too long before timing out, then the service will be robust but with higher than necessary latency. If it does not wait long enough before timing out, then valid responses from databases will be lost.

Q2. Answer

(a) CS is a very popular architecture for distributed systems and is well understood. This two-tier approach works well at low scales or with limited complexity applications. The two types of component have different functionality and behavior; a key aspect that affects performance and scalability is the way in which the functionality is divided across the component types.

(b) Peer-to-peer applications have a single-component type. Many components can connect together, often on an ad hoc basis, to achieve application-level goals, which are often related to data or resource sharing. A main benefit is dynamic run-time configuration flexibility. Connectivity in peer-to-peer applications can become a performance bottleneck, which thus affects scalability.

(c) The three-tier architecture facilitates separation of the three stands of functionality (user interface, business logic, and data access logic) such that a middle tier can be dedicated to business logic. This is more flexible and potentially more scalable and robust than the two-tier CS architecture but is also more complex (in terms of structure and behavior, thus requiring greater design and testing effort).

(d) Multitier is an extension of three-tier; it facilitates multiple middle tiers so that the business logic can be subdivided. This not only extends the flexibility and scalability advantages of three-tier designs (compared, e.g., with two-tier) but also further increases the complexity.

(e) The distributed objects approach is a fine-grained technique by which the application's logic is distributed at the object level. This means that there can be a large number of relatively simple objects distributed across a system, each providing quite limited but clearly defined functionality. The main advantage is the flexibility it offers. However, there is potentially high complexity, and if poorly designed, there can be large numbers of component-component dependencies and high interaction intensity, which impacts on robustness. Distributed objects applications rely on supporting infrastructure such as middleware to facilitate object location and also communication between objects.

Q3. Answer

(a) CS applications are directly coupled (in the common case where the client identifies the server explicitly) and loosely coupled when middleware is a communication intermediary.

(b) The use of hard-coded addresses implies design time-decided connectivity. The components in adjacent tiers connect directly to each other; hence, in this case, the coupling is tight and direct. The nonadjacent tiers (the user interface and the data access tier) connect indirectly to each other, through the middle tier, which acts as an intermediary, so in this case, the coupling is tight and indirect.

(c) The adjacent components are directly coupled, and the nonadjacent components are indirectly coupled (as in the answer to part (b) above). The directory service introduces loose coupling in that the location of components can be found at run time.

(d) The ad hoc connectivity is a form of loose coupling (the communication partners were not decided at design time). The components connect directly to each other, so the coupling is also direct.

(e) Clients connect indirectly (via the online service) and to any other clients (not known at design time) so the coupling between clients is indirect and loose. The connection between a specific client and the service itself is direct and tight (it was decided at design time).

(f) The use of a service advertisement mechanism implies loose coupling. The resulting connection is directly between a client and a server and thus is an example of direct coupling.

Refer to Section 5.5.1 for further explanation.

Q4. Answer

(a) It is possible that there is no heterogeneity present in this case. However, purchasing different batches of computers over an extended time period is likely to lead to resource differences, for example, the later batches may have larger memory, larger hard disk storage, or different variants of the CPU. Thus, it is likely that there is some performance heterogeneity present. In addition, it is possible that different versions of the Windows operating system are in use, potentially giving rise to operating system heterogeneity.

(b) The hardware platforms are likely to be compatible (the laptops should provide the same hardware interface as the PC), and thus, the platforms may offer the same interfaces to the processes and operating systems. It is likely that the platforms offer different levels of resource, so the system will exhibit performance heterogeneity. Operating system heterogeneity may arise if different versions of the Windows operating system are in use.

(c) Performance heterogeneity has been introduced purposefully to ensure the server process has sufficient resource to achieve the appropriate performance. Operating system heterogeneity is also present.

(d) This system exhibits all three forms of heterogeneity (performance, platform, and operating system). Different executable versions of the game will be needed for the various different devices, and the interoperability between the devices is achieved by using a standard communication mechanism.

(e) This system may exhibit all three forms of heterogeneity, although it is possible that the three platforms are compatible. Performance heterogeneity and operating system heterogeneity will be present, and in general, the different computers will be used for executing different applications (or components thereof).

5.20.4 LIST OF IN-TEXT ACTIVITIES

Activity number	Section	Description
A1	5.8	Exploring architecture, coupling, connectivity, and transparency with two-tier and three-tier versions of a database application
A2	5.9.3	Exploring peer-to-peer architecture and behavior, using a peer-to-peer music-sharing application with ad hoc automatic configuration
A3	5.16.3	Exploring replication, using a master-backup database application with service advertisement, heartbeat-based dynamic configuration of component roles, and update propagation among service instances

5.20.5 **LIST OF ACCOMPANYING RESOURCES**

The following resources are referred to directly in the chapter text, the in-text activities, and/or the end of chapter exercises.

Program	Availability	Relevant sections of chapter
DB_Arch_AppClient Two-tier architecture (model A)	Executable file Source code	Activity A1 (Section 5.8)
DB_Arch_DBServer_DB1_Direct Two-tier/three-tier architectures (models A, B, and C)	Executable file Source code	Activity A1 (Section 5.8)
DB_Arch_DBServer_DB2_Direct Two-tier/three-tier architectures (models A, B, and C)	Executable file Source code	Activity A1 (Section 5.8)
DB_Arch_AppClient_for_AppServer1and2 Three-tier architectures (model B)	Executable file Source code	Activity A1 (Section 5.8)
DB_Arch_AppServer_for_DB1 Three-tier architectures (model B)	Executable file Source code	Activity A1 (Section 5.8)
DB_Arch_AppServer_for_DB2 Three-tier architectures (model B)	Executable file Source code	Activity A1 (Section 5.8)
DB_Arch_AppClient_for_SingleAppServer_DB1andDB2 Three-tier architectures (model C)	Executable file Source code	Activity A1 (Section 5.8)
DB_Arch_AppServer_for_DB1andDB2 Three-tier architectures (model C)	Executable file Source code	Activity A1 (Section 5.8)
MediaShare_Peer (peer-to-peer) Exploring peer-to-peer architecture and behavior (peer-to-peer—original version)	Executable file Source code	Activity A2 (Sections 5.9.3 and 5.13.1)
MediaShare_Peer_Refactored (Peer-to-peer—refactoring example)	Executable file Source code	Section 5.13.1
MediaShare_Peer_UsesLibrary (Peer-to-peer—library example, application)	Executable file Source code	Section 5.13.1
DemonstrationLibrary_for_MediaShare_Peer (Peer-to-peer—library example, library code)	Executable file Source code	Section 5.13.1
MediaShare_Peer_Disconnect Extended version of peer-to-peer application supporting automatic detection of peer disconnect (solution to end of chapter programming task #A3) (The sample solution is based on the refactored version of the application)	Executable file Source code	Section 5.20.2
Replication_Client An implementation of replication (Also serves as example solution to end of chapter programming tasks #A1 and #A2)	Executable file Source code	Activity A3 (Sections 5.16.3 and 5.20.2)

Program	Availability	Relevant sections of chapter
Replication_Server An implementation of replication (Also serves as example solution to end of chapter programming tasks #A1 and #A2)	Executable file Source code	Activity A3 (Sections 5.16.3 and 5.20.2)
Replication_Server_DB_Transfer Extends the replicated database server to support full-database transfer between server instances (solution to end of chapter programming task #A4)	Executable file Source code	Section 5.20.2

APPENDIX THE PEER-TO-PEER APPLICATION-LEVEL PROTOCOL MESSAGE SEQUENCE

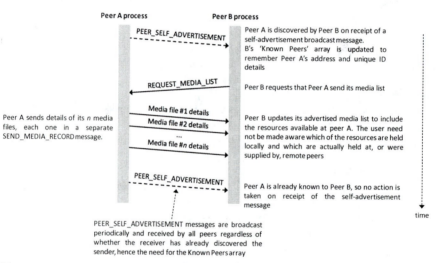

FIGURE 5.47

The peer-to-peer application-level protocol message sequence diagram.

Activity A2 part C sets the challenge of determining the application-level protocol message sequence of the sample peer-to-peer application. The message sequence is shown in Figure 5.47 so that you can check your answers.

CHAPTER CONTENTS

6.1 RATIONALE AND OVERVIEW

This chapter takes a systems-level approach to the three main focal areas: transparency, common services, and middleware.

Distributed systems can comprise many different interacting components and as a result are dynamic and complex in many ways relating to both their structure and behavior. The potentially very high complexity of systems is problematic for developers of distributed applications and also for users and is a major risk to correctness and quality. From the developer's perspective, complexity and dynamic behavior make systems less predictable and understandable and therefore make application design, development, and testing more difficult and increase the probability that untested scenarios exist that potentially hide latent faults. From the user's perspective, systems that are unreliable and difficult to use or require the user to know technical details of system configuration are of low usability and may not be trusted.

Transparency provision is a main influence on the systems' quality and is therefore one of the main focal themes of this chapter. The causes of complexity and the need for transparency to shield application developers and users from it have been discussed in the earlier chapters in their specific contexts. The approach in this chapter is to focus on transparency itself and to deal with each of its forms in detail, with examples of technologies and mechanisms to facilitate transparency.

In keeping with the systems-level theme of this chapter, a second main focal area is common services in distributed systems. There are many benefits that arise from the provision of a number of common services, which are used by applications and other services. These benefits include standardization of the main aspects of behavior and reduction of the complexity of applications by removing the need to embed into them the commonly required functionalities that these services provide; this would be inefficient and not always possible. This chapter explores a number of common services in-depth.

The third main focus is on middleware technologies that bind the components of the systems together and facilitate interoperability. Middleware is explored in detail, as well as a number of platform-independent and implementation-agnostic technologies for data and message formatting and transport across heterogeneous systems.

6.2 TRANSPARENCY

It is no accident that transparency has featured strongly in all of the four core chapters of the book. As has been demonstrated in those chapters, distributed systems can be complex in many different ways.

To understand the nature and importance of transparency, consider two different roles that humans play when interacting with distributed systems. As a designer or developer of distributed systems and applications, it is of course necessary that the various internal mechanisms of the systems are understood. There are technical challenges that relate to the interconnection and collaboration of many components, with issues such as locating the components, managing communication between the components, and ensuring that specific timing or sequencing requirements are met. There may be a need to replicate some services or data resources while ensuring that the system remains consistent. It may be necessary to allow the system to dynamically configure itself, automatically forming new connections between components to adjust in order to meet greater service demand or to overcome the failure of a specific component. A user of the system has a completely different viewpoint. They wish to use the system to perform their work without having to understand the details of how the system is configured or how it works.

A good analogy is provided by our relationship with cars. Certainly, there are some drivers who understand very well what the various mechanical parts of the car are and how these parts such as the engine, gearbox, steering, brakes, and suspension work. However, the majority of drivers do not understand, and do not want to spend effort to learn, how the various parts work. Their view of the car is as a means of transport, not as a machine. During use, events can happen quickly. If someone steps into the path of the car, the user must press the brake pedal immediately; there is no time to think about it, and understanding the mechanical details of how the brake works is of no help in actually stopping the car in an emergency. The user implicitly trusts that the braking system has been designed to be suitable for purpose, usually without question. When the user presses the brake pedal, they expect the car to stop.

The designer has a quite different view of the car braking system. The designer may have spent a lot of effort ensuring that the brakes are as safe as possible. They may have built-in redundant components, such as the use of dual-brake pipelines and dual hydraulic cylinders to ensure that even if one component should fail, the car will still stop. In the designer's view, the braking system is a work of art, but one that must remain hidden. The user's quality measure, i.e., the measure of success, is that the car continues to stop on demand, throughout its entire lifetime.

The car analogy helps illustrate why transparency is considered to be a very important indicator of quality and usability for distributed systems. Users have a high-level functional view of systems, i.e, they have expectations of the functionality that the system will provide for them, without being troubled by having to know how that functionality will be achieved. If a user wishes to edit a file, then they will expect to be able to retrieve the file and display its contents on their screen without needing to know where the file was stored. When the user makes a change to the file and saves it, the file system may have to update several replica copies of the file stored at different locations: The user is not interested in this level of detail; they just want some form of acknowledgment that the file was saved.

A phrase often used to describe the requirement of transparency is that there should be a "single-system abstraction presented to the user." This is quite a good, memorable way of summing up all the various more specific needs of transparency. The single-system abstraction implies that users (and the application processes that run on their behalf) are presented with a well-designed interface to the system that hides the distribution of the underlying processes and resources. Resource names should be human-friendly and should be represented in ways that are independent of their physical location, which may change dynamically in some systems; of course, the user should not be aware that such reconfigurations are occurring. When a user requests a resource and service, the system should locate that resource and pass the user's request to the service, respectively, without the user having to know where the resource and service are located, whether it is replicated, and so forth. Problems that occur during use of the system should be hidden from the user (to the greatest extent possible). If one instance of a service crashes, then the user's request should be routed to another instance. The bottom line is that the user should get a correct response to their service request without being aware of the failure that occurred; it should not matter which actual instance dealt with the request.

The reason why transparency is so prominently discussed throughout this book is that it must be a first-class concern when designing distributed systems if the resulting system is to be of high quality and high usability. Transparency requirements must be taken into account during the design of each component and service. Transparency is a crosscutting concern and should be considered as an integral theme and certainly not as something that can be bolted on later. A flawed design that does not support transparency cannot in general be patched up at a later stage without significant reworking, which may lead to inconsistencies.

As transparency is such an important and far-reaching topic and with a great many facets, it is commonly divided into a number of transparency forms, which facilitates greater focus and depth of inquiry of the key subtopics.

6.2.1 ACCESS TRANSPARENCY

In a distributed system, it is likely that the users will routinely use a mix of resources and services, some of which are locally held at their own computer and some of which are held on or provided by other computers within the system. Access transparency requires that objects (this includes resources and services) are accessed with the same operations regardless of whether they are local or remote. In other words, the user's interface to access a particular object should be consistent for that object no matter where it is actually stored in the system.

A popular way to achieve access transparency is to install a software layer between applications and the operating system that can deal with access resolutions, sending local requests to the local resource provision service and remote requests to the corresponding layer at some other computers where the required object is located. This is described as resource virtualization because the software layer makes all resources appear to be local to the user.

Figure 6.1 shows the concept of resource virtualization. The process makes a request to a service instead of the resource directly. The service is responsible for locating the actual resource and passing the access request to it and subsequently returning the result back to the process. Using this approach, the process accesses all supported objects via the same call interface, whether they are local or remote, regardless of any underlying implementation differences at the lower level where the resources are stored.

An example of resource virtualization is Unix's virtual file system (VFS) that transparently differentiates between accesses to local files that are handled by the Unix file system and accesses to remote files that are handled by the Network File System (NFS).

Figure 6.2 shows how the VFS layer provides access transparency. When a request for a file is received, the VFS layer finds where the file is and directs requests for files that are held locally to the local file storage system. Requests for files that are held on other computers are passed to the NFS client program that makes a request for the file to the NFS server on the appropriate remote computer. The file

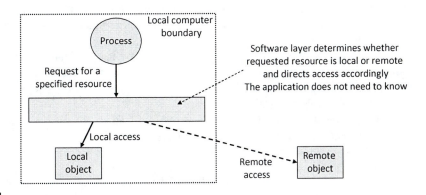

FIGURE 6.1

Generic representation of resource virtualization via a software layer or service.

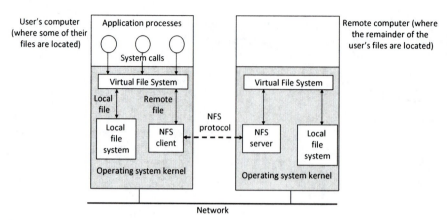

FIGURE 6.2

Access transparency provided by the virtual file system.

is then retrieved and passed back to the user through the VFS layer, such that the user is shielded from the complexity of what has gone on; hence, they just get access to the file they requested.

6.2.2 LOCATION TRANSPARENCY

One of the most commonly occurring challenges in distributed systems is the need to be able to locate resources and services when needed. Some desirable capabilities of distributed systems actually increase the complexity of this challenge: such as the ability to replicate resources, the ability to distribute groups of resources so that they are split over several locations, and the ability to dynamically reconfigure systems and services within, for example, to adapt to changes in workload, to accommodate larger numbers of users, or to mask partial failures within the system.

Location transparency is the ability to access objects without the knowledge of their location. A main facilitator of this is to use a resource naming scheme in which the names of resources are location-independent. The user or application should be able to request a resource by its name only, and the system should be able to translate the name into a unique identifier that can then be mapped onto the current location of the resource.

The provision of location transparency is often achieved through the use of special services whose role is to perform a mapping between a resource's name and its address; this is called name resolution. This particular mechanism is explored in detail later in this chapter in the section that discusses name services and the Domain Name System (DNS).

Resource virtualization using a special layer or service (as discussed in "Access transparency") also provides location transparency. This is because the requesting process does not need to know where the resource is located in the system, it only has to pass a unique identifier to the service, and the service will locate the resource.

Communication mechanisms and protocols that require that the address of the specific destination computer be provided are not location-transparent. Setting up a TCP connection with, or sending a UDP datagram to, a specific destination is clearly not location-transparent (unless the address has been automatically retrieved in advance using an additional service), but nevertheless, the underlying mechanisms of TCP and UDP (when used in its point-to-point mode) are not location-transparent.

Higher-level communication mechanisms such as remote procedure call (RPC) and Remote Method Invocation (RMI) require that the client (the calling process) knows the location of the server object (this is usually supplied as a parameter to the local invocation). Therefore, RPC and RMI are not location-transparent. However, as with socket-level communication discussed above, these mechanisms can be used in location-transparent applications by prefetching the target address using another service such as a name service.

Middleware systems provide a number of forms of transparency including location transparency. The whole purpose of middleware is to facilitate communication between components in distributed systems while hiding the implementation and distribution aspects of the system. This requires built-in mechanisms to locate components on demand (usually based on a system-wide unique identifier) and to pass requests between components in access and location-transparent ways. An object request broker (ORB) is a core component of middleware that automatically maps requests for objects and their methods to the appropriate objects anywhere in the system. Middleware has been introduced in Chapter 5 and is also discussed in further detail later in this chapter.

Group communication mechanisms (discussed later in this chapter) provide a means of sending a message to a group of processes without knowing the identity or location of the individuals and thus provide location transparency.

Multicast communication also permits sending a message to a group of processes, but there are several different implementations. In the case that the recipients are identified collectively by a single virtual address that represents the group, then it is location-transparent. However, in the case where the sender has to identify the individual recipients in the form of a list of specific addresses, it is not location-transparent.

Broadcast communication is inherently location-transparent as it uses a special address that causes a message to be sent to all possible recipients. A group of processes can communicate without having to know the membership of the group (such as the number of processes and the location of each).

6.2.3 REPLICATION TRANSPARENCY

Distributed systems can comprise many resources and can have many users who need access to those resources. Having a single copy of each resource can be problematic; it can lead to performance bottlenecks if lots of users need to access the same resource and it also leaves the system exposed to the risk of one of the resources becoming unavailable, preventing work being done (e.g., a file becomes corrupted or a service crashes). For these reasons, among others, replication of resources is a commonly used technique.

Replication transparency requires that multiple copies of objects can be created without any effect of the replication seen by applications that use the objects. This implies that it should not be possible for an application to determine the number of replicas or to be able to see the identities of specific replica instances. All copies of a replicated data resource, such as files, should be maintained such that they have the same contents, and thus, any operation applied to one replica must yield the same results as if applied to any other replica. The provision of transparent replication increases availability because the accesses to the resource are spread across the various copies. This is relatively easy to provide for read-only access to resources but is complicated by the need for consistency control where updates to data objects are concerned.

The focus of the following discussion is on the mechanistic aspects of implementing replication. The need for resources to be replicated to achieve nonfunctional requirements in systems, including robustness, availability, and responsiveness, has been discussed in detail in Chapter 5. There is also an activity in that chapter that explores replication in action.

The most significant challenge of implementing replication of data resources is the maintenance of consistency. This must be unconditional; under all possible use scenarios, the data resources must remain consistent. Regardless of what access or update sequence occurs, the system should enforce whatever controls are needed to ensure that all copies of the data remain correct and reflect the same value, such that whichever copy is accessed, the same result is achieved. For example, a pair of seemingly simultaneous accesses to a particular resource (by two different users) may actually be serialized such that one access takes place and completes before the other starts. This should be performed on short timescales so that users do not notice the additional latency of the request and thus have the illusion that they are the only user (see also "Concurrency transparency" for more details).

When one copy of a replicated data resource is updated, it is necessary to propagate the change to the other copies (maintaining consistency as mentioned above) before any further accesses are made to those copies to ensure that out-of-date data are not used and that updates are not lost.

There are several different update strategies that can be used to propagate updates to multiple replicas. The simplest update strategy is to allow write access at only one replica, limiting other replicas to read-only access. Where multiple replicas can be updated, the control becomes more complex; there is a trade-off between the flexibility benefits of allowing multiple replicas to be accessed in a read-write fashion and the additional control and communication overheads of managing the update propagation.

Access to shared resources is usually provided via services. Application processes should not in general access shared resources directly because, in such a case, it is not possible to exercise access control and therefore maintain consistency. Therefore, the replication of data resources generally implies the replication of the service entities that manage the resources. So, for example, if the data content of a database is to be replicated, then there will need to be multiple copies of the database service, through which access to the data is facilitated. Figure 6.3 illustrates some models for server replication and update propagation.

Figure 6.3 shows three different models for server replication. The most important aspect of these models is the way in which updates are performed after a process external to the service has written new data or updated existing data. The fundamental requirement is that all replicas are just that (exact replicas of each other) a service is inconsistent if the different copies of its data do not hold identical values. Part A of the figure shows the primary-backup model (also called the master-backup model). Here, only the primary instance is visible to external processes, so all accesses (read and write) are performed at the primary, and thus, there can be no inconsistency under normal conditions (i.e., when the primary instance is functioning). Updates performed at the primary instance are propagated to the backup instance at regular periods or possibly immediately each time the primary data are changed. The backup instance is thus a "hot spare"; it has a full copy of the service's data and can be made available to external processes as soon as the primary node fails. The strength of this approach is its simplicity, while it has the weaknesses of only providing one instance of the service at any given time (so is not scalable). There is a small window of opportunity for the two copies to become inconsistent, which can arise if the primary updates its database and then crashes before managing to propagate the update to the backup instance. Primary-backup (master-backup) replication has been explored in detail in activity A3 in Chapter 5.

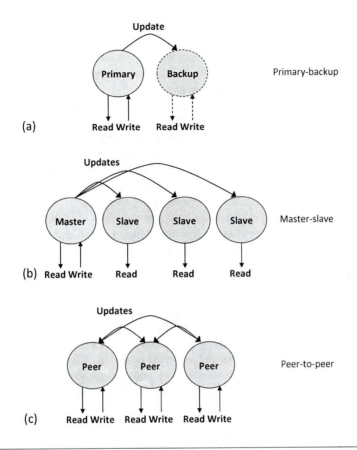

FIGURE 6.3

Some alternative models for server replication.

Figure 6.3 part B shows the master-slave model. All instances of the service can be made available for access by external processes, but write requests are only supported by the master instance and must be propagated to all slave instances as soon as possible so that reads are consistent across the entire service. This replication model is ideal for the large number of applications in which read access is more frequent than write access. For example, in file systems and database systems, reads tend to be more common than writes because updates tend to require a read-modify-write sequence, and thus, writing incorporates a read (the exception being when new files or records, respectively, are created), but reading doesn't incorporate a write. There is no absolute limit to the number of slave instances so the model is very scalable with respect to read requests. A large number of write requests can become a bottleneck because of the requirement to propagate updates, and this becomes more severe as the number of slaves (whose contents must be kept consistent) becomes higher. Mechanisms such as the two-phase commit (see below) should be used to ensure that all updates are either completed (at all nodes) or rolled back to the previous state so that all copies of the data remain consistent even when one instance cannot be updated. In the case of a rollback, the affected update is lost; in which case, the external process that submitted the original request must resubmit it to the service. The slave instances are all potential "hot spares" for the master, should it fail. An election algorithm (see later) is required to ensure that failure of the master is detected and acted upon quickly, selecting exactly one slave to be promoted to master status. The existence of multiple master instances would violate the consistency of the data as multiple writes could occur at the same data record or file at the same time but at different instances, leading to lost updates and inconsistent values held at different nodes.

Figure 6.3 part C shows the peer-to-peer model. This model requires very careful consideration of the semantics of file updates and the way that the data are replicated. It is challenging to implement where global consistency is required at the same time as requiring that each replica has a full copy of the data. This service can however be very useful where the data are fragmented and each node only holds a small subset of the entire data, and thus, the level of replication is lower (i.e., when an update must be performed, it only has to be propagated to the subset of nodes that have copies of the particular data object). This replication model is ideally suited to applications where most of the data are personalized to particular end users, and thus, there is a naturally low level of replication. This approach has become very popular for mobile computing with applications such as file sharing and social networking running on user's portable computing devices such as mobile phones and tablets.

6.2.3.1 Invalidation

Caching of local copies of data within distributed applications is a specialized form of replication to reduce the number of remote access requests to the same data. Caching schemes tend to not update all cached copies when the master copy is updated; this is because of the communication overhead involved, coupled with the possibility that the process holding the cached copy may not actually need to access the data again (so propagating the update would be wasted effort). In such systems, it is still necessary to inform the cache holders that the data they hold are out of date; this is achieved with an invalidation message. In such case, the application only needs to rerequest the data from the master copy if it needs to access the same again.

6.2.3.2 Two-Phase Commit (2PC) Protocol

Updating multiple copies of a resource simultaneously requires that all copies are successfully updated; otherwise, the system will become inconsistent. For example, consider that there are three copies of a variable named X, which has the value 5 initially. An update to change the value to 7 occurs; this requires that all three copies are changed to the value 7. If only two of the values change, the consistency requirement is violated. There could however be reasons why one of the copies cannot be updated: perhaps the network connection has temporarily failed. In such a case where one copy cannot be updated, then none of them should be, once again preserving consistency. In such a situation, the requestor process wanting to perform the update will be informed that the update failed and will be able to resubmit the update later.

The two-phase commit protocol is a well-known technique to ensure that the consistency requirement is met when updating replicas. The first of the two phases determines whether it is possible to update all copies of the resource, and the second phase actually commits the change on an all-or-none basis.

Operation: A commit manager (CM) coordinates a transaction that may involve several participating processes to update replicated data at several sites (see Figure 6.4):

- Phase 1. An update request is sent to each participating process and each replies with an acknowledgment that they have managed to perform the update (or otherwise that they are not

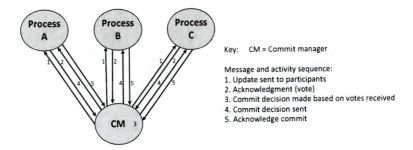

Key: CM = Commit manager

Message and activity sequence:
1. Update sent to participants
2. Acknowledgment (vote)
3. Commit decision made based on votes received
4. Commit decision sent
5. Acknowledge commit

FIGURE 6.4

The two-phase commit protocol.

able to). Updates are not made permanent at this stage; a rollback to the original state may be required. The acknowledgments serve as **yes** or **no** votes.

- Phase 2. The CM decides whether to commit or abort based on the votes received. If all processes voted yes in phase 1, then a commit decision will be taken; otherwise, the transaction is aborted. The CM then informs participating nodes whether to commit the transaction (i.e., make the changes permanent or rollback).

Figure 6.4 shows the behavior and sequence of messages that constitute the two-phase commit protocol.

The first two messages 1 and 2 represent the first phase of the protocol in which the update is sent to each participating process and they send their votes back (informing of their ability to perform the update). The CM then decides whether or not to commit, based on the votes (step 3). The final two messages 4 and 5 represent the second phase in which the processes are told whether to commit or abort, and each sends back an acknowledgment to confirm their compliance.

6.2.4 CONCURRENCY TRANSPARENCY

Distributed systems can comprise many shared-access resources and can have many users (and applications running on behalf of users), which use those resources. The behavior of users is naturally asynchronous; this means that they each perform actions when they need to without knowing or checking what others are doing. The resulting asynchronous nature of resource accesses means that there will be occasions where two or more processes attempt to access a particular resource simultaneously.

Concurrency transparency requires that concurrent processes can share objects without interference. This means that the system should provide each user with the illusion that they have exclusive access to the resource.

Concurrent access to data objects raises the issue of data consistency, but from a slightly different angle to that discussed in the context of data replication (above). In the case of replication, there are multiple copies of a resource being updated with the same value, whereas with concurrent access, there are multiple entities updating a single resource. These are different variations of the same fundamental problem and equally important.

In a situation where two or more concurrent processes attempt to access the same resource, there needs to be some regulation of actions. If both processes only read the resource data, then the order of the two reads does not matter. However, if one or both of them write a new value to the resource, then the sequence with which the accesses take place becomes critical to ensuring that data consistency is maintained. Typically, updating a data value follows a read-update-write sequence. If each whole sequence is isolated from other sequences (e.g., by wrapping them inside a transaction mechanism or by locking the resource for the duration of the sequence so that one process has temporary exclusive access), then consistency is preserved. However, where the access sequences of the two processes are allowed to become interleaved, the lost update problem can arise and the system becomes inconsistent (the lost update problem was introduced in Chapter 4 and is discussed further below).

Figure 6.5 illustrates the lost update problem, using an airline booking system as a case example. The application must support multiple concurrent users who are unaware of the existence of other users. The users should be presented with a consistent view of the system, and even more importantly, the underlying data stored in the system must remain consistent at all times. This can be difficult to achieve in highly dynamic applications. For the airline booking application, we consider the consistency requirement that (for a specific flight, on a specific aircraft) the total number of seats available plus the total number of seats booked must always be equal to the total number of seats on the aircraft. It must not be possible for two users to manage to book the same seat or for seats to be "lost," for example, a seat is booked and then released, but somehow is not added back to the available pool.

The scenario shown in Figure 6.5 starts in a consistent state in which there are 170 seats available. In step 1, client1 reads the number of seats available and caches it locally. Soon after this, in step 2, client2 does the same. Imagine that this activity is somehow linked to users browsing an online booking system, taking a while to decide whether to book or not and then submitting their order. Client1 then books 2 seats and writes back the new availability, which is $170-2=168$ (step 3 in the figure). Later, client2 books 3 seats and writes back the new availability, which is $170-3=167$ (step 4). The true availability of seats is now $170-(2+3)=165$. The sequence of accesses in the scenario has led to the creation of two seats in the system that do not actually exist on the plane; therefore, the system is inconsistent.

It is important that you can see where the problem lies in this scenario: it arises because the sequences of accesses of the two clients were allowed to overlap. If client2 had been forced to reread the availability of seats after client1's update, then the system would have remained consistent.

In addition to the consistency aspect of concurrency transparency, there is also a performance aspect. Ideally, user requests can be interleaved on a sufficiently fine-grained timescale that they do not notice a performance penalty arising from the forced serialization occurring behind the scenes. If

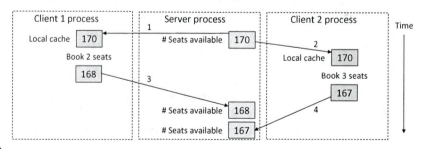

FIGURE 6.5

The lost update problem (illustrated with an airline seat booking scenario).

resources are locked for long periods of time, the concurrency transparency is lost, as users notice that transaction times increase significantly when system load or the number of users increases.

Important design considerations include deciding what must be locked and when and ensuring that locks are released promptly when no longer needed. Also important is the scope of the locking; it is undesirable to lock a whole group of resources when only one item in the group is actually accessed. To put this into context, consider the options for preserving database consistency: locking entire databases during transactions temporarily prevents access to the entire database and is highly undesirable from a concurrency viewpoint. Table-level locking enables different processes to access different tables at the same time, because their updates do not interfere, but still prevents access to the entire locked table even if only a single row is being accessed. Row-level locking is a fine-grained approach that increases transparency by allowing concurrent access at the table level.

6.2.4.1 Transactions

A transaction is an indivisible sequence of related operations that must be processed in its entirety or aborted without making any changes to system state. A transaction must not be partially processed because that could corrupt data resources or lead to inconsistent states.

Transactions were introduced in Chapter 4. Recall that there are four mandatory properties of trans-actions (the ACID properties):

- Atomicity. The transaction cannot be divided. The whole transaction (all suboperations) is carried out or none of it is carried out.
- Consistency. The stored data in the system must be left in a consistent state at the end of the transaction (this leads on from the all-or-nothing requirement of atomicity). Achieving the requirement of consistency is more complex if the system supports data replication.
- Isolation. There must be no interference between transactions. Some resources need to be locked for the duration of the transaction to ensure this requirement is met. Some code sections need to be protected so that they can only be entered by one process at a time (the protection mechanisms are called MUTEXs because they enforce mutual exclusion).
- Durability. The results of a transaction must be made permanent (stored in some nonvolatile storage).

Figure 6.6 relates together the four properties of transactions in the context of a multipart transaction in which partial results are generated but must not be made visible to processes outside of the transaction.

The transaction properties are placed into the perspective of a banking application example:

The banking application maintains a variety of different types of data, in a number of databases. These data could include customer accounts data, financial products data (e.g., the rules for opening different types of accounts and depositing and withdrawal of funds), interest rates applicable, and tax rates applicable. A variety of different transactions can occur, depending on circumstances. Transaction types could include open new account, deposit funds, withdraw funds, add net interest, generate annual interest and tax statement, and close account. Each of these transactions may be internally subdivided into a number of steps and may need to access one or more of the databases.

Consider a specific transaction type: add net interest. This transaction may need to perform the following steps: (1) read the account balance and multiply by the current gross interest rate to determine the gross interest amount payable; (2) multiply the gross interest amount by the tax rate to determine

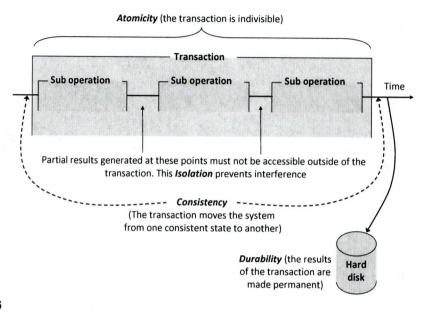

FIGURE 6.6

The four properties of transactions.

the tax payable on the interest; (3) subtract the tax payable from the gross interest amount to determine the net interest payable.

Prior to the transaction, the system is in a consistent state and the following three values are stored (in three separate databases): account balance=£1000; interest rate=2%; tax rate=20%. Figure 6.7 illustrates the internal operation of the transaction.

Figure 6.7 places the ACID transaction properties into the perspective of the mechanics of the banking application transaction. The transaction operates in three steps leading to temporary internal states (partial results), which must not be visible externally. When the transaction completes, the system is in a new consistent state, the account balance having been updated to the value £1016.

The isolation property of transactions is particularly important with respect to concurrency transparency because it prevents external processes accessing partial results generated temporarily as a transaction progresses. In the example illustrated in Figure 6.7, a temporary value of £1020 is written to the account, but the transaction is only partially complete at this stage, and tax is yet to be deducted. Therefore, the user never actually has that amount to withdraw. If the value were exposed to other processes, then the system could become inconsistent. If the user were to check their balance in the short time window while the temporary value was showing on the account, they would think they had more money than they actually do have. Worse still would be if the user were allowed to withdraw £1020 at this point because they do not actually have that much money in the account. When the transaction finally completes, the system is left in a consistent state with £1016 in the account; this value can now be exposed to other processes.

A further example is provided by re-presenting the airline seat booking system (seen earlier in this section) as a series of transactions. The forced serialization (and thus isolation) overcomes the inconsistency weakness of the earlier design.

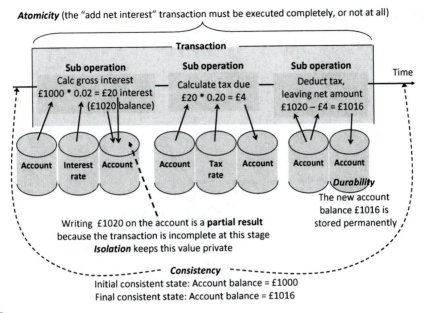

FIGURE 6.7

The internal operation of the "add net interest" transaction of the banking application.

Figure 6.8 presents a transaction implementation of the airline seat booking system. This approach serializes the two seat booking operations that would lead to an inconsistent state if allowed to become interleaved. The system is left in a consistent state after each transaction, in which the number of seats available and the number of seats booked always are equal to the total number of seats on the aircraft.

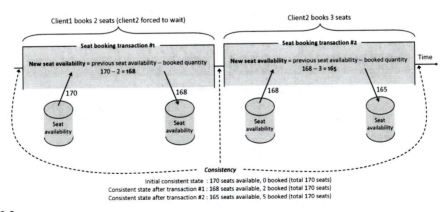

FIGURE 6.8

A transaction implementation of the airline seat booking system.

6.2.5 MIGRATION TRANSPARENCY

Distributed systems tend to be dynamic in a number of ways including changes in the user population and the activities they carry out, which in turn leads to load-level fluctuations on different services at various times. Systems are also dynamic due to the addition and relocation of physical computers, continuous changes in network traffic levels, and the random failure of computers and network connections.

Due to the dynamic nature of these systems, it is necessary to be able to reconfigure the resources within the system, for example, to relocate a particular data resource or service from one computer to another.

Migration transparency requires that data objects can be moved without affecting the operation of applications that use those objects and that processes can be moved without affecting their operations or results.

In the case of migration of data objects (such as files) in active use, access requests from processes using the object must be transparently redirected to the object's new location. Where objects are moved between accesses, techniques used to implement location transparency can suffice. A name service (discussed later) provides the current location of a resource; its history of movement is of no consequence as long as its current location after moving is known. However, there is a challenge in keeping the name service itself up to date if resources are moved frequently.

Process transfers can be achieved preemptively or nonpreemptively. Preemptive transfers involve moving a process in midexecution. This is complex because the process' execution state and environment must be preserved during the transfer. Nonpreemptive transfers are done before the task starts to execute so the transfer is much simpler to achieve.

6.2.6 FAILURE TRANSPARENCY

Failures in distributed systems are inevitable. There can be large numbers of hardware and software components interacting, dependent on the communication links between them. The set of possible configurations and behaviors that can arise is too great in general that every scenario can be tested for; therefore, there will always be the possibility of some unforeseen combination of circumstances that leads to failure. In addition to any built-in reliability weaknesses they may have, hardware devices and network links can fail due to external factors; for example, a power cut may occur or a cable is accidentally unplugged.

While it is not possible to prevent failures outright, measures should be taken to minimize the probability of failures occurring and to limit the consequences of failures when they do happen.

Good system-level design should take into account the reality that any component can fail and should avoid having critical single points of failure where possible. Software design should avoid unnecessary complexity within components and in the connectivity with, and thus dependency upon, other components (see the section on component coupling in Chapter 5). Additional complexity increases the opportunities for failure; and the more complex the system, the harder it is to test. This leads to undertesting where not all of the functional and behavioral scope is covered by tests. Even where testing is thorough, it cannot prove that a failure will not take place. Latent faults are present in most software systems. These are faults that have not yet shown up; faults in this category often only occur in a particular sequence or combination of events so they can lurk undetected for a long time.

Once we have exhausted all possible design-time ways to build our systems to be as reliable as possible, we need to rely on runtime techniques that will deal with the residual failures that can occur.

Failure transparency requires that faults are concealed so that applications can continue to function without any impact on behavior or correctness. Failure transparency is a significant challenge! As mentioned above, many different types of fault can occur in a distributed system.

Communication protocols provide a good example of how different levels of runtime failure transparency can be built in through clever design. For example, compare the TCP and UDP. TCP has a number of built-in features including sequence numbers, acknowledgments, and a retransmission-on-time-out mechanism that transparently deal with various issues that occur at the message transmission level, such as message loss, message corruption, and acknowledgment loss. UDP is a more lightweight protocol and, as a result, has none of these facilities and, hence, is commonly referred to as a "send and pray" protocol.

6.2.6.1 Support for Failure Transparency

A popular technique to provide a high degree of failure transparency is to replicate processes or data resources at several computing hosts, thus avoiding the occurrence of a single point of failure (see "Replication transparency").

Election algorithms can be used to mask the failure of critical or centralized components. This approach is popular in services that need a coordinator and can include replicated services in which one copy is allocated the role of master or coordinator. On the failure of the coordinator, another service member process will be elected to take over the role. Election algorithms are explored in detail later in this chapter.

In all replicated services or situations where a new coordinator is elected when a failure occurs, the extent to which the original failure is masked is dependent on the internal design of the service, in particular the way in which state is managed. The new coordinator may not have a perfect copy of the state information that the previous one had (e.g., an instantaneous crash can occur during a transaction), so the system may not be in an identical situation after recovery. This scenario should be given careful consideration during the design effort to maximize the likelihood that the system does remain entirely consistent across the handover. In particular, the use of stateless server design can reduce or remove the risk of state loss on server failure, as all state is held on the client side of connections (see the discussion on stateful versus stateless services in Chapter 5).

Even when stateless services are used, problems can still arise. For example, if a single requested action is carried out multiple times at a server, the correctness or consistency of the system could be disrupted. Consider, for example, in a banking application, the function "Add annual interest" being executed multiple times by accident. This could happen where a request is sent and not acknowledged; the client may resend the message on the assumption that the original request was lost, but in fact, the message had arrived and it was actually the acknowledgment that was lost; the outcome being that the server will receive two copies of the request. One way to resolve this is to use sequence numbers so that duplicate requests can be identified. Another approach is to design all actions to be idempotent.

An idempotent action is one that is repeatable without having side effects. The use of idempotent requests contributes to failure transparency because it hides the fact that a request has been repeated, such that the intended outcome is correct. There is no side effect of requesting the action more than once, whether the action is actually carried out multiple times or not. Another way to think of this is that the use of idempotent actions allows certain types of fault to occur while preventing them from having any impact and therefore removing the need to handle the faults or recover from them.

Generic request types that can be idempotent include "set value to *x*," "get value of item whose ID is *x*," and "delete item whose ID is *x*."

Generic request types that are not idempotent include "add value *y* to value *x*," "get next item," and "delete item at position *z* in the list."

A specific example of a nonidempotent action is "add 10 pounds to account number 123." This is because (if we assume the initial balance is 200 pounds) after being executed once, the new balance will be 210 pounds, and after two executions, the balance will be 220 pounds and so on.

However, the action can be reconstructed as a series of two idempotent actions, each of which can be repeated without corrupting the system's data. The first of the new actions is "get account balance," which copies the balance from the server side to the client side. The result of this is that the client is informed that the balance is 200 pounds. If this request is repeated multiple times, the client is informed of the balance value several times, but it is still 200 pounds. Once the client has the balance, it then locally adds 10 pounds. The second idempotent action is "set account balance to 210 pounds." If this action is performed once or more times in succession, the balance at the server will always end up at 210 pounds. In addition to being robust, the approach of shifting the computation into the client further improves the scalability of the stateless server approach. However, this technique is mostly useful for nonshared data, such as the situation in the example above in which each client is likely to be interested in a unique bank account. Where the data are shared, as in the earlier airline seat booking example, transactions (which are more heavyweight and less scalable) are more appropriate due to the need for consistency across multiple actions and the need to serialize accesses to the system data.

Idempotent actions are also very useful in safety-critical systems, as well as in systems that have unreliable communication links or very high latency communication. This is because the role of acknowledgments is less critical when idempotent requests are used and the not uncommon problem of the time-out being too short (causing retransmission) does not result in erroneous behavior at the application level.

Checkpointing is an approach to fault tolerance that can be used to protect from the failure of critical processes or from failure of the physical computers that critical processes run on.

Checkpointing is the mechanism of making a copy of the process' state at regular intervals and sending that state to a remote store (the state information that is stored includes the process' memory image, such as the value of variables, as well as process management details such as which instruction is to be executed next, and IO details such as which files are open and what communication links are set up with other processes.

If a checkpointed process crashes or its host computer fails, then a new copy of the process can be restarted using the stored state image. The new process begins operating from the point the previous one was at when the last checkpoint was taken. This technique is particularly valuable for protecting the work performed by long-running processes such as occur in scientific computing and simulations such as weather forecasts that may run for many hours. Without checkpointing, a failed process would have to start again from the beginning, potentially causing the loss of a lot of work and causing delay to the user who is waiting for the result.

6.2.7 SCALING TRANSPARENCY

For distributed systems in general, as the system is scaled up, a point is eventually reached where the performance will begin to drop; this could be noticed, for example, in terms of slower response times or service requests timing-out. Small increases in scale beyond this point can have severe effects on performance.

Scaling transparency requires that it should be possible to scale up an application, service, or system without changing the system structure or algorithms. Scaling transparency is largely dependent on efficient design, in terms of the use of resources, and especially in terms of the intensity of communication.

Centralized components are often problematic for scalability. These can become performance bottlenecks as the number of clients or service requests increases. Centralized data structures grow with system size, eventually causing scaling problems in terms of the size of the data and the increased time taken to search the larger structure, impacting on service response times. A backlog of requests can build up rapidly once a certain size threshold is exceeded.

Distributed services avoid the bottleneck pitfalls of centralization but represent a trade-off in terms of higher total communication requirements. This is because in addition to the external communication between clients and the service, there is also the service-internal communication necessary to coordinate the service and, for example, to propagate updates between server instances.

Hierarchical design improves scalability; a very good example of this is the DNS that is discussed in detail later in this chapter. Decoupling of components also improves scalability. Publish-subscribe event notification services (also discussed later) are an example technique by which the extent of coupling and also the communication intensity can be significantly reduced.

6.2.7.1 Communication Intensity: Impact on Scalability

Interaction complexity is a measure of the number of communication relationships within a group of components. Because systems scale can change, interaction complexity is described in terms of the proportion of the other components in the system each component communicates with, rather than absolute numbers (see Table 6.1).

Communication intensity is the amount of communication that actually occurs, which results from the interaction complexity combined with the actual frequency of sending messages between communicating components and the size of those messages. This is a significant factor that limits the scalability

Table 6.1 Example Interaction Complexities for a System of N Components

Typical proportion of other components that each of the N components communicates with	Interaction complexity	Typical interpretation
1	$O(N)$	Each component communicates with another component. This is highly scalable as the communication intensity increases linearly as the system size increases
2	$O(2N)$	Each component communicates with two other components. Communication intensity increases linearly as the system size increases
$N/2$	$O(N^2/2)$	Each component communicates with approximately half of the system. This represents an exponential rate of increase of communication intensity and thus can impact on scalability
$N-1$	$O(N^2 - N)$ also written $O(N(N-1))$	Each component communicates with most or all. This is a steep exponential relationship and can severely impact on scalability

of many systems. This is because the communication bandwidth is finite in any system and the communication channels become bottlenecks as the amount of communication builds up. Communication is also relatively time-consuming compared with computation. As the ratio of time spent communicating (including waiting to communicate due to network congestion and access latency) to computation time increases, the throughput and efficiency of systems fall. The reduction in performance eventually becomes a limiting factor on usability. If the performance cannot be restored by adding more resource while leaving the design unchanged, then the design is said to be not scalable or to have reached the limit of its scalability.

Some diverse examples of interaction complexity are provided below:

- The bully election algorithm in its worst-case scenario during an election has $O(N^2 - N)$ interaction complexity (the bully election algorithm is discussed in "Election algorithms" later in this chapter).
- A peer-to-peer media sharing application (as explored in activity A2 in Chapter 5) may have typical interaction complexity of between $O(2N)$ and $O(N^2/2)$ depending on the actual proportion of other peers that each one connects to.
- The case study game that has been used as a common point of reference throughout the book has a very low interaction complexity. Each client connects to one server component regardless of the size of the system, so system-wide interaction complexity is $O(N)$ where N is the number of clients in the system.

Figure 6.9 shows two different interaction mappings between the components of similar systems. Part A illustrates a low-intensity mapping in which each component connects with on average one other, so the interaction complexity is $O(N)$. In contrast, part B shows a system of highly coupled components in which each component communicates with approximately half of the others, so the interaction complexity is $O(N^2/2)$.

Figure 6.10 provides a graphic illustration of the way in which interaction complexity affects the relationship between the size of the system (the number of components) and the resulting intensity of communication (the number of interaction relationships). The steepness of the curves associated with the more intense interaction complexities illustrates the relative severity of their effect on scalability.

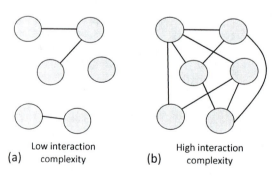

(a) Low interaction complexity (b) High interaction complexity

FIGURE 6.9

Illustration of low and high interaction complexity.

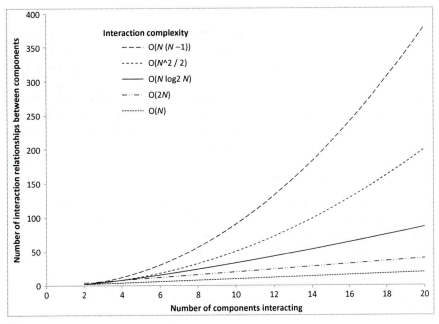

FIGURE 6.10

The effect of various interaction complexities on the relationship between the size of the system and the resulting intensity of communication.

6.2.8 PERFORMANCE TRANSPARENCY

The performance of distributed systems is affected by numerous aspects of their configuration and use.

Performance transparency requires that the performance of systems should degrade gracefully as the load on the system increases. Consistency of performance is a significant aspect of the user experience and can be more important than absolute performance. A system that has consistent good performance is better received than one in which the performance is outstanding some of the time but can degrade rapidly and unpredictably, which leads to user frustration. Ultimately, this is a measure of usability.

6.2.8.1 Support for Performance Transparency

Performance (an attribute of the system) and performance transparency (a requirement on performance) are affected by the design of every component in the system and also by the collective behavior of the system that itself cannot be predicted by knowing the behavior of each individual component, due to the complex runtime relationships and sequences of events that occur.

High performance cannot therefore be guaranteed through the implementation of any particular mechanism; rather, it is an emergent characteristic that arises through consistently good design technique across all aspects of the system. Performance transparency is an explicit goal of load-sharing schemes that attempt to evenly distribute the processing load across the processing resources so as to maintain responsiveness.

6.2.9 DISTRIBUTION TRANSPARENCY

Distribution transparency requires that all details of the network and the physical separation of components are hidden such that application components operate as though they are all local to each other (i.e., running on the same computer) and therefore do not need to be concerned with network connections and addresses.

A good example is provided by middleware. A virtual layer is created across the system that decouples processes from their underlying platforms. All communication between processes passes through the middleware in access-transparent and location-transparent ways, providing the overall effect of hiding the network and the distribution of the components.

6.2.10 IMPLEMENTATION TRANSPARENCY

Implementation transparency means hiding the details of the ways in which components are implemented. For example, this can include enabling applications to comprise components developed in different languages; in which case, it is necessary to ensure that the semantics of communication, such as in method calls, are preserved when these components interoperate.

Middleware such as CORBA provides implementation transparency. It uses a special interface definition language (IDL) that represents method calls in a programming language-neutral way such that the semantics of the method call between a pair of components are preserved (including the number parameters and data type of each parameter value and the direction of each parameter, i.e, being passed into the method or returned from the method) regardless of the combination of languages the two components are written in.

6.3 COMMON SERVICES

Distributed applications have a number of common requirements that arise specifically because of their distributed nature and of the dynamic nature of the system and platforms they operate on. Common requirements of distributed applications include

- an automatic means of locating services and resources,
- an automatic means of synchronizing clocks,
- an automatic means of selecting a coordinator process from a group of candidates,
- mechanisms for the management of distributed transactions to ensure consistency is maintained,
- communications support for components operating in groups,
- mechanisms to support indirect and loose coupling of components to improve scalability and robustness.

It is therefore sensible that a group of support services are provided generically in systems, which provide services to applications in standard ways. Application developers can integrate calls to these services into their applications instead of having to implement additional functionality within each application. This saves a lot of duplicated effort that would be costly, would significantly extend lead times, and could ultimately reduce quality as each developer would implement different variations of services leading to possible inconsistency.

In addition to specific functionalities such as those mentioned above, common services also contribute to the provision of all transparency forms discussed earlier in this chapter and also to the nonfunctional requirements of distributed applications discussed in Chapter 5.

Common services are generally regarded as an integral part of a distributed systems infrastructure and are invisible to users. These support services are usually distributed or replicated across the computers in the system and therefore have the same quality requirements (robustness, scalability, responsiveness, etc.) as the distributed applications themselves. Some of the common services are exemplars of good distributed application design; DNS is a particular example.

There are a wide range of possible services and mechanisms that can be considered in the common services category, so this chapter focuses on some of the most significant and frequently used services. The common services and mechanisms explored in the following sections of this chapter are

- name services and directory services,
- the DNS (a very important example of a name service, treated in-depth),
- time services,
- clock synchronization mechanisms,
- election algorithms,
- group communication mechanisms,
- event notification services,
- middleware.

6.4 NAME SERVICES

One of the biggest challenges in a distributed system is finding resources. The very fact that the resources are distributed across many different computers means that there needs to be a way to automatically find the resources needed and to be able to do this very quickly and reliably.

Consider the situation where one software component needs to find the location of another, so that a message can be sent to it. Keeping at the very highest level, there are only two approaches: Information that is already known is used and there is a way to look up the information needed on demand. There are several parallels with the way people find resources: two good examples are phone numbers and Web sites. You probably know the phone numbers and Web site addresses that you use regularly. These are memorized, so this is the equivalent of built-in or hard-coded, if you were a software component. One pertinent issue here is that if one of your friends changed their number, then your memorized data are of no use and you would need a way to get hold of the new number and then rememorize it. For the phone numbers and Web sites that you cannot remember, which realistically is most of them, you need some way to be able to find them; you need a service that searches for them based on a description. Your mobile phone has a database built into it, into which you can store your regularly needed phone numbers, using the name of the phone number owner as a key. You then type in the person's name when you need to phone them (you don't need to remember the number), the database is searched, and the phone number is retrieved; this is essentially a simple form of name service (more specifically, this is an example of a directory service; see discussion below).

Consider the number of resources in a system as large as the Internet. There are thousands of millions of computers connected to the Internet. There are hundreds of millions of Web sites and some of these Web sites have hundreds of pages. The numbers are staggering, but how many can you remember? You probably don't remember very many at all, but you have ways to find out, using services that you probably use many times a day without necessarily thinking about how they operate.

Search results

Council services- Havering
https://www.**havering**.gov.uk/Pages/**Services**.aspx

Havering Council
https://www.**havering**.gov.uk/

A-Z of Council services- Havering
https://www.**havering**.gov.uk/Pages/AtoZ.aspx?AtoZindex=A

Contact the Council- Havering
https://www.**havering**.gov.uk/Pages/Category/Contact-us.aspx

FIGURE 6.11

The first four results returned by the search engine, for my search string.

To illustrate, let me set you a typical day-to-day information-retrieval task (try to do this right away without thinking too much about it): find the Web site for your local government office (such as your local council) where you would get information about local services such as weekly rubbish collections.

Did you manage to get the Web site displayed on your computer? If so, then I expect you probably used two different services. Firstly, you probably used a search engine (such as Bing, Google, and Yahoo), where you submitted a textual query such as "Havering council services" and were presented with a number of uniform resource locators (URLs; these were introduced in Chapter 4). The results I get after this first stage include those shown in Figure 6.11.

The next step requires you to choose one of the search results that appears to describe the Web site that you are actually looking for and to click on the provided hyperlink (these are the underlined sections of text, and when clicked, the associated Web page will automatically be opened in a browser). Modern search engines are very good at contextually ordering the results of the search, and in this particular case, the first result in the list does seem the most promising, so I would now click on the first link in the list.

This is the point where the second service (a name service) comes into play, and because you are using it automatically, it is quite possible that you are not even aware that you are using it. Several things must happen in sequence, in order to display the Web page. First, the URL must be converted to an IP address (the address of the host computer where the relevant Web server is located), and then, a TCP connection can be made to the Web server. Once the TCP connection is set up, then a request for the Web page can be sent to the Web server, and the Web page contents are sent back to my computer. Finally, the Web page is displayed on my screen. The name service is the part of the system that converts the URL into the IP address of the Web server's host computer's address. The actual name service used in the Internet is the DNS, which is discussed in detail later in this chapter.

6.4.1 NAME SERVICE OPERATION

A name service is a network service that translates one form of address into another. A very common requirement is to translate a human-meaningful address type, such as a URL, into the type of address used to actually communicate with components within a system (such as an IP address).

The fundamental need for name services stems from several factors:

- Networks can be huge, containing many computers, and the IP addresses of computers are logical, not physical. This means that a computer's IP address is related to its logical connection into the network. If the computer is moved to a different subnet, then its IP address will change; this is a necessity for routing to operate correctly (see the discussion in Chapter 4).

- Distributed applications can span across many physical computers. The configuration of the application can change, such that different components are located on different computers at different times.
- Networks and distributed systems are dynamic; resources are added, removed, and moved around. Even if you know where all of the resources are at one point in time, your list can be out of date soon after.
- The means to locate resources needs to be standardized for a particular system and externalized from the application software components. It is not desirable to have to embed special mechanisms into each component separately as this represents a lot of effort (design and also testing) and increases the complexity of components significantly.

A fundamental part of name service functionality is to look up the name of a resource (which has been provided in a request message) in a database and to extract the corresponding address details. The address details are then sent back to the requestor process, which uses the information to access the resource. This subset of name service functionality can be described as a directory service (which is discussed in more detail later).

A name service is differentiated from a directory service by the additional functionality and transparency it provides. A name service implements a namespace, which is a structured way to represent resource names. To achieve scalability, a hierarchical namespace is necessary in which a resource name explicitly maps onto its position in the namespace and thus assists in locating the resource (see the discussion on hierarchical addressing in Chapter 3).

In the context of name services, the most important example of hierarchical names is URLs, in which the structure of the resource name relates to its logical location. Consider your e-mail address as a simple example. The URL might have the format: A.Student@myUniversity.Academic.MyCountry. This achieves three important requirements. Firstly, it represents the resource, your e-mail inbox, in a human-friendly way so that people can describe it easily and hopefully remember it. Secondly, it contains an unambiguous mapping of the resource (the e-mail inbox named A.Student) to the e-mail server that hosts the resource, which has the logical address myUniversity.Academic.MyCountry. Thirdly, it is globally unique as there are no other e-mail addresses the same as your one anywhere in the world.

A name service may need to be distributed to enhance scalability and to achieve performance transparency by spreading the namespace, and the work of resolving names within the namespace, across multiple servers. To achieve failure transparency, the name service may also need to be replicated, so that there is no single critical instance of the service (i.e., so that each name can be resolved by more than one service instance).

6.4.2 DIRECTORY SERVICE

As explained above, a directory service provides a subset of name service functionality; it looks up resources in a directory and returns the result. It does not implement its own namespace, and the directory structure is usually flat rather than hierarchical.

Figure 6.12 illustrates how a directory service is used. The application client passes the name of the required application server to the directory server, which responds with the details stored in its database. A directory service is suitable for use within specific applications or for local resource

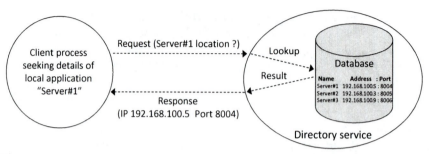

FIGURE 6.12

Overview of directory service operation.

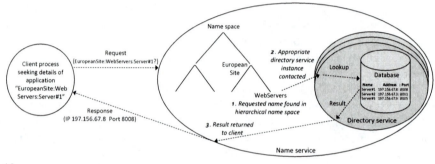

FIGURE 6.13

A directory service as a subcomponent of a name service.

address resolution in small-scale systems; in which case, the size and complexity of the database storage and lookup are limited.

Figure 6.13 shows how a name service wraps a more sophisticated service around the core directory service functionality. In particular, the name service implements a hierarchical namespace and distributes the resource details logically across different directory instances based on the logical position of those resources in the namespace.

Activity D1 uses the directory service that is integrated into the Distributed Systems Workbench to investigate the need for, and behavior of, name and directory services. The directory service has been designed to work in local, small-scale systems, and therefore, it does not support replication and is not distributed, features you would expect in a scalable and robust name service. Significantly, as the directory service operates locally with a limited number of application servers, it stores their names in a flat addressing scheme, that is, it only uses a single-layer textual name such as "server1" or "AuthenticationServer."

Figure 6.14 shows the basic interaction between application components and the directory service, as will be explored in activity D1. The client of an application does not initially know the location of its service counterpart so it passes the name of the required service to the directory service (step 1 in the figure). The directory service looks up the application server name and returns its address if found (step 2 in the figure). Once the client has got the server address, it can make a connection in the usual way (steps 3 and 4 in the figure).

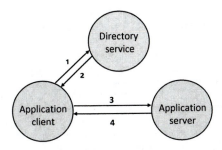

Message sequence key:
1 Client asks directory service for location of server
2 Directory service responds with address if known
3,4 Client and server communicate

FIGURE 6.14

Basic interaction with the directory service.

ACTIVITY D1 EXPERIMENTATION WITH A DIRECTORY SERVICE

This activity uses the directory service that is integrated into the Distributed Systems Workbench to investigate the need for, and behavior of, name and directory services.

The directory service runs as a process on one of the computers in the local network. Application servers can be registered with the directory service when they are initiated. When a client process needs to access a particular application server, it can request the address details from the directory service, identifying the application server by its textual name. The directory service returns the IP address and port number that the client process needs in order to connect to the application service.

Note that name services and directory services perform essentially the same function, namely, to resolve the name of a resource into its location details that can be used to access the resource. The particular service used in this activity is classified as a directory service. It maintains a database of resources that have registered with it, and upon request, it searches the database for the supplied name and returns to the requestor the relevant location details. The simple directory service demonstrates the essential behavior of a name service without implementing a namespace and without itself being distributed; hence, it has not only limited scalability but also limited complexity. Such a service is ideally suited to automatic resource discovery in small-scale local network systems, but is not appropriate for large-scale systems. The low complexity of the directory service makes it ideal for exploring the fundamental mechanism of resource location.

Prerequisites: Copy the support materials required by this activity onto your computer (see activity I1 in Chapter 1).

Learning Outcomes
1. To gain an appreciation of the need for name/directory services
2. To gain an understanding of the operation of an example directory service
3. To gain an appreciation of the transparency benefits of name/directory services
4. To investigate problem scenarios for the use of directory services
5. To explore service autoregistration with a directory service

This activity uses the set of programs found under the "Directory Service" drop-down in the Distributed Systems Workbench top-level menu. The programs include a directory service, four application servers, and an application client. All of the components can be run on a single computer to get a basic idea of the way the directory service operates, but the activity is best performed in a network of at least three different computers if possible, so that the application servers have different IP addresses and separate the client process from the various server processes it connects to in order to make the experimental scenarios realistic.

ACTIVITY D1 EXPERIMENTATION WITH A DIRECTORY SERVICE—Cont'd

Method Part a: Understanding the Need for Name or Directory Services

In this part of the activity, you will run the application client on one computer and the Application Server1 on another. **Do not start the directory server on any computer at this stage**.

Part A1. Start Server1 on one computer. Directory Service → Application Server1, and then, click "Start server."

Part A2. Start the client on a second computer (ideally, but, otherwise, you can use the same computer for both client and server). Directory Service → Client.

Note that the client sets a default address for the server to be the same as its own address and sets a default port number of 8000. Even if the address is correct (i.e., you have started the server on the same computer as the client), the port number is wrong. Try sending a request string to the server with these settings (place some text in the "Message to send" box and press the Send button); it should not do anything.

Part A3. Manually configure the client (enter the correct server address and server port details) so that it can communicate with server1 (confirm that the client and server are actually communicating by sending a request string; the server should send back a reversed-order copy of whatever string you typed).

Part A4. Repeat parts A2 and A3 using server2 on a third computer (ideally, otherwise, use the same computer as earlier).

Part A5. Repeat 1.2 and 1.3 using server3 on a fourth computer (ideally, otherwise, use the same computer as earlier).

Expected Outcome for Part A

By now, you should be able to comment on the suitability (especially in terms of the low usability) of this manual client-server binding approach for commercial distributed systems. Try to identify alternative ways that the client could use to locate the required application server.

The screenshots below show the client, on a computer with IP address 192.168.0.2, manually configured to connect to server3, which is on a computer with IP address 192.168.0.3, using port 8006. Note that the "Server required" field is not used at this stage.

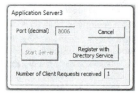

Method Part B: Using the Directory Service

Part B1. Start the directory server **on one computer only**. Note that the directory service does not support replication. If multiple copies of the directory service exist, they will all respond to a client request; this will confuse the results of the experiment.

Part B2. Run the application client on a second computer (if available) and run the application server1 on a third computer.

Part B2. Press the button on server1 to register the server with the directory server. Observe the directory service information boxes.

Part B4. Use the directory service (the client has a button labeled "Contact Directory Service") to get server1's address and port details). Observe the "Server details" boxes in the client and the directory server information boxes.

ACTIVITY D1 EXPERIMENTATION WITH A DIRECTORY SERVICE—Cont'd

Part B5. Start sever2 and server3 also (on any of the computers available). Register these with the directory service. Contact all three services in sequence, using the client. Each time you wish use a new service, change the name of the service in the "Server required" text box on the client, and then, use the Contact Directory Service button to get the details.

Expected Outcome for Part B

You should now be able to see the benefit of having an automatic name resolution service (as provided by the directory service) to facilitate automated component-to-component binding using only textual component names.

The set of screenshots below shows the system configuration once all of the steps of part B of the activity have been completed. The client and server2 (shown of the left below) were running on a computer with IP address 192.168.0.2, while the directory server and application server1 and server3 (shown on the right below) were running on a computer with IP address 192.168.0.3.

The three application servers have been started and have been registered with the directory service, as can be seen in the "Directory Database" listing within the directory server dialog box. The client has requested the address and port details for each server in turn, from the directory service, as can be seen in the "Request History" listing within the directory server dialog box.

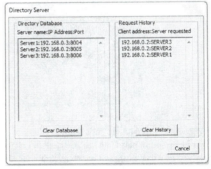

Method Part C: Investigate the Impact of Problem Scenarios on the Behavior of the Directory Service

For this part of the activity, you are encouraged to carry out your own experiments to investigate what happens under a range of scenarios that include the following:

- An application server is not registered when the client asks for its details.
- An application server was registered but has crashed since then.
- An application server was registered at one location but has since been relocated.
- The directory service is running on two different computers simultaneously.
- The directory service is not running at all.
- The directory service crashes after application servers have registered and is then restarted.

Expected Outcome for Part C

Some of the problem scenarios will reveal limitations of the quite simple design of the example directory service. For any problems you discover, repeat experiments to make sure you appreciate the mechanism of the problem (i.e., what is the

---

ACTIVITY D1 EXPERIMENTATION WITH A DIRECTORY SERVICE—Cont'd

actual cause of the problem behavior and how/why does it affect the overall system behavior). Identify any modifications that you think might solve the problem.

The screenshot below shows the "Not Found" response from the directory service when the client requests details of an application server that is not registered.

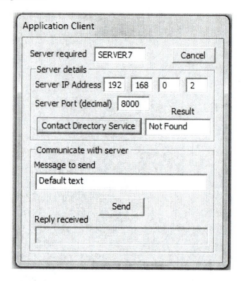

Method Part D: Investigate Service Registration

The problem scenarios identified in part C above do occur in real systems: Application services get relocated within systems, and directory services can crash and recover (with possibly out-of-date information). This means that manually registering services or one-off automated service registration is insufficient in terms of continuously meeting nonfunctional requirements such as usability, robustness, and responsiveness.

Part D1. To appreciate the problem, repeat part C above and move a service (any of application server1, server2, or server3) AFTER you have registered it. Note that the directory service now provides incorrect details. Alternatively shutdown and restart the directory service AFTER an application had registered; the directory service is stateless and thus (after restarting) does not know about the previously registered server.

Part D2. Repeat part D1, but this time, use application server4 (instead of server1, server2, or server3). Notice that there is no button to register the application server with the directory service because it is self-registering. Move server4 as many times as you like. Restart the directory service too. Each time you change something, wait a few seconds and then see if the client can get the server4 details from the directory server.

Expected Outcome for Part D

From your experiments, you should have noticed some distinctly different behavior when using application server4 than when using the other ones.

Question 1. What differences do you notice with respect to server registration?
Question 2. How is the directory service updated?
Question 3. To what extent are the problem scenarios identified in section C overcome?
Question 4. How appropriate is this behavior for large-scale distributed systems?

Reflection

From carrying out this activity, you should have a basic understanding of the behavior of the directory service and appreciate that it is very powerful in terms of transparency and usability. Once the application servers have registered with the directory service, the user only needs to know the textual name of the service they require in order to contact and use the

---

ACTIVITY D1 EXPERIMENTATION WITH A DIRECTORY SERVICE—Cont'd

---

service. Even this aspect could be automated where it is implicitly known, such that the client automatically requests the service it needs, by name upon start-up. In addition to the significant usability benefits, this also achieves location and migration transparency.

Further Investigation

How does the client locate the directory service itself? You may have already worked this out from the experiments you have done, but if not, try a few further experiments to determine it. Try placing the directory server on the same computer as the application servers and on different ones and also investigate having the client process on the same computer as the directory server and on a different one. Here is a clue: do you ever have to provide the address of the directory server?

6.4.3 CHALLENGES OF NAME SERVICE DESIGN AND IMPLEMENTATION

A name service has many of the common nonfunctional design requirements of distributed applications that were identified and discussed in Chapter 5. In particular, the following apply: robustness (because applications rely on the name service for their own operation, any failures will have a ripple effect across other parts of the system; scalability (the name service must be able to scale to meet the needs of the host system and should not become a limiting factor as the system grows; responsiveness, (name resolution is one of the many steps in application execution, and the latency added by the name service should be as low as possible.

In addition to the nonfunctional requirements, there are a number of specific challenges associated with the design, implementation, and use of name services, which affect the correctness of the data held within the service itself, as well as the robustness and scalability of the service. Some of these challenges have been revealed during activity D1.

Server registration: When should application servers register with the name service? Should one-off registration be performed automatically when a service is started? Or should it be performed periodically (to protect against the situation where the name server crashes and restarts, losing details of previous registrations)? If registration is periodic, then how frequently should it occur? (There is a trade-off between the communications cost of doing it too frequently and the latency of the service being updated if the interval between registration events is too long).

Server deregistration: Should application servers deregister as part of their shutdown procedure? If so, what happens if they crash without shutting down correctly? (This will lead to out-of-date information being held by the name service, which will still think the application is present and will continue to advertise it). Could the lack of periodic reregistration activity be used as an automatic indicator that the application is no longer running?

Relocation of application servers: How is the name service updated if an application server is moved? (In many systems, it will be adequate to use an existing deregistration facility prior to the move and then reregister the application after the move.)

The name service's interaction with replicated application servers: If there are many instances of the same application service present, how does the name service determine which instance to direct client requests to? Some possibilities include round-robin, always returning the first instance found in the database, or implementing some form of load-sharing scheme.

Client caching of lookup results: Should application clients cache lookup results, or should they query the name service every time? There is a trade-off between always getting the latest information from the name server (at the cost of higher communication and more work for the name service) and using cached information that could be out of date (in which case, the client may waste time trying to contact an application server at the wrong location). This trade-off needs to be managed based on the extent of dynamism in the system; more static systems are better suited to longer caching periods.

What happens if the directory service crashes: Name services are a vital link in establishing communication within applications and facilitating access to remote resources. The extent to which a system can continue to operate while the name service is down depends on a number of factors that include the frequency with which new connections are made between application components (connections already established are not affected by failure of the name service); whether clients' cache lookup results (in which case they don't always need to contact the name service when establishing connections with application components); and the likelihood that components connect to the same set of other components or different ones each time (thus impacting on the usefulness of the cache contents).

Replication of the name service: Replication can be used to improve the robustness and scalability of a name service. However, if two independent copies of the name service coexist without some form of control or delegation in place, then client requests might be answered by both instances leading to unpredictable behavior, especially if the data held at the two name server instances become inconsistent.

Locating the name service: How do clients find the name service itself? If a name service is needed to find resources and the name service is itself a resource, then a circular problem arises. Organization-specific or application-specific name services could be fixed at a known location or found by broadcast query messages (this approach has been implemented in the directory service used in Activity D1). Such an approach is adequate for small systems but cannot work in large-scale and highly dynamic environments such as the Internet. The name service of the Internet is the DNS, which is described in the next section. DNS is organized hierarchically and solves the "finding the name service" problem by having a local DNS component at the organizational level, which can be found by broadcast communication. This component is part of the wider DNS system and can pass messages up through the DNS hierarchy as necessary.

6.5 DOMAIN NAME SYSTEM (DNS)

The most commonly used name service is the DNS, because it is the name service of the Internet. Every time someone carries out any one of a vast number of common activities such as opening a Web page or sending an e-mail, a URL-based resource name has to be translated into an Internet address, which requires service from DNS. Therefore, there are thousands of DNS service requests being made every second.

DNS is a critical component of the Internet. How critical? If it were shutdown, then only resources for which the IP address were already known would be accessible; this would be disastrous for the information-dependent society we live in (could you imagine not being able to access your social media for a whole hour!). Serious problems would occur for business and commerce, university students and researchers performing information searches, people needing travel updates or weather updates or wanting to access their bank accounts, etc. The Internet, as you perceive it, would shrink to only those resources whose IP address was already cached in your computer.

Yet, despite the large-scale global deployment of DNS and the very high workload it handles, it is extremely robust. If it failed outright, then we would all know about it very quickly. The fact that DNS has been operating for longer than almost any other service you can imagine, without system-wide failures, is testimony to its incredibly good design, which is discussed in detail in this section.

DNS is simultaneously one of the most robust, scalable, and responsive computer applications of all time. The databases maintained within DNS contain massive amounts of dynamic data relating to resources and their addresses. I have studied a great many distributed applications and am still impressed by how well the design of DNS suits its purpose. This is especially significant when you realize that DNS was designed in times when the Internet was much smaller in many ways, for example, in terms of the number of connected computers, the number of users, the physical extent of cables and connections, the amount of traffic flowing, and the transmission speeds of data. DNS was designed in 1983, and despite the exponential growth of the Internet ever since, DNS still performs its original function, so well in fact that most users don't even know it is there.

There are a number of key features that contribute to the success of DNS. These include hierarchical organization of the namespace, distribution of DNS servers that maps onto the logical distribution of the namespace, replication of servers at each logical domain, and different server types, leading to robustness at the domain service level without excessive complexity. Each of these features is investigated in the subsequent sections.

6.5.1 DOMAIN NAMESPACE

The naming structure of a system is called its namespace. What this means is that there are a set of possible names that can occur and each of these is somehow mapped or located in some sort of structure.

A flat (unstructured) namespace is suitable only for the smallest systems, for example, caravans at a holiday park might be arranged in a grid but numbered linearly, say, from 1 to 90. Once an arriving family has found their holiday home the first time, they remember its physical location: there is no real need for a more complex structure or search scheme. Of course, if the caravan site owners wanted to facilitate such a scheme, then a matrix might be suitable in this case, with letters indicating the south-north position and numbers running from east to west. A caravan labeled B3 would be near the southeast corner of the site.

Systems with very many resources require organization into a hierarchical mapping in order that the resources can be logically grouped and thus facilitate finding those resources when needed. The Internet has billions of resources, and therefore, a hierarchical resource naming scheme is essential.

An example is used to illustrate hierarchical mapping. An easy to understand example of a namespace is the telephone numbers scheme used in the United Kingdom in which the very large range of possible numbers follows a rigid tree structure that provides information in addition to the actual value of the phone number itself. Almost all numbers have 11 digits of which the first one is always 0 so there are 10 significant digits. However, these are not organized as a simple flat list; there is a structure in which the number is divided into sections and these sections have different meanings. Numbers contain a code part that signifies either a type of service or an area code and then a unique subscriber part. This has several consequences including that not all of the 10 to the power of 10 possible number sequences are available, as the first part of any number must be one of the allocated codes. Another consequence of the structure is that any number in the scheme can be mapped onto the tree of all usable numbers, starting from the most significant (left-hand) part of the number. So, for example, I know that any number starting with 020 belongs to a phone somewhere in London. If the next digit is 7, then I know it is in inner London, while if the digit were 8, it would be in outer London.

The namespace of the Internet is called the domain namespace. DNS implements a hierarchical domain-based naming scheme, in which the namespace is organized as an inverted tree structure with the root at the top. Starting at the top of the tree and working down the layers step by step, it must be possible to reach every possible allowed domain name by EXACTLY one path.

The tree has a single root to which every domain connects within a few steps. The tree is wide rather than deep, which allows for many branches at each level and avoids the need for many levels. This is very important from the point of view of usability. Humans need to be able to remember domain names, so shorter paths are more helpful. There are also times when domain names have to be typed or read out over the telephone, so again, short names with few levels are far better for usability.

As the root is always present in every path, it can be ignored when describing the path (but it is always there by implication). The next level down the tree is called the top level, containing what are called the top-level domains. This layer is so called top because it is the highest discriminating layer in the path name. Famous top-level domains include com, org, gov, net, and the country-named domains such as uk, de, and fr. Figure 6.15 shows a fraction of the domain namespace hierarchy, in which four of these top-level domains are shown.

Figure 6.15 shows a tiny fraction of the domain namespace, including the root, four top-level domains, and a couple of lower branches. The leftmost of these two branches shows the gre.ac.uk domain that is a subdomain of the ac.uk domain that in turn is a subdomain of the uk domain. Similarly, the right branch shows the bbc.co.uk domain that is a subdomain of the co.uk domain that in turn is also a subdomain of the uk domain.

There have been several implementations of DNS. Berkeley Internet Name Domain (BIND) is the most popular and thus the most important. BIND is the implementation on which the following discussion is based.

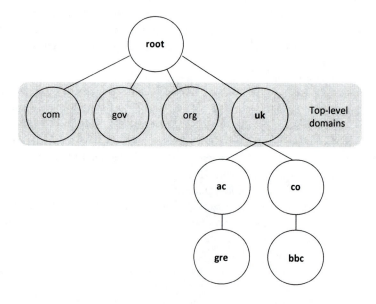

FIGURE 6.15

The inverted tree structure of the domain namespace.

BIND's implementation limits the namespace tree's depth to 127 levels, and each node in the tree has a simple label (name) that can be up to 63 characters in length and must not contain dots. This is a massive namespace and it is difficult to imagine it ever being exhausted. However, as mentioned previously, short names and short paths are more desirable because they are more memorable and usable for humans.

The domain name of a node is the sequence of labels on the path from the node to the root, moving up the tree, with dots separating the names in the path. The root label is often "silent." For example, in Figure 6.15, the node labeled "gre" has a domain name of gre.ac.uk while the node labeled "bbc" has bbc.co.uk as its domain name.

If the root domain does appear, the name is written with a trailing dot, i.e, the root is signified by a null final label. For example, gre.ac.uk. could be used to represent the domain name of the gre node in Figure 6.15. Names that are written with this trailing dot notation are termed absolute, as the name is relative to the root and thus unambiguously specifies the node's position in the tree. Absolute domain names are also known as fully qualified domain names (FQDNs).

6.5.2 DNS IMPLEMENTATION

DNS consists of the hierarchical domain-based naming scheme (discussed above) and a database to hold the naming information. The database is distributed due to a number of factors that include the vast size of the namespace and the massive amount of data that must be held to relate the names of resources to their position in the namespace and also to their IP address.

The distribution is performed in a way that mirrors the structure of the namespace itself, so, for example, (referring to Figure 6.15) there would be a part (segment) of the database held at the root level, which contains the details of the top-level domains (i.e., the next level down the tree). The information held in this root segment of the database includes the address details of the database component in each of the top-level domains, so the queries can be directed to them if necessary. It is important to realize that due to the vastness of the namespace, it is not feasible to hold the entire database at the root (or at any other node) as it would take too long to search and thus impact on responsiveness. Instead, if a query to the root node requires information for the domain gre.ac.uk, as an example, then the query will be passed down to the uk top-level domain (because the database segment at that level will contain data relating to the ac.uk domain and the root node does not). The uk domain database segment would be searched to find the address of the ac.uk domain database segment, and the query is then passed down another level (because the ac.uk domain database segment will hold details of the gre.ac.uk domain, and the uk domain database segment does not). The ac.uk domain database segment is used to lookup the address of the database segment within the gre.ac.uk domain and the query is passed down yet again. As the gre.ac.uk domain is a leaf node in the namespace tree, the database segment within the gre.ac.uk domain should contain details of all the resources within the domain such as specific computers, e-mail inboxes, and Web pages.

The example above illustrates the very important way in which the namespace structure is used to achieve name resolution: the actual domain name itself describes how to find the required data, i.e, by working down the tree in the reverse order of the components in the domain name. So for gre.ac.uk, it is possible to start at the root and then visit the uk domain, the ac.uk domain, and finally the gre.ac.uk domain.

However, DNS would be inefficient if every query had to go to up to the root database. Referring once again to Figure 6.15, consider what would happen if a user in the gre.ac.uk domain requested to open a Web page held in the bbc.co.uk domain (such as bbc.co.uk/weather). The query (for bbc.co.uk) is first passed to the user's local DNS component (which is located at gre.ac.uk in this case). The gre. ac.uk database segment does not contain details of the target domain, so the query is passed up a level, to the ac.uk domain. The ac.uk database segment also does not contain details of the target domain so the query is passed up again, this time to the uk domain. The uk domain database segment does contain details of the co.uk domain, which is the topmost portion of the target path, so the query is this time passed down the tree to the co.uk domain and subsequently to the bbc.co.uk domain. The very important point here is that the query did not travel up to the root level; it was only passed up the tree until a common point in the path was found in which case the target was known to be lower than that point in the tree. This is very significant in terms of understanding the way searches are performed across the distributed database and also in terms of understanding the way in which the tree structure contributes to scalability.

The distribution of the database facilitates scalability of the DNS service (because each segment of the database is restricted in size as it only needs to contain information for the domains connected to it at the next level down the tree and also extensibility of the namespace itself (because the addition of new domains only incurs the registration of the domain at one level above; the new subtree of data relating to the new subtree of namespace will be held in new database segments at the nodes in the new tree itself).

The tree structure by which the distribution is performed facilitates local control of the database segments within specific domains while also allowing the data in each segment to be available across the entire DNS service and allowing for searches to be performed efficiently across multiple database segments.

The localization of control in turn facilitates replication of database segments at the domain level. That is, a particular database segment can be replicated to achieve robustness and enhance performance. The replication factor can differ from one domain to another, to match the name resolution workload of the domain.

DNS has a client-server architecture. A name server is a program that manages a segment of the DNS database. A DNS client (called a Resolver) is an entity requiring the name resolution service of DNS. The name servers make their database segments available to the resolvers through a request-response protocol.

A resolver is usually a library routine used by application developers and is built into end-user applications (such as a Web browser) so that DNS functionality can be accessed automatically when needed from within applications. gethostbyname is a popular DNS resolver for C and C++ (see footnote for Java and C#[1]), provided as a library routine as part of the Berkeley sockets API.

Figure 6.16 illustrates the use of a DNS resolver called gethostbyname, which is a library routine that can be embedded into applications so that they can directly make DNS requests to resolve the names of computers or other resources into IP addresses. Activity D2 (below) provides an opportunity to explore the behavior of this resolver in action.

The scenario illustrated in Figure 6.16 works as follows: (1) A user application executes up until a point where it requires a domain name to be resolved. (2) At this point, the gethostbyname routine is called, passing in the required domain name as a parameter. (3) A DNS request is sent to a DNS name server. (4) A DNS response, containing the IP address corresponding to the supplied domain name, is returned.

---

[1]The DNS_Resolver example application used in this activity is written in C++ and uses the gethostbyname method. For C#, there is the equivalent Dns.GetHostByName method or Dns.GetHostEntry method, both of which are part of the.net framework. For Java, see the various methods of the java.net.InetAddress class, including getAllByName and getLocalHost.

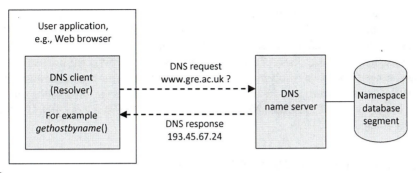

FIGURE 6.16

A resolver (the DNS client side) can be embedded into a user application.

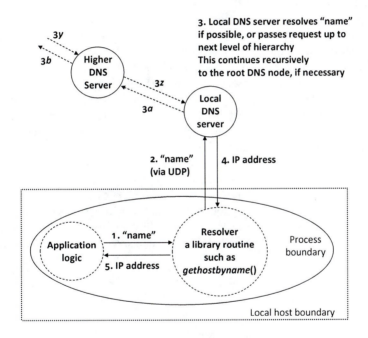

FIGURE 6.17

Hierarchical name resolution in DNS.

The behavior is more complex if the local name server cannot resolve the name requested, as depicted in Figure 6.17.

Figure 6.17 illustrates the behavior that occurs when the local DNS server is not able to resolve a DNS request. In step 1, the application logic makes a local function call to the gethostbyname resolver. In step 2, a DNS request is issued to the local DNS server instance. If this server could resolve the requested name, it would send back a DNS response directly to the resolver. However, in this case, it is unable to resolve the request so has to pass it up to a DNS server at the next highest level in the tree (this is shown as step 3a in the figure). This passing up procedure is repeated as many times as necessary (see step 3b) until a point is reached where the DNS server can resolve the name. The resolved address is passed back down the levels until it reaches the original DNS server (steps 3y and 3z). The local DNS server then sends a DNS response back to the resolver (step 4). The internal behavior of the DNS system is transparent to the resolver, such that it does not know that the request was passed up to additional DNS servers; the response from the local DNS server to the resolver is the same whether it was resolved locally or not. Finally, the gethostbyname function returns the required IP address details to the application logic (step 5).

6.5.3 DNS NAME SERVERS: AUTHORITY AND DELEGATION

Zones: A zone is part of the domain namespace and is associated with a particular named domain. A DNS name server generally has complete information about a particular zone; in which case, the name server is said to be authoritative for that zone. Being authoritative means that it holds the original data for the resources in the zone (i.e., that the information has been configured by the domain administrator or through dynamic DNS methods that support automatic update of records, as opposed to being data that have been supplied through queries to another name server).

Delegation: A zone is a subset of a domain. The difference between a zone and a domain is that a zone contains only the authoritative subset of domain names and not the domain names that are delegated elsewhere (i.e., another name server has authority over that portion of the domain).

Delegation involves assigning responsibility for part of a domain to another organization or assigning authority for subdomains to different name servers. Figures 6.18 and 6.19 illustrate the difference between zones and domains where delegation is present.

Figures 6.18 and 6.19 show the way in which the zone boundary reflects the limit of authority of the respective name servers. In Figure 6.18, the com name server has delegated responsibility of the subdomains to the organizations that own those domains. This is the most common approach as it prevents the size of the higher-level zone becoming too large, which would increase the workload of its name servers and potentially impact on performance and scalability. In Figure 6.19, the org zone extends to include the def.org subdomain; this means that the org name server remains authoritative for the def.org domain.

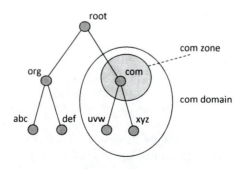

FIGURE 6.18

Delegation example 1: the responsibility for the uvw.com and xyz.com subdomains of the com domain has been delegated to their owner organizations.

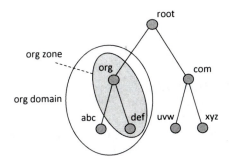

FIGURE 6.19

Delegation example 2: the responsibility for the abc.org subdomain of the org domain has been delegated to the abc owner organization. However, the org domain remains responsible for the def.org domain.

6.5.4 REPLICATION

DNS name servers (and therefore the domain name data they hold) are replicated for three main reasons:

- Robustness. As mentioned earlier, almost all Internet activity is in some way dependent on DNS to resolve resource names into IP addresses. The distribution of the DNS namespace across multiple domains, each with their own name server, protects against any single failure of a name server affecting the entire system. However, failure of any name server would render the part of the namespace that it was authoritative for unobtainable. Replication is therefore performed at the domain level to provide resilience against failure of any single DNS server.
- Performance. A name server must deal with all requests that require an authoritative answer for its zone. This can become a performance bottleneck, especially in large or very popular zones. Replication shares the lookup burden over two or more name server instances.
- Proximity. The closer a name server to the requestor, the shorter the round-trip network journey and thus the shorter the resolve time. Domains are logical concepts (more obviously near the root of the tree, consider.com that has no geographic basis), and there is no requirement that the replicas of a particular domain's name server are geographically close to each other. .com name servers could be located in the United States and Europe, reducing average round-trip times for service. Leaf domains are more likely to be linked to specific organizations with a physical footprint and thus a link to a specific geographic location. Even so, for international organizations, it may still be beneficial to host multiple replicas of the domain's name servers at different offices around the world.

There two types of name server: primary master servers and secondary servers (also called slave servers). Once running, the secondary server is a replica of the master server, enhancing robustness (through redundancy) and enhancing performance (by sharing the zone's name resolution workload with the master server).

A primary master name server gets its data (for the zones that it's authoritative for) from the host it runs on, i.e., a locally stored file (this is the master copy of the data for the zone). A secondary name server gets its zone data from another server that is authoritative for the zone (such as the primary master or another secondary server). When a secondary server initializes, it contacts an authoritative name server and pulls the zone data over; this is known as a zone transfer. The zone transfer concept can greatly reduce administrative load; the secondary name server may not need any direct administration as it (indirectly) shares the master copy of the zone data.

6.5.5 NAME RESOLUTION IN MORE DETAIL

There are two forms of name resolution query:

- Iterative queries require the name server to give the best answer it already knows. There is no additional querying of other name servers. The best answer might not be the actual address required, but instead, the name server may refer the requester to a closer (in the logical tree) name server that it knows of. Referring back to Figure 6.15 for an example, if the uk zone name server were asked to resolve the name gre.ac.uk, it would refer the requester to the ac.uk zone name server, as this is closer to the target domain and the uk server does not know how to resolve the whole name.
- A recursive query is one where the recipient name server asks other name servers for help in resolving a request (these requests must be iterative queries). The name server originally receiving the recursive query must return the final answer, i.e., the resolved IP address; this is to prevent excessive complexity and latency if recursive queries could be answered with referrals. Any referrals received must be followed, resulting in further iterative queries being sent to other name servers. Recursive queries place most of the burden of resolution on a single name server, as illustrated in Figure 6.20.

Figure 6.20 depicts the usage of the two types of query, in an example to resolve the address of the domain finance.yahoo.com, in 8 steps:

Step 1.A resolver embedded inside an application issues a recursive query to its local name server. This implies that the local name server must return the required address and cannot send back a referral.

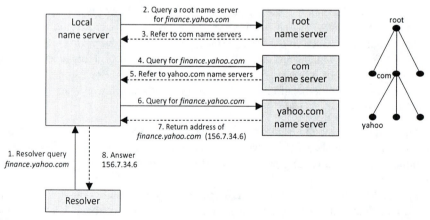

FIGURE 6.20

Resolving a domain name request using a mix of recursive and iterative queries.

Step 2.The local name server does not know any part of the domain name in the request so it issues an iterative query to a root name server.

Step 3.The root name server does not know finance.yahoo.com but it does know com, which is logically closer in the domain name tree than the root, so it refers the requesting local name server to a com name server.

Step 4.The local name server issues an iterative query to a com name server.

Step 5.The com name server does not know finance.yahoo.com but it does know yahoo.com, which is logically closer in the domain name tree than the com, so it refers the requesting local name server to a yahoo.com name server.

Step 6.The local name server issues an iterative query to a yahoo.com name server.

Step 7.The yahoo.com name server knows finance.yahoo.com, because it is within the zone for which the name server is authoritative, so it returns the corresponding IP address to the local name server.

Step 8.The local name server returns the IP address to the resolver (this is the result of the original recursive query).

6.5.6 CACHING IN DNS

Caching can be implemented at either the client or server side of DNS (or both) to improve performance:

- DNS caching name servers store the results of DNS queries so that if requested again, the answer can be provided immediately from the cache storage, cutting down on the amount of communication occurring between servers and reducing the latency of the request. Caching servers store results for a limited period of time, which is indicated in the domain name record. This means that the cache-holding time is based on the resource itself and thus can be made shorter for more dynamic resources that may be relocated.
- DNS clients can also keep a cache of name-to-address mappings, avoiding the need for repeat queries to name servers for the same resource in a short period of time. This can significantly reduce the load on the local DNS server and enhance responsiveness, since cache access time is much shorter than the time it takes to get a name resolved by contacting a name server.

6.5.7 EXPLORING ADDRESS RESOLUTION

Activity D2 investigates the use of local name resolvers. Specifically, the use of the gethostbyname library method is explored, using the DNS_Resolver example application. The activity is concerned with the way in which the gethostbyname resolver is used to find the IP address of the application's host computer.

Several of the sample applications that accompany the book (in C++, Java, and C#) provide further examples of the use of DNS resolvers such as gethostbyname. Server components make use of a local resolver to find the IP address of their host computer; this address is used to bind a local port so that clients can subsequently make connection requests. In some client components, the local host address is found using a resolver and is used as a default address with which to attempt to connect to the server, as many of the applications can be run for experimental purposes with both client and server on the same computer.

ACTIVITY D2 EXPLORING THE GETHOSTBYNAME DNS RESOLVER

The gethostbyname library method enables a software engineer to make DNS lookup requests from within applications. In this activity, we shall first run an application to see the use of gethostbyname in action. We then inspect the relevant section of the application's source code to marry up the behavior with the program logic.

This activity is based on the DNS_Resolver application that has been designed specifically to explore the way in which the gethostbyname DNS resolver can be embedded into user applications.

The DNS_Resolver application demonstrates two main uses of gethostbyname: firstly, to enable an application to find its own IP address (the IP address of its host computer) and, secondly, to enable an application to find the IP address of a computer or domain, based on its textual name.

Learning Outcomes

1. To gain an appreciation of the need to embed name resolvers into application programs
2. To gain an introductory understanding of function of the gethostbyname name resolver
3. To gain an appreciation of the way in which gethostbyname is used to find out the local computer's IP address details
4. To gain an appreciation of the way in which gethostbyname can be used to find out the IP address details of a named computer or the IP address associated with a domain name

Method Part A: Appreciating the Need to Embed Name Resolvers into Application Programs

Run the DNS_Resolver application on several different computers. Note that in each case, the application detects and displays the list of IP addresses of the host computer.

Use the built-in name-to-IP address resolver to resolve the names of other computers in your local network or try external domain names.

Expected Outcome for Part A

You should see the correct IP address(es) displayed. Your home computer will typically only have one IP address. However, many computers have several IP addresses depending on their configuration and use. A computer may, for example, be configured to work with two different networks, one wired and one wireless, in which case it will have two IP addresses.

The screenshot below shows the program running on a computer with the computer name RICH_MAIN and IP address 192.168.100.2. You can also see that the IP address resolver has been used to find the IP address associated with the domain name bbc.co.uk.

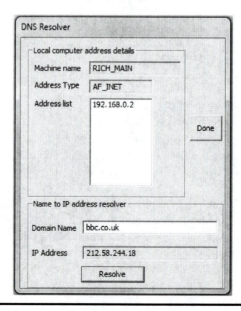

ACTIVITY D2 EXPLORING THE GETHOSTBYNAME DNS RESOLVER—Cont'd

Method Part B: Using gethostbyname to Find the IP Address of the Local Host (Computer)

Look at the source file named DNS_ResolverDlg.cpp. Study the code and locate the part where the local hosts' IP address is obtained.

Expected Outcome for Part B

The relevant code is contained within the method GetLocalHostAddress_List(). Here is the code:

```
char szStr[80];
DWORD lLen = sizeof(szStr);
GetComputerNameA(szStr,&lLen);
hostent* pHost;
pHost = gethostbyname(szStr);

m_pHostName->SetWindowText(pHost->h_name);// Display host name

CString csStr = "Other";                   // Display address type as string
switch(pHost->h_addrtype)
{
   case AF_UNSPEC:
   csStr = "AF_UNSPEC";
   break;
   case AF_UNIX:
   csStr = "AF_UNIX";
   break;
   case AF_INET:
   csStr = "AF_INET";
   break;
}
m_pAddressType->SetWindowText(csStr);

int iAddressCount = 0;
IN_ADDR addr;
char **ppChar = pHost->h_addr_list;    // Initialise outer pointer (point to 1st byte of 1st address in list)
char * pChar;                          // Inner pointer (addresses do not follow on in sequential memory after each other)
                                       // Each address is in a separate memory area, so cannot simply increment the inner
                                       // pointer to next address, after end of current address. Instead, increment outer
                                       // pointer, then re-initialise inner pointer to 1st byte of new address

while(ppChar != NULL && *ppChar != NULL && iAddressCount < MAX_NUM_IP_ADDRESSES)
{
   pChar = *ppChar;                        // (re) Initialise inner pointer to start of current address
   addr.S_un.S_un_b.s_b1 = (unsigned char) *pChar++;
   addr.S_un.S_un_b.s_b2 = (unsigned char) *pChar++;
   addr.S_un.S_un_b.s_b3 = (unsigned char) *pChar++;
   addr.S_un.S_un_b.s_b4 = (unsigned char) *pChar;
   ppChar++;                               // Advance outer pointer, point to next IP address (or NULL if no more addresses)

   // Display the local address value
   csStr.Format("%d.%d.%d.%d", addr.S_un.S_un_b.s_b1, addr.S_un.S_un_b.s_b2,
                               addr.S_un.S_un_b.s_b3, addr.S_un.S_un_b.s_b4);

   WriteStatusLine(csStr);
}
```

This code works as follows:

First, the computer's textual name is found. A character array is declared as a buffer, of size 80 bytes, to hold the computer's host name. The variable lLen is initialized with the size of the buffer. The GetComputerNameA() method is called, which places the computer's textual name in the character array (the lLen parameter prevents overrun of the buffer if a very long computer name has been used).

Second, the computer's IP address is found by passing the computer's name as a parameter to the gethostbyname method. The result of the gethostbyname() call is a special hostent structure that contains the computer's name, address-type code, and a list of IP addresses (if there are more than one).

Next, the computer's host name and address type are displayed.

Finally, the while loop iterates over the address list (which is part of the hostent structure) and each of the local computer's IP addresses is displayed.

Method Part C: Using gethostbyname to Find the IP Address of a Computer or Domain

Look again at the source file named DNS_ResolverDlg.cpp. Find the section of code where a computer's IP address is obtained based on its textual name.

ACTIVITY D2 EXPLORING THE GETHOSTBYNAME DNS RESOLVER—Cont'd

Expected Outcome for Part C

This functionality is achieved by the event-handler method OnBnClickedResolveButton(). The key part of the code is shown below:

```
CString csStr;
m_pLookupHostName->GetWindowText(csStr);  // Get the textual name provided by the user
hostent* pHost;
pHost = gethostbyname(csStr.GetString()); // Use gethostbyname to populate the hostent structure
```

The main difference here is that the name of the computer is provided by the user and not implicitly as in part B of the activity. The computer name is retrieved from the user-interface control and then passed as a parameter to gethostbyname(). The rest of the code works in a similar way to that of part B except that in this case, only the first IP address in the list of addresses is displayed and also that error handling is needed because the user may enter nonexistent computer names or the names of other resources to which IP addresses are not mapped.

Reflection

The DNS resolver gethostbyname enables you to leverage the power of the DNS service within your application. This is a very important concept for distributed applications. If you look at the sample applications provided as support resources for the book, you will find that many of them use gethostbyname.

6.5.8 REVERSE DNS LOOKUP

There are occasions when it is necessary to map a known IP address to an unknown domain name. For example, with eCommerce and online services, it is often desirable to validate that the source of a message is actually where it claims to come from. The ability to trace a source IP address back to a domain name can also be very useful for systems administration and maintenance purposes and is an important part of a computer-forensics tool kit.

Reverse DNS lookup is supported through the provision of two special domains named in-addr.arpa for IPv4 addresses and ip6.arpa for IPv6 addresses. All possible values of Internet address are mapped appropriately in one of these domains.

For explanation purposes, IPv4 will be considered. At the level below in-addr.arpa (level three), there are 256 domains labeled 0 to 255 (i.e., 0.in-addr.arpa to 255.in-addr.arpa). At level four, there are 256 domains for each level three domain (0.0.in-addr.arpa to 255.0.in-addr.arpa up to 255.555.in-addr.arpa). At level five, there are 256 domains for each level four domain. At level six, there are 256 domains for each level five domain. This allows every combination of IPv4 address in the range 0.0.0.0 to 255.255.255.255 to be represented in a corresponding entry in the range 0.0.0.0.in-addr.arpa to 255.255.255.255.in-addr.arpa.

Therefore, each possible Internet address maps directly onto a level six domain in the in-addr.arpa domain space. The Internet address is written backward so that the most significant byte of the address is closest to the root of the tree. For example, IP address 212.58.244.20 is represented in the in-addr.arpa domain space as 20.244.58.212.in-addr.arpa. When a query for a domain in the in-addr.arpa domain space is received by a name server, data describing the domain to which the supplied IP address relates are returned.

Here is a simple reverse DNS lookup experiment to try: Step 1, use the DNS_Resolver application (see activity D2) to resolve a domain name that you are familiar with (e.g., the domain name bbc.co.uk was resolved to IPv4 address 212.58.244.20). Step 2, identify one of the freely available online reverse DNS lookup tools and request a reverse lookup for the domain name constructed in the form reversed-IPv4-address.in-addr.arpa (for the bbc.co.uk example, this is 20.244.58.212.in-addr.arpa). The result should be the original domain name you started with (for the bbc.co.uk example, the query returned fmt-vip71.telhc.bbc.co.uk, which is indeed within the bbc.co.uk domain).

6.6 TIME SERVICES

A general requirement for many distributed applications is that processes each have access to an accurate local clock or can otherwise get an accurate time value when necessary (e.g., through a time service). The following section describes time services such as NTP; these provide a time value that can be used however needed by applications (this could include setting the physical clock at the local computer). Subsequent sections deal with physical and logical clock synchronization, respectively, and also discuss the various ways in which time values are used in distributed applications.

6.6.1 TIME SERVICES

The Internet Time Service (ITS) is a collection of time service protocols provided by the National Institute of Standards and Technology (NIST). The NIST services are hosted on a moderate number of computers around the world, primarily in the United States, owned by commercial organizations and universities. The replication of the service over numerous geographically distributed sites ensures that the service is robust, and because the time service load is shared across the servers, it is responsive.

NIST currently supports the DAYTIME protocol, the TIME protocol, the Network Time Protocol (NTP), and the Simple Network Time Protocol (SNTP), a simplified version of NTP. Of these, the popularity of the first two is in decline as they are less accurate and less efficient with respect to communication resources than NTP. At the time of writing, NIST is encouraging users of those protocols to migrate to NTP.

Externally, the NIST servers offer the time services mentioned above. Lists of NIST time servers are available on the Internet, and users either can request time services directly from a geographically local server or can use the global address time.nist.gov, which is resolved to different physical time server addresses in sequence to share out the load on the time servers. Using this address also has the advantage of reliability as it will always be resolved to a currently working server, whereas contacting a specific server by its address runs the risk that the server is unavailable.

6.6.1.1 TIME Protocol

The TIME protocol is currently supported by NIST time servers but has several weaknesses when compared with NTP and thus is included here briefly for comparison purposes only.

This protocol provides a 32-bit value that represents the time in seconds since January 1, 1900. Due to the 32-bit resolution, the format can represent dates in an approximately 136-year range; i.e., it will be redundant by design in 2037. The simple data format does not allow the transmission of additional information such as daylight saving time or information about the health status of the server.

6.6.1.2 DAYTIME Protocol

This protocol provides significantly more information than the TIME protocol. Designed in 1983, it is inferior to NTP. Brief details are included here for comparison purposes.

The time is sent using standard ASCII characters with a simple code format. In addition to the actual time and date information, it also includes a code to signal daylight saving time and an advance warning code that a leap second is to be added at the end of the current month. There is also a code to signal the health of the server, which is important for time-critical applications to be able to have confidence in the accuracy of the time service values.

The DAYTIME protocol adds a fixed offset (currently 50 milliseconds) to the advertised time value to partially compensate for network transmission delay.

6.6.1.3 Network Time Protocol (NTP)

In use since 1985, the NTP is the most popular Internet time protocol. It is based on UDP, therefore having low networking overheads and low service response latency because it does not need to establish a TCP connection.

An NTP client periodically requests updates from at least one server. When multiple servers are used, the client averages the received time values, ignoring any outlier values (in a similar way to that used by the master server in the Berkeley algorithm; see later text).

NTP provides greater precision than the TIME and DAYTIME protocols. It uses a 64-bit time stamp value representing the time in seconds since January 1, 1900, and has a resolution of 200 picoseconds (although this level of precision cannot generally be leveraged due to dynamic network delays that can fluctuate by values significantly larger than this).

The use of NTP within distributed applications has been discussed in Chapter 3, where it is also used as an example of a request-reply protocol and explored in a practical activity using an NTP client application that has been built into the Distributed Systems Workbench.

An alternative to the continual operation of NTP is the similar but more lightweight SNTP that supports single time requests when needed (as opposed to the periodic nature of NTP usage).

Figure 6.21 illustrates infrastructural features of the NIST time service provision, showing the differentiation between the internal and external aspects of the service. The internal service configuration synchronizes the NIST internal time value to UTC/GMT and also synchronizes the NIST time servers to each other. Externally, NIST provides a number of time services that each serves the same time value but in different formats and with different levels of precision. Of these services, NTP and SNTP are the most important due to communication efficiency and precision of time values.

All of the NIST time services provide transparency to clients in the sense that clients do not need to be aware of the internal configuration and behavior of the NIST system, of the multiplicity of time services, or of the replication of NIST time servers.

6.6.2 PHYSICAL CLOCK SYNCHRONIZATION

Each computer has an electronic clock that keeps track of wall-clock time (time in the real world, as shown by a clock). These electronic clocks (called physical clocks) tend to be accurate to within a few seconds each day, but can drift over longer periods, such that the clocks on different computers in the same system show significantly different times. Physical clock drift can be problematic for any applications whose behaviors are time-dependent or need to record the time at which events occur.

Factors that affect the rate of clock drift include the quality of the electronics that constitutes the clock circuit and the ambient temperature of the clock's environment (which can fluctuate significantly

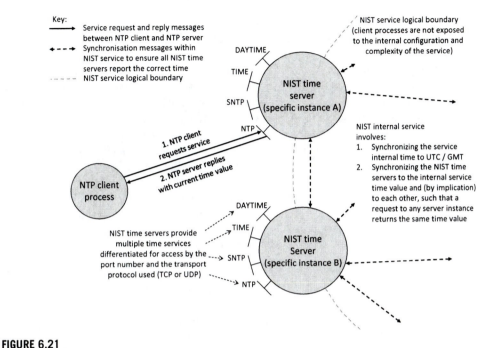

FIGURE 6.21

Infrastructural aspects of the NIST time service provision.

if the clock is contained within the casing of a computer with a heat-generating CPU and cooling fans running). Therefore, even with the best-quality clock circuitry, it is not possible to precisely predict drift and thus compensate for it by software techniques.

A wide variety of types of distributed applications require that the clocks at each processing node within a distributed system must be synchronized to ensure consistency and accuracy. Clocks are used for various purposes:

- To define an ordering of events (e.g., when constructing models of real-world systems based on sensed data collected from many sites, such as weather prediction).
- To coordinate events to occur at the same wall-clock time (e.g., to start processes simultaneously or with a specific time offset, in a controlled physical environment such as an automated production facility).
- To record the passing of wall-clock time (e.g., measuring the interval between events in systems, such as network message arrival, and another example is transport display systems where the expected time of arrival (of busses, trains, or aircraft) has to be computed and displayed alongside current time or displayed as an offset from current time).
- As a measure of performance (this is achieved by comparing the beginning and end times of a particular activity; this could be a system activity such as measuring how long the system takes to perform a particular task or a real-world activity such as measuring the acceleration of a vehicle based on multiple samples from speed sensors or a reaction timer as part of a game).

- Time values as a signature, or identity (e.g., for indicating the creation and modification times of resources such as files and a second example is the within-security schemes, where message time stamps are used to prevent message replay).
- To permit reasoning about the global state of the system based only on local information (e.g., within heartbeat-based systems to determine if another process is present, such as within election algorithms (see earlier section) in which heartbeats are awaited only for a limited time window).
- To provide globally unique values (a precise time stamp is a component in a globally unique identifier (GUID). The GUID also contains a location-based component (IP or MAC address) and a large random component. This combination of values yields a number that cannot occur again. This is because if generated on the same computer, the new GUID will have a different time component (or even if performed in rapid succession such that the time stamp does not change, the random component will) and if generated on two computers at the same time, it will have different location components). GUIDs are thus vital in systems such as distributed databases and distributed object-based applications where resource identifiers must be guaranteed unique system-wide yet need to be locally generated without having a central ID issuing service).

In some distributed applications, the wall-clock time accuracy is of prime importance, while in others, the actual precision by which the clocks are synchronized is more important than the wall-clock time accuracy.

The crux of the challenge for synchronizing physical clocks in loosely coupled distributed systems (i.e., those that consist of independent computers that communicate over computer networks) is that any message sent across the network encounters delay, and the delay has some fixed and some variable components. An example of a fixed delay component is the propagation delay that is directly related to the distance the signal has to travel through cables, and an example of variable delay is the queuing time that a message spends in routers, which is traffic-dependent. The variable components of the message delay mean that it is not possible to precisely know the arrival time of any message sent between two computers even if its transmission time is known precisely.

The fact that message delays cannot be precisely known means that it is not possible to transmit a time value between two computers while preserving its wall-clock meaning, so as to accurately set the clock at the recipient computer. For example, consider that at exactly 12 noon, a time stamp is sent from computer A (whose clock accurately reflects wall-clock time) to computer B, across a computer network. When the time stamp arrives, its value will still be 12 noon but its meaning is now no longer accurate because the actual time is a little bit past 12 noon; but the recipient does not know how much time has elapsed while the message was in transit, so they cannot make the adjustment required. If the time stamp is used literally, then some error creeps in. For systems connected over physically short distances with few intermediate routers, this error value may be on average much less than one second and the resulting small time difference between clocks may be acceptable for some systems.

There are various ways to improve on this basic starting position of simply sending the wall-clock time and using the resulting value literally. However, since network delay is nonconstant, whatever technique is performed, the outcome is described as a loose synchrony.

6.6.2.1 Physical Clock Synchronization Techniques

A time service must synchronize the clock of the local computer with that of other computers in a network. One approach is to designate some time servers as "reference" servers that provide an accurate, stable time source to clients on the network. In order to do this, the reference servers must synchronize their own host's physical clocks to agree with some real-world clock aligned with UTC/GMT (see the discussion on NIST time services above). Clients and nonreference time servers adjust their clocks to agree with the time reported by a reference server.

The problems involved in this synchronization process are that clocks can drift, which can lead to differences between local clock times, network delays are unpredictable (these points are explained above), and also processing delays (due to the presence of other processes) at both the sending and receiving computers of a network message further introduce a variable delay in reading a clock value or writing a clock value, respectively.

6.6.2.2 Cristian's Algorithm

This technique uses a time server that is synchronized to Coordinated Universal Time (UTC). The clocks of other computers in the local network are set by querying the server. The distinguishing feature of Cristian's technique is the way it takes account of network latency. The round-trip delay (d) is measured. The assumed one-way latency ($d/2$) is added to the time value when sent to a requesting computer, to improve the accuracy of the value upon arrival ($d/2$ time later) (see Figure 6.22).

Figure 6.22 shows the principle of estimating network delay used in Cristian's algorithm. The concept is simple: measure the round-trip time for a message to be sent to another computer and a reply to be sent back; this takes into account the delay in each direction in the network and also the processing delay at the two computers themselves when dealing with sending and receiving the messages. This approach uses the same clock to measure the start time and end time of the round trip; this is the clock of host X in the figure, hence avoiding any inaccuracies arising from the fact that the clocks are not yet synchronized. Therefore, the assumption is that if the total delay is halved, then this is representative of the delay in one direction. This halved value can thus be added as an offset when sending the time stamp so that when it arrives, having suffered the equivalent delay, it is realigned with wall-clock time, and thus, the recipient can set its clock accurately. However, while being generally sound and an improvement over not adjusting for network delay, there are still three sources of error with this technique that can affect the accuracy of the $d/2$ delay assumption: (1) Network delays are time-varying; (2) network delays can be different in each direction, even on the same link; and (3) the processing delay on each computer is also time-varying.

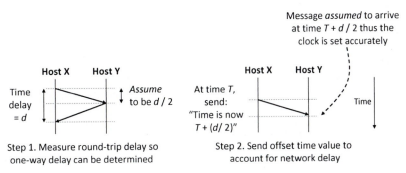

FIGURE 6.22

Cristian's algorithm for physical clock synchronization.

6.6.2.3 The Berkeley Algorithm

The Berkeley algorithm aims to synchronize all clocks in a group of time servers. The first step is to elect a master, which coordinates the synchronization activity (see the earlier section "Election algorithms"). The master polls the other time servers, who respond by sending their current time values back to the master. During this step, the master also determines the round-trip time between itself and each of the respondents, in the same way that Cristian's algorithm does it.

Based on all of the received values and its own clock value, the master computes the average time (significant outlier values are ignored to prevent distortion of the result). There is an assumption that errors cancel out to a certain extent; however, if all clocks are fast or all are slow, the resulting average will also be fast or slow, respectively.

The master calculates the amount by which each individual time server process must adjust its clock. This takes into account the current time difference (between the specific server's current clock and the computed average time value) and also adds an adjustment equivalent to half of the round-trip delay measured for the specific time server. The resulting clock offset values are then sent to each time server process, and the master updates its own clock locally. Upon arrival of these offsets, the recipient computer knows how much to adjust its clock to bring it to the same value as the group average (because the network delay has already been compensated for). The Berkeley algorithm is illustrated in Figure 6.23.

Figure 6.23 shows the operation of the Berkeley algorithm, contextualized with an example. The scenario assumes that the master has already been elected (this is realistic as the election of a master should be a rare event occurring only when a previous master has crashed). The Berkeley algorithm operates periodically. The figure shows one of these periodic clock update episodes.

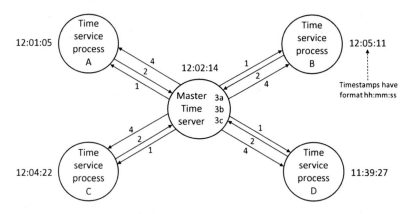

Message and activity sequence:
1   The elected master time server polls other time servers for their current time value
2   Time servers reply with their current time value
3a Compute the average time (ignore outliers e.g., 11:39:27). Average is 12:03:13
3b Compute round trip communication delay individually for each time server
3c Compute offset value for each clock including its own
    For other time servers:- include the network delay component
4   Send individual update offset to each time server

FIGURE 6.23

The Berkeley clock synchronization algorithm.

In step 1, the master polls all time servers in the group for their current time values; they respond in step 2. The master then computes the average time of all clocks including its own but excluding any that is significantly different from the average value, to avoid distortion by unreliable clocks (step 3a). In step 3b, the master estimates the network delay to each specific time server (using the half round-trip delay technique as used in Cristian's method). The master then combines the results of step 3a and 3b to provide a unique clock offset value for each time server (step 3c) and sends these values to the time servers in step 4.

There are two update scenarios that occur at time servers when applying the received offset value:

- When the clock adjustment is forward (e.g., time server A in Figure 6.23 moving its clock value from 12:01:05 to 12:03:13), the adjustment can be applied immediately. This is because the clock has never showed the time values that are being skipped, and thus, no events could have occurred and been time-stamped with those values. Therefore, moving the time forward cannot confuse the representation of the ordering of events that have already happened.
- When the required clock adjustment is backward (e.g., time server B in Figure 6.23 moving its clock value from 12:05:11 to 12:03:13), the situation is more complex. Actually, moving clocks backward is undesirable in systems where events are time-stamped and where the history of event ordering is important. The problem is that the clock has already held time values in the range of times that will be repeated, and by setting the clock back could lead to inconsistency in the event order history.

For example, consider a scenario in which an event E1 has already occurred at time 12:04:17 on a computer that gets its time updates directly from time server B (in Figure 6.23). When the time gets to 12:05:11 (as perceived by that specific time server), the server receives a time update from the master, requiring it to set its clock back to a time earlier than the stored time stamp of E1. Shortly afterward, some of the computers that get their time updates from server B have updated their local clocks. An event E2 then occurs at one of those computers, at the time 12:03:55. Now, the system is inconsistent because event E1 actually happened before event E2, but their time stamps indicate that E2 happened first. An example of how this inconsistency could materialize into a real problem is a distributed file system in which there are multiple versions of the same file. Let events E1 and E2 represent the last modification events of two versions of the same file, and thus, the most recent time stamp implies the latest version of the file. A particular application may inspect the time stamps and wrongly assume that the file version with the E1 time stamp is the most up-to-date copy of the file.

Rather than adjusting the clock backward, there are two better alternatives: (1) Halt the clock from updating, for a period equivalent to the offset sent from the master, so that wall-clock time catches up with the time shown by the clock, and (2) slow down the physical clock's tick rate (which is described as clock slew), so that the correction is applied over a longer period of time rather than instantly. Both of these solutions avoid the inconsistency that can arise when previously shown clock values reoccur.

6.6.3 LOGICAL CLOCKS AND SYNCHRONIZATION

Event ordering can be achieved without the use of real-time clocks. If real-world time values are not required, then a simple mechanism can be devised for event ordering. The only requirement in such a case is the need to know the sequence with which the events occur.

A logical clock is a monotonically increasing integer value. In other words, it is a number that increases by one increment each time an event occurs. Logical clocks do not capture the passing of wall-clock time; instead, they are used to indicate the relative time at which events occur. The "time" values are a simple sequence of numbers.

Consider a set of three events that occur at different times, as shown in Table 6.2.

By looking at the wall-clock times of the events shown in Table 6.2, we can see that the events occur in the sequence A first, then B, and finally C. We can convert this to a logical clock numbering, as shown in Table 6.3.

As illustrated in Table 6.3, the logical clock increases monotonically each time a new event occurs. Notice that the logical clock representation is purely concerned with sequence; it shows that event A happened before event B and that event B happened before event C. In Table 6.2, where a wall-clock sequencing is used, it is possible to see the relative timing of the actual events (event B follows soon after event A, and then, there is a relatively long interval before event C). The time element is discarded when using a logical clock representation.

6.6.3.1 Event Ordering Using Logical Clocks

When two events a and b occur in the same process and a occurs before b, then event a is said to have happened before event b.

Message sending is split into two events: when a message is sent from one process to another, the "message sent" event happened before the "message received" event. This is a fundamental requirement to represent the fact that all messages have some transmission delay, and this is a very important concept when considering the correctness of distributed algorithms. In a distributed system, it is possible for two processes to each send a message to the other process and for both send events to have occurred before either of the receive events. This is just one of the possible orderings that could occur; another could be that one process sends a message to the other process that receives that message before sending a reply message back.

When two events are related together in some application-meaningful way (e.g., in a banking application, they could both be transactions on the same bank account), then they are said to be causally related. However, using the same banking example, events that update different bank accounts are not causally related; their relative ordering has no consequence to the banking application itself.

Table 6.2 Wall-clock Event Times

Event	Wall-clock time
A	02:05:17
B	02:05:19
C	07:49:01

Table 6.3 Logical Clock Event Values

Event	Logical clock value
A	1
B	2
C	3

For a pair of causally related events a and b, if event a happened before event b, then we express this using the "happened before" relation written as $a \rightarrow b$. This is also described as causal ordering. New causal orderings can be built up from existing causal ordering knowledge. For example, a simple but very important rule is:

$$\text{if } a \rightarrow b \text{ and } b \rightarrow c \text{ then } a \rightarrow c$$

This states that if event a occurs before b and b occurs before c, then a occurs before c.

Groups of causally related events can overlap other groups of causally related events, but each group of events is not causally related to the events in the other groups. In such cases, the global ordering of the entire system must respect the causal ordering sequences that exist. To clarify, consider, for example, sequences of ATM cash withdrawals for two unrelated customers a and b. Each customer makes two cash withdrawals on the same day. The events generated are labeled $a1$ and $a2$ (for customer a) and $b1$ and $b2$ (for customer b).

If $a1 \rightarrow a2$ and $b1 \rightarrow b2$, then $a1$ and $a2$ are causally ordered, and $b1$ and $b2$ are causally ordered, but $a1$ and $b1$, for example, are not. In such a scenario, the following actual event orderings are possible because they respect the causal orderings:

$$\{a1 \; a2 \; b1 \; b2\}, \{a1 \; b1 \; b2 \; a2\}, \{a1 \; b1 \; b2 \; a2\}, \{b1 \; a1 \; a2 \; b2\}, \{b1 \; a1 \; b2 \; a2\}, \{b1 \; b2 \; a1 \; a2\}$$

However, $\{a1 \; b2 \; a2 \; b1\}$ is not possible because it violates the $b1 \rightarrow b2$ relationship. Similarly, $\{b1 \; a2 \; a1 \; b2\}$ is not possible because it violates the $a1 \rightarrow a2$ relationship.

6.6.3.2 *Logical Clock Implementation*

Ordering of events at a process can be achieved by defining a *logical clock* mechanism. Each process maintains a local variable LC called its *logical clock* that relates each event occurrence to a unique integer value. Before the initial event, all processes must set their logical clocks to zero. For consistency across the system, logical clocks must always increase in value as events occur.

An event occurrence causes the logical clock to be updated. Newly created events (e.g., sending a message) are assigned the resulting updated value of the logical clock (this value can be considered the time stamp of the message). For example, if the logical clock has an initial value 4, when a message is sent, the clock will increment to 5 and the message will be sent with a time stamp of 5.

When a message is received, the receiving process updates its logical clock to be greater than the maximum of its current logical clock value and the time stamp of the incoming message, as illustrated in Figure 6.24. The effect of this is to (loosely) synchronize the local logical clock of the process that received the message with that of the remote process that sent the message.

Example scenarios	Current LC = 7	or	Current LC = 14
	Message timestamp = 9		Message timestamp = 11
	New LC = 10		New LC = 15
Rule	New LC = maximum (Current LC, Message timestamp) + 1		

FIGURE 6.24

Logical clock update scenarios on receipt of a message from another process.

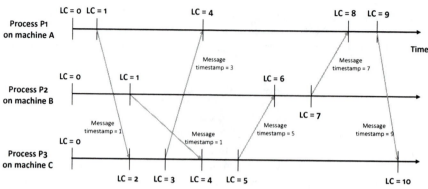

FIGURE 6.25

Logical clock-based event ordering across a distributed system.

Figure 6.24 shows the rule that is applied when a message arrives from another process causing the local logical clock value to be updated and provides two example scenarios. In the scenario on the left, the message arrives with a time stamp value of 9 and is higher than the logical clock value of 7. The new logical clock value is thus $9 + 1 = 10$. In the scenario on the right, the message arrives with a time stamp value of 11 but the logical clock value is already higher, at 14. The new logical clock value is thus $14 + 1 = 15$.

The progression of logical clock values in a system of three communicating processes is illustrated in Figure 6.25. Notice that for each process, the logical clock values are always increasing according to the "happened before" relationship between events, and the clock update rule is illustrated in Figure 6.24.

Figure 6.25 shows how the logical clock values progress in a scenario involving three communicating processes. The logical clocks are maintained locally by each process, and therefore, they are not tightly synchronized. Instead, a loose synchronization is achieved in which processes only get a hint as to the value of the clocks at other processes when they receive a message from those processes (the time stamp of the message indicating the sender's logical clock at the point when the message was sent). Logical clock values remain static between event occurrences, as the passing of wall-clock time is of no concern.

6.7 ELECTION ALGORITHMS

There are many scenarios in distributed systems where it is necessary to automatically select one process from a group, so that it can perform some specific role. An election algorithm provides the means to do this.

Scenarios where election algorithms are employed include

- replicated services in which coordination is necessary,
- reliable services in which continuation of service despite failures is important,
- self-organizing services in which processes may need to know their status relative to others,
- group communication mechanisms (see later text) in which there is a need to establish a group coordinator.

Election algorithms are therefore a fundamental requirement for many distributed applications. As an example, a replicated database system may require that a single coordinator is maintained, to ensure that updates are propagated to all copies of the database. In such an application, there must always be exactly one coordinator, despite variations in the number of database server instances (e.g., additional servers might be automatically started when the system load increases) and node failures. If there are no coordinators, or multiple coordinators, then the database could become inconsistent. Therefore, if the system enters an illegal state, e.g., no coordinator or multiple coordinators, it must be returned to a legal state as quickly as possible.

6.7.1 OPERATION OVERVIEW

Most election algorithms have a two-state operation, in which instances assume the slave state by default. From this starting point, a single instance is elected to be the master (sometimes called coordinator, or leader). Once elected, the role of the master is to coordinate a particular distributed or replicated service or application. The role of the slaves is to monitor the presence of the master, and upon detection of its failure, they must elect a single new master from the pool of slaves.

Figure 6.26 shows an election occurring after the original master has failed. There are two critical stages to this: firstly, the means by which the remaining processes detect that the master has failed (any delay here impacts on the overall time required to establish a new master) and, secondly, critical stage, the means by which the election takes place (i.e., the negotiation as shown in part c of the figure). It is important that the negotiation is not too communication-intense because that would impact on scalability, as well as wasting valuable network bandwidth resource.

Each of the processes involved in the election algorithm runs the algorithm locally. There cannot be a central controller; that would be self-defeating because the central controller could fail, so how would that be replaced? The whole point of the election algorithm is to elect a leader in a distributed way. There are some implications of this: Any of the processes present should be able to become the leader, and even if there is only a single process, there should still be a single leader (the single process must elect itself in such a case).

Figure 6.27 shows a simplified state transition diagram for a generic election algorithm (it does not show the slave negotiation aspect of the behavior). Each participatory process must operate this algorithm and keep track of its own individual state. The diagram shows the only states and transitions between those states that are allowed to occur. This is a very useful way to represent algorithms because it is easy to translate the diagram into program logic. Even though this is a somewhat simplified representation of a generalized algorithm, it illustrates how you can almost read off the program logic from

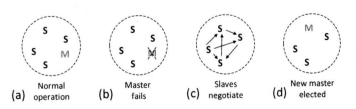

FIGURE 6.26

General operation of election algorithm, showing an election taking place.

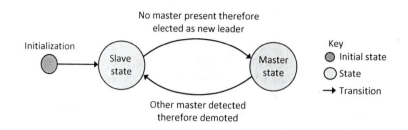

FIGURE 6.27

Generic state transition diagram for 2-state election algorithm.

```
Initialise
    Set state = Slave
End

Periodic_SystemStateCheck
    If (State = Slave  AND  OtherMasterPresent = false)
        Set state = Master
    If (State = Master  AND  OtherMasterPresent = true)
        Set state = Slave
End
```

FIGURE 6.28

Simplified pseudocode elicited from the state transition diagram in Figure 6.27.

the transition descriptions. Figure 6.28 presents a simplified pseudocode that can be elicited from this particular state transition diagram.

Election algorithms are distributed algorithms that operate within distributed applications. They have a number of specific design requirements arising from both their distributed nature and the key behavioral requirement that they ensure a single master is maintained.

The nonfunctional requirements are generally the same for all election algorithms and include the following:

- Scalability. The algorithm should operate correctly regardless of how many processes are involved.
- Robustness. This is implied by the very nature of an election algorithm, i.e., to recover from the failure of the master process.
- Efficiency. There should not be excessive communication, particularly in the negotiation phase.
- Responsiveness. There should be low latency in detecting the absence of a master process and subsequently initiating an election.

See also the more detailed discussion of nonfunctional requirements in Chapter 5.

The various election algorithms differ in their design and thus in their internal function. This means the functional requirements can differ from one algorithm to another but generally include the following:

- The proportion of time that a master exists should be very high.
- A replacement must be found quickly if the current master is removed.

- Multimaster scenarios must be detected and resolved quickly.
- Spurious elections caused by falsely detecting master failure should be avoided.
- Normal-mode communication intensity (the number of messages sent under master-present conditions) must be low.
- Election-mode communication intensity (the number of messages and the number of rounds of messages required to elect a new master) must be low.
- Communications overhead (the mean total communication bandwidth required by the election algorithm) must be low.

6.7.2 THE BULLY ELECTION ALGORITHM

A number of different election algorithms have been designed. The bully election algorithm is probably the best-known election algorithm. It works as follows:

- Each node is preallocated a unique numeric identifier.
- During an election, the highest ID node available will be elected as master.
- When the master fails, the nodes communicate, in rounds, to elect a new master.
- The nodes enter the election state when they are a candidate for the master role.
- The nodes are eliminated if they receive an election message from a higher-ID node.

By negotiation, they must

- determine which node has the highest ID,
- reach consensus (all nodes must agree).

Figure 6.29 shows the operation of the bully election algorithm. Part a shows the normal single-master scenario. In part b, the master fails, leaving a system of zero or more slave nodes (in this example, there are 4). In part c, the first slave node (1) to notice the absence of the master (by the absence of its heartbeat signals) initiates an election by sending a special message (which also serves to inform all other slaves of its unique ID). In part d, slave 4 joins the election, sending its special election message that causes slaves 1 and 2 to be eliminated (because ID 4 is higher than ID 1 and ID 2). In part e, slave 5 joins the election, eliminating slave 4. If slave 5 does not hear any further election messages in

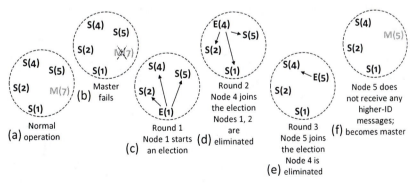

FIGURE 6.29

Operation of the bully leader election algorithm.

a given short time frame, it assumes that it has won the election (as a result of it having the highest ID) and it elevates itself to master status (part f).

Notice that the number of rounds needed to complete an election is dependent on the sequence by which the slaves join the election. The election would be over very quickly if the highest ID slave happens to be the one that first notices the failure of the master, as it would eliminate all other slaves in a single round. In the worst case, the slaves join the election in ascending order, requiring one round per slave (i.e., $N-1$ rounds, where N is the size of the original system before the master failed).

6.7.3 THE RING ELECTION ALGORITHM

The ring election algorithm is similar to the bully election algorithm, but the nodes are arranged in logical ring, and the nodes only communicate with their logical neighbors.

When the master is lost, its neighbors (in the ring) will notice (due to a lack of periodic heartbeat messages). The negotiation phase is achieved by the nodes passing messages around the ring (in several rounds) to establish which is the highest numbered node and to ensure consensus.

Figure 6.30 shows the operation of the ring election algorithm. Part a shows the normal single-master scenario; the nodes are connected in a logical ring that is maintained by periodically sending messages from node to node. The message informs the recipient of the identity of its upstream neighbor and that the neighbor is alive. In part b, the master fails, which breaks the ring. In part c, node 1 notices the absence of the master (by the absence of the expected messages) and initiates an election by sending a special message to its logical neighbor (node 2). In part d, the election message propagates around the ring until the highest numbered remaining node has been identified and all nodes are aware of its identity. In part e, slave 5 elevates itself to master status.

6.7.4 LEADER PREELECTION

Leader preelection is a technique where a backup master is selected while the system is operating normally. If the master fails, the backup detects the failure and takes over as master.

Selection of the backup is still performed by an election algorithm, but the election is done during normal operation (i.e., in advance of the master failing) so the system is leaderless for a shorter time.

Note that the backup can fail before an election occurs; therefore, there is the possibility of wasteful elections to select backup master nodes that are survived by the current master.

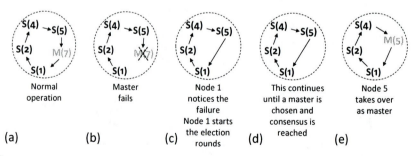

(a) Normal operation

(b) Master fails

(c) Node 1 notices the failure Node 1 starts the election rounds

(d) This continues until a master is chosen and consensus is reached

(e) Node 5 takes over as master

FIGURE 6.30

Operation of the ring election algorithm.

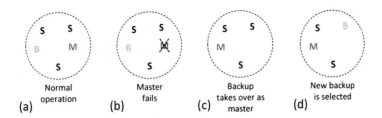

FIGURE 6.31

The leader preelection technique.

As illustrated in Figure 6.31, the purpose of the leader preelection is to preselect a backup leader in advance of any problem with the master, such that under normal operation, both the master and the backup master exist (as in part a of the figure) and both send heartbeat messages to inhibit slaves electing further nodes. When the master node fails (part b), the backup is rapidly able to take over leadership of the service (part c). The latency is only the time needed to detect that the master has failed, the main component of which is the time waiting for the next heartbeat from the master (which never arrives). There is no requirement for additional message transmission or the negotiation associated with elections. As soon as the backup node has elevated itself to master status, it can initiate an election of a replacement backup node (part d). Thus, the amount of time the system is leaderless is very small (the one tuning parameter being the interval between heartbeat messages).

6.7.5 EXPLORATION WITH AN ELECTION ALGORITHM

Activity D3 explores the behavior of election algorithms. It uses a specific election algorithm, the "Emergent Election Algorithm," which is built into the Distributed Systems Workbench.

The Emergent Election Algorithm is a two-stage algorithm for electing leaders in large systems. It has been designed specifically to be highly scalable and efficient. It achieves this by introducing two additional states not usually found in traditional algorithms:

The idle state is used to separate out a majority of processes (on average, it is all except four processes) that only listen to messages sent by the master and slaves. Processes in the idle state never send any messages.

The candidate state is a transient state that is only used during elections. A process that determines it is a candidate for being the master moves into the candidate state from slave state, prior to becoming master. The process must remain in the candidate state long enough to ensure that there are no other processes still involved in the election. This is used to enforce the rule that there must only be a single-master process present at any time.

The four states of the Emergent Election algorithm are described in Table 6.4. As mentioned above, the algorithm operates in two stages, as this enables a design that is simultaneously highly scalable and also very efficient in terms of the number of messages sent (which is near constant regardless of the system size).

The first stage employs the idle state. This stage separates the majority of processes away from a small active pool of slaves. The idle processes (the majority) never transmit messages; they simply monitor the size of the slave pool. Each slave state process sends periodic slave-heartbeat messages, so by listening for these and counting them over a specific time period, an idle-state process can determine

Table 6.4 The Four States of the Emergent Election Algorithm

State	State persistence	Description of behavior when in the state
Master	Stable state	Coordinate the host service
		Send regular beacon messages to inhibit elections and thus ensure stability
Candidate	Transient state	Election participant. After negotiation based on IP address, exactly one candidate node will elevate to master status
Slave	Stable state	Monitor the presence of master. Contender for master status (via candidate state) if the current master fails
Idle	Stable state	Monitor slave population. Contender to become slave if the pool of slaves is diminished beyond some threshold

the number of slaves present (i.e., the size of the slave pool). If an idle process' local perception of the slave pool size falls below a lower threshold, the process will elevate to slave state.

Slave-state processes also listen to the slave-heartbeat messages to determine the slave pool size. If a slave process' local perception of the slave pool size rises above an upper threshold, it will demote to idle state. Both the idle and slave state listening periods contain random components to ensure that each process has a slightly different perception of the state of the system, thus ensuring stability (because the processes don't all suddenly switch to either the slave or the idle state, instead a gradual and self-regulating effect is achieved).

The candidate state is used in the second stage of the algorithm to ensure that elections are deterministic, i.e., that only one process elevates to master status, regardless of how many slaves are in the slave pool. The candidate state also plays an important role in preventing false elections, for example, if a master's heartbeat message is lost in the network. This is because a process must remain in the candidate state for a time long enough for several master heartbeat messages to occur, so that even if several were lost, there is a high probability that the candidate will eventually detect a master heartbeat if the master is present.

Figure 6.32 shows how the two stages of this particular algorithm are coupled together by the slave pool, as an idle process must move through the slave state to become master, and vice versa. The composition of the slave pool and thus its size also are emergent properties arising from all of the local interactions between slave and idle processes, whereby the behavior of each is determined by the number of slave messages received in a short time interval. Hence, the algorithm is described as "emergent."

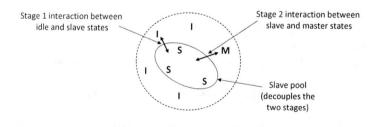

FIGURE 6.32

The two-stage operation of the Emergent Election Algorithm.

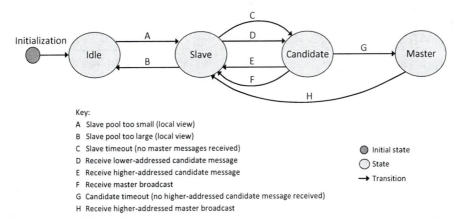

Key:
A Slave pool too small (local view)
B Slave pool too large (local view)
C Slave timeout (no master messages received)
D Receive lower-addressed candidate message
E Receive higher-addressed candidate message
F Receive master broadcast
G Candidate timeout (no higher-addressed candidate message received)
H Receive higher-addressed master broadcast

● Initial state
○ State
→ Transition

FIGURE 6.33

The state transition diagram for the Emergent Election Algorithm.

The first stage of the algorithm serves the purpose of enabling a very large population of processes to participate but most are passive at any time (i.e., they are in the idle state and do not send messages; they only listen).

The slave-master interaction occurs in the second stage of the algorithm and must be deterministic, that is, during an election, only a single slave can become master. This requires that the slaves have some means of negotiating between themselves. Slaves use timers to monitor the presence of the master by listening for its periodic heartbeat messages. When a master heartbeat is received, the timer is restarted, but if the end of the time period is reached without hearing from the master, the particular slave elevates to candidate status and broadcasts a candidate message. The candidate message informs slaves that the master has failed and also provides the address of the candidate. Higher-addressed slaves then also elevate to candidate status and transmit candidate messages. Lower-addressed slaves remain in the slave state. Candidate nodes that receive higher-addressed candidate messages withdraw their candidacy (they revert to slave status). Eventually, only the highest addressed candidate remains. It elevates to master status and the election is complete.

The corresponding state transition diagram for the Emergent Election Algorithm is shown in Figure 6.33.

ACTIVITY D3 EXPLORING THE BEHAVIOR OF AN ELECTION ALGORITHM AND USING AN AUTOMATED LOGGING TOOL

This activity uses the Emergent Election Algorithm that is built into the Distributed Systems Workbench. The activity explores the behavior of the election algorithm, in terms of the elections that occur, the state sequences of the individual instances, and the messages sent by those instances, under various conditions.

You will need at least two computers in the same local network to experiment with the election algorithm; only one copy will run on each computer because all instances use the same ports.

There is also an optional event logger utility that monitors all message events and state changes of the election algorithm processes and writes these to a logfile for subsequent analysis. The use of the logger is recommended for

ACTIVITY D3 EXPLORING THE BEHAVIOR OF AN ELECTION ALGORITHM AND USING AN AUTOMATED LOGGING TOOL—Cont'd

experiments where large numbers of election algorithm instances are used or where complex state change sequences are induced (e.g., by purposely starting additional instances in master state). The logger also uses the same ports as the election algorithm so it has to be run on an additional computer that does not have an instance of the election algorithm running.

Learning Outcomes

1. To gain experience of using an election algorithm.
2. To gain an appreciation of the behavior of an election algorithm.
3. To appreciate that a system may comprise a single process at the limit case and all behavioral rules must be respected in this case.
4. To gain an understanding of the mechanics of an election, including the state changes that occur at individual instances and the messages that are transmitted between instances.
5. To gain an appreciation of the usefulness of independent logging processes to capture dynamic event behavior in distributed applications.

Method Part A: Experimentation with a Single Instance of the Election Algorithm

The election algorithm should work correctly even if there is only one instance; this is the limit case (it is important to realize that the concept of a limit case also applies to other applications such as clock synchronization services, in which a single instance should "synchronize to itself"). The universal requirement for the election algorithm is that there should always be exactly one master, so a single instance should move to the master state and stay in that state.

Run the application called "Emergent Election Algorithm" from within the Distributed Systems Workbench on a single computer. Make sure the initial state is selected as "Idle" and press the Start button.

Expected Outcome for Part A

The screenshot below shows the election algorithm process; having started in the idle state, it has progressed through the other states in sequence to the master state. The process was left running and remained in the master state, which is the expected correct behavior.

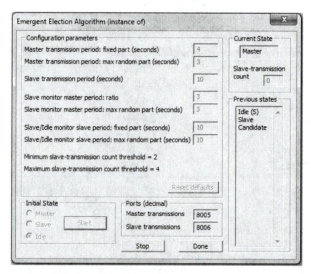

Method Part B: Use of a Logging Utility for Diagnostics

This part of the activity introduces a separate utility for logging the behavior of the election algorithm so that it can be analyzed precisely, later. This is very important when evaluating the algorithm in large systems or when gathering

ACTIVITY D3 EXPLORING THE BEHAVIOR OF AN ELECTION ALGORITHM AND USING AN AUTOMATED LOGGING TOOL—Cont'd

statistics, for example, in terms of efficiency measured as the number of messages per unit time, which is a measure of communication complexity and can impact scalability. To fully understand the internal behavior of the algorithm, it is important to capture the ordering of the events and key information such as which instances change from one particular state to another particular state.

In addition to the specific use of this logging utility, it is also intended that you gain an appreciation of the usefulness of independent logging processes to capture dynamic event behavior in distributed applications in the more general case. When complex scenarios arise, such as when many messages are being sent between components, or when there are large numbers of components, or when the relative timing of events is critical, then it is not possible to manually collate the information in a useful manner for subsequent analysis. The distributed nature of the system itself means that only by actually capturing the messages themselves can you identify the actual sequence of events and thus ensure correctness of the system or find complex timing-related problems.

First, create an empty logfile in a convenient location, for example, ElectionAlgorithm_Log.txt in the C:\temp directory (a simple editor such as Notepad can be used to create this file).

Once you have created the empty logfile, run the logger application called "Emergent Election Algorithm event logger" from within the Distributed Systems Workbench; this must be on a computer in the local network that is not running the election algorithm itself. Enter the path and filename of the logfile in the provided text box, and then press the "Start logging" button.

Expected Outcome for Part B

The screenshot on the left below shows the event logger running while a single instance of the election algorithm was running on another computer in the local network. You can see from the log trace that one election algorithm instance initialized in the idle state, and because it did not detect any messages from other instances, it elevated to slave state, then to candidate state, and then to master state. When in the slave state, it transmitted slave messages. Once in the master state, it transmitted master messages (these serve to prevent other instances elevating to candidate or master state).

The generated logfile content is shown on the right below. It shows the same information as the logger screen, as well as start time and the listening periods for master and slave messages (the periods over which messages are collated for logging and display purposes). The logfile is particularly useful for long-running experiments and for tracing sequences of node states when large numbers of nodes are used in experiments.

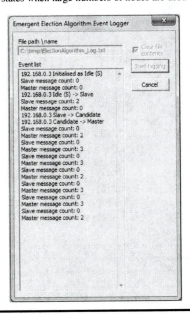

```
**Started 28/8/2014 14:37:52
**Configuration- Listen4Master period:15 Listen4Slave period:15
192.168.0.3 Initialised as Idle (S)
Slave message count: 0
Master message count: 0
192.168.0.3 Idle (S) -> Slave
Slave message count: 2
Master message count: 0
192.168.0.3 Slave -> Candidate
192.168.0.3 Candidate -> Master
Slave message count: 0
Master message count: 2
Slave message count: 0
Master message count: 3
Slave message count: 0
Master message count: 3
Slave message count: 0
Master message count: 2
Slave message count: 0
Master message count: 3
Slave message count: 0
Master message count: 3
Slave message count: 0
Master message count: 2
```

ACTIVITY D3 EXPLORING THE BEHAVIOR OF AN ELECTION ALGORITHM AND USING AN AUTOMATED LOGGING TOOL—Cont'd

Method Part C: Experimentation with Multiple Instances of the Election Algorithm

The expected behavior is that an election occurs and a single instance enters the master state. A slave pool should be established with this particular algorithm; therefore, there should be between (typically) two and four slave state instances in larger systems. Additional instances should end up in the idle state.

Run multiple copies of the Emergent Election Algorithm each on separate computers (at least two computers are needed to perform this part adequately). Make sure the initial state in each case is selected as "Idle" and press the Start button.

Expected Outcome for Part C

One master instance was established (the user interface resembles the result for part A above). In my experiment, I only ran two instances, so the second instance settled in the slave state, which is the correct and expected behavior. The screenshot below shows the slave state process.

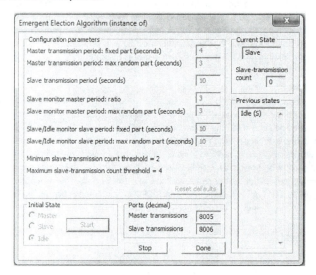

Method Part D: Stress Testing the Election Algorithm

Parts A and C above explored the election algorithm under stable conditions. However, in distributed systems, there can be highly dynamic, and unstable behavior where processes are started stopped or crashed unpredictably. This part of the activity explores the resilience of the election algorithm under some of these circumstances.

Experiment with a wide range of different starting conditions and interventions such as killing the master-state process or killing all the slave state processes and restarting them in the idle state.

Here is one particular experiment where the system is forced into an illegal state and left to recover:

Run multiple copies of the Emergent Election Algorithm each on separate computers. Let the system stabilize to where there is a single master.

Now, start one further instance of the election algorithm. In this case, make sure the initial state is selected as "Master" and press the Start button (thus creating a situation where there are two masters present).

Expected Outcome for Part D

Under any starting conditions and with any combination of starting and stopping instances and starting them in any state, the algorithm should work correctly and the system should settle to a steady state of one master, between two and four

---

ACTIVITY D3 EXPLORING THE BEHAVIOR OF AN ELECTION ALGORITHM AND USING AN AUTOMATED LOGGING TOOL—Cont'd

slaves and the remainder in the idle state. The screenshot below shows the behavior of a process that had previously elevated to master status. Another instance was started directly in master state, which is an illegal condition. This leads to a race in which the first master to hear a master message from the other will demote itself to slave status. In this case, the original master demoted (as can be seen in the screenshot, look at the previous state sequence and the current state) and the new instance stayed in master role.

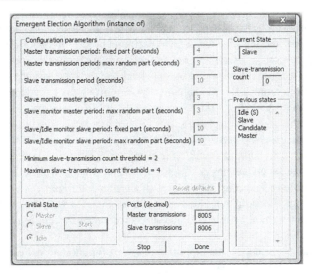

Reflection

This activity has explored the behavior of an election algorithm under a range of system conditions. It also introduced the use of automated logging utilities to capture the dynamic behavior of systems in a way that facilitates postmortem study of behavior and to check for correctness, enhance understanding, or identify problems.

Further Exploration

If you have access to a computer laboratory with moderate or large number of computers connected in the same broadcast domain (i.e., without separation by a router), try running the election algorithm on as many computers as you can.

Carry out some simple experiments to investigate characteristics of behavior such as the following:

- Does the number of process instances affect the time to reach a steady state?
- How many slave state instances are there on average? How steady is this value?
- What happens if you start ten or more instances in master state at the same time? (I found that by carefully positioning the keyboards, I can start four instances at the same time; use Tab to highlight the Start button and then you can start them all at once by simultaneously pressing the carriage return key. You can do at least two per person, so you may need a few helpers).

6.8 GROUP COMMUNICATIONS

Many distributed applications require that processes work together in groups to solve particular problems or to provide a particular service. Externally, i.e., to their clients, these applications and services appear as a single process (this is a main transparency goal when designing such systems). However, internally, there can be complex behavior arising from the number of individual processes and the interactions between these processes. In particular, there need to be a means of control or coordination of the group and a means for messages from outside the group to be delivered to each member of the group in a way that is transparent to the external sender. In other words, the client should not need to identify the individual group members and send the message to each one in turn. In fact, the client should not need know the number of processes in the group or even that there are multiple processes.

Group communication mechanisms and protocols facilitate the maintenance of a group of processes that cooperate to perform some service. Typically, service groups will need to have dynamic membership, so that they can be scaled up and down as necessary to meet service demand. For example, consider a replicated database. The database servers may be organized as a group for the purpose of managing replication and ensuring consistency. Externally, a client may send an update request to the database service, unaware that internally within the group, an update propagation must take place. Only a single confirmation that the update has completed will be sent back to the client.

If the external interface to the group is by means of a group communication protocol, the client will see the same interface regardless of the number of processes in the group. The client should be unaware of internal complexities, for example, if additional servers are added when the request load increases or that some servers crash from time to time.

Group communication protocols can support a range of functionalities related to dynamic group maintenance and membership including

- group creation and destruction,
- process join and leave actions,
- send-to-group messaging,
- intra-group messaging.

There are two main approaches to group structure; hierarchical groups and peer groups, as illustrated in Figures 6.34 and 6.35, respectively.

Figure 6.34 shows the structure of a hierarchical group, in which a coordinator process manages the group. The main role of the coordinator is to distribute service requests to the worker processes. The client is presented with a single-entity view of the group and the group-send method of the group communication protocol should hide details of the membership of the group and also the structure, so the client is unaware of the size of the group and the presence of the coordinator. The reply to a group-send message could be generated by the worker process that handled the request or by the coordinator.

The coordinator represents a single point of failure, and therefore, it may be necessary to implement an election algorithm (discussed earlier) to automatically select a replacement if the coordinator should fail.

Figure 6.35 shows the structure of a peer group, which by implication does not have a coordinator. Therefore, peers negotiate (or vote) to determine which one will deal with an incoming request. In some applications, this may be decided by the location of a specific resource (i.e., not all peers may be capable of providing the required service).

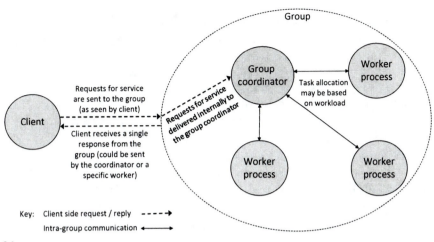

FIGURE 6.34

Hierarchical group structure.

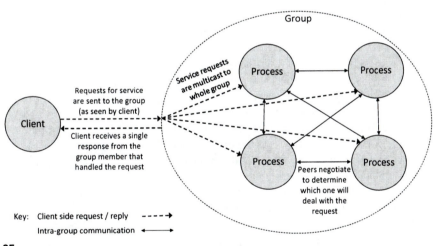

FIGURE 6.35

Peer group structure.

Peer groups are useful in dynamic and ad hoc applications. The difference between a peer-to-peer application and a peer group application is that in the former, the client is a peer (e.g., see the media sharing example and activity in Chapter 5). In the case of a peer group application, the peer group itself is a closed or bounded service and the client is an external entity. This has significant implications in terms of transparency, because the internal dynamic configuration of the peer group may be complex, but the client is shielded from it.

6.8.1 TRANSPARENCY ASPECTS OF GROUP COMMUNICATION

For both types of groups, external clients of the group should be presented with a single-entity view of the group. Internally, groups can have complex structure and/or behavior, for example, the membership may change dynamically, processes may fail, and there may be a need to elect a new coordinator process. The fact that it is a group is known to the programmer, because messages are sent using primitives called, i.e., group-send or send-to-group. However, specific details of the group, such as group size, the identities of specific member processes, and the structure (whether or not there is a coordinator), are hidden from external processes.

6.9 NOTIFICATION SERVICES

There are many scenarios in distributed systems where a particular application (or process thereof) is concerned with knowing details of events that occur elsewhere in the system.

A notification service tracks events centrally and informs client applications when an event that is of interest to them occurs. For this to operate, the applications need to register with the notification service and provide details of which subset of events they are interested in. Such a service is most effective in systems where there are large numbers of events occurring (or that could occur) and individual clients are each only interested in a small subset of these. In contrast, if a process is interested in all (or a clear majority) of the events occurring, it may be more efficient for that process to monitor those events directly, removing the need for the notification service and the interaction with it.

Take, for example, automated stockbroking. A particular trading process may wish to buy shares in the company GlaxoSmithKline, but only if the price dips below 1200 pence per share, while another trading process may wish to sell shares in the same company, but only if the share price rises above 1600 pence per share. The actual market prices are held by a central brokerage system and change continuously throughout the day. As the prices can change quickly and dramatically and thus are not predictable, it is necessary for the trading processes to somehow keep track of the actual prices.

One option is for the brokerage system to continuously send out the prices of the stock, as they change. However, there are many thousands of different stocks listed on the exchange, and with price changes occurring at intervals of less than one second for many stocks, there are a lot of data to send out, and each trading process is only actually interested in a fraction of the information. This is quite inefficient and requires very high network bandwidth.

Another option is for the trading processes to repeatedly request the price of the particular stocks that they are interested in. This is called polling and would have to be done at a high rate to keep up with the fast price fluctuations that can occur. It is important to take into account that there can be a great many trading processes running simultaneously and each may be interested in a few tens or even hundreds of different stocks. Therefore, the polling approach could overwhelm the brokerage system or the communication network.

A more sophisticated approach for this situation would be to arrange that the trading processes register their interest in particular stocks, and the threshold prices they are waiting for, with a special notification service. This service would keep track of the stock prices, and whenever a prenotified target threshold is reached, the particular trading process would be notified. This approach cuts down on a lot of duplicate processing as each individual trading process is not continuously performing price comparisons, and also of course, there are significantly lower levels of network traffic.

6.9.1 **PUBLISH-SUBSCRIBE SERVICES**

Notification services can also be used as a form of middleware between processes within the same application. This is useful for applications where the various processes are each interested in certain subsets of events being generated by other processes. In such a scenario, the notification service is an example of what is called a publish-subscribe system; this is so named because some processes generate (publish) events that the notification service then forward to other processes that have preregistered their interest in (subscribed to) those events.

As an example, consider an online conferencing system with an integrated virtual whiteboard facility so that participants can draw diagrams to assist their discussions during a conference. Each user's computer has a local conferencing manager that manages the input and output resources of the system and maps these into a suitable user interface.

The conference manager registers with the notification service for the specific conferences that its user wishes to participate in; and for each of these conferences, it subscribes to the subset of events that the user requires (e.g., some users may have a voice-only interface and thus are not interested in the virtual whiteboard events).

Once the conference manager components have registered and subscribed to certain event types, the notification service will inform the managers when events of interest to them occur. Examples of events in this application include another user joining a conference and a user adding content to the virtual whiteboard. This scenario is illustrated in Figure 6.36.

Figure 6.36 shows the way in which a notification service decouples two application components such that they communicate indirectly. The notification service forwards only those events that each conferencing manager component has previously subscribed to, i.e., registered an interest in.

The figure shows the interaction taking place in the following sequence: steps 1 and 2; each conference manager registers with the conference event notification service. They each provide details of the actual conference, as well as the type of events within the conference that they are interested in. In this

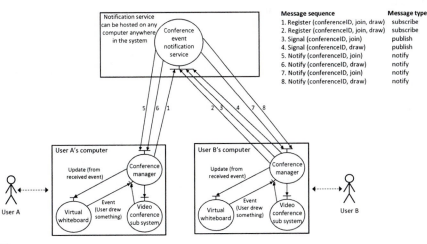

FIGURE 6.36

Notification service illustrated in the context of an online conferencing scenario.

case, the event types are join events (when other users join the conference) and draw events (when existing conference members draw on the virtual whiteboard). User B then joins the conference and draws on the virtual whiteboard (steps 3 and 4, respectively). The notification service sees that both managers have subscribed to these event types, so each event is forwarded to each manager (steps 5, 6, 7, and 8).

The publish-subscribe mechanism is important because it decouples components both at the design time and at the runtime and therefore facilitates flexible dynamic configuration. A notification service provides loose coupling (because the relationships between different components are decided by runtime needs and thus not fixed at design time) and also provides indirect coupling (because the components only need to communicate with the intermediary, the notification service, and do not need to communicate directly with each other). There is an activity based on an event notification service in Chapter 7 (see also the detailed discussion on component coupling in Chapter 5).

6.10 MIDDLEWARE: MECHANISM AND OPERATION

Middleware has been introduced in Chapter 5 in the form of an overview of its operation and a discussion of the ways in which middleware supports software architectures.

This section deals with the mechanistic and operational aspects of middleware and the ways in which it provides transparency to applications.

Middleware comprises the addition of a "middle" virtual layer between applications and the underlying platforms they run on. The layer is conceptually continuous across the entire system such that all processes sit above it and all platform resources are conceptually below it. By communicating through the layer, all aspects of location, the network, and computer boundaries are abstracted away (see Figure 6.37).

Figure 6.37 provides an overview of the middleware concept. Processes communicate only via the middleware layer; they are not concerned with physical aspects of the system such as which platform they are running on or the addresses of other processes they are communicating with.

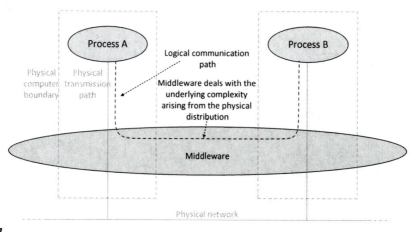

FIGURE 6.37

Middleware represented as a virtual layer connecting processes across the system.

The virtual layer architecture of middleware provides significant transparency, in several of its forms, to processes. To achieve this, the middleware itself is quite complex internally. To achieve the illusion of the virtual layer, the middleware consists of processes and services located on each participating computer and special communication protocols connecting these components together so that collectively, they act like a continuous "layer" or "channel" that is spread across all computers. The middleware communication is typically based on top of TCP connections between the participating computers and may also use higher-level constructed forms of communication such as RMI to support remote method calls to application processes. The middleware hides differences in the underlying platforms from processes, but the middleware components must themselves be implemented specifically for their respective platforms and operating system. Figure 6.38 shows a physical system view of middleware.

Figure 6.38 shows in a generic way the main internal components of middleware. There are three main types of interface that must be supported: (1) The application interface through which process-to-process communication is facilitated—Processes are given the illusion that they are sending messages directly to other processes, but actually, they send and receive messages to/from the middleware, which forwards the messages on to the other processes on their behalf, therefore providing location and access transparency. (2) The middleware internal interface through which the middleware components communicate and are managed—The various middleware service instances work together internally through a special protocol (which is defined by the middleware) to provide externally the illusion that the middleware is a single continuous layer, therefore achieving distribution transparency (the network is hidden). The middleware internal interface is used to pass control and configuration messages between middleware instances to maintain the middleware structure itself, as well as to forward messages from application components between parts of the system so that they reappear at the destination component's site as if the sender were a local process. (3) The platform-specific interface enables the middleware to work across a number of different platform types in the same system, therefore overcoming heterogeneity. This interface is the only part of the middleware that has to change to move the middleware across to a new platform; all of the middleware services and transparency provision are unchanged.

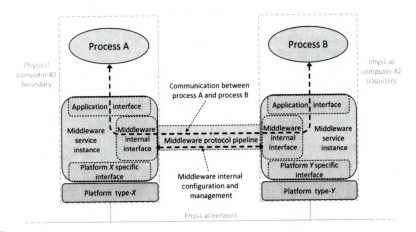

FIGURE 6.38

Middleware under the hood: a physical system view of middleware.

6.11 MIDDLEWARE EXAMPLES AND SUPPORT TECHNOLOGIES
6.11.1 THE COMMON OBJECT REQUEST BROKER ARCHITECTURE (CORBA)

There are many types of middleware; CORBA is a standard defined by the Object Management Group (OMG) and is one of the best-known and historically most widely used examples. CORBA has been around since 1991 and is therefore considered to be a legacy technology by some practitioners, in some opinions superseded by other technologies such as Web services (see later). However, it still has many strengths and is still is in use.

CORBA serves as a useful reference model by which to explain some of the mechanics of middleware operation and some of the transparency aspects of middleware.

6.11.1.1 Motivation for CORBA

Distributed systems represent highly dynamic environments in which significant complexity stems from a wide variety of sources, some of which are inherent in the nature of distribution. Complexity challenges include a large location space in which it is necessary to find resources; communication latency; message loss; partial failures of networks; service partitioning (e.g., the functional split between client and server); replication, concurrency, and consistency control; and the requirement of consistent ordering of distributed events. In addition to these inherent forms of complexity, there are some accidental or avoidable forms of complexity that include the continuous rediscovery and reinvention of core concepts and components and lack of a single common design or development methodology. Distributed systems are also subject to various forms of heterogeneity that have been discussed in detail in Chapter 5.

CORBA was created as an answer to the problems of complexity and heterogeneity in distributed systems. With no consensus ever likely on hardware platforms, operating systems, programming languages, or application formats, the goal of CORBA was to facilitate universal interoperability. In this regard, CORBA allows application components to be accessed from anywhere in a network, regardless of the operating system they are running on and the language they are written in.

In CORBA systems, the communicating entities are objects (which are themselves part of larger applications). Dividing into separate entities at the object level allows for flexible fine-grained distribution of services, functionality, data resources, and workload, across the processing resources of the system.

The ORB is the central component of CORBA. An ORB provides mechanisms to invoke methods on local and remote objects, as illustrated in Figure 6.39.

Figure 6.39 shows a simplified representation of a client object making two calls to methods on other objects, showing only the ORB aspects and not other components of the middleware. The client object does not know where the host objects of these methods (the implementation objects) are located. The figure shows that it does not matter whether the implementation objects are local or remote to the client; the ORB handles the method invocation transparently.

As indicated by the example in Figure 6.39, the ORB provides several forms of transparency. When an object (the client) makes a method request, the ORB automatically locates the host object and calls the requested method. The middleware layer hides platform and operating system heterogeneity that may be present when the called object is remote (the so-called object may be hosted on a physical platform of a different hardware type and/or running a different operating system to the client object's platform). The middleware uses a special IDL format when passing arguments to methods, which means that the objects can be written in different languages that use different call semantics; this will not affect the method call.

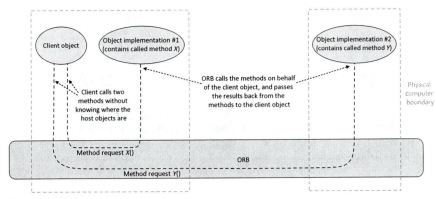

FIGURE 6.39

The object request broker provides a transparent connectivity service supporting method calls.

The transparency provided by the ORB (achieved with support from other components of CORBA) is summarized as follows:

- Access transparency. The calling object does not need to know if a called object is local or remote. Object methods are invoked in the same manner whether they are local or remote to the calling object.
- Location transparency. The location of a called object is not known and does not need to be known by the client object when invoking that object's methods. The called object does not need to know the location of the calling object when passing back results.
- Implementation transparency. Objects interoperate together despite possibly being written in different languages or residing in heterogeneous environments with different hardware platforms or operating systems.
- Distribution transparency. The communications network is hidden. The middleware takes care of setting up low-level (transport-layer) connections between the involved computers and manages all object-level communication using its own special protocols that sit above TCP. At the object-level, a single platform illusion is provided such that objects see all other objects as if they are local.

Figure 6.39 hides a lot of detail as to the actual architecture of CORBA and the actual mechanisms used to invoke method calls. In addition to the ORB, there are several other components and interfaces as shown in Figure 6.40.

Figure 6.40 shows the architecture of CORBA, from the perspective of the ORB and its support components. Also shown are the various interfaces, which are in two categories: those between internal components and also the external interfaces to application objects. Two alternative forms of method invocation are supported—static and dynamic—which each involve different groups of components; the alternative paths are represented by the dotted arrows in the figure.

The subsections below provide details of the roles and behavior of the various components of CORBA and the interactions that occur between the components.

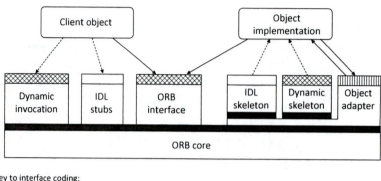

Key to interface coding:

▮ ORB-dependent internal interface

▨ External interface identical for all ORB implementations

☐ Object-specific interfaces (a stub and skeleton for each object type, created by the IDL compiler)

▥ There may be multiple object adapters. The basic object adapter (BOA) is generic and simple. The portable object adapter (POA) is more sophisticated.

FIGURE 6.40

The ORB-related components and interfaces.

6.11.1.2 Object Adapter and Skeleton

An object adapter is a special component used to interface the CORBA mechanisms to an implementation object (i.e., an object on which a method is to be called). In addition to actually invoking the requested method, the object adapter performs some preparatory actions that include the following:

- Implementation activation and deactivation. The requested application component (the one hosting the object that contains the called method) may not be running (instantiated) when a request arrives to the ORB. If this were to happen in nonmiddleware-based applications in which a client component attempts to connect to a nonrunning server, the call would fail. With CORBA, there is an opportunity for the object adapter to actually instantiate the service component in such circumstances, prior to actually making the method request. It is also possible to leave the application component running after the method has been called or for the object adapter to deactivate it, depending on the server activation policy (see below).
- Mapping object references to implementations. A mapping of which object IDs are provided by each instantiated application component is maintained.
- Registration of implementations. A mapping of the physical location of instantiated application components is maintained.
- Generation and interpretation of object references. When a request to invoke a particular method is received, the ORB locates the particular service instance needed. It does this by relating together the mapping of the required object ID to an instantiation of a specific component and the mapping of instantiated components to locations.
- Object activation and deactivation. Once an object's service host component is instantiated, it may be necessary to separately instantiate specific objects (essentially by creating an instance of the object and calling its constructor).

Once all preparatory steps have been completed, the requested method is invoked (called), with the aid of the object's skeleton.

The skeleton is a server-side object-specific interface that actually performs the method invocation. The skeleton performs three functions: (1) It preserves the semantics of the object request and of the response, by translating the arguments from the IDL representation into the necessary object representation (which is dependent on the implementation language of the server object) and back into IDL for the response; (2) it makes the remote call appear as a local call from the point of view of the server object; (3) it takes care of the network connectivity aspects of the call so that the server application logic need not do so.

The combined operation of the object adapter and the skeleton is portrayed in an example application context in Figure 6.41.

Figure 6.41 illustrates the object adapter's management of method invocation, including the usage of the skeleton, placed into the context of a robot arm application example. In the scenario shown, the client object makes a request to open the robot arm's gripper, by calling the open-gripper method, without knowing the activation status of the server implementation component that hosts the object that contains this method. In the scenario, the server implementation is not already instantiated so the object adapter must first activate (instantiate) an instance of the application component that contains the Robot-Arm-Control object (step 1 in the figure). In step 2, the newly started component is now registered in a repository so that future service requests can be directed to it (otherwise, each new request could result in the instantiation of a dedicated component instance). In step 3, the Robot-Arm-Control object is activated (essentially, this means that an actual object instance of the appropriate class is created and its constructor called). In step 4, the open-gripper method is called using the precreated custom skeleton interface for the object (the skeleton actually performs a local method call on behalf of the remote client object). The server object responds by passing the result of the call back to the skeleton as though the skeleton were the client. This is an important aspect of distribution transparency from the application developer's viewpoint: the fact that the server object thinks it is being called locally means that no special communication considerations need to be made by the server's developer.

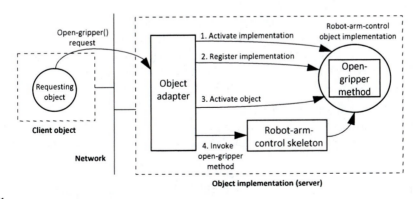

FIGURE 6.41

Object adapter management of method invocation.

6.11.1.3 CORBA Object Servers and Activation Policy

There are several types of object server that can be implemented in CORBA, differentiated by the activation policy that describes the ways the object implementation and object activation are achieved. The different activation policies are as follows:

- Shared server policy. An object adapter activates a given server process the first time that one of its objects receives a request. The server then remains active. A server may implement multiple objects.
- Unshared server policy. The same as a shared server policy except that a server may implement only one object.
- Per-method server policy. Each method request causes a new server process to be started dynamically. Servers terminate once they have executed a method.
- Persistent server policy. Servers are initiated outside of the object adapter. The object adapter is still used to route method requests to the servers. In this situation, if a method request occurs for an object whose server is not already running, the call will fail.

6.11.1.4 CORBA's Repositories

CORBA uses two databases to keep track of the state of the system:

- The implementation repository is used by the ORB and object adapter to keep track of object servers and their runtime instances. In other words, it is a dynamic database of whether or not server applications are actually instantiated (running) and the location details of those that are running, so that requests can be forwarded to them.
- The interface repository is a database that contains descriptions of the methods associated with each class. Details are held in the form of IDL descriptions of each method's interface (which are programming language-independent). This database is used during dynamic method invocation to find a suitable server object for a dynamic request by matching the IDL definition of each of the server's method prototypes against the IDL description in the request message.

6.11.1.5 Static Method Invocation

Static invocation is used when the client object wants to send a request message to a specific design-time-known object. The mechanism of static invocation is illustrated in Figure 6.42.

Figure 6.42 illustrates how static invocation takes place. The sequence of steps shown in the figure begins at the point where a client identifies a particular implementation object that it wishes to send a method invocation request to. The steps are as follows:

1. The client object sends the request message.
2. The message is passed to the client stub (associated with the client object's application) that represents the server object (an application has one such stub for each remote object that it may access).
3. The message is converted into IDL representation.
4. The IDL code is passed via the client-side ORB (for the client platform) to the network. The client-side ORB consists of local services that the application may use (e.g., it may convert an object reference to a string for type-safe transmission over the network).

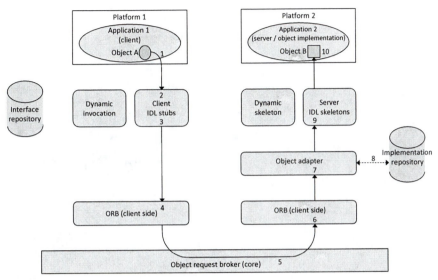

FIGURE 6.42

The mechanism of static method invocation.

5. The message is passed over the network through the ORB core. CORBA enforces strict syntax and the mode of transport for messages passed over the network to ensure interoperability between CORBA implementations. The required syntax is the General Inter-ORB Protocol (GIOP) and the mode of transport is the Internet Inter-ORB Protocol (IIOP), which operates over TCP.

6. Once the message arrives at the server object's platform, it is picked up by the client-side ORB (which may perform local services such as object reference format conversion) and passed to the object adapter.

7. The object adapter provides the runtime environment for instantiating server objects and passing requests to them.

8. The object adapter searches the implementation repository to find an already running instance of the required server object or, otherwise, instantiates and registers the newly instantiated server object with the repository.

9. The object adapter passes the message to the appropriate server skeleton, which translates the IDL message into the message format of the specific server object.

10. The server object receives the message and acts on it.

6.11.1.6 Dynamic Method Invocation

Dynamic method invocation is used when the client object requests a service (by description) but does not know the specific object ID or class of object to satisfy the request. This supports runtime-configured applications where the relationships between components are not determined at design time, that is, components are not tightly coupled (see the discussion on component coupling in Chapter 5).

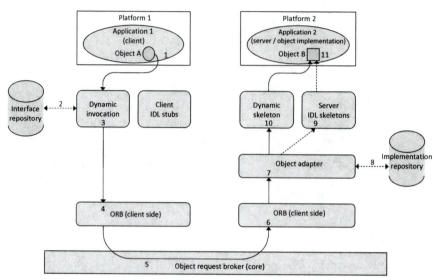

FIGURE 6.43

The mechanism of dynamic method invocation.

Figure 6.43 illustrates how dynamic method invocation takes place. The sequence of steps shown in the figure begins at the point where a client identifies a particular implementation object that it wishes to send a method invocation request to. The steps are as follows:

1. The client object sends the message to the dynamic method invocation utility.
2. The dynamic method invocation utility accesses an interface repository (a runtime database) that contains IDL descriptions of the methods associated with various objects. The dynamic method invocation utility identifies one or more objects that have methods that could satisfy the request.
3. The request is converted to IDL code and routed to those objects.
4. The IDL code is passed via the client-side ORB (for the client platform) to the network.
5. The message is passed over the network through the ORB core, using the GIOP and IIOP as with the static invocation mechanism.
6. The message is received by the client-side ORB (this time on the server-object's platform).
7. The message is passed via the object adapter to the appropriate object (which may need to be instantiated).
8. The object adapter searches the implementation repository to find an already running instance of the required server object or, otherwise, instantiates and registers the newly instantiated server object with the repository.
9. If the appropriate object on the server has an IDL skeleton, the message is passed via the server skeleton and thereby translated from IDL code into the message format of the target (server) object.
10. In the more complicated case, when the server object does not have an appropriate skeleton, the dynamic skeleton utility dynamically creates a skeleton for the server object and translates the IDL code into the message format of the target (server) object.
11. The server object receives the message and acts on it.

6.11.1.7 OMG Interface Definition Language (IDL)

The use of an IDL in middleware such as CORBA is a very powerful concept for application interoperability and in particular solves the problem of interoperability between objects written in different programming languages (and thus achieves implementation transparency). CORBA uses the OMG IDL, which is a specific instance of an IDL with support for several target languages including C, C++, and Java.

The OMG IDL is used to describe the interfaces to objects so that method calls can be made to them. IDL descriptions completely and unambiguously define all aspects of component call interfaces, including the parameters, their types, and the direction in which each parameter is passed (into the method or returned from the method). Using these interface definitions, a client component can make a method call on a remote object without knowing the language the remote object is written in and also without needing to know how the functionality is implemented; the IDL description does not include the internal behavior of the method.

The IDL interface definitions are needed during the automatic generation of the code (see below) in order that stubs and skeletons can automatically be generated and compiled into the application code. This removes the need for application developers to be concerned with communication and interoperability aspects and instead focus only on the business logic of components, as if all calls were between local objects.

See also the further discussion on IDL in a later section.

6.11.1.8 CORBA Application Development

Middleware such as CORBA provides design-time transparency to application developers and runtime transparency to applications and objects. The use of CORBA simplifies the application developer's role in building distributed applications because it facilitates interoperability between components and also provides mechanisms to take care of the networking and connectivity aspects.

The application development approach encouraged that developers write their code as if all components were to run locally and therefore not require any networking support. The developer must still take care of the separation of concerns and distribute the application logic across the components appropriately. Where there are static design-time-known relationships between components, these are built-in (this implies the use of the static invocation mechanism at runtime). So if, for example, a particular component X is known to need to contact component Y to perform some specific function, then this relationship will be built into the application logic, in the same way as static relationships between objects are embedded in nondistributed applications.

The application developer must however perform an additional step, which is to describe the interfaces between the components using OMG IDL.

6.11.1.9 Automatic Code Generation in CORBA

The user-provided IDL code specifies the interfaces of objects and thus defines how their methods are invoked. Based on the IDL definitions, the IDL compiler generates the client stubs and server implementation skeletons.

The stub and skeleton provide an object-specific interface between the object and the ORB, as shown in Figure 6.40. Significantly, this removes the need for the application developer to write any communication code, and because of transparencies provided by the various CORBA components and mechanisms, the application developer does not need to be concerned with any aspects of distribution

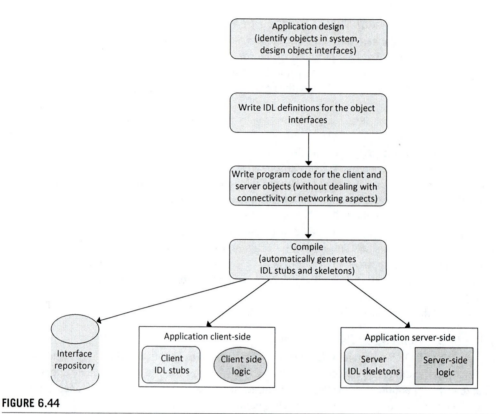

FIGURE 6.44

The sequence of steps to develop a CORBA application.

such as the relative locality or remoteness of objects and network addresses. The stubs and skeletons automatically include the necessary links between the objects and the CORBA mechanisms that deal with the actual network communication automatically.

The server implementation skeleton is used by the ORB and object adapter to make calls to method implementations. The IDL definitions provide the object adapter with the required format of each specific method call.

Figure 6.44 illustrates the basic sequence of steps in the development of CORBA applications. The developer's role is simplified because the complexity of the distribution, networking, and connectivity is handled automatically by CORBA's mechanisms that are driven by the IDL.

6.11.2 INTERFACE DEFINITION LANGUAGE (IDL)

The IDL approach separates the interface part of program code from the implementation part. This is very significant for distributed systems because these are two types of concern that should ideally be treated in different ways. Application developers need to focus on the business logic aspects of application behavior (i.e., the implementation). The separation of interface from implementation facilitates automation of interface-related aspects such as connectivity and communication functionality, through middleware services.

There are various IDLs, used in specific middlewares, but they tend to be similar in terms of the role they perform, the ways in which they are used, and their syntax. CORBA uses the OMG IDL, for example, while Microsoft defined the Microsoft IDL (MIDL) primarily for use with its other technologies such as OLE, COM, and DCOM.

An IDL is designed to be programming language-independent, that is, it defines the interface of a component only in terms of the names of methods and the parameter types that are passed in and out of the method, regardless of whether the method is implemented in C++, C#, Java, or some other language. An IDL explicitly identifies the type and direction of each parameter. The type values supported are the same in general as most languages and include int, float, double, bool, and string. The direction is defined explicitly (as being an input to the method (in), an output from the method (out) or a parameter that is passed in and modified, and the new value output (in, out)) instead of implicit representation in which the position of the parameter in addition to the use of special symbols (such as * and &) indicates the way the parameters are used. An example of an (in, out) parameter in conventional C usage is a value passed into a method by reference, whereby the called method may modify the variable (this is the same instance of the variable that is visible to the calling method, so the change in value will be seen when the call returns). In addition to the basic description of parameters, IDL can provide additional constraints (such as maximum and minimum values). Figure 6.45 puts the use of IDL into context with a simple example.

Figure 6.45 provides a very simple example of the OMG IDL syntax. Part A shows part of the C++ header file for a simple class called simple MathUtils. There are two simple member function declarations shown. Part B of the figure shows the equivalent OMG IDL representation. Notice that the IDL representation is quite similar to the C++ header file format; this is not surprising when you consider that the header file is essentially an interface specification and does not contain implementation detail. In the particular example shown (for C++), the IDL uses the term interface to replace class and places the parameter direction ahead of each listed parameter, to avoid any language-specific implied meaning. IDL does use implication in regard to the parameter to the left of the method name, which is implied to be an out parameter by its position (as with many high-level languages).

Part of a C++ class header showing two function prototypes	`class SimpleMathUtils`
	`{`
	`...`
	`int Add2(int iFirst, int iSecond);`
	`float Add3f(float fFirst, float fSecond, float fThird);`
	`...`
	`}`

(a)	

The equivalent representation in OMG IDL	`interface SimpleMathUtils`
	`{`
	`...`
	`int Add2(in int iFirst, in int iSecond);`
	`float Add3f(in float fFirst, in float fSecond, in float fThird);`
	`...`
	`}`

(b)	

FIGURE 6.45

Comparison of programming language-specific interface definitions and IDL.

The implementation of the application logic is contained within the components themselves and is not exposed at its interfaces; therefore, IDL does not need to represent the implementation. So for the example shown in Figure 6.45, the IDL representation does not show how the addition methods work. This detail is not required by the calling component, which only needs the information shown in the interface definition in order to invoke the methods; for this reason, IDL does not have language constructs to represent the implementation.

The most significant difference between the two representations of the same interface in Figure 6.45 is that the C++ specific one is only understood by a C++ compiler, and therefore, only another component written in C++ could call the methods. The IDL representation can be used with any of the supported languages (which are many) so the fact that the simple MathUtils server object has been developed in C++ does not place any restrictions on the language used to develop a client object that calls its methods.

6.11.3 EXTENSIBLE MARKUP LANGUAGE

Extensible Markup Language (XML) is a standard, platform-independent markup language that defines format rules for encoding data. A main strength is that it provides an unambiguous way to represent structured data for use within applications, in particular as a format for storage and for communication in messages.

XML's portability across different platforms makes it ideal for representing data in distributed systems, overcoming heterogeneity. The XML is also extensible, which enables application-specific and application domain-specific variations of the basic language to be created, a classic example of which is the Chemical Markup Language (CML); this is used to describe complex molecular structures in a standardized and unambiguous document format. XML's characteristics have led to its popular use in many applications, as well as being the data representation method of choice in other protocols such as SOAP and Web services. A simple example of the use of XML to encode structured data is provided in Figure 6.46.

```
<?xml version="1.0" encoding="UTF-8"?>
<CUSTOMER_LIST>
  <CUSTOMER>
    <CUST_ID> 000129365</CUST_ID>
    <CUST_NAME>John Jones</CUST_NAME>
    <CUST_ADDR>Victoria British_Columbia Canada</CUST_ADDR>
    <CUST_DOB>10_February_1976</CUST_DOB>
  </CUSTOMER>
  <CUSTOMER>
    <CUST_ID> 000031348</CUST_ID>
    <CUST_NAME>Mary Smith</CUST_NAME>
    <CUST_ADDR>Leeds Yorkshire England</CUST_ADDR>
    <CUST_DOB>22_May_1954</CUST_DOB>
  </CUSTOMER>
  <CUSTOMER>
    <CUST_ID> 000245170</CUST_ID>
    <CUST_NAME>Pierre Vert</CUST_NAME>
    <CUST_ADDR>Paris France</CUST_ADDR>
    <CUST_DOB>17_October_1982</CUST_DOB>
  </CUSTOMER>
</CUSTOMER_LIST>
```

FIGURE 6.46

XML encoding in a simple application example.

Figure 6.46 illustrates how XML provides a simple way in which to encode complex data structures in an unambiguous way. The data representation format not only is easy to parse within a computer program but also is human-readable, which contributes to usability significantly. Compare, for example, with simpler formats that could be considered alternatives, such as a comma-separated file in which each data field is separated by a delimiter such as a comma and the position in the list denotes the meaning of each field; this is illustrated in Figure 6.47.

Figure 6.47 presents the same data as encoded in Figure 6.46, but in a simple comma-separated list format. In this example, the field delimiter is a comma and the row delimiter is a semicolon. The comma-separated list format serves to illustrate the relative benefits of XML. The comma-separated list format is more efficient, but XML has several advantages: (1) It preserves the structure of the data. (2) It names each field explicitly, which makes the format more readable. (3) It supports repetition of several data items of the same type within a single data record; for example, consider extending both the XML and comma-separated representations of the customer data to encode customers' phone numbers. The XML format can easily deal with situations where a customer has zero, one, or more phone numbers, because each entry is explicitly labeled. However, the comma-separated format uses position to represent meaning so repeating or omitted fields are not so simple to encode.

6.11.4 JAVASCRIPT OBJECT NOTATION (JSON)

JSON is an efficient data-interchange format based on a subset of JavaScript and is both human-readable and straightforward for programs to create and parse. JSON is suitable for use in distributed systems because it uses a programming language-independent textual representation of data and thus provides implementation transparency in systems where multiple programming languages are used. JSON is a popular format for data interchange in Web applications.

A JSON script is organized in two levels. The outer level comprises a list of objects. Within this, each object is represented as a set of records, each expressed as an unordered list of name-value pairs delimited by commas. JSON is generally more concise than XML, a compromise between the simpler (raw) formats such as a comma-separated list and the highly structured XML. An application example of the JSON format is provided in Figure 6.48, using the same customer application as in Figures 6.46 and 6.47.

```
*CUSTOMER_LIST;
000129365,John Jones,Victoria British_Columbia Canada,10_February_1976;
000031348,Mary Smith,Leeds Yorkshire England,22_May_1954;
000245170,Pierre Vert,Paris France,17_October_1982;
```

FIGURE 6.47

Comma-separated list format—for comparison with XML.

```
JSON example
{" CUSTOMER_LIST ":[
    {"CUST_ID":"000129365", "CUST_NAME":"John Jones", "CUST_ADDR":"Victoria British_Columbia Canada", "CUST_DOB":"10_February_1976"},
    {"CUST_ID":"000031348", "CUST_NAME":"Mary Smith", "CUST_ADDR":"Leeds Yorkshire England", "CUST_DOB":"22_May_1954"},
    {"CUST_ID":"000245170", "CUST_NAME":"Pierre Vert", "CUST_ADDR":"Paris France", "CUST_DOB":"17_October_1982"}
]}
```

FIGURE 6.48

JSON encoding in a simple application example.

Figure 6.48 shows a JSON script that defines a single CUSTOMER_LIST object, which contains an array of 3 customer records. The example illustrates how JSON shares some efficiency characteristics with the comma-separated list format while also retaining the explicit labeling of XML, making it flexible with respect to the representation of complex data with repeating fields or omitted field values and enhancing human readability. The JSON usage of arrays and lists more naturally matches the data model used in most programming languages than XML does, and therefore, it is more efficient to parse.

6.11.5 WEB SERVICES AND REST

A Web service is a communication interface that supports interoperability in distributed systems using standard Internet protocols used widely in the World Wide Web (Web) and as such is naturally platform-independent. The Web Services Description Language (WSDL) is used to describe the functionality of a Web service (WSDL is a type of IDL based on XML).

Clients communicate with the Web service using the Simple Object Access Protocol (SOAP), which is also a platform-independent standard (see later text). The SOAP messages themselves are encoded using XML and transmitted using the http, two further standards. The service is addressed using its URL, which describes the specific service and also represents the address of the host computer.

A main class of Web services is those that are REST-compliant. These Web services use a fixed set of operations—PUT (create), GET (read), POST (update), and DELETE—to manipulate XML representations of Web resources (see "Representational State Transfer (REST)" below). There are also arbitrary Web services, which are not constrained by the rules of REST and can thus expose an arbitrary set of operations. A simple example of a Web service application is shown in Figure 6.49.

Figure 6.49 illustrates a simple Web service following the same Customer Details application scenario as the previous sections. The example shows a single stateless Web service with three GET methods {GetCustomerName, GetCustomerAddress, GetCustomerDOB}. The method requests are parameterized by the string value CustomerID. In other words, the Web service does not need to store any state concerning the client or the client's request; all the necessary information is self-contained in the request message. This is an important aspect that contributes to the scalability of Web services.

6.11.5.1 Representational State Transfer (REST)

REST is a set of guidelines that are designed to ensure high quality in applications such as Web services, in terms of simplicity, performance, and scalability. REST-compliant (or RESTful) Web services must have a client-server architecture and use a stateless communication protocol such as http.

The design of RESTful applications should respect the following four design principles:

1. Resource identification through URI: Resources that are accessible via a RESTful Web service should be identified by URIs. URIs represent a global Web-compliant-related address space.
2. Uniform interface: A fixed set of four operations—PUT, GET, POST, and DELETE—are provided to create, read, update, and delete resources, respectively. This restriction ensures clean, uncluttered, and universally understood interfaces.
3. Self-descriptive messages: Resources need to be represented in various formats, depending on the way they are to be manipulated and how their content is to be accessed. This requires that the representation of a resource in a message is decoupled from the actual resource itself and that the request and response messages identify the resource itself and either which operation is to be performed or the resulting value of the resource after the operation, respectively.

```
<%@ WebService language="C" class="CustomerDetails" %>

using System;
using System.Web.Services;
using System.Xml.Serialization;

[WebService(Namespace="http://www.widgets.org/customerdetails/WebServices/")]
public class customerdetails : WebService
{
  [WebMethod]
  public String GetCustomerName (String CustomerID)
  {

    ...
    return CustomerName;
  }
  [WebMethod]
  public String GetCustomerAddress (String CustomerID)
  {

    ...
    return CustomerAddress;
  }
  [WebMethod]
  public String GetCustomerDOB (String CustomerID)
  {

    ...
    return CustomerDOB;
  }
}
```

FIGURE 6.49

A simple Web service application example.

4. Stateful interactions through hyperlinks: The Web service itself, and thus each server-side interaction with a resource, should be stateless. This requires that request messages must be self-contained (i.e., the request message must contain sufficient information to contextualize the request so that it can be satisfied by the service without the need for any additional server-side-stored state concerning the client or its specific request).

6.11.6 THE SIMPLE OBJECT ACCESS PROTOCOL (SOAP)

The SOAP facilitates connectivity in heterogeneous systems and is used to exchange structured information in Web services. It uses several standard Internet protocols to achieve platform and operating system-independent message transmission and message content representation. Message transmission is usually based on either hypertext transfer protocol (http) or Simple Mail Transfer Protocol (SMTP).

http and the XML are used to achieve information exchange in a format that is both universally recognized and unambiguous in interpretation. SOAP defines how an http header and an XML file should be encoded to create a request message and the corresponding response message so that components of distributed applications can communicate. Figure 6.50 illustrates the use of SOAP with a simple application example.

SOAP request
(get customer name from ID)

```
POST /customerdetailsHTTP/1.0
Host: www.widgets.org
Content-Type: application/soap+xml; charset=utf-8
Content-Length:nnn

< ?xml version="1.0"?>
< soap:Envelope
xmlns:soap="http://www.w3.org/2001/12/soap-envelope"
soap:encodingStyle="http://www.w3.org/2001/12/soap-encoding">

  <soap:Bodyxmlns:m=" http://www.widgets.org/customerdetails ">
    <m:GetCustomerName>
      <m:CustomerID>000129365</m: CustomerID>
    </m: GetCustomerName>
  </soap:Body>
</soap:Envelope>
```

(a)

SOAP response
(return the requested
customer name)

```
HTTP/1.1 200 OK
Content-Type: application/soap+xml; charset=utf-8
Content-Length: nnn

< ?xml version="1.0"?>
< soap:Envelope
xmlns:soap="http://www.w3.org/2001/12/soap-envelope"
soap:encodingStyle="http://www.w3.org/2001/12/soap-encoding">

  <soap:Bodyxmlns:m=" http://www.widgets.org/customerdetails ">
    <m: GetCustomerNameResponse>
      <m: CustomerName>John Jones</m: CustomerName>
    </m: GetCustomerNameResponse>
  </soap:Body>
</soap:Envelope>
```

(b)

FIGURE 6.50

SOAP encoding in a simple application example.

Figure 6.50 provides a simple application example to illustrate the way in which SOAP combines HTML and XML to define unambiguous request and response message formats. Part A of the figure shows the SOAP request to get the name of a customer, based on a provided customer ID value. This is an http POST request type. Within the message, XML coding format is used to represent the structure of the request message data. Part B of the figure shows the corresponding response message.

6.12 DETERMINISTIC AND NONDETERMINISTIC ASPECTS OF DISTRIBUTED SYSTEMS

Deterministic behavior essentially means predictable. If we know the initial conditions of a deterministic function, we can predict the outcome, whether it be a behavior or the result of a calculation.

Nondeterministic behavior arises in systems in which there are sufficient numbers of interacting components and sources of randomness that it is not possible to predict the future states precisely. Natural systems tend to be nondeterministic; examples include behavior in insect colonies, weather systems, and species population sizes. Human-oriented nondeterministic system examples include economies and crowd behavior. These systems are sensitive to their starting conditions and the actual sequences of interactions that occur within the system and possibly even the timing of those interactions. For such systems, it is usually possible to predict an expected range of outcomes, with varying confidence levels, rather than a knowable particular outcome. Computer simulations of nondeterministic systems may have to be run many times in order to gain usable results, with each run having slightly different starting conditions and yielding one possible outcome. Patterns in the set of outcomes may be used to predict the most likely of many possible futures.

For example, a weather forecasting algorithm is very complex and uses a large data set as its starting point in order to forecast a weather sequence. It is actually a simulation, computing a sequence of future states based on current and recent conditions. There may be some tuning parameters that affect the algorithm's sensitivity to certain characteristics of the input data. As there are so many factors affecting the accuracy of the weather forecast and also the fact that we cannot capture all the possible data needed with equal accuracy across all samples (sensors and/or their placement may be imperfect), there is always an element of error in the result. If we run the simulation just once, we may get a very good forecast, but it may also be poor (because of the varying sensitivity to specific weather histories and varying extents of dynamism in the weather systems). So although we may have the best forecast we are going to get, we cannot be confident that that is the case. If we change the tuning parameters very slightly and run the simulation again, we may get a similar or distinctly different result. Running the simulation many times with slightly different settings will give us a large number of outcomes, but hopefully, they are clustered together such that if somehow averaged, they provide a good approximation of what the weather will actually do. This is an example of a nondeterministic computation that hopefully yields a valuable result.

Distributed computer systems are themselves complex systems with many interacting parts. Nondeterministic behavior arises due to a large number of unpredictable characteristics of systems. For example, network traffic levels are continuously fluctuating, and this leads to different queue lengths building up, which in turn affects the delay to packets and also the probability of packets being dropped because a queue is full. Even a single hardware component can contribute nondeterministic behavior; consider the operation of a hard disk. Disk seek time is dependent on the rotation delay, which depends on where the disk is (in an angular sense) at the point of starting the seek and also the relative distance between the current track and one the head has to move to. These variations in starting conditions affect every block read from the disk so it is more likely that disk read times will vary each time than they will be exactly the same. The runtime of even a simple process depends on the sequence of low-level scheduling decisions made by the operating system, which in turn depend on the set of other processes present and the behavior of those processes. Therefore, executing a single process multiple times can lead to different runtimes, arising from the combination of differences in scheduling decisions, disk access latency, and communication latency.

The message for designers and developers of distributed applications and systems is that even if your algorithms are entirely deterministic in their operation and even if your data are complete and accurate, the underlying computing systems and networks are not perfect and not perfectly predictable. A component failure can happen at any time, a network message can be corrupted, the load on a processing host computer can change suddenly leading to increased latency of service, and so on. Seeking to eradicate all unpredictable behavior is futile, and the assumption of determinism is dangerous. You cannot prevent certain types of faults, and you cannot in general predict them. Instead, focus your design effort on making applications robust and fault-tolerant.

6.13 END OF CHAPTER EXERCISES

6.13.1 QUESTIONS

Q1. Scalability and interaction complexity

    (a) What is the level of interaction complexity in a system in which each component interacts with approximately half of the other components in the system?

    (b) What is the formula for calculating the number of separate interactions that occur?

    (c) How many separate interactions occur if there are 10 components in the system?

    (d) How many separate interactions occur if there are 50 components in the system?

    (e) How many separate interactions occur if there are 100 components in the system?

Q2. Scalability and interaction complexity

    (a) What is the level of interaction complexity in a system in which each component interacts with approximately four other components in the system?

    (b) What is the formula for calculating the number of separate interactions that occur?

    (c) How many separate interactions occur if there are 10 components in the system?

    (d) How many separate interactions occur if there are 50 components in the system?

    (e) How many separate interactions occur if there are 100 components in the system?

Q3. Scalability

Comment on the relative scalability of the two systems described in questions 1 and 2.

Q4. Implementation transparency

    (a) How does IDL contribute to implementation transparency?

    (b) Why does IDL contain only interface definitions and not implementation detail?

Q5. Concurrency transparency

    (a) What is the main challenge when facilitating concurrent access to shared resources?

    (b) How do transactions contribute to concurrency transparency?

Q6. Location transparency

    (a) Why is location transparency one of the most common requirements of distributed applications?

    (b) How does a name service contribute to the achievement of location transparency?

Q7. Replication transparency

    (a) What are the main motivations for replication of data and/or services?

    (b) What is the main challenge when implementing replication?

    (c) How does the two-phase commit protocol contribute to the achievement of robust replication mechanisms?

6.13.2 PROGRAMMING EXERCISES

Programming Exercise #D1: This programming challenge relates to the use of directory services to provide location transparency. In particular, it involves the use of the directory service used in activity D1 (which is built into the Distributed Systems Workbench).

    The task: Modify the client and server components of the use-case game so that the server can be registered with the directory service and the client can subsequently use the directory service to obtain the IP address and port details of the game server:

- For the server side: You need to consider at what point the game server is registered with the name service. This is best done automatically during the game server initialization.

- For the client side: There are two ways you could do this—you could have a button "contact directory service" on the client user interface; alternatively, a more transparent approach is for the client to contact the directory service automatically when the game client is started.

Note: the directory service can be run from within the Distributed Systems Workbench.

The interface to the directory service is defined as follows:

Protocol

UDP

Port number allocations

From_DIRECTORY_SERVICE_PORT 8002The port the application client must listen on for DirectoryServiceReply messages sent in response to RESOLVE request messages.

To_DIRECTORY_SERVICE_PORT 8008The port that application clients use to send RESOLVE messages to the directory service (broadcast is used).

The port that application servers use to send REGISTER messages to the directory service (broadcast is used).

Message Structures

The message structure returned by the directory service in response to RESOLVE request messages is shown in Figure 6.51.

Message Formats

Client RESOLVE request messages are encoded as a character string containing "RESOLVE:server_name" where server_name can be a maximum of 30 characters. An example is RESOLVE:GameServer.

Server REGISTER messages are encoded as a character string containing "REGISTER:server_name:port" where server_name can be a maximum of 30 characters and the port number is expressed in text form. An example is REGISTER:GameServer:8004.

Note that for both message types, the IP address of the sending process is extracted by the directory service, directly from the header of the received message; the game component does not have to explicitly send it.

An example solution is provided in the programs: CaseStudyGame_Client_DS and CaseStudyGame_Server_DS.

Programming Exercise #D2: This programming challenge relates to the use of election algorithms to provide robustness and failure transparency. In particular, it is related to the election algorithm activity D3.

The task: Implement the bully election algorithm.

```
struct DirectoryServiceReply {      // Requested service address
        unsigned char a1;           // IP address byte 1
        unsigned char a2;           // IP address byte 2
        unsigned char a3;           // IP address byte 3
        unsigned char a4;           // IP address byte 4
        unsigned int port;          // Port
};
```

FIGURE 6.51

The directory service reply message format.

The operation of the bully election algorithm has been discussed earlier in the chapter, the most important aspect of behavior being that there must only be one master-state instance present at any time. Here are some specific implementation details for guidance:

1. Assume that the elections will occur between processes in a local network, and therefore, broadcast communication can be used.
2. Assume that only one participating process will be present on each computer, and therefore, the IP address of the host computer can be used as the process' ID for the purposes of the election (as this is a simple way to ensure that IDs are unique).

An example solution is provided in the program BullyElectionAlgorithm.

6.13.3 ANSWERS TO END OF CHAPTER QUESTIONS

Q1. (Answer)

(a) Each of N components interacts with $N/2$ components, so interaction complexity is $O(N*N/2)$.
(b) The formula for the number of separate interactions is $N*N/4$. The number of interactions is half of the interaction intensity because each interaction involves two components.
(c) If there are 10 components in the system, there are 25 separate interactions.
(d) If there are 50 components in the system, there are 625 separate interactions.
(e) If there are 100 components in the system, there are 2500 separate interactions.

Q2. (Answer)

(a) Each of N components interacts with 4 components, so interaction complexity is $O(4N)$.
(b) The formula for the number of separate interactions is $2N$. The number of interactions is half of the interaction intensity because each interaction involves two components.
(c) If there are 10 components in the system, there are 20 separate interactions.
(d) If there are 50 components in the system, there are 100 separate interactions.
(e) If there are 100 components in the system, there are 200 separate interactions.

Q3. (Answer)

The system described in question 1 has a steep exponential interaction complexity, which potentially has a severe impact on scalability. The system described in question 2 has a linear interaction complexity and therefore is more scalable.

Q4. (Answer)

(a) IDL facilitates interoperability when components are developed using different programming languages. It does this by providing a universal intermediate representation of method call interfaces, which is language-independent.
(b) IDL only needs to represent call requests in a language-independent way and thus is only concerned with component interfaces. IDL does not define the behavior or internal logic of the communicating components, so there is no need for IDL to express any implementation detail.

Q5. (Answer)

    (a) The main challenge is maintaining consistency.

    (b) Transactions prevent overlapped access to shared resources. The properties of atomicity, consistency, isolation, and durability collectively ensure that the system is left in a consistent state after each access and/or update event has completed.

Q6. (Answer)

    (a) Components need to communicate with other components regardless of where they are located. There needs to be either an automated way to find the location of a component or alternatively a means of sending a message to another component through an intermediate service without the sender knowing the location of that component.

    (b) A name service resolves a component name (or a resource name) into its address. Therefore, the sender of a message only needs to initially know the identity of the target component and not where it is located.

Q7. (Answer)

    (a) Replication of data and/or services contributes to robustness, availability, responsiveness, and scalability.

    (b) Replication involves creating multiple copies of data resources and state information. This introduces the potential for the different instances of a replicated resource to become inconsistent. Therefore, maintaining consistency is the main challenge when implementing replication.

    (c) The two-phase commit protocol ensures that updates are performed at all replica instances of a data resource or at none of them, thus maintaining consistency.

6.13.4 LIST OF IN-TEXT ACTIVITIES

Activity number	Section	Description
D1	6.4.2	Experimentation with a Directory Service
D2	6.5.7	Exploring address resolution and the gethostbyname DNS resolver
D3	6.7.5	Exploring the behavior of an election algorithm and using an automated logging tool

6.13.5 LIST OF ACCOMPANYING RESOURCES

The following resources are referred to directly in the chapter text, the in-text activities, and/or the end of chapter exercises:

- Distributed Systems Workbench ("Systems Programming" edition)
- Source code
- Executable code

Program	Availability	Relevant sections of the chapter
Directory Service—Directory Server	Executable (application is built into the Distributed Systems Workbench)	Activity D1 (Sections 6.4.2 and 6.13.2)

Program	Availability	Relevant sections of the chapter
Directory Service—Application Server1	Executable (application is built into the Distributed Systems Workbench)	Activity D1 (Section 6.4.2)
Directory Service—Application Server2	Executable (application is built into the Distributed Systems Workbench)	Activity D1 (Section 6.4.2)
Directory Service—Application Server3	Executable (application is built into the Distributed Systems Workbench)	Activity D1 (Section 6.4.2)
Directory Service—Application Server4	Executable (application is built into the Distributed Systems Workbench)	Activity D1 (Section 6.4.2)
Directory Service—Client	Executable (application is built into the Distributed Systems Workbench)	Activity D1 (Section 6.4.2)
DNS_Resolver	Executable file Source code	Activity D2 (Section 6.5.7 and 6.5.8)
Emergent Election Algorithm	Executable (application is built into the Distributed Systems Workbench)	Activity D3 (Section 6.7.5)
Emergent Election Algorithm— event logger utility	Executable (application is built into the Distributed Systems Workbench)	Activity D3 (Section 6.7.5)
CaseStudyGame_Client_DS Extension of the case study game to use a directory service to facilitate client discovery of server. Solution to programming exercise D1	Executable file Source code	Section 6.13.2
CaseStudyGame_Server_DS Extension of the case study game to use a directory service to facilitate client discovery of server. Solution to programming exercise D1	Executable file Source code	Section 6.13.2
BullyElectionAlgorithm Solution to programming exercise D2	Executable file Source code	Section 6.13.2

CASE STUDIES: PUTTING IT ALL TOGETHER

7.1 RATIONALE AND OVERVIEW

The purpose of this chapter is to present two complete and detailed case studies, which place the various sections of theory and practice covered in the earlier parts of the book into application perspectives. The new case studies, in addition to the multiplayer distributed game case study, which has been used as a common thread throughout the earlier parts of the book, serve to integrate the four viewpoints (process, communication, resource, and architecture) to give a complete big-picture view of distributed applications animated through a series of diverse examples.

The case studies are (1) time service client and (2) event notification service. These have been chosen to so as to collectively provide wide coverage of the concepts discussed in the earlier chapters; each case study provides unique opportunities to demonstrate specific structural and behavioral characteristics and techniques to overcome the earlier identified challenges of distributed applications design and development.

For each use case, the design and development process is documented in detail with annotations to help the reader follow the various steps and understand the choices available and decisions taken. The full program code is provided.

7.2 INTRODUCTION TO THE USE CASES

The first case study is a client-side application for the Network Time Protocol (NTP) service provided by the National Institute of Standards and Technology (NIST). NTP has been described in Chapter 6.

This case study provides an interesting example of a situation where a developer must design an application that integrates with a preexisting service with a predefined interface. In such cases, the developer must ensure strict conformance to the prepublished interface specification. In the case of NTP, the communication protocol operates on a request-reply basis with a fixed message format. This request-reply nature of the protocol implicitly defines the interaction mechanism.

The case study also demonstrates the use of a DNS resolver to locate the IP address of the required NTP server instance, an example of refactoring, the creation of a software library to modularize the logic and facilitate code reuse, and the creation of two different user front-end components, which change the user interface but use the same library methods and thus have the same underlying functionality.

The second case study is an event notification service (ENS), complete with a set of application components, which serve as publisher clients and consumer clients of the ENS. The ENS decouples the application components (the publishers and consumers) such that they never communicate directly. The ENS does not need to know which events will be published or the meaning of those events; it simply stores event type-value pairs. When a new event type or new value of an existing event type is published, the ENS updates its tables. Event values are pushed out to all clients that have subscribed to (registered an interest in) the respective event type. The ENS is a service that can be employed by multiple different applications simultaneously; it does not need to know which applications are using it or what their purpose is.

The use of an ENS has design-time benefits in that a consumer component does not need to know the identity of a publisher that will generate the event data and vice versa. Component design is thus simpler, faster, and safer in the sense that it will not have built-in dependencies on specific other components. The ENS provides runtime flexibility and facilitates dynamic logical configuration in terms of publisher-consumer relationships between components.

The second case study also demonstrates the use of a directory service (DS) to facilitate dynamic binding of components and thus provides an example of a hierarchical service model (the ENS server self-registers with the DS, and ENS clients then contact the DS to get the address of the ENS server), interoperability between heterogeneous components developed in multiple different languages, and serialization of language-specific representations of data structures into implementation-neutral (byte array) representations of the same data structure.

7.3 CASE STUDY #1: TIME SERVICE CLIENT (WITH LIBRARY)

This case study is concerned with the design and development of a client-side application, which obtains a current timestamp value, on demand, from a trusted time service hosted on the Internet.

7.3.1 LEARNING OUTCOMES ASSOCIATED WITH THE CASE STUDY

This case study encompasses several important aspects of distributed applications design, structure, and behavior. Subject matter includes the following:

- A practical example of the client-server architecture
- A practical example of a request-reply protocol
- A practical example of refactoring to separate business logic and user interface logic
- The development of a code library
- Incorporation of library codes into application projects
- An example of the use of a DNS resolver to resolve domain names into IP addresses
- A detailed example of documentation of the design and development processes
- An example of the use of the UDP communication protocol at the transport layer
- An example of the use of the NTP communication protocol at the application layer

Note that this case study has been implemented in three phases and that the documentation presented relates to the third phase, in which the business logic for the client-side interaction with the time service is separated from the user interface front end and placed into a software library. The three phases of development are described later, in Section 7.3.7.

7.3.2 REQUIREMENTS ANALYSIS

This section identifies the functional and nonfunctional requirements of the time service client application.

- Trustable, reliable, and future-proofed. The application must use a standard, popular, and well-supported time service. NIST provides the Internet Time Service (ITS), which comprises several different time services. Some of these, such as TIME and DAYTIME, are outdated and depreciated to some extent; the currently recommended network time protocol of choice is NTP. The case study example will thus use NTP.
- Flexible and loose-coupled. The application must not be dependent on any specific NIST time server. The application must be able to use different time server instances if any particular one is not available or has had an IP address change. The case study example will thus embed a DNS resolver so that NIST servers can be selected based on their domain name URL.
- Responsive. There must be low-latency end-to-end, that is, from when the timestamp is requested to when it is displayed to the user. This is because the data (being the current time value) are highly delay-sensitive. The client's operation and especially the way the communication aspect is managed in the library component must be designed accordingly.
- Robust. The NTP client side should be able to continue functioning despite a number of server-side problems, as well as communication problems. Examples of problems that could occur are as follows: the NTP server crashes, the service domain name used is incorrect and cannot be resolved to the IP address of an NIST server, the UDP-transported NTP request message is lost or corrupted, and the NTP server response message is lost or corrupted.
- Modular architecture. There is a need to support the integration of the time service client behavior into a variety of applications that require accurate timestamps. This suggests that the core NTP client functionality should be deployed in the form of a library. It is also necessary to be able to build simple self-contained NTP client applications for testing and evaluation of the library functionality.
- Efficient. As the NTP client side will be developed as a library module, it is very important that the NTP client logic should be implemented with the lowest possible complexity code, with only the required functionality and using the least possible resources in terms of processing time and also network bandwidth. The library module interface must be as simple as possible, exposing only a minimal set of methods required to configure the module and to instigate NTP timestamp requests.

7.3.3 ARCHITECTURE AND CODE STRUCTURE

The application is designed around a library component, which deals with the core behavior. This comprises setting up the local communication resources (i.e., creating a socket and configuring it to operate in nonblocking mode), resolving the domain name of an NIST time server to its IP address (this requires the use of a DNS resolver), and the actual communication with the NTP server instance located at the resolved IP address. The communication methods within the library that perform sending an NTP request and receiving an NTP response must always return a result within a short time frame; even when the NTP server does not respond, the library module must continue to operate and must not crash or freeze. The library logic has been kept as simple as possible and comprises a single class as shown in Figure 7.1.

Figure 7.1 shows the CNTP_Client class template. The NTP client library component is initialized when the constructor CNTP_Client() is called; this initializes the socket that will be used to communicate with the NTP server. There are two internal state variables: (1) the IP address of a specific

```
CNTP_Client

m_TimeService_SockAddr : SOCKADDR_IN
m_NTP_Timestamp : NTP_Timestamp_Data

CNTP_Client(pbSocketOpenSuccess : bool*)
ResolveURLtoIPaddress(cStrURL : char*) : SOCKADDR_IN
Get_NTP_Timestamp(pNTP_Timestamp : NTP_Timestamp_Data*) : unsigned int
Send_TimeService_Request() : bool
Receive(pNTP_Timestamp : NTP_Timestamp_Data*) : bool
```

FIGURE 7.1

The CNTP_Client class (the core of the NTP client library).

```
struct NTP_Timestamp_Data {
    unsigned long lUnixTime;   // Seconds since 1970 (secsSince1900 - Seventy Years)
    unsigned long lHour;
    unsigned long lMinute;
    unsigned long lSecond;
};
```

FIGURE 7.2

The NTP_Timestamp_Data structure returned by the Get_NTP_Timestamp() method of the library.

NTP server, which is set when the application component calls the ResolveURLtoIPaddress() method with the URL of an NIST server as the passed-in parameter, and (2) the timestamp data structure NTP_Timestamp_Data (see Figure 7.2), which is created in the library based on received NTP time-stamps, which are encoded in a raw format as the number of seconds since the beginning of the year 1900. This structure is returned from the library as the result of an application component making a timestamp request by calling the Get_NTP_Timestamp() method. The Send_TimeService:Request() and Receive() methods are used internally to structure the communication logic and handle the NTP server connectivity side of the library. These two methods are not exposed on the application component interface of the library.

The case study includes two application components, either of which can be combined with the NTP client library component to build a specific time service client application program. The application components differ in terms of the user interface they provide but use the library functionality internally in the same way. The external connectivity to the NTP service is managed by the library component and not the application components, and therefore, this aspect is identical in both of the resulting application programs.

The first of the two application components provides a graphical user interface (GUI); see Figure 7.3. The template of the core class of this application component is shown in Figure 7.4.

Figure 7.4 shows the template of the CCaseStudy_TimeServiceClient_GUIDlg class. This is the core class of the GUI application component. Only the key detail that relates to the integration with the library component is included; user interface-specific details such as controls (buttons, list boxes, etc.) are omitted. The m_pNTP_Client variable is a pointer to an instance of the library module, which is initialized when the class constructor CCaseStudy_TimeServiceClient_GUIDlg() runs. Whenever the user selects an NIST server domain name from the provided list of URLs (see Figure 7.3), the

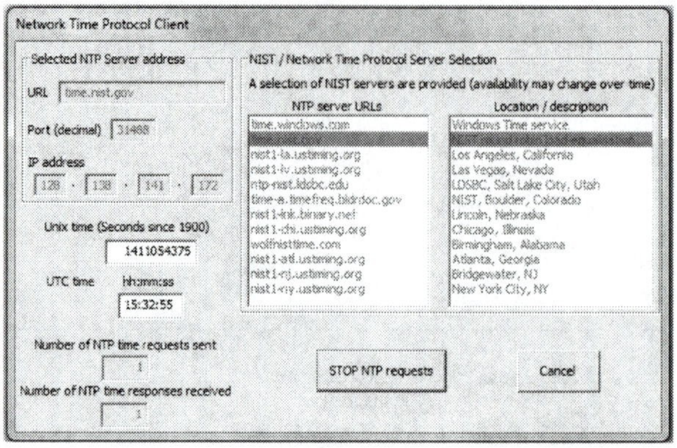

FIGURE 7.3

The GUI time service client user interface.

```
CCaseStudy_TimeServiceClient_GUIDlg
-----------------------------------------------------------
m_pNTP_Client : CNTP_Client*
m_NTP_Timestamp : NTP_Timestamp_Data
-----------------------------------------------------------
CCaseStudy_TimeServiceClient_GUIDlg(pParent : CWnd*)
OnLbnSelchangeNtpServerUrlList()
OnTimer(nIDEvent : UINT)
```

FIGURE 7.4

The CCaseStudy_TimeServiceClient_GUIDlg class.

OnLbnSelchangeNtpServerUrlList() event handler method is called, which passes the domain name to the library to be resolved to its respective IP address. NTP time requests are made (via the NTP client library) at 5 s intervals in the OnTimer event handler method, which is controlled by a programmable timer.

The second application component provides a textual user interface; see Figure 7.5. This procedural application component is represented in a class template-like format in Figure 7.6.

Figure 7.6 shows the key aspects of the console time service client user interface component, in terms of its interface with the NTP client library. The m_pNTP_Client variable is a pointer to an instance of the library module, which is initialized in the InitialiseLibrary() function. The ResolveTimeServiceDomainNameTOIPAddress() function passes the URL of the user-chosen NIST time server to the library. NTP time requests are made (via the NTP client library) at 5 s intervals from the _tmain() function.

Figure 7.7 shows the sequence diagram for the GUI application, which comprises the GUI front-end component and the NTP client library. Compare this with Figure 7.8, which shows the sequence diagram for the textual interface-based application, which comprises the console front-end component and the NTP client library.

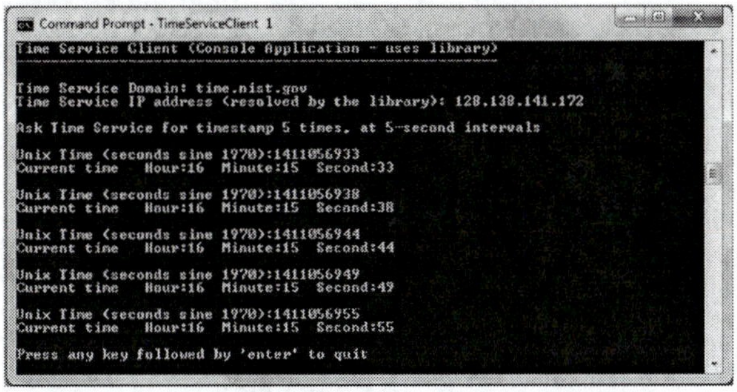

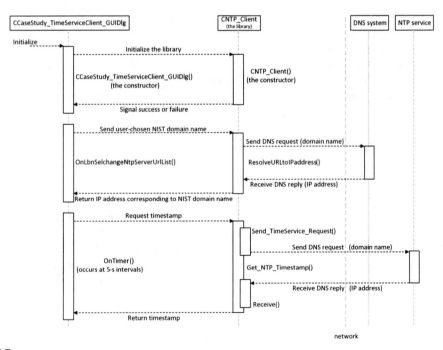

FIGURE 7.5

The console (text-based) time service client user interface.

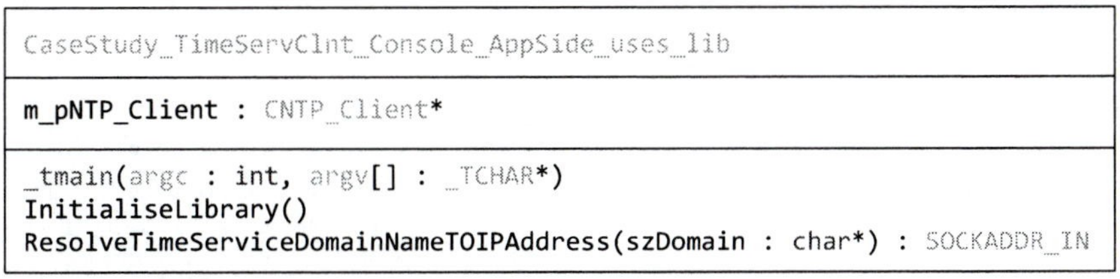

```
CaseStudy_TimeServClnt_Console_AppSide_uses_lib

m_pNTP_Client : CNTP_Client*

_tmain(argc : int, argv[] : _TCHAR*)
InitialiseLibrary()
ResolveTimeServiceDomainNameTOIPAddress(szDomain : char*) : SOCKADDR_IN
```

FIGURE 7.6

The console version of the time service client.

FIGURE 7.7

Sequence diagram for the GUI front-end interaction with the NTP client library.

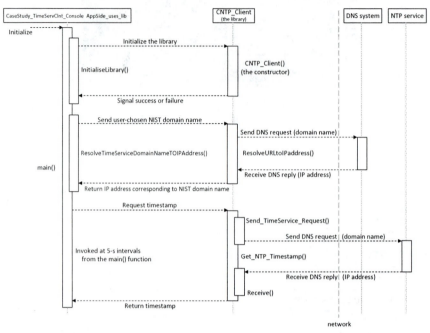

FIGURE 7.8

Sequence diagram for the console front-end interaction with the NTP client library.

Figures 7.7 and 7.8 show the interactions between each of the two client application front ends and the NTP client library. The front-end applications are different in terms of their code structure and their internal behavior. The most significant difference is that the GUI-based front end is event-driven (i.e., its behavior is driven by events such as the user's mouse clicks or keyboard entries, as well as by timer-driven events), while the console application is procedural (i.e., it begins with a main function, from which other functions are called in a sequence to carry out the logic of the program). Despite the differences in the two front ends, it is clear from these diagrams that the library is used in the same way in each case:

- The library is first initialized (its constructor method is invoked). This involves setting up the communication socket, which will be used to send requests to, and receive responses from, the NTP service. This socket is set to work in nonblocking mode.
- The library resolves the domain name of the NIST service, within the ResolveURLtoIPaddress() method. It uses gethostbyname (which is a DNS resolver) internally and contacts the external DNS service automatically (see Chapter 6 for details of how DNS works).
- The library makes NTP timestamp requests, from the Get_NTP_Timestamp() method to the external NTP service.

The sequence diagrams also illustrate an important aspect of transparency; the two external services that are used, DNS and NTP, are represented as single objects that respond to requests. This is the external view that the developer is presented with although each of these services is internally quite complex. A component diagram is provided in Figure 7.9 to further reinforce this point.

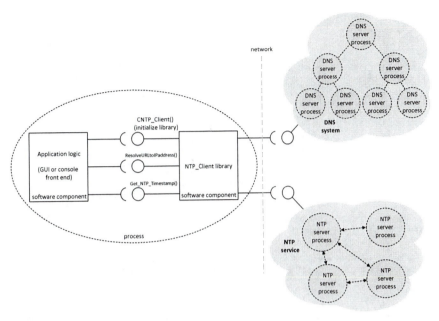

FIGURE 7.9

Component diagram showing the process—internal and external connectivities.

Figure 7.9 (left-hand side) shows how the client application is composed of two software components: one of the front-end user interfaces and the NTP client library, which deals with all of the external connectivity and communication with the two external services used (DNS and NTP). The figure (right-hand side) also depicts the external services as pseudocomponents; essentially, the entire DNS service is abstracted as a single method on a single component (and likewise for NTP). In reality, these two services have high complexity in terms of the number of server entities and the way they interconnect and synchronize. However, the whole point of transparency provision is to make services such as these accessible without knowing any of the details of their internal workings.

7.3.4 SEPARATION OF CONCERNS

Careful separation of concerns along component boundaries contributes benefits in terms of clear design and ease of implementation (especially in terms of reducing the extent of coupling and interaction between software components). It also facilitates modular reuse of functionality and can simplify testing.

The NTP service provides a clearly defined function, and in the use case scenario presented here, the client side is a user interface front end, the functionality of which is limited to displaying the timestamp value provided by the NTP service. However, the client-side application functionality can be broken down at a finer level. There are two software components, one of which provides the user interface and the other (the NTP_Client library) provides the business logic necessary to locate and connect to the NTP service, to make NTP requests to the service, and to receive and interpret the responses from that service. Figure 7.10 puts this two-level view of the separation of concerns into perspective.

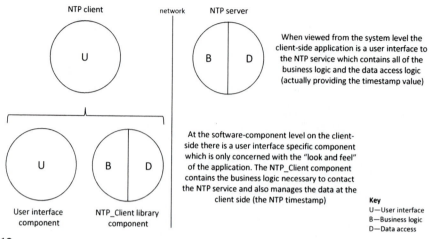

FIGURE 7.10

Mapping the strands of functionality at the system level and the software component level.

Figure 7.10 shows that the mapping of the different functional strands is dependent on the level at which it is applied. At the highest level, the NTP client application only provides user interface functionality, but internally, the logic is split between two components, and at this finer level, we can separate out the purely user interface-related logic from the business logic of managing the communication with external services and managing the data resource, which in this case is the timestamp.

7.3.5 COUPLING AND BINDING BETWEEN COMPONENTS

The coupling between the NTP client and NTP service can be described as loose (because the client can connect to any instance of the NTP service, based on a runtime-provided NIST service domain name) and direct (because once the service instance is decided, the communication takes place directly between the client and server components).

7.3.5.1 Client Binding to Time Servers

NIST has a number of time servers deployed with well-known domain names, but this does not mean that the IP addresses of servers are fixed, and thus, a chosen domain name must be resolved to an IP address, rather than hard coding or long-term caching. Binding can be considered to occur in two phases. Firstly, a user-selected URL is resolved to the IP address of the respective NTP time server, courtesy of the DNS service, and then the IP address is used to send point-to-point UDP segments containing NTP request messages to the NTP server.

7.3.6 COMMUNICATION ASPECTS OF THE DESIGN

NTP uses a request-reply protocol. A fixed well-known port number 123 is used to identify the NTP server process on a particular computer. The host computer is identified by its IP address (which is in turn derived from a NIST-publicized domain name; see preceding section).

7.3.6.1 Message Types and Semantics

There are two message types: an NTP request and an NTP response. The NTP request is only valid when sent to an NTP server, and an NTP response is only valid when received from an NTP server as a response to an NTP request that was sent a short time earlier. The communication semantics are thus simple.

7.3.6.2 NTP Protocol Definition Unit (PDU)

Both the NTP request message and NTP response message are encoded as fixed-size arrays of 64 bytes. The NTP PDU format overlays the linear byte array with a structure that collects the bytes into various fixed length fields and thus maps out the application meaning of the message content. Figure 7.11 shows the NTP PDU, which defines the format of NTP request and response messages.

	Bits 0-7			Bits 8-15	Bits 16-23	Bits 24-31
Bytes 0-3	LI	VN	Mode	Stratum (8 bits)	Poll (8 bits)	Precision (8 bits)
Bytes 4-7	Root delay (32 bits)					
Bytes 8-11	Root dispersion (32 bits)					
Bytes 12-15	Reference identifier (32 bits)					
Bytes 16-19	Reference timestamp (64 bits)					
Bytes 20-23						
Bytes 24-27	Originate timestamp (64 bits)					
Bytes 28-31						
Bytes 32-35	Receive timestamp (64 bits)					
Bytes 36-39						
Bytes 40-43	Transmit timestamp (64 bits) in format :- whole seconds (32 bits) : fraction of second (32 bits)					
Bytes 44-47						
Bytes 48-51	Authenticator (optional, 128 bits)					
Bytes 52-55						
Bytes 56-59						
Bytes 60-63						

FIGURE 7.11

The PDU format of the NTP protocol. LI = Leap Indicator: A 2-bit code, which indicates that a leap second will be inserted or deleted in the last minute of the current day. This field is significant only in an NTP server response message. VN = Version Number: A 3-bit code that indicates the NTP version number. Mode: A 3-bit code indicating the protocol mode. When sending an NTP request, the NTP client sets this field to 3 (which signifies the message originated on the client side). When responding to a client request, the NTP server sets the mode value to 4 (which signifies the message originated on the server side). When operating in broadcast mode, the NTP server sets the mode value to 5 (which signifies broadcast). Stratum: An 8-bit value indicating the type of reference clock (1 means primary reference, such as synchronized by a radio clock, and values 2-15 mean a secondary reference, which is synchronized by NTP). Poll: An eight-bit value expressed as an exponent of two, indicating the maximum interval between successive messages. Values are from 4 to 17, meaning maximum intervals of 16, 32, 64, 128 ... seconds up to 131,072 s (which is approximately 36 h). Precision: An 8-bit value representing the clock's precision, expressed as an exponent of two. Values are from −6 to −20, meaning precision values of one sixty-fourth of a second or better. Root Delay: A 32-bit value indicating the round-trip delay to the primary reference source in seconds. Root Dispersion: A 32-bit unsigned value indicating the maximum error, which can be up to several hundred milliseconds. Reference Identifier: A 32-bit value identifying the particular reference source. For stratum 1 (primary server), the value is a four-character code, and for secondary servers, the value is the IPv4 address of the synchronization source. Reference Timestamp: The time the system clock was last set or corrected. Originate Timestamp: The time at which the request message was sent from the client (to the server). Receive Timestamp: The time the request arrived at the server (or the time the reply arrived at the client, depending on the message direction). Transmit Timestamp: The time the reply message was sent from the server (to the client). Authenticator: An optional value used with NTP authentication.

The NTP request message is populated as follows: The entire 48-byte array is zeroed out, and then the LI, Version, and Mode fields are set to the values 3, 4, and 3, respectively; this indicates that the message is an NTP version 4 message sent from the client (i.e., a request), with a currently unsynchronized clock (i.e., the timestamp values in the message are not meaningful). See Figure 7.12.

Figure 7.12 shows the program code that sets the NTP request message content and sends the message, in the time service client library component. Only the first byte is configured to inform the recipient that the type of message is a request (from a client) and is conformant to NTP version 4.

Figure 7.13 shows the receive method of the library component. This method is called when an NTP request message has been sent (over UDP) to the NTP time server and an NTP response is expected (also over UDP). The combined use of a short time delay and a single call to recvfrom (i.e., not repeated periodically in a loop) with the socket configured in nonblocking mode meets a useful compromise between the three potentially conflicting requirements of low-latency responsiveness, robustness, and

```
bool CNTP_Client::Send_TimeService_Request()
{
    memset(SendPacketBuffer, 0,  NTP_PACKET_SIZE ); // Zero-out entire 48-byte array
    // Initialize values needed to form NTP request
    SendPacketBuffer[0] = 0xE3;   // 0b11100011;
                                  // LI bits 7,6     = 3 (Clock not synchronised),
                                  // Version bits 5,4,3  = 4 (The current version of NTP)
                                  // Mode bits 2,1,0     = 3 (Sent by client)

    m_iSendLen = sizeof(SendPacketBuffer);

    int iBytesSent = sendto(m_TimeService_Socket, (char FAR *)SendPacketBuffer, m_iSendLen, 0,
        (const struct sockaddr FAR *)&m_TimeService_SockAddr, sizeof(m_TimeService_SockAddr));
    if(INVALID_SOCKET == iBytesSent)
    {
        return false;
    }
    return true;
}
```

FIGURE 7.12

The Send_TimeService:Request method of the CNTP_Client class in the library.

```
bool CNTP_Client::Receive(NTP_Timestamp_Data* pNTP_Timestamp)
{
    Sleep(500);     // Wait for a short time (500 milliseconds) for the time service response.
    // In combination with non-blocking receive this prevents the application freezing if the time service does not
    // respond but waits long enough for the reply RTT so mostly avoids missing an actual reply and avoids the need
    // for a timer within the NTP_Client class
    // Tested with the following values:
    // 100ms(unreliable) 200ms(highly dependent on network RTT) 400ms(generally reliable) 500ms(adds margin of safety)

    // The process inspects its buffer to see if any messages have arrived
    int iBytesRecd = recvfrom(m_TimeService_Socket, (char FAR*)ReceivePacketBuffer, NTP_PACKET_SIZE, 0, NULL, NULL);
    if(SOCKET_ERROR == iBytesRecd)
    {
        return false;
    }
    // Receive succeeded (response received from Time server)
    // The timestamp starts at byte 40 of the received packet and is four bytes,
    unsigned long secsSince1900 = (ReceivePacketBuffer[40] << 24) + (ReceivePacketBuffer[41] << 16) +
                                  (ReceivePacketBuffer[42] << 8) + ReceivePacketBuffer[43];
    const unsigned long seventyYears = 2208988800UL;       // Unix time starts on Jan 1 1970 (2208988800 seconds)
    pNTP_Timestamp->lUnixTime = secsSince1900 - seventyYears;  // Subtract seventy years:
    pNTP_Timestamp->lHour = (pNTP_Timestamp->lUnixTime  % 86400L) / 3600;
    pNTP_Timestamp->lMinute = (pNTP_Timestamp->lUnixTime  % 3600) / 60;
    pNTP_Timestamp->lSecond = pNTP_Timestamp->lUnixTime  % 60;
    return true;
}
```

FIGURE 7.13

The receive method of the CNTP_Client class in the library.

simple design. The nonblocking socket mode ensures reliability in the sense that the call will return regardless of whether the NTP server responds or not. This is essential to prevent the NTP client library code from blocking indefinitely if the NTP server crashes or if either the request or response message is lost or corrupted in the network.

The use of the 500 ms delay allows for the round-trip time (RTT) of sending the request message and receiving the response. Network delay is continuously changing, and therefore, there can never be a perfect statically decided time-out value for long-haul network transmissions (as in the case of contacting NTP time servers). The 500 ms-delay value was found experimentally to be a good compromise between waiting long enough so that NTP responses are caught in almost all cases and on the other hand not inserting too much additional latency. Even if the RTT was near instantaneous, this approach only inserts half a second of latency.

The timestamp is held in bytes 40-47 of the response message (the Transmit Timestamp field). The timestamp value is 64 bits wide, the most significant 32 bits representing the number of seconds and the least significant 32 bits representing the fraction of seconds. For the case study application, it was deemed adequate to only consider the whole seconds part of the timestamp (hence, the values of bytes 40-43 are used as can be seen in the code in Figure 7.13). In applications where greater precision is needed, the fractional part of the timestamp can also be taken into account.

7.3.6.3 URL Resolution with DNS

The gethostbyname DNS resolver has been embedded into the library code such that the DNS system is automatically contacted to resolve an NIST time server domain address into an IP address; see Figure 7.14.

7.3.6.4 Rationale for the Chosen Communication Design

The fixed-latency receive mechanism was chosen to keep the code simple while also ensuring a predictable response and preventing the call from blocking if certain faults occur. The mechanism is simple in design and operation: a short time delay is used in combination with a nonblocking socket call.

```
SOCKADDR_IN CNTP_Client::ResolveURLtoIPaddress(char* cStrURL)
{
    DWORD dwError;
    struct hostent *TimeServiceHost;
    TimeServiceHost = gethostbyname((const char*)cStrURL);

    if(NULL == TimeServiceHost)
    { // gethostbyname failed to resove time service domain name
      dwError = WSAGetLastError();
      m_TimeService_SockAddr.sin_addr.S_un.S_un_b.s_b1 = 0;
      m_TimeService_SockAddr.sin_addr.S_un.S_un_b.s_b2 = 0;
      m_TimeService_SockAddr.sin_addr.S_un.S_un_b.s_b3 = 0;
      m_TimeService_SockAddr.sin_addr.S_un.S_un_b.s_b4 = 0;
      m_bTimeServiceAddressSet = false;
    }
    else
    { // gethostbyname successfully resoved time service domain name
      m_TimeService_SockAddr.sin_addr.S_un.S_addr = *(u_long *) TimeServiceHost->h_addr_list[0];
                            // Get first address from host's list of addresses
      m_TimeService_SockAddr.sin_family = AF_INET;      // Set the address type
      m_TimeService_SockAddr.sin_port = htons(NTP_Port); // Set the NTP port (Decimal 123)
      m_bTimeServiceAddressSet = true;
    }
    return m_TimeService_SockAddr;
}
```

FIGURE 7.14

The ResolveURLtoIPaddress method of the CNTP_Client class in the library.

There are however additional approaches that could be used if the 500 ms fixed latency were problematic in some applications.

A self-tuning system could be built in which a short delay of 50 ms is first tried, and if the recvfrom times out, the delay is doubled and the request message sent again. This doubling would be repeated until the NTP response is received without timing out (thus auto-adjusting the RTT wait time on the client side). There are three issues with this approach. (1) It increases complexity. (2) NTP clients are not supposed to make NTP requests more frequently than once every 4 s (callers making requests at a higher rate may be interpreted as performing a denial of service attack on the NTP service). To conform with this requirement, the self-tuning approach would have to wait 4 s in between each attempt and thus could introduce a significant delay before a timestamp value is received (although the latency in the timestamp itself will be potentially less than the currently fixed 500 ms). (3) Network delay is continuously varying, so the RTT can change even after the self-tuning has completed.

Another way to increase responsiveness of the client side is to invoke the nonblocking recvfrom call at shorter intervals (such as 50 ms), driven by a programmable timer mechanism. This requires a stopping condition in case the NTP server never responds; a cutoff point has to be decided, perhaps after 10 invocations (i.e., keeping the upper limit latency to 500 ms). This approach increases complexity and uses more runtime resource than the current design.

7.3.7 IMPLEMENTATION

The time service client application has been implemented in three phases, all of which are available as full sample code examples.

The first iteration was to develop a monolithic application, which contained the full NTP client functionality, integrated with the user interface logic. This approach represents a form of rapid prototyping-based development and is only really suitable in applications with quite narrow functionality, as in this case. The phase 1 monolithic project is CaseStudy_TimeServiceClient_GUI Phase1 Monolithic.

The second phase was to refactor the code to place the NTP client-side business logic into a separate class from the user interface-related functionality. The phase 2 refactored project is CaseStudy_TimeServiceClient_GUI Phase2 Refactored.

The third phase was to create a library that contains the NTP client-side functionality and enables the reuse of this functionality by embedding the library into applications. The phase 3 library project is CaseStudy_TimeServiceClient Phase3 Library.

To demonstrate the benefit of the library approach, two separate front-end applications are developed. The first of these provides the same GUI interface as the phase 1 and phase 2 projects. The second front end provides a text-based interface; since it uses the library, it has exactly the same time service-related functionality, but with a totally different user interface. The phase 3 (part a) GUI application project is CaseStudy_TimeServiceClient_GUI Phase3 App-side uses library. The phase 3 (part b) text-based application project is CaseStudy_TimeServClnt_Console AppSide uses lib.

This implementation route is mapped out in Figure 7.15.

7.3.8 TESTING

Testing is a continual process of checking the correctness of the requirements and the design and ensuring that the design actually reflects the requirements and that the implementation actually reflects the design. In the case of the NTP client application, it was decided to implement the core functionality in

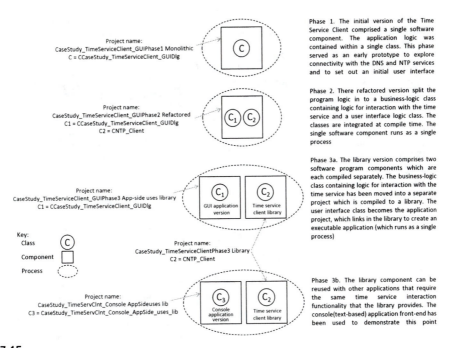

Phase 1. The initial version of the Time Service Client comprised a single software component. The application logic was contained within a single class. This phase served as an early prototype to explore connectivity with the DNS and NTP services and to set out an initial user interface

Project name:
CaseStudy_TimeServiceClient_GUIPhase1 Monolithic
C = CCaseStudy_TimeServiceClient_GUIDlg

Phase 2. There refactored version split the program logic in to a business-logic class containing logic for interaction with the time service and a user interface logic class. The classes are integrated at compile time. The single software component runs as a single process

Project name:
CaseStudy_TimeServiceClient_GUIPhase2 Refactored
C1 = CCaseStudy_TimeServiceClient_GUIDlg
C2 = CNTP_Client

Phase 3a. The library version comprises two software program components which are each compiled separately. The business-logic class containing logic for interaction with the time service has been moved into a separate project which is compiled to a library. The user interface class becomes the application project, which links in the library to create an executable application (which runs as a single process)

Project name:
CaseStudy_TimeServiceClient_GUIPhase3 App-side uses library
C1 = CCaseStudy_TimeServiceClient_GUIDlg

Key:
Class
Component
Process

Project name:
CaseStudy_TimeServiceClientPhase3 Library
C2 = CNTP_Client

Phase 3b. The library component can be reused with other applications that require the same time service interaction functionality that the library provides. The console(text-based) application front-end has been used to demonstrate this point

Project name:
CaseStudy_TimeServClnt_Console AppSideuses lib
C3 = CaseStudy_TimeServClnt_Console_AppSide_uses_lib

FIGURE 7.15

The implementation roadmap.

the form of a library. The most important aspects of behavior in this particular application case are that the NTP protocol is being used correctly, and that the correct results are returned from the NTP service, and also that the results are properly interpreted in the application code. There are various faults that can occur, and one particular perceived problem that was to be avoided was that the application should not crash or freeze if a problem occurs with the NTP service itself or as a result of the communication with the service. The approach taken was to build an application, which served as a test-bed for getting the NTP protocol interaction correct, and then to subsequently refactor and extract the library as secondary phases. The user interface aspect was not the primary concern of the first phase, but since it turned out to be quite suitable for purpose, it was not changed for the sake of doing so, when moving through phases 2 and 3.

The formal test plan is used as a final sign-off that the application meets its functional, behavioral, and correctness requirements, but as stated above, this does not reveal the true extent of the testing that actually occurs, due to its continuous nature. The test plan and the test outcomes are provided in Table 7.1.

7.3.9 **TRANSPARENCY ASPECTS OF THE USE CASE**

Transparency to the user. The NTP client-side library deals with the connectivity and communication with the NTP service, thus hiding the communication aspect from the user regardless of the front-end user interface. Depending on how it is designed, it is possible that the user interface hides or reveals

Table 7.1 The Test Plan and Outcomes for the Time Service Client Application

Test no.	Characteristic or behavior under test	Test conditions (test conditions and outcomes reported relate to the GUI version of the application)	Outcome	Deviations or other comments
1	Allow user to select an NTP service instance based on NIST domain names	The various NIST time service domains in the list box are selected in turn	The user-highlighted choice domain name was selected and displayed in the selected server URL text box	None
2	Resolve selected NIST time service domain name to the appropriate IP address silently and reliably	The various NIST time service domains in the list box are selected in turn	Each domain name was resolved to the correct IP address	Additional dynamic debugging experiments were carried out to observe the sequence of steps within the program code
3	Establish a connection with the appropriate NTP server instance silently and reliably; the user should be unaware of the details of this activity	The various NIST time service domains in the list box are selected in turn	The appropriate NTP time servers were contacted	This was confirmed in some cases where a response was received back. In other cases, this was confirmed through dynamic debugging to observe that the correctly formatted network message was generated and sent
4	Get NTP timestamp from the NTP time service. Get the correct timestamp regardless of which NTP server instance contacted	The various NIST time service domains in the list box are selected in turn	The correct NTP timestamp was returned in cases where the contacted NTP server returned a response, except in one case where the NTP server gave a time value that was wrong by approximately 40 min	The client-side behavior was found to be correct in all cases. The situation where there was no response from a server is covered in a subsequent test
5	Silently handle situations where the NIST domain name is incorrect	The code was modified to facilitate this test. A fictitious NIST domain name was embedded into the provided list and then selected during the test	The fault was handled silently. The DNS resolver failed to resolve the domain name to an IP address and the NTP client-side action was canceled	Additional dynamic debugging experiments were carried out to observe the sequence of steps within the program code

Test no.	Characteristic or behavior under test	Test conditions (test conditions and outcomes reported relate to the GUI version of the application)	Outcome	Deviations or other comments
6	Silently handle situations where the NTP server does not respond to a request (or where either the request message or response message are lost)	The various NIST time service domains in the list box are selected in turn	Some NTP servers did not respond when a request was sent to them. The receive method timed out as expected and the NTP client-side action was canceled	Additional dynamic debugging experiments were carried out to observe the sequence of steps within the program code
7	UI appearance. The user interface must be clear and uncluttered	The user interface was observed, both as a static design and in use with live data	The UI was found to have acceptable appearance	This is a somewhat subjective result since in this case, the tester and the designer were the same person
8	UI functionality. The user interface controls must function correctly and data values must be displayed correctly	The user interface was observed in use with live data	The controls functioned correctly and data values were displayed correctly	The correctness of the NTP timestamp data was confirmed by comparison with the local computer clock and an external satellite-controlled clock

Table 7.1   The Test Plan and Outcomes for the Time Service Client Application—Cont'd

different levels of detail, for example, the user may be asked to select a name service instance by its domain name and/or IP address. The library could be embedded into an application such that the NTP connection is handled silently from the user's perspective and thus there is no need for the user to be aware that the NTP service is used. The library provides location transparency, distribution transparency, and access transparency (the time value is a resource, which is accessed via the NTP service, regardless of which service instance is used or its underlying platform).

Transparency to the developer. The internal clock synchronization of the NTP service is hidden from developers. Applications need only resolve one of the published NIST service domain names to get a server IP address and then send an NTP request message to well-known port 123 at that address. All server instances should provide the same time value, thus hiding the distributed nature of the service as well as the structure and organization including details of the clock strata and the synchronization that goes on between the servers.

7.3.10 CASE STUDY RESOURCES

The full source code and project files for each of the three phases of the case study implementation, as well as both of the user interface variants used in phase 3 (the library version), are provided as part of the support resources that accompany the book (five complete code projects).

7.4 CASE STUDY #2: EVENT NOTIFICATION SERVICE

This case study focuses on the design and development of an ENS. In addition, it provides a demonstration of the use of a DS to support dynamic binding between clients of the ENS and the ENS server itself. The various components have been developed in a variety of languages to illustrate interoperability within a heterogeneous distributed application.

Applications that use the ENS comprise two types of components: publisher components, which publish events via the ENS, and consumer components, which use the event values received from the ENS.

The case study uses the DS that is built into the Distributed Systems Workbench to facilitate dynamic binding between the application components (which are clients of the ENS) and the ENS. To facilitate this, the ENS server auto-registers its name and address details with the DS, and the client components send resolve request messages to obtain the IP address and port of the ENS server from the DS.

The ENS is a form of middleware that supports applications, which operate on a publish-subscribe basis. The ENS provides logical connectivity between application components while they remain fully decoupled from each other. Figure 7.16 provides a simplified view of the interaction that occurs between the ENS and the application components.

Figure 7.16 shows how the ENS serves as a form of middleware between the application components. Events published by components are automatically passed to other components that have registered an interest in those event types.

7.4.1 LEARNING OUTCOMES ASSOCIATED WITH THE CASE STUDY

This case study covers a wide range of topics, which include the following:

- A practical example of an ENS
- A practical example of a publish-subscribe application
- A practical example of loose-coupled components and runtime configuration
- Dynamic binding of components using a DS
- An example of the combined use of TCP and UDP transport layer protocols in the same application

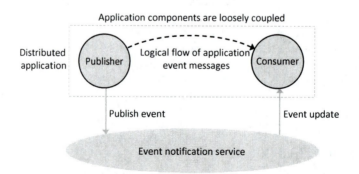

FIGURE 7.16

High-level illustration of the role of the event notification service.

- An example of the use of UDP in broadcast mode to perform service location
- An example of TCP connections and a server component maintaining an array of connected clients
- Interoperability across heterogeneous components developed in different languages
- Serialization and deserialization of language-specific data representations into an implementation-neutral byte array format

Note that the application components (the event publishers and event consumers) have each been implemented in three different languages (C++, C#, and Java), and therefore, there are six different sample client component types, which can connect to the ENS and interact through event publishing and consumption.

The differently implemented components have different user interfaces, with a different "look and feel" but with the same underlying behavior. In particular, they all interact with the ENS with the same, single interface it provides. This means that through the ENS, the components can interoperate regardless of the language they are written in; for example, a C++ publisher can create events, which are consumed by a Java consumer (any of the combinations of the six component types will work). For this to be possible, all messages are serialized into a specific ENS PDU, which comprises four fixed length fields, and transmitted as a flattened byte array (a contiguous block of bytes).

All messages have the same standard format when they reach the ENS; thus, it can correctly extract the message content from these messages and construct replies as appropriate, without needing to know the implementation of the sender.

7.4.2 REQUIREMENTS ANALYSIS

This section identifies the functional and nonfunctional requirements of the ENS:

- Automatic location and connection. The ENS server should automatically register with the DS so that other components can query the DS to obtain the address of the ENS server on demand. When a client component starts, it should automatically discover the ENS address details by querying the DS. Clients should then automatically establish a TCP connection with ENS.
- Support for publish-subscribe-based applications. Such applications comprise some components that publish events and others that consume events. The ENS should maintain a database of event types and their values and the address details of the most recent publisher for each particular event.
- Facilitate dynamic logical association between components based only on named event types. Consumer clients will subscribe to events that they are interested in. Publisher components will publish events that they generate. The ENS will make implicit associations by automatically forwarding to each client updates of the events the specific client has subscribed to.
- Application-independent and extensible. The ENS server must create new event type categories when they are either subscribed to or published, if they don't already exist.
- Low-latency. The ENS server must pass the current value of an event (if known) to a subscriber, immediately upon receiving a subscription request. That is, it sends the instantaneously available cached value; it must not contact the publisher requesting an update, which would add latency and increase the overall communication intensity. Event updates are propagated on a state-change basis to the set of registered subscriber components thereafter.

- Scalable and efficient. The ENS must use resources effectively. In particular, the communication intensity must be low; event updates should only be sent to the subset of clients that have subscribed to them.
- Availability. The use model assumes that the ENS server is long-lived and runs continually. This requires that it is robust.

7.4.3 ARCHITECTURE AND CODE STRUCTURE

The ENS and DS fall into the category of common services discussed in Chapter 6. The combined use of these services facilitates full decoupling between application components, as shown in the interaction diagram in Figure 7.17; the application components do not communicate directly.

Figure 7.17 shows a typical interaction involving the ENS, the DS, and a pair of application components: one publisher and one consumer. In this sequence, the ENS first registers with the DS. The publisher component is then started and obtains the address details of the ENS from the DS and using this information connects to the ENS. The publisher then publishes a new event type "E" with value "27." The consumer component is then started, and it too obtains the address of the ENS from the DS, and it also establishes a connection with the ENS. The consumer subscribes to event type "E," and the ENS sends back its cached value for this event type, which is "27." The publisher then publishes a new value of "33" for event type "E." The ENS responds by pushing the new value for the event type to the consumer. The consumer now unsubscribes to event type "E." Subsequently, the publisher publishes a new value of "47" for event type "E." The ENS does not push the new value for the event type to the consumer.

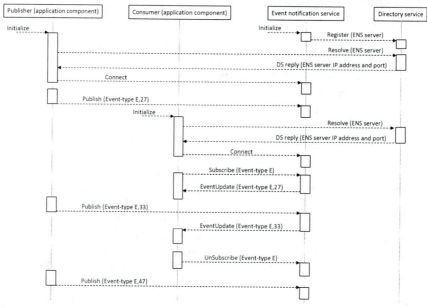

FIGURE 7.17

Sequence diagram representation of ENS interaction.

7.4.4 SEPARATION OF CONCERNS

The ENS is designed to support distributed applications, which consist of two categories of components (publishers and consumers); both of these categories of components are seen as clients from the ENS system perspective. Within the application itself, publishers may be effectively the server side and consumers are effectively the client side. These have quite specific application-dependent behavior with respect to a particular type of event, and in this regard, the functional and behavioral concerns are naturally separated. However, the design can be more complex when one component is a publisher of some event types and a consumer of others or where a component consumes an event, modifies the underlying data values, and then publishes a new version of the same event. The ENS is stateless, that is, its design assumes that publish and subscribe activities are independent, asynchronous, and unordered. It is possible that there are multiple subscribers to a particular event type; this situation is not problematic. However, where a particular consumer subscribes to multiple event types, the relative ordering of updates may be an issue in some applications (and should be resolved in the application logic). In the case that there are multiple publishers of a specific event type, there may be application-specific restrictions needed, for example, creating variations of event types with additional naming information, which differentiates between them without creating a dependency on a specific publisher component. For example, one publisher may publish an event type temperature_01, which could indicate a temperature value with an accuracy of $1°$, while another publisher could publish an event type temperature_03, which could indicate a temperature value with an accuracy of $3°$. A consumer could subscribe to both event types but use the value of temperature_01 with preference if it is available.

7.4.5 COUPLING AND BINDING BETWEEN COMPONENTS

The coupling between ENS clients (either an application's publisher or consumer component) is loose (because the DS is used to find the address details of the ENS server dynamically at runtime) and direct (because once the ENS server address details are known, a TCP connection is established directly between the client component and the ENS server).

The coupling between the application components themselves, that is, the coupling between the event publishers and event consumers, is loose (because the ENS provides a logical connectivity based on event types and not addresses) and indirect (because there is no direct connection or messaging between these components; all communication is brokered by the ENS server).

The avoidance of tight coupling ensures that the entire system comprising the ENS service and the applications that use it can be flexibly configured at runtime, and no components need any prior knowledge of the location of others. This also contributes to robustness since publisher components can be substituted without consumers being affected and that consumers can be added or removed without publishers being affected.

7.4.5.1 Application-Level Coupling

Application components are logically coupled solely by the event relationships they share. An event type is dynamically created whenever a publisher publishes a new event type or a consumer subscribes to a new event type not already in the ENS database. This aspect is totally runtime-configured.

Application components therefore have no direct dependencies on other components; a publisher can publish a new event type regardless of whether there is any consumer for that event type, and similarly, a consumer can subscribe to an event type regardless of whether a publisher for that event type is present.

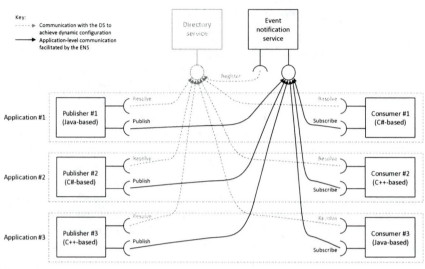

FIGURE 7.18

Loose coupling of application components, facilitated by the ENS.

This lack of direct dependency is important for scalability and also extensibility because new features of applications, or even new applications, can be supported by the ENS without it having to know what event types exist a priori. The complete application-level decoupling allows publish and subscribe actions to occur asynchronously and in any order, for example, it is not an error to subscribe to an event type that has not yet been published. The loose coupling achieved is illustrated in Figure 7.18.

Figure 7.18 shows how the ENS decouples application components such that they do not have any direct dependencies and do not communicate directly. This allows systems to scale up without having to redesign components. For example, new consumers can be added for a particular event type without having to modify the publisher component, which generates the events. The lack of direct dependencies is also very powerful in terms of fault tolerance; a consumer can fail without the publisher needing to know about it. A publisher can fail without crashing the consumer (although the events will no longer be published by the particular failed publisher, another publisher may be started or the consumer will wait but will meanwhile still be capable of responding to other event types it has subscribed to).

Figure 7.18 also shows the separation of concerns at two levels. All components shown below the ENS in the figure are clients from the point of view of the ENS service. However, when viewed from the perspective of specific applications, the components on the left are essentially servers and those on the right are essentially clients.

7.4.6 COMMUNICATION ASPECTS OF THE DESIGN

Figure 7.19 shows the port assignments used in the ENS and the DS.

All components must interact with the DS interface using the ports shown in Figure 7.19. However, the client components do not need to know the ENS port number a priori; the purpose of using the DS is to allow the clients to find the ENS address and port details at runtime.

```
#define From_DIRECTORY_SERVICE_PORT  (u_int) 8002  // UDP, Defined by Directory Service
#define To_DIRECTORY_SERVICE_PORT    (u_int) 8008  // UDP, Defined by Directory Service
#define ENS_APPLICATION_PORT         (u_int) 8003  // TCP, ENS_Server Binds to this port
```

FIGURE 7.19

ENS and DS ports.

The ENS uses a combination of UDP and TCP transport layer communications. UDP is used for communication with the DS. UDP broadcasts are used to send register messages to the DS (in the case of the ENS Server) and to send resolve request messages to the DS (in the case of clients of the ENS, in order to obtain the address of the ENS Server). The DS responds to resolve requests with a directed UDP message to the specific client component. TCP is used for communication between the ENS server and its clients (the publishers and consumers of events). Each client, publisher, or consumer establishes a dedicated TCP connection with the ENS server, over which the ENS application messages are passed. There are four ENS message types, which are discussed later. Figure 7.20 maps out the ENS connectivity in the form of a socket-level view of the communication.

Figure 7.20 provides a socket-level view of the communication that occurs between the various components. The diagram illustrates several important points:

- The ENS is a service that makes use of another service (the DS) to facilitate connectivity. This is a useful example of the use of common services as building blocks to achieve higher functionality while at the same time limiting the complexity of components. In this case,

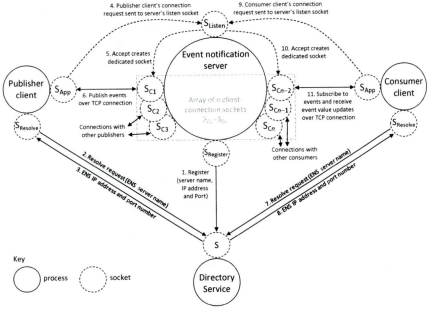

FIGURE 7.20

Socket-level view of ENS communication.

the clients of the ENS can automatically locate the ENS server and connect to it at runtime. Communication with the DS is implemented using UDP because it supports broadcasts.

- The ENS is a form of middleware. The user-level applications comprise the application event publisher components and the application event consumer components. The ENS is not actually part of the user-level applications; its role is to provide a loosely coupled connectivity between the application-level components such that they never communicate directly. This facilitates runtime configuration and leads to flexible and robust outcomes.

- The ENS supports multiple concurrent TCP connections with clients. These can be either consumers or publishers (in fact, a single component can play both roles, as it can subscribe to some event types and also publish some event types). The ENS therefore maintains an array of all client sockets (and hence, connections); it does not differentiate between the roles of clients at the connection level.

Figure 7.21 shows the TCP connection structure used in the ENS. An array of these structures are maintained. The bInUse flag is set to true for entries in the array that relate to currently connected client components.

Figure 7.22 shows the structure that the ENS uses to hold details of event types. The ENS maintains an array of these structures.

For each event type, there can be many subscribers, and it cannot be predicted how popular the various event types are. Using a large array to hold subscribers, details for each event type would be inefficient in cases where there are only a small number of actual subscribers, and no matter how large the array is, there is no certainty that it is large enough in all cases. Therefore, a linked list of subscribers is attached to each event type (as can be seen in Figure 7.22); this can grow and shrink dynamically as necessary. Figure 7.23 shows the format of a subscriber linked list entry. Note that the linked list entry only contains a single piece of data relating to the subscriber, the index into the connection array. This approach is efficient because it is concise and avoids duplication of data.

```
struct Connection {
    SOCKET m_iConnectSock;
    SOCKADDR_IN m_ConnectSockAddr;
    bool bInUse;
};
```

FIGURE 7.21

The ENS TCP connection structure.

```
#define MAX_EVENT_TYPE_NAME_LENGTH 50
#define MAX_EVENT_VALUE_LENGTH 50

struct Event_Type {
    char cEventType[MAX_EVENT_TYPE_NAME_LENGTH];
    char cEventValue[MAX_EVENT_VALUE_LENGTH];
    SubscriberListItem* pSubscriberList_Head;// Linked list of subscribers
    SOCKADDR_IN PublisherAddress;            // IP address and Port of most recent publisher
    bool bInUse_ValueValid;                  // Has the event been published
    bool bInUse_SubscriptionExists;          // Are there consumer(s) waiting for this event
};
```

FIGURE 7.22

The Event_Type structure.

```
struct SubscriberListItem {
        int iConnectionIndex; // Index into connection array to identify the subscriber
        SubscriberListItem* pSubscriberList_Next;
};
```

FIGURE 7.23

The subscriber linked list entry structure.

7.4.6.1 ENS Message Types

The ENS application interface comprises four message types, which are defined in the form of an enumerated type in all of the components, regardless of the component's role and the language it is developed in (see Figure 7.24). This is a key aspect of achieving universal interoperability.

The various ENS message types share a single PDU format, shown in Figure 7.25, which simplifies design and development. A couple of the fields are not used in some message types representing slight inefficiency (e.g., the cEventValue field is not valid in subscribe messages), but this is not considered to be significant enough to warrant a more complex design in the sense that message serialization and deserialization would be dependent on the message type.

Figure 7.25 shows the ENS PDU (the representation as defined in C++). This PDU format is an invariant across all the component implementations, although the structure cannot be defined in exactly the same way in each of the three languages that were used in the example application. The equivalent flattened byte array format that is achieved when this structure is serialized is shown in Figure 7.26. This forms a linear buffer of 117 bytes and is the format in which the message is actually transmitted within the TCP segment and thus is the format that must be achieved when serializing from the internal representations in the other languages.

7.4.6.2 ENS Communication Semantics

Communication with the ENS operates on a one-way basis with regard to each of the four message types. No acknowledgment is necessary at the application protocol level because the reliable TCP transport layer protocol is used, which automatically takes care of retransmissions if a message is lost

```
enum EventNotificationService_Message_Type {
    SubscribeToEvent,       /* value 0, sent from Consumer component to ENS */
    UnSubscribeToEvent,     /* value 1, sent from Consumer component to ENS */
    PublishEvent,           /* value 2, sent from Publisher component to ENS */
    EventUpdate             /* value 3, sent from ENS to Consumer component */
};
```

FIGURE 7.24

The ENS message type codes enumeration.

```
struct EventNotificationService_Message_PDU {
    byte iMessageType;
    char cEventType[MAX_EVENT_TYPE_NAME_LENGTH];
    char cEventValue[MAX_EVENT_VALUE_LENGTH];  // Not valid in Subscribe messages
    SOCKADDR_IN SendersAddress;
};
```

FIGURE 7.25

The ENS PDU.

Index positions in byte array	Field length	Field name	Data type
Byte 0	1	iMessageType	Unsigned integer value in range 0-255
Bytes 1-50	50	cEventType	8-bit ASCII character values, in ASCIIZ string format (i.e., terminated with a "\0" character)
Bytes 51-100	50	cEventValue	8-bit ASCII character values, in ASCIIZ string format (i.e., terminated with a "\0" character)
Bytes 101-116	16	SendersAddress	Unsigned integer values in range 0-255. Each component of the IP address is encoded as a single 8-bit value. The port number is encoded as a 16-bit number spread across two adjacent bytes

FIGURE 7.26

The flattened byte array representation of the ENS PDU.

or corrupted. Conceptually, subscribe might be considered to operate on a request-reply basis (as it is answered by zero or more event update messages), but since these are asynchronous, and may never occur, it is more accurate to consider the subscribe and update messages as separate activities from a communication semantics viewpoint.

7.4.6.3 DS Message Types

The DS has a simple interface comprising two request messages, which are each encoded as a string of 8-bit ASCII character values, in ASCIIZ format (i.e., terminated with a "\0" character) and a single reply PDU format. See Figures 7.27 and 7.28.

Figure 7.27 shows the two DS request message types. Note that in the case of register request messages, the DS automatically determines the IP address of the sender from the recvfrom socket API call, which extracts this information from the UDP packet header. Hence, there is no need to explicitly encode the address in the register request message; its omission represents a slight efficiency improvement in terms of processing time and communication bandwidth usage. The port must be stated explicitly however because it cannot be assumed that the registering service wants to use the same port that it used to connect to the DS for receiving application messages.

Figure 7.28 shows the DS reply message PDU, which contains the IP address and port number of the requested service.

REGISTER:<*Service name*>:<*Port*>
For example the ENS sends "REGISTER:Event_NS:8003"

RESOLVE:<*Service name*>
For example a client of the ENS sends "RESOLVE:Event_NS"

FIGURE 7.27

The DS request message formats with ENS usage examples.

```
struct DirectoryServiceReply {
    unsigned char a1;
    unsigned char a2;
    unsigned char a3;
    unsigned char a4;
    unsigned int iPort;
};
```

FIGURE 7.28

The DS reply message PDU.

7.4.6.4 *DS Communication Semantics*

The DS has been designed to be lightweight with respect to communication overhead and also to operate with low latency. As such, it has a simple communication interface as discussed above and also simple communication semantics. DS register messages operate on a one-way basis without acknowledgment. DS resolve messages operate on a request-reply basis: When the requested service name is matched by the DS, an appropriately populated DirectoryServiceReply PDU is returned (see Figure 7.28); if the requested service name is not found in the DS database, the DS returns a PDU containing the address:port values 0.0.0.0:0.

7.4.7 AN APPLICATION USE SCENARIO TO ILLUSTRATE THE USE OF THE ENS

An application that comprises temperature and humidity monitoring components (which are effectively application servers) and display components (which are effectively application clients) has been created to illustrate the use and behavior of the ENS in a realistic application setting. The environmental monitoring components need to send messages containing temperature and humidity values to the display components. The application has been designed to make use of the ENS to achieve a decoupled and runtime configurable architecture. In this scheme, the application components never communicate directly with each other; the ENS acts as a message broker, based on event types. The environmental monitoring components publish events (which are the values of temperature or humidity when they change). The display components are said to be consumers of these events. They each register their interest in certain event types by sending a subscribe message to the ENS. Thereafter, the ENS sends event update messages to each of the consumers, when new values are published.

To illustrate interoperability across components written in different programming languages, the environment monitoring application has been developed with publisher component variants and consumer component variants developed in three different languages (C++, C#, and Java).

A use scenario in which one of the publisher variants (the C# one) publishes events that are consumed by all three consumer components is used to illustrate the operation of the ENS and the transparency it provides. See the following four figures in which the activity of this scenario is broken down into four stages.

Figure 7.29 shows the first stage of activity in the environment monitoring application use scenario.[1] The sequence of actions in this stage occur in five steps: (1) The DS is started if not already running (the DS is an application provided by the Distributed Systems Workbench); (2) the ENS server registers its name, IP address, and port number with the DS; (3) The ENS client components (which are the environment monitoring application event publishers and event consumers) send resolve requests to the DS, containing the name of the ENS server "Event_NS"; (4) the DS replies to each request with the IP address and port number of the ENS server; and (5) each of the ENS clients then makes a TCP connect request based on the ENS server's address and port details.

Figure 7.30 shows the second stage of activity in the environment monitoring application use scenario, in which the consumer clients subscribe to the event types they are each interested in. Working down from the top on the right-hand side of the figure, the C#-based consumer client subscribes to "TemperatureChange" events, the C++-based consumer client subscribes to both "TemperatureChange" and "HumidityChange" events, and the Java-based consumer client subscribes to "HumidityChange"

---

[1] For the purpose of simple presentation and annotation, all components were running on a single computer in the scenario illustrated.

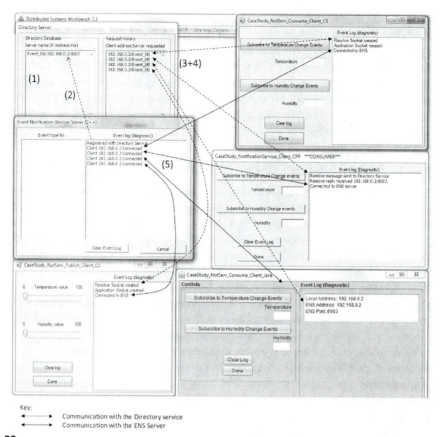

FIGURE 7.29

Stage 1: Automatic binding and connectivity facilitated by the directory service.

events. Note that the buttons on the user interfaces toggle between "Subscribe" and "Unsubscribe" actions, and their labeling is updated accordingly when pressed.

Note that in the specific application scenario sequence illustrated in this section, the three consumers all subscribe to event types before any events have been published. The publish and subscribe actions are however completely asynchronous, and the ENS does not enforce or expect any particular ordering. For example, one of the consumers could have delayed subscribing to the event types until some values had already been published; in which case, upon receiving the subscription message, the ENS server would immediately send back to the client the latest already stored value of the respective event type.

Figure 7.31 shows the third stage of activity. The C#-based publisher publishes a series of four TemperatureChange events, each of which is pushed out to the relevant subscribers in the form of event update messages. Notice that only the consumer clients that have subscribed to the particular event type receive the updates, in this case, the C#-based consumer and the C++-based consumer.

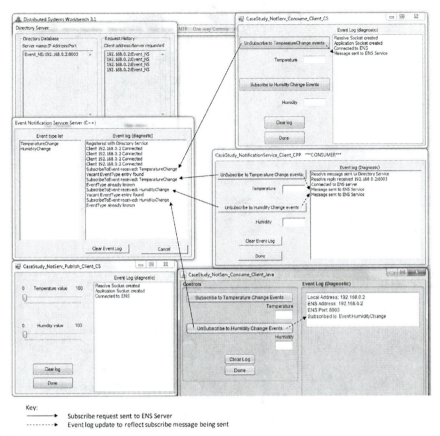

Key:
⟶ Subscribe request sent to ENS Server
----▶ Event log update to reflect subscribe message being sent

FIGURE 7.30

Stage 2: Consumer clients subscribe to event types they are interested in.

Figure 7.32 shows the fourth stage of activity. The C#-based publisher publishes a series of four HumidityChange events, each of which is pushed out to the relevant subscribers in the form of event update messages. Only the consumer clients that have subscribed to the HumidityChange event type receive the updates, in this case, the C++-based consumer and the Java-based consumer.

7.4.8 TESTING (TABLE 7.2)

The test plan and test outcomes are shown in Table 7.2.

7.4.9 TRANSPARENCY ASPECTS OF THE ENS

Access transparency is provided because the application data are transmitted in a platform-independent and language-independent serialized byte stream format. All event type names and event values are represented in simple 8-bit ASCIIZ character string format, hence avoiding encoding anomalies that can arise when data formats such as integers and floating point numbers are used with different

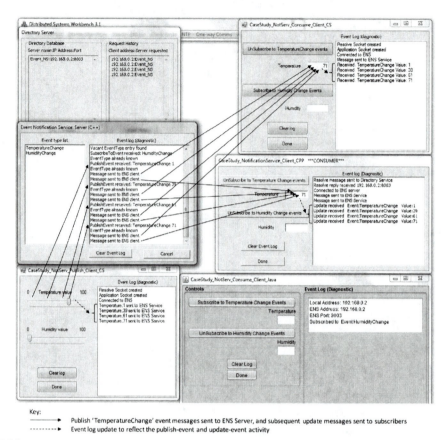

Key:

———▶ Publish 'TemperatureChange' event messages sent to ENS Server, and subsequent update messages sent to subscribers

‑ ‑ ‑ ‑ ▶ Event log update to reflect the publish-event and update-event activity

FIGURE 7.31

Stage 3: Publisher client publishes a series of TemperatureChange events.

encodings and precisions in different systems. The character string approach also means that any event type name and value can be encoded and managed by the ENS in a totally application-agnostic manner.

Location transparency is provided by the fact that the DS is used to resolve the ENS address from its name when clients need to connect.

Migration transparency is achieved in the sense that the ENS server self-registers with the DS on a 10s periodic basis, which means that it can be moved between computers, and any newly started client components will receive the new location details when they subsequently issue resolve requests to the DS.

Implementation transparency. The use of the standard TCP communication protocol, in combination with the simple data representation as described above (see access transparency), means that the ENS supports clients operating on any platform and developed in any programming language. This does however require great care when performing the message serialization and deserialization actions

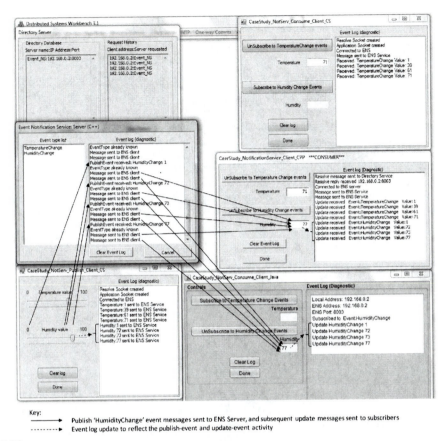

FIGURE 7.32

Stage 4: Publisher client publishes a series of HumidityChange events.

within application code (see the different techniques used in each of the C++, C#, and Java examples included in the supporting materials).

The loose coupling between application components, facilitated by the ENS, contributes to failure transparency because there are no direct dependencies between components. One component can crash without causing others to crash, thus achieving fault tolerance. The extent to which this is actually transparent is application-dependent. For example, while a consumer can fail without affecting the behavior of the publisher components, the role of the consumer is not necessarily being performed elsewhere in the system. Similarly, if a publisher were to fail, the events it generates are no longer published; this will not cause the consumers to crash, but they may wait indefinitely for the missing events. The asynchronous nature of the event updates means that the consumer may still be capable of responding to other events it has subscribed to (this depends on the application-specific interpretation of events).

In addition, the operation of the ENS has been designed to be application-independent; that is, it can support any publish-subscribe-based application. This contributes to flexibility and future-proofing.

Table 7.2 The Test Plan and Outcomes for the ENS

Test no.	Characteristic or behavior under test	Test conditions	Outcome	Deviations or other comments
1	The ENS must register with the DS automatically upon start-up and must reregister on a 10 s periodic basis	The ENS was started before the DS in one test and after the DS in another test	In both cases, within ten seconds of both processes running, the ENS had registered with the DS	
2	Clients of the ENS (which are the application publisher and consumer components) must be able to obtain the address and port details of the ENS, from the DS	Client components issued resolve messages to the DS, both when the ENS was already registered and when it was not	When the ENS was registered with the DS, the client components did obtain the ENS address and port details	The DS retains server address details until overwritten. Therefore, if the ENS registers and then is abruptly terminated, the DS will continue to supply the ENS address details. If the ENS remains absent, this is an issue. However, the problem is automatically resolved if the ENS is restarted (whether on the same computer or another one) and sends a new register message
3	Clients of the ENS should use the address details obtained from the DS to establish a TCP connection with the ENS	Publisher and consumer components were tested to determine whether they automatically connect to the ENS	Client components do establish TCP connections with the ENS	
4	The ENS server must accept multiple TCP connections, up to the maximum level supported by the design	The code was modified to facilitate this test. The maximum level (defined in the constant MAX_CONNECTIONS) was artificially lowered to the value 5 and then to 1 to test the accept/refuse behavior	Connections were accepted up to the limit and details retained in the form of entries in the connection array (m_ConnectionArray)	Additional dynamic debugging experiments were carried out to observe the sequence of steps within the program code
5	Application components must be fully decoupled and have independent behavior and lifetimes	Publisher and consumer components related by event associations were started and stopped in different sequences	Component behavior, including abrupt termination, had no adverse affects on other components	No messages are ever sent directly from one application component to another

Table 7.2   The Test Plan and Outcomes for the ENS—Cont'd

Test no.	Characteristic or behavior under test	Test conditions	Outcome	Deviations or other comments
6	ENS messages must be fully asynchronous	Publisher and consumer components performed publish, subscribe, and unsubscribe actions in various sequences and orders	In all cases, the ENS pushed event update messages to consumers where a subscription was present and not otherwise	
7	The ENS must accept new (previously unknown) event types that are published or subscribed to	A publisher generated a new event type E1 A consumer subscribed to a new event type E2	In both cases, the new event type was added to the event type array in the ENS	The components' source code was modified to facilitate these tests
8	Application components must be able to publish multiple types of event and must be able to publish new values for an existing event type	A publisher was used to generate multiple event types and also to generate multiple updates for each event type	The ENS received all event type-value pairs correctly and updated its event type array accordingly	
9	Components must be able to subscribe to multiple event types and receive multiple value updates for each event type	A consumer was used to subscribe to multiple event types	The component did receive a sequence of updates for each event type that corresponded with the sequences published	
10	Consumer components must be able to unsubscribe to event types and the ENS should no longer push updates for the relevant event types to the consumer	A consumer was used to subscribe to two event types, both of which were being actively published by other components. After receiving several updates for each event type, the consumer unsubscribed to one of the event types	The consumer received event updates for the subset of event types it was subscribed to. The semantics of unsubscribe operated correctly and the consumer continued to receive updates for only the one remaining event type it was subscribed to	
11	Multiple components must be supported, in any combination of roles (part a: publishers)	Multiple publishers were used to publish the same event type	The ENS always pushed out the latest value for a given event type regardless of the identity of the publisher	

Continued

Table 7.2   The Test Plan and Outcomes for the ENS—Cont'd

Test no.	Characteristic or behavior under test	Test conditions	Outcome	Deviations or other comments
12	Multiple components must be supported, in any combination of roles (part b: consumers)	Multiple consumers were used to subscribe to the same event type	The ENS pushed out event updates to all consumers that had subscribed to the event type	
13	The ENS must be application-independent	The event type strings were changed in some components to determine if multiple different publisher-consumer application pairings could be simultaneously supported	The ENS treated each event type independently and pushed out the correct event updates to the correct consumers without any configuration or knowledge that multiple applications were present	The source code of some components was modified to facilitate this test
14	ENS applications must be supported regardless of their implementation language	Consumer and publisher components have been developed in C++, C#, and Java (six sample components in total)	All combinations of the various publishers and consumers were tested. All combinations worked correctly	This demonstrates the interoperability support provided by the ENS approach and reinforces the concept that the ENS is a form of middleware

7.4.10 CASE STUDY RESOURCES

The ENS server has been developed in C++. The environment monitoring application has been developed with three publisher component variants (developed in C++, C#, and Java) and three consumer component variants (also developed in C++, C#, and Java).

The full source code and project files for the ENS server and all of the application components of the environment monitoring system (which are clients of the ENS) are provided as part of the support resources that accompany the book. The Distributed Systems Workbench (which provides the DS necessary to run the ENS system) is also provided as part of the supporting resource materials.

7.5 GOOD DESIGN PRACTICE FOR DISTRIBUTED APPLICATIONS

This section summarizes some main design concepts that have been identified in the book and relates them to the case studies where relevant. Guidelines are provided which identify the key considerations and decisions that must be taken when designing a distributed application, accompanied by discussion of the significance of the various issues.

7.5.1 **REQUIREMENTS ANALYSIS**

Get the requirements analysis right. Take great care to ensure that you understand what is required, what features are needed, and how it should work. You should also consider the feasibility and form initial plans of how you are going to build and test the application. If you unknowingly make mistakes at this stage, they will propagate through the design and build. Many systems effectively fail at this stage, but the failure does not become apparent until much later, by which point it has cost time and other resources and is more difficult to put right.

Requirements fall into two categories: functional and nonfunctional. Both are equally important, but the functional requirements are easier to identify and usually a lot easier to test. The nonfunctional requirements can be overlooked, or sometimes, the intention is to add them on later. However, in general, it is not possible to add on support for nonfunctional requirements effectively, as by their nature, they are not provided by a specific software function (consider, e.g., transparency and scalability). Instead, they are resultant of good design practice across all aspects of the functional behavior, the underlying software architectures, and the mechanistic aspects. Therefore, it is important to make the nonfunctional requirements a first-class concern at every stage of the project.

7.5.2 **ARCHITECTURAL ASPECTS**

Pay attention to separating concerns on a logical basis. This applies at the level of classes within the same software component as well as at the level of software components, which execute as separate processes. For example, in a client-server application, pay attention to the split of functionality between the client and the server. Consider, for example, the distributed game use case in which the server manages the game logic and holds the game state and the client provides the user interface. Separation of concerns leads to a number of benefits, which include cleaner design, especially in terms of interfaces, less interaction across interfaces, easier to understand code structure, and behavior (and thus easier to test, validate, and document). In particular, clear separation of concerns can reduce the intensity of interprocess communication and thus less network bandwidth is used and less latency is incurred. Separating the logical or behavioral scope of components on clear functional boundaries can also reduce the occurrence of direct dependencies as components are less tightly integrated than when a particular function is spread across several components.

Avoid direct coupling wherever possible. Direct coupling risks fault propagation where one component cannot operate because of the failure of, or absence of, another component. Direct coupling also projects a design-time vision of connectivity (which cannot in general foresee the full set of configuration scenarios that can occur) into the runtime. Loose coupling is more flexible and robust; it allows runtime connectivity associations between components to be based on actual availability and other contextual aspects such as system workload and resource reconfiguration to overcome platform-level failures.

The components should be right-sized. Coarse-grained designs, having larger components, can reduce the total number of components and thus also reduce the amount of communication necessary to link the application together. However, if this approach is taken too far, it reduces the benefits of distribution in regard to being able to separate functionalities and spread load across processing resources, facilitate sharing, and meet nonfunctional requirements such as availability, robustness, and scalability. The larger components are also more complex and therefore more challenging to test. Fine-grained systems with many small components are more flexible and the individual components are easier to understand and test. However, if the system is too fine-grained, there is a risk of excessive connectivity and higher communication overhead. The configuration complexity of systems increases as the number of communicating components rises, and this is traded with the reducing complexity of the individual components. Therefore, it is very important that a balance is reached in which components are right-sized for the particular application in terms of their functionality and connectivity requirements.

Use common services to provide generic functionality and thus keep application components as simple as possible. Application functionality should focus on the business logic mainly and where possible should not provide additional services such as resource locating. The use of common services permits standardized behavior across applications and entire systems. Common services themselves can be used in modular ways; as, for example, in the second case study in this chapter in which an ENS makes use of an external DS. It would have been possible to build the DS functionality into the ENS or to use some form of service advertising broadcast mechanism. However, this would add extra complexity to the ENS and possibly detract from the development of its core functionality. Other applications and services are likely to require the DS functionality in most systems, and in such cases, there is effectively no additional cost of providing the DS (i.e., it is not for the exclusive use of the ENS).

7.5.3 COMMUNICATION ASPECTS

Communication is fundamental to all distributed applications. It is also a cause or factor in many different classes of problems relating to performance, latency, resource limitations, and the occurrence of errors. In general, it is best to minimize the frequency of communication and also to keep the actual messages as short as possible, based on careful analysis of application requirements. Messages must be serialized and transmitted in language-independent and architecture-independent formats to ensure consistency and correctness in heterogeneous systems (see the Event Notification Service case study).

Blocking IO mode communication is efficient because a process (or thread) does not use CPU resource while waiting for message arrival. However, this can lead to unresponsive behavior of processes when they wait indefinitely (see Chapter 3). This can be overcome by using multithreaded designs such that some threads continue to be responsive while others wait on the IO. Alternatively, single-threaded components can be designed to be responsive without the additional complexity of threads, by using nonblocking IO mode sockets and an appropriately chosen time-out (see, e.g., the technique used in the time service client case study). This level of detail can only be sensibly considered in the context of specific application requirements, but it is important to flag up this aspect as it can have a significant impact on efficiency. Situations where both sides of a connection use blocking IO mode sockets should be avoided because of the risk of communication deadlock (see Chapter 3).

7.5.4 REUSE CODE WHEN OPPORTUNITIES ARISE

Code reuse has many benefits. Most obviously, you don't have to write so much code. However, it also has other benefits, which are perhaps more important, as identified:

- Better readability of code. Extracting classes and methods when opportunities arise has the effect of reducing the size of methods, or blocks of code, making them easier to understand. This has the additional benefit of making it more likely that certain errors or inefficiencies will be noticed at the time of code writing.

- Better structure of code. Refactoring improves the structure of code, and the avoidance of duplication (through extracting methods) makes code more maintainable as any modifications in the future only need to be applied in one place; this also prevents inconsistency creeping in through incremental updates where there are multiple sections of code where changes need to be synchronized.
- Reduced testing effort. The reuse of code blocks, which have already been unit tested, saves testing effort, both in terms of avoiding the need to write additional tests and also by not having to run those additional tests each time the full test suite is run.

7.5.5 CREATE LIBRARIES OF TESTED AND TRUSTED CODE

Code libraries are a means of achieving code reuse across different software components and projects.

Libraries are a means of preserving your effort so that it can pay off again in the future. For example, suppose you have spent significant effort developing a class that deals with some complex numerical formulas, which are specific to your company's line of business. Encoding of these formulas turned out to be quite error-prone and has required a disproportional testing effort compared to more routine aspects of the code. This is a good example of a situation where placing the class in a library could have high benefits: It provides a means of encapsulating the test cases and also the documentation needed to explain the complex formulas, and it has the potential to avoid a repetition of the hard effort in the future should another application require using the same formulas.

Modularize code (and thus, the development process) where opportunities arise. This leads to a cleaner division of functionality (separation of concerns), better code structure, and also better documentation.

Create libraries wherever possible. Refactor code to separate different aspects of business functionality or to separate business functionality from UI functionality as a precursor step to splitting off a library. See the example in Chapter 5 and also the time service client case study.

7.5.6 TESTING ASPECTS

As the earlier chapters have illustrated and emphasized, distributed systems represent complex environments in which many components interact with unpredictable timing artifacts and the ever-present possibilities of hardware failures, message loss, and software component crashes. This provides a challenging backdrop for the design and development of distributed applications and places high importance on testing.

Test plans are vital and should be established, to the extent possible, as part of the analysis and design stages of a project. However, it is very difficult to formally capture the full set of testing activities that an experienced developer carries out throughout the development life cycle.

Testing is often documented as a primarily postdevelopment step; this is partly due to the way in which the various development methodologies describe the software life cycle as a series of stages, which are typically as follows: analysis → design → development → testing.

Some methodologies such as the spiral model repeat these steps in a series of shorter cycles but essentially show testing at the end of each block of activity. While this sequence makes sense to a theorist (you cannot test something that you have not yet developed), it does not reflect what really needs to happen to ensure high-quality outcomes and efficient development progress.

Your perception of the role of testing and the way you apply it is linked to your mind-set with regard to building systems; it is about the extent to which you value having a quality outcome. You need to consider testing as a continual activity and to integrate testing throughout the entire development process.

As part of a quality-oriented mind-set, consider that every step of the development life cycle is an opportunity to make good or bad decisions. It can be difficult to elicit the full set of requirements of a system at the outset of a project and to express these in unambiguous ways. It may not be possible to capture every single nuance of behavior in the requirements statements; it may be necessary to retain some flexibility in their interpretation and to ensure that the consequences of any subsequent changes are considered across all levels of the design.

You should check that requirements do not conflict with one another such that they cannot all be satisfied, and if such a situation occurs, it must be resolved before moving on to design. You can evaluate the correctness and feasibility of the requirements by asking carefully thought-out questions to the would-be users of the system. You can also consider building partially functioning early prototype systems to check that your design concepts are well aligned with the requirements and also as a means for users to be able to see the consequences of the stated requirements and thus to revisit the requirements stage to ensure they correctly reflect and describe the desired system.

During development, you should test regularly. I have had many discussions with students about testing where their initial viewpoint has been that testing is somehow additional work. The reality is that if testing is performed on a continuous basis, it actually saves time and effort because problems are found and their causes understood before they propagate through the design; undoing a bad design decision is usually a lot easier in the earlier stages of development.

I find that an incremental iterative approach to testing with the basic premise that only one feature is added or modified between tests is most productive. This can on the face of it seem a slow way to progress, but it does lead to quality outcomes, and it ensures that the effects of one change can be understood before further additions are made, and it also provides regular opportunities for reflection on the overall goals and progress toward them.

7.6 END OF CHAPTER PROGRAMMING EXERCISES

1. Integrate the NTP client-side functionality into an application. This programming challenge relates to the time service client use case.
   The task. Build an NTP client functionality into any application of your choice. You are recommended to use the NTP library provided as part of the support materials. Start by studying the program code of the two provided NTP application client programs, which integrate the library and then mimic this library integration in your own application.
   Note that the two application clients already discussed in the time service case study serve as sample answers for this exercise.
2. Develop a publish-subscribe application, which uses an external ENS as a means of decoupling the application components. You are recommended to use the ENS presented in the second case study in this chapter.
   The event types and values will depend on the theme of the application you choose; for example, in a distributed game application, there may be event types such as new-player-arrival and new-game-started. Begin by studying the program code of the sample application publisher and consumer components provided as part of the supporting resources for the book. Consider developing your publisher in one language and your consumer in another, to experiment with the heterogeneity and interoperability aspects.
   Note that the application clients already discussed in the ENS case study serve as sample answers for this exercise.

7.7 LIST OF ACCOMPANYING RESOURCES

The following resources are referred to directly in the chapter text and/or the end of chapter exercises:

- Distributed Systems Workbench, "systems programming" edition (specifically the DS application)
- Source code
- Executable code

Case study	Program	Availability	Comments
#1 TimeServiceClient	CaseStudy_ TimeServiceClient_GUI Phase1 Monolithic	Source code Executable	Business logic and GUI logic integrated in single class
	CaseStudy_ TimeServiceClient_GUI Phase2 Refactored	Source code Executable	Refactored, business logic and GUI logic in separate classes
	CaseStudy_ TimeServiceClient Phase3 Library	Source code Executable	The phase 3 TimeServiceClient library
	CaseStudy_ TimeServiceClient_GUI Phase3 App-side uses library	Source code Executable	The phase 3 GUI application project (statically links the TimeServiceClient library)
	CaseStudy_TimeServClnt_ Console AppSide uses lib	Source code Executable	The phase 3 text application project (statically links the TimeServiceClient library)
#2 Event notification server	CaseStudy_ NotificationService:Server_ CPP	Source code Executable	The ENS server
	Directory service (DS)	The DS is provided as an application in the Distributed Systems Workbench	Necessary to support ENS client components locating the ENS
#2 Sample application components for testing and demonstration of event notification Server	CaseStudy_NotServ_ Publish_Client_CPP	Source code Executable	Sample application publisher component (C++ version)
	CaseStudy_NotServ_ Consume_Client_CPP	Source code Executable	Sample application consumer component (C++ version)
	CaseStudy_NotServ_ Publish_Client_CSharp	Source code Executable	Sample application publisher component (C-sharp version)
	CaseStudy_NotServ_ Consume_Client_CSharp	Source code Executable	Sample application consumer component (C-sharp version)
	CaseStudy_NotServ_ Publish_Client_JAVA	Source code Executable	Sample application publisher component (Java version)
	CaseStudy_NotServ_ Consume_Client_JAVA	Source code Executable	Sample application consumer component (Java version)

Index

Note: Page numbers followed by *b* indicate boxes, *f* indicate figures, *t* indicate tables, and *np* indicate foot note.

CPSIA information can be obtained
at www.ICGtesting.com
Printed in the USA
FFOW01n1643030315
11533FF

9 780128 007297